The Cistercian abbey of St Mary Graces, East Smithfield, London

MOLA Monograph Series

For more information about these titles and other MOLA publications visit the publications page at www.museumoflondonarchaeology.org.uk

1 Excavations at the priory and hospital of St Mary Spital, London

2 The National Roman Fabric Reference Collection: a handbook

3 The Cross Bones burial ground, Redcross Way, Southwark, London: archaeological excavations (1991–8) for the London Underground Limited Jubilee Line Extension Project

4 The eastern cemetery of Roman London: excavations 1983–90

5 The Holocene evolution of the London Thames: archaeological excavations (1991–8) for the London Underground Limited Jubilee Line Extension Project

6 The Limehouse porcelain manufactory: excavations at 108–116 Narrow Street, London, 1990

7 Roman defences and medieval industry: excavations at Baltic House, City of London

8 London bridge: 2000 years of a river crossing

9 Roman and medieval townhouses on the London waterfront: excavations at Governor's House, City of London

10 The London Charterhouse

11 Medieval 'Westminster' floor tiles

12 Settlement in Roman Southwark: archaeological excavations (1991–8) for the London Underground Limited Jubilee Line Extension Project

13 Aspects of medieval and later Southwark: archaeological excavations (1991–8) for the London Underground Limited Jubilee Line Extension Project

14 The prehistory and topography of Southwark and Lambeth

15 Middle Saxon London: excavations at the Royal Opera House 1989–99

16 Urban development in north-west Roman Southwark: excavations 1974–90

17 Industry in north-west Roman Southwark: excavations 1984–8

18 The Cistercian abbey of St Mary Stratford Langthorne, Essex: archaeological excavations for the London Underground Limited Jubilee Line Extension Project

19 Material culture in London in an age of transition: Tudor and Stuart period finds *c* 1450–*c* 1700 from excavations at riverside sites in Southwark

20 Excavations at the priory of the Order of the Hospital of St John of Jerusalem, Clerkenwell, London

21 Roman and medieval Cripplegate, City of London: archaeological excavations 1992–8

22 The royal palace, abbey and town of Westminster on Thorney Island: archaeological excavations (1991–8) for the London Underground Limited Jubilee Line Extension Project

23 A prestigious Roman building complex on the Southwark waterfront: excavations at Winchester Palace, London, 1983–90

24 Holy Trinity Priory, Aldgate, City of London: an archaeological reconstruction and history

25 Roman pottery production in the Walbrook valley: excavations at 20–28 Moorgate, City of London, 1998–2000

26 Prehistoric landscape to Roman villa: excavations at Beddington, Surrey, 1981–7

27 Saxon, medieval and post-medieval settlement at Sol Central, Marefair, Northampton: archaeological excavations, 1998–2002

28 John Baker's late 17th-century glasshouse at Vauxhall

29 The medieval postern gate by the Tower of London

30 Roman and later development east of the forum and Cornhill: excavations at Lloyd's Register, 71 Fenchurch Street, City of London

31 Winchester Palace: excavations at the Southwark residence of the bishops of Winchester

32 Development on Roman London's western hill: excavations at Paternoster Square, City of London

33 Within these walls: Roman and medieval defences north of Newgate at the Merrill Lynch Financial Centre, City of London

34 The Augustinian priory of St Mary Merton, Surrey: excavations 1976–90

35 London's Roman amphitheatre: excavations at the Guildhall

36 The London Guildhall: an archaeological history of a neighbourhood from early medieval to modern times

37 Roman London and the Walbrook stream crossing: excavations at 1 Poultry and vicinity, City of London

38 The development of early medieval and later Poultry and Cheapside: excavations at 1 Poultry and vicinity, City of London

39 Burial at the site of the parish church of St Benet Sherehog before and after the Great Fire: excavations at 1 Poultry, City of London

40 London's delftware industry: the tin-glazed pottery industries of Southwark and Lambeth

41 Early and Middle Saxon rural settlement in the London region

42 Roman Southwark settlement and economy: excavations in Southwark 1973–91

43 The Black Death cemetery, East Smithfield, London

44 The Cistercian abbey of St Mary Graces, East Smithfield, London

45 The Royal Navy victualling yard, East Smithfield, London

46 St Marylebone Church and burial ground in the 18th to 19th centuries: excavations at St Marylebone School, 1992 and 2004–6

47 Great houses, moats and mills on the south bank of the Thames: medieval and Tudor Southwark and Rotherhithe

48 The Rose and the Globe – playhouses of Shakespeare's Bankside, Southwark: excavations 1988–91

49 A dated type series of London medieval pottery: Part 5, Shelly-sandy ware and the greyware industries

50 The Cluniac priory and abbey of St Saviour Bermondsey, Surrey: excavations 1984–95

The Cistercian abbey of St Mary Graces, East Smithfield, London

Ian Grainger and Christopher Phillpotts

MOLA MONOGRAPH 44

MUSEUM OF LONDON ARCHAEOLOGY

Published by Museum of London Archaeology

A CIP catalogue record for this book is available from the British Library

Production and series design by Tracy Wellman
Typesetting and design by Sue Cawood
Reprographics by Andy Chopping
Copy editing by Simon Burnell
Series editing by Sue Hirst/Susan M Wright

Printed by the Lavenham Press

Front cover: St Mary Graces on Wyngaerde's panorama of London of c *1540 (centre left), with the Tower of London in the foreground; tenements on St Katherine's Lane (later Way) and East Smithfield are shown converging to the far left by the abbey gatehouse and Tower Hill (© Ashmolean Museum, University of Oxford)*

CONTRIBUTORS

Principal authors	Ian Grainger, Christopher Phillpotts
Stratigraphic sequence	Ian Grainger, Duncan Hawkins
Documentary research	Christopher Phillpotts
Architectural fragments	Mark Samuel
Floor tiles and brick	Naomi Crowley, †Elizabeth Eames
Stove-tiles	Lyn Blackmore, David Gaimster, Richenda Goffin
Pottery	Lyn Blackmore (imported wares), Richenda Goffin (medieval assemblages), Roy Stephenson (Dissolution-period assemblages), with David Gaimster (stonewares)
Vessel glass	John Shepherd
Window glass	Jill Channer
Accessioned finds	Richenda Goffin (antler and bone artefacts), Judy Stevenson (metal artefacts), Alison Nailer (leather items)
Plant remains	John Giorgi
Textiles	Frances Pritchard
Small mammal and amphibian bones	†Helen Hibberd
Fish bones	Alison Locker
Eggshell	Jane Sidell
Parasite remains	Clare de Rouffignac
Human bone	Jelena Bekvalac, Tania Kausmally
Graphics	Caroline Caldwell, Peter Hart-Allison, Sue Hermon, Sophie Lamb, Carlos Lemos, Faith Vardy
Photography	Andy Chopping, Paul Falcini, Ian Grainger, Duncan Hawkins, Peter Mills, David Pritchard
Academic adviser	Glyn Coppack
Project management	Richard Malt, Peter Mills, Barney Sloane, with David Bowsher
Editor	Susan M Wright, with Robert Cowie, Sue Hirst

CONTENTS

FIGURES

TABLES

SUMMARY

The Cistercian abbey of St Mary Graces was founded in 1350 by Edward III in East Smithfield, London, and was suppressed in 1539. St Mary Graces was the last of 62 Cistercian abbeys to be founded in England. It was also established in the immediate aftermath of the Black Death in what was, unusually for an English Cistercian house, an urban setting, and to a non-standard Cistercian plan that was nevertheless typical of many other 14th-century monastic constructions. All these factors combine to make the monastery of international significance, certainly in terms of Cistercian studies and monastic and medieval archaeology in general. The circumstances of the foundation of St Mary Graces are comparable to those of the slightly later London Charterhouse, having much to do with the increased piety of Edward III's court. Both began as mortuary chapels and continued as mausolea for wealthy patrons, and both brought traditionally rural orders to the urban environment – introducing to England for the first time a trend that began before the Black Death on the Continent.

The excavations on the site of the former Royal Mint took place between 1983 and 1988. A fully integrated report has been written to take into account all the strands of evidence for the development of the abbey. This approach aims to achieve a greater understanding of the site's history through a combination of stratigraphic, documentary, finds and environmental evidence. This volume is the second in a trilogy on the archaeology of the site. Its publication follows that of MoLAS/MOLA monographs on the Black Death cemetery of 1348–50 (Grainger et al 2008) and on the later Royal Navy victualling yard of 1560–1785 (Grainger and Phillpotts 2010).

Following the introduction (Chapter 1), a fully integrated chronological narrative sets out what is known of the site before and during the lifetime of the abbey and immediately after the Dissolution when the buildings were used as a manor house. Chapter 2.1–2.2 summarises the geology and outlines the history and archaeology of the site up to the Black Death, putting the layout of the abbey into context. Chapter 2.3 attempts to show how and why the monks used the Black Death chapel of Holy Trinity as their first church. Chapter 2.4 covers the main period of construction, showing that the bulk of the church and the conventual buildings were built between 1361 and 1392. The 15th and 16th centuries (Chapter 2.5) were a period of little apparent building activity, beyond the construction of two small chapels, but do account for the majority of the 131 burials in the church and cloister, and the 305 burials in the external cemetery areas. The final stratigraphic chapter-section covers the suppression of the abbey and the conversion to a manor house, when it appears that the church and many other buildings stood derelict.

A series of thematic essays then examines the abbey in a wider context. Chapter 3.1 considers the foundation of the abbey and suggests reasons why the Cistercians established a new abbey so close to the city, some 70 years after their last foundation in England. A study of the layout of the abbey is undertaken in Chapter 3.2, which clearly demonstrates the influence of contemporary friary designs along with more traditional Cistercian elements and simple adaptation to the constraints of the site. The essentially Perpendicular architecture of the church and the major conventual buildings is analysed in Chapter 3.3. The politics and endowment of the abbey are also covered (Chapter 3.4), looking at what is known of the financial base and history of the abbey and the factors which affected them. Chapter 3.5 examines what is known of the monastic economy as the house struggled to survive in the post-Black Death environment. In Chapter 3.6, the personnel of the abbey are studied on the basis of the documentary sources and the skeletal assemblages from the church and burial areas; evidence for health and disease is considered, and the imbalance of male to female burials, usual on a monastic site, is discussed. Burial practices and the many well-defined areas of burial are described and the problematic issue of identifying the various elements of the monastic and lay populations is addressed. Of particular interest is the 'Visitations of Clarenceux', a document naming and to a certain extent locating a number of lay burials within the church. The final thematic section (Chapter 3.9) attempts to place St Mary Graces in its wider context to assess the impact it had on London and vice versa, and to gauge the importance of the abbey for the Cistercian Order.

The conclusion (Chapter 4) summarises the significance of the findings in the light of current academic debate, suggests further areas where research is needed and indicates the potential for further excavation. The specialist appendices (Chapter 5) provide data to support the arguments advanced in earlier chapters.

ACKNOWLEDGEMENTS

This publication is the product of a joint venture between English Heritage and Museum of London Archaeology (MOLA, formerly MoLAS, the Museum of London Archaeology Service) to publish backlog sites identified in the London post-excavation review (DGLA 1989; see now Hinton and Thomas 1997). MOLA would like to thank English Heritage for their generous funding of the post-excavation analysis and resulting publication.

The archaeological excavation programme was managed throughout by Peter Mills. He and MOLA would like to thank City Merchant Developers, particularly Ray Pearse, and the Crown Estate Commissioners for their generous funding of the archaeological investigations. Particular thanks are also due to the architects involved: Paul Watkins and Virginia Newman (née Goldstone) of Sheppard Robson, and Henry Brown (now of Henry Brown Associates) and Geoff Watkins, both formerly with RMJM.

Thanks also go to the staff of the Museum of London's former Department of Greater London Archaeology (DGLA) who worked on the site – in all more than 150 archaeologists were employed there between 1983 and 1988 – in particular the site supervisors, Paul Falcini, Duncan Hawkins and David Pritchard. Many members of the public helped process the hundreds of skeletons and artefacts that were excavated at the Royal Mint, working in unpleasant surroundings, with minimal facilities, yet doing so stalwartly and with humour. Specialists who assisted with the work on this part of the site in the late 1980s, but who are not listed as contributors, were: Jayne Baxter, John Cherry, John Clark, Wendy Evans, Hazel Forsyth, Sandra Garside-Neville, Jenny Hall, Michael Hammerson, Josephine Higson, Christine Jones, John Letts, Glynis Lloyd-Morgan, Nick Merriman, Andrea Milburn, Tony North, Frances Palmer, Andrew Prescott, James Rackham, Tom Richardson, Mark Robinson, Peter Stott and Guy Wilson.

Particular thanks are also due to Tony Waldron for his work on the human bone assemblage during the late 1980s and early 1990s, and for his input into the present publication. Richard Lea (English Heritage) advised on the reconstruction of architectural features from the fragments. Mark Samuel would also like to thank the Very Reverend Patrick Mitchell for granting access to the Dean's Cloister, Windsor Castle, for research connected with the project, and for drawing his attention to Harvey's 1961 article.

Help and advice were provided by many individuals during the course of the project, including Brian Kerr and Tim Williams of English Heritage, Geoff Egan, Anna Heywood, Jackie Keily, Fiona Macdonell, Louise Rayner and Bill White (all of MOLA), and Eleanor Lanyon and Alan Thompson (of MOL's London Archaeological Archive and Research Centre). The post-excavation phase of the project was monitored by Brian Kerr and Barney Sloane for English Heritage and the post-excavation programme was managed for MOLA by Gordon Malcolm.

1

Introduction

1.1 The Royal Mint: the three-volume approach

The site of the former Royal Mint in East Smithfield, London, contained within its boundaries a Black Death cemetery and chapel (1348–50), the Cistercian abbey of St Mary Graces (1350–1539) and a Royal Navy victualling yard (1560–1785). The objectives of the Royal Mint excavations were:

- to locate and quantify the documented emergency burial ground, established in 1348–9;
- to recover the ground plan of the Cistercian abbey of St Mary Graces, founded in 1350, and information on the economic and ritual life of the abbey, and to examine the effect of the Dissolution on the abbey and its reuse as a Tudor manor house;
- to recover the ground plan of the Royal Navy victualling yard, established in 1560, and archaeological evidence for its industrial functions.

Given the size of the project, the diverse nature of the three major phases of archaeological interest (Black Death cemetery, abbey and manor house, and Royal Navy victualling yard) and the likely differences in academic interest in them, the excavation is published in three separate volumes. The first in the sequence is *The Black Death cemetery, East Smithfield, London* (Grainger et al 2008), which is followed by this monograph about the abbey of St Mary Graces, and then by *The Royal Navy victualling yard, East Smithfield, London* (Grainger and Phillpotts 2010).

1.2 The abbey of St Mary Graces

The medieval Cistercian abbey of St Mary Graces stood on Tower Hill in London, just beyond the city wall, to the north-east of the Tower of London itself. The past tense, however, is not entirely accurate when applied to St Mary Graces, for, though it was buried for most of the 19th and 20th centuries by the Royal Mint and thought to be largely, if not wholly, lost, substantial remains of the abbey which were excavated and recorded in the 1980s do survive today and can be viewed. Admittedly their setting is less than ideal, being locked away beneath the Royal Mint Court complex which now occupies the site, and only partly visible to the public from a pedestrian subway. Those lucky enough to see the remains, which include parts of the church, chapter house, infirmary and refectory, are unlikely to be able to identify them without prior knowledge. They are not signposted and do not feature in tourist guide books for either London or abbeys and monasteries.

Those who know something of Cistercian monasteries might also be surprised that St Mary Graces existed so close to England's capital city, the location scarcely being 'far from the concourse of men' as traditionally required by the Order (Robinson 1998, 11). If the stricture concerning remoteness was never completely adhered to, even in the early days of Cistercian reforming zeal in the 12th century, St Mary Graces' suburban location makes it unique among English Cistercian houses, as does the fact that it was the only new British Cistercian house to be constructed in the 14th century, and the last one to be founded before the Dissolution.

Established in 1350 by Edward III, there are many other aspects to the abbey that are highly unusual for a Cistercian house, if not unique. Though ostensibly in fulfilment of a vow made by Edward after being saved from drowning at sea, the abbey was also founded as a memorial to all those who had recently died in the Black Death, and, indeed, only a few short months before, the site had been used as an emergency burial ground for many of the Londoners who had succumbed to the terrifying disease (Grainger et al 2008). The Black Death's shadow loomed over the abbey's early years: the monks used the chapel of Holy Trinity, attached to the burial ground, as their first church, and it is likely that part of the burial ground – now within the monastic precinct – continued to be used for victims of later epidemics until 1400.

Although originally planned by Edward as a grandiose double house of 24 monks, it is doubtful that St Mary's ever achieved half this number (*Cal Close R*, 1396–9, 85–6; *Cal Pat R*, 1388–92, 364; TNA: PRO, E 328/344; SC 8/E711A and B). For much of its short 189-year history the house was troubled by poor finances, and the construction of its necessary buildings stretched over 50 years, not being near completion until the 1390s (TNA: PRO, SC 6/1258/1, ms 1, 2, 5). The abbey which this building programme produced was certainly no rival to the great Cistercian houses like Rievaulx or Fountains in Yorkshire, and it was small and often utilitarian in appearance. Yet when finally suppressed in 1539 along with the other, greater houses, St Mary Graces had the third-highest surrender value of all the English Cistercian houses (*Val Eccl*, i, 398–9), and the excavated *ex situ* architectural stone hints at some beauty lost. Its royal connections and location in the capital also meant that it briefly played a pre-eminent role in the affairs of the Order, hosting the general chapter from 1394 to 1400 (Graham 1929, 378–9, 383; Knowles 1955, 169; *Cal Pap Letters*, v, 9). It also became the burial place of Sir Simon Burley, royal favourite of Richard II, who was executed in 1388 (Lewis 1937, 668–9), and by the 15th century attracted the patronage of prominent families, most notably of the Stafford dukes of Buckingham and the de Vere earls of Oxford, serving as the burial place of minor members of those families (Wagner 1956, 143–4). Among other prominent 15th-century people buried there were Sir Lewis John and Sir Thomas Montgomery, both powerful Essex landowners (ibid). Montgomery funded the construction of the Lady chapel and was subsequently buried in it (TNA: PRO, PROB 11/10/22). The abbey appears to have derived much income from the sale of burial space in the church.

The excavations of 1983–8 revealed a ground plan that was both traditionally Cistercian yet incorporated elements that made it look overall like no other British Cistercian house. The abbey had a large north–south aligned refectory, a defining feature of Cistercian houses from the 12th century onwards. However, the church was not cruciform: it included an aisled nave and a simple rectangular presbytery without transepts, and was similar in all respects to a contemporary 14th-century friary church (Butler 1984, 123–36; Clapham and Godfrey 1913, 247) (Fig 60). Similarly, there was no identifiable dormitory, and the complex included a second, subsidiary cloister, the church cloister having only a timber pentice for the north aisle, all reminiscent of a friary. For some of these features – such as the subsidiary cloister – there were reasons peculiar to the location and history of the house itself, but others show the influence of the secular masons employed by the king (*Cal Pat R*, 1358–61, 567) and schooled in contemporary 14th-century design, rather than that of the Cistercians themselves.

After the Dissolution the abbey suffered a fate common to many monasteries. It became the grand house of one of the officials who oversaw the suppression of the monasteries for the Court of Augmentations, in this case Sir Arthur Darcy who bought the abbey in 1542 (*L and P Hen VIII*, xvii, no. 714(18)). However, it did not remain so for long, and was sold back to the Crown in 1560 to become the Royal Navy's principal victualling yard or food supply depot, serving in that capacity until 1785. Many of the abbey buildings survived well into the 18th century as part of the yard, and this portion of the site's story is dealt with in the third monograph on the Royal Mint excavations (Grainger and Phillpotts 2010).

1.3 The excavation

The study area

The Royal Mint is a two-hectare (4.94 acre) site to the north-east of the Tower of London, lying between Royal Mint Street to the north, East Smithfield to the south, Cartwright Street to the east, and Mansell Street and Tower Hill to the west (Fig 1). The site now contains Royal Mint Court and St Mary Graces Court. After the closure of the victualling yard in 1785, the buildings became government warehouses before the Royal Mint was moved to the site from the Tower of London in 1806. Monastic building foundations and a doorway were exposed in 1900 during excavations to build new Medal and Die Offices in the Royal Mint (*The Builder Magazine*, 21 April 1900). The Royal Mint was gradually transferred to its present home in Llantrisant, Wales, between 1967 and the late 1970s. A period of demolition and dereliction followed, until the only buildings of the old Royal Mint to remain standing were the central administration block or Johnson Smirke Building, built in 1806–11 (Fig 21), the main gatehouse, the courtyard and the Seaman's Registry building. All of these structures are Grade 2* listed and were incorporated into the Royal Mint Court redevelopment that began in 1986.

The circumstances of excavation

In 1972 Brian Davison carried out the first archaeological work on the site. This excavation consisted of two small trenches in

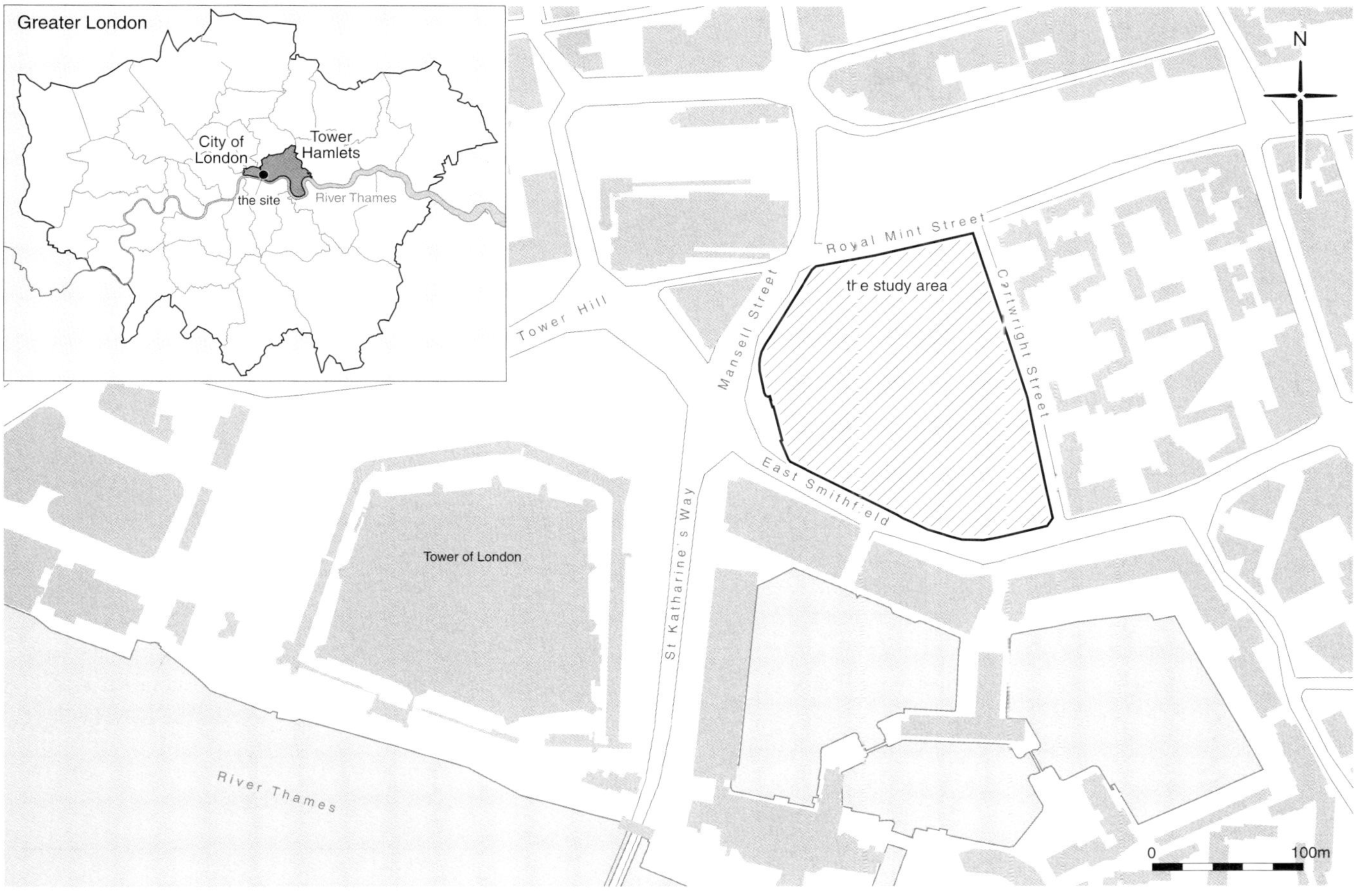

Fig 1 Map showing the location of the study area (scale 1:5000)

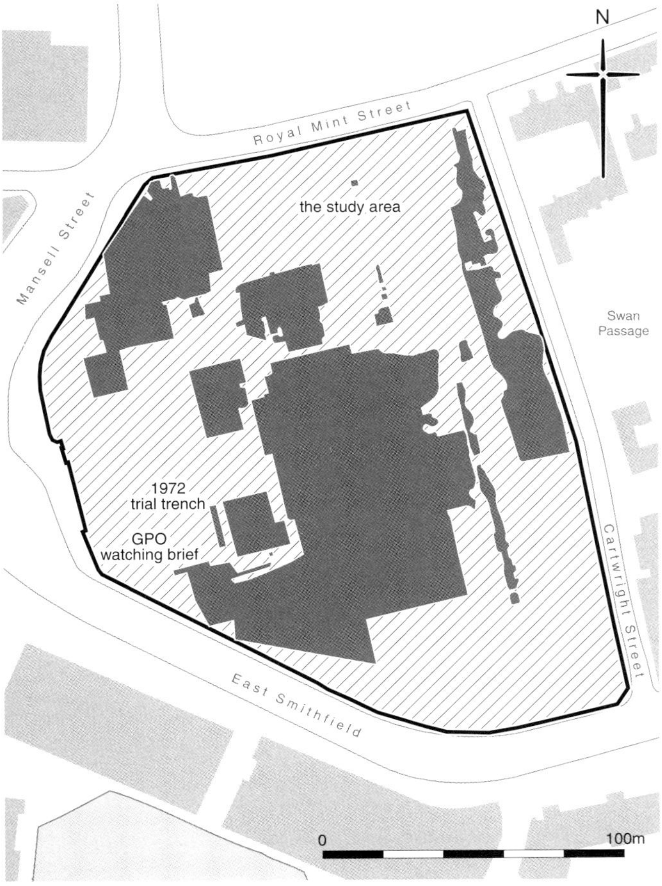

Fig 2 The study area: the areas excavated are shown in grey (scale 1:2500)

the south end of the listed courtyard (Davison 1972). The Museum of London's Department of Greater London Archaeology (DGLA) – one of the precursors to Museum of London Archaeology (MOLA) – carried out further work in the early 1980s, comprising a watching brief on a GPO trench in East Smithfield (in the street, revealing the south-west corner of what was later identified as Building 2) and work under the direction of Peter Mills which began in 1983. In 1984 more extensive trial work (MIN84) funded by the Crown Estate Commissioners established the ground plan of the south range of the abbey and indicated a number of areas of burial. This trial work was published in interim form (Mills 1983; 1985).

In June 1986 the DGLA began a full excavation of the site (MIN86), funded by City Merchant Developers. The project lasted approximately two years – it finished in June 1988, having employed around 150 staff, used 16,000 context numbers, produced 8000 plans, and taken 24,000 colour and black-and-white film exposures. Approximately four-fifths of the site was either eventually excavated, or written off as archaeologically negative, in a rolling programme which consisted of 17 areas (Fig 2). This work has also been reported in interim form (Grainger and Hawkins 1988).

1.4 The organisation of the report

The chronological narrative

The Royal Mint archaeological data have been organised chronologically by means of a system of dated periods (Table 1). Each volume is devoted to a period (A, B or C) that deals with a readily definable large-scale land use in the archaeology of the site. The first volume deals with period A, the medieval occupation up to and including the Black Death cemetery (Grainger et al 2008); this, the second, volume deals with period B, which covers the abbey and manor house; and the final volume (Grainger and Phillpotts 2010) deals with period C, the victualling yard. These periods have been formed from the basic ceramic and stratigraphic phasing, combined with other evidence for clear changes to the layout or function of elements of the study area. The sub-periods are described in detail in Chapter 2 of each volume. Each section of the period chapters, where appropriate, begins with the documentary evidence for that sub-period. Archaeological events within each land-use zone are then described chronologically (and, in so far as is compatible, in land-use numerical order), and each period concludes with a discussion.

Several problems arise in any attempt to interpret the excavated remains of St Mary Graces. The abbey had a relatively short lifespan of only 189 years. The documentary sources indicate that much of the construction work, particularly on the domestic buildings, was confined to the first 40 years of the abbey's history. This time-frame is too tight for many of the archaeological dating techniques applicable to the site to be of use in refining the sequence of events. The majority of the non-residual pottery recovered from the definite monastic strata simply has a date of *c* 1350+; only very rarely does a sherd suggest a date of later than *c* 1380. Both the amount of surviving monastic deposits and the quantity of datable finds recovered from those deposits were extremely limited. The surviving walls of the domestic buildings were of a distinctly utilitarian nature, and no datable architectural features were found in them. A constructional sequence based on the surviving butt joints and variations in wall construction can be established for much of the complex; however, the significance of this in terms of phasing is difficult to judge. With the exception of the church, none of the internal features can be used to build up a long occupational sequence within a particular building, and certainly the excavated sequence in one room can at no point be reliably related to that in another. Even within the church the internal phasing is at best tentative. Thus, in this instance, as with the companion monograph on the Black Death cemetery (Grainger et al 2008), because the sub-periods under discussion are of short duration, the dating tables normally presented to support the stratigraphic analysis in MOLA publications are omitted. However, the descriptions of artefacts and environmental material relating to the stratigraphy are incorporated into the narrative.

Each sub-period is accompanied by a plan showing the major features of each land use for that sub-period. Illustrations of individual archaeological features or finds are presented alongside the description of the building or open area from which they came. Items that can be intrinsically dated to a particular sub-period, but which were recovered from later features, are illustrated as part of a corpus of material within the sub-period to which they originally belonged. The intention is to form a cumulative catalogue of finds following the chronology of the site. This is fully cross-referenced to allow the reader to check at once the archaeological provenance of each object.

Table 1 The chronological periods used in the Royal Mint reports

Period	Description	Date range	Publication
A1	pre-Black Death	*c* 1050–1348	Grainger et al 2008
A2	Black Death cemetery	1348–50	Grainger et al 2008
B1	abbey	1350–61	this volume
B2	abbey	1361–*c* 1400	this volume
B3	abbey	*c* 1400–1539	this volume
B4	Dissolution and manor house	1539–60	this volume
C1	victualling yard	1560–*c* 1660	Grainger and Phillpotts 2010
C2	victualling yard	*c* 1660–1785	Grainger and Phillpotts 2010
C3	post-victualling yard	1785–1970	Grainger and Phillpotts 2010

The thematic sections

Chapter 3 consists of a series of essays wherein debate and interpretation of the archaeological evidence find wider expression. The themes to have emerged from the descriptive narrative in Chapter 2 are discussed here in the light of current understanding.

The specialist appendices

In order to provide a flowing text, much of the necessary 'technical support' for conclusions and interpretations is gathered towards the back of the volume in individual sections in Chapter 5.

The research archives

In accordance with the principles laid out in *Management of archaeological projects* (MAP2) (English Heritage 1991), analysis of the material from the site resulted in a series of specialist research archives, all of which are lodged with the Museum of London. Most of this work was carried out in the early 1990s, with only limited subsequent updating.

Much of the detailed data and all the major themes from each specialist research archive have been integrated into this volume. There remains, however, a large corpus of material that is inappropriate for publication in this present format. This information includes detailed identification, quantification, measurement and description of the various assemblages, and it is stored in a series of research archives, one for each specialist discipline. Researchers wishing to intensify the scope of their studies are directed to these archives, references to which are detailed in the bibliography. They, along with the site records, are accessible to the public in the archive of the MOL's London Archaeological Archive and Research Centre (LAARC), Mortimer Wheeler House, 46 Eagle Wharf Road, London N1 7ED, and may be consulted by prior arrangement with the Archaeological Archive Manager.

This and the companion volume on the Black Death burials at the Royal Mint site (Grainger et al 2008) draw upon the first skeletal data to be recorded on the Wellcome Osteological Research Database ('WORD') at the Museum of London and analysed under the auspices of the Wellcome project. The data are directly accessible through the Museum of London website, access to which will be sustained for the foreseeable future: www.museumoflondon.org.uk/English/Collections/OnlineResources/CHB/Database/. Not all the excavated individuals were analysed for the Oracle WORD database, some remains being unsuitable due to truncation or contamination, and not all burials were planned in detail. The data concerned with this volume may be located by searching online, using the site code: MIN86. Earlier unpublished reports, skeletal recording, and other human bone data are located in the paper archive in the LAARC. However, it needs to be pointed out that for historical reasons these records relate to an earlier, smaller sample from MIN86 that is now superseded by work carried out in the 21st century.

Textual and graphical conventions

The basic unit of cross-reference throughout the research archive for this project is the context number. This is a unique number given to each archaeological event on the site (such as a layer, wall, grave cut etc), presented within square brackets, thus:

[100] representing context 100 from the site;
[+] representing unstratified and unrecorded material.

The vast majority of the published contexts come from the main phase of excavation (MIN 86). However, a limited number of contexts from the MIN84 trial work are also referred to and, where this occurs, the context is prefixed thus: MIN84 [100].

The land-use units are described as Building (B), Structure (S), Open Area (OA) and Drain (D). A single system of land-use numbers (B1–00, S1–00 etc) has been adopted throughout the three companion volumes. Thus the first 'new' building number in this volume is Building 2, but reused Building 1, first described in the preceding volume (Grainger et al 2008), also appears here.

Several categories of finds have been numbered for publication. These are referred to within angled brackets by an appropriate letter prefix (indicating material) and a catalogue number, thus:

<A1> refers to Architectural fragment no. 1;
<G2> refers to Glass object no. 2;
<GW3> refers to Window Glass fragment no. 3;
<P4> refers to illustrated Pottery object no. 4;
<S5> refers to accessioned Small find no. 5;
<T6> refers to Tile no. 6.

Catalogued objects are also referred to by their original accession number in the catalogues, thus: <3124>. A continuous published find numbering system is used throughout the three volumes so that with some categories the numbering in this volume will not start at 1. Thus, for example, the accessioned small finds begin at <S41> in this volume because 40 objects have been catalogued in the preceding volume (Grainger et al 2008), and the glass and pottery series also commence there with a small number of items.

This publication employs standard Museum of London reference codes for ceramics; these codes were developed by the MOL for recording purposes. Expansions of pottery codes are given at the first mention in a text section. Detailed descriptions of the building material fabrics and complete lists of the pottery codes, their expansions and date ranges are available from the LAARC as part of the research archive and are also posted on the LAARC and MOLA pages of the MOL website: www.museumoflondonarchaeology.org.uk. Details of the illustrated pottery discussed in this volume (<P3>–<P37>) may be found in Table 20.

Weights and measures are sometimes quoted in the text in the units used before metrication in the late 20th century. These include feet (1ft equals 0.305m; 12 inches (in) to 1ft, 3ft to 1 yard) and ells (an ell was often as long as 45 inches (1.1m)). An acre is 0.4 hectares, or alternatively 1ha equals about 2.5 acres. A pound (1lb equals 0.45kg) comprises 16 ounces (1oz equals 28g); a hundredweight (cwt) equals 112lb, and a quarter correspondingly equals 28lb, while a fother was 19.5cwt. Sums of money are quoted in the text as cited in £, s and d, where 12 pence (d) made one shilling (s) and 20 shillings (or 240d) a pound (£), since modern equivalents would be misleading. Dyer (1989, xv) provides the following reminder on which to base an approximation to current values: 'A skilled building worker earned 2d per day in 1250, 4d per day in 1400 and 6d in 1500'. The definitions of Kentish ragstone and Reigate stone for the purposes of this study are given in Chapter 3.3 ('Materials'). County names in the text refer to historic counties.

The graphical conventions used in this report are shown in Fig 3.

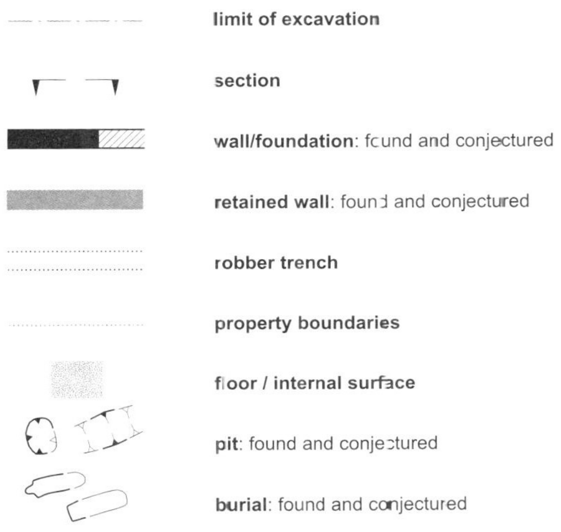

Fig 3 Graphical conventions used in this report

2

The archaeological sequence

2.1 Drift geology and topography

The drift geology comprised Quaternary second river floodplain terrace deposits, consisting of gravel with some sand and clay. These overlay the London Clay. The highest surviving gravels were in the centre of the site where they occurred at approximately 9.7m OD. To the south and east the surviving gravels were lower, at a maximum of 9.00m OD. In the south-east these deposits did not survive above 8.20m OD. To the west the gravels did not survive above 8.50m OD. In many cases the surviving height was clearly the result of truncation. However, those heights from the north, centre and south may suggest the original topography, and that the central and western parts were slightly higher, forming a low rise.

2.2 Summary of the pre-cemetery and Black Death cemetery sequence (periods A1–A2)

The evidence summarised here is reported in detail in the companion volume on the Black Death cemetery (Grainger et al 2008).

Prehistoric and Roman

Nearly all the prehistoric and Roman finds recovered were from medieval and post-medieval deposits. No prehistoric or Roman features were positively identified. The apparent absence of prehistoric and Roman contexts cannot be explained entirely by later truncation; it suggests that the site was open and possibly in agricultural use during these periods.

Pre-Black Death cemetery evidence, *c* 1050–1348 (OA1) (period A1)

In the late 9th century AD a ward was formed to guard the Aldgate. In the middle of the 10th century AD, the extra-mural part of this ward was transferred to the new ward of Portsoken. The land was then said to be derelict. In 1125 the Portsoken was transferred to Holy Trinity Priory, Aldgate. The parish of St Botolph without Aldgate was then created under the priory's control to serve the Portsoken (*Cart Holy Trinity*, 168, nos 871, 875; Stow 1603, i, 122; Haslam 1988, 35–6, 40–1). It originally stretched from Bishopsgate ward around the city walls, down to the river to the east of the Tower.

The bulk, if not the whole, of the site formed one agricultural holding or toft in the 12th and 13th centuries. The land appears to have been ploughed north–south in strips or selions. The common field immediately to its east (through which Cartwright Street now runs (Fig 2)) was certainly ploughed in this direction (TNA: PRO, E 40/2212). The boundary of the toft with this field was an 'earth wall' or bank. Another 'earth wall' marked the northern boundary along

Hoggestrete (later Hogg Lane and now Royal Mint Street (Fig 2)) (TNA: PRO, C 66/250, m 3). The western frontage along Tower Hill was separated, probably in the late 13th or early 14th century, to form a number of tenements and gardens. Shops and at least one brewhouse were built along the street frontage. Some of the gardens were exploited for gravel or brickearth quarrying, and ample archaeological evidence for this quarrying was found on all parts of the site, together with a number of 13th- and 14th-century pits and postholes. The southern frontage along the way to Ratcliff (now East Smithfield (Fig 2)) was split up into tenements and gardens by the 1320s, and possibly before (TNA: PRO, E 210/3437; E 326/9431; *Cal Feet of Fines*, i, 49, 65, 72, 73, 77, 80, 97, 118). Some shops were built along this street too. After parts of the property were divided from the toft to the west and south, the irregular piece of ploughed land that was left was called 'Horseleggesfurlong' (TNA: PRO, C 66/305, m 37; E 40/2643; Grainger et al 2008, 7, fig 5; see Fig 5).

The Black Death cemetery and chapel, 1348–50 (OA2 and OA3, and B1) (period A2)

The Black Death cemetery was established in late 1348 or possibly early 1349 (Fig 4). The cemetery at East Smithfield (the Royal Mint site) was one of two emergency burial grounds established for this purpose, the second being at West Smithfield. John Corey established the East Smithfield cemetery at 'the instigation of substantial men of the City' according to the cartulary of Holy Trinity Priory, Aldgate (*Cart Holy Trinity*, 186–8). The dimensions of the cemetery, as recorded in the cartulary, seem to correspond with those of the Horselegge furlong and an adjacent plot to the south-west, and it was almost entirely within the limits of the site. The cemetery was organised in two separate burial areas (OA2 and OA3), employing a mixture of individual graves and mass burial trenches. During the excavations 759 burials were found, and it is estimated that up to *c* 2400 people were interred there. Some of the deceased were accompanied by copper-alloy annular buckles/brooches, which seemed to indicate that they were buried in everyday clothes rather than shrouds, but other burials were clearly within coffins, some lined with charcoal. Two burials produced groups of silver coins that were closely datable to the mid 14th century, and these individuals had clearly been buried in their everyday clothes. In 1350 Corey bought the lands and tenements of Henry Cros and Nicholas Bedyngton as an extension to the cemetery (Fig 4). On this plot of land the chapel of Holy Trinity (B1) was built from 1350 onwards to serve the cemetery.

2.3 The first church and cloister, 1350–61 (period B1)

Documentary evidence

Edward III may have been expressing his thanks to God for the victory at Crécy in 1346, for his escape from shipwreck in 1347, and for surviving the Black Death of 1348–9 when he founded St Mary Graces in 1350 (Honeybourne 1952, 16–17). Certainly Edward left Calais on about 12 October 1347, accompanied by Queen Philippa, the Black Prince and much of his army. The crossing was very stormy and several of the ships were lost. The king and his party landed at London on 14 October (Barber 1978, 80) and this is the most likely occasion for Edward to have made his vow to found the abbey of St Mary Graces in thanks for deliverance from the storm. Nevertheless, some contemporary sources indicate an explicit connection between the foundation of the abbey and the commemoration of the Black Death on the site of the recent cemetery and chapel (TNA: PRO, E 40/13839; E 42/447).

In choosing the Cistercians, Edward III was following a family tradition stretching back to the Empress Matilda in the 12th century. He may have particularly valued an order with such strong international connections (Holdsworth 1992, 142, 149). The story of the vow may be apocryphal but John Corey, the king's agent, was buying land on the site as early as 1346, possibly for the king with a religious foundation in mind (TNA: PRO, E 40/2643; E 210/1661, 1692, 1681; E 326/9933, 2307, 2310, 2311, 2316, 2317; E 315/47, no. 110; Grainger et al 2008, 9–12, 18–19, 29) (Chapter 3.1). Corey was still buying houses, gardens and yards for the site of the abbey at Tower Hill and East Smithfield in March 1353, from John atte Ree, filling in the gaps left by previous purchases (LMA, CLA/023/DW/01/81/44). In 1353 the ownership of both the Black Death cemetery and the chapel of Holy Trinity, planned from as early as 1349 and probably built from 1350 onwards, passed to the king who granted both to St Mary Graces on 2 August of that year (*Cal Pat R*, 1350–4, 488). In the same year he also gave them the Basing and Henewode tenements (immediately to the south of Bedyngton's) and John Craunstoke's tenement to the south of that (*Cart Holy Trinity*, no. 958; *Cal Pat R*, 1350–4, 487–8) (Fig 5). The monks were occupying these in 1359, and by March 1364 they were apparently in the next houses to the north, behind the gatehouse – recorded for the first time that year – but there is no documentary evidence to suggest where they lived prior to 1353 (*Cart Holy Trinity*, no. 958).

As the first president of the new house, Edward chose Walter de Sancta Cruce, the former abbot of Garendon in Leicestershire. In February 1351 he asked Beaulieu (Hampshire) to send some of its monks to form the first community, and subjected the new foundation to Beaulieu as mother house and visitor (*Cal Close R*, 1349–54, 283, 370–1; 1354–60, 22; *Cal Pat R*, 1422–9, 89; TNA: PRO, E 210/1982).

Like all Cistercian houses this abbey was dedicated to St Mary the Virgin, but during the course of its history it was known by a confusing variety of names and seems to have retained some 'residual' dedications. Edward III founded it as 'the royal free chapel of St Mary of Graces' and this was what it was called during the first decade of its life (*Cal Close R*, 1349–54, 283; 1354–60, 22; 1360–4, 5; *Cal Pat R*, 1348–50, 484, 560; 1358–61, 34). Once, in June 1351, it was referred to as 'the royal free chapel of the Holy Trinity and of St Mary of

Fig 4 The principal features of the Black Death cemetery: the cemetery (OA2 and OA3) and chapel (B1) and documented boundaries by 1350 (Grainger et al 2008, period A2) (scale 1:1000)

Graces', a name derived from the dedication of the chapel in the preceding burial ground (*Cal Close R*, 1349–54, 370). By 1360 it began to be called 'the abbey of St Mary of Graces by the Tower of London', which remained the normal official formula for the rest of the medieval period (*Cal Pat R*, 1358–61, 34, 457; 1388–92, 364). The name 'Eastminster' has also occasionally been used to describe the abbey, but this appears to be a purely post-medieval invention (Clapham 1915, 353).

The Cistercians probably used the chapel of Holy Trinity as their first church during the early part of the monastery's life (Clapham 1915, 354). This is suggested by Edward III's early – from 1350 onwards – name for the abbey and by a reference in April 1358 to the abbot and five monks in the chapel (*Cal Pat R*, 1358–61, 34). There was also a bequest in October 1358 to the chapel of St Mary (*Cal Husting Wills*, ii, 131). There is no specific mention of work on the 'new'

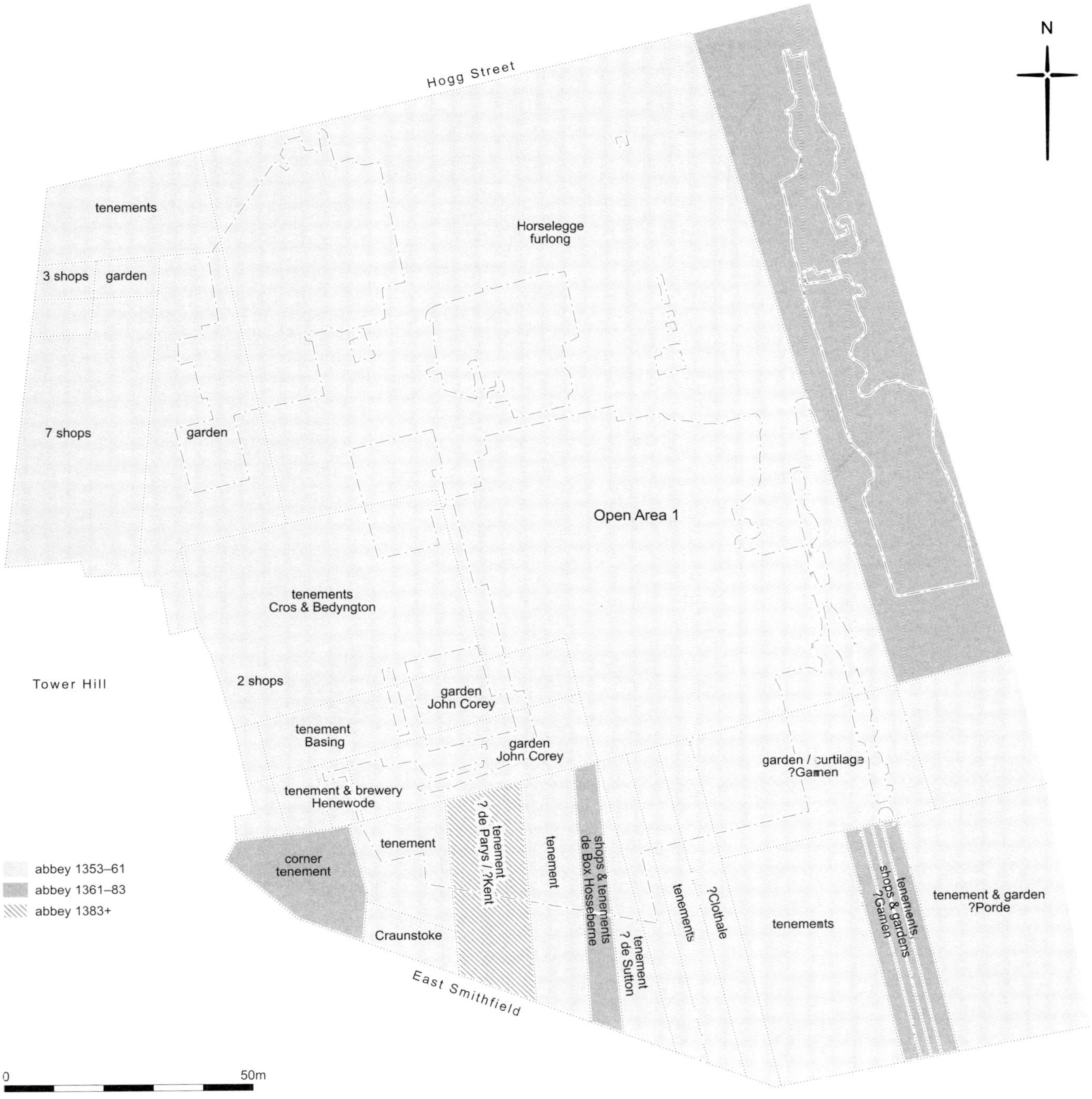

Fig 5 Probable documented boundaries of property held by the abbey of St Mary Graces and others on Tower Hill and East Smithfield, 1353–83 (scale 1:1250)

church before 1361 (*Cal Close R*, 1360–4, 179). In June 1353, two months before the abbey formally acquired the property on which the chapel of Holy Trinity stood, John Tyrington, a royal mason who had worked on St Stephen's Chapel, Westminster, the Tower postern and Kennington Palace, was appointed to start work on the monastery buildings with 12 carpenters, masons and tilers (Harvey 1984, 304; *Cal Pat R*, 1350–4, 465, 471).

Archaeological evidence

Prior to the construction of their church, which apparently took place from 1361 onwards – certainly from 1353 onwards, and possibly before – the Cistercians used the chapel of Holy Trinity, identified as Building 1, as their first church, constructing a 'temporary' or 'transitional' monastic complex immediately to the south of the chapel, which consisted ultimately of a stone cloister (B3) and possibly a refectory with dormitory above (B2) (Fig 6). Unusually, these initial buildings, here constructed of stone, would survive until the suppression in 1539. It is also possible that a number of other stratigraphically early features (in OA1) represent further, even earlier temporary monastic structures, this time of timber, which were soon superseded.

The Henewode tenement (OA1)

A number of levelling layers in the area of the Henewode tenement and brewery (Fig 5) were truncated by the foundations of the south-west corner of the cloister (B3) (Fig 6). They may represent the backfilling of a depression left by the underlying pre-Black Death quarrying (period A1: Grainger et al 2008, 7–9). Three small trenches cut these layers and were themselves cut by the walls of the cloister and Building 2. They were truncated to 9.22m OD or below, the internal ground surface in the east cloister alley having been lowered in the post-medieval period. To the east, truncated by the east garth wall, was a well. This survived only to a maximum upper level of 8.91m OD because of post-medieval landscaping in the garth. The well shaft was in excess of 2.3m deep and had a diameter of 1.0m. No evidence was found to suggest how the well was lined. Most of the medieval pottery from these contexts was coarse Surrey-Hampshire border ware (CBW), with small amounts of south Hertfordshire-type greyware (SHER), London-type ware (LOND) and Mill Green ware (MG).

The ? chapel of Holy Trinity (B1)

This building has been described and discussed in the preceding monograph as part of the Black Death cemetery (Grainger et al

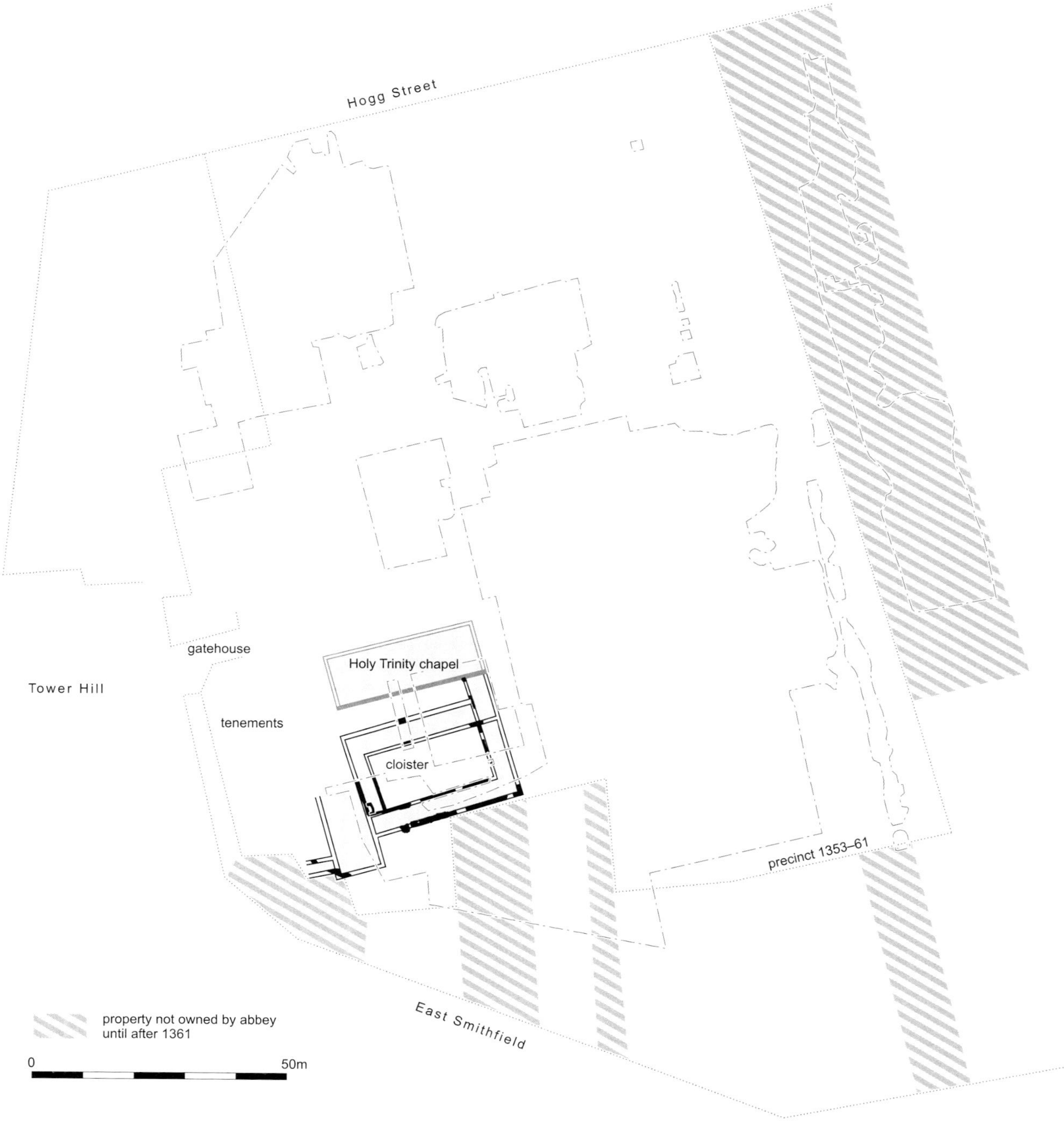

Fig 6 The principal archaeological features, 1350–61 (period B1): above – overall (scale 1:1250); facing page – detail (scale 1:400)

N
Building 1
Holy Trinity chapel
Building 3
cloister
Building 2
refectory/dormitory
precinct 1353–61
0
10m

2008, 18), but a brief description is included here. A short length of wall foundation was clearly earlier than the east garth wall of the cloister (B3) that abutted it to the south (Fig 6). The structure represented by this foundation may not have been particularly substantial: though the foundation reached a depth of 8.78m OD, it was only 0.6m wide and would have carried a wall slightly thinner than this. The later truncation removed all further trace of Building 1 as originally built within the areas excavated, although a brick-edged tile floor, clearly of a later date (below, 2.5), was found to the north of the projected line of this wall.

The ? first dormitory and refectory (B2)

The west wall of the west cloister alley (B3) was formed by an earlier building (B2) (Fig 6). Only 5.9m of its length survived, but its overall original length may have been at least 22.0m. The foundations reached a depth of 8.86m OD, over a metre shallower than the other, outer, cloister alley walls. The offset between the foundations and the wall proper was at 9.60m OD, approximately 0.2m below that of the corresponding east garth wall. One course of the east face survived; this was of small hammer-dressed Kentish ragstone blocks, which suggests an external face intended to survive weathering.

To the south-west of this wall, beyond the limit of the site and beneath the East Smithfield modern pavement, were a group of foundations. These were found, and hastily recorded, in a British Telecom trench in 1985 (Mills 1985). They were apparently medieval, conceivably part of Building 2 and thus grouped with it.

The first cloister (B3)

The well and the three trenches (above, OA1) were backfilled with a compact mixture of clay and tile fragments, the similarity of the fills suggesting a single operation. A number of layers were found above the earlier quarry pits of Open Area 1 in the north of the garth and beneath the north and west cloister alleys. One layer contained eight pottery sherds suggesting a late 13th-century or later date, and one layer sealed the backfilled trenches and well. These layers were probably laid to prepare the ground surface for construction. Some of the material may have been upcast from the foundation trenches of Buildings 1–3.

Despite the fragmentary nature of the remains, the overall dimensions of the cloister can be given with some confidence (Fig 6). Internally, the cloister enclosure measured 29.0m east–west and 20.0m north–south. The dimensions of the garth were 10.6m x 22.0m. The north alley was approximately 3.8m wide, the south alley 3.25m wide, the west alley 2.85m wide, and the east alley between 2.75m and 3.0m wide. The space between the north alley and Building 1 was 4.25m wide.

The depth of the foundations was considerably greater than for buildings further north such as the presbytery and the nave (below, 2.4; Fig 9). The bases of the outer walls were found between 7.15m and 7.79m OD and of the inner between 8.11m and 8.60m OD. This foundation depth was noted for all the buildings of the south range (below, 2.4; Fig 9) and is in excess of what might be expected for the natural slope of the site. The medieval ground surface here was in general at 9.70m OD as opposed to 10.20m OD in the centre. The depth of these foundations may reflect a greater depth of the natural sands and gravels – on to which the better foundations were usually bedded – caused by the underlying quarrying or the need to counter problems caused by poor drainage.

The foundations of the outer walls of the cloister (B3) were generally between 1.1m and 1.3m wide, while those of the garth walls averaged 0.7m. The south and east outer walls survived above foundation level to a height of approximately 0.5m. The north and west faces of these walls were of roughly dressed chalk blocks, suggesting interior faces, while the south and east faces respectively were of coursed hammer-dressed Kentish ragstone designed to withstand weathering. Only the lowest course of the west garth wall survived. The west face of this wall had been removed in the post-medieval period and replaced by brick patching; the east face was composed of coursed hammer-dressed Kentish ragstone. The remainder of the cloister walls survived only as foundations, and the north alley outer wall had been largely robbed while a post-medieval wall replaced the garth wall. There may have been a buttress or sleeper wall across the north end of the east alley. A foundation was also laid across the east end of the north alley, and a similar foundation was inserted across the south end of the west alley. These two foundations may have carried walls above them, but it is more likely that they were sleeper walls used to strengthen the foundations, perhaps to help carry the load of first-floor chambers or to counter problems caused by poor drainage. Another wall, continuing the line of the east garth wall, abutted the south wall of the chapel of Holy Trinity (B1). This would indicate that there was a short passage connecting the cloister to the chapel and that an open area – a passage or 'lane' – possibly separated the cloister from the chapel.

In the angle created by Building 2 and the inserted wall across the south end of the west alley, an L-shaped foundation was inserted. Its overall length was 2.7m, it had walls 0.7m wide, and it reached a depth of 8.14m OD – well below that of the two walls. The interior edges were rough and undressed, and created a cavity 0.5m wide and 1.7m long. Since this foundation cut well down into the natural sands and gravels, it may have been a soakaway for water.

Only Brian Davison's trial work (Davison 1972, 21) revealed any possible evidence of monastic stratification in the north alley. A mortar surface, which carried the faint impressions of tiles laid parallel with the alignment of the cloister, was found at approximately 9.0m OD, 0.85m lower than the probable surface found in the south alley described below. If this was medieval it may have been the base of a tomb or possibly a storage chamber.

In the south alley, make-up layers of sand, silt, chalk and mortar rubble were laid to raise the level to approximately

9.85m OD. These were cut by a number of postholes. The postholes and the underlying make-up produced only four sherds, of late 13th- to mid 14th-century date. The postholes were sealed by a further layer of levelling which in turn was cut by a second series of postholes. The layers contained coarse Surrey-Hampshire border ware (CBW) and a jug sherd in late medieval Hertfordshire glazed ware (LMHG). As a whole, more CBW was found in this building than in any other of period B1 (total 325g). This was sealed by the remnants of a thin compact layer of mortar [3939] (Fig 7) which showed considerable signs of wear. This layer also contained medieval pottery, including a sherd of Saintonge whiteware (SAIN) and a sherd of Cheam whiteware (CHEA). This sequence of layers and postholes represents the preparation of the interior with scaffolding to facilitate work on the superstructure of the south alley. Both sets of postholes formed lines running parallel to the south wall. It is unclear whether this activity was confined to the initial phase of construction in the building or whether it, all or in part, represents subsequent refurbishment. The mortar surface clearly represents a floor level, although it is unclear if this was merely a temporary surface laid to facilitate building work or bedding for a floor proper.

Within the west alley only a number of apparently medieval levelling layers survived the post-medieval remodelling. Only one of these layers, an extensive make-up [4542], produced medieval pottery dating from *c* 1350–*c* 1500. A number of dump layers were also found within the garth, clearly abutting the west inner wall and raising the interior to 9.70m OD; these layers were undated.

Fig 7 The south cloister alley (B3) under excavation, showing floor [3939], looking west

Discussion, 1350–61 (period B1)

The pre-existing cemetery chapel of Holy Trinity, built in 1350–3, was probably used as the first church. The chapel may have been under construction from early 1350 onwards, when the land that it was apparently built on, the Cros/Bedyngton tenement, was acquired by John Corey; however, there is some documentary evidence from wills of the period to suggest that the chapel was at least planned from April 1349, well before the foundation of the monastery in 1350 (*Cal Husting Wills*, i, 651, 679). The first monks did not arrive until after February 1351, while construction work on the first 'temporary' cloister (B3) and the possible dormitory/refectory (B2) in Open Area 1 could not begin until August 1353, when the king granted the abbey the Basing, Henewode and Craunstoke tenements with the chapel and cemetery. It is unknown where the monks lived before this date, whether in pre-existing tenements or purpose-built temporary structures, since there is no documentary evidence for it. The features excavated in Open Area 1 may be the remains of earlier, probably timber, temporary buildings occupied by the monks or masons, but, if they are associated with the monastic occupation, this cannot have occurred before 1353. Equally the features could relate to the pre-monastic tenements.

The later layout of the abbey suggests that the chapel (B1) is likely to have been a maximum of 30m long by 12m wide, taking the form of a simple rectangular structure with a main door originally on the west or north side. This would have made it similar to the cemetery chapel established by Sir Walter Manny on Spitalcroft at the West Smithfield Black Death cemetery site, a rectangular building 29.6m long and 11.6m wide which became the conventual church of the Charterhouse (Barber and Thomas 2002, 14).

The documentary evidence appears to contradict such an early construction date for any cloister on the site. The two references to cloisters suggest that they were not built by 1368 or by 1383 (*Reg Sudbury*, 83; *Cal Pat R*, 1381–5, 306). However, the 1368 reference is specifically to the 'church cloister and necessary houses not yet built', which may suggest a programme of construction associated with the later church. There is no specific reference to work on the church before 1361, but masons under Tyrington were at work on the site in 1353. Conceivably they were working on the cloister described above (Harvey 1984, 304; *Cal Pat R*, 1350–4, 465, 471). The land required for the cloister (B3) – but not for the kitchen (B11) and storeroom (B12), constructed with the refectory (B13) (below, 2.4; Fig 9) – had been acquired as early as 1353. The use of Kentish ragstone on the south face of its south wall strongly suggests that the cloister was built some time before all the property required for the construction of the south range was acquired (Fig 5). The de Parys tenement to the south of the cloister may not have been acquired until after 1383 (TNA: PRO, E 326/2324; SC 6/1258/1, m 2). The south cloister wall follows the west–east boundary between John Corey's garden to the north and the de Parys and other East Smithfield tenements to the south (Fig 6). The alignment of the first cloister, and the first dormitory/refectory (B2), diverges fractionally from that of the other, stratigraphically later buildings of the south range such as the refectory (B13) which are associated with the later church and chapter house in a fairly traditional Cistercian manner

The cloister, Building 3, was a very unusual shape for a Cistercian cloister, forming a small rectangle rather than a square, and being separated from the chapel by an open area. Although the archaeological evidence for the extent of this cloister complex is perhaps equivocal, the 1635 plan (Fig 58) shows and describes it as a cloister with chambers above. The use of possible sleeper foundations across the north and west alleys may suggest that these chambers were medieval in origin and that strengthened foundations were required to support a first floor. Possibly this first floor would have contained private chambers. The narrowness of the cloister alleys, particularly that of the northern alley, suggests that this cloister was not used for study but functioned as simple passageways, as proposed for the Austin Friars, Leicester (Mellor and Pearce 1981, 23). The probable use of a passage to the north of the cloister is a unique feature in a British Cistercian monastery, and appears slightly odd here as it reduces the already limited space available for the cloister for no readily apparent reason. Although lanes were commonly constructed on the west sides of cloisters for the use of lay brothers, this can hardly have been the case here. Such passages were often constructed in friaries where the public used the preaching nave, as at Walsingham and London, to provide greater seclusion for the cloister (Fig 60) (Clapham and Godfrey 1913, 247; Butler 1984, 123–36). It is possible that the laity did have access to the chapel of Holy Trinity, as it was founded in the first instance to serve the Black Death cemetery, but there is no documentary record of this.

The identification of Building 2 as originally a temporary, combined dormitory and refectory seems most probable, since the monks were apparently occupying the area of the de Henewode tenement in June 1359 (TNA: PRO, E 40/13839).

2.4 The church and claustral complex, 1361–*c* 1400 (period B2)

Documentary evidence

The chronology of the abbey's acquisition of land to complete the precinct after 1361 can to some extent be mapped (Fig 5). On 7 May 1361 the corner tenement at the junction of Tower Hill and East Smithfield was acquired by the abbey via a Crown purchase (*Cal Pat R*, 1361–4, 20; TNA: PRO, E 210/5125, 5843, 7824, 8920; E 326/2313). At various dates in 1362 tenements on the opposite, south, side of East Smithfield, stretching east from Tower Hill and on both sides of the entrance to St Katherine's Lane, were bought by the abbey via purchases by the Crown and Corey (*Cal Pat R*, 1361–4, 176–7, 246, 272–3; TNA: PRO, E 210/1661, 5239, 6811). These were never included in the precinct. In August 1363 Corey was still buying up quitrents in parishes in the east part of the city, perhaps to contribute to the income of the abbey (LMA, CLA/023/DW/01/91/140). On 8 November 1365 the stone hall to the north-west of the cemetery and other adjacent tenements and gardens extending south to the gatehouse were acquired from John Corey who had bought all these in 1350 (*Cal Close R*, 1364–8, 211–12; *Cal Pat R*, 1364–7, 180–1; *Cat Anc Deeds*, ii, 105; TNA: PRO, E 40/2640; E 210/9098, 9368; E 326/2318, 2326; E 315/47, no. 110). On 12 October 1370, two tenements were acquired from William Gamen, filling a gap in the East Smithfield frontage (TNA: PRO, E 326/9431). Then on 1 March 1372 the tenements of Hosseberne and Clothale filled further gaps in the East Smithfield frontage, to be followed on 22 May 1376 by a strip of land on the east side of the toft (ie the Horselegge furlong) (*Cat Anc Deeds*, iv, 160; *Cal Close R*, 1364–8, 490; TNA: PRO, C 66/305, m 37; E 40/2212). Later, probably between 1383 and 1391, the tenement of Richard de Parys to the east of the abbot's garden completed the East Smithfield street frontage (TNA: PRO, E 326/2324; SC 6/1258/1, m 2).

In March 1361 Tyrington and Corey were appointed to supervise the work of 24 men at the abbot's wages; the commission stated that the king wished to hasten on the work as much as possible (*Cal Pat R*, 1358–61, 567). Edward III granted £100 for the work on the new church in March 1361, but in 1368 it was still not built (*Cal Close R*, 1360–4, 179; *Reg Sudbury*, 83). In 1361 and 1364 the monks were said to be 'in their monastery', but there was evidently no chapter house (TNA: PRO, E 42/447; E 210/5843). In February 1368 they were living in poverty on alms from Edward III; the church, cloister and necessary houses for the abbot, monks and their servants were not yet built (*Reg Sudbury*, 83). In May 1368 a chantry was founded in the 'chapel of Holy Trinity at the new cemetery' (*Cal Husting Wills*, ii, 160). In 1374 the monks were granted a papal relaxation of penance for contributors in aid of their building. In November 1379 John of Gaunt and the other feoffees granted the abbey 100 marks per annum from the income of the Kent manors (Chapter 3.4), until the endowment was properly arranged. This money was intended to support the abbot and monks, and to fund the construction of buildings necessary for their practice of religion (TNA: PRO, E 329/412). In November 1380 they were said to have few possessions and buildings (*Cal Pap Letters*, iv, 199; *VCH* 1909, 462, n25; TNA: PRO, E 210/9947).

Throughout the 1380s and 1390s the foundation and endowment were regarded as incomplete (*Cal Close R*, 1385–9, 16; 1388–92, 236; *Cal Pat R*, 1396–9, 389; TNA: PRO, SC 8/E711A; SC 8/989; SC 8/9443). The south range of the main cloister (consisting of the dormitory, refectory and infirmary) and the southern boundary wall of the precinct could not have been built until all the properties along the East Smithfield frontage had been acquired in the 1380s (Fig 5). In August 1383 the abbey received the grant of the Gravesend houses (Chapter 3.4) to build the dormitory, refectory, cloister and other buildings (*Cal Pat R*, 1381–5, 306). In April 1391 it was pardoned for felling and selling trees at Wateryngbury (only newly acquired) to build new houses and buildings in the abbey (*Cal Pat R*, 1388–92, 397). Evidently some of the most fundamental structures of the abbey had not been completed more than 40 years after the foundation.

There is a paucity of detailed information about the monastic layout at the time of its fullest extent. There are hardly any surviving leases and only one account, dated 1391–2, which gives much idea of the building programme (TNA: PRO, SC 6/1258/1, ms 1–3) However, this account and other documents provide some detail about the church itself. It was able to receive burials by 1375 (*Cal Husting Wills*, ii, 182) but work was still continuing in 1380 (TNA: PRO, E 210/9947), and it was not until 1391–2 that it was paved and doorways were added to it: 650 new 'pavements' and 3700 paving tiles were bought for the choir and laid, while further pavements were bought for the choir, the vestry and the area around the high altar (1450 pavements) and freestone doorways with wooden doors were made for the vestry in this year (TNA: PRO, SC 6/1258/1, ms 2, 3). Iron candlesticks were also provided for the church that year. The west door was directly behind the gatehouse (TNA: PRO, SC 6/HenVIII/2396, m 1). The nave was probably five or six bays in length, as is implied in Wyngaerde's view (Fig 56).

The high altar is probably to be identified with the altar of St Mary the Virgin mentioned in 1365, though this may have been in the earlier chapel of Holy Trinity during the 1350s and 1360s, while the church was being built (TNA: PRO, E 326/5595). In 1391 the high altar had images of the Holy Trinity and St Mary; two little wooden altars were made in front of them and two stools in front of the whole altar. Also provided for the choir in 1391–2 were a 'roundel' (perhaps a bundle or disc?) of white rods, benches with footrests, and a psalter; the silver 'tribulis' (censer) was also mended and cleaned (TNA: PRO, SC 6/1258/1, ms 2, 3). By 1529 there was a rood screen, at least on the south side of the church (TNA: PRO, PROB 11/23/10).

The pope's statement that the church was founded in honour of St Anne suggests that the chapel of St Anne existed by 1374 (*Cal Pap Letters*, iv, 199). In 1383 the abbey was said to contain the head of St Anne, but this is the only reference (*Cal Pat R*, 1381–5). The chapel was on the south side of the church (Wagner 1956, 143–4). Also in the church were altars to All Saints in 1375 and St Katherine in 1400 (*Cal Close R*, 1399–1401, 326; *Cal Pat R*, 1399–1401, 457; TNA: PRO, E 326/5599; GL, MS 25121/953).

A new ladder was bought for the bell tower in 1391 (SC 6/1258/1, ms 2, 3). At the Dissolution it contained four bells weighing 39cwt 1 quarter 14lb (TNA: PRO, SC 6/HenVIII/2427). It seems likely that much of the church roof and the spire were covered with lead, for at the suppression 16 fothers of lead were melted down at the abbey, probably in 1540 (TNA: PRO, SC 6/HenVIII/2427; 2383, m 42v).

By the end of the 14th century the church contained a tomb for Sir Nicholas Loveyne (d 1375), the lord of East Smithfield, on the south side of the choir (Wagner 1956, 143–4). The contract for Loveyne's tomb (Chapter 3.8; Fig 71) was granted to Henry Lakenham, a London marbler, in 1376 (TNA: PRO,

E 210/6436; Blair 1980). In January 1376 a chantry was endowed in the abbey for Loveyne (ibid, 68). One of Loveyne's two wives, either Margaret de Bereford or Margaret de Vere, who died before 1370, was noted in 1533 as being 'beside him on the floor' (Sheppard 1965–8; Wagner 1956, 143–4). Sir Simon Burley, a tutor and favourite of Richard II, was executed by the Merciless Parliament on 5 May 1388 and buried in the presbytery (Lewis 1937, 668–9). In 1392 John of Gaunt, Duke of Lancaster, contributed £10 towards the cost of Sir Simon Burley's tomb (TNA: PRO, DL 28/3/2). Another documented early burial was that of Sir Andrew Cavendish, interred in the chapel of St Anne in 1396 (TNA: PRO, PROB 11/2/45). Burials were in the charge of the sacristan, who collected burial fees and offerings in the church. In 1391 this office was farmed out to Brother Roger (TNA: PRO, SC 6/1258/1, m 1).

An indenture of February 1365 was sealed 'in the place of chapter' (*in loco capitulari*) at the monastery, implying that there was no chapter house as yet (TNA: PRO, E 326/5595). The first deed dated in the chapter house is from July 1375, and it was used regularly for this purpose from then on (GL, MS 25121/953; TNA: PRO, E 326/5599; *Cal Pat R*, 1391–6, 138; 1396–9, 330; TNA: PRO, E 135/12/14; E 210/9947; E 326/5712; E 329/7; E 303/10/294, 354). Mats were bought for it in 1391 (TNA: PRO, SC 6/1258/1, m 1).

The infirmary was entirely built in the year 1391–2 in the south-east corner of the precinct. Its foundations were made of chalk and it was paved with tiles (6000 for this and other houses). It had freestone chimneys in chambers and Walter Tyler tiled the roof. The doors and windows were made with 'estrichebord' (imported Baltic planking), two batches of 400 being bought for this and the new tenements (TNA: PRO, SC 6/1258/1, ms 2, 3). The monks may have lived in the chambers in the infirmary rather than together in the dormitory (TNA: PRO, C 1/9/358). References to the hospice in 1425 may refer to the infirmary or to a guesthouse by the abbot's lodging (TNA: PRO, SC 6/917/16). A dormitory was in existence by 1402 (*Cal Pap Letters*, v, 517, 602).

The refectory is probably to be identified with the building called the 'halle'. Bowls were bought for this in 1425, and a refectory is also mentioned (TNA: PRO, SC 6/917/16). A kitchen was operating by 1391 when masons did some work in it, and pewter vessels, iron candlesticks and food were bought for it. It had a staff of three cooks and several pages (TNA: PRO, SC 6/1258/1, ms 1, 2, 5).

In 1391 there are references to the abbot's chapel (in which a cupboard was made), the abbot's hospice and the abbot's garden on the west side of the monastery (TNA: PRO, SC 6/1258/1, ms 1, 2, 3). In 1516 Richard Pest died in the abbot's chamber (TNA: PRO, C 1/426/49).

The gatehouse was to the west of the church by 1359. In 1391 William Ketel and his wife were the keepers of the postern (TNA: PRO, SC 6/1258/1, m 1). A house and chamber were built to the east of the abbot's garden in 1391–2 and a common store house was clearly in existence before 1425, as were a number of tenements in the precinct (TNA: PRO, SC 6/1258/1, m 2; SC 6/917/16).

Archaeological evidence

The establishment of the permanent claustral complex commenced after 1361 with the construction of the monastic church (Fig 9). A long rectangular presbytery (B4) was built first, including a central tower but no transepts, and an aisled nave was then added (B6). All three elements – presbytery, tower and nave – were probably part of a single design concept, the execution of which was completed in rapid stages and which was mendicant in style (below, and Chapter 3.2). The church included a porch (B8) and vestry (B7), both to the south of the presbytery. Traces of possible masons' lodges (B5) pre-dating the nave and chapter house were found to the south of the presbytery. The interior of the nave included evidence for the position of the rood screen and at least two chapels, one tentatively identified as the chapel of St Anne (room 6a). The chapter house (B9) was built to the south of the church together with a cloister enclosure (OA4) into which were later inserted the east and possibly south alleys (B10) of the cloister itself, but, significantly, no north alley; the west side of the cloister garth was formed by the east wall of the retained Holy Trinity chapel (B1). The construction programme for the south range incorporated the earlier cloister (B3) and ? first dormitory and refectory (B2), and included the abbot's garden (OA5), a kitchen (B11), a cellared storeroom (B12), a refectory (B13), a kitchen yard (OA6) and a refectory yard (OA7). This period of construction was completed with the building of the infirmary (B15) and what may have been a house and chamber, or the abbot's hospice (B14). A burial area (OA2) to the north-west of the church is also assigned to this period. It may have contained later 14th-century epidemic burials and gone out of use early in the 15th century.

The ? chapel of Holy Trinity (B1)

This ceased to be the monastic church between 1361 and *c* 1380, but continued in use as a chapel still called the chapel of Holy Trinity (Fig 9).

The ? first dormitory and refectory (B2), now the ? abbot's lodging

At some point during this period, this building may have become part of the abbot's lodging, situated near the gatehouse to the west and subsequently reused after the Dissolution as a house by Sir Arthur Darcy (Fig 9).

The first cloister (B3), now secondary cloister

The first cloister remained in use throughout the monastic period, probably as a secondary cloister, and possibly with sleeping accommodation above for some if not all of the monks. The 1635 plan (Fig 58) records the cloister with chambers above, which may have been medieval in origin (Fig 9).

The presbytery (B4)

The presbytery was not constructed as a true rectangle. The walls survived only as fragments of foundations and a series of later robber trenches, but the general outline can be traced (Fig 8).

The foundations reached a depth of 9.00m OD and were 1.3–1.4m wide where measurable. They were cut from a medieval ground surface at approximately 10.00–10.20m OD, probably the highest point on the site in the medieval period. Post-Dissolution robber trenches had largely removed the south wall; at only one point did the wall survive above medieval ground level, in the form of a south-facing square buttress 0.7m long positioned 3.0m from the eastern end of the wall. The west end of the presbytery had been removed by a robber trench, which was itself cut by a number of graves within the nave (B6); this represents the demolition of the western end prior to the construction of the nave. The east end survived only below foundation level, but the form is clear. The eastern buttresses were 1.75m long and the southern ones 1.25m long. The north wall was severely truncated, with only two small fragments of foundation, together with the foundations of a buttress which corresponded to that on the south wall, indicating its line. The north buttress was 1.5m long, somewhat larger than its southern counterpart.

An internal pilaster buttress foundation along the south wall may have been an original feature. The main wall line survived only as a robber trench, destroying the relationship, although to the east of this the foundation including the south buttress did suggest a similar internal pilaster on its north face, and the thickening of the foundations here was an original feature. A later internal robber trench at 90° to the south wall represents a respond *c* 3m from the west end, indicating the location and foundations of the tower.

Only next to the south wall line did medieval floor surfaces survive. Immediately to the east of the robbed respond, make-up layers were laid for a tile floor at 10.08m OD. This floor was extremely abraded, with few of the tiles remaining *in situ*, none surviving whole, and most of them only represented by impressions left in the mortar bedding. Two postholes cut this floor. A third posthole and two stakeholes may also have cut the floor but the relationship was no longer extant. To the west of the respond, rubble make-up was laid for a tile floor at 10.06m OD. This floor [13679] was again badly abraded, but was clearly composed of two types of tile laid square on to the alignment of the building. Immediately to the north of and abutting the surviving tiles were two fragmentary tiles set on edge and corresponding to the north edge of the underlying burial [13545].

A limited number of burials in the presbytery may be 14th-century in date (Fig 9). Only in the case of burial [13545] (not analysed) was a relationship with an interior floor surface evident, and only in the case of burials [16052] and [16076] was there any intercutting between the burials, with burial [16052] slightly cutting burial [16076]. Burial [16052], of an adult (otherwise of unknown age and sex) is of particular interest. This individual had been decapitated at the fourth cervical vertebra (Chapter 5.10; Fig 115) and was almost certainly Sir Simon Burley, excecuted on 5 May 1388 (Lewis 1937). This means that burial [16076], of a possible male aged ≥46 years, was interred before 1388. This individual had an unhealed fracture of the clavicle, which had later developed osteoarthritis (Chapter 5.10; Fig 113). A further coffined burial [13554] (not analysed) was found close to the south wall of the choir between the internal pilaster buttresses.

A small quantity of pottery was recovered, including a sherd of London-type ware (LOND) from a posthole. The pottery from two of the graves comprises Kingston-type ware (KING) and LOND, the date ranges of which reach *c* 1350. These sherds must be derived from the pre-monastic ground surface.

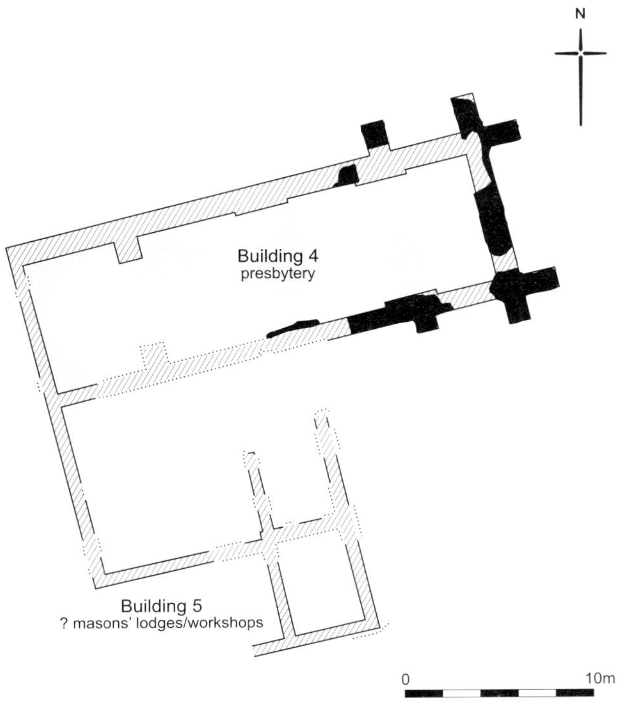

Fig 8 Detailed plan of the presbytery (B4) and ? masons' lodges/workshops (B5) (period B2) (scale 1:400)

? Masons' lodges/workshops (B5)

To the south of the presbytery (B4) a number of silt layers overlay the earlier medieval ground surface. They had no direct relationship with the presbytery but clearly pre-dated the robber trenches described below. These layers may have been the upper fills of the quarry pits, but could have been levelling prior to, or the upcast from, the digging of the presbytery foundations. The robber trenches cutting these layers pre-dated the construction of the nave (B6) and the chapter house (B9) and were aligned on the presbytery (Fig 8); they represent parts of a structure, or structures, contemporary with the presbytery but subsequently demolished prior to the construction of the nave. These trenches were not of uniform depth and width: none was deeper than 9.40m OD, and only one was wider than

1.0m, with most being between 0.7m and 0.9m wide. All contained a high concentration of fine chalk and mortar rubble with occasional fragments of Reigate stone. One trench was some distance to the south of the other trenches and was heavily truncated by a 19th-century wall, but its appearance and alignment suggested that it belonged to this group. No features associated with the interiors of these structures survived.

The trenches may have been workshops or lodges for the masons, carpenters and labourers employed on the site. If so, they are one of only two sets of later medieval lodges known, the other, dated *c* 1398–1400, being at the Carthusian Mount Grace Priory in Yorkshire (G Coppack, pers comm).

The nave (B6)

Only the eastern end of the nave survived within the area of excavation (Fig 9; Fig 10). The robber trench that removed the western end of the presbytery (B4) indicates that the (primary) west wall of the presbytery was largely demolished prior to or during the construction of the nave, the east walls of which then abutted the presbytery.

The north wall of the nave had been entirely robbed by a trench which suggested that the foundations had reached an approximate depth of 9.3m OD and were less than 1.2m wide. No trace remained of the nave east wall north of the presbytery. To the south of the presbytery, the line of the east wall was

*Fig 9 The principal archaeological features, 1361–*c *1400 (period B2): above – overall (scale 1:1250); facing page – detail (scale 1:400)*

N
church
room 6d
[12480]
[16052]
Building 4
presbytery
room 6b
room 6c
Building 6
nave
Building 8
porch
Building 7
?vestry
room 6a
Building 9
chapter house
Open Area 4
cloister enclosure
Building 15
infirmary
Building 1
Holy Trinity chapel
Building 10
cloister
Building 15
infirmary
Open Area 7
Building 13
refectory
Open
Area 6
Building 3
cloister
Building 11
kitchen
Building 2
? abbot's lodging
Open Area 5
? abbot's garden
Building 12
Building
14
0
10m

Fig 10 The piers and south wall of the nave (B6) from above, with the porch (B8) and east cloister alley (B10) to the south, looking east (2.0m scales)

represented by a further robber trench and a stub of wall to the south. The foundations of the east wall stub reached a depth of 9.40m OD and were 0.9m wide. The last vestiges of the lowest course of the wall above this survived, and were sufficient to indicate an internal face of chalk blocks and an external face of Kentish ragstone blocks. A buttress projected eastwards here and was original but did not survive above ground level. The south nave wall had not been robbed but an 18th-century drain had largely removed what remained up till then (Fig 10). This wall was of continuous build with the east wall stub but more substantial: the foundations reached a depth of 8.98m OD and were 1.4m wide. There were two original substantial south buttresses. The lowest course of the west buttress survived above ground level and was faced in roughly dressed Kentish ragstone blocks.

The west wall was not found within the area of excavation, and might have lain beneath the Johnson Smirke Building (Fig 21). Excavation in the north basement wing of this building failed to locate any trace of this or of the north wall, or of any other features that could be associated with the nave. Enough stratification survived along the western edge of the basement to indicate that the nave had not extended that far. This suggests an east–west length of *c* 25m or less. The internal width would have been approximately 18.5m north–south.

Four pier bases were part of the original construction of the surviving eastern end of the nave (Fig 10). Only the foundations remained, and only the south-east pier base survived to medieval ground level at 10.16m OD. All were approximately 2m square and cut to a depth of just over 9.00m OD. The pier bases give the width of the nave north and south aisles as approximately 4.25m, making the central portion of the nave approximately 7m wide. Two and a half bays of each aisle remained in the area of excavation. The easternmost bay was approximately 5.5m east–west, the next bay *c* 5m, and the westernmost surviving bay in excess of 3.5m. (The intermediate bay, at *c* 5m, probably represents the standard interval corresponding to one perch, or 16.5ft (5.029m).) Architectural fragments from the nave arcade (<A36>–<A42>) found in post-Dissolution layers and structures, and comparable to nave arcades constructed at Canterbury and Arundel in the late 14th century, are shown in Fig 63 and Fig 77 (Chapters 3.3 and 5.1).

Two probable respond foundations for an arch to support the central tower were constructed, set at the junction between the presbytery and the nave. These were of similar construction to the four pier bases, though they were shallower, reaching only to approximately 9.4m OD. The south foundation, at the junction of the nave east wall and the presbytery south wall, was the better preserved of the two, though even here only the lowest course survived. The tiny fragment of foundation to the north possibly indicates a similar arrangement there. This foundation lay 0.25m to the west of the line of the south foundation, suggesting that the junction between the two buildings was asymmetrical and mimicked the original line of the western end of the presbytery (Fig 9).

A chalk foundation and robber trenches (which removed much of the foundation) were found in line with, and between, the pier bases and were much disturbed by later burials in the nave. The depths of the trenches varied considerably, the base of the shallowest being at 9.50m OD and the deepest at 8.96m OD, and they were a maximum of 1.3m wide. The trenches probably represent the removal of benches or, less probably, screen walls inserted into the nave arcade but not keyed into the pier bases, before the rood screen was constructed. Any such walls appear to have been destroyed at an early date.

A posthole and a number of dump layers represent stratigraphically early activity within the nave. Only one of the layers ([13781]) contained dating evidence in the form of two pottery sherds, one of which, of Cheam whiteware (CHEA), suggests that this layer at least was deposited later than *c* 1380. A number of burials are considered to be reasonably early, that is, probably late 14th-century in date. These burials were at the base of, or low down in, an intercutting sequence and/or do not appear to fit the later pattern of burial outlined for those partitioned areas of the nave identified below (2.5). This is admittedly a somewhat arbitrary division, and many of the burials could be later.

Burials [12342], [12377], [12455],[12480], [16017], [16023] and [16045] (the latter two not analysed) formed a compact cluster in the north aisle which does not apparently conform to the pattern of burial established for the nave west of the rood screen (room 6c) and the ?chapel in the north aisle (room 6d). Burial [12377] was that of an unclassified subadult. Burial [12342] was of a probable female aged 26–35 in a coffin, as was burial [12455] but without a coffin. Burial [12480], a male aged 36–45, was the only burial within the church which indicated the use of charcoal or ash as a coffin lining, similar to those found in the Black Death cemetery (Grainger et al 2008, 20) and external cemeteries (Chapter 3.8). The charcoal contained two eel and six herring vertebral centra. This individual also suffered from diffuse idiopathic skeletal hyperostosis (DISH) (Chapters 3.7 and 5.10). The remaining burials were a ?male adult [16017] or not analysed ([16023] and [16045]).

A similar cluster of burials – [13663], [13928], [13931] and [13943] – existed in the south aisle. Burial [13663] was that of a male aged ≥46 years; the rest were unclassified adults (ie of indeterminate sex and age category).

In the central part of the nave, burial [13906] was cut in half by [13831] (room 6b) and the skeleton survived only as a stain. Burial [13830], a male aged ≥46 years, was not severely truncated by any later burial, but clearly pre-dated the construction of a beamslot. This slot marked the position of a screen, which is interpreted as the rood screen dividing the area immediately to the west of the choir – the choir entry or 'retrochoir' (room 6b) – from the nave (room 6c).

THE CHAPEL OF ? ST ANNE (ROOM 6a)

To the east of the rood screen, the easternmost bay of the south aisle of the nave was separated from its neighbour to the west by a beamslot, which represents the position of a screen, a partition removed in the post-Dissolution stripping of the nave. Two small layers of sand, mortar and tile fragments were found to the west of the screen slot, and two floor tiles were laid on edge to strengthen the side at that point. To the east of the slot, make-up layers were laid in preparation for a tiled floor. This floor was laid at approximately 10.3m OD, with the tiles square on to the north–south and west–east axes of the building. The south-eastern fragment of this floor which survived *in situ* abutting the south wall of the nave almost certainly retained the original pattern (Fig 11). Immediately adjacent to the south wall was a row of 11 plain glazed tiles arranged alternately light and dark. Towards the eastern end of the next row to the north were two examples of Penn design <T52>; and to the west of these was a double row of 15 examples of Penn design <T20> (Fig 12; Table 15). Both designs consisted of four-tile repeating patterns. The other two surviving areas of flooring to the north and west of this original area had been disturbed by burials (Fig 33; Fig 34) and relaid in a slightly careless manner with some disregard for the decorative design of the original floor. Here the flooring was made up of a mixture of decorated and plain glazed tiles. The decorative Penn designs present were <T11>, <T34>, <T39>, <T40>, <T47> and <T60> (Fig 12; Table 16). The plain tiles are identified as Low Countries imports or English products. The English examples include a number of small tiles in MOL fabric 1810, a fabric normally associated with tiles, decorated and plain glazed, manufactured at Penn in Buckinghamshire during the 14th century. These tiles were very worn and it is not possible to tell if they were once decorated. Also present were small tiles in fabric 2318 with traces of yellow glaze. The imported tiles are in fabrics 2850, 2323 and 2504; these fabrics stand out because of their silty or calcium carbonate inclusions, and nail holes are visible in the corners of all these tiles. Although many of the tiles have worn surfaces, traces of green and yellow glaze are visible on the tile edges. Two sizes of tile are present in fabrics 2323 and 2850, while some of the tiles in fabrics 2323 and 2504 appear to have been deliberately broken into smaller sizes and may possibly represent repairs (Table 17).

The north limit of room 6a was defined by a distinct break between this tile floor and the tile floor to the north in room 6b, and the remains of what may have been a later standing tomb or monument [13856] between the two rooms (below, 2.5; Fig 33; Fig 34). Though no cut for a beamslot was found, it seems likely that a partition existed between the south-east nave pier base and the tomb or monument, as well as to the east of the latter.

Burial [13727] (not analysed) occupied a central position within room 6a. Though the burial itself was not disturbed, most of its grave had been removed when grave [13542] was superimposed above it (below, 2.5).

THE WESTERN CHOIR ENTRY OR 'RETROCHOIR' (ROOM 6b)

The line of the beamslot seen in room 6a continued 1.25m to the north of the south-east nave pier base, and would have

Fig 11 The surviving undisturbed floor in the chapel of ? St Anne (B6, room 6a), looking south (0.2m scale)

Fig 12 Decorated Penn floor tile designs <T11>, <T20>, <T39>, <T40>, <T47>, <T52> and <T60>, from the floor of the chapel of ? St Anne (B6, room 6a) (scale 1:6 diagrammatic, 1:3 pictorial (<T60>))

provided the base for a screen – interpreted as the rood screen – on the west side of room 6b. The south side of room 6b was bounded by the monument/tomb [13856] (below, 2.5). The two arch responds defined the east limit of this area against the presbytery (B4). To the north, heavy truncation had removed all floor surfaces, and only the pattern of burial, particularly a distinct drop in density to the north (in room 6d), suggested a division there. Two small postholes were found within this room, one sealed by the tile floor described below and the other sealed by the later floor (below, 2.4); both were probably scaffolding holes.

One patch of tiled floor survived, laid on a make-up of silty clay. The floor, badly abraded, consisted of both floor tiles and bricks. The bricks were possibly laid as a border, but only two (each measuring 280 x 350mm) survived. The line of bricks apparently did not match any underlying grave cuts. One plain glazed floor tile was recovered, in fabric 1678 and measuring 280 x 280 x 40mm (Table 17).

THE NAVE WEST OF THE ROOD SCREEN (ROOM 6c)

In the central part of the nave west of the rood screen, and to the south of the north-west nave pier base and apparently abutting it, was a highly compacted mortar surface. This had a maximum height of 9.24m OD, at least 0.8m below any other recorded surface in the nave. It was sealed only by unstratified material and may have been a post-medieval intrusion, but

<T7>

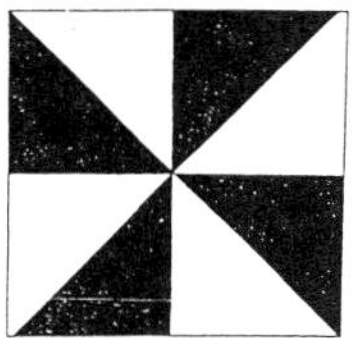
<T10>

<T29>

<T59>

Fig 13 Decorated Penn floor tile designs <T7> (which reads 'Signum Sce Crucis' ('the Sign of the Holy Cross')) and <T10>, both ex situ, *and <T29> and <T59> from the floor of the central part of the nave (B6, room 6c) (scale 1:6)*

might instead have been the base of a burial vault or tomb. A small and highly abraded patch of tiled floor [12321] also survived in the central vessel. Two of the tiles were designs <T29> and <T59> on tiles slightly larger than the average size of the main products of the Penn kilns; *ex situ*, similar, larger-size tiles with designs <T7> and <T10> may also have originated from this area (Fig 13).

The nave to the west of the screen retained no definite floor surface in the south aisle prior to the late floor [13903] (below, 2.5). The layers associated with the screen beamslot and described above under room 6a, together with a small patch of broken roof tiles, may, however, have been make-up layers for a surface.

A ?CHAPEL IN THE NORTH AISLE (ROOM 6d)

No surface layers survived the modern truncation in the north aisle east of the line of the rood screen extended northwards, so the division between the easternmost part of the north aisle (room 6d) and that to the west (room 6c) can only be surmised from the pattern of burials, as can the boundary with the retrochoir (room 6b). It is clear that the later burials within the western part of the north aisle (room 6c) respected the extended line of the screen. It is also clear, despite some modern truncation, that burial was far more intensive west of the screen line, in the nave proper (room 6c), than in the north aisle ?chapel (room 6d), which contained only three burials (below, 2.5).

The church ?vestry (B7)

The walls of this building were heavily robbed (Fig 9). Nevertheless, parts of the east wall survived below foundation level and abutted the south buttress of the presbytery (B4); and a heavily truncated stub of the corner of the east and south walls remained. Both foundations reached a depth of around 9.02m OD and were a maximum of 1.0m wide. Much of the south wall had been truncated and only a robber trench indicated its line. However, a surviving fragment attests to foundations 1.14m wide and just over 1.0m deep. Similarly, the west wall had been almost completely robbed. A fragment of foundation remained but this was too small to be of use in determining the nature of the wall. The robber trench suggested that this wall was comparable in size and depth to the east wall. The overall internal measurements of Building 7 were 6.5m x 3.75m.

Within this building were a number of make-up layers which included no dating evidence. These abutted the east wall and were cut by three postholes, which in turn were sealed by more levelling. A second series of postholes then cut the levelling. None of the layers were floor surfaces and the postholes appear to have been for scaffolding. Levelling [13772] contained a small quantity of Kingston-type (KING) and London-type (LOND) ware sherds, which probably came from the pre-monastic ground surface.

The church cloister enclosure (OA4)

The construction of the church cloister appears not to have been a single operation but piecemeal and protracted (Fig 9). An enclosure for the cloister was constructed first to the south of the church. Some 6.0m to the west of the ?vestry (B7), a north–south wall was built to the south of the presbytery (B4). The northern end survived only as a robber trench and the relationship with the south wall of the presbytery was lost. The foundations were a maximum of 1.0m wide and just over 1.0m deep. The depth of the foundations increased slightly to the south, following the natural slope of the site, from 9.16m to 8.60m OD. Part of the fabric of the wall survived to a height of 1.3m above the medieval ground level, on a slight offset from the foundations. Both faces were of coursed, hammer-dressed Kentish ragstone blocks, suggesting that both were external and that this section of wall was designed to 'stand alone' against weathering (prior to the construction of the later, east, cloister alley).

The wall enclosed the area to the south of the nave (B6) and to the east of the chapel of Holy Trinity (B3), and may have been continuous with the north wall of the refectory (B13) which formed the south boundary of the enclosed area (and secondarily the south wall of the south cloister alley).

In a second stage, the construction of east and south cloister alleys (B10; below) reduced the size of the enclosed area (OA4) and created a formal cloister garth.

To the south of the nave a large, shallow subcircular pit cut the ? masons' lodges/workshops (B5) and was in turn cut by graves within the timber pentice (B18) that formed the later north cloister alley (below, 2.5, period B3). This pit contained some demolition material and produced one sherd of pottery later than the mid 13th century.

Two heavily truncated burials within Open Area 4 have been tentatively assigned to period B2, primarily because they do not fit the pattern of later burials in the east cloister alley (B10) or within the later pentice (B18) (below, 2.5, period B3). One burial, to the south of the pentice, was in an exceptionally shallow grave. The second ([14395]) was in a particularly deep grave against the east wall of Open Area 4, beneath those within the east cloister alley (B10). Both burials were fragmentary and of unknown age and sex (not analysed).

The church south porch (B8)

A porch was constructed to the south of the presbytery (B4) by inserting a wall between the east-facing buttress at the south-east corner of the nave (B6) and the west face of the east wall of the cloister enclosure (OA4) (Fig 9). The foundations reached a depth of 9.44m OD and were 0.8m wide. They supported the threshold and east jamb of a doorway surviving to a height of 11.57m OD; the west door-jamb did not survive (Fig 14). The threshold was laid on a bed of Kentish ragstone rubble and mortar and was composed of Kentish ragstone slabs and a reused Purbeck marble grave slab [13808]. This slab (left *in situ* on the site) had some decoration on its upper surface but showed considerable wear (Fig 15). The much-worn decoration, incised into the surface, may show parts of a canopy above a no longer extant figure and the head of a staff held in the left hand, but could also represent practice decoration on the reverse of a slab or on one not intended for use above a burial. Above the threshold the door-jamb was constructed of moulded Reigate stone blocks, two of which survived *in situ*. This was backed by a short length of wall composed of coursed, hammer-dressed Kentish ragstone blocks with dressed Reigate stone blocks on the south face. The north face was composed of similar, smaller and less well-cut blocks, and it is probable that the rendering here was original and intended to disguise this. The room created by the insertion of this wall measured approximately 4.0m x 5.0m.

A shallow west–east cross-wall was inserted 1.0m from the north end of the building. Its foundations reached a depth of only 9.75m OD and were 0.45m wide; no trace of the wall survived above foundation level. This was probably the remains of a step: it would have been necessary to step down into the west tower bay of the presbytery as there was a difference of some 0.3m between the maximum heights of the two floor levels. At the south end of the building, abutting the threshold of the doorway, were the remnants of a tiled floor at a maximum height of 10.35m OD. It was composed of reasonably large (200 x 240mm) tiles laid square on to the building's alignment. The floor was heavily abraded and had been partially robbed.

The chapter house (B9)

The walls of the chapter house were constructed in a single operation and abutted the cloister enclosure east wall (OA4) to the west (Fig 9). The foundations had a maximum width of

Fig 14 The south door of the south porch (B8), looking north (0.2m and 0.1m scales)

Fig 15 Detail of the tomb-slab threshold [13808] of the south door of the porch (B8) looking east, showing the decoration (0.1m scale)

1.15m. Those of the north wall reached a depth of 9.10m OD and those of the south wall a depth of 8.66m OD; the foundations of the east wall sloped from north to south to accommodate this difference. The foundations were trench-built, but a number of cross-sections through the walls revealed an earlier trench. The base of this trench conformed to that of the foundations, but one edge was visible 0.5m beyond the internal edge of all the foundations. The foundations of the south-east corner were loose rubble, sand and silt in a visible cut that truncated the earlier trench (Fig 16). Perhaps an earlier attempt to dig foundation trenches for the chapter house was abandoned, and they were backfilled before this building was constructed. The overall length of the chapter house was 14.25m and its width 8.15m, with interior measurements of 12.75m x 6.0m (Fig 17).

The chapter house walls were constructed with a 0.02–0.05m offset on the interior edge above the foundations. The walls survived to a maximum height of 0.5m above medieval ground level, or approximately 10.2m OD. The external faces were of hammer-dressed, randomly coursed

Fig 16 A cross-section through the chapter house (B9) foundations, looking south (0.5m scale)

Fig 17 The chapter house (B9) from above, showing the surviving footpaces/benches and with the east wall of the infirmary (B15) to the south (top right), looking south-east (2.0m scale)

Kentish ragstone blocks. On the south-east corner was a large dressed Reigate stone block; the north-east corner did not survive above foundation level. The interior faces were of randomly coursed chalk blocks. No attempt was made to dress the chalk on the interior faces, as they lay behind the remnants of stone footpaces for benches constructed of uncoursed mortared chalk rubble and would have been hidden from view. The footpaces were constructed to a width of 1.1m. All were heavily truncated, with the largest surviving fragment occupying the south-east corner of the building and surviving to 10.88m OD. The upper surface of this fragment suggested that there was a step, at least 0.3m high, in the footpace (Fig 40).

A tiled floor abutting a fragment of footpace was laid at the west end of the building, at 10.32m OD, on three layers of make-up. This floor was badly abraded and possibly robbed, and much of it survived only as mortar bedding. No complete tiles survived *in situ* except for a line of plain tiles to the south, laid square-on. These were imported floor tiles with yellow and green glaze in fabric 1678 (Table 17), and with nail holes where corners are present. The north face of the footpace or bench was rendered with mortar after this floor was laid. The last vestiges of a vertical-sided flat-bottomed cut, containing one iron nail, pierced the floor. This may have been the remnants of a burial, but the cut is undated and could easily have been post-medieval.

The east and south alleys of the church cloister (B10)

Evidence was found for the construction – secondary to that of the cloister enclosure (OA4) – of the east and possibly the south alleys of the church cloister (Fig 9). Any trace of the west alley was either lost to truncation or lay beyond the areas excavated, but it was clear that, in this period and later, no attempt was made to construct a north alley in stone.

The east alley of the cloister was constructed immediately to the south of the porch (B8) which gave access to the west (tower) bay of the presbytery. The new garth wall abutted the easternmost south-facing buttress of the nave (B6), while the existing cloister enclosure wall (OA4) became the east outer wall. No trace of the southern limit of this alley was found: the garth wall survived southwards for 5.2m before being truncated. The foundation reached a maximum depth of 8.98m OD and was a maximum of 0.9m wide. On its west side was a large buttress which was apparently original, though this was difficult to verify because the buttress had been extensively remodelled (below, 2.5). A second west-facing foundation fragment at the south (truncated) end may have been the remains of a second buttress or a return. Only the last vestiges of the wall above the foundation survived. At the north end of the wall, fragments of the south jamb of a doorway survived; these were, unusually for the site, composed of yellow sandstone. A second doorway was cut through the cloister enclosure wall. This had been largely dismantled and the opening blocked in the post-medieval period, but the lowest course of each jamb survived, consisting of a single shaped block of green sandstone and approximately 1m apart. Within the alley a number of undated rubble- and silt-filled pits or hollows may have been associated with preparation of the ground surface for a floor level.

The last vestiges of an east–west footing may have been part of the garth wall of the south alley. It ran parallel to the north wall of the refectory (B13). This foundation had two (truncated) southern returns and reached a depth of 8.65m OD. It is unclear whether the recorded length of 3.48m represents the complete original length or the truncated length. To the north of this was a very fragmentary chalk rubble foundation in the base of a large cut measuring 1.9m x 1.32m; it reached a depth of 8.22m OD, and one piece of 13th-century pottery was recovered from it. This feature may have been the heavily robbed base of a chalk-lined grave within the cloister garth, but no human bone was found.

The ? abbot's garden (OA5)

This area extended further east in its primary phase than subsequently. The original east wall of the garden clearly abutted the south wall of the earlier cloister (B3) (above, 2.3) to the north, and was in turn clearly abutted by the south walls of each of Buildings 11 and 12 to the east (Fig 9). However, within Buildings 11 and 12 the east side of the wall had an internal facing of coursed chalk blocks, indicating that Buildings 11 and 12 were constructed immediately after the east wall as part of the same building campaign. The west face of the wall was of hammer-dressed Kentish ragstone blocks, and where the wall continued south beyond Building 12 to the limit of excavation both the west and east faces were of Kentish ragstone, indicating a free-standing wall. The acute angle at which the wall was constructed conformed to the pre-existing property boundary of the de Parys tenement (Fig 5; Fig 18).

There was no evidence of any intention to construct the building to the west of the wall (B14, below) at this stage. This wall appears, then, originally only to have defined the eastern limit of the abbot's garden, while the south cloister wall defined its northern side and all other edges were lost to truncation or not excavated.

The kitchen (B11)

The internal measurements of the building interpreted as the kitchen were approximately 13m x 3.5m (Fig 9). No evidence survived for a butt joint between the south wall of the first cloister (B3) and the east wall of the kitchen: much of both walls here had been rebuilt and the foundations strengthened

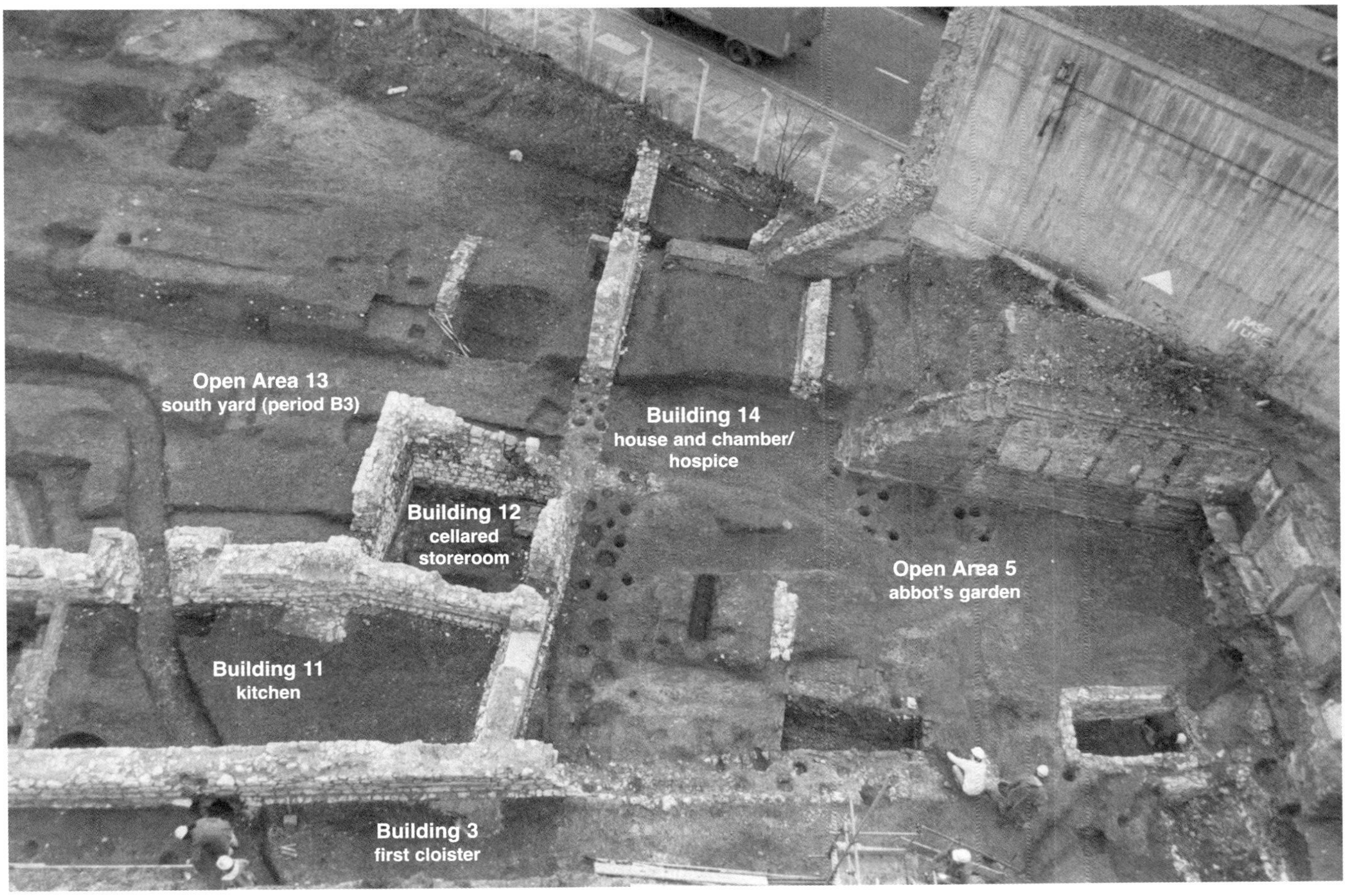

Fig 18 The abbot's garden (OA5) with the kitchen (B11), storeroom (B12), and house and chamber or hospice (B14) under excavation, from above looking south

after the Dissolution. However, given that the south face of the cloister wall was of Kentish ragstone and that a joint clearly existed between this and the east wall of the abbot's garden (OA5) – which formed the west wall of the kitchen – it is probable that such a joint existed to the east too. The east and south walls were of continuous construction and had internal faces of coursed, dressed chalk blocks. The south wall included the base of an original chimney-stack, 2.75m long and projecting 1.25m south; unfortunately, a later drain had removed any evidence of the associated hearth (Fig 18). Chamfered Reigate stone blocks were used on the south face at the base of the stack.

Two doorways were inserted into the south cloister wall to provide access to the kitchen. The western doorway had a threshold composed of two slabs, one a plain slab of Kentish ragstone but the second a reused early 14th-century Purbeck marble grave slab with an indent for a brass (Fig 19; preserved *in situ* on site). Neither slab showed significant wear, and the door-jambs above the threshold had been removed and the opening blocked with Kentish ragstone rubble. This blocking may have occurred at an early date. The second doorway to the east had only plain Kentish ragstone slabs for a threshold, and there was no evidence that it was ever blocked. A later drain truncated it

Fig 19 The early 14th-century tomb-slab threshold in the kitchen (B11) with oblong indent for a brass, looking south (0.5m scale)

and neither door-jamb remained (Fig 18). Conceivably it was a replacement for the west doorway.

The kitchen contained several features associated with its construction. A large number of dump layers were deposited to level the interior to 9.70m OD. A silty layer [4789] contained more or less equal amounts of south Hertfordshire-type greyware (SHER) and coarse Surrey-Hampshire border ware (CBW), with a slightly smaller amount of London-type ware (LOND) and a fragment from a Cheam whiteware (CHEA) biconical jug. Taken together, these suggest a date of *c* 1350–*c* 1450 for this deposit. The dump layers were sealed by small layers of chalk and mortar rubble cut by postholes for scaffolding. No evidence for a medieval floor surface was found in the building; all the features above these layers were clearly of mid 16th-century or later date.

A cellared storeroom (B12)

The internal measurements of this room (B12), interpreted as a storeroom, were 3.25m x 3.5m. The east and south walls were contemporary with those of the kitchen (B11) to the north (Fig 9). Both had internal faces of coursed chalk blocks, as did the south face (within the storeroom) of the south wall of the kitchen. The interior faces of the foundations were constructed of coursed, roughly dressed chalk blocks down to 8.30m OD, creating a cellar with a floor at least 1.4m beneath the adjacent external medieval ground surface. These faces were roughly rendered in mortar, though this need not have been original. A doorway only 0.8m wide was incorporated into the south wall with a threshold at 9.00m OD, at least 0.7m below medieval ground level (Fig 20). No trace of a threshold or jambs was found; they may have been removed when the doorway was later blocked, but on the other hand they would have made the doorway exceedingly narrow if they had existed. The remains of three square slots cut into the walls at the top of the foundations, at 9.50m OD, indicated the presence of joists for a timber floor. It was impossible to determine whether either the doorway or the timber floor was original to the building, or if they were in contemporary use. There was no evidence for a doorway connecting the storeroom to the kitchen at ground-floor level, although this may have been possible at an upper, first-floor level if the room was two-storeyed.

Two very shallow cuts and a dump of chalk rubble were found at the base of the apparently otherwise unfloored cellar. These features are undated and may have come about in the course of construction work.

The refectory (B13)

Situated roughly midway along, and running south of, the south cloister alley (B10), Building 13 is interpreted as the refectory. Its overall internal dimensions were approximately 19.4m north–south by 7.25m east–west (Fig 9). The foundations were trench-built of mortared chalk rubble, in this case roughly coursed rather than uncoursed. Those of the south wall were 2.15m wide and reached a maximum depth of

Fig 20 The storeroom (B12) (left foreground) showing the doorway (with later blocking [4629]), looking north (2.0m and 1.0m scales)

8.20m OD. This south foundation was 14.25m long, extending west of the refectory to abut the south-east corner of the kitchen (B11) and carry the south wall of the kitchen yard (OA6, below). The foundations of the east wall of the refectory were 1.25m wide and reached a maximum depth of 8.97m OD. The junction between the east and south walls had been removed. At the north end of the east wall the truncated stub of a buttress foundation or east–west wall projected east. If this was intended to be a wall, the stratification to the east indicated that it did not reach the east side of the refectory yard (OA7, below). The foundations of the west wall were 1.6m wide and reached a depth of at least 8.66m OD. There was a butt joint between the foundations of the west and south walls, but above this their fabric was continuous. Some 2.5m from the south end of the west wall foundation a substantial foundation for the pulpit projected 1.25m to the west. This was in excess of 4.0m long, its north end being truncated. It survived only to the top of foundation level, but could be traced to the surviving height of the wall via a scar left on the face by its demolition. Only the lowest 0.3m of the foundations of the north wall remained; these were 1.0m wide and reached a depth of 8.95m OD. Neither of the junctions with the east and west walls survived. This foundation continued east beyond Building 13 for 2.15m before being truncated; conceivably, it had formed the base of the wall delimiting a south side to the primary enclosed cloister area (OA4, above). The foundations of the west and east walls were thicker than those of the north wall, suggesting that the other foundations of the refectory were constructed later.

The surviving walls of the refectory were laid in a single operation above the foundations. The survival of the east wall was the poorest but, where traces survived, it was set flush with the east edge of the foundations, leaving an internal ledge 0.2m wide. Only 0.5m height survived, so only parts of the lower plinth of the wall – shown to exist on the more complete south wall – were actually available for study. The internal face was of dressed chalk blocks while the external face was of hammer-dressed Kentish ragstone blocks. The south wall survived to 2.2m above medieval ground level (Fig 21). Again the wall was set flush with the external edge of the foundations, leaving an internal ledge 1.05m wide. A plinth 1.1m wide and 0.6m high was laid above the foundations. This was faced to the north with dressed chalk blocks and to the south with coursed hammer-dressed Kentish ragstone blocks. Above this the wall proper was set flush with the north face of the plinth but with a slight offset on the south face. The north face was again constructed of dressed chalk blocks. The south external face was composed largely of courses of roughly dressed Kentish ragstone blocks interspersed at semi-regular intervals by bands of black flint. At the corners larger blocks of dressed Kentish ragstone were used for the returns. The west wall was constructed in the same fashion and was clearly

Fig 21 The south face of the south wall of the refectory (B13) with the Johnson Smirke Building behind, looking north-west (0.5m and 0.2m scales)

continuous with the south wall; it had an internal foundation ledge of 0.45m.

On the internal face of the west wall was a scar where the chalk rubble core was exposed up to the surviving height of the wall at 11.46m OD. This scar is interpreted as the result of the removal down to ground level of the pulpit foundation after the suppression. Within the scarring an opening 1.4–1.7m wide at the south end was later blocked, and there was a second opening, also later blocked, 1.6m to the north. Between these the internal face had been repaired with brick.

Internally a rubble base for a dais abutted and partially covered the foundations of the south wall. The interior of the building was levelled up to 10.30m OD. The levelling included within it a patch of burnt clay, mortar and tile which may have been the base of a hearth. Perhaps a workmen's hearth used during the construction work, it was severely damaged; archaeomagnetic dating suggests that it had been disturbed by later intrusions (both dates obtained are too early for the foundation of the abbey: Linford and Linford 1991, 1–11). This was sealed by further levelling. Rubble layer [4175] contained coarse Surrey-Hampshire border ware (CBW) and Cheam whiteware (CHEA) dated *c* 1380–*c* 1500, and [4063] also contained CBW (*c* 1350–*c* 1500). Above the levelling two distinct areas of tiled floor were laid at 10.33m OD. To the south was a patch of mortar bedding which bore the faint impressions of small tiles, possibly measuring *c* 110 x 100mm, laid square-on. To the north of this a second patch of mortar bedding carried the impressions of larger tiles, possibly measuring *c* 200 x 200mm, laid diagonally to the axis of the building. It is probable that these floors were contemporary but it is impossible to ascertain whether they represent functional divisions within the building.

The ?kitchen yard (OA6)

The refectory was constructed, most unusually, with two open spaces or yards to the west and east of it, respectively the ?kitchen yard (OA6) and the ?refectory yard (OA7, below) (Fig 9).

The south wall of the ?kitchen yard (OA6), between the kitchen (B11) and the refectory (B13), was carried by a contemporary continuation westwards of the south foundation of the refectory (B13). It was built in a similar fashion to that of the refectory but on a smaller scale. The plinth was only 0.75m wide, leaving an internal ledge 1.4m wide, and it was faced on both sides with hammer-dressed Kentish ragstone blocks, as was the wall proper above. The offset between the wall and the plinth was less than 0.02m and was this time on the north side. The wall survived in two fragments, one at each end; the central section had been removed to below foundation level by post-Dissolution drains. The east fragment abutted the refectory, but scarring on the external west face of that building, above the wall fragment, may suggest that it replaced an earlier build integrated into the refectory. Alternatively, the scarring may have resulted from an over-zealous demolition of the wall during the post-medieval period. The west fragment abutted the kitchen. The use of Kentish ragstone on both sides of the wall suggests a yard wall.

Approximately 14m to the north was an isolated fragment of a second east–west wall. This survived only below foundation level and was truncated at both ends. The foundation reached a maximum depth of 8.38m OD and was 1.3m wide. This wall may have been the north wall of the yard, in which case the yard measured 13.5m north–south by 5.0m east–west.

The ?refectory yard (OA7)

This yard (OA7) was constructed to the east of the refectory (B13) (Fig 9). Either immediately before or during that construction, an east–west drainage ditch was dug in line with the wall stub on the east side of the refectory. Surviving for a length of 9.0m and with a maximum width of 0.9m, it sloped down to the east from 8.17m to 7.71m OD. It had near-vertical sides and a concave base, and the eastern end was truncated. This feature probably drained water away from the refectory. It was backfilled with clean sand and gravel [3055], and there was little evidence of slumping. Three sherds of medieval pottery found in it date to after the mid 13th century. They include a

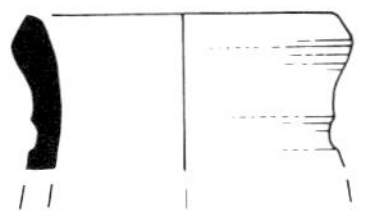

Fig 22 Spanish green-glazed ware (SPGR) or Maghrebi-type ware (MAGR) jar <P3> from the drain in the ?refectory yard ([3055], OA7) (scale 1:4)

sherd from a green-glazed jar (<P3>, Fig 22), possibly Spanish green-glazed ware (SPGR) or Maghrebi-type ware (MAGR) from North Africa. Although rather small, this might have contained sugar, manna, treacle, spices or other exotic products used in the abbey (Childs 1993, 37). The ditch almost certainly pre-dated the construction of the yard, but the lack of slumping from the sides indicates that it was comparatively short-lived and may only have been in use while the foundations of the refectory were being constructed.

The overall internal dimensions of the yard were approximately 19.5m north–south by 9.5m east–west. The foundations of the south wall abutted the refectory, and were a maximum of 1.0m wide and reached a maximum depth of 8.20m OD. There was a slight offset between the foundations and the wall, which was faced on both sides with hammer-dressed Kentish ragstone blocks. A Kentish ragstone plinth similar to that employed in the refectory was also a feature here, as was decorative flint banding on the north face, though with a rougher appearance than that in the refectory. The lower parts of the wall proper also abutted those of the refectory, but above 11.00m OD only the rubble cores of both walls survived and at the junction they were indistinguishable. This may suggest that the upper walls of both were rebuilt later, or that the start of construction of the yard's enclosing walls rapidly followed that of the refectory and was, after a certain point, simultaneous.

Truncation had removed the junction between the south and east walls. The foundations and walls were similar save that the Kentish ragstone plinth appeared to be absent from the east wall; traces of rough black flint banding were also found on the east face of the east wall. Truncation had also removed the north wall, which was probably a continuation of the north refectory wall and the southern cloister enclosure wall (OA4).

A house and chamber, or the ? abbot's hospice (B14)

This building was internally 4.25m wide east–west and at least 19.5m long north–south (Fig 9); the south end lay beyond the area of excavation beneath East Smithfield. Building 14 reused the south wall of the first cloister (B3) as its north wall and the east wall of the abbot's garden (OA5) as its east wall. A new wall was constructed to the west of and parallel with that of the abbot's garden. This survived in two separate fragments, of which only the southern one still carried part of the wall above the foundations, which were 0.75m wide and reached a maximum depth of 9.13m OD. To the south, where the wall proper survived to a height of 0.45m, it was offset from the foundations with an internal ledge 0.15m wide. This offset was at 9.75m OD, 0.3m higher than that on the east wall. The west face was of coursed hammer-dressed Kentish ragstone blocks; the east, internal, face was a mixture of coursed hammer-dressed chalk and Kentish ragstone blocks, which was atypical for a purpose-built internal building face on this site. The west face of the pre-existing east wall was roughly rendered.

Some 6.9m from the north end of the building, foundation fragments from an east–west internal wall were found. One of the fragments clearly abutted the east wall; the relationship to the newer west wall was lost but the internal wall may have been of contemporaneous construction. Within the area to the north of this was a second, north–south, robbed internal wall, possibly a stair base. This was 1.2m to the east of, and ran parallel with, the west wall; it was a maximum of 0.55m wide and reached a maximum depth of 9.44m OD. Once again it may have been part of the original fabric of the building. This wall would have created a space to the east 2.5m wide and another to the west only 1.2m wide (Fig 18).

A doorway was inserted into the east wall to provide access to the kitchen (B11). There was a distinct cut for the doorway through the fabric of the wall. The threshold was composed largely of a Purbeck marble grave slab. The door-jambs were 1.07m apart, and were constructed of brick and tile rather than the more usual dressed Reigate stone. This may suggest that the doorway was a later feature, but the provision of a doorway to the monastic kitchen is significant. While the northern part of the building may have had an upper floor, the lack of any evidence for a latrine argues against such an upper floor being a chamber and the whole being a private house within the monastery. The southern part of the building may have been a hall, and the whole building part of the abbot's hospice. The suggestion of a hall is supported by the insertion of a fireplace in the south part of the east wall. The size of the chimney-stack can only be judged from the foundations, as only one dressed Reigate stone block of the north corner of the stack survived above ground level. The stack was 1.0m long and projected 0.4m to the east.

No internal stratification of monastic date survived, the medieval floor levels having been stripped out during the post-Dissolution period.

The infirmary (B15)

The west wall of the infirmary was formed by the pre-existing east walls of the church cloister enclosure (OA4) and the ?refectory yard (OA7) (Fig 9); this resulted in a west wall which 21.0m from the south end was then offset 2.0m to the west. The internal dimensions of the infirmary, allowing for the offset, were 20.3m x 11.3m south of the offset and 13.1m x 9.1m north of it. The north wall was formed by the south wall of the chapter house (B9). The infirmary was completed by a south wall which extended the ?refectory yard's (OA7) south wall, and by an east wall abutting the east end of the chapter house. The junction between these south and east walls was truncated, but the surviving sections suggest that the building was erected in a single operation. The foundations of the south wall reached a maximum depth of 8.35m OD and were a maximum of 0.75m wide. Those of the east wall reached a maximum depth of 8.35m OD to the south but rising to 8.72m OD where they abutted the infirmary, and were 0.75m wide. The foundations incorporated two unusual features. At the east end of the south wall a foundation arch 3.8m long and 1.1m high was constructed to span undisturbed quarry pit fills. This was the only foundation arch recorded on the site; they were usually used to counter problems caused by poorly drained land or a shortage of building material. At the north end of the east wall, the lowest 0.4m of the foundations was composed of loose chalk rubble, sand and silt, rather than the mortared chalk blocks used elsewhere; this was also used on the south-east corner of the chapter house, which this wall abutted (Fig 17). The walls proper survived at all points to a height of at least 0.5m and, in the case of the east wall, 2.0m above the medieval ground level (Fig 23). The internal faces were of dressed, coursed, mortared chalk blocks, and the external faces consisted of courses of mortared, hammer-dressed Kentish ragstone blocks. Patches of mortar rendering survived on the internal faces.

The east wall included three features of note. To the south an oblong recess measuring 0.86m x 0.73m and 1.0m above foundation level in the internal face was filled with several courses of red brick in the post-Dissolution period (Fig 23). The bricks remained *in situ* so the depth of the recess could not be determined. To the north of this an original fireplace was incorporated into the wall. The chimney-stack was 2.8m long and projected 0.4m to the east. It was faced largely with hammer-dressed Kentish ragstone blocks, but larger dressed Kentish ragstone blocks were used on the south corner (the north corner was too heavily truncated for this to be verified there). The interior was lined at the base with moulded Reigate stone blocks. The hearth was composed of mortared peg tiles, stacked vertically, and was 1.6m long by 0.65m deep (Fig 24). To the north of the fireplace the threshold and south jamb of a doorway were found in the wall. Only three blocks of dressed Reigate stone survived of the jamb, but they did appear to be original to the wall. Midway along the south wall was the edge of the western side of a doorway, but it was impossible to establish whether this was an original feature.

The infirmary was evidently divided at ground-floor level. It is assumed that the structure was partitioned east–west at the offset (Fig 9). In the southern half of the structure, the stub of an east–west internal foundation of continuous build with the east wall survived but was truncated; however, a slight scar visible on the west face of the east wall indicated that it had been a full partition wall. To the south of this partition a large pit or butt of a trench was dug (Fig 9). It had near-vertical sides and a flat base, was at least 5.0m long (its western end was truncated) and 2.6m wide, and reached a maximum depth of 7.78m OD. It was backfilled largely with sand and gravel, but contained some demolition material. There was little slumping, and pottery recovered from the fill suggests a late 14th-century or later date. This feature may have pre-dated the building and may have been for an aborted set of foundations or dug as a soakaway for ground water during construction; it should perhaps be compared to the ditch in the refectory yard (OA7, above). Another possibility is that it was a sawpit.

A number of other internal wall foundations in the southern

Fig 23 The east wall of the infirmary (B15) with later Royal Mint walls behind, looking north-east (2.0m scales)

Fig 24 The infirmary (B15) fireplace showing the stacked roof-tile hearth, looking down (0.5m scale)

half may or may not have been original to the building (Fig 9). A north–south wall was constructed to the south of the integral east–west partition described above, cutting the large pit. This was 0.5m wide and reached a maximum depth of 9.03m OD to the south, where it survived to a height of 9.55m OD, rising to 9.68m OD to the north. It had been robbed for part of its length and truncated elsewhere. To the south was the truncated east–west stub of another partially robbed and truncated foundation which reached a maximum depth of 8.83m OD and was 0.4m wide. It was possibly of continuous build with the north–south wall but the junction was truncated. A second east–west wall to the south of the first survived only as a truncated robber trench, reaching a maximum depth of 9.02m OD and 0.4m wide. These further foundations appear to have divided up the southern half of the infirmary as shown in the plan (Fig 9). It is possible that they supported timber partitions rather than full stone walls.

A number of undated postholes survived between 9.45m and 9.63m OD, but formed no discernible patterns. They cut only the underlying quarry pits, so some or all could pre-date the building, but many probably derived from scaffolding used in the construction or repair of the building.

Later 14th-century ?epidemic cemetery (OA2)

This burial area overlay the Black Death cemetery (Grainger et al 2008) (Fig 9). As with the eastern burial area (OA9; below, 2.5), it is impossible archaeologically to date these burials other than to the lifetime of the abbey. However, there is sufficient documentary evidence to suggest that this area was closed to burials by 1410 when part of the cemetery became a garden (below, 2.5). Certainly there are differences regarding the osteological assemblages between the two cemetery areas (Chapter 3.7 and 3.8) and it is conceivable that this area was used, at least in part, to inter further epidemic burials in the second half of the 14th century.

Stratigraphically overlying the Black Death burials were 12 north–south rows of east–west aligned graves. These graves contained 221 burials, and the rows appeared initially to infill the gaps between the underlying graves of the Black Death cemetery and to follow the line of the mass burial trenches. However, these rough rows became less distinct as time passed, as the graves in some rows would cut those in adjacent rows; but there was no coherent pattern to this intercutting. In some cases a later grave or even series of graves lay directly over a Black Death burial. To the west there was a noticeable concentration of infant and juvenile burials, in the same area previously favoured for such burials during the Black Death. An absence of burials on the eastern edge of the area probably reflects the difficulties of digging through the London Clay levelling deposits found there (OA1) (Grainger et al 2008, 9).

All the burials were interred supine and extended with their heads to the west and feet to the east. One hundred and two burials were interred in coffins, identified either by wood stains or fittings. Nine burials produced copper-alloy buckles. Of these, four (found in pairs on the skeleton) are catalogued (Chapter 5.6, <S96> and <S97>). The pair of buckles <S97> both had traces of textile on them; their positions suggest that they may have been used to secure a hose to linen under-breeches or an undershirt rather than to fasten a shroud. One of the coffined burials, an adult ([9650], Fig 9), was interred with a deposit of charcoal. Three graves contained two burials each. Grave [6258] contained burial [6260], of an unsexed child, and burial [7102] of a male aged ≥46 years, and grave [8002] contained burial [8004], of an unsexed adult aged 36–45, and burial [8005] (not analysed); all four individuals were apparently interred in coffins. Grave [11035] contained a possible male aged 26–35 (burial [11033]) and an adolescent (burial [11034]), neither of whom was apparently interred in a coffin.

Three grave fills produced further copper-alloy objects: from [9890] a small cruciform mount <S48> (Fig 25), from [12674] a small circular brooch with twisted wire decoration <S95> (Fig 25), and from [11895] a small single-loop buckle and buckle plate <S98> (Fig 25).

One group of burials ([8320], [8385] (Fig 9), [12677], [12680] and [12683]) on the southern edge of the area consisted almost exclusively of infants and juveniles, with the exception of an unclassified adult ([12805]). One female ([12648]) aged 36–45 had a primary infection of her maxillary sinus (sinusitis)

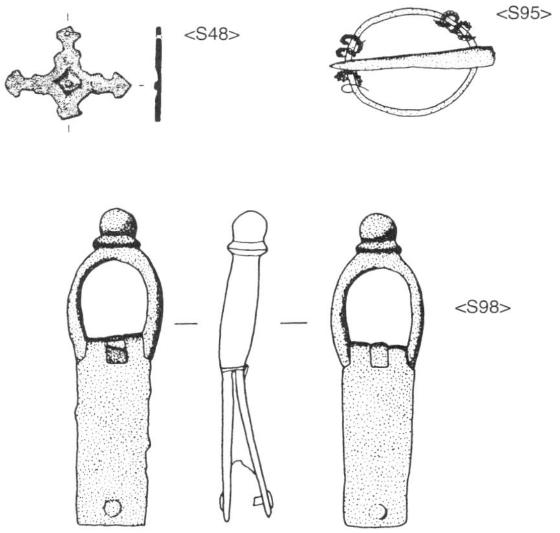

Fig 25 Copper-alloy finds from graves in the later ?epidemic cemetery (OA2): cruciform mount <S48>, brooch with wire decoration <S95>, and buckle and buckle plate <S98> (scale 1:1)

that produced new bone. One case of tuberculosis was noted in the vertebrae of a *c* 15-year-old adolescent ([12696]). There were four cases of cribra orbitalia which may possibly indicate iron deficiency anaemia. One of these was in an unsexed child ([6213]), two in adolescents ([9659] and [12696]) and one in a female aged 18–25 years ([8157]). A 'parry' fracture to the left radius and ulna of a male aged ≥46 years ([7102]) was found with evidence for other injuries to the knee and tibia, while a second similarly aged male ([7314]) had a possible arrowhead embedded in his spine. One case of spondylolysis was found in a female aged ≥46 years ([12687]).

Close to the western edge of Open Area 2 was a cesspit [12836] (Fig 26). The walls were composed entirely of peg tiles laid flat and bonded with clay, while the base was a layer of loose peg tiles above the natural sands and gravels. The pit measured 1.12m x 1.1m at the top but sloped in slightly towards the base at 7.19m OD. It appeared to contain rubbish and faecal deposits. There was a fairly high concentration of parasite eggs of both *Trichuris* and *Ascaris* (the total egg count was 1120 opg) which suggests primary use as a cesspit. Waterlogged fruit seeds (small numbers of grape, wild strawberry and fig, and larger numbers of blackberry/raspberry) were found in fill [12872], with a few seeds from other plants (goosefoot, henbane, elder).

The pottery assemblage from this feature (total 2436g) is of interest in that over half of it comprises Mill Green ware (MG) (Table 2). This includes a substantial part of a squat jug with

Table 2 Pottery from cesspit [12836] in the north-west part of the precinct (OA2, period B2)

Fabric	Form	Weight (g)	Weight %	EVEs
MG	bowl	405	16.6	0.1
MG	jug	1283	52.7	0.5
LOND	jug	20	0.8	-
KING	?bowl	717	29.4	0.1
KING	misc	3	0.1	-
SHER	misc	8	0.3	-
Total		**2436**		**0.7**

Fig 26 Cesspit [12836] constructed of peg tiles in the north-west part of the precinct (OA2), viewed from above from the north-east (0.5m scale)

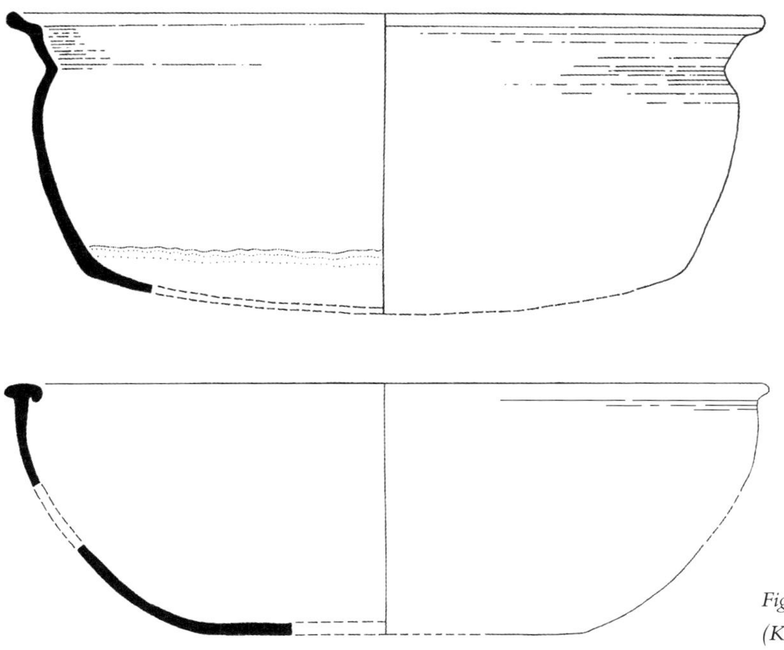

Fig 27 Mill Green ware (MG) bowl <P4> and Kingston-type ware (KING) bowl <P5> from cesspit [12836] (scale 1:4)

white slip, green glaze and combed decoration which is probably early 14th-century in date (Pearce et al 1985), and a deep bowl or cooking pot (<P4>, Fig 27). The latter has a slightly lid-seated rim and sagging base, and is also in the fine variant of this ware (ibid, nos 54, 294). It is unglazed apart from a slight clear glaze inside the base, and is heavily sooted over the whole of the outside. A large Kingston-type ware (KING) bowl with a hammerhead rim was also found, and probably dates to the mid 14th century (<P5>, Fig 27). A rowel spur <S163> also came from this feature, which seems to have been backfilled in the mid to late 14th century.

Discussion, 1361–*c* 1400 (period B2)

The attempt to establish the permanent claustral complex must have begun within a decade or so of the foundation if, as suggested, work began on the new church in 1361 and on the chapter house before 1375 (*Cal Pat R*, 1358–61, 567; GL, MS 25121/953; TNA: PRO, E 326/5599). The new building programme was clearly not without problems, and much had to wait on the acquisition of the de Parys tenement in the 1380s which completed the abbey's holdings on the East Smithfield frontage and allowed the construction of the south range. The archaeological sequence indicates that the kitchen (B11) and storeroom (B12) were built first, on the de Parys tenement, followed perhaps quite quickly by the refectory (B13) and its yard (OA6) abutting the kitchen, and then by the infirmary (B15) abutting the refectory yard (OA7) (cf Fig 5 and Fig 6 with Fig 9).

The choice of a contemporary friary ground plan for the monastic church is not unusual for the mid 14th century (as discussed in detail in Chapter 3.2). The archaeological evidence, though fragmentary, indicates that the presbytery (B4) was constructed before the nave (B6) as a free-standing structure, albeit probably with a temporary wall at the west end before the nave was constructed. The possible masons' lodges (B5) associated with the presbytery clearly did pre-date the nave. The long rectangular form of the presbytery is very un-Cistercian, and even as a free-standing structure clearly shows contemporary mendicant influence (eg Walsingham Friary, Norfolk; Fig 60).

As with friaries, the church had no transepts, the choir was contained entirely within the presbytery, and a tower was constructed on arches above a central walking place or, in this Cistercian context, the 'retrochoir' (Fig 59; Fig 60). Building 7, given the absence of burials within it and its position on the south side of the presbytery, may have been the vestry documented in 1391 rather than a chapel (TNA: PRO, SC 6/1258/1, ms 2, 3), while the porch (B8) simply gave entry to the choir proper, via the retrochoir, from the monastic cloister (B10). The lack of a definable pulpitum (the screen closing the west end of the choir stalls and so dividing the choir from the retrochoir and nave in standard Cistercian church plans (eg Roche Abbey, Yorkshire; Fig 60) also conforms to contemporary Franciscan and Carthusian church design, as evidenced by Coventry and Mount Grace Charterhouses (G Coppack, pers comm; Coppack 1991, 2–3 (plan), 10–11; 2006, 59–60): the formal west end of the choir lay beyond the retrochoir and was defined by the west (not east) arch responds supporting the tower.

Within the nave, the early, robbed, foundations between the nave arcade pier bases probably represent the position of benches removed to make way for the rood screen and burials between the piers of the nave arcade. It is uncertain whether this occurred as a single operation or in piecemeal fashion as the demand for burial space in these desirable locations grew. It is also uncertain who these benches were intended for: they may have been for monastic servants and patrons, and perhaps – given the abbey's incorporation of the chapel of Holy Trinity and the Black Death cemetery – other members of the laity seeking solace in piety after the recent, and recurring, catastrophe. This is certainly likely during the church's early history if, as suggested, the Black Death cemetery (OA2) was still being used for epidemic burials until *c* 1400. One other possibility for the use of these benches in the late 14th century exists. The brief period in the 1390s when St Mary Graces was ordered to convoke the general chapter of the Order at the monastery (Chapter 3.9) may have necessitated the installation of the benches in the nave for the use of the assembled abbots at meetings. The brevity of St Mary Graces' supremacy in this regard may also explain the subsequent removal of the benches at a relatively early date.

It is clear from the documentary evidence that there was a multiplicity of altars and chapels in the church. It is probable that altars existed to the west of the rood screen, in the north and south aisles, and to the east in the chapels (rooms 6a and 6d), but only the intensity of the burials west of the screen in this period (period B2) and later (period B3) suggests it. Two chapels are known to have existed on the south side of the church, the chapel of St Anne and a 'chapel without the quire door' (Wagner 1956, 143–4). Room 6a was clearly a chapel and, given that it was within the main body of the church, it seems unlikely that it would have been the chapel beyond the choir door, which appears to have been a later addition (below, 2.5). The chapel of St Anne may have existed by 1374, and was certainly receiving burials by 1396 (*Cal Pap Letters*, iv, 199; TNA: PRO, PROB 11/2/45). The tiled floor of room 6a was of late 14th-century date; indeed, a number of the Penn tiles found in the undisturbed portion of the floor may have come from a pre-*c* 1350 production period, indicating that they were still available, either from existing stocks or continued production.

The northern church cloister enclosure (OA4) pre-dated the construction of the chapter house (B9), documented as existing by 1375, indicating the creation of the enclosure – but not necessarily of the cloister – before that date. It may have been contemporary with the nave in construction, and certainly the masons' lodges (B5) associated with the presbytery were demolished before the construction of both the enclosure and the chapter house.

The chapter house was a rather small, simple, square-ended aisleless building of a standard Cistercian type. If, as suggested, there was more than one attempt to construct this building, the precarious finances of this period may provide the reason. It was constructed projecting eastwards parallel with the presbytery, with an open space between. This arrangement finds parallels in other Cistercian houses where the chapter house projects eastwards beyond the east range, as at Fountains and Rievaulx in Yorkshire, but again is not uncommon in friaries like Walsingham, Norfolk (Fig 60), to which this arrangement looks remarkably similar. It allowed for the later construction of a number of buildings between the church and chapter house. The inclusion of this space between the church and chapter house also indicates that there was no dormitory-over arrangement. There is no firm evidence to suggest that burials ever took place in the chapter house.

In 1383 the abbey received a grant of houses in Gravesend to construct the dormitory, refectory, cloister and other buildings (*Cal Pat R*, 1381–5, 306), which implies that construction of the new buildings, either entirely new or as replacements for the 'temporary' structures of 1350–61 (period B1), was either in progress but still not complete, or had possibly not yet begun. It is significant that the monks never intended to construct a church cloister entirely of stone. There was a full stone east alley (B10), and possibly a south alley with lavatorium, but there was never more than the later timber pentice (B18) serving as the north alley which, as discussed below (2.5), should perhaps be regarded more as another aisle of the nave than as a cloister alley. There was no surviving evidence for a west alley, although it is clear that the earlier stone cloister (B3) to the west – with which a west alley could have connected – was retained and used. By the 14th century the monastic cloister had lost many of its traditional functions. The north alley was often no longer used for readings or study.

Despite a number of butt joints, it is reasonable to regard the kitchen, storeroom and refectory as part of a unified programme of construction between 1383 and 1391. The property on which the kitchen (B11) stood was probably not acquired until the 1380s, and the refectory (B13) was constructed after it. This suggests that the kitchen could be considered in relationship either to the refectory or to the earlier structures of the 'temporary' claustral complex associated with the chapel of Holy Trinity (B1) which it lies immediately south of, or else that it could be considered in relationship to both – in other words that it was the monastic kitchen, but served both the old refectory/dormitory (B2) and the new refectory (B13) via the cloister (B3). That the old refectory/dormitory had probably become the abbot's lodging by the end of this period (B2) need not affect this.

There is certainly no other convincing candidate for the monastic kitchen among the excavated remains. The strongest argument against this interpretation is that there would have been no direct link with either refectory (B2 or B13), with no provision for a serving hatch to pass food and utensils from one to the other. However, simple problems of space created by the existing buildings such as the first cloister (B3) may also have dictated this less convenient position. It is also probable that the new refectory was not used regularly as a communal dining hall, but only on special occasions. In the 14th century monks frequently ate in the *misericorde* (meat-kitchen), where meat could be eaten, or in private chambers, making the traditional arrangement less vital. However, the grand and traditional nature of the refectory's construction, with its north–south alignment, a wall pulpit, a dais, and open to the roof, clearly indicates that it was meant as a main communal refectory, which was highly optimistic and unusual for the late 14th century. It was without doubt the most impressive building in the south range and was referred to as a 'chapel' as late as 1726 on a plan of the Tower (TNA: PRO, MPHH 1/56). It was also the only building in the south range referred to on the 1635 plan as a hall with no upper floor (Fig 58). The building called the 'halle' in 1425 probably refers to the refectory (TNA: PRO, SC 6/917/16). The south doorway shown in the 1589–92 picture plan (Fig 64) was probably a later post-medieval insertion, as it is unlikely that a refectory would originally have had such a feature. However, the two multi-light windows shown above this door were almost certainly medieval features (TNA: PRO, MPB 1/4).

Building 12 was clearly part of the same building programme as the kitchen, and the cellar described above was original to it. A storeroom remains the safest identification for this structure, though a pantry, buttery or scullery are possibilities. It may even be the 'common store' referred to in 1425 (TNA: PRO, SC 6/917/16). Although it seems rather small for this purpose, there was evidence of joists for the timber floor mentioned in the documentary sources for the common store.

There was no other evidence for adjacent buildings either side of the refectory immediately to the south of the church cloister (B10), where, conventionally, the kitchen would be expected to the west and the warming room to the east. Instead, what have been designated the ?kitchen and ?refectory yards (OA6 and OA7) were created as open spaces on either side of the refectory. Although the buttress or wall stub to the east of the refectory may indicate an intention to construct a warming house, this would be highly unusual in the late 14th century, and if it was intended to construct any building here, this plan appears to have been abandoned before or during the construction of the refectory yard. This yard arrangement is highly unusual, but probably reflects the positioning of the kitchen further to the west, the lack of any need for a warming house, and the absence from the completed monastic plan of a traditional dormitory to the east.

The Kentish ragstone used on the east face of the east wall of the ?refectory yard suggests that the programme of construction which included the kitchen, the storeroom, the refectory and two associated yards had come to an end, and that there was a significant hiatus before the infirmary (B15) was built to the east. The accounts of 1391–2 deal principally with the construction of the infirmary (TNA: PRO, SC 6/1258/1, ms 2, 3). Building 15 is referred to as the 'farmery' on a plan of the victualling yard dated 1623 (TNA: PRO, MPF 1/158) and is one of the last two buildings constructed in the south range (the other being B14). Although this building occupies the space reserved for the dormitory in previous centuries, there is only one reference to the existence of the dormitory (rather than the need or intention to build it, as in 1383): an unruly monk prevented the abbot from entering it in 1402 (*Cal Pap Letters*, v, 517, 602). No mention is made of it in the 1391–2 accounts. The only dormitory built at St Mary Graces may be that suggested as part of the earlier 'temporary' phase of occupation to the west, Building 2. Building 15 also lacked any drains or garderobes, or any evidence to indicate a reredorter. That said, it also lacks many elements that would indentify it archaeologically as an infirmary, for example the provision of aisles partitioned off to create individual cubicles, with a central vessel. More conventionally, the infirmary would have been further to the south and/or east of the church and chapter house. However, here those areas were occupied by tenements, the Black Death cemetery (OA3) (Grainger et al 2008) and marshy ground.

By the late 14th century there was an increasing tendency for the monks to abandon their communal accommodation for private chambers, and the infirmary had become a favourite location for such chambers. There is evidence both archaeological and documentary to show that, from the outset, the infirmary was constructed to house individual chambers. The excavated internal walls in the southern half strongly suggest this, while the chimney referred to in the new chamber for the 'monks' farmery' (TNA: PRO, SC 6/1258/1, ms 2, 3) is almost certainly the excavated fireplace (Fig 24). The 1635 plan (Fig 58) indicates that this building had a first floor, which was probably medieval in origin. The same plan describes the first cloister (B3) as having chambers above, and these may also possibly have been used to accommodate the monks.

The bursar's accounts of 1391–2 also mention the construction of a house and chamber to the east of the abbot's garden. This may refer to Building 14 on the east side of Open Area 5 and suggests that further private accommodation was being built. However, the excavated remains and the 1635 plan (Fig 58) indicate the great length of this structure. The plan also notes that it had a first floor, and the archaeological evidence suggests a set of medieval stairs in the north end for access to a first floor. It is unclear whether this first floor originally ran the length of the building or was confined to the northern part, with the southern being an open hall, as the presence of the fireplace may suggest. The building may therefore be the abbot's hospice also referred to in 1391–2 and likewise probably to the west of the claustral complex. St Mary Graces may also have had facilities for the care of sick and poor lay people, given the Dissolution-period petition for it to be kept open along with three London hospitals for this purpose (BL, Cotton MS Cleopatra E.iv, fo 222) (below, 2.6). Building 14 extended south to the East Smithfield street frontage and, as a long hall, could have been used for the care of the sick. The building is also, in relation to the early cloister (B3) and the chapel of Holy Trinity (B1), in a position equivalent to that of a refectory in a Cistercian house and, although it was clearly not the main refectory, the doorway through to the kitchen may be significant in this respect.

It is possible that burial in Open Area 2 ceased at some point before 1410; certainly by that date a tenement belonging to William and Katherine Somers existed to the north of the church, and part of the cemetery stretching north to Hogg Street became the garden (*Cal Close R*, 1422–7, 211; TNA: PRO, SC 6/917/16). The tenement can probably be equated with those buildings shown to the north of the 'great court' on the 1635 plan (Fig 58) and Building 21 (period B3; below, 2.5). The extent of the medieval garden is unknown; although the 17th-century plan suggests a large one, the medieval version may have been smaller.

2.5 Later additions to the abbey, *c* 1400–1539 (period B3)

Documentary evidence

Grants were still being made for the fabric of the church as late as 1447 (TNA: PRO, E 326/5591). Two chapels were added in the 15th century. A chapel beyond the south choir door was noted in the heraldic visitation of Clarenceux King of Arms on 27 March 1533 as containing the burial of Sir Thomas Charles who had died by 1475 (Wagner 1956, 143–4; *Cal Pat R*, 1467–77, 449). Sir Thomas Montgomery funded the construction of a Lady chapel on the north side of the presbytery before 1489. In that year he left £20 to 'garnish' it, and bequeathed it a white testament, a mass-book, a silver candlestick and a 'chales' (most likely a chalice); he was buried there in 1494 (Wagner 1956, 143–4; TNA: PRO, PROB 11/ 10/22). A bequest by John Sedley in 1528 mentions the altar of St Anne and orders the building of a partition across the chapel (TNA: PRO, E 303/10/354). A number of other burials within the church are known; they are listed in Table 13 and Table 14 and discussed fully in Chapter 3.7. In 1425–6 Kentish ragstone was bought for the chapel in the monks' cemetery (*capell' in cimiterio monachorum*) (TNA: PRO, SC 6/917/16).

There is a reference to the 'lavatory' in 1528 (TNA: PRO, E 303/10/354). In the 1530s several tenants paid their rents in the 'halle' (TNA: PRO, E 303/10/303, 314, 334, 340; BL, Harley Ch 75.G.7). In 1425 knives, bowls and baskets were bought for the kitchen (TNA: PRO, SC 6/917/16). A tenement existed by 1410 within the precinct to the north of the 'great court' and the church door, as described above (2.4, 'Discussion'); part of the cemetery stretching north to Hogg Street became its garden. ('Hoggestrete' seems to be the earlier form and 'Hoggelane' the later, occurring in 1539 (TNA: PRO, E 315/233, fo 339v)). Lewis John also had a tenement on the east side of the cemetery between the 1420s and the 1440s (*Cart Holy Trinity*, no. 995; TNA: PRO, SC 2/191/56, m 2; PROB 11/1/14). New buildings were made in the tenements in the precinct before 1425, and in this year a joist was fitted in the common storeroom (*communi promptuar*) (TNA: PRO, SC 6/ 917). The boundaries shown on the plan of the principal archaeological features in period B3 (Fig 28) derive from the authors' interpretation of the 1635 plan of the victualling yard (Fig 58).

Archaeological evidence

Burials continued to take place in both the nave (B6) and presbytery (B4) of the monastic church throughout this period, while two more chapels for burials were added to the church, one probably the Lady chapel (B17) to the north and the other possibly the 'chapel without the quire door on the south side' (B16) (Fig 28). Additionally, a timber pentice (B18) was constructed to the south of the nave, where traditionally the north alley of the cloister would be found, and this too was used for burials, as was a modified east cloister alley (B10). The vestry (B7) was extended and the area between it and the chapter house (B9) enclosed as a yard (OA8). The kitchen yard (OA6) was extensively modified and cesspits and storage pits found there were similar to examples dug in the abbot's lodging (B2), garden (OA5) and the first cloister (B3). The kitchen yard modifications included a chalk-walled drain (D1), while a well house (B19) was constructed to the north of this, possibly to serve the drain. In the refectory yard (OA7) a chamber (B20) was constructed to the north, probably as a lean-to. Features excavated in the precinct (B21–B23, OA10–OA13) have been included in this period, as has a burial area immediately to the north of the church (OA9) which could have been open for the lifetime of the abbey.

The ? chapel of Holy Trinity (B1)

The 1972 trial work (Davison 1972, 21) revealed a small area of brick-edged tile floor slightly to the north of the projected line of the south wall identified in period B1 (above, 2.3). This floor, though clearly of a later date than the foundation of the chapel of Holy Trinity, may – if not part of the floor of the chapel – have been the base of a tomb, similar to that found in the Lady chapel (B17, below).

The presbytery (B4)

The later burials were isolated and in many cases truncated (Fig 28). Three of the graves ([12477], [16106], [16108]) contained no skeleton. In the case of grave [12477] this was the result of immediate post-Dissolution robbing, but in the other two it may simply have been the result of more modern disturbance. In the central presbytery area, grave [12477] contained the remains of a cist-type lining composed of chalk fragments set in mortar (Fig 29). The later robber cut contained parts of a tomb canopy <A56>–<A58> suggesting an expensive monument (Fig 30), although not necessarily over this grave.

Immediately to the east of [12477] and probably originally below a tomb chest was burial [16042], of a male aged 36–45 years who had osteoarthritis both of his hips and thumb joints. Two small, truncated chalk-and-mortar foundations were found either side of the eastern end of the grave, but modern disturbance had removed any evidence for similar foundations at the western end. These reached 0.5m below floor level, and there was a rough roof-tile surface at their base overlying the fill of the grave, sealed only by loose debris. This suggests a cavity between the grave fill and a structure above (Fig 31). The central west–east line of burials was completed by [12297], that of a possible female aged 26–35 years, and [12427], of a possible male also aged 26–35 years.

There were no burials to the south of this line adjacent to the south wall. This absence reflects the position of the choir stalls. To the north, no archaeological deposits survived to confirm a similar situation there. Between the internal pilasters, and including burial [16042] (above), a number of rough rows of burials were suggested by the positions of burials from this and the earlier period: [16052] of an adult (period B2: probably Sir Simon Burley, executed in 1388; above, 2.4), [16063] of a 26–35-year-old of indeterminate sex, [16068] (not analysed), [16073] of a male aged ≥46 years, [16076] (period B2) of a possible male aged ≥46 years, [16104] of an individual of indeterminate sex aged ≥46 years, and [16106] and [16108] (both empty graves; see above). No burials were found at the east end of the presbytery where the high altar is likely to have been (Fig 28).

A brick-walled vault [16011] was inserted into the north wall of the presbytery to the south of the buttress and cut the foundations to such an extent that an arch above the vault is likely (Fig 32). The west wall survived almost intact to the medieval floor level, but only the lowest course of bricks of the south wall survived, and only a stub of the lowest course of the east wall. The north side was a simple cut through the foundations of the presbytery and the underlying sands and gravels. The tomb measured 2.2m x 2.2m and was approximately 1.5m deep. The walls were composed of coursed, mortared red brick with occasional use of chalk rubble in the west wall. The base was the natural sands and gravels on which the coffined burials rested. These were covered by fine silt, which is undated and may have been deliberately deposited over the coffins at interment, or have accumulated gradually within the vault, or else have been introduced after the Dissolution. Burial [16098], of a male adult aged 36–45 years and suffering from diffuse idiopathic skeletal hyperostosis (DISH) and hyperostosis frontalis interna, conditions possibly associated with obesity, and burial [16102], of a female aged 26–35 years, were together in this vault (Fig 32).

The nave (B6)

Activity recorded within the nave in the 15th and early 16th centuries was largely confined to burial within the areas (rooms 6a–d) already defined under period B2 (above, 2.4; Fig 9). These burials are poorly dated. Much of the medieval pottery was residual (south Hertfordshire-type greyware (SHER), London-type ware (LOND) and Mill Green ware (MG)) and derived from the pre-monastic ground surface. However, later medieval wares such as 'Tudor Green' (TUDG), coarse Surrey-Hampshire border ware (CBW) and Cheam whiteware (CHEA) were well represented (41.7% of the medieval assemblage) and indicate graves dug in the late 14th or 15th centuries. These finds include the handle of a large red-slipped cistern made in CBW and the lower part a baluster jug made in TUDG-type ware with a sparse green glaze; the latter may be of 15th-century date.

THE CHAPEL OF ? ST ANNE (ROOM 6a)

There were eight further burials in six graves, with two graves containing two burials each (Fig 28; Fig 33). Four of the graves occupied a single row at the western end of the room, and a fifth was immediately to the east of this row at the north end. A sixth grave occupied a position in the north screen of the chapel. There was some peripheral intercutting between these graves but otherwise they appeared to respect each other carefully.

Burial [13765], a 6–11-year-old child with possible spondylolysis, was the most southerly of the four burials to the west. Immediately to the north of this was burial [13518], of a female aged ≥46 years with DISH, which occupied a much larger cut, similar in size to those of graves [13542] and [13667] to the north. The grave cut had a squared western end, which may suggest the original presence of a slab above. To the north of this was the grave cut [13542], a large rectangular cut 2.25m long by 1.25m wide. Burial [13633], of an unclassified adult, was the primary interment in this grave; following the interment the cut was backfilled with loose silts. The second interment [13724], of a female 36–45 years old, was inserted through the loose silts above [13633], partially disturbing that burial so that the skull and a number of other bones were pushed to one side. The disarticulation of primary burial [13633] suggests that the second interment occurred several years later, though the presence of the earlier burial appears to have been known. The square-ended appearance of the cut again suggests a large slab or monument. Grave [13667] was similar in all respects to grave [13452], and cut that grave slightly to the north. The primary interment was [13747], of a male aged ≥46 years, which was placed in the north side of the cut and then sealed with loose silt up to floor level. The secondary interment was [13670], a female aged ≥46 years, which was again inserted directly above the primary burial, slightly disturbing it but this time with no major bones being displaced. A badly decayed lead papal bulla <S46> was found on the breast of [13670]. The busts of St Peter and St Paul and their accompanying inscription 'SPASPE' can be made out on the reverse, and a number 'VIII' on the obverse. From a comparison of seal formats, anti-pope Clement VIII (?1424–9) emerges as the most likely candidate. Once again the grave cut for these two burials was square-ended in appearance, suggesting a slab or monument. The placing of the two burials in the north of the cut may suggest that further interments were intended to the south.

Immediately to the east of grave [13667] was burial [13624], of a possible male 26–35 years of age. This burial slightly cut the east end of grave [13667].

Burial [13525], of a male aged 36–45 years, occupied a large rectangular grave cut similar to those described above, positioned on the line of the north screen of the chapel. An extensive layer of mortar measuring 2.2m x 1.6m sealed and partially slumped into the grave. On this were the remains of the base of a possible tomb chest or other monument [13856] in the form of two east–west strips of mortar 0.95m apart either side of the burial (Fig 33; Fig 34). The southern mortar strip had three large tiles set on edge within it, on its internal (north) edge, with a mortar backing which carried the possible impressions of a timber beam to the south, suggesting a timber slot or emplacement.

THE WESTERN CHOIR ENTRY OR RETROCHOIR (ROOM 6b)

Burials [13831] of a male aged ≥46 years, [13872] of a female aged 18–25 years, and [13898] of another female aged 26–35, formed a well-defined row to the north of the monument or tomb [13856] (room 6a) (Fig 28). Burial [13898] was slightly cut by burial [13872], which in turn was slightly cut by burial [13831], the row being completed from north to south. The careful positioning of these three graves may suggest a personal relationship. Burial [13831] was square-ended; a fragment of Purbeck marble grave slab was found in the north-west corner of the grave, but although it appeared to be lying in the correct position, it was found to be in the fill of a post-Dissolution posthole. A male aged 36–45 years (burial [12400]) may possibly have suffered from leprosy.

It appeared to the excavators that the burial of a child [16081] (not analysed) was dug in the retrochoir to the north of and slightly cutting the upper grave fill of burial [12473], a probable male. This relationship between an adult and a child burial was also recorded in the chapel outside the choir door (B16, below). It may reflect a familial relationship, a non-related adult burial 'accompanying' the child, or simple space saving. The adult grave had a square-ended grave cut which may suggest the presence of a slab above the burial.

A tiled floor was laid in the retrochoir on two make-up layers of sand, mortar and chalk rubble, diagonally relative to the alignment of the building. It was composed of a variety of tile types and sizes, and possibly represents an assortment of tiles relaid above burial [16122] in order to roughly match floor [13902] in the rest of the nave to the west (room 6c). However, the floor itself extended beyond the edges of the grave and

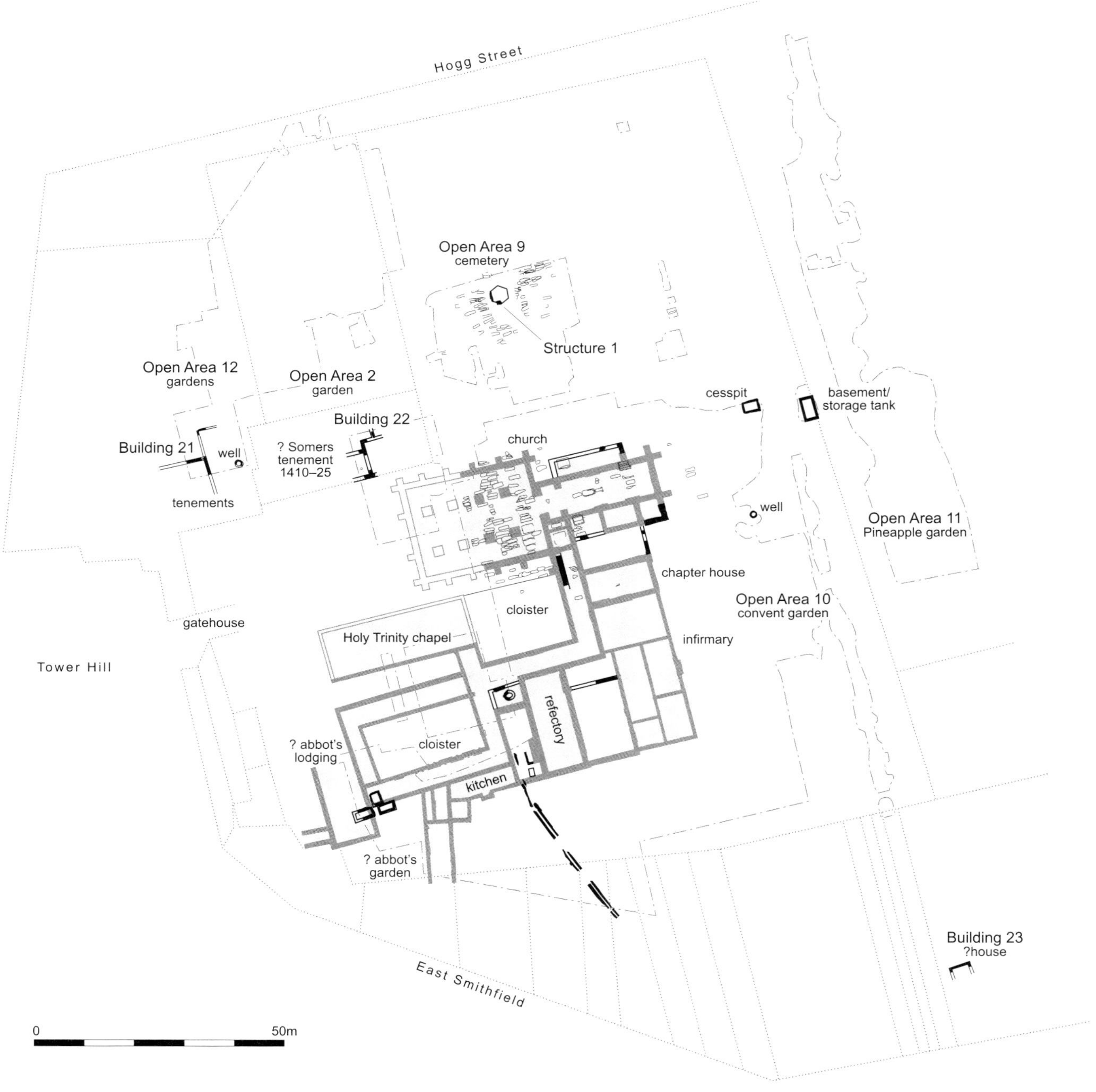

Fig 28 The principal archaeological features, c *1400–1539 (period B3): above – overall (scale 1:1250); facing page – detail (scale 1:400)*

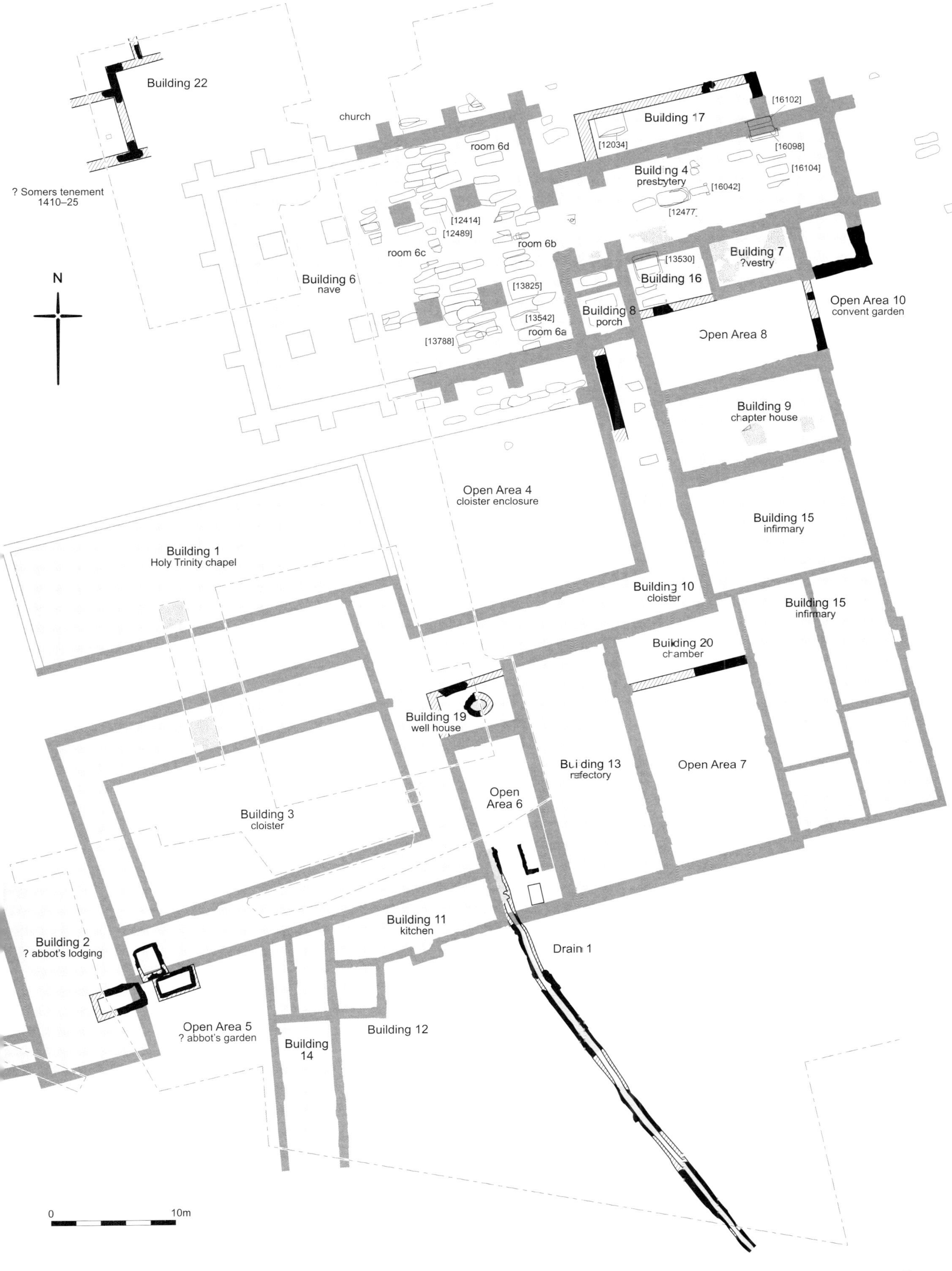
Building 22
church
Building 17
[16102]
[12034]
[16098]
room 6d
Building 4
presbytery
[16104]
[16042]
? Somers tenement
1410–25
[12477]
[12414]
[12489]
room 6b
room 6c
[13530]
Building 7
?vestry
N
Building 6
nave
Building 16
[13825]
Building 8
porch
Open Area 10
convent garden
[13542]
room 6a
[13788]
Open Area 8
Building 9
chapter house
Open Area 4
cloister enclosure
Building 15
infirmary
Building 1
Holy Trinity chapel
Building 10
cloister
Building 15
infirmary
Building 20
chamber
Building 19
well house
Building 13
refectory
Open Area 7
Open
Area 6
Building 3
cloister
Building 11
kitchen
Drain 1
Building 2
? abbot's lodging
Open Area 5
? abbot's garden
Building
14
Building 12
0
10m

Fig 29 The chalk and mortar cist-type lining [12478] of grave [12477] in the presbytery (B4), looking west (1.0m scale)

there was no evidence for a cut through the floor. The floor consisted of small English tiles and fragments of imported floor tile. The English tiles are small green-glazed tiles in fabric 1810, a Penn tile fabric, measuring 105 x 105 x 20mm. The imported tiles are in fabrics 1678, 1977 and 2497, and have nail holes where corners survive and traces of yellow, green, or dark green glaze (Table 17). The floor was cut by a posthole which was backfilled and the floor then made good with mortar.

THE NAVE WEST OF THE ROOD SCREEN (ROOM 6c)

There were a considerable number of burials here (Fig 28). The marked concentration of burials described in the previous period in the south aisle (period B2; above, 2.4) was continued in this period by burials [13774] of a possible male adult, [13777] of an unclassified adult, [13840] of a 36–45-year-old male, [13843] (not analysed), [13848] of a male aged ≥46 years, [13887] of a child, [13913] of a child, [16302] of an adolescent, [16308] (not analysed), [16311] of an unclassified adult with DISH, [16313] (not analysed), and [16316] of a male aged 26–35. Burials [13774], [13840], [13843], [13848] and [13887] in particular formed a tight cluster of only peripherally intercutting graves between the piers of the south nave arcade in the eastern bay. The grave cut or charnel pit [13788], also in this group, contained only redeposited human bone from more than one individual (not analysed), and probably from burials disturbed by later burials or construction work in the church.

Several burials in the central vessel of the nave were – with the exception of [13830], a male aged ≥46 years in a coffin – truncated by later burials. Burial [12410], an adolescent, was superimposed above burial [12424], a male aged 36–45, before it in turn was superimposed by burial [12403] of another male aged 36–45, forming a compact cluster. A similar relationship

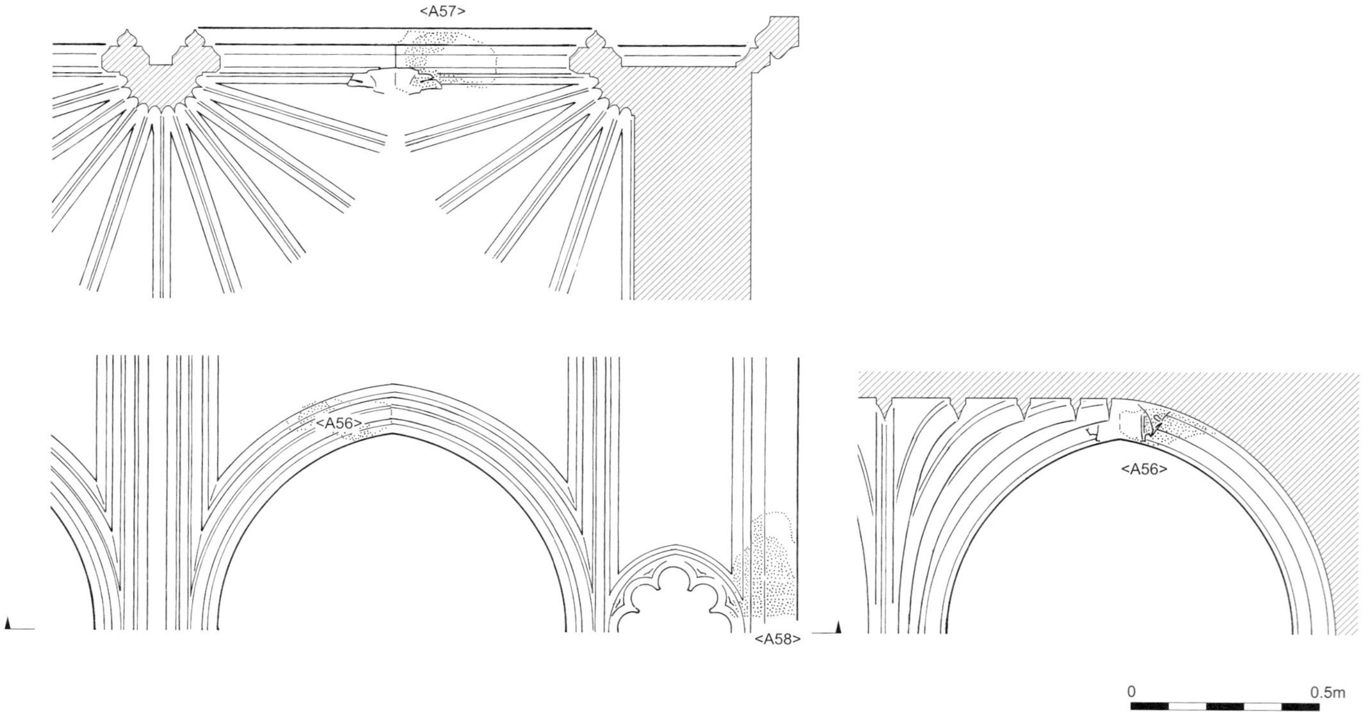

Fig 30 Part of a tomb canopy <A56>–<A58> from the 16th-century robber cut of grave [12477] in the presbytery (B4) (scale 1:20)

Fig 31 Burial [16042] in the presbytery (B4), showing (right) the surviving north foundation for a ? tomb chest (the south foundation was lost to weathering in 1987 before this photograph was taken), looking west (0.5m scale)

existed between burials [13970] and [16253], both of unclassified adults, and the later burial [13257] (not analysed), as well as between burial [16344], a male aged 26–35 with DISH, and burial [16122] of an unclassified adult. This may suggest a personal relationship between the deceased, or just indicate the relative popularity of the location where they were buried. Later burials in this area were [12345], an unsexed 18–25-year-old, [12365] of an unclassified adult, [12485] of a female aged ≥46 years, [13622] of a male aged 26–35, [13678] of a male aged 36–45, [13697] of a male aged ≥46 years, [13975] of a possible male aged 36–45, [13984] of an unclassified adult, and [13257] (not analysed). Only burial [13257] extensively cut other burials, [13970] and [16253]. A number of burials may represent contemporary pairs in that they were buried alongside one another with only peripheral intercutting. Such potential pairs were [12365], of an unclassified adult, and [12485] of a female aged ≥46 years; [13622], a male aged 26–35, and [13697], a male aged ≥46 years; and [13678], a male aged 36–45, and [13975], a probable male aged 36–45. These may or may not be

Fig 32 The brick vault [16011] in the north wall of the presbytery (B4), close to the high altar, looking west (0.5m scale)

Fig 33 The chapel of ? St Anne (B6, room 6a) from above, showing the layout of the later burials and floors, with other parts of the nave (B6) and porch (B8) visible, looking east (2.0m scale)

significant in terms of family relationships. A grave-shaped cut [13682] contained no burial. Burials [16320] (not analysed), [16326] of an unsexed adult, [16328] of a 36–45-year-old male, [16332] of a male adult with DISH, and [16338] of a subadult, formed a reasonably uniform row of burials to the west of the more westerly of the two excavated pier bases of the north nave arcade (ie west of the second nave arcade pier from the east).

Two burials, [12414] of a male aged 36–45 and [12489] of an unclassified adult, which may represent a husband and wife, were found between the two excavated pier bases of the north nave arcade. A post-Dissolution robber trench cut them, perhaps indicating a tomb or monument above or possibly a later screen wall. The spacing of the burials itself suggests the existence of a structure that precluded the dense pattern of burial found in the corresponding bay of the south arcade. Burial [12489] was cut slightly to the north by burial [12414]. The male was buried in a substantial timber coffin, surviving as a heavy stain, which had been lined with crushed chalk or lime (Fig 35).

Two or possibly three rough rows of burials survived in the north aisle. Burial [16060] was a single unclassified adult burial perhaps representing the start of a row in line with the more westerly pier base of the north nave arcade. East of this, burials [12382] of a child, [12432] of an adolescent, [12493] of a male aged ≥46 years, [12497] of a female aged 36–45, [16005] of a probable male aged 36–45, and [16119] of a child, formed one row in the western half of the bay. Burials [12339] of a female aged 26–35, [12403] of a male aged 26–35, and [12450] and [16009] each of a male aged ≥46 years, formed a row in the eastern half of the bay. Each slightly cut a burial in the row to the west, but in no case were the skeletons disturbed. These burials continued the intense burial activity already outlined for the preceding period in the north aisle (above, 2.4), and the density of burial here should be compared to that found in the corresponding bay of the south aisle (above). The square-ended appearance of the grave cut for burial [12339] suggests the presence of a slab above.

Fig 34 The remains of the base of a possible tomb chest [13856] above burial [13825] in the chapel of ? St Anne (B6, room 6a), looking east (0.5m scale)

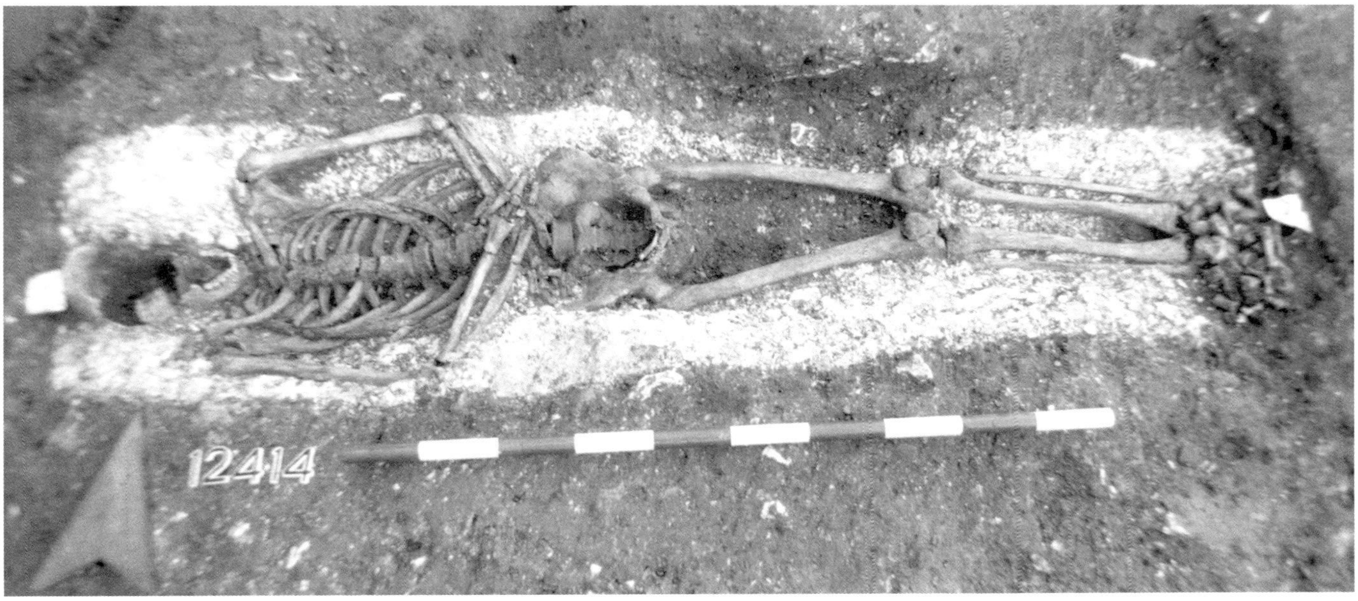

Fig 35 Burial [12414] in the nave (B6, room 6c), with crushed chalk or lime lining the coffin, looking north (1.0m scale)

Returning more to the southern part of room 6c, two small irregular-shaped pits or postholes cut burial [13848] and were partially sealed by a new floor [13902] (below). Two dump layers sealed a shallow pit cutting the top of burial [13887]. These features post-dated at least several of the burials, and it is possible that they were associated with the laying of the floor. Make-up layers of mortar and sand were laid in preparation for a tiled floor. The floor tiles were large (280 x 280mm) and laid diagonally relative to the alignment of the nave at approximately 10.26m OD. The imported tiles are very worn, large, plain glazed examples, but the edges show traces of yellow and green glaze; all have nail holes in the corners. They are in fabrics 1678 and 2324, except for a triangular tile in fabric 2850 which was cut from a square tile measuring 275 x 270 x 50mm scored diagonally before firing (Table 17; Fig 28; Fig 34; Fig 36).

Two burials, [13711] of a 1-year-old child with signs of vitamin C deficiency, and [13959] of a 26–35-year-old female, appeared to post-date this floor, cutting the make-up but not the tiles, which suggests that the tiles were relaid; however, the burials could have been inserted immediately before the primary laying of the tiles. The juvenile burial slightly cut the south side of the larger grave. Though these burials were separated from the earlier interments by the floor construction and were superimposed over a number of earlier burials, they did not greatly disturb these. There is no reason to suppose, therefore, that the floor or burials heralded a significant change in layout or pattern of burial. The small amount of pottery from the later features within the nave again includes 'Tudor Green' (TUDG) of 14th- or 15th-century date and the base of a coarse Surrey-Hampshire border ware (CBW) rounded jug found in the fill of one of the burials.

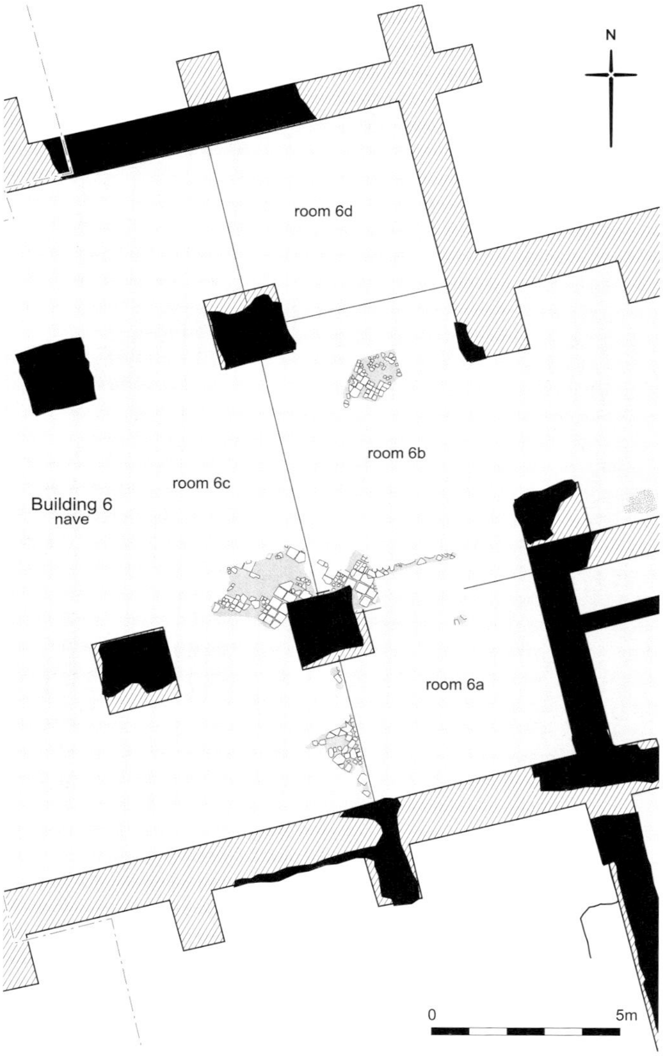

Fig 36 The late (period B3) tiled floor in the nave (B6) (scale 1:200)

A CHAPEL IN THE NORTH AISLE (ROOM 6d)

This area contained three well-spaced burials in a single irregular row (Fig 28). No floor levels survived the modern truncation in this area, although the square-ended appearance of the cut for [12331], the burial of a female aged 36–45, may indicate the former presence of a slab. The two remaining burials were [12323] (not analysed), and [12356] of a male aged ≥46 years.

Changes to the church ?vestry (B7)

The ?vestry (B7) was increased in size by about a third by extending the south wall 4.75m to the east with an L-shaped wall abutting the south-east corner of the presbytery (B4) (Fig 28). Only the foundations of this survived. They reached a maximum depth of 9.45m OD, approximately 0.5m shallower than the earlier walls they abutted, and had a maximum width of 1.3m. The original east wall of the vestry was reduced to floor level and the foundations partly robbed. The south-facing buttress of the presbytery was also cut down to floor level. This was replaced by a pilaster strip inserted against the south wall of the presbytery in a wide, shallow construction cut backfilled with chalk rubble and mortar. Only the chalk rubble foundations of the pilaster survived. Its function appears to have been cosmetic, that is to disguise the scar left by the removal of the buttress. A similar pilaster was inserted against the south wall. This was truncated but survived to its full width of 0.36m.

Several layers of make-up were laid for a tiled floor at 10.07m OD which occupied at least the west end of the building (ie the area bounded by the original east wall). Residual London-type ware (LOND) was recovered from layer [13577]. This floor sealed the construction cuts of the two pilasters and abutted their surviving foundations. The floor could not be traced beyond the original east wall. Only the mortar bedding survived, and the tile positions were inferred from impressions left in it. The tiles were laid square on to the alignment of the building and were approximately 300 x 300mm in size. Two tiles of similar size and alignment were found bedded on to the foundation of the south wall of the presbytery, and perhaps represent a continuation of the floor beyond a doorway or arch into the presbytery.

? A 'chapel without the quire door on the south side' (B16)

This chapel was constructed by enclosing the area to the south of the presbytery between the church porch (B8) and the vestry (B7) with an east–west wall (Fig 28). Only 1.24m length of foundation survived, which was a maximum of 0.64m wide and reached a maximum depth of 9.33m OD. Mortared into it was a processional marker or, more likely, a station of the cross (G Coppack, pers comm) lying face up. This complete ashlar <A1> (*c* 480 x 302mm), dressed from Reigate stone, is fresh and unweathered (Fig 37; Chapter 5.1). The carving on its face is shallow (*c* 1mm) and picked out in red paint. The style of the inscription is 'blackletter', conventionally dated after *c* 1350. The inscription is the Greek 'IHCOYC' ('Jesus') and 'INRI', the

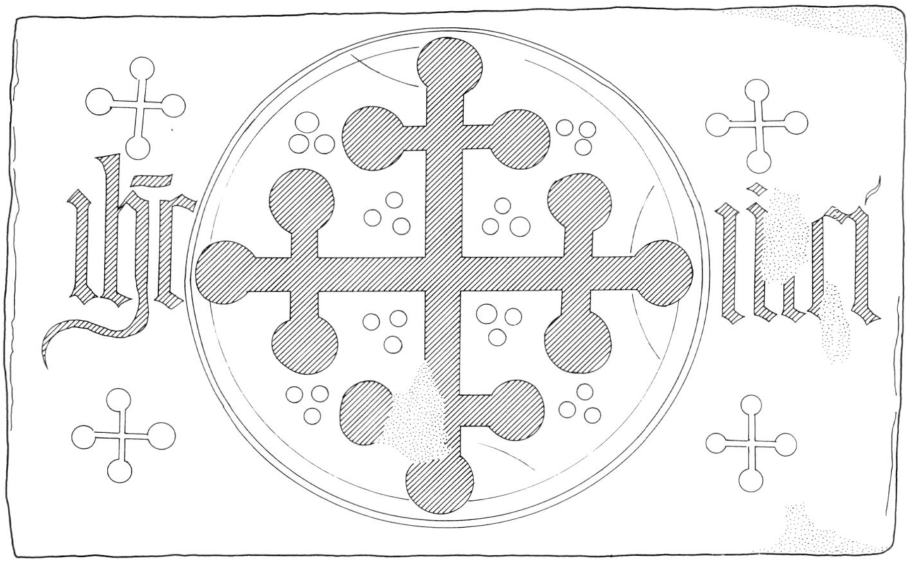

<A1>

Fig 27 The station of the cross or processional marker <A1> (scale 1:2)

abbreviation of 'Iesus Nazarenus Rex Iudaeorum' ('Jesus of Nazareth, King of the Jews'). The circles represent eternity and the groups of three balls probably signify the Trinity, further alluded to by the circles at the ends of the central cross. The central cross and the four smaller crosses probably symbolise the five wounds of Christ with the red paint further signifying the Passion (G Coppack, pers comm). An alternative possibility is that the quartering of the central cross may suggest the four quarters of the world, and the smaller crosses the Evangelists (Boyle 1951). It is probable that the ashlar originally formed part of the internal facing of the presbytery. The insertion of a later chapel to the south may have involved removing part of the south wall – for example to create an entrance directly from the choir – and the disturbed masonry could have been used in the new chapel. The ritual use of the stone would have been preserved by sealing it within the new chapel foundations.

The 'quire door' described was probably the door at the north end of the porch (B8) constructed in the preceding period (period B2; Chapter 2.4). The chapel could thus have had an entrance in its west wall and been accessible from the porch. The new south wall did not have the load-bearing capacity of the surrounding walls, and the chapel was probably constructed as a 'lean-to' structure against existing walls. Its internal dimensions would have been 6.0m x 3.75m.

Only one small patch of possible floor remained. This was laid at only 9.87m OD, which was rather low for a medieval floor immediately to the south of the church, and consisted largely of mortar. One floor tile was conceivably *in situ* but the whole may instead have been a Dissolution dump layer. Pottery from this floor or dump includes 'Tudor Green' (TUDG) or early Surrey-Hampshire border whiteware (EBORD), probably of late 15th- or early 16th-century date.

Burial [13530] was a male aged ≥46 years showing DISH and/or scoliosis of the spine, interred in a chalk-walled vault set into and below the foundations of the south wall of the presbytery (Fig 28; Fig 38). The vault measured 2.16m x 2.16m at the top, narrowing slightly at the base, and was 1.5m deep. Its walls were constructed of roughly coursed mortared chalk and Kentish ragstone rubble with the occasional use of brick. No floor was found; the whole vault was dug out to 0.25m below the base of its walls and the burial placed on natural gravel. The burial was sealed with the redeposited natural sands and gravels removed to inter it. It was in a substantial wooden coffin which barely fitted the vault at its base and which was lined with crushed chalk/lime. The skeleton was badly cramped and in its turn barely fitted the coffin, even allowing for the deformity of the spine. A group of cloth fragments <3765> and <3829> (Table 23) were preserved through contact with the crushed chalk. The textile, a medium-grade linen fabric woven in tabby from Z-spun yarn, is of similar character to that recorded on the buckles from the Black Death cemetery (Grainger et al 2008, 37–41) but this time there is little doubt that the cloth was part of a shroud. The sealing of the coffin in sand and gravel below the base of the vault may have been an attempt to counter the smell of putrefaction. It is clear that the tomb was designed for more than one interment, but no trace of further burials was found. The fill contained a sherd of Tudor brown ware (*c* 1500–*c* 1600), which could be accounted for by grave robbing.

To the south of the vault a small group of burials survived. The grave cut for [13762], a juvenile, had a square-ended appearance, as did that of burial [13909] of an unsexed adult, which may suggest the earlier presence of slabs. Burial [13805] was that of an infant which slightly cut the north side of the cut for [13909] (cf [16081], B6 room 6b). Burial [13805] was also partially sealed by the possible floor.

The ? Lady chapel (B17)

A 2.2m long north–south wall was constructed abutting the north-facing buttress of the presbytery (B4) and survived only as foundations (Fig 28). With the buttress the wall was 3.75m long. The foundations were trench-built of random, uncoursed, mortared chalk and Reigate stone rubble but also included

Fig 38 The vault for burial [13530] within the ? 'chapel without the quire door on the south side' (B16), looking down and to the south (0.1m scale)

occasional roof and floor tile fragments. These foundations reached a maximum depth of 9.27m OD and were a maximum of 0.75m wide. At the north end was a truncated stub of a return to the west, and here the lowest course of the wall survived, built of Kentish ragstone blocks. To the west was another truncated fragment of the north wall, 1.2m long, of which only the lowest 0.3m of the foundations survived. Within the corner formed by these walls a mortar floor or make-up level survived at 10.02m OD.

A walled tomb or vault [12000] was potentially within the area encompassed by these walls and may even have been set into the north wall in a similar fashion to the vaults in the presbytery and chapel (B16) (Fig 28; Fig 39). The vault was severely truncated, so that only part of the lowest course of the south wall, the stub of the east wall, and several tiles forming the base of the tomb remained. The floor was of unmortared imported tile consisting of green-glazed examples in fabric 1678 measuring on average 220 x 220 x 30mm (Table 17). Within the vault was the disarticulated burial [12034] (not analysed). The vault south wall survived to a length of 2.2m,

Fig 39 The fragmentary remains of vault [12000] for burial [12034], ?within the ? Lady chapel (B17), looking west (0.5m scale)

and was composed of a mixture of roughly coursed Kentish ragstone, flint and red brick rubble. The north side was entirely missing so that its original size can only be conjectured. It need not have been of comparable size to the others in the church, nor even have been within this chapel originally, and it is possible that it was constructed in the external cemetery (OA9).

Two other burials may also have been within the building, or perhaps immediately to the west of it as part of the external cemetery (and are shown thus on Fig 28): [12005] of a possible male 18–25 years old, and [12110] also of a male aged 36–45 years.

The church south porch (B8)

Four burials were found in three graves in the south porch (Fig 10; Fig 28). South of the internal sleeper wall were two graves, the more southerly of which, similar in form to those described in the chapel of ? St Anne (room 6a), contained two burials. Burial [13778], of an indeterminate adult, was the primary interment, with burial [13675], a male aged 36–45, inserted above and partially disturbing the first burial. The grave was partially sealed by the mortar bedding of the tile floor (above, 2.4) but as there were no tile impressions in the mortar the use of a slab is possible. Burial [13849], of an unclassified adult, was in a similar square-ended cut which may suggest the presence of another slab. Burial [13935], a male aged 26–35, occupied the area to the north of the internal sleeper wall.

The chapter house (B9)

A second tiled floor was laid at the eastern end of the building at 10.13m OD (Fig 28; Fig 40). This floor was composed of several plain tiles measuring 230 x 230mm laid square on to the alignment of the building and bedded only loosely with sand and gravel. No make-up layers were found; the floor was laid directly over the underlying quarry pits (Grainger et al 2008, 7). Despite the lower level, this floor did not appear to the west beneath the earlier floor (above, 2.4) and there was no evidence there that it had been removed prior to the laying of that floor. The tiles also had no relationship to the bench or footpace foundations or any other part of the chapter house. The two floor areas may have been in contemporary use and there was possibly – although it is extremely unlikely – a step down into the eastern half of the building. More likely is that this floor was the base of a tomb, storage chamber or strongbox; it was, however, less than 0.2m below the western floor.

The chapter house yard (OA8)

A north–south wall was inserted between the original (period B2) east end of the vestry (B7) and the north-east corner of the

Fig 40 The lower tile floor and stone footpace/bench in the chapter house (B9), looking south (1.0m and (top right) 2.0m scales)

chapter house (B9) (Fig 28). The foundations reached a maximum depth of 9.10m OD and were a maximum of 0.8m wide. The wall survived in two fragments. The first abutted the chapter house and survived to a height of 11.33m OD. The east face was composed of coursed hammer-dressed Kentish ragstone blocks, while the west had been removed and repaired in brick in the post-Dissolution period. To the north of this, the second surviving wall fragment was 0.9m long north–south. Here, above foundation level, no fabric survived except a south door-jamb composed of squared Reigate stone blocks, one of which still retained an iron staple for the hinge. A thin layer of soil beneath the door-jamb suggests that the door was a later insertion. This doorway in the yard's east wall may have been post-medieval but reusing medieval materials. The overall area of the yard, after the chapel (B16) was constructed to the north-west, was 13.5m east–west by 6.15m north–south.

Several pits were found within the yard cutting the robber trenches of the period B2 masons' lodges/workshops (B5) (above, 2.4). These pits varied in size and shape, the deepest being 1.03m below a highest surviving surface of 9.86m OD. All contained fairly high proportions of clay in their backfills, which otherwise consisted of a relatively clean sandy silt. There was little evidence of slumping, suggesting that they were open for only a limited amount of time. None cut the underlying natural sand and gravels significantly. One pit produced two residual sherds of medieval pottery later than the mid 13th century.

The east alley of the church cloister (B10)

The foundations of the west wall of the east alley were strengthened at the north end by the addition of a parallel sleeper foundation to the east (Fig 28). Possibly the foundations had proved inadequate for their original purpose, or a second storey was added to the cloister alley. This sleeper foundation reached a maximum depth of 9.00m OD and was a maximum of 0.8m wide. The buttress of the west wall was extensively remodelled, perhaps at the same time. A wide construction cut was dug around the buttress so that its foundations could be strengthened. The base of the new foundation was far wider than at ground level: in effect a very rough cone shape was constructed (Fig 41). This may have involved the clasping of

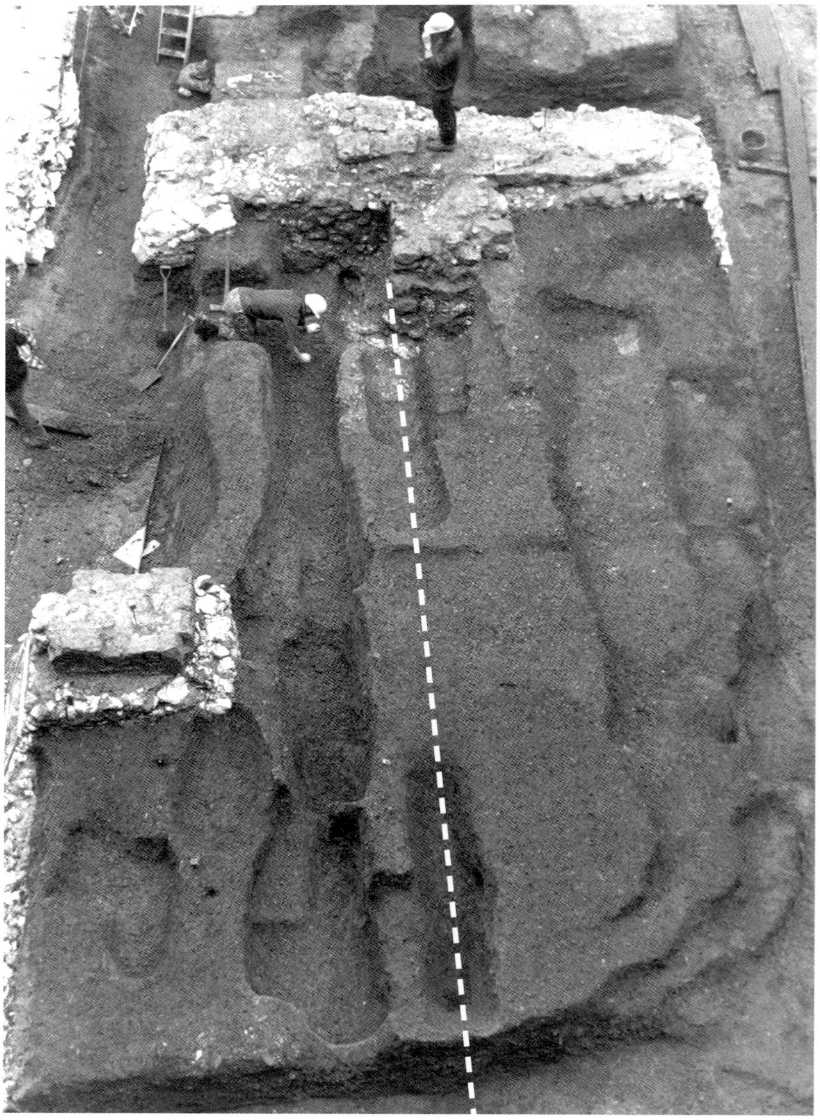

Fig 41 The west wall of the east cloister alley (B10, top) viewed from the west, showing the rebuilt buttress, with (below) the timber pentice (B18) to the south of the nave, fully excavated; the line of post trenches is indicated by a dashed line

material around the existing buttress or substantial rebuilding. Then, oddly, and not necessarily when the foundations were being altered, the buttress was rebuilt to the south of the foundation so that it rested partially on unconsolidated ground. Possibly this was done when the timber pentice (B18, below) was constructed, that is, the buttress was shifted south to accommodate it.

The sleeper foundation and the threshold of the doorway (above, 2.4) were sealed by the remnants of a tiled floor which was laid at 10.20m OD. The size and orientation of the tiles could only be deduced from impressions left in the mortar bedding. They measured approximately 200 x 200mm and were laid square on to the alley. A second fragment of mortar floor laid at 10.21m OD was found abutting the east wall of the building.

The second patch of mortar floor partially sealed burial [14321] of an unclassified adult and may also have sealed burial [14340], likewise of an unclassified adult. The three burials found here were heavily truncated and, in the case of burial [15200] (not analysed), heavily contaminated by chemicals from the Royal Mint workshops.

A timber pentice attached to the south of the nave (B18)

An east–west line of post trenches was dug to the south of the nave (B6) for a timber pentice attached to the nave (Fig 28), with access to the east cloister alley (B10) via the doorway in that building's west wall (above, 2.4). The trenches were narrow and steep-sided with concave bases, and were backfilled with compact rubble. They varied considerably in length, depth and width (Fig 41), and though all were probably associated with a single structure, these variations suggest that it was repaired and added to at different times. The three trenches to the east suggest that a timber post was replaced and a trench was then cut at right angles to the line for a prop to the pentice. One trench was perhaps too wide and shallow to have been a post trench and may represent repairs to the pentice, or else a rubbish pit. A small amount of pottery from the fills comprises 12th- to earlier 14th-century material, but with some Cheam whiteware (CHEA) and part of a 'Tudor Green' (TUDG) jug dated to the 15th century also present; two post-medieval sherds may be intrusive.

Between the post trenches and the nave was a strip of ten burials (Fig 28). Eight burials were in a single line: [14398] (not analysed), [14432] of an adult of indeterminate sex aged 36–45 years, [14405] of a *c* 11-year-old child, [14411] and [14418] (both not analysed), [14421] and [14424] both of adolescents, and [14427] (not analysed). In several cases one burial was superimposed over another, but only in one instance did a later burial disturb the skeleton from an earlier interment, with [14398] removing the skull of [14432]. Burial [16304], a male aged ≥46 years showing DISH, was an isolated burial to the north of this line, close to the south wall of the nave, and burial [14429] was a similarly positioned infant interment. This may hint at an unusual concentration of younger individuals being buried here, but the sample is a small one.

The church cloister garth (OA4)

To the south of the pentice (B18) a single grave cut the construction cut of the remodelled buttress of the east cloister alley (B10) (Fig 28). It contained the remains of one disarticulated skeleton (not analysed), and suggests the reburial of an individual disturbed by construction work.

A well house (B19)

Some 4m to the north of the north wall of the kitchen yard (OA6; above, 2.4) was a second, much slighter, truncated east–west foundation (Fig 28). It reached a maximum depth of 8.67m OD and had a maximum width of 0.6m. A chalk-lined well was inserted in the centre of the area defined by these walls and walls of the early cloister (B3) and refectory (B13), suggesting the construction of a well house (Fig 42). The well had an internal diameter of 1.0m and reached a depth of 6.09m OD. The lining was composed of random, uncoursed, mortared chalk rubble with the internal face of coursed, dressed chalk blocks. The decayed remains of timber planking associated with the construction of the well were found at the base of the lining. The well was backfilled only with rubble of late 16th- or early 17th-century date, including large fragments of Purbeck marble paving which may have come from the demolished church (Fig 86). It is possible that the well was used in connection with the drain (D1, below) to the south.

Drain 1 (OA6 and OA13)

A chalk-vaulted drain (D1) was constructed within the kitchen yard (OA6) and to the south through the south yard (OA13) (Fig 28; below, 2.6). It was extensively rebuilt with a brick vault during the post-medieval period, so that little of the original drain above its base and lower sides survived. Nevertheless, the course of the drain could be traced for a distance of *c* 40m, from where it emerged at the northern limit of the kitchen yard (OA6) to where it vanished beyond the southern limit of the excavation (OA13). The base was constructed of mortared, dressed chalk slabs, and the sides largely of mortar 0.4m thick and faced internally with chalk blocks roughly dressed on their internal edge. The original upper vault, where it survived, was composed of two curved chalk slabs resting on the sides and meeting at the apex to form a rounded arch above the base (Fig 43). Internally this vault was 0.4m wide and 0.5m high. Drain 1 drained to the south: at the northern limit of excavation its base was at 9.02m OD, and at the southern limit at 8.09m OD, a drop of nearly a metre over a distance of 40m. The drain was not recorded in the well house (B19) immediately to the north, but no archaeological stratification survived there above 8.80m OD; if the drain had reached this point, its base would have been at approximately 9.2m OD.

Within the kitchen yard the drain was constructed against the foundations of the east wall of the kitchen (B11), but the relationship with the south wall of the yard is less well understood. The foundations of the wall appeared to have been

Fig 42 The well in the well house (B19), looking down and to the north (1.0m scale)

Fig 43 Detail of Drain 1 showing the vault and base (0.2m scale)

disturbed, and the base of the drain roughly bedded on to them, with fragments of the foundations projecting through the base of the drain. A hole may have been punched through the wall to insert the drain, removing much of the wall fabric or possibly only disturbing the foundations. This may explain the scarring on the face of the west wall of the refectory (B13; above, 2.4), if it represents a south wall which pre-dated the excavated wall rebuilt over the drain. However, the scarring could also have resulted from the post-Dissolution demolition of the excavated south wall.

The ?kitchen yard (OA6)

A number of undated chalk and mortar rubble layers were associated with the construction of Drain 1, and cutting these rubble layers were two north–south aligned pits (Fig 28). To the north a probable cesspit, possibly with an overflow to Drain 1, was lined with unmortared Kentish ragstone, chalk and brick, and was at least 2.5m long (the north wall was lost) by 1.7m wide. This pit reused the west face of the refectory pulpit (B13) as an east wall, and a number of slots cut into the pulpit foundation suggest a timber floor above the pit. The pit had a chalk and Kentish ragstone rubble base at 8.89m OD. The lower fill [4132] contained faecal material including parasite eggs, with a total concentration of just over 1000 opg for both *Trichuris* and *Ascaris*. A large number of fish bones were found (850 fragments from [4132]; included in the fragment count by period in Table 25), of which 91% were eel, largely vertebral centra but with some skull fragments from which total lengths could be calculated, with a range of 0.15–0.28m (n=9). These were all rather small specimens compared with males in general reaching 0.5m and females 1.0m (Libois et al 1987; Wheeler 1978). In fact all the calculations for the size of eel from this site show them to be fairly small specimens of below average size (Table 26). The fills [4132] and [4156] also produced amphibian remains (Table 24), possible chicken eggshell fragments, terrestrial and marine molluscs, and charred grain and calcified fruit seeds (Table 21).

A clay-floored storage tank or pit was constructed approximately 1m to the south of the first pit. This was 1.7m long by 0.9m wide, with its base at 9.24m OD. It was largely backfilled with relatively clean silt layers and some demolition rubble and domestic refuse. The fills [2544], [2546] and [2777] produced a few fish bones (26 fragments; Table 25) and eggshell fragments (Chapter 5.9). Waterlogged fruit seeds, plus a few seeds from other plants, as well as some carbonised grain and mineralised fruit seeds, also came from the fills (Table 21). The construction of cesspits and storage pits in this yard should be compared with similar activity in the ? abbot's garden (OA5) and lodging (B2) (below).

A wall was keyed into the east wall of the kitchen (B11), in line with the south-west corner of the refectory pulpit. Only a fragment of this, 0.5m wide, survived attached to the wall. This was composed of mortared Kentish ragstone rubble and did not descend below the top of the kitchen's foundations at 9.75m OD. It may have been the last vestige of a suspended wall or arch keyed into the refectory pulpit and spanning the 3.25m between the buildings. Such a wall or arch would have divided the cesspit and storage pits into separate areas.

A chamber (B20) in the refectory yard (OA7)

A wall enclosed the north end of the refectory yard (OA7, Fig 28). With a maximum depth of 9.30m OD, this foundation was considerably shallower than the surrounding walls of the refectory (B13) and refectory yard, and had a maximum width of 0.6m. The construction trench was substantially deeper and wider than the wall foundation, and the trench was partially backfilled with sand, gravel and mortar before the wall was constructed along the south edge. The foundation trench contained three sherds of medieval pottery, including a sherd of coarse Surrey-Hampshire border ware (CBW). The wall followed the same east–west alignment as the earlier ditch in the yard (OA7; above, 2.4) but was offset slightly to the south and was considerably shallower. The wall abutted the east wall of the yard but was truncated to the west. This was not a major load-bearing foundation, and suggests a pentice structure, possibly with only a dwarf wall above the foundation. Only one course of the south face of the wall survived, consisting of hammer-dressed Kentish ragstone blocks. The maximum internal measurements of the building were 4.25m x 10.0m.

A chalk-walled pit in the ? abbot's lodging (formerly the dormitory/refectory) (B2)

An east–west chalk-walled pit [98] was found within the projected area of Building 2, adjacent to the similar pits (described below) in the first cloister (B3) and the ? abbot's garden (OA5) (Fig 28; Fig 44). The pit reached a maximum depth of 7.71m OD. It had a heavily green-stained lining and the fills produced some parasite eggs, although the egg count was low at 320 opg and no intact eggs of *Trichuris* were noted. The fills also produced fish bone (eg fill [100], 50 fragments; Table 25), mainly smelt vertebral centra reflecting a seasonal fishery pursued in the Thames. Eel and plaice/flounder vertebral centra were also recovered. Waterlogged fruit seeds, with a few seeds of other plants, were likewise found (fill [100], Table 21). Unfortunately, none of these fills produced dating evidence. Later fills, possibly associated with demolition, produced a cup and bottle (?costrel) in 'Tudor Green' (TUDG), along with some Tudor wares (London-area early post medieval redware (PMRE) and slipped redware (PMSR)). The imports comprise a sherd from a north French-style jug and part of an Italian floral vase with 'ladder' medallion dated to *c* 1500–75.

A chalk-walled pit in the first cloister (B3)

A chalk-walled pit [1724] was constructed at right angles to the pit in in the ? abbot's lodging (B2), and cut the foundations and the south alley of the first cloister (B3) (Fig 28; Fig 44). The pit reached a depth of 6.98m OD. There were no staining or waste deposits to indicate that it had been used for waste disposal; it may originally have been a water storage tank or soakaway and should probably be compared with that noted in period B1 (Chapter 2.3). It was backfilled only with rubble which contained a small quantity of Kingston-type ware (KING), a barrel-shaped jug in Cheam whiteware (CHEA), and a CHEA biconical jug and pipkin. Also present were nine sherds from a standing costrel in Iberian red micaceous ware (SPAM). This small assemblage appears to represent kitchen refuse, as it consists of jugs and cooking vessels.

A chalk-walled pit in the ? abbot's garden (OA5)

Another chalk-walled pit [100] was dug adjacent to and in line with that found in the abbot's lodging (B2) (Fig 28; Fig 44), reaching a maximum depth of 8.03m OD. Its walls were not stained but its lowest, undated, fill appeared to be a waste

Fig 44 The chalk-walled pits in the first cloister (B3) and ? abbot's garden (OA5), looking north (0.5m and 1.0m scales)

deposit. It was capped by a thick layer of clay which had clearly been used to seal the waste deposit after the pit had gone out of use. This layer [1930] was in turn sealed by silt and rubble, which contained some late 14th- or 15th-century pottery as well as a small, hinged pendant strapend of 13th- to 15th-century date (<S117>, Fig 103).

The eastern cemetery (OA9)

Nine rows of graves containing 91 burials were recorded here, cutting the quarry pits of Open Area 1 (Fig 28; Grainger et al 2008, 9). Graves in some rows cut ones in adjacent rows, but there was no coherent pattern to this intercutting. As with the western cemetery, this burial area appears to have evolved from a pattern of reasonably well-defined rows into a less orderly pattern. Relatively few infant and juvenile burials were recorded here.

All the burials were interred supine and extended, with heads to the west and feet to the east. In all, 28 were identified as having been in coffins, either from wood stains or fittings. One burial (fill [9386]) produced a small oblong copper-alloy ?shoe buckle (<S102>, Fig 102), and a coffined burial ([12102], not analysed) was interred with a deposit of charcoal close to the north wall of the nave. In one grave, although there was an individual inhumation at the base, the upper part of the grave had been utilised as a charnel pit which yielded the remains of at least 47 individuals. A second grave may also have been a charnel pit, and another appeared to be partly lined with tile.

The majority of the pottery from the eastern cemetery comprises residual London-type ware (LOND) and south Hertfordshire-type greyware (SHER). The rarity of 14th- and 15th-century fabric types, other than coarse Surrey-Hampshire border ware (CBW), is notable, although 'Tudor Green' (TUDG), Cheam whiteware (CHEA), late medieval Hertfordshire glazed ware (LMHG), some possible late London-type ware (LLON), Dutch red earthenware (DUTR) and Siegburg stoneware (SIEG) were present.

CEMETERY CROSS OR CALVARY (S1)

A truncated plinth of chalk blocks bonded with mortar (S1) was found in roughly the middle of Open Area 9 (Fig 28). The untruncated part of this plinth suggested that it was hexagonal in plan. The structure does not appear to have been part of a building, and likely interpretations of it are a shrine, a cemetery cross, or a Calvary. A number of the burials within the eastern cemetery approached close to it and appeared to be partly aligned on it.

Tenement to the north of the gatehouse (B21)

Two truncated chalk rubble foundation fragments formed the eastern edge of a building on the Tower Hill street frontage (Fig

28). They were a maximum of 0.7m wide and reached deeper than 9.45m OD.

The ? tenement of William and Catherine Somers (B22)

Slightly to the north and west of the nave (B6) were two fragments of chalk rubble foundation (B22), which may have been part of the documented tenement of William and Katherine Somers to the north of the 'great court' (Fig 28). To the north was a north–south foundation 0.6m wide and reaching a maximum depth of 8.98m OD, which had one possible west-facing return to the south and a probable east buttress to the north. Directly to the south of this was a foundation of similar construction, width and depth. This appeared to be the truncated stub of the south end of the first foundation, making a north–south wall approximately 8m long. It had a truncated eastern return but did not appear to be truncated to the west.

The convent garden (OA10)

In part of what was the eastern Black Death cemetery area (OA3: Grainger et al 2008, 17–18) four stratigraphically late graves were identified (Fig 28). To the north-east, burial [5325] was that of a ?male adult interred with a deposit of charcoal in a coffin. East of the church were burial [5787], of an unclassified adult, and two empty graves. Apparently contemporary with these graves was a large charnel pit. These graves may represent late additions to the Black Death cemetery, or the continued short-lived or occasional use of the area for burial in the monastic period.

To the east of the three latter burials was a heavily truncated chalk-walled basement or storage tank measuring 5.5m x 4.0m (Fig 28). Only the base of the walls remained; they reached a depth of 8.60m OD and were 0.6m wide. A fragmentary clay floor and make-up levels survived, from which was recovered a small quantity of pottery including coarse Surrey-Hampshire border ware (CBW) and a Raeren stoneware (RAER) drinking jug (*c* 1480–*c* 1550).

A chalk-lined cesspit measuring 3.5m x 2.5m was also found immediately to the east of these burials (Fig 28). It was severely truncated and reached a maximum depth of 7.97m OD. The walls were stained with cess but no cess fills remained. It had been backfilled with demolition rubble which produced CBW and a base sherd of an Italian tin-glazed ware (ITGW) jug dated to *c* 1450–80. To the south of this and in line with the west end of the pit was the truncated fragment (surviving length 0.7m) of a north–south chalk wall foundation reaching a maximum depth of 8.47m OD and in excess of 0.5m wide (not illustrated). A chalk-lined well (Fig 28) nearby, and lying some 20m south of the cesspit, had a diameter of 1.5m and reached a maximum depth of 7.08m OD.

The Pineapple garden (OA11)

The name Pineapple garden refers to the late Middle English term for a pine-cone, rather than the fruit itself, which was named, in this country, for its resemblance to the pine-cone in the 17th century, according to the *Oxford English Dictionary*. The name here implies the presence of pine trees in this area on the eastern edge of the site. The only feature of note here was a chalk-lined well (not illustrated). This was built with shaped mortared chalk blocks and an internal timber framework; it had a maximum diameter of 1.0m and reached a maximum depth of 7.05m OD. The well was extensively rebuilt in the post-medieval period.

A ? house on East Smithfield (B23)

A chalk-walled basement was found in the south-east corner of the site close to the East Smithfield street frontage (Fig 28). Only the north wall remained with the stubs of two southern returns. The north wall was 4.14m long, surviving to a width of 0.46m and reaching a depth of 8.02m OD. Its south face was constructed of coursed dressed chalk blocks. No internal medieval stratification survived.

Gardens in the north-west part of the precinct (OA2, OA12)

Some 5m to the east of the tenement (B21) to the north of the gatehouse was a well [9649] (OA12, Fig 28). This had a diameter of 1.0m and reached a depth of 6.73m OD. The lining was of mortared chalk, Kentish ragstone and green sandstone blocks. Putlog holes in the fabric suggest either a timber framework or scaffolding used in the construction. Two fills ([9649] and [9671]) produced parasite eggs, with [9671] yielding the most – a count of around 500 opg in total; there were no complete *Trichuris* and also very few intact *Ascaris* eggs. The same fills also produced some waterlogged fruit seeds and a few seeds of other plants (Table 21).

A large pit [9589] in the northern part of the later 14th-century ?epidemic cemetery (OA2, period B2), measuring 4.2m x 1.9m and reaching a depth of 8.82m OD, was used for the disposal of domestic rubbish (OA2/OA12; not illustrated). This produced a number of mouse and rat bones, a large quantity of chicken eggshell fragments (Chapter 5.9), and a number of molluscs (Wilkinson 1991), as well as some waterlogged fruit seeds from fill [9592] and a few seeds of other plants (Table 21). Fill [9592] also produced a large number of fish bones (588 fragments; Table 25) from a variety of species, particularly herring, sprat (48%), cod and whiting. Apart from 22 eel vertebral centra and a few freshwater species (cyprinids and pike), the sample is marine-orientated.

The pottery is characterised by a large quantity of Surrey whitewares. The most unusual vessel is the greater part of a puzzle jug in a fine version of coarse Surrey-Hampshire border ware (CBW) (<P6>, Fig 45). The jug has a thick tubular handle and spout, and the remains of a frilled base reminiscent of a German stoneware drinking jug. The top part of the vessel is covered with a green glaze spread over applied discs of red clay stamped with a rosette design (positioned on the shoulder of the jug). One rectangular hole is pierced through the underside of the handle at the top, and a second, smaller, rectangular

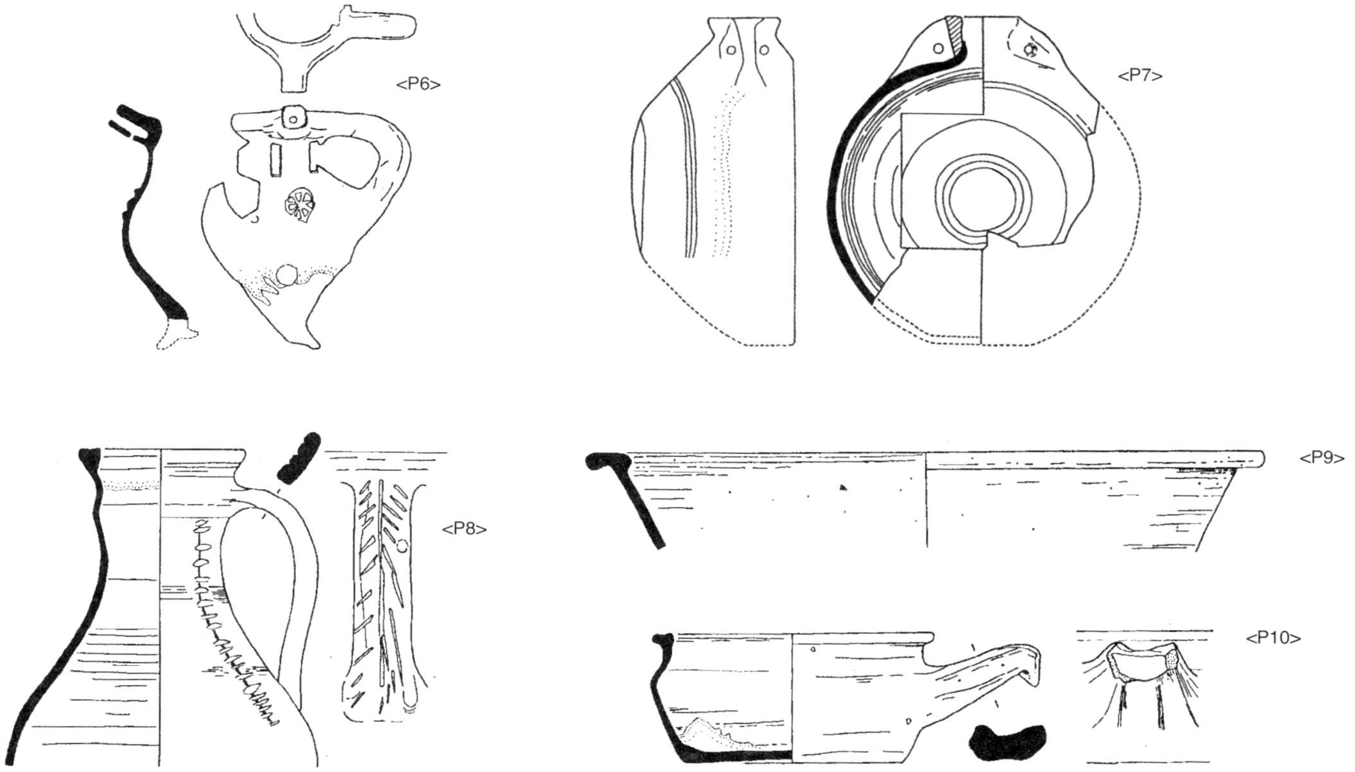

Fig 45 Coarse Surrey-Hampshire border ware (CBW) puzzle jug <P6>, Surrey whiteware (?CBW) mammiform costrel <P7> and baluster jug <P8>, CBW bowl <P9> and Cheam whiteware (CHEA) pipkin <P10> from fill [9592] of rubbish pit [9589] (OA2/OA12) (scale 1:4)

perforation has been cut under the spout; these would be covered with fingers when using the jug. Inside, the hollow tubular handle extends nearly to the bottom, where it is knife-trimmed flush with the angle of the vessel wall. Vessel sherds of this type have been found elsewhere in London in this fabric, but such a complete example is unusual (Pearce and Vince 1988, 56).

A second vessel in fine Surrey whiteware is a mammiform costrel (<P7>, Fig 45). In style it is very similar to 'Tudor Green' (TUDG), although it would perhaps be more accurate to describe it as a fine variant of CBW. There is also a baluster jug made in a similar fabric with vertical notched decoration and slashed strap handle (<P8>, Fig 45). It is possible that this is part of an anthropomorphic vessel, since it is very similar to excavated examples from London with stylised faces moulded round the pouring lip (Pearce and Vince 1988, 151). The pit fill also yielded the top half of a conical jug in a fine whiteware, perhaps a product of the late Kingston-type industry (J Pearce, pers comm). The jug is covered with a lustrous green glaze and has a band of pronounced rilling halfway down the body. Other vessels include a bowl made in a more traditional CBW fabric (<P9>, Fig 45) and a fragment of late London slipware (LLSL) cooking pot with lid seating. Cheam whiteware (CHEA), the dominant fabric by weight, includes a pipkin (<P10>, Fig 45) and four barrel-shaped jugs of different sizes dated to after 1430. The pit also produced a Siegburg stoneware (SIEG) *Jacobakanne* jug base and Raeren stoneware (RAER).

The group contains examples of fine whitewares of a transitional character (Table 3). Although they are products of the late medieval Surrey whiteware industries, most are not quite fine enough for TUDG and not yet the Surrey-Hampshire border wares (BORD and its variants) of the 16th and 17th centuries. Some of the fine white sherds with a lustrous glaze, however, have been called 'Tudor Green'. As in many mid 14th- to mid 15th-century assemblages, CBW and CHEA dominate this group. There is a marked absence of late medieval Hertfordshire glazed ware (LMHG), but the presence of several CHEA barrel-shaped jugs, the LLSL and the SIEG nevertheless indicates that the bulk of the assemblage is of early to mid 15th-century date. The pit may, however, have been filled over a long period of time, as earlier material such as Kingston-type ware (KING) and Mill Green ware (MG) is well represented. The latest finds comprise a small amount of early post-medieval redware (CHEAR, PMRE, PMSR) along with sherds of RAER and Frechen stoneware (FREC). The latter should date to after *c* 1550 and may be intrusive, but it is clear that the pit was finally filled at the time of the suppression or in the aftermath.

The pit also produced several glass flask or bottle fragments <G18>–<G19> of 13th- to 16th-century date (Chapter 5.4).

Discussion, *c* 1400–1539 (period B3)

The ?vestry (B7) was extended at an uncertain date (Fig 28). The documentary evidence indicates that the vestry and choir received a tile floor in 1391, and Building 7 was extended before the only surviving floor was laid. This may represent the

Table 3 Pottery from fill [9592] of rubbish pit [9589] in the north-west part of the precinct (OA2/OA12, period B3)

Period	Fabric	Form	Weight (g)	Weight %	EVEs
Medieval	AHFA	ll	35	0.8	0.2
	CBW	bowl	59	1.3	0.8
	CBW	jug	409	9.0	1.0
	CBW	misc	7	0.2	
	CBW	misc	164	3.6	
	CBW	costrel	80	1.7	
	CBW	jug	618	13.6	1.2
	CHEA	jug	1011	22.2	0.7
	CHEA	misc	46	1.0	
	CHEA	pipkin	299	6.6	0.2
	KING	jar	27	0.6	0.1
	KING	jug	297	6.5	
	KING	misc	5	0.1	
	KING	jug	161	3.5	0.4
	LANG	misc	2	<0.1	
	LLON	jug	292	6.4	
	LLSL	jar	54	1.2	0.2
	LOND	misc	11	0.2	
	MG	misc	35	0.8	
	SHER	jar	16	0.3	
	SHER	misc	8	0.2	
	SIEG	drinking jug	5	0.1	<0.1
	SIEG	jug	459	10.1	0.3
	TUDG	cup	1	<0.1	
	TUDG	jug	19	0.4	
	TUDG	misc	286	6.3	
Post-medieval	CHEAR	misc	5	0.1	
	FREC	jug	58	1.3	
	PMRE	misc	12	0.3	
	PMSR	misc	34	0.7	
	RAER	jug	40	0.9	
Total			4555		5.1+

documented floor of the vestry and choir, but the surviving tiles and the general size of the tile impressions suggest a later date. If the identification of the vestry is correct, this suggests the removal and replacement of the documented floor in the 15th century. The enclosure of the chapter house yard (OA8) and the construction of the chapel (B16) may have occurred before or after the vestry was extended.

Two chapels have approximate documented locations, and appear to have been of late construction. The chapel 'without the quire door on the south side' mentioned in the 'Visitations of Clarenceux' in 1533 (Wagner 1956, 143–4) was probably Building 16, given the relationship to the choir and the retrochoir at the north end of the porch (B8). This chapel was in existence by 1475, when Sir Thomas Charles was buried there (*Cal Pat R*, 1467–77, 449). The documentary evidence also indicates a Lady chapel (B17) on the north side of the church (Wagner 1956, 143–4), which appears to have been constructed shortly before 1489 (TNA: PRO, PROB 11/10/22). Lady chapels were popular in the 14th and 15th centuries, and although Cistercian churches were already dedicated to the Blessed Virgin Mary most of the greater Cistercian churches would have additional altars dedicated to her (G Coppack, pers comm). A much earlier Lady chapel is recorded at St Mary Stratford Langthorne (Barber et al 2004, 37–8), so St Mary Graces may also have been influenced by local example. The Lady chapel was also of course constructed in deference to the wishes of the patron, Sir Thomas Montgomery, and served as a mortuary chapel for his family and friends (Chapter 3.7; Table 13). The documentary sources do not indicate whether the Lady chapel lay to the north of the nave (B6) or the presbytery (B4), although the 'Visitations of Clarenceux' suggests that it was close to the high altar and thus the choir (Chapter 3.7). Building 17 is the only likely excavated candidate, added to the north because the presbytery was not aisled and lacked an eastern chapel group. The surviving remains hardly indicate an impressive size, as might be expected of a 15th-century Lady chapel, but instead perhaps only a small extension to the north with an open arcade to the presbytery.

The internal arrangements of the chapter house (B9) present a problem. If the two tile floors evidenced in periods B2 (above, 2.4) and B3 were in contemporary use, then either there was a step down at the east end of the building, which is highly unlikely, or the later floor was the tiled base of a tomb or storage chamber. A tomb seems most likely, but by the 14th and 15th centuries it had become much less common for abbots and senior obedientiaries to be buried in the chapter house. The west ends of a number of Cistercian chapter houses contained the library, but it seems unlikely that significant space would have been devoted to this at so small a house. Shrines existed in the chapter houses of both Rievaulx, Yorkshire, and Melrose, Roxburghshire (Coldstream 1986, 158), but there is no documentary evidence to suggest that this was the case here.

The building (B20) adjacent to the south cloister alley (B10), between the refectory (B13) and the infirmary (B15), is unlikely, given its insubstantial nature and the late date, to have been a warming house, despite occupying the position traditionally reserved for this building. It may have been a meat kitchen or misericord associated with the infirmary. It is also possible that it was a small chapel, a storeroom, or a private chamber.

Drain 1 and the other modifications to the ?kitchen yard (OA6) represent a considerable alteration to the structure of the yard between the refectory (B13) and the kitchen (B11). The 'drain' may have been a conduit carrying fresh water from the well house (B19) to buildings beyond the southern limit of excavation where the abbey held several properties. However, there was no proof that the drain and well/cistern were associated, and the drain's proximity to the cesspit in the yard suggests that it carried foul water. Drain 1 could have served either latrines or the kitchen. Small latrines, confined to the north end of the yard and serving private chambers above the first cloister (B3), are a possibility, but there was no evidence here or elsewhere on site for a communal reredorter and large main drain. The chalk-walled pits found in the yard, the abbot's lodging and garden (B2 and OA5) and the first cloister (B3) were probably associated with water management in one form or another, and suggest an increase in or changes to domestic accommodation around this cloister. Although two produced evidence of waste disposal, and in one case sufficient parasite eggs to suggest a latrine, they may have only subsequently been used for this purpose, having originally been soakaways or storage tanks. The disuse fills of two produced a small amount of imported pottery, which may again suggest association with private chambers, perhaps of the more important monks, corrodians or servants, and with the abbot's lodging, as do the early 16th-century ceramic stove-tiles found in demolition deposits (Chapters 2.6 and 5.2).

The household waste from the other 15th-century tenements (OA12) also hints at comparatively well-off households owning good-quality tableware items like the puzzle-jug bought for amusement, and with fish served often.

There is no evidence to suggest that the eastern burial area – or churchyard, surrounded as it was by property boundaries – directly to the north of the church was ever closed during the lifetime of St Mary Graces, unlike the western cemetery (OA2) (above, 2.4). The osteological assemblage suggests a male to female burial ratio more akin to that of other monastic cemeteries, as opposed to parish cemeteries or that of the western cemetery which was potentially for later 14th-century epidemic burials.

2.6 The Dissolution and manor house, 1539–60 (period B4)

Documentary evidence

The abbey was suppressed in 1539, although this had clearly been foreseen for some years. As early as 1528 it was considered likely that the monastery would be suppressed and that alternative arrangements would have to be made for chantries (TNA: PRO, E 303/10/354). Support for St Mary Graces had been drawn partly from London's merchant community, and it had attracted donations from London merchants in their wills to fund chantries.

At the time of the Dissolution the abbey's contribution to London's spiritual and social needs was recognised by the mayor, Richard Gresham. In August 1538 he petitioned Henry VIII to keep the abbey and three of the London hospitals open because of their good work on behalf of the poor and sick, proposing that henceforward they should be governed by the mayor and aldermen (BL, Cotton MS Cleopatra E.iv, fo 222). This did not meet with royal approval. Late in 1538 the abbey granted several life annuities to royal officials (including Thomas Pope, treasurer of the Court of Augmentations) and lawyers, presumably for services in connection with the impending dissolution (TNA: PRO, E 315/94, p 93; E 315/100, fos 223, 240–240v, 343; SC 6/HenVIII/2396, m 52). The monastery was finally dissolved on 31 March 1539 (not in September 1538 as suggested by Clapham and the *Victoria County History*), on the same day as the nunnery of the Poor Clares in the Minories, and the monks and nuns were turned out (*VCH* 1909, 463 and n49; Clapham 1915, 356).

Royal commissioners arrived to assess the monastery and its tenements, and also the tenements of the manor of Poplar. The lead from the roof was melted down; the bells, jewels, plate, vessels and other goods taken away; and timber was taken from Gomshull wood for the king's building work at Hampton Court (TNA: PRO, SC 6/HenVIII/2383, m 42–42v; 2427; SC 12/29/22, fo 2). The rents ceased to be paid to the abbot and were paid to the Crown instead. Hugh Losse, the abbey's last rent-collector, accounted for the monastery lands to the king and paid the profits to the Court of Augmentations (TNA: PRO, SC 6/HenVIII/2382; 2383, m 1; 2396, m 53; 2427). A list of debts owed to and by the abbey was drawn up (TNA: PRO, SC 12/29/22).

In August 1536, Abbot Henry Moore had been licensed to receive Coggeshall Abbey *in commendam* (*L and P Hen VIII*, xi, nos 385(37), 392; TNA: PRO, E 303/10/323, 328). It was probably envisaged that the king would soon gain possession of both of Moore's abbeys through his death or surrender. By November 1537 Coggeshall was expected to pass to Sir Thomas Seymour (*L and P Hen VIII*, xii(2), no. 1151). Moore surrendered it to the Crown in February 1538 and it was granted to Seymour six weeks later. Seymour was obliged to pay Moore a pension of 100 marks per annum for life and reimburse his expenses in obtaining the abbey (*L and P Hen VIII*, xiii(1), nos 221, 646(61); TNA: PRO, E 211/344).

Eight former monks of St Mary Graces were granted life pensions of 8 marks (£5 6s 8d) per annum each, and the sub-prior 10 marks (£6 13s 4d). These were paid by the treasurer of the Court of Augmentations from 25 March 1539, not from 29 September 1538 as stated in the *Victoria County History*. Abbot Henry Moore also received a gift of 50 marks (£33 6s 8d) (*L and P Hen VIII*, xiv(1), no. 688; TNA: PRO, SC 6/HenVIII/2427; E 315/233, fos 262–263v; *VCH* 1909, 463 and n49). He continued to be paid the Augmentations pension for the remainder of Henry VIII's reign (*L and P Hen VIII*, xiv(2), no. 236; xvi, no. 745; xvii, no. 258; xviii(1), no. 436; xviii(2), no. 231; xix(1), no. 368; xx(1), no. 557; xxi(1), no. 643; xxi(2), no. 775).

Immediately after the suppression the site was under the control of Sir Christopher Morice, the king's Master Gunner, on the king's behalf (TNA: PRO, SC 6/HenVIII/2382; 2383, m 1). In July 1539 (with effect back-dated to 25 March) Morice was granted the monastery site and precinct for life, together with adjacent tenements and enclosures and the abbey's Kentish manors of Gravesend, Parrock and Lynches (TNA: PRO, SC 6/HenVIII/2396, ms 42, 50–50v, 52v; 2397, m 40–40v; E 315/233, fos 339v–340).

In August 1542, Sir Arthur Darcy was granted the abbey brewhouses along the Thames bank and the reversion of Morice's grant of the monastery precinct with the adjacent tenements and enclosures (*L and P Hen VIII*, xvii, no. 714(18); xix, no. 278(76); Rosenfield 1961, 317). He probably bought out Morice's interest straight away, and was certainly in possession before the end of Henry's reign (TNA: PRO, LR 2/262). Morice had died in September 1544 (*DNB* 1894, 988–9). Darcy also acquired former abbey land to the south of East Smithfield in 1543 and Well Close in 1546 (*L and P Hen VIII*, xviii(1), nos 802(1), 623(43); Rosenfield 1961, 300, 301, 303; TNA: PRO, SC 11/455; SC 6/HenVIII/2398; E 210/4857; ADM 114/14).

John Stow describes the monastery as 'being clean pulled down' by Darcy and others (Stow 1603, i, 116). Darcy occupied the former abbot's lodging as his dwelling, and his wife died there in December 1559 (TNA: PRO, SC 12/26/32). Stow says that Darcy too died there in 1561 and was buried in St Botolph's Aldgate (Stow 1603, i, 116). But Darcy had already sold the site to Queen Elizabeth in February 1560 and there is no mention of it in his will (TNA: PRO, PROB 11/44).

The suppression may have seen the dispersal of the monastic property but the precinct remained intact. The cemetery was divided up into orchards and gardens (TNA: PRO, CRES 38/1683; E 178/1364). Numerous grants and leases relating to property changes after the suppression are extant, including some comprehensive surveys of parts of the site. Houses and gardens let to tenants were well established to the north-west of the precinct, on the north side of the courtyard, and along the Tower Hill and East Smithfield frontages. One of these, to the north of the gatehouse, had a 'great cellar'. Several gunners from the Tower of London lived in the vicinity of the precinct (eg Anthony of Naples on the north side of the courtyard) as well as many brewers and coopers (Clapham 1915, 358; TNA: PRO, CRES 38/1683; SC 2/191/59, m 1; SC 6/HenVIII/2396, m 42; SC 11/455, ms 1–2; SC 12/11/13; E 310/19/94, no. 13; E 315/100, fos 232–3; E 315/233, fo 339v; E 303/10/295, 300, 303, 314, 318, 320, 330, 331, 335; E 178/1364; E 178/2986; E 211/160; C 1/714/32; C 66/712, m 15; C 66/723, m 2; *Cat Anc Deeds*, vi, 446; *L and P Hen VIII*, xix(2), no. 340(12)).

The land to the north and east of the precinct was used as pasture and gardens (TNA: PRO, MPB 1/4; Honeybourne 1929, 200; Clapham 1915, 358; Honeybourne 1930, 256–7; TNA: PRO, CRES 38/1683; SC 6/HenVIII/2396, m 44; E 310/3/17/107; E 311/29/225; E 178/1364; E 178/1374; E 178/2986; E 178/2988; E 211/160; DL 25/1032, i, ii, iii; E 303/10/310; E 210/4857; *HMC Salisbury*, 505). The former monastic land stretching from East Smithfield down to the River Thames alongside Nightingale Lane was divided up into gardens and meadows (Honeybourne 1929, 202–3; 1930, 259–60; 1952, 19, 21–2; Jeaffreson 1886–92, i, 230, 260; *L and P Hen VIII*, xix(1), no. 278(76); TNA: PRO, SC 6/HenVIII/2396, m 43; SC 12/11/13; C 66/712, m 15; C 66/723, m 3; C 66/742, m 33; E 178/1374; ADM 114/14; E 135/22/48). Along the riverbank between the Crash Mills to the east and St Katherine's Dock to the west, a series of brewhouses had been built from the late 15th century onwards (Stow 1603, ii, 71; Honeybourne 1929, 200, 202–3; 1952, 21–2; 1930, 260; Clapham 1915, 358; Fry 1896, i, 201; ii, 30–1, 254–5; *L and P Hen VIII*, xv, no. 282(36); xix(1), nos 278(76), 812(45), 1035(137ii); xx(1), no. 846(93); xxi(2), no. 476(107); TNA: PRO, SC 6/HenVIII/2396, ms 42, 44–5; 2397, m 42v; 2398, m 54v; SC 11/455, ms 1–7; SC 12/11/13; C 66/712, m 15; C 66/723, m 3; C 66/742, m 33; E 178/1356; E 178/1374; E 178/1413; E 303/10/313; BL, MS Sloane 3254A, no. 1).

Archaeological evidence

Period B4 was of extremely short duration, lasting only 22 years, and was almost impossible to define archaeologically (Fig 46). The demolition of the church was a well-defined archaeological event, but the date at which it occurred is less clear. The available dating evidence suggests that it took place some time after the mid 16th century, and the documentary evidence allows this to be narrowed down to the middle years of the century. It is suggested that full demolition of the church did not occur until 1560–70, during the victualling yard period (Grainger and Phillpotts 2010, 12), and that prior to this the church was only rendered unusable for worship. Thus the demolition of the church is discussed for the most part in the final companion volume (ibid, 33) and only earlier acts of lesser destruction, vandalism, rubbish disposal and possible squatter occupation are described here. The Tudor manor house existed for barely 20 years, and any changes to the claustral complex wrought by either Morice or Darcy were not readily indentifiable as such. The conversion of the kitchen (B11) and refectory (B13) could belong in period C1, 1560–*c* 1660 (ibid, 17–21), even though they appear to represent the conversion of the complex to domestic rather than industrial use and thus would belong here. Other, more isolated, features in the former monastic precinct appear to belong to the mid 16th century, but again many could properly belong to period C1.

The land uses are described here in approximately chronological groupings: first, pre-demolition activities, namely disuse, the disinterring or robbing of burials, and minor acts of demolition or vandalism, in the former chapter house yard (OA8) and church; and, second, larger-scale demolition and conversion to domestic use.

The former chapter house yard (OA8)

A large number of silt layers were deposited, raising the yard's interior level to *c* 10.2m OD, through which a small number of rubbish pits were dug. The pottery recovered is mid 16th-century or later in date, and one layer produced part of a 14th- or 15th-century horseshoe <S157> and a possible iron knife blade <S132>. Above these layers, a pathway of compact crushed chalk and mortar was laid. On the south side of this was a gutter composed of clay and reused medieval floor tiles. The pathway abutted the doorway in the west wall (the east wall of the east cloister alley (B10; above, 2.4)) and probably led to the doorway in the east wall of the yard (above, 2.5). The provision of a gutter suggests that the pathway was not intended as a temporary measure, for example during demolition of the church, and the first demolition layer (period C1: Grainger and Phillpotts 2010, 15) sealed the pathway so that it pre-dated the demolition of both the church (B4, B6) and the chapter house (B9).

The presbytery (B4)

The burial in grave [12477] (above, 2.5) was robbed, or distintered for relocation, leaving a rectangular pit with steep, near-vertical sides and a flat base. It contained no redeposited human bone and only two sherds of pottery dated *c* 1550–*c* 1650. Also found in it were fragments of a tomb canopy <A56>–<A58> (Fig 30) which may have come from the tomb above this grave.

The nave (B6)

A number of features dated to the mid 16th century within the nave pre-date the demolition of the church, and represent minor acts of demolition and vandalism. The tile floors in the south aisle of the nave (in the chapel of ? St Anne and the next bay to the west, respectively rooms 6a and 6c; above, 2.4 and 2.5) were covered by silt and rubble patches. These contained some demolition material in small quantities and a large iron implement <S147> possibly associated with demolition, but also domestic refuse. One deposit ([13395]) sealed the demolished tomb [13856] (in room 6a; above, 2.5) and produced part of a late Andalusian lustreware (ANDAL) dish (<P11>, Fig 47). Several pits probably represent attempts to rob or disinter and relocate other graves or monuments. A layer containing large quantities of animal bone and domestic refuse sealed one such pit. A number of postholes probably come from scaffolding erected during the stripping of the nave roof. One posthole cut the north-west corner of burial [13831] (in the retrochoir, room 6b; above, 2.5) and contained a fragment of Purbeck marble

Fig 46 The principal archaeological features, 1539–60 (period B4): above – overall (scale 1:1250); facing page – detail (scale 1:400)

N
Building 22
church
Building 17
Building 4
Building 6
Building 16
Building 7
Building 8
Open Area 8
Building 18
Building 9
Open Area 4
Building 15
Building 1
Building 10
Building 15
Building 20
Building 19
Open Area 7
Building 13
Open Area 6
Building 3
Building 11
Drain 1
Building 2
Building 12
Building 14
Open Area 5
0
10m
structure survives: but no longer in use

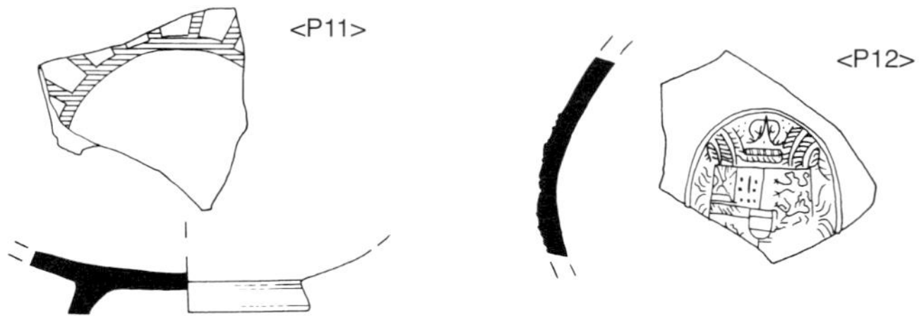

Fig 47 Late Andalusian lustreware (ANDAL) dish fragment <P11> and Frechen stoneware (FREC) sherd <P12> from the disused church (period B4) (scale 1:4)

tomb slab apparently laid in the correct position to cover the grave. A number of Purbeck marble tomb slab fragments and paviors were found in later demolition contexts and reused in later wall foundations. Of particular note are several fragments of a late 15th-century Purbeck marble slab with indents for shroud brasses and a coat of arms (Fig 48) recovered from the area of the nave during machining in 1984. Another pit was dug to remove the south-east pier above the base and may have been part of a more general removal of the south nave arcade in period C1. The timbers were removed from the beamslots of the chapel of ? St Anne and the retrochoir (rooms 6a and 6b; above, 2.5), destroying the rood screen and chapels. The floor there was probably badly damaged at this time. Within the truncated north aisle only two examples of minor destruction were found: a robber trench was dug above burials [12414] and [12489], between the two pier bases of the north nave arcade (above, 2.5), apparently to demolish the monument above.

The church ?vestry (B7)

Within the ?vestry no features could be dated to the immediate post-suppression period, but the tile floor (period B3; above, 2.5) was systematically stripped of tiles before any demolition occurred in period C1 (Grainger and Phillpotts 2010, 12–14).

The church south porch (B8)

Any tile floor within the north end of this building was stripped out and the interior perhaps slightly lowered before a number of small pits and postholes were dug. One pit may represent the robbing of the upper part of a grave, possibly only to remove the slab above. The postholes probably derived from scaffolding used for stripping the porch roof and/or adjacent roofs.

? A 'chapel without the quire door on the south side' (B16)

Demolition layers found within the burial vault of [13530] in this former chapel (above, 2.5) contained several fragments of pre-mid 16th-century lead window cames <S71> and an iron knife blade <S136> (Chapter 5.6). They also produced a fragment of a substantially intact non-reused window mullion <A23> (Chapter 5.1; Fig 75). The layers contained a range of weed seeds indicative of a variety of habitats: arable (eg stinking camomile, sheep's sorrel, corn spurrey), ruderal (eg common nettle, goose-foots) and wet ground (eg celery-leafed crowfoot, sedges). These layers represent the possible robbing or removal of later burials from the vault and the destruction of any monument above it.

Fig 48 A 15th-century tomb slab found in the area of the former church nave (period B4, MIN84 [+] <87>) (scale c 1:10) (12in/0.3m ruler as scale)

Pottery from the disused church (B4, B6–B8, B16) and chapter house yard (OA8)

This activity – the disinterring or robbing of burials, and minor acts of demolition or vandalism – produced a total of 6469g of pottery, the breakdown of which is shown in Table 4. The composition of the group is typical of the mid 16th century and reflects the nature of the phase. The dominant fabrics by weight are locally produced plain and slipped post-medieval redwares, which together comprise *c* 75% of the group. These large catch-all categories cover late 15th- to16th-century redwares whose sources cannot easily be differentiated. The presence of residual pottery (9%) across the whole of the area is to be expected at such a time of disruption and change, but there seems to have been a particular concentration in the pits in the former chapter house yard (OA8). The occurrence of a quantity of later post-medieval pottery is possibly indicative of the fact that these buildings and yards were left open for some time, allowing sherds of Surrey-Hampshire border ware (BORD etc), post-medieval redwares (PMR etc), Frechen stoneware (FREC) and tin-glazed ware (TGW) to be incorporated in the groups. This is most noticeable in the nave (B6). The proportion of prestigious imported and non-local pottery is small, and the bulk of the Rhenish stonewares consist of the Raeren/Langerwehe types (RAER/LANG), with only a sherd each of FREC (<P12>, Fig 47) and Siegburg unglazed stoneware (SIEG). The most notable import is the late Andalusian lustreware (ANDAL) dish (<P11>, Fig 47).

Table 4 Pottery from the disused church (B4, B6–B8, B16) and chapter house yard (OA8)

Period	Fabric	Weight (g)	Weight %
Roman	misc	66	1.0
Medieval	CSTN	527	8.1
Post-medieval			
English	BORD	118	1.8
	MISC	7	0.1
	PMRE	2502	38.7
	PMR	179	2.8
	PMSR	2430	37.6
	TGW	15	0.2
Imports	stonewares	530	8.2
	others	95	1.5
Total		6469	

The former ? abbot's garden (OA5)

Sixteenth-century pottery sherds were recovered from the upper rubble fill of the chalk-walled pit [100] (above, 2.5) associated with its demolition.

The former ?kitchen yard (OA6)

The upper fills of the partly brick-lined cesspit (above, 2.5) were composed of demolition material and dated after *c* 1550. Upper fill [4132] yielded charred grain and waterlogged seeds (Table 22). Fragments of two further brick-walled pits (not illustrated) were found to the south of the clay-floored pit (above, 2.5). These may have been cesspits although this is not certain; no organic deposits were found in them and no staining of the walls was noted. Both were backfilled in the later 16th century or later.

The former kitchen (B11)

At the western end of Building 11 were three small irregular-shaped cuts. These contained ash and charcoal, and were fires or the debris from fires. If they were *in situ* fires they were insubstantial and may have been lit by workmen converting the building. One ([4603]) contained a fragment from a vase in south Netherlands maiolica (SNTG) on which the design incorporates the hindquarters of a hare (<P13>, Fig 49). Animal motifs such as this are more typical of the later 16th century, and so this piece could date to *c* 1550–60 (Korf 1981, pl opp p18; Hurst et al 1986, 121, col pl VIII). Another fill ([4553]) produced a large copper-alloy domed stud (<S64>, Fig 99). The fill [4554] contained almost entirely charred arable weed seeds (corncockle, brome). These plants may have been imported incidentally with the cereals and used as tinder.

These cuts were sealed by a spread of crushed chalk. This rough surface was possibly a hard standing. A small amount of debris was allowed to build up on it, with one layer producing an iron chest key <S86>. A small cellar was then constructed by digging out 4.6m of the east end of the building to a depth of 7.40m OD, or 2.45m below the contemporary floor. A chalk, Kentish ragstone and brick wall 0.5m wide retained the western side of the cut. This wall had two rectangular recesses of differing sizes in it (Fig 50). The wall did not rise above the contemporary floor surface but no evidence was found to suggest how, if at all, the cellar was roofed. The base of the cellar was sealed by a clay damp course *c* 1m thick and capped by thin layers of mortar and sand, before a brick floor was laid at 8.43m OD, making the depth of the cellar only 1.4m. This floor contained both 15th/16th- and 17th-century brick types. The pattern of the floor suggested that parts were relaid and repaired in the early 17th century when a drain was inserted (period C1: Grainger and Phillpotts 2010, 21). A doorway was cut through the south wall of the building centrally to the cellar at 9.50m OD, slightly below the level of the foundation offset

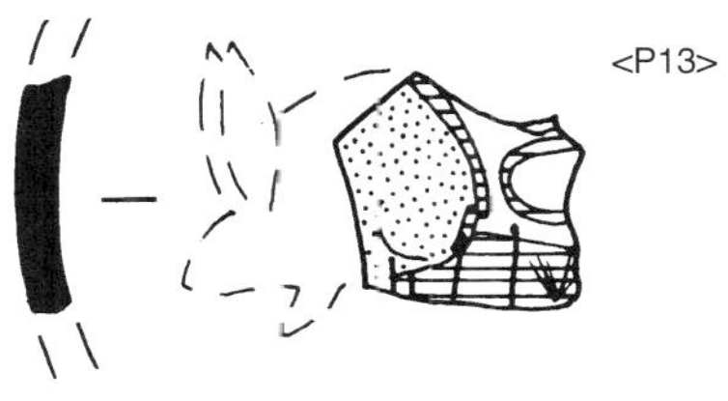

Fig 49 South Netherlands maiolica (SNTG) sherd decorated with a hare <P13>, from the former kitchen (311, period B4) (scale 1:2)

Fig 50 The early post-medieval cellar in the former kitchen (B11, period B4), looking west, showing the brick floor and wall recesses (2.0m and 1.0m scales)

and 1.1m above the cellar floor. This doorway was exceptionally narrow at 0.7m, and was probably intended to provide access to the cellar from below the building's ground-floor level. There was no evidence to suggest that the north doorway of the building went out of use at this time. The internal faces of the cellar, including the exposed medieval foundations, were rendered with mortar. Later demolition layers (period C1: Grainger and Phillpotts 2010, 23) in this cellar contained a large number of early 16th-century stove-tile fragments which may have come from a stove in a nearby building, rather than from the former kitchen itself (Fig 88).

To the west of the cellar, above the crushed chalk an extensive make-up layer was laid for a tile floor abutting the west side of the cellar. The floor was laid at 9.85m OD with reused medieval tiles (Fig 51). Only a few tiles adjacent to the south wall retained glaze, and the surface was very heavily worn. The tiled area was complete from wall to wall, consisting of 17 rows parallel to the building. The floor was composed of green- and yellow-glazed tiles in fabrics 2323 and 2497 in two sizes, and with nail holes, similar to those in Building 14 (below). In addition there were four green-glazed triangular tiles in fabric 2323, cut from two square tiles with dimensions of 206 x 206 x 28mm. An oblong area at the western end of the building was not covered by the floor, and appeared never to have been. This measured 1.75m x 2.75m and appeared to represent the position of a large object – possibly a stove or other structure – that the floor abutted. Conceivably it was during this period that the west doorway (above, 2.4) was blocked with brick and mortar.

Almost half the pottery from features in this building is residual, being mostly coarse Surrey-Hampshire border ware (CBW) which could have still been in use in the early 16th century, and Kingston-type ware (KING). The post-medieval wares are dominated by redwares. Imports are rare, but include types characteristic of Dissolution-period groups, notably Italian and Dutch tin-glazed wares and Beauvais whiteware (Table 5).

The former storeroom (B12)

Two organic deposits [3998] and [4594] sealed the base of the cellar, both being the result of deliberate rubbish disposal. Deposit [4594] contained no pottery but [3998] was extremely rich in both finds and environmental data, though it did not appear – despite the presence of several fragments of glass urinals of 13th- to 16th-century date (<G7>–<G9> and <G13>–<G17>, Fig 52; Chapter 5.4), recovered along with a fragment of a glass hanging lamp of similar date (<G4>, Fig 52) – to be the result of

Fig 51 The early post-medieval floor in the former kitchen (B11, period B4), looking south-west

Table 5 Quantification of the pottery from the former kitchen (B11), storeroom (B12) and house and chamber or abbot's hospice (B14) (period B4), by weight and percentage weight of fabrics

Period	Fabric	Building 11		Building 12		Building 14	
		Weight (g)	Weight %	Weight (g)	Weight %	Weight (g)	Weight %
Medieval							
English	CBW	197	22.0	53	0.2	488	43.4
	CHEA	15	1.7	126	0.4		
	EMS					37	3.3
	ESUR					5	0.4
	KING	117	13.1			232	20.6
	LMHG	2	0.2			18	1.6
	LOND	10	1.1	2	<0.1	73	6.5
	MG/MGCOAR	14	1.6	5	<0.1	115	10.2
	SHER	20	2.2			33	2.9
	TUDG	8	0.9	154	0.5		
Imports	DUGR	30	3.4				
	SAIM/SAIP					<1	
Post-medieval							
English	BORD	9	1.0	580	1.9	9	0.8
	PMRE	335	37.5	10683	34.5	98	8.7
	PMR	62	6.9				
	PMSR	27	3.0	15254	49.2	4	0.4
Imports	BEAU			1161	3.7		
	DUTR			8	<0.1		
	FREC	8	0.9	3	<0.1		
	RAER	31	3.5	2882	9.3	13	1.2
	SNTG	9	1.0	82	0.3		
	WESE			10	<0.1		
	Total	894		31003		1125+	

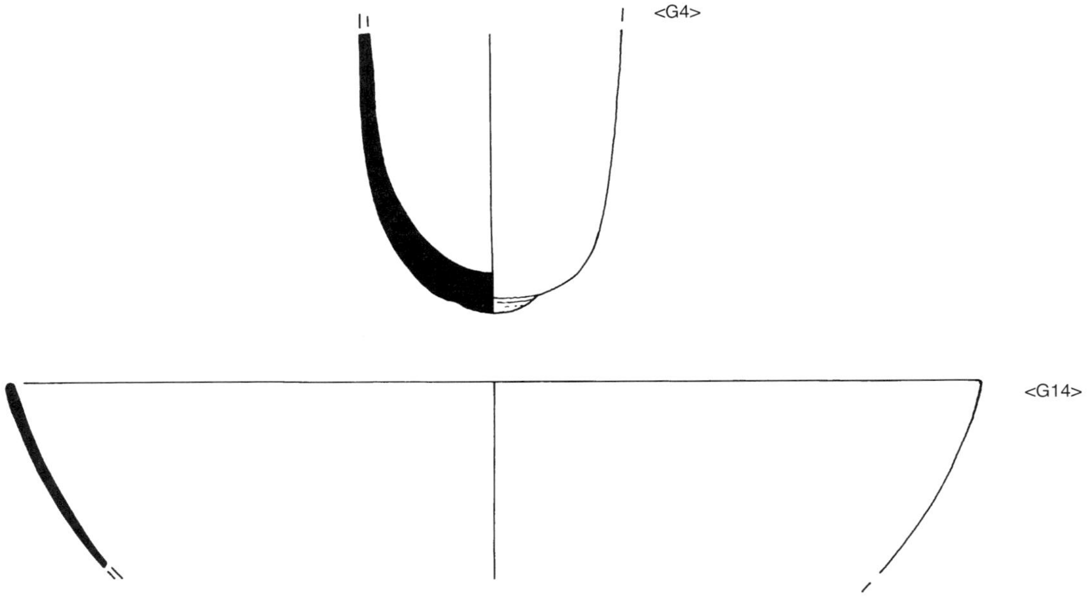

Fig 52 Vessel glass from organic rubbish deposit [3998] in the former storeroom (B12, period B4): hanging lamp <G4> and urinal or bottle <G14> (scale 1:1)

use of the cellar as a cesspit. A number of metal objects, including a copper-alloy book clasp <S44>, some lead plating <S77> and lead window cames <S67>–<S70>, and part of an iron box <S57> and scissors <S145>, were also found (Chapter 5.6).

The large assemblage of pottery recovered from deposit [3998] seems to be typical of rubbish disposed of from an upper-class household with some displayable pieces. From the total estimated vessel equivalents (EVEs) present in each form type, it is clear that the bulk of the pottery falls into form categories that are usually associated with display and with the serving of food rather than its preparation, that is, jugs and drinking vessels (Table 6). The bulk of the pottery comprises locally produced coarse wares such as the 'Tudor' redwares – both London-area early post-medieval redware (PMRE) and London-area early post-medieval slipped redware (PMSR). These include the slipped jugs <P14>–<P16> (Fig 53). A small but significant number of other fabrics, such as Surrey-Hampshire border whiteware (BORD), including a plate (<P17>, Fig 53) and a compartmented condiment dish <P18>, and Frechen stoneware (FREC), suggest that the group dates to after *c* 1550. A small amount of residual pottery, mostly Cheam whiteware (CHEA) and 'Tudor Green' (TUDG), dates to the 15th century. There is an absence of sanitary ware forms, apart from what appears to be a PMRE chamber pot (possibly similar to London-area post-medieval redware (PMR) forms of chamber pots) (<P19>, Fig 53). The proportion of imported pottery in this group is the highest for this phase (Table 5), with Raeren stoneware (RAER) and Beauvais *sgraffito* ware (BEAU1) being the most common types. The latter includes a jug handle and sherds from up to four single slipware dishes with *sgraffito* designs. Two of these have the 'IHS' insignia at the centre, suggesting that they should date to before 1539 (<P20>, <P21>, Fig 53). Five sherds of south Netherlands maiolica (SNTG) vase or altar vase were found, including a body sherd with ring handle. Several examples of the standard RAER drinking jug were found (eg <P22>, Fig 53), and of note is a near-complete RAER jug with collared rim form (<P23>, Fig 53). The former are not usually regarded as a prestigious item (unless they had added silver lids) and occur frequently on all types of sites across the country. The Beauvais wares, however, are less common in London, and were probably used for display. It is likely that a skillet recorded as PMSR is in fact a Dutch redware (<P24>, Fig 53).

A number of leather items were also recovered from deposit [3998]. Most notable among these is <S65>, part of a thick

Table 6 Quantification of the fabrics and forms of the pottery from organic rubbish deposit [3998] in the former storeroom (B12, period B4)

Form	Fabric (EVEs)					
	BORD	PMRE	PMSRY	BEAU	RAER	WESE
Jug			0.1			
Bowl		0.7				
Chamber pot		0.1				
Candlestick	1.0					
Condiment dish	0.5					
Costrel			1.0			
Dish				0.1		<0.1
Drinking jug/mug					5.0	
Jar		2.3				
Jug		0.5	7.4		0.5	
Pancheon		0.5	0.4			
Pipkin		0.3	<0.1			
Pitcher			0.2			
Plate	0.6			1.5		
Skillet			1.0			
Total EVEs	2.1	4.4	10.1+	1.6	5.5	<0.1
EVEs %	8	18	41	7	23	<1

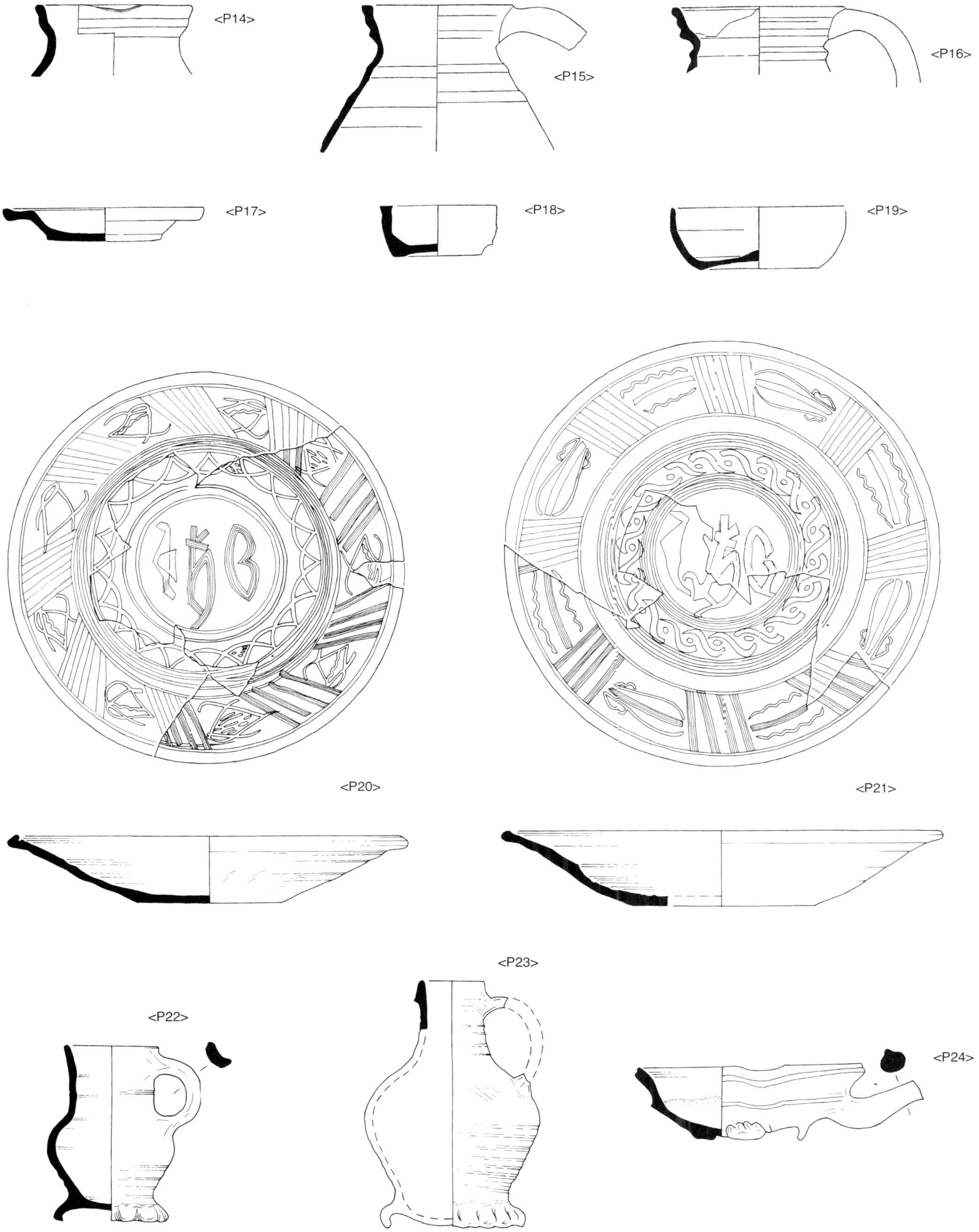

Fig 53 Pottery from organic rubbish deposit [3998] in the former storeroom (B12, period B4): London-area early post-medieval slipped redware (PMSR) jugs <P14>–<P16>, Surrey-Hampshire border whiteware (BORD) plate <P17> and condiment dish <P18>, London-area early post-medieval redware (PMR(E)) chamber pot <P19>, Beauvais single sgraffito ware (BEAU1) dishes <P20> and <P21>, Raeren stoneware (RAER) jugs <P22> and <P23>, and post-medieval slipped (?Dutch) redware (?DUTSL) skillet <P24> (scale 1:4)

leather strap most probably used for heavy work. The deposit also produced a quantity of shoe leather <S91> (Chapter 5.6). Six textile items were recovered from the layer (Table 23). The most distinctive of these is part of the crown of a knitted cap worked in stocking stitch from double, S-twisted yarn <2027> (Table 23). Knitted caps were a popular form of male headwear in England in the late 15th and 16th centuries, and caps of many different styles have been found on building sites in London, particularly around Moorfields in the late 19th and early 20th centuries (Baily 1868; Lambert 1921, 94; Levey 1968, 188; Ponting 1979, 79; Rutt 1987, 59–61). More recent London examples come from Baynard's Castle and Cutler Street, and there are others from Newcastle upon Tyne, Exeter, Southampton and the wreck of the *Mary Rose* (Crowfoot 1979, nos 15–18; Pritchard 1991; Hedges 1984, 335; Rutt 1987, 64, fig 60). By the latter part of the 16th century knitted caps had become outmoded, and it is probable that this cap was made no later than the third quarter of the 16th century. The woven textiles found also conform to types recorded elsewhere as dating to the 16th century, although none is diagnostic of the period. The three wool cloths included a fine-grade 2.2 twill made from worsted (combed) yarn, a lightweight fabric identified as a 'new drapery' (<2042>), and two heavier woollen cloths that underwent prolonged finishing processes to be hard-wearing and of good raping quality (<2008>, <2405>) (Table 23). Both these latter pieces preserve traces of sewing in the form of stitch holes and were presumably worn-out offcuts from clothing, whereas the twill is a long strip cut from the edge of a length of cloth and tied in a knot. The two other textiles are brittle scraps woven from cellulosic fibres, the finer probably linen (<2125>) and the coarser a type of canvas (<2125>) (Table 23). They are too small to determine what they derived from.

Waterlogged seeds (fruits and other plants) make up the bulk of the plant remains from [3998], both in terms of seed frequency and species diversity (21 samples analysed; Table 22). Single charred grains of bread wheat and rye were recovered, with one darnel seed. The mineralised remains consist nearly entirely of a low diversity of small-seeded fruit species with a surprisingly diverse collection of seeds from other plants in low frequencies. Grape, fig, blackberry/raspberry (these three being particularly abundant), elder, apple/pear and strawberry were present. Other fruit species include barberry, mulberry, and the larger fruit stones of plum/bullace and sloe/blackthorn. An interesting find was a single peach stone, the only evidence for this species from the site. The fruits may have been grown on site or imported, or both. The larger fruit stones and cereal grains suggest the dumping of other food refuse.

Henbane was recovered in moderate quantities, suggesting possible use for its narcotic properties. A moderate number of corn spurrey seeds may represent the residues from collection as a fodder plant. The seeds of other plants, found for the most part in low numbers and in mixed assemblages, were probably simply weeds rather than residues from utilised plants. The moderate seed frequency of several high-seed-producing species such as stinging nettle and goosefoots may be down to single plants. Present also were blinks, sun spurge, maple-leaved goosefoot and petty spurge. These include a surprisingly high number of potential arable weeds, and their predominance in the samples, supported by other characteristic arable weeds (eg fumitory, fool's parsley and corncockle), suggests the residues associated with crop processing, such as the cleaning of imported crops in the vicinity. The other weed seeds came from a range of habitats; among the wetland plants, the sedges were found in very low quantities for such a high-seed-producing plant.

Eel remains (1091 fragments; Table 25) formed 57% of the fish assemblage. A total of 23 skull bones (largely branchial arcs) could be measured to estimate total lengths (Libois et al 1987, 6; Table 26). The generally consistent size of the eels both in this period and others reflects a very seasonal fishery in the Thames, implying fish at the same stage of maturity caught at the same time and place on their seaward migration every year. The quantity of smelt is evidence of another seasonal fishery in the Thames. Herring are well represented; they were a staple food and the subject of a highly developed fishing industry from the 14th century.

The deposit also contained quantities of chicken eggshell, the remains of frogs, toads and the warty newt, small mammals like mice, rabbits and hares, and a limited number of aquatic molluscs (Wilkinson 1991; Chapter 5.9).

The former house and chamber or ? abbot's hospice (B14)

Two long, shallow cuts were found at the base of the excavated sequence within this building, each parallel to one of the walls. They perhaps represent the stripping-out of medieval floor levels. One contained two copper-alloy toilet instruments of 14th- to 16th-century and definite 16th-century date (<S151>, <S152>, Fig 107; Chapter 5.6). The cuts produced a small assemblage of mostly residual medieval pottery but sherds from a London-area post-medieval redware (PMR) colander indicate that these features were cut in the late 16th or 17th century. Small amounts of London-area post-medieval slipped redware (PMSR) and Surrey-Hampshire border whiteware (BORD) were also found in this area (Table 5). Several layers of levelling capped with a thin mortar spread raised the level to 9.90m OD. The mortar may have been a temporary surface. Set into this surface, 0.2m away from and aligned with the west wall of the building, was a narrow channel or gutter. This had a mortar bedding on which was set a single course of chalk, tile, brick and Kentish ragstone fragments forming the east side of the structure, which was filled with a relatively clean layer of silt. The mortar surface was covered by two further thin layers of sand and silt which abutted the gutter, before four postholes were cut parallel to the gutter. Possibly these were related to the gutter, but are more likely to represent scaffolding used on the upper parts of the building.

All previous features were then covered by further levelling to approximately 10.0m OD in preparation for a tile floor. The tiles were laid square on to the alignment of the building and occupied its full width (Fig 54). Most were plain glazed, either light or almost black and laid in an alternating pattern. Only in the south-eastern corner were these tiles well preserved; elsewhere, particularly towards the west wall, they were badly worn and broken. The southern surviving area of floor was composed of two types of tile. A panel of smaller decorated tiles, 11 wide and three tiles long, broke the regular arrangement of dark and light plain tiles. Most of the decorated tiles were very worn but it is possible to identify three different designs, all Penn: design <T11> (Fig 12) on three tiles, design <T57> or <T58> (Fig 87) on two, and design <T60> (Fig 12) on two others (Table 16). The northern section of floor was severely damaged, showing signs of secondary burning, and the tiles were badly cracked. To the east were six rows of larger tiles laid parallel to the walls. These were plain glazed light and dark but were not laid in any regular pattern. The rest of the tiles were plain glazed yellow or green tiles, which were not as heavily worn but badly cracked and laid in a chequerboard pattern. There were three distinct sizes of tile in fabric 2194. Some had very worn surfaces with no surviving glaze. They had nail holes in each corner although the fabric suggests an English origin. Many of the small tiles in Penn fabric 1810 were very worn and may once have been decorated, while some retained traces of green glaze. Of the imported tiles, all the fabrics contained varying amounts of silty inclusions (2322, 2324, 2850), except 1678 and 2497 containing calcium carbonate (Table 17).

At the northern end of the building a third fragment of tile floor survived against the east wall. This overlay the brick blocking of the east doorway (into the former kitchen, B11) and was at the same level as the two more extensive areas to the south. It was probably during this period that the internal walls of the building (above, 2.4) were removed.

The former cemetery (OA9) and gardens in the north-west part of the former precinct (OA12)

These areas were sealed in places by a number of levelling deposits, which produced a copper-alloy buckle <S106>, Fig 102; Chapter 5.6) dated *c* 1350–*c* 1450, a Nuremburg jetton of late 15th- or early 16th-century type (B Cook, pers comm) and a fragment of 16th- or 17th-century glass jug or tazza <G21> (Fig 92; Chapter 5.4). The most notable iron object is a door key <S87>. Another context ([4132]) produced an exotic shell, *Monetaria moneta* or money cowrie, which is found in Indo-Pacific waters, either in shallow water or on coral reefs. They are easily collected, very attractive, and were extensively used as currency in the past, hence the common name (Buglass 1991).

Much of the pottery from the levelling and pits is of medieval date. The dominant medieval ware is coarse Surrey-Hampshire border ware (CBW) although London-type ware (LOND) is also common, including some fragments of dripping

Fig 54 The tile floors in the former house and chamber or abbot's hospice (B14, period B4), looking east (2.0m scales)

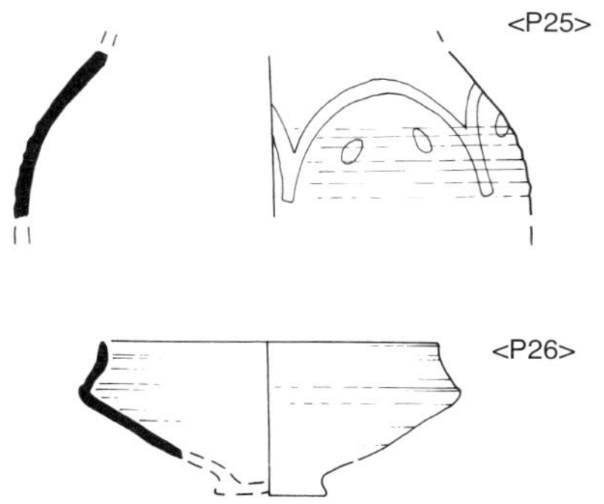

Fig 55 Dutch red earthenware (DUTR) pipkin <P25> and Siegburg stoneware (SIEG) bowl <P26> (period B4) (scale 1:4)

dishes. The quantity of local post-medieval pottery (ie a fairly high proportion of early post-medieval redwares including slipped ware) is more characteristic of the mid-to-later 16th than the mid 16th century. There is a large amount of post-medieval redware (PMR etc) and a small amount of tin-glazed ware (TGW). These could indicate a deposition date in the late 16th or early 17th century, or represent later intrusive disturbance and the mixed nature of garden deposits. The date of the group is also reflected in the nature of the imports, dominated by stonewares and including a significant amount of Frechen stoneware (FREC), although the remainder of the Rhenish stonewares would be consistent with a mid 16th-century date. The pottery also includes a Dutch red earthenware (DUTR) pipkin with arcaded slip decoration <P25> (Fig 55; cf Hurst et al 1986, fig 60, no. 191).

Plant remains from the pits included charred material and some waterlogged seeds but few potential foodstuffs except fig, *Rubus* and elder. Fill [9798] contained charred cereal grains, plus a range of plants of disturbed and waste ground (Table 22). The pits also produced black rat bones and bird remains like sparrow, house martin and redwing, chicken eggshell, and molluscs indicating dry conditions (West 1992; Wilkinson 1991; Chapter 5.9). The assemblage from [11852], a rubbish pit, indicates that cod, haddock, whiting and other gadid remains are dominant numerically for the first time, and is perhaps more typical of later deposits associated with period C1 (Grainger and Phillpotts 2010, 24–5).

The south yard (OA13)

Ten of a group of 21 quarry pits here produced pottery, amounting to 46 sherds in all (846g), of which 38 are medieval. There was little or no evidence for slumping from the sides of these pits, suggesting that they were backfilled soon after they were opened. The medieval fabrics are dominated by Surrey whitewares, with ten sherds each of Kingston-type ware (KING) and coarse Surrey-Hampshire border ware (CBW). Together with four sherds of Siegburg stoneware (SIEG), these could point to a late 14th- or 15th-century date for the fill, although there is also a mix of earlier material: in addition to six sherds of London-type ware (LOND) and five of Mill Green ware (MG), there are single sherds of early medieval sand-tempered ware (EMS) and south Hertfordshire-type greyware (SHER). Roman pottery was also present in quarry pits [3120], [3134] and [3339]. In addition, there are eight post-medieval sherds, of which six are CBW and two are of London-area early post-medieval slipped redware (PMSR). These suggest that quarry pit [3145] was open or disturbed some time after *c* 1480, while [3077] and [3321] were open and/or disturbed after *c* 1550, and the sherds were perhaps introduced by garden activity in the upper fills of the quarry pits. The stonewares include a SIEG *Jacobakanne* drinking jug (cf Hurst et al 1986, 179, fig 88, no. 263) and a SIEG shallow drinking bowl dating to after 1450, <P26> (Fig 55; cf ibid, 178, fig 88, no. 257).

Discussion, 1539–60 (period B4)

The date of the demolition of the church cannot be determined archaeologically other than to suggest that it occurred at some point in the mid to late 16th century, and that it was a rather long-drawn-out process which was not fully complete until some time after *c* 1550, given the rather limited evidence from period C1, 1560–*c* 1660 (Grainger and Phillpotts 2010, 12). The documentary sources allow a little more precision. The church does appear on Wyngaerde's panorama of London drawn in *c* 1540 (Fig 56) but does not appear on the Braun and Hogenberg map of London, published in Cologne in 1572 and probably drawn a year or two before that (Fig 57). John Stow, in his survey of London first published in 1598, states that Sir Arthur Darcy and 'others … clean pulled down' the monastery. As Darcy had sold his holdings on the site to the Crown by 1560 and was dead by 1561, any work carried out by him must have been done before this date (Stow 1603, i, 116). The 'others' almost certainly refers to Sir Christopher Morice, who owned the site between 1539 and 1542, and to Edward Basshe, the first General Surveyor of the Victuals and active on the site between 1560 and 1575 (Rosenfield 1961, 317; Oppenheim 1896, 140–1).

Some demolition work was carried out immediately after the suppression in 1539. The lead from the roof was taken away and melted down, and the bells from the tower removed along with other valuables (TNA: PRO, SC 6/HenVIII/2383, m 42–42v; 2427). This does not prove that the full demolition occurred at this date. The archaeological stratification suggests, rather, a period of dereliction and vandalism immediately after 1539. The domestic refuse found in the nave suggests that the shell of the church survived for some time and that squatters occupied it, or other nearby residents used it as a rubbish dump. The commissioners were required to 'pull down to the ground all the walls of the churches …' but this frequently meant no more than 'inwardly' defacing 'the church and dormitory', as Dr London reported that he had done at the Franciscan friary of Reading, to render the buildings unusable (Platt 1984, 229–30). Some demolition of the church could have occurred during the time of Morice and Darcy. The floors in particular may have been partially removed both to make the building 'unusable' and to tile the former kitchen (B11) and house and chamber or abbot's hospice (B14). A number of walls may have been

Fig 56 Wyngaerde's panorama of London of c *1540 with St Mary Graces circled, showing the central church tower with the presbytery and nave of approximately equal length (© Ashmolean Museum, University of Oxford; reproduced in Colvin and Foister 1996, ix)*

partially stripped for stone. With the roof removed, the fabric of the church would decay, and parts may have either fallen over or been pulled down for safety. Nevertheless, the limited dating evidence available and presented in period C1 (Grainger and Phillpotts 2010, 12) suggests that it was Basshe who delivered the *coup de grâce* between 1560 and *c* 1570, probably before *c* 1565.

In all probability Morice intended to use the suppressed monastery as the core of a new manor house, and it is clear that Darcy achieved this, living there between 1542 and 1560. This fate befell a number of other suburban London monasteries: Bermondsey Abbey became the house of Sir Thomas Pope, treasurer of the Court of Augmentations (Beard 1986, 188; Dyson et al 2011, 153–4), the London Charterhouse became the property of Sir Edward North (Bettey 1989, 209; Barber and Thomas 2002, 73), Sir Richard Rich acquired St Bartholemew's Priory, Smithfield, and Holy Trinity Priory, Aldgate, passed to Thomas Audley (Bettey 1989, 210; Schofield and Lea 2005, 164–9, 181–5). Darcy, himself a commissioner for the Court of Augmentations, also acquired two other former Cistercian abbeys, at Jervaulx in Yorkshire and Sawley in Lancashire, for

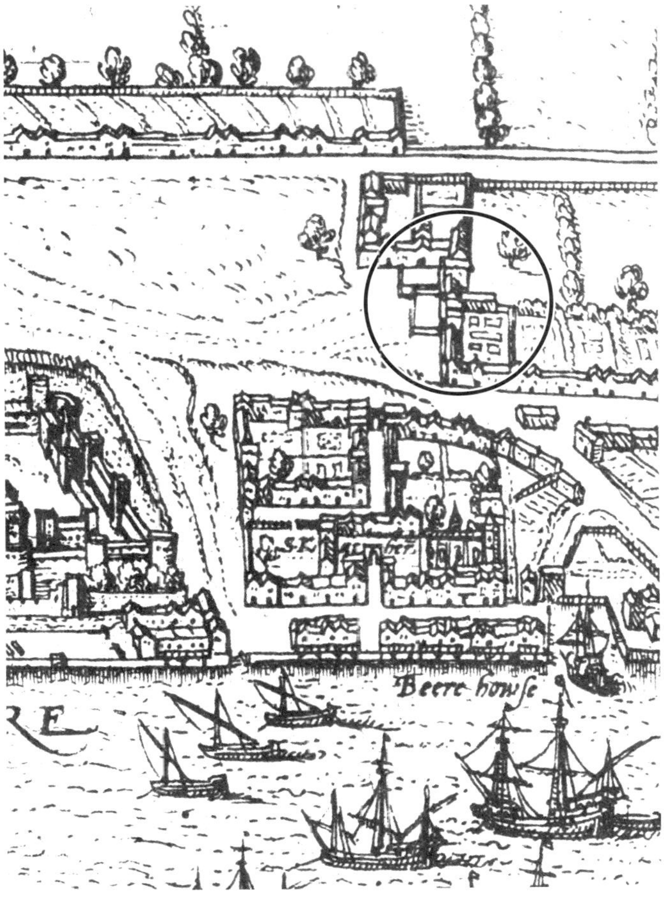

Fig 57 Braun and Hogenberg's map of London of c *1572, with the site of St Mary Graces circled, showing the church demolished (reproduced from Margary 1981)*

use as private houses (Knowles 1976, 266; *VCH* 1974, 156–8; Coppack et al 2002). In common with other Tudor magnates, Darcy used the old abbot's lodgings of St Mary Graces to the west, beyond any area yet excavated, as the core of his new house. The abbot's lodgings would have been the most comfortable of the surviving monastic buildings and the most attractive to the new private owner. Darcy clearly also did this at Sawley, where he converted the lodgings in the west range and built or extended a kitchen at its northern end (ibid). Such conversions also occurred at Milton Abbey in Dorset and Battle Abbey in Sussex (Bettey 1989, 144). It is impossible to be certain whether the conversions of the former kitchen, storeroom, and house and chamber or abbot's hospice (B11, B12 and B14) were undertaken by Darcy, but the buildings were close to the former abbot's lodgings and connected to them by the first cloister (B3), which may have been reused as the inner court of the new structure. The cloister clearly survived the suppression, and the second storey marked on the 1635 plan (Fig 58) may have been constructed at this date rather than earlier. The church cloister of Bermondsey Abbey was converted in this fashion by Pope, as were those at Newstead Abbey, Nottinghamshire, by Sir John Byron and at Lacock, Wiltshire, by Sir William Sharington (Dyson et al 2011, 165; Bettey 1989, 150–1). Overall, the available archaeological evidence does not suggest that the kitchen changed use; indeed, the evidence of the cellar and tiled floor may simply indicate extensive modernisation. The floors of the former kitchen and chamber (B11 and B14), though considerably worn, were of a reasonably high quality, and do not accord with the earliest recorded use of these buildings after 1561 as salt houses. Nevertheless, they became the floors of these salt houses, and it is possible that the conversion may represent early victualling yard activity (period C1: Grainger and Phillpotts 2010, 21–4).

The rubbish dumped in the former storeroom (B12) suggests a reasonably high-status household in the immediate vicinity, and the clearance of rubbish either towards the end of this period (period B4) or throughout it. The latter seems less likely if there were high-status buildings adjacent (above). The pottery includes several imported vessels. The large number of rare, imported, early 16th-century stove-tile fragments (Chapter 5.2; Fig 88) found in the cellar backfill of the former kitchen (B11) (period C1: Grainger and Phillpotts 2010, 23) also suggests a higher-status usage for this general area. A glazed and highly decorated stove or stoves had, it seems, stood nearby, but not within a working kitchen since such stoves were designed for living accommodation and also intended for show. Given the long gap between manufacturing date, *c* 1500–25, and deposition date, *c* 1600, the stove(s) could have been constructed in the pre-Dissolution period (B3) and continued in use after. The purpose of the post-Dissolution cellar (Fig 50) is unclear; it could have been a buttery or pantry. If a stove had been relocated to this building (B11) it suggests that the kitchen was converted to another use, possibly to that of a parlour or dining room (but see above). The general absence of mortar adhering to the excavated tile fragments may suggest that these surviving tiles remained unused at the end of the construction process; this is a common occurrence in the archaeological record. In the 16th century, clergy, aristocracy and richer merchants undertook frequent cross-Channel travel and were aware of Continental customs of interior heating and decoration; ceramic tile-stoves are a physical expression of Continental cultural influence from across the Channel (for the full cultural significance of this find, see Gaimster et al 1990; Gaimster and Hughes 1999). Any of the last three abbots could have commissioned the stove(s). Morice (who had himself travelled in Germany: *DNB* 1894, 988–9) and thereafter Darcy could have reused a stove or stoves installed before the suppression. The abbot's house at Fountains in Yorkshire, disused by 1539, produced a number of stove-tiles of similar quality (G Coppack, pers comm; Coppack 2003, 101–2).

In all probability the chapter house (B9) survived until later in the century and was only destroyed in the 1590s (in period C1, 1560–*c* 1660: Grainger and Phillpotts 2010, 13–14). The church cloister and the timber pentice (B10 and B18) to the south of the nave also survived this period, there being no evidence that they were demolished before the 17th century. However, there is no clue as to how these buildings were used in the new scheme, and they may simply have stood derelict. The infirmary (B15) survived into the 18th century and possibly the early 19th century (periods C1–C2: Grainger and Phillpotts 2010, 81), but the period C1 stripping of the interior left no clue as to what it was used for in the mid 16th century. Similarly, the refectory (B13) survived into the 18th and possibly the 19th century, but the preservation of the interior was poor. Probably the floor levels described above (2.4) continued in use after the suppression in an increasing state of disrepair, before being replaced in the 17th century. One of the essential features of the Tudor magnate's house was a large hall. Where the house was a converted monastery, this could be constructed out of the nave, which clearly did not happen here, or one of the larger claustral buildings such as the dormitory or refectory. Here the refectory may have served Morice or Darcy in this fashion. Drain 1 (above, 2.5) continued in use until the later 17th century (period C1: Grainger and Phillpotts 2010, 46). The 1635 plan (Fig 58) suggests that the well house (B19) was removed at some point before the early 17th century.

The former burial areas (OA2 and OA9) were no longer part of the precinct and consisted largely of private gardens and orchards, a land use compatible with the number of rubbish and charnel pits found. In fact, as previously noted (above, 2.5), Open Area 2 may entirely or in part have been a garden since the turn of the 15th century.

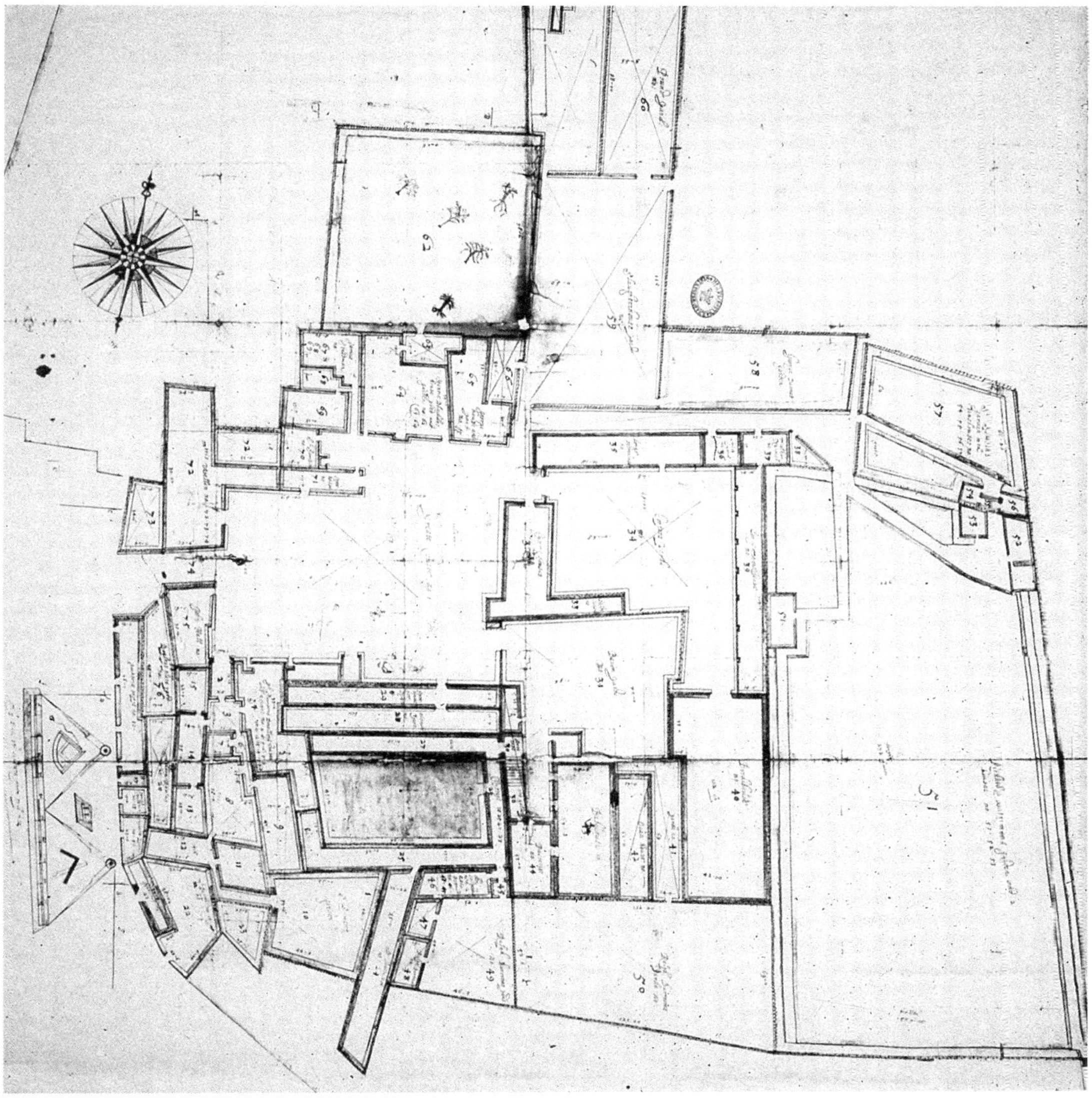

Fig 58 The 1635 plan of the victualling yard, showing (lower half, from right to left) the former infirmary (B15), refectory (B13), early cloister (B3), kitchen (B11), storeroom (B12) and house or hospice (B14) still standing (TNA: PRO, MR 1/106)

3

Aspects of the Cistercian abbey

3.1 The foundation of the abbey

The reasons for the foundation

The foundation of St Mary Graces raises a number of questions which revolve around two principal issues: why, as late as 1350, the Cistercians were chosen to found the monastery, and why a Cistercian monastery was founded so close to a major city, in contravention of their earlier practice. The answer to both these questions appears to be that it was the will of the king, Edward III, the monastery's founder. The vast majority of Cistercian foundations in Britain were made before 1152, when the general chapter forbade further expansion (Robinson 1998, 19). Although this did not prevent further foundations, these were few in comparison, and after the turn of the 13th century only another handful were made. Of these, two of the principal later foundations were also (like St Mary Graces) daughter houses of Beaulieu, Hampshire (founded 1204): Netley, Hampshire (1239) and Hailes, Gloucestershire (1246). Vale Royal, Cheshire (1274) was arguably the last traditional foundation of a Cistercian monastery, with only Rewley, founded as a college for Cistercian monks near Oxford, coming slightly later in 1281. No other Cistercian house was founded in England in the 69 years between Rewley and St Mary Graces, and the Cistercians as an order were no longer generally popular in England. However, the Cistercians, like the Carthusians, were very much an international order and founded abbeys in Spain, Poland, France, Italy, Denmark and Germany throughout the 14th century. More significantly, the impetus for the foundation of St Mary Graces came from Edward III; no surviving documents suggest that the Cistercians initiated the project as they had done with earlier lay patrons. The king's motives for choosing the Cistercians are unclear, but in doing so he was also following earlier examples set by his family. Beaulieu was founded by King John, Hailes by John's son Richard, Earl of Cornwall, Rewley by Richard's son Edmund, also Earl of Cornwall, and Vale Royal by Edward I, while Netley was founded by a royal servant, although Henry III rapidly became the patron. Coincidentally, an almost identical tradition of a vow to found an abbey exists for Vale Royal, where Edward I is said to have made such a vow in 1263–4 when he suffered a similar stormy voyage to that endured by his grandson, Edward III (Robinson 1998, 192). It is possible that Edward III was following his grandfather's publicly pious example. Edward III also had some personal experience of the Cistercians and stayed at Beaulieu on a number of occasions (Honeybourne 1952, 16). He may have particularly valued an order with such strong international connections (Holdsworth 1992, 142, 149).

The story of the king's vow to found the monastery after being saved from drowning in 1347 appears from contemporary documents to be true; similarly, the story that the abbey was founded to give thanks to God for his victory at Crécy in 1346 may also have an element of truth in it. However, as Marjorie Honeybourne has pointed out, a number of years separate both the victory at Crécy and the escape from shipwreck from the foundation of the abbey in 1350, and this suggests that the intervening Black Death, an even more immediate and overpowering cause for so conspicuous an act of piety, may have been the crucial factor in the king's decision (Honeybourne 1952). She also attributes a more personal reason than simple overriding horror and sorrow at the scale of the catastrophe of 1348–50. In 1349 the Black Death claimed the life of his friend and confessor, Thomas Bradwardine, who had recently been made Archbishop of Canterbury after the plague had also taken his two predecessors in rapid succession. Thus the abbey, founded on the site of a large Black Death cemetery and chapel, becomes in part a memorial or mausoleum – to all who died of the plague, to those buried in the cemetery, and to a dead friend. In this respect the foundation of St Mary Graces closely parallels the foundation of the London Charterhouse by Edward's good friend and courtier Sir Walter Manny, both in the founding of a monastery on and around a Black Death cemetery and chapel (in this case at West Smithfield), as a memorial to the dead, and in the choice of, by the 14th century, an unfashionable but international order – in this case the Carthusians. Ultimately, whatever specific reasons are proposed for the foundation of St Mary Graces and the London Charterhouse, both foundations are almost certainly best viewed as acts of extreme piety on the part of the Court in the post-plague environment, and part of a general return to favour of the 12th-century reforming orders among the upper echelons of society.

The suburban location of St Mary Graces has also been the subject of some debate. This was not 'far from the concourse of men' (Robinson 1998) but very much in their midst, and the only such siting of an English Cistercian house. The next closest Cistercian house to London, the Savigniac foundation of St Mary Stratford Langthorne, was a few miles to the east (Barber et al 2004). The Cistercian quest for solitude, to found their abbeys in remote places, may not have been strictly observed even in their heyday of the early 12th century; the early foundations were often within a few miles of a settlement or castle, though all were in distinctly rural locations (Robinson 1998, 14–17). Honeybourne has stressed the marshy and marginal nature of the area to the east of Tower Hill in 1350 (Honeybourne 1952, 19). It is true that in 1368 the monks petitioned the Bishop of London to appropriate All Hallows Staining because the abbey stood in a barren and uncultivated spot and they were poor (*VCH* 1909, 462), and that the marshes to the east and south were sparsely populated at that date, but the argument is strained at best. Uneconomic agriculturally and suitably bleak the site may have been, but remote and isolated it certainly was not. The abbey was a stone's throw from the Tower and a few hundred yards from the city wall. St Katherine's Hospital, founded in 1148, was just to the south of East Smithfield, and both the Tower Hill and East Smithfield street frontages were already occupied. St Mary Graces was very much a suburban, if not an urban, monastery.

But it is not necessary to attempt to reconcile Cistercian tradition with St Mary Graces' suburban setting. Overriding all else, Edward III as founder chose the location for his commemorative church, just as he chose the Cistercians. Added to this, the Cistercians of the 14th century were not their early 12th-century forebears: the Order that had begun as a protest against wealth and money had even by the end of the 12th century 'acquired for itself an unenviable reputation for avarice and group acquisitiveness' (Lawrence 1984, 161). As the 13th century progressed they gradually abandoned their ideals and their self-denying ordinances. In the 14th century the lay brothers, their agricultural labour force, disappeared, rural properties were leased not farmed directly, urban properties were bought and rented out, and income from chantries became increasingly important – particularly relevant for a memorial church like St Mary Graces. The abbots of Beaulieu, Kirkstead, Stratford Langthorne and Waverley had town houses in London, just like many abbots from other orders. The Cistercians were an international order, who had by the 14th century long since moved into the urban and suburban environment on the Continent. Even in England, the late foundation of Rewley in 1281, close to the University of Oxford, was criticised in 1344 for being too far from the town (Robinson 1998, 160). And if no other English Cistercian houses were in or quite so close to urban centres, there are examples from the Continent, mostly in Italy (Jamroziak 2006, 153).

The foundation process

If the story of Edward III's vow is taken as the inception of the scheme to found the abbey, then the earliest that the process leading to the foundation in 1350 could have begun was late 1347. This rules out any association of the foundation with the victory at Crécy in 1346, but still pre-dates the Black Death, which arrived in England late in 1348 (Grainger et al 2008, 9–10). However, despite the story of the vow, there is no unequivocal evidence that Edward made any move to actually found the abbey before the plague had struck.

John Corey, who bought the land on which the Black Death cemetery and chapel, and subsequently the abbey, were laid out, had been buying land on the site in general as early as 1346 (TNA: PRO, E 40/2643; E 210/1661, 1692, 1681; E 326/9933, 2317, 2307, 2310, 2311, 2316; E 315/47, no. 110). Corey was a highly placed royal clerk in the service of Edward III's eldest son Edward the Black Prince, Prince of Wales, working for him principally in London and Westminster. In November 1346, when the king and prince were on campaign in France, he oversaw repairs to the Prince's Wardrobe at Ironmonger Lane in the City of London, and at his residence at Kennington; and he also deputised for the prince's Receiver General, John de Pirie, at the prince's exchequer at Westminster, while Pirie was on a tour of the Principality lands in Cheshire and Wales (*Reg Edward Black Prince*, i, 27, 28). In January 1347, Corey was with the prince at the siege of Calais and was sent back to England to make arrangements concerning the prince's lands in Devon. In March he was again working in the prince's exchequer at Westminster, where he was paid as an auditor (ibid, i, 42, 61). It is likely that Corey accompanied the king and the prince on the crossing that occasioned the royal vow, since he is known to have been in Calais on 4 October and in London on 29 October (ibid, i, 123, 137). He would therefore probably have been chosen to be the king's agent for the purchase of land for the foundation on the spot. In London at the end of October, he was presented with the church of Mertherkeler in the diocese of St Davids, perhaps as a reward for his endeavours.

Corey, however, was also active in the London property market on his own behalf. He purchased houses in the City in Fenchurch Street and Trinity Lane in 1339 and 1340, and in October 1346 in *Margerylane* in the parish of St Dunstan in the East (LMA, CLA/023/DW/01/66/113; 67/102; 73/124), and there is no suggestion at this stage of any involvement of the Court in any of Corey's purchases on the site. Corey's first purchase on Tower Hill in 1346 was small, comprising only the Henewode and Basing tenements, and may have been for personal reasons.

Similarly, although the king and the Court may have been involved in Corey's purchase of the land that made up the Black Death cemetery in 1348, it is only recorded as being 'at the instigation of substantial men in the city' (*Cart Holy Trinity*, 186). He did not in fact sell the land on which the Black Death cemetery and chapel stood to the king until 1353, and the abbey did not, so far as is known, formally acquire that property or any property on the site from the king until August of that year.

Nevertheless, Corey was very much a royal servant, and the Black Death may simply have interrupted a nascent royal scheme to purchase sufficient land for the foundation of the abbey. Certainly, Corey was the royal agent buying land on the site for the abbey and overseeing work there after 1350 (*Cal Pat R*, 1358–61, 567). By February 1351 an abbot had been selected and monks from the mother house of Beaulieu requested, and the master mason, John Tyrington, was appointed two months before the purchase in 1353; all this suggests a scheme in progress, and that the Cistercians were already involved and present somewhere on the site.

3.2 The layout of the abbey

St Mary Graces was the only Cistercian abbey built in Britain in the 14th century, but in many respects the process of construction followed that mapped out elsewhere for earlier Cistercian houses, with two or sometimes three stages evident. This involved the construction first of temporary, often timber, structures for worship and domestic use until such time as the new monastery achieved sufficient financial stability (*stabilitas*) to build a permanent church and claustral complex in stone. In earlier centuries the temporary structures generally were not constructed around a cloister, but by the 14th century a cloister had become a requirement for the Sunday procession (G Coppack, pers comm). The achievement of *stabilitas* could, given the uncertain finances of many houses, take a long time – in some cases centuries. Despite the documented evidence for precarious finances in the late 14th century (Chapter 2.3), St Mary Graces appears to have more or less achieved *stabilitas* and construction of a purpose-built stone church and cloister within the first 40 years of its existence. It would also appear that the majority of the early 'temporary' buildings were of stone not timber and survived from foundation to suppression, being incorporated into the permanent layout. East Smithfield was not a virgin site, and the early layout of the abbey was as much influenced by the site's recent history and pre-existing property boundaries as by traditional practice (Fig 5). The first, stone, cloister (B3) was attached to the chapel of Holy Trinity (B1) and the monks probably lived to the west on Tower Hill, in the dormitory/refectory (B2), or nearby (Fig 6). The use of a pre-existing church or chapel as the first church during the 'temporary' phase of site occupation is not unusual for a monastic house, and here closely parallels the use of the West Smithfield cemetery chapel by the Carthusians at Charterhouse (Barber and Thomas 2002, 18). It does not seem ever to have served as a charnel chapel, in contrast to the near-contemporary cemetery chapel at St Mary Spital (Harward et al in prep). No unequivocal evidence for early timber buildings associated with this phase of stone construction was found. A number of features excavated in the south-west corner of the site and elsewhere may represent the fragmentary remains of early monastic timber buildings, but they could equally have pre-dated monastic occupation of the site. The monks of St Mary Graces may not in any case have needed to make extensive use of new purpose-built timber structures given the existence already of extensive tenements on the East Smithfield and Tower Hill street frontages. Indeed the monks are documented as living in a tenement to the *north* of the gatehouse as late as 1359. The first stone structures apparently limit the monastery to the south-west corner of the site when, by 1353, the abbey already owned enough of the land (the Horselegge furlong) to construct the new church and conventual buildings where it would soon do so, and it would not acquire one vital property in the south-west, the de Parys tenement, until after 1383, effectively blocking expansion south until then (Fig 5; TNA: PRO, E 326/2324; SC 6/1258/1, m 2). Even after the Cistercians acquired all the properties on the East Smithfield and Tower Hill frontages, they appear to have been unwilling to expand the precinct there, preferring instead the rental income from the properties.

Given that the monks did begin construction of their new church and chapter house to the north-east within a decade or two, it is probable that there was always an intention to do so and that the buildings to the south-west were seen merely as a necessary stop-gap measure. A crucial factor in this decision may have been the presence of the two Black Death burial areas (OA2 and OA3, Fig 4). These areas certainly limited the greater expansion of the monastery to the north and east from the 1360s onwards, particularly if Open Area 2 was still in use until *c* 1400 for epidemic burials as suggested (Chapter 2.4). Their presence did not prevent later expansion in the unused cemetery area, but during the 1350s the Cistercians probably considered it a good idea to let the bodies decay for a few years before building near them. They were perhaps afraid that the burial areas would need to be used again and even extended. The Black Death of 1348–50 was the first outbreak of the second pandemic of the plague; nobody alive had ever encountered it before or had knowledge of it from the recent past. The survivors had just suffered an inexplicable and terrifying catastrophe; and for all they knew it might be back again in 1351, 1352, and so on. This realistic fear may have induced excessive caution and caused the Cistercians to limit their monastery to the south-west corner for a while. That the plague did unfortunately return to London as the *Pesta Secunda* in 1361, just as the Cistercians were beginning construction of the new church, may be ironic; but any new epidemic interments appear to have been confined to Open Area 2, well away from the new church.

The influence of friary church design on the church of St Mary Graces is clear (Fig 59). The lack of structural transepts is without parallel in a completed British Cistercian church, but was common in 13th- and 14th-century friaries. The design of a monastic church came from three sources in the medieval period: the wishes of the patron, the needs of the community, and the advice of the master mason. The first and last of these factors tended to be influenced by contemporary fashion, and given that the patron in this case was the king, and the mason, John Tyrington, a royal master mason, the needs of the community may have had less influence than might be expected. There was clearly no attempt to copy the magnificent church of the mother house, Beaulieu (Fig 60), nor was there any attempt to produce the more standard late Cistercian plan of Beaulieu's daughter houses at Hailes (first church) and Netley (Fig 60). However, over 70 years separate even the next latest Cistercian foundation, Vale Royal (1274) from St Mary Graces, whereas, for example, Ware Greyfriars in Hertfordshire was founded in 1338, Coventry Whitefriars, Warwickshire, in 1342, Walsingham Greyfriars, Norfolk (Fig 60) in 1347, Ludlow friary, Shropshire, in 1350, and the Isle of Man friary in 1368. The church of the London Blackfriars (Fig 60) was constructed during *c* 1275–80 and that of the London Whitefriars during the mid 14th century (Clapham and Godfrey 1913, 255, 265; Watson and Thomas 2010, 276). But in the late 14th century the Cistercians themselves were replanning their existing churches to non-standard plans, as at Sawley, Lancashire, and Warden, Bedfordshire (Robinson 1998, 170,198; Coppack et al 2002, 73, 106–7, fig 4). These churches were by no means like St Mary Graces and contemporary friary churches, but they show a willingness on the part of the Cistercians to abandon the old model.

St Mary Graces church probably had a five-bay (Fig 59) or possibly six-bay nave, and was similar in form to that of several Franciscan churches, at Cardiff, Lichfield, Reading, Walsingham (Fig 60) and Winchelsea (Martin 1937, 22). The evidence indicates a structural arrangement similar to that of the friary walking-place, in this Cistercian context the retrochoir, with the bell tower above at the junction of the nave and presbytery. It is difficult to envisage what use the Cistercians would have had for a true walking-place, though access from the choir to the monastic cemetery may have been desirable for conducting funerals.

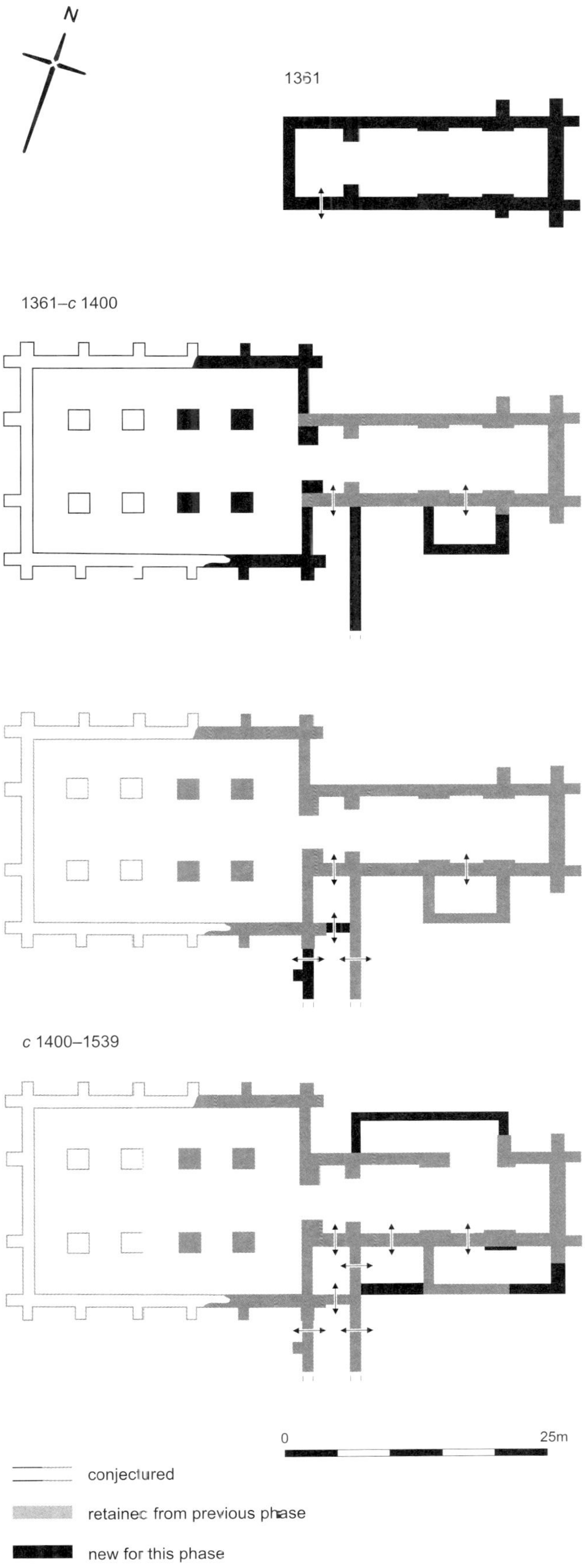

Fig 59 The development of the church of St Mary Graces (scale 1:650)

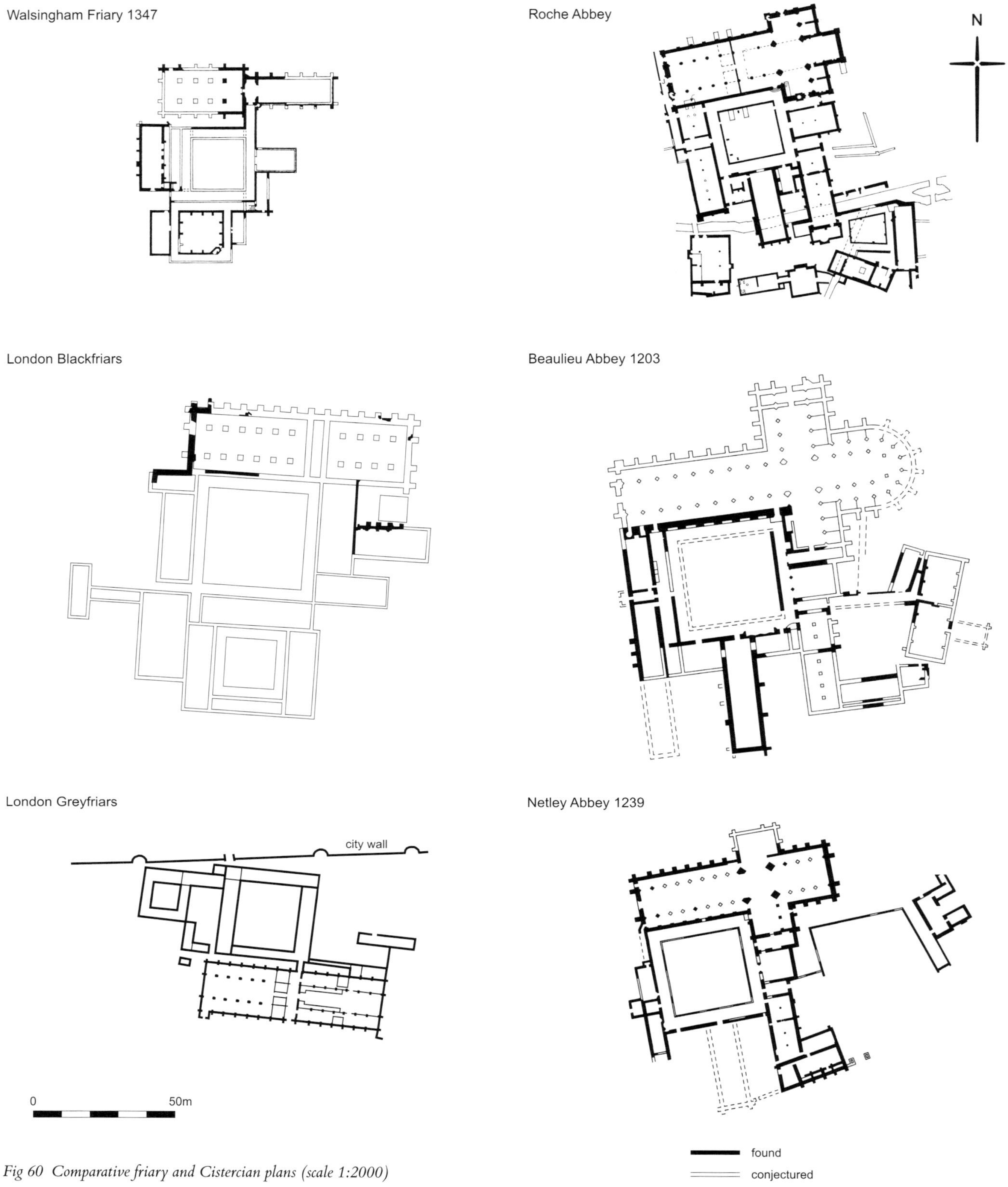

Fig 60 Comparative friary and Cistercian plans (scale 1:2000)

The adoption of such a friary-style plan does not imply that the Cistercians had adopted the liturgy and outlook of the friars. The church would have served the Cistercians' needs as adequately as their more usual cruciform plan (eg Roche Abbey, Yorkshire: Fig 60). The square-ended aisleless presbytery was a common feature of many early Cistercian churches (eg Roche Abbey: Fig 60), and the removal of choir stalls entirely into the presbytery was not a serious change in ritual arrangements and had occurred at Rievaulx (Coldstream 1986, 147). The monks would clearly have had little use for a preaching nave. The area to the west of the rood screen may have been used by the *seculares* or lay clerks mentioned (below, 3.6), but the primary function of the nave was probably to provide space for chantry chapels and secular burials, both of which brought much-needed income. The lack of structural transepts limited the space available for further chapels, making the use of the space to the north and south of the presbytery imperative. The addition of what were essentially mortuary chapels, the Lady chapel (B17) and the 'chapel without the quire door on the south side' (B16), to the north and south of the presbytery in the 15th century, followed the pattern set by the friars in similar circumstances. Here again the small number of monks at St Mary Graces (below, 3.4) would have limited the number of priests available to officiate at altars, thus restricting the need for chapels and making the design of the church therefore more than adequate in this respect.

The influence of the friars and the late medieval general disintegration of the monastic plan can also be seen in the rest of the complex. Though relatively little of London Whitefriars or Blackfriars has been excavated, Clapham's reconstructed plans show similarities to St Mary Graces, and Watson's work on the Blackfriars has to some extent confirmed the reliability of his reconstruction (Clapham and Godfrey 1913, 255, 265; Watson 1990; see now Watson and Thomas 2010, 266–72).

The space to the south of the chapel of Holy Trinity (B1), postulated as used as a passage, reflects a feature seen in friaries (Fig 60), but is otherwise unknown in Cistercian abbeys. The use of two cloisters where the second is not an infirmary or lay brothers' cloister was also common in friaries (Fig 60) but not in Cistercian abbeys. The south-western cloister (B3), despite its early construction, may have eventually been treated like the secondary cloisters in a number of friaries, providing space for the accommodation of corrodians, the more important monastic servants, and guests (Butler 1984, 123–6). St Mary Graces undoubtedly had a number of corrodians appointed by the king from at least 1391 onwards (Table 11), servants (Table 10) and probably important guests from time to time. The secondary cloister was also adjacent to the abbot's lodging, which may further suggest a connection. Its proximity to the kitchen (B11), which may have been serving the abbot, corrodians, servants and guests, as well as the refectory, may also be relevant here. The relationship of the chapter house to the church, with a large yard between the two, though not unknown in Cistercian monasteries, is also reminiscent of a number of friaries (eg Walsingham (Fig 60) and Norwich).

The church cloister (B10) appears to have been incapable of serving its traditional function, even if it had had a complete set of full walkways, which it clearly did not. The northern walkway was a narrow timber pentice which should perhaps be regarded rather as an additional aisle or mortuary space for burial tacked on to the south side of the nave, rather than a cloister passage. The eastern walkway was also fairly narrow though made of stone, and appears to have functioned purely as a corridor. However, this arrangement is hardly surprising in the late 14th century: the monastic cloister was no longer used as it had been, for example for the instruction of novices, and there was therefore no need to build a traditional cloister to the south of the nave. Equally there was no need to build a warming room or dormitory (for which there was no excavated evidence) in a century when such facilities had long since been replaced by private heated chambers. Building 2 at the south-west corner of the first cloister (B3) may have been a small communal dormitory used in the early years to provide accommodation for the monks as a temporary solution, but it was probably converted into the abbot's lodging long before the close of the 14th century and the monks moved to more private accommodation. The documented infirmary, here occupying the position usually reserved for the dormitory, would more normally have been further to the south and east. At St Mary Graces the plague burials (OA3, Fig 4) and marshes to the east hindered construction there, but it is probable that the lack of any need for a large formal communal dormitory also allowed the infirmary to be sited here. The infirmary had long since become a place for the construction of private heated chambers for the monks, and unsurprisingly both the archaeological and documentary evidence for St Mary Graces indicate that there was never any intention to build the communal infirmary of earlier centuries. Both indicate that private chambers were constructed here from the outset.

What is perhaps surprising amid the pervasive and understandable adaptation of contemporary mendicant design, and abandonment of the communal life, is the Cistercians' construction of a large and rather lavish traditional refectory in the south range – without, it should also be noted, a kitchen immediately adjacent to the west. The construction of a building usually designed for regular communal meals in a monastery built without most other communal facilities, at a time when most monks would have eaten meals in their private chambers, may suggest the triumph of hope over experience, but given the clear non-communal intentions shown elsewhere, perhaps requires further examination. The building may be that referred to as the 'halle' in 1425 when a refectory is also mentioned (TNA: PRO, SC 6/917/16). It may never have been intended for the daily communal meals of the monks but rather only for irregular, more important meals, perhaps with and/or entirely for invited guests. Equally the building may have been used for other events such as meetings, conferences, or performances. The refectory was constructed *c* 1383–91. During the Great Schism of 1378–1409, and in or before 1394, the pope ordered the chapter of England to convoke at St Mary Graces; and the English chapters continued to meet there until 1400. Moreover, in 1392 the parish clerks of London performed a stage play at St Mary Graces, and once in 1419 a royal council met there (below, 3.9). Some need may therefore have been felt in the 1380s for a large hall structure within the abbey, even if none was felt for a communal refectory. From the excavated remains, the refectory was most suitable, the chapter house being too small and the nave – though certainly containing some evidence for early benches which may have been used during general chapters *c* 1394–1400 – was needed for burial and the income it generated. The fact that the kitchen (B11) was some distance from the refectory, was built before it, and apparently served other parts of the monastery via the secondary cloister (B3), may support the idea of an intended intermittent use of the refectory for such purposes. St Mary Graces' tiny suburban precinct also contained a number of private tenements, further fragmenting it. This, though unknown in earlier centuries, was again not uncommon from the 14th century onwards. By the early 16th century, parts of the precinct of Stratford Langthorne had been leased out to lay people, while at Beaulieu late leases show at least 35 copyhold tenants in the Great Close, and the Carmelites in London had private dwellings in their precinct by 1385 (Barber et al 2004, 93; Hockey 1976, 169; Clapham 1910, 20). So in this, as in so much else, St Mary Graces, built from the mid 14th century onwards, was simply exemplifying current trends. Another aspect of secular encroachment concerns the usage of the chapel of Holy Trinity after the construction of the church. This may have functioned simply as another mortuary chapel or still been open to the public, given its original function of serving the Black Death cemetery and commemorating the victims of the epidemic. This, as mentioned above (3.1), clearly parallels the Black Death cemetery at West Smithfield, where the chapel later became the conventual church (Barber and Thomas 2002, 18). The inclusion of such public places of worship within Cistercian precincts was not unknown: at Stratford Langthorne, originally a Savigniac foundation, an existing parish church was incorporated (Barber et al 2004, 71).

For the first ten years at least, construction was controlled by John Tyrington, a royal master mason of considerable experience and standing (Harvey 1984, 304). Though it is not known who replaced Tyrington after 1361, the continued interest of Edward III and Richard II would suggest that a royal mason continued to guide the work. The study of the *ex situ* architectural fragments shows a number of parallels with the work on other London projects of the time (below, 3.3). It is not unreasonable to suggest that the pool of skills and ideas responsible for these buildings in and around London in the 14th century contributed significantly to the construction of St Mary Graces.

3.3 The architecture of the abbey

St Mary Graces suffered severe financial hardship many times, not least during the first decades of construction. The conventual buildings have a small and utilitarian look to them, and there is evidence for false starts (the chapter house (B9)), interrupted building campaigns (the presbytery (B4) and nave (B6)) and shoddy work (the foundations of the chapter house (B9) and infirmary (B15)) (above, 2.4). The great size and magnificence of earlier Cistercian houses is lacking; as reconstructed, the church of St Mary Graces fits easily into just the nave of Byland or Rievaulx. Yet, particularly with the church, the *ex situ* Perpendicular-style architectural fragments hint at some beauty lost. When considering the architectural history of the abbey it is important to remember its relative brevity; the abbey was founded in 1350 and suppressed in 1539, yet the vast majority of the church and the conventual buildings were probably complete by the turn of the 15th century, having been built largely between 1360 and 1391. Before this period, the chapel of Holy Trinity (B1) and the south-west cloister (B3) were probably constructed; after it, only two small chapels are thought to have been built: the chapel 'without the quire door on the south side' (B16), which appears to have been in existence by 1475, and the Lady chapel (B17) which was in existence by 1489. A remarkable decrease in moulding variety occurred in the early Perpendicular period. The contrast between the sole occurrence of Decorated-style work (group <A61>–<A70>: below and Chapter 5.1; Fig 61; Fig 85) and the uniformity of the remainder is striking, and shows how St Mary Graces straddled a true watershed in style. A reduced emphasis on the moulding and a simplification of the orders meant that there was a corresponding increase in the area of glass; builders now chose to experiment with geometric patterns and light rather than the strongly three-dimensional receding planes that were a feature of Decorated architecture.

The chapel of Holy Trinity (B1)

Sufficient documentary references exist to put the existence of this building beyond doubt; however, its location, size and appearance are more debatable. The later layout of the abbey suggests that Building 1 is likely to have been the chapel, in the form of a simple rectangular structure at most 30m long by 12m wide. This would have been similar to the chapel established by Sir Walter Manny on Spitalcroft at the West Smithfield Black Death cemetery site, a rectangular building 29.6m long and 11.6m wide which became the conventual church of the Charterhouse (Barber and Thomas 2002, 18). The chapel of Holy Trinity was apparently built between 1350, the nominal date of St Mary Graces' foundation, and 1353, when the abbey acquired the chapel and building work on the abbey began. It was not constructed as part of the abbey, but as part of a short and separate building campaign.

The chapel is unlikely to have been the work of John Tyrington, who first appears to have supervised work in 1353 and was probably responsible for much of the form of the abbey church. A number of window mouldings might stylistically be early enough to have come from this building, but most seem to be part of a unified larger-scale campaign associated with the church, and thus withTyrington. Architectural fragments <A61>–<A70>, uncompromisingly Decorated in style and distinct from any other mouldings found, may have come from the chapel rather than the church (Chapter 5.1; Fig 85). The panel tracery and the elaborate window (Fig 61) must come from an important and early structure, perhaps an east window set within the gable end. However, there is no reason why this could not have been the east window of the presbytery of the church and thus part of Tyrington's scheme. Although now destroyed, St Stephen's Chapel, Westminster, was built to one design of extreme opulence (Alexander and Binski 1987, 337) between 1292 and 1348. The decorative use of continuous mullions that ran down the walls below the sills to frame panel tracery is common to both. The ornamental brattishing resembles work at St Stephen's Chapel, although it is hard to judge how widespread this form was.

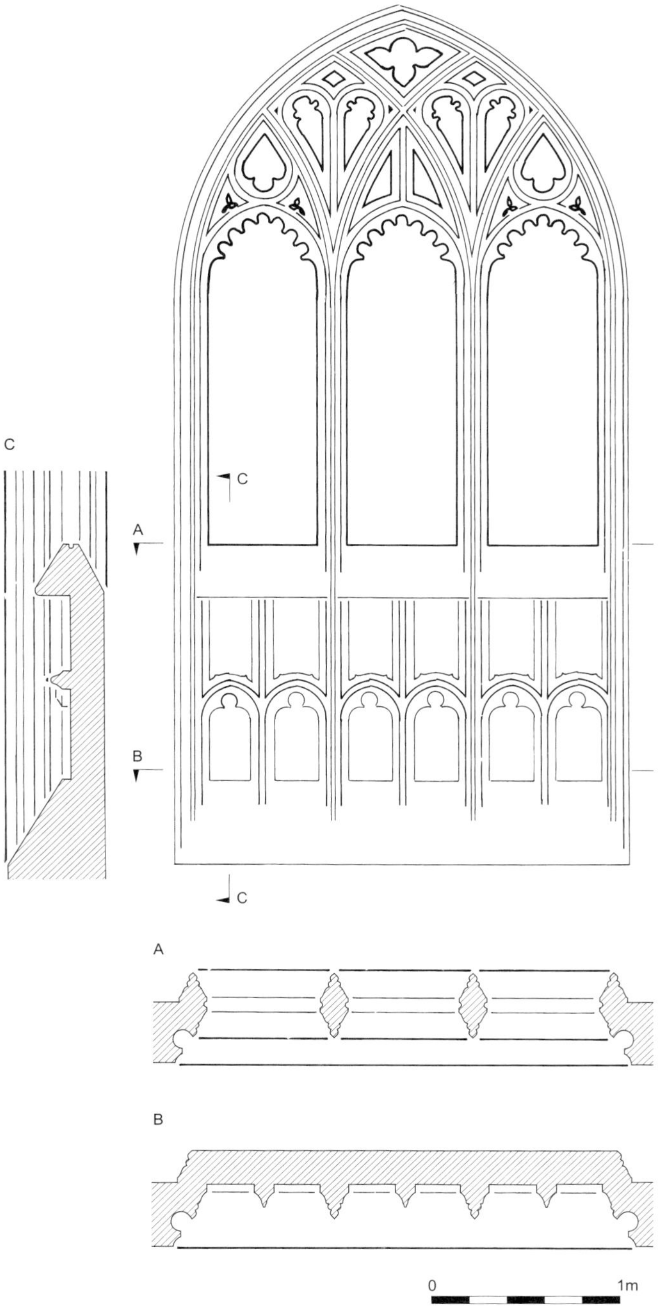

Fig 61 Reconstruction of the Decorated-style window, possibly from the chapel of Holy Trinity or the presbytery, based on architectural fragments (group <A61>–<A70>) (scale 1:40)

The church (B4, B6–B8, B16–B17)

The church was substantially complete by 1391 (Clapham 1915, 354). Though the remains are fragmentary and incomplete, the overall appearance of the eastern end of the church can be reconstructed, and that of the western end at least inferred. The internal measurements of the presbytery were 24.0m x 7.0m. The positions of the tower arch respond and the pilaster buttresses indicate four bays of uneven length. Counting from west to east, they were approximately 4.5m (retrochoir/ walking-place), 5.5m (choir stalls), 3.5m, and 3.5m (high altar) long respectively (Fig 59). The high altar would have been at the east end of the presbytery, to the east of the final row of burials. The choir stalls were in the second bay from the west of the presbytery, where no burials were recorded against the south wall. The central strip of burials suggests that the stalls were no more than 3.0m wide on each side and probably less, with a length of 5.5m, but sufficient to serve a community of a dozen or fewer monks and even the double monastery of 24 originally planned by Edward III.

There is evidence to suggest that some of the plain window mouldings (group <A2>–<A10>: Chapter 5.1; Fig 72) derive either from the building campaign associated with the chapel of Holy Trinity (1350–3: Chapter 2.2) or were used in the presbytery (from 1361: Chapter 2.4). Fragments <A2>–<A6> closely resemble window mouldings employed in the inner court of Edward III's great house at Rotherhithe (Samuel 2009, 160–4, esp figs 127, 130). There were close royal and institutional links between Edward III's Rotherhithe palace and manor and the abbey he founded (Dyson 2009, 17). The Rotherhithe works can be closely dated by royal accounts to 1353–61 (Allen Brown et al 1963, 993). It is plausible that similar mouldings at St Mary Graces formed part of the earliest abbey buildings commenced under the supervision of Tyrington in either 1353 or 1361, although their simplicity makes them rather non-specific. It is equally possible that masons named in 1353 at Rotherhithe such as William of Hemel Hempstead, Roger Stephen and Thomas Cook (ibid, 990, 992; Blatherwick and Bluer 2009, 20, 155) were responsible. The two contemporary royal works were in very close proximity to one another. The heavy buttressing at the east end of the building suggests the presence of a large east window and possibly two smaller side windows, as well as a presbytery vault. As noted for the chapel of Holy Trinity (above), it is possible that the window including <A61>–<A70> formed the main east window of the presbytery. Equally, the window mouldings <A22>–<A32> may also belong to the presbytery as a single unified building campaign with the windows represented by <A13>–<A21>. These appear to have come from the nave (Chapter 5.1; Fig 62; Fig 74; Fig 75), which may again suggest that windows <A2>–<A10> belong rather to the earlier phase of work associated with the chapel of Holy Trinity.

The overall size of the nave can be estimated. The width can be determined as *c* 18.5m, but the length is more problematical. The nave could have occupied much of the 'great court' marked on the 1635 plan (Fig 58), with the west front aligned to the west end of the south-west cloister (B3). This would have produced a nave of nine bays and approximately 45m long. Nevertheless, the excavations suggested, but did not prove, that the nave could not have been longer than six bays, or *c* 30m, and was more probably only five bays long, or *c* 25m (Fig 59). Wyngaerde's 16th-century panorama (Fig 56), showing a central tower, may be a reasonably accurate sketch of the church, in which case five or six bays would appear to be the correct length for the nave. A smaller nave would also accord with the relative poverty of the house and the absence of any sizeable contingent of lay brothers, but a larger nave would have provided more space for burials and thus more revenue.

The position of the documented bell tower was clearly at the junction of the nave and presbytery, as shown by the fragmentary remains of the arch responds in the nave and presbytery there (Fig 59). Wyngaerde's view of the church (Fig 56) shows a relatively large bell tower projecting centrally from the church roof. However, he had a tendency to exaggerate the size of church towers in his panorama. It is more likely, bearing in mind the size of the foundations, that the tower was much smaller than depicted and that, given the external buttressing on both, the roof of the presbytery and nave were unvaulted and of timber. Only one true stone vaulting element (<A52>–<A54>: Chapter 5.1; Fig 82) has been identified; the vault rib (<A53>, <A54>) was found in a very late 18th-century context (period C3: Grainger and Phillpotts 2010, 84), which strongly suggests that it did not come from the church, which was demolished *c* 1560 and its stone apparently reused in earlier post-medieval structures. If the use of stone vaulting had been extensive, more should have been found.

The nave may have employed a single type of window in three orders of size (group <A13>–<A21>: Chapter 5.1; Fig 62; Fig 74). The light moulding with ogival axial terminations is an early example of a type which saw widespread use over more than a century and a half. Early examples can be seen at Norwich Cathedral in the presbytery clerestory of *c* 1362, and at Worcester Cathedral in the east walk of the cloister of *c* 1385–1404 (Harvey 1978, 254, 259). The analogy with the closely related Arundel collegiate church suggests that these windows lit the aisles. The heavy buttressing on the south wall of the St Mary Graces nave suggests that the south aisle had large multi-light windows on the south side. Window glass found in the second bay from the east in the south aisle among demolition debris of *c* 1560 (period C1: Grainger and Phillpotts 2010, 12) is dated to the 15th century; stylistically this glass is typical of that date in being figurative,

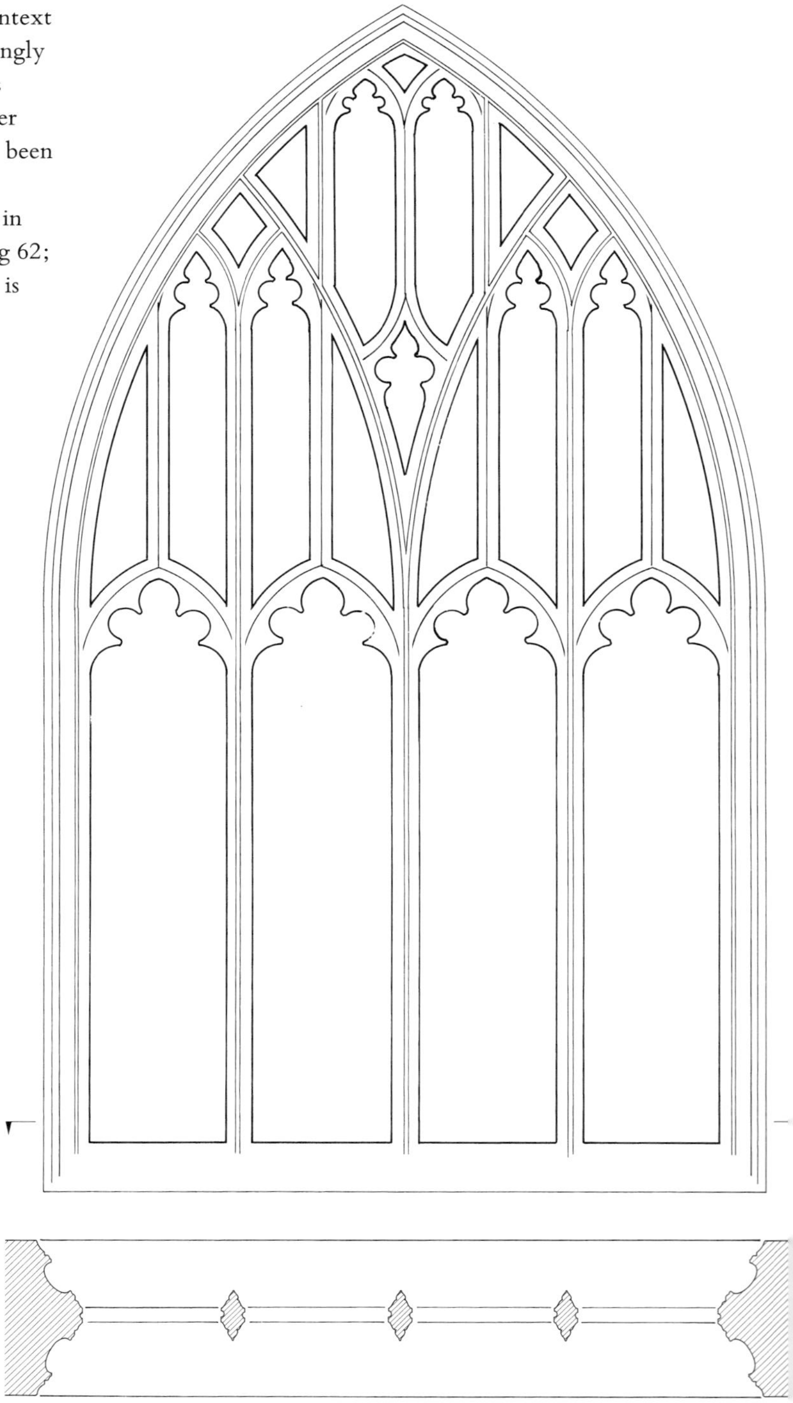

Fig 62 Reconstruction of a Perpendicular-style window, possibly from the nave, based on architectural fragments (group <A13>–<A21>) (scale 1:40)

although of disappointing quality (Chapter 5.5; Fig 95). The smaller windows appear to have had two different tracery patterns and may have lit clerestories because of the need for brightness. The mouldings are similar to recently excavated material from St Mary Spital in London (Samuel in prep) where chapel dedications support a reconstruction of the presbytery in the 1390s (Thomas et al 1997, 68).

The arcade group <A36>–<A42> (Chapter 5.1; Fig 63; Fig 77) derives from the nave of the church and is paralleled by Arundel collegiate church and the nave of Canterbury Cathedral, but the style was very long-lived. The nearest surviving London parallels are at St Andrew Undershaft and St Olave Hart Street. Similar bases were used in the nave at Canterbury Cathedral (*c* 1391, thought to have been built by Henry Yevele). Although the Canterbury piers were far larger than those of St Mary Graces, the mouldings were only slightly bigger. The arcade is also paralleled at Arundel collegiate church (*c* 1390), attributed on stylistic grounds to Yevele and William Wynford (Harvey 1978, 117) and again at St Mary Spital (Samuel in prep). The late occurrence (*c* 1520) of the type at St Mary in Beverley, Yorkshire, shows that it is impossible to date such piers too closely (R Lea, pers comm). The uniformity of the pier in the Perpendicular style is striking, even over a period of more than 150 years.

A quatrefoil screen, <A34>–<A35> (Chapter 5.1; Fig 76), could have been built in front of the sill of the great western window of the nave and would have extended the width of the nave.

The chapter house (B9)

The chapter house was apparently built between 1365 and 1375 (TNA: PRO, E 326/5595; GL, MS 25121/953), before Edward III's bequests and the relative affluence of the last years of the 14th century. The overall length of the chapter house was 14.25m and its width 8.15m, with interior measurements of 12.75m x 6.0m (Fig 17). It was a simple square-ended rectangular building of a standard Cistercian type. Its small size almost certainly reflects the more modest ambitions of the monastery after the poverty of the early years, and the

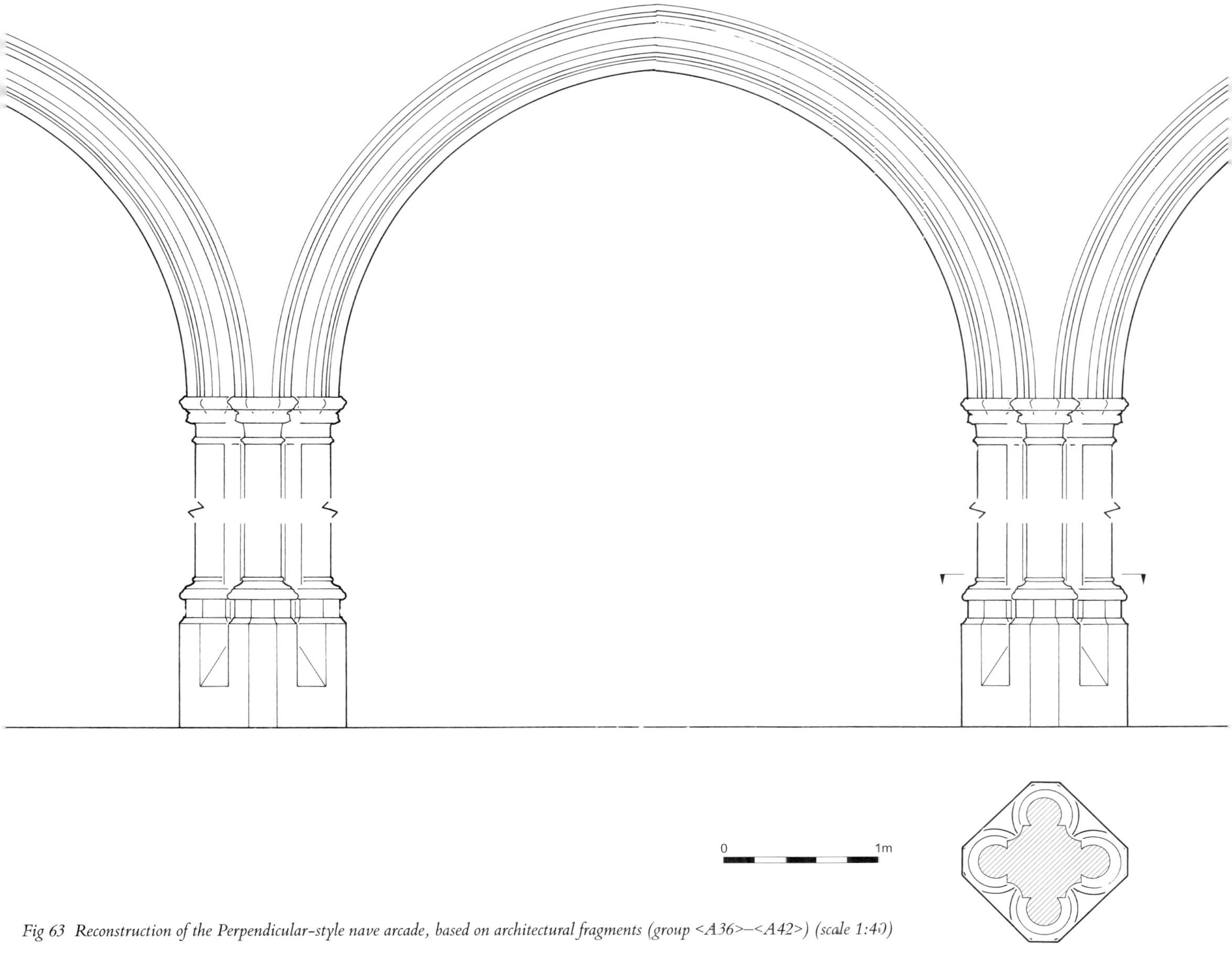

Fig 63 Reconstruction of the Perpendicular-style nave arcade, based on architectural fragments (group <A36>–<A42>) (scale 1:40)

apparent plainness of the structure may also be indicative of early poverty.

The refectory (B13)

The refectory was the most impressive building in the south range, with overall internal dimensions of 19.4m x 7.25m. It had a raised dais at the southern end and a large pulpit to the west. The south wall was offset on a plinth above the foundation, cornered with chamfered Reigate stone and decorated with flint banding. The south doorway shown in the 1589–92 picture plan (Fig 64; Fig 65) was almost certainly a later insertion (TNA: PRO, MPB 1/4), as it is unlikely that a medieval refectory would have had such a feature. Two multi-light windows are shown above this door, which were almost certainly medieval features. The distinctive moulding of the

Fig 64 Picture plan of 1589–92 showing the former monastic refectory and (to the right of this) the monastic infirmary (TNA: PRO, MPB 1/4)

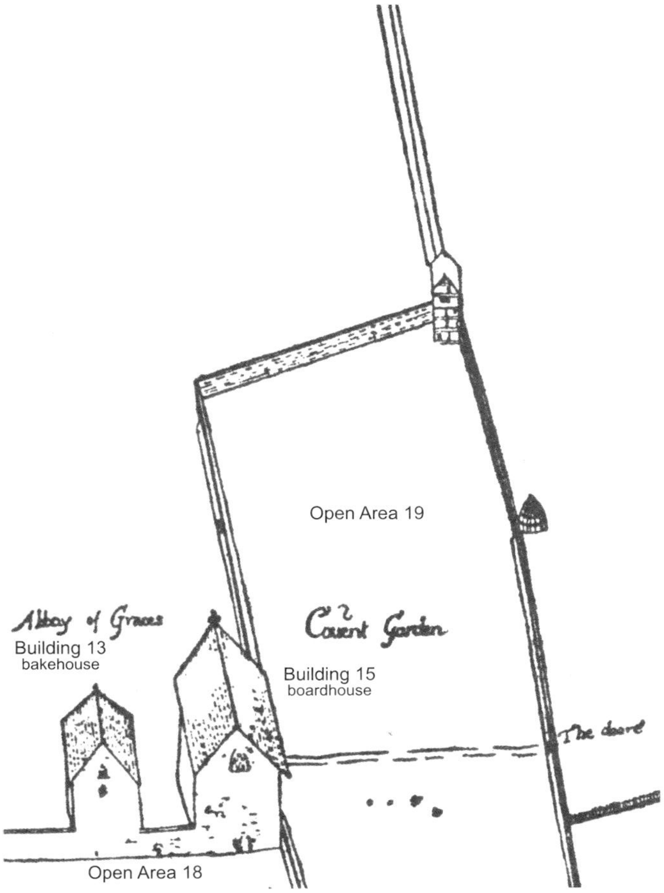

Fig 65 Detail from Marjorie Honeybourne's tracing of the 1589–92 picture plan (see Fig 64) showing the former monastic refectory and (to the right of this) the monastic infirmary (then, respectively, the bakehouse (B13) and the boardhouse (B15) of the Royal Navy victualling yard: Grainger and Phillpotts 2010) (Honeybourne 1929, 200)

window mullion <A43> (Chapter 5.1; Fig 78) is similar to the Westminster Hall Great Window built in 1394 by Henry Yevele (Harvey 1978, fig 30). At Westminster, the great size of the window required a much heavier section, but the stylistic similarity is otherwise apparent. The St Mary Graces fragment appears to have come from an important precinct building which may have survived the suppression; both the refectory and the infirmary had long post-suppression lifespans.

The infirmary (B15)

Building 15 was the last major south range building to be constructed, almost certainly in 1390–2 (TNA: PRO, SC 6/1258, ms 1, 2, 3). Its overall internal dimensions were, allowing for the offset in the west wall, 20.3m x 11.3m to the south of the dogleg and 13.1m x 9.1m to the north of it. The 1635 plan (Fig 58) indicates that this building had a first floor that may have been medieval in origin. The 1589–92 picture plan (Fig 64; Fig 65) shows a south doorway which may be a later insertion, and a large multi-light window which was probably original. The <A43> window mullion (Fig 78) could also have been appropriate for this building.

The south-west (first) cloister (B3)

Internally the cloister enclosure measured 29.0m east–west and 20.0m north–south. The dimensions of the garth were 10.6m x 22.0m. The north alley was approximately 3.8m wide, the south alley 3.25m wide, the west alley 2.85m wide, and the east alley between 2.75m and 3.0m wide. The open space or passage between the north alley and the chapel (B1) was 4.25m wide. In 1635 this cloister had a first floor above, which may have been an original feature. The possible cloister mullion <A46>–<A47> (below; Fig 66) may be relevant to this structure. However, this cloister complex is known from cartographic evidence to have remainded standing, as a recognisable cloister, until after 1635 (Fig 58) and probably stood until at least *c* 1680 (period C2: Grainger and Phillpotts 2010), long after the victualling yard buildings were constructed in which these architectural fragments and <A33> (below; Fig 66) were reused. Hence it is more likely that any moulded stone found that may relate to a cloister derives from the church cloister (B10) which appears to have been demolished in the late 16th century.

The church cloister (B10)

The unglazed tracery fragment <A33> (Chapter 5.1; Fig 66) may derive from a cloister; its pattern is similar to the tracery patterns of the groups possibly used on the nave (<A17>, <A19>–<A21>, <A22>–<A26>; above and Chapter 5.1; Fig 62; Fig 74). The general appearance of the tracery resembles that of the west end of the antechapel at New College, Oxford, thought to be the work of William Wynford (Harvey 1984, 353). The unglazed window mullion <A46>–<A47> (Chapter 5.1; Fig 66) may also derive from this cloister, which may not have been built in a single operation and was clearly remodelled (above, Chapter 2.4 and 2.5). Although the moulding is less elaborate, the mullion capitals resemble Yevele's north cloister walk at Canterbury Cathedral (1397–1414), where they are restricted to the internal elevation. On the St Mary Graces fragments no evidence of the tracery survives, but broken lines suggest the general form (Fig 66). The single iron bar at the level of the springing line is also paralleled. At Canterbury the cloisters were partially glazed. The simple moulding was used over a long period, and a very similar unglazed moulding was used by John Croxtone for the courtyard/street screen (1442–55) at the Leadenhall garner (Samuel 1989). The moulding parallels the (restored) moulding used in the Dean's Cloister, Windsor, by John Sponlee in 1353 (Harvey 1961, fig 2).

The masons

The builders who worked on the abbey seem to have been hired on an ad hoc basis for particular jobs. Only John Tyrington is known for work elsewhere (Harvey 1984, 304). He learnt his trade in the prestigious royal chapel of St Stephen, Westminster, where he was well schooled in the Decorated style. He held an important position in the London mystery of masons by the middle of the century, and was called upon by the king to

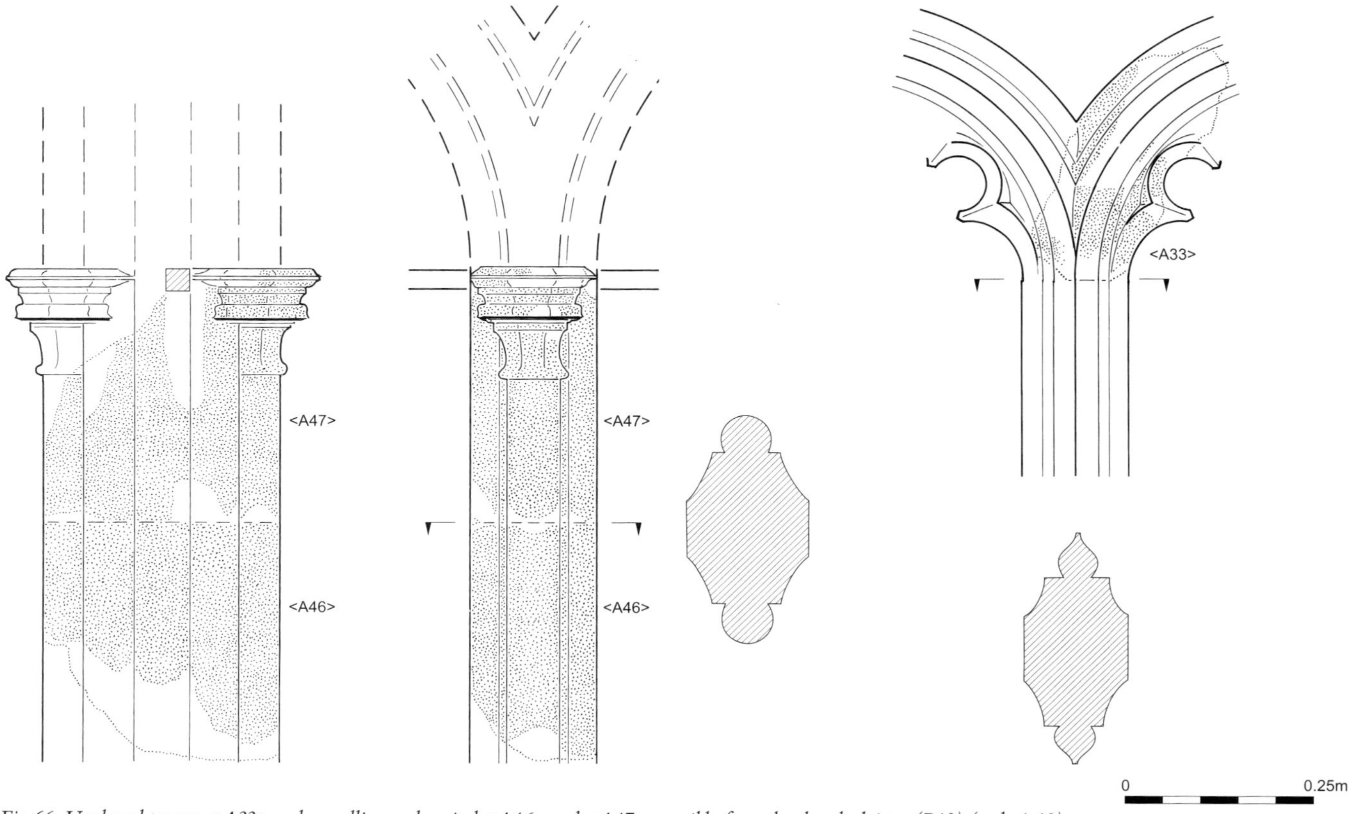

Fig 66 Unglazed tracery <A33> and a mullion and capital <A46> and <A47>, possibly from the church cloister (B10) (scale 1:10)

'impress' masons for St Mary Graces on two occasions in 1353 and 1361 (*Cal Pat R*, 1350–4, 465, 471; 1358–61, 567). The names of some otherwise unknown masons working on the abbey in the 14th century are known from the bursar's accounts of 1391–2 (TNA: PRO, SC 6/1258/1). There were two types of masons: hewers and 'leggers' (layers). Labourers, carpenters, tilers and 'daubers' were also hired. One John Prophete is mentioned as a 'stone man' and supplier of five loads of freestone for 18s. Richard Olyver, another mason at St Mary Graces, may be related to the better-known Adam Oliver, who was active as a carpenter at Carisbrooke Castle on the Isle of Wight in 1384–5 (Harvey 1984, 220). Richard seems to have been a mason in the broad sense of the term, because he acted as a contractor for the abbey and the abbey's tenements in the City, hiring labour and buying stone, timber and other materials for these buildings. His 'job description' is consonant with that of head mason, where negotiating skills were as important as technical ability. In 1425 the abbey supported Walter Myddilton, a mason, as a pensioner (TNA: PRO, SC 6/917/16) (Table 11). He may have been related to John de Middleton who was active at Durham Cathedral Priory from 1398 to 1401 (Harvey 1984, 204). Walter had been awarded his pension under Abbot Roger (1412–15). It is not clear whether the mason was old or disabled, or if he was simply a full-time employee of the abbey.

The influence of the well-known royal masons William Wynford (active 1360–1405) and Henry Yevele (active 1353–1400) was ubiquitous throughout southern England. At the time of the abbey's construction, both were at the height of their careers. Yevele's royal office made him (for the last 22 years of his life) hugely influential (Harvey 1978, 121). Harvey favoured the attribution of buildings of unknown authorship to these two architects, but it is likely that any mason who was successful would be widely imitated.

At St Mary Graces there is an exact repetition of features found at St Mary Spital. These similarities comprise the nave arcade, the chief window mouldings and even, it would appear, the tracery patterns. Can a common mason for these two churches be identified? The nave at St Mary Spital must have been very extensively remodelled if not entirely rebuilt before a chantry was added to it by 1379, and the Lady chapel was part of a building campaign completed before *c* 1370 (Samuel in prep). Tyrington could have been the master mason of the nave at St Mary Spital as well as the mason for St Mary Graces, although this would have required him to be an old man by the standards of the time (he was probably born around the turn of the century).

Another possible candidate is the younger mason Thomas Cook. He was a working mason at Edward III's great house at Rotherhithe in 1349 and was the probable author of the remarkable facade at Rotherhithe which survived into the early 20th century; he rose to the position of warden of masons at Eltham Palace by 1360 (Allen Brown et al 1963, 992; Blatherwick and Bluer 2009, 20, 155). Edward III endowed St Mary Graces with the manor of Rotherhithe on his death (ibid, 17). Cook's career working on royal projects suggests that he could have been involved at St Mary Graces, perhaps working for Tyrington. He would have been in a good position to re-employ much of his expertise gained at St Mary Graces on St Mary Spital. This is pure conjecture, but something of this nature could have occurred.

Materials

The two main stone types identified visually on site were 'Reigate stone' and 'Kentish ragstone'. (No systematic scientific geological study has been undertaken.) The 'freestone' employed at St Mary Graces was almost all the glauconitic sand/limestone, with no oolitic structure, usually described as 'greensand' (Sherlock 1960, 18) but very commonly referred to as 'Reigate stone' because the North Downs in the area of Merstham and Reigate in Surrey are the most well-documented and probable source for the London basin. Three varieties of 'Reigate stone' are apparent at St Mary Graces, and several quarries seem to be indicated. The earliest phase of construction used a hard, coarse, unusually dense variety, excellent as a building stone. It is an over-simplification to say that Reigate stone was always poor and vulnerable to the weather. The main phase used a soft, dust-shedding, fine-grained absorbent variety, prone to serious weathering, though St Mary Graces did not last long enough for this to become a problem. The stone was whitewashed outside and in, to avoid weathering. A third variety, of excellent quality, was used for the small 'veneer' elements applied to internal monuments. This was a fine-grained, dense variety, capable of being very finely dressed, but entirely unsuitable for external use, and all surfaces were sealed by paint or gilt.

The fabric of the church walls, like the excavated claustral buildings, was probably composed of coursed, hammer-dressed Kentish ragstone laid as 'random rubble'. The wall core would have consisted largely of poured mortar and stone waste, and the wall surface would probably have been rendered over and limewashed. The 'Kentish ragstone' identified on site and referred to in the text would have been Kentish limestone ragstone and Hassock sandstone, from the Maidstone area of Kent. The interior surfaces of the claustral buildings were usually of coursed, dressed chalk blocks, which would also have been rendered over and limewashed. Random, uncoursed, mortared chalk rubble was also usually used for the foundations, though these were sometimes skimped on, using loose mixtures of sand, gravel and building debris.

A number of paviors (paving slabs) or tomb slabs of Purbeck marble were also found in the course of the excavations. Purbeck 'marble' is not a true marble but a hard fossiliferous limestone; it is quarried on the Isle of Purbeck in Dorset along with Purbeck limestone, a shelly limestone.

3.4 Endowment and politics

Edward III's original vow was to found a monastery for an abbot and a double convent (24 monks) with a landed endowment worth 1000 marks (£667 6s 8d) a year. Before his death he granted the abbey property in and around London worth 205 marks (£137 6s 8d) per annum (*Cal Close R*, 1396–9, 85–6; *Cal Pat R*, 1388–92, 364; TNA: PRO, E 328/344; SC 8/E711A and B). He had also earmarked several groups of manors to be granted to the abbey, and his will left instructions to fulfil these intentions (Nichols 1780, 59–64). The success of these provisions depended on his successors, Richard II and Henry IV.

The bulk of the abbey's London property was received between 1365 and Edward's death in 1377. It consisted mostly of tenements scattered across about 30 City parishes. A substantial proportion of them came to the king through the Court of Chancery: their owners had used them to fund chantries in City churches, but had neglected to obtain licences to alienate in mortmain (*Cal Pat R*, 1361–4, 84; 1364–7, 156, 253, 298–9, 335, 348, 393, 407; 1367–70, 323–4; 1370–4, 83, 347; 1374–7, 109, 276, 429; *Cal Close R*, 1360–4, 179; TNA: PRO, E 210/8264; E 210/9839; SC 8/9443; BL, Add Ch 39405; Harley Ch 43.E.7; GL, MS 25121/953). These holdings had little geographical coherence, though there was some rationalisation by the Dissolution, when the abbey held property in about 20 parishes. The abbey was also left the manor of East Smithfield, including the Crash Mills and the Swan's Nest hermitage, by Sir Nicholas Loveyne in 1375 (*Cal Pat R*, 1374–7, 213–14; *Cat Anc Deeds*, ii, 94; LPL, Reg Sudbury, fo 87v). In 1397 Loveyne's widow granted the manor of Poplar to the abbey, consisting of messuages, tofts, mills, pasture and arable land in Stepney, East Ham, Stratford, Edmonton, Hackney, Bromley, Old Ford and Woolwich (*Cal Close R*, 1413–19, 509; TNA: PRO, E 315/154, fos 63–72).

There were three main blocks of property which Edward III purchased in the shires to endow St Mary Graces: the reversion of three Hertfordshire manors held by Marie de St-Pol (*Cal Pat R*, 1374–7, 374; *Cal Close R*, 1374–7, 502–3); part of the Leybourne inheritance consisting of the manors of Gravesend, Lynches, Bikenore, Parrock, Leybourne, Wateringbury and Gore in Kent, and Gomshall and Rotherhithe in Surrey (Tuck 1973, 75–6; *Cal Close R*, 1396–9, 85–6); and the reversion of eight manors of Sir James d'Audley in Somerset, Devon and Cornwall (*Cal Pat R*, 1388–92, 364). St Mary Graces received the Hertfordshire manors shortly before the death of Edward III and held them until the Dissolution, when they were worth 88 marks (£59 6s 8d) per annum (*Cal Pat R*, 1374–7, 374; *Cal Close R*, 1374–7, 502–3; 1381–5, 286; 1422–7, 211; 1435–41, 114; *Cat Anc Deeds*, i, 545; iii, 312; vi, 293; *L and P Hen VIII*, i, no. 4766; xiii(2), nos 410, 967(33); xiv, no. 1027(6); xvi, no. 305(12); TNA: PRO, SC 6/1258/1, ms 1, 3; SC 6/917/16; SC 12/29/22, fo 4; LR 14/724; E 303/10/323; E 314; E 321/17/83).

Edward granted the other properties to a panel of feoffees, headed by his eldest surviving son John of Gaunt, with the intention that they should execute his plans for these manors after his death (Dugdale 1655–73, v, 718; *Cal Pat R*, 1388–92, 364; *Cal Close R*, 1392–6, 503). Unfortunately, the abbey could not gain possession of the Audley manors while Audley was alive, and Robert de Vere, Earl of Oxford, seized them on his death (TNA: PRO, SC 8/989). Another of Richard II's favourites, Sir Simon Burley, persuaded the king to make the Kent manors over to him and his family in 1383–5 (Lewis 1937, 664–5; Tuck 1973, 75–6; *Cal Pat R*, 1381–5, 305, 343, 367–8; 1385–9, 37, 109–10; TNA: PRO, SC 8/989; Given-Wilson 1978, 327, 329). After de Vere's exile and Burley's execution in 1388, St Mary Graces successfully petitioned Parliament for the restitution of its rights and gained control of the Kent manors, including Bikenore and Parrock. Ironically, the abbey church became the recipient of the decapitated body of the man who had defrauded it (Chapter 2.4; below, 3.7). Since it had never possessed Parrock before the grant to Burley, in November 1393 the abbey agreed with Baldwin de Raddington, Burley's last surviving nephew, that their hold on Parrock be guaranteed in return for masses said for Burley's soul (Lewis 1937, 664–8; *Cat Anc Deeds*, ii, 285, 448). In July 1398 Richard II finally granted all the Kent and Surrey manors to the abbey in perpetual alms, and thereafter it possessed them undisturbed until the Dissolution, when their value was about 210 marks (£140) per annum (Dugdale 1655–73, v, 719; *Cal Pat R*, 1396–9, 389; 1399–1401, 326; 1401–5, 122, 266; *Cal Close R*, 1402–5, 469–71; *Cat Anc Deeds*, ii, 320; *L and P Hen VIII*, xiii(2), nos 410, 967(330); xiv(1), no. 1354(50); TNA: PRO, E 303/10/307, 328, 354; E 314/55; E 315/233, fo 340; SC 6/HenVIII/2382; 2396, ms 49v–51v). Rotherhithe was leased to Bermondsey Priory in May 1397, and later to Ramsey Abbey (TNA: PRO, SC 6/HenVIII/2396, m 51v; *Cal Pat R*, 1396–9, 108).

Meanwhile, St Mary Graces lost the Audley manors to Richard II's half-brother John Holand, Earl of Huntingdon. Following Robert de Vere's forfeiture, Holand received these manors in July 1388 (TNA: PRO, SC 8/6082; SC 8/E711A; SC 8/E658; SC 8/E1320; *Cal Pat R*, 1385–9, 494–5). The abbey's petition to regain them was unsuccessful. In January 1400 Holand's estates in turn were forfeited, following his rebellion against Henry IV, and in March the Audley manors were restored to the abbey (*Cal Pat R*, 1399–1401, 274–5, 284, 397, 457; 1401–5, 122, 266–7; 1405–8, 227; *Cat Anc Deeds*, i, 294; iii, 486, 488; BL, Campbell Ch X.iv.27; TNA: PRO, E 328/380, 381; E 303/10/293; SC 8/E711A; SC 8/E658; SC 8/E1320). But Holand's son John, Duke of Exeter, continued to make claims on them, leading to a case in Chancery in 1417–18. This time the abbey reinforced its title to the manors by forging a deed, but Exeter took forcible repossession of them in 1426–7 (*Cal Pat R*, 1446–51, 109; *Cal Close R*, 1392–6, 503; TNA: PRO, E 328/343; E 211/380; C 81/666/864, 865, 880, 881; E 135/22/46; SC 8/E1320; C 1/9/357–61). Not until after Exeter's death in 1447 did the abbey regain these manors, and then only during the minority of his heir, though it had petitioned for their restitution in perpetuity (Graham 1929, 377–8; Knowles 1955, 168–9; *Cal Pat R*, 1391–6, 557). In the end St Mary Graces could not withstand the power of the Holands, and the Audley lands were lost.

St Mary Graces seems to have been favourably regarded by Richard II in the 1390s, perhaps because its church was the burial place of his favourite, Burley. In August 1391 the king granted it the leper hospital of St Giles in the Fields, with the advowson and property, including Feltham church (*Cal Pat R*, 1396–9, 47–8). Richard had previously confirmed possession to the master of Burton Lazars, who disputed the grant to St Mary's (*Cal Close R*, 1399–1402, 450). The City authorities were also reluctant to recognise its validity and had to be ordered by Richard to assist the abbot in collecting the St Giles rents (TNA: PRO, E 135/22/44). The abbey was in possession by October 1391, though not securely, and the abbot's agents stripped the hospital of most of the movable property (Flower 1923, 66; TNA: PRO, E 303/10/292, 294; E 326/4417; E 326/5712; E 329/7; E 42/443; SC 6/1258/1, ms 1, 2, 3, 4; SC 2/190/17). The master of Burton Lazars maintained his claims, however, and renewed them at Richard's deposition. In 1399 he drove the abbot's men out of St Giles by force and St Mary Graces submitted to arbitration, the profits being held by a neutral party in the interim (TNA: PRO, E 326/6759, 12431, 12432, 12433, 12435). In 1401 the case was brought to the Court of Chancery but Henry IV was still ordering judgement to be delivered in October 1402 (*Cal Close R*, 1399–1402, 450–1; 1402–5, 16–17). Meanwhile, in September, he had restored the hospital to the master of Burton Lazars, allegedly on the personal petition of Richard made at his deposition (*Cal Pat R*, 1401–5, 120).

3.5 The monastic economy

Despite the lateness of the foundation, the absence of a sizeable contingent of lay brothers and its suburban setting, St Mary Graces practised a certain amount of demesne (or direct) farming. This appears to have been the case with the manor of Poplar, which was held directly as part of the temporalities of the house in 1419 (*Rot Parl*, iv, 312). The customary tenants inherited their tenures of marsh, arable, or meadowland by a system of gavelkind, as in the parent manor of Stepney (TNA: PRO, LR 11/78/904, fo 1; SC 2/191/48–53; SC 6/1258/1, m 4). In the 16th century the property associated with the manor house included a dairy house, a gatehouse, a barn, a granary, a dove house, stables, woods, gardens, meadows, arable land, and fishing and fowling rights (*Val Eccl*, i, 398; *L and P Hen VIII*, i(3), no. 5378; xv, no. 1032; TNA: PRO, E 210/10916; E 178/1364, 2988; E 303/ 10/321; E 310/3/18, no. 48; E 315/191, p 117; E 315/222, fos 304v–305; E 318/38/2042; LR 14/784; SC 12/11/13; SC 12/29/22, fo 7; SC 6/HenVIII/2382; 2383, m 42; 2383, m 6; 2396, m 49; 2397, m 49). The abbey had a grange at Rotherhithe in 1397, but leased it a few years later to Bermondsey Priory (*Cal Pat R*, 1396–9, 108). It also possessed a ruinous grange at Little Hormead in Essex during the reign of Edward IV, but this may always have been leased out (BL, Harley Roll N.18). A number of rural properties were clearly leased out and not exploited directly for demesne farming. The Audley manors (above, 3.4) were in the West Country, an impractical distance away for demesne farming, and in 1408 Holsworthy and Northleigh, Devon, and Tackbeare, Cornwall, were let on a 20-year lease (TNA: PRO, E 303/10/293; BL, Campbell Ch X.iv.27). By the 16th century these had been lost, and all the Kent, Surrey and Hertfordshire manors had been farmed out; and this may have been the situation for some time. Rotherhithe was let to Bermondsey Priory in 1397 (above), but the earliest known lease in these counties was made in 1493 (*Cal Pat R*, 1396–9, 108, 330; TNA: PRO, E 303/10/354).

The abbey owned a considerable amount of non-agricultural rural property. By 1535 it owned 360 acres of woodland in Kent, at Henhurst, Leybourne and Wateringbury, where the abbey felled and sold 26 acres of trees in 1391 for the building programme, as well as a 28-acre wood in Bikenore (*Val Eccl*, i, 398; TNA: PRO, E 314/55; E 315/233, fo 340; *Cal Pat R*, 1388–92, 397). Two small woods were sold at Little Hormead in 1439 (*Cat Anc Deeds*, iii, 312). At Gomshall it retained the King's Wood and Cumbes Wood in its own possession when the manor was leased in 1521, though they were sold to the lessor a few years later (TNA: PRO, E 303/10/298, 352). In 1481 and 1501 the Poplar tenants were fined for taking elm and walnut from a 5-acre wood called the Grove (TNA: PRO, E 315/222, fos 404v–405; SC 2/191/49, m 3; SC 2/1919/50, m 8; SC 6/HenVIII/2396, m 49; SC 12/29/22, fo 7). During the abbey's short-lived tenure of St Giles it was able to exploit the hospital's wood; 6cwt of firewood was taken from it in 1391 (TNA: PRO, SC 6/1258/1, m 3). The abbey's marshlands were more extensive still. In Kent it owned Slayhill Marsh near Sittingbourne, estimated at 600 acres, and Elmeley Marsh near Tunbridge (*Val Eccl*, i, 399; TNA: PRO, SC 12/29/22, fo 7; E 303/10/299, 316; SC 6/HenVIII/2396, m 51; 2397, m 51). The manor of Poplar included Poplar Marsh and marshes at Bromley and Woolwich. Poplar Marsh included a 40-acre piece known as 'Wetemersh'. Much of this flooded in March 1448 and remained partly underwater until well into the next century (*Val Eccl*, i, 399; TNA: PRO, E 303/10/321; E 318/38/2042; SC 2/191/48, m 9; SC 2/191/50, ms 1, 5v; SC 12/11/13; SC 6/HenVIII/2396, ms 44, 49). Sir Lewis John bequeathed Woolwich Marsh to the abbey in 1440 and it became part of Poplar manor (TNA: PRO, SC 6/HenVIII/2396, m 49; 2397, m 49; PROB 11/1/14). Even the immediate vicinity of the abbey was marshy. In the 1530s there was an osier-bed off Nightingale Lane (now Thomas More Street) leased to a basket weaver, and the Pineapple garden (OA11: Fig 28; Fig 64) was waterlogged (TNA: PRO, SC 6/HenVIII/2396, m 43v; E 135/22/48; E 178/1374). The abbey – despite the Cistercians' reputation for developing marginal land – does not appear to have done a great deal to reclaim the marshland, contrary to Marjorie Honeybourne's suggestion (Honeybourne 1952, 20–2). The marshes of Woolwich and Poplar were already enclosed by a river wall and drained by ditches before the abbey obtained them. The abbey never succeeded in draining the land adjacent to their precinct, and the river walls of Poplar needed repair soon after the Dissolution, in 1540 and 1541 (TNA: PRO, SC 6/HenVIII/2384, m 6; 2397, m 53v).

The abbey also exploited the Thames river frontage. It had a wharf at Gravesend and several on Thames-side properties in Wapping, which might have been used to transport agricultural produce from the Kent manors to the abbey (TNA: PRO, E 315/233, fo 340; SC 6/HenVIII/2383, m 30; 2396, ms 42, 44v, 50). The properties in Wapping included several breweries: the Swan's Nest with a wharf and several gardens, the Abbey, the Hartshorn, the Katherine Wheel, the Three Kings and the Lyon. The abbey's milling was done at the Crash Mills, also on the Thames at the boundary between Wapping Marsh and the parish of St Botolph Aldgate. These mills were held as part of the temporalities of the abbey in 1419, and consisted of two watermills under one roof, driven by the tides and supplied by ditches from East Smithfield down Nightingale Lane to the Thames. These ditches needed frequent scouring and in 1391 the mill was repaired, with a new millstone and spindle provided (TNA: PRO, E 40/14033; E 135/22/48; SC 6/1258/1, ms 1, 2, 3; GL, MS 25121/1761; *Cal Feet of Fines*, i, 43; *Rot Parl*, iv, 312; Honeybourne 1952, 22–3). The mills were leased in 1528 in return for a daily supply of wheat-flour to the abbey, but by 1540 they were in ruins and this had been commuted to a cash payment to the manor (TNA: PRO, SC 12/29/22, fo 7; E 315/212, fo 7; SC 6/HenVIII/2384, m 6; 2396, m 44v; 2397, m 53v; 2398; *Val Eccl*, i, 398). There was a granary next to the Katherine Wheel brewhouse (TNA: PRO, E 303/10/313; Fry 1896, iii, 254).

Property held in the City was probably leased out as soon as it was acquired, though only a few of the leases survive (*Cal Close R*, 1381–5, 521; *Cat Anc Deeds*, ii, 254; BL, Royal MS 17.B.xlvii, fo 131v; TNA: PRO, E 326/5712; SC 6/1258/1, m 1; E 303/10/294). The City rent-collector's account of 1425 implies that all the City properties then held were rented out, except some that were vacant but normally worth £14 per annum (TNA: PRO, SC 6/917/16). A cluster of leases survives from June and December 1538, several of which were for 99 years, and several other existing leases were lengthened. The last abbot, Henry Moore, appears to have been providing tenants with long leases that would be recognised by the Court of Augmentations, probably to the profit of himself and the monks (Rosenfield 1961, 244–9; BL, Harley Ch 111.C.36; GL, MS 10890; TNA: PRO, E 303/10/296, 301, 304, 305, 308, 311, 312, 315, 317, 324, 325, 326, 329, 332, 333, 334, 336, 338, 339, 340, 341, 344, 345, 346, 349, 350, 351, 353; E 315/96, pp 140–1; E 315/100, fo 213; SC6/HenVIII/2396, ms 42, 49; SC 12/1/13). In 1540 rents were received from 20 City parishes, the highest incomes coming from St Botolph Billingsgate, St Margaret Moses and St Sepulchre without Newgate (TNA: PRO, SC 6/HenVIII/2396, ms 45v–48v; *Val Eccl*, i, 399). The value of urban properties to the abbey's economy appears to have been sufficient to warrant considerable repairs and construction over time. In 1391 it was repairing and re-tiling tenements in Fenchurch Street and elsewhere, building a new brewhouse in Aldgate Street, and three new tenements to the south of the precinct and five to the south of East Smithfield. Twenty-four thousand roof tiles were required for this work, and a painter was employed on the Tower Hill tenements (TNA: PRO, SC 6/1258/1, ms 1, 2, 3). In 1425 a latrine was mended in St Anthony's parish (TNA: PRO, SC 6/917/16). The abbey built the Hartshorn brewery by 1472 and the Katherine Wheel by

1491 (TNA: PRO, SC 2/191/56, m 9; SC 2/191/58, m 3). Newly-built tenements in Thames Street were leased out in 1528, and in Timberhithe Street in 1534 (TNA: PRO, E 303/10/329, 346). At the Dissolution tenements were being repaired on Tower Hill and East Smithfield, paving was laid in Houndsditch and elsewhere, and a latrine was mended (TNA: PRO, SC 6/HenVIII/2397, m 53v; 2382; 2384, m 6).

One source of income which required no investment and was normally retained when a manor was leased out was the manorial court. The abbey held such a court at Shenfield in 1391 (TNA: PRO, SC 6/1258/1, m 2). Courts were held at Little Hormead in Edward IV's reign and at Meesdon and Westmill in 1508–11 (BL, Harley Roll N.18). In the 1520s the leases of Gomshall and Gravesend allowed for the abbey steward to hold courts there (TNA: PRO, E 303/10/337; E 321/41/262). The abbot also possessed a court baron for Poplar and a court leet with a view of frankpledge at East Smithfield. The earliest known meeting of the latter was in February 1422 (TNA: PRO, SC 6/HenVIII/2396, m 53; SC 2/190/18; SC 2/191/55–9; CRES 38/1683).

The abbey kept cattle near the precinct. Bullocks were fed in the Rose garden and a vacant tenement on Tower Hill in 1524–5, and in the Pineapple garden (OA11: Chapter 2.5; Fig 28) in the 1530s (TNA: PRO, E 178/1374; SC 12/11/43, fos 8, 25). The monks kept chickens and doves; in 1501 a Poplar tenant retained a servant to kill the abbot's doves with limestones. There were two dovecotes, one of which was in the Pineapple garden and was probably the birdcage structure depicted in the picture-plan of 1589–92 (Fig 64; Fig 65) (TNA: PRO, SC 2/191/50, m 8; SC 2/191/52, m 2; SC 6/917/16; E 315/233, fo 339v; MPB 1/4).

Horses were bought for the abbot in 1391 and 1425, and additional horses were hired as needed (TNA: PRO, SC 6/1258/1, ms 1, 2, 3, 5; SC 6/917/16). The accounts of 1391, 1425 and 1539 give some indication of diet and food consumption in the abbey. The foodstuffs included bread, beer, ale, fish, spices, salt, wheat-flour, honey, oil, walnuts, cheese, mustard and barley for 'polayle'. Meat and wine were bought, but may have been reserved for the abbot and his guests in the abbot's hospice (TNA: PRO, SC 6/917/16; SC 6/1258/1, ms 1, 2, 3, 5; SC 12/11/43, fo 8; SC 12/29/22, fo 3). The abbot and monks were allowed to eat meat outside the abbey in certain circumstances by a papal dispensation of 1402 (*Cal Pap Letters*, v, 545). One boar was eaten annually on the feast of St Katherine, supplied by Meesdon under the terms of its lease (TNA: PRO, LR 14/724). In 1411 precinct tenants, Henry Somers and his wife, received 14 loaves a week (seven of white 'convent' bread and seven 'seconds') (*Cal Close R*, 1422–7, 211). The weekly supply of wheat-flour to the abbey in 1528 from the Crash Mills was too much for the monastic community, but extra amounts were to be supplied for feast days (TNA: PRO, E 315/212, fos 7–8). The excess was probably distributed as alms at the abbey gates.

It is difficult to evaluate the success of St Mary Graces' finances from the paucity of financial information available. Only the bursar's account of 1391–2 gives a complete but snapshot picture of the monastery's income and expenditure, and there are some puzzling aspects to the arithmetic. However, it is clear that the abbey was taking advantage of the recent acquisition of the Kent manors late in 1388 to push forward the building programme. Out of the year's income of £505, the largest expenditure by far was £238 on construction work. This burden was leading to an accelerating deficit: of £243 at Michaelmas 1391, increasing to £330 at Michaelmas 1392 (TNA: PRO, SC 6/1258/1). The abbey probably remained in debt throughout the 1390s and beyond. In May 1400 Abbot William arranged a loan of 160 marks (£107 6s 8d) to be repaid over a term of 20 years (*Cal Close R*, 1399–1402, 130, 133–4, 181). In 1426–7 Abbot John wrote to the king that the house was in debt and impoverished by the mismanagement of his predecessors (TNA: PRO, SC 8/6733). The abbey's problems of finance and discipline led to it being taken into royal custody several times. In the 1380s the abbey petitioned to be taken into the king's hands because of impoverishment through the loss of London properties; the petition is endorsed as accepted, though no order for taking custody is known (TNA: PRO, SC 8/9443). In November 1410 the custody of the abbey was given to a panel of members of the royal council and Cistercian abbots, and again in February 1427 (*Cal Pat R*, 1408–13, 268; TNA: PRO, C 1/75/80; *Cal Pat R*, 1422–9, 394; TNA: PRO, SC 8/6733). This was probably a direct consequence of Abbot Paschal's intrusion the previous year (below, 3.6). The abbey also had problems with the Exchequer claiming the income during the vacancies following the deaths of Abbots Ranulph and John Pecche (*Cal Pat R*, 1436–41, 483–4; *Rot Parl*, iv, 312).

The abbey's financial position stabilised somewhat during the 15th century as problems over endowment and construction faded into the past. In 1522 Henry VIII was able to force a loan of 100 marks (£67 6s 8d) from it for his campaign in France (*L and P Hen VIII*, iii(2), no. 2483). At the suppression the gross receipts were worth £603 per annum. The London property was the most valuable, followed by Poplar and the Kent manors. With the fixed annual expenses subtracted, the *Valor Ecclesiasticus* gave it an annual net value of £547 in 1535, the third-highest among the English and Welsh Cistercian houses (*Val Eccl*, i, 398–9). However, the fixed expenses did not take into account the bulk of monastic expenditure. Against this were arrears of £220 owing to the abbey and the debts it owed for goods and services, amounting to £610, more than one year's gross annual income (TNA: PRO, SC 12/29/22).

3.6 The people

The abbots

The head of the house was initially called the president, but only rarely after he is first referred to as abbot in 1353 (*Cal Close R*, 1349–54, 283; 1354–60, 22; 1364–8, 259; 1399–1402, 325; *Cal Pat R*, 1348–50, 484, 560; 1350–4, 397; 1358–61, 34;

1399–1401, 457). The names of a number of abbots of St Mary Graces are known and it is possible to suggest a chronology for them (Table 7). The first abbot was Walter de Sancta Cruce, a former abbot of Garendon, Leicestershire, who appears to have been brought in at the request of the king, but to have only lasted a year or so and to have had little impact on the construction of the abbey. During the 1350s Abbot Walter was followed by one or possibly two men, John de Gloucester (which may be an error) and Peter de Luffegrove, a monk from the mother house, Beaulieu, who may have been among the first monks sent for in 1353. These men also appear to have had little impact on the abbey, but may have overseen the construction of the first cloister (B3) to the south of the chapel of Holy Trinity (B1) (*Cal Close R*, 1354–60, 22; TNA: PRO, E 210/1982).

The third or fourth abbot was William de Warden, a monk from Woburn, Bedfordshire, who is first recorded in August 1360. Abbot William, it would appear, remained in office for at least 51 years, being attested again in July 1411, and presided over the construction of most of the church and the conventual buildings (*Reg Sudbury*, 58; *Cal Pat R*, 1358–61, 457; 1408–13, 340; TNA: PRO, E 210/1982). His longevity in office suggests a relatively young man in 1360, and it is possible that he was the driving force behind the abbey's somewhat improved fortunes from the 1360s to the 1390s, coinciding with renewed interest on the part of the king and the utilisation of the unused Black Death cemetery area for construction.

Whatever his strengths, Abbot William did have to deal with a number of disciplinary problems in later life. In 1401, when William was likely to have been at least in his sixties, a monk called Ralph de Byker (Table 8) was convicted and imprisoned for theft and violence committed against the abbot at Swineshead Abbey. He left the Cistercian Order but came to London and re-entered the Order at St Mary Graces. Abbot William absolved him of his crimes and allowed him to stay; but in 1402 the unruly Byker reverted to his old ways, doing violence to William, ejecting him from the dorter and appropriating abbey goods for his own use (*Cal Pap Letters*, v, 346–7, 517, 602). On 28 November 1410, the king granted the abbot of St Mary Stratford Langthorne and others the keeping and governance of St Mary Graces (*Cal Pat R*, 1408–13, 224). In July 1411 there were more problems when a commission was issued to arrest two monks of the house, Nicholas Sampson and Thomas Broun (Table 8), who had rejected their obedience to the abbot and were wandering abroad. They were to be delivered to the abbot for punishment (*Cal Pat R*, 1408–13, 320). By then William would have been an extremely old man, and it is tempting to see these problems in part as the result of his failing grasp at a time when the abbey's fortunes were once again in decline after the deposition of Richard II.

William de Warden's death does not appear to have resolved any of the problems that his dotage may have caused. He was followed in fairly rapid succession by Abbots Roger Ykham or Greeneway and Ranulph or Rancolf (*Cat Anc Deeds*, iii, 488; *Cal Close R*, 1409–13, 509; TNA: PRO, C 1/9/358; *Rot Parl*, iv, 312; *Cal Close R*, 1413–19, 509). Neither of these men was from outside, but a former sub-prior and prior respectively of the abbey (Table 8). After William's long tenure, the abbey was

Table 7 Abbots of St Mary Graces

Abbot	Origin	Dates	References
Walter de Sancta Cruce	abbot of Garendon	1350–1	*Cal Close R*, 1354–60, 22; TNA: PRO, E 210/1982
? John de Gloucester	(possibly erroneous)	1354	*Cal Close R*, 1354–60, 22
Peter de Luffegrove	monk of Beaulieu	?	TNA: PRO, E 210/1982
William de Warden	monk of Woburn	1360–1411	*Reg Sudbury*, ii, 58; *Cal Pat R*, 1358–61, 457; 1408–13, 340; TNA: PRO, E 210/1982
Roger Ykham or Greeneway	sub-prior	1412–15	*Cat Anc Deeds*, iii, 488; *Cal Close R*, 1409–13, 328–9, 344; TNA: PRO, C 1/9/358
Ranulph	prior	1417–19	*Rot Parl*, iv, 312; *Cal Close R*, 1413–19, 509; TNA: PRO, C 1/9/358
Paschal Gilot		1419–22	*Cal Pap Letters*, vii, 319; *Rot Parl*, iv, 312; *Cal Pat R*, 1446–51, 50; TNA: PRO, SC 8/6733; SC 6/917/16; C 1/9/357–61; BL, Campbell Ch X.iv.27
William		1423	*Cat Anc Deeds*, ii, 259
John Pecche		1424–30	*Cal PM R*, iv, 248; *Cal Pat R*, 1436–41, 483–4; 1446–51, 109; *Cal Close R*, 1422–9, 211; TNA: PRO, SC 8/6733; SC 2/191/43, ms 1–2; E 213/31
Robert Wellys		1432–57	*Cal Feet of Fines*, i, 237; *Cat Anc Deeds*, iii, 312; vi, 293; *Cal Close R*, 1435–41, 114; *Reg Chichele*, ii, 688; TNA: PRO, SC 2/191/48, m 3; /55, ms 2–4; /56, ms 22–3; SC 6/972/11; E 326/9046.
Thomas Been		1457–75	*Cal Close R*, 1468–76, nos 767, 985; TNA: PRO, SC 2/191/48, m 10; /55, m 5; /56, ms 5–9
John		1476–7	TNA: PRO, SC 2/191/57, m 1
Edmund		1478–82	*Cal Pat R*, 1476–85, 215; TNA: PRO, SC 2/191/49, ms 1–5; /50, m 1; /57, ms 2–5; E 326/9046
John Langton (Gerves)		1483–1513	*Cal Pap Letters*, xvi, 166–7; *L & P Hen VIII*, i, no. 438(3), m 16; *Cat Anc Deeds*, i, 545; ii, 320; *Cal Pat R*, 1476–85, 466; TNA: PRO, SC 2/190/18; SC 2/191/50, ms 2–11; /51, ms 2, 3; /52, ms 1–2; /57, m 6; /58, ms 1–4; E 303/10/307, 354; BL, Harley MS 6953, pp 10, 30; Add Ch 39405
Richard Prehest or Pest		1514–16	*L & P Hen VIII*, ii(1), no. 1861; TNA: PRO, SC 2/191/52, m 3; E 303/10/297; C 1/426/49
Henry Moore		1516–38	*L & P Hen VIII*, xi, no. 392; TNA: PRO, SC 2/191/59, ms 1–4; E 303/10/354; C 1/426/49; BL, Harley MS 6955, p 74; GL, MS 9531/9, fo 64

well-established and internal candidates could be appointed. Both men were in the abbey during the last years of Abbot William. Roger Ykham is recorded as sub-prior in 1379 and as sacristan in 1391–2; Ranulph is recorded as prior in 1400 and 1417, when he succeeded Roger as abbot (McHardy 1977, no. 13; *Cal Pat R*, 1399–1401, 397; *Cat Anc Deeds*, i, 212: *VCH* 1909, i, 463; TNA: PRO, E 303/10/354; BL, Royal MS 17.B.xlvii; TNA: PRO, SC 6/1258/1). As officers of the abbey they were in part responsible for the maintenance of a discipline that had failed at least twice in a decade. In 1415, during Roger's abbacy, the pope granted the abbots their only major privilege: the use of the mitre, ring and other pontifical insignia, which gave the abbot of St Mary Graces an equivalent status to the most important abbots of England (*Cal Pap Letters*, vi, 425). After two years Abbot Ranulph was succeeded in 1419 by the most colourful of St Mary Graces' abbots, Paschal Gilot. Paschal is first mentioned as a monk in 1412, the year after William de Warden's death, but may have been there earlier (*Cal Close R*, 1409–13, 344, 400; TNA: PRO, C 1/9/358). In about 1422 Abbot Paschal was forced to resign following a period of mismanagement. Though in receipt of a pension in 1425–6, in May 1426, while Abbot John Pecche – who became abbot in 1424 after a briefly mentioned William (*Cat Anc Deeds*, ii, 259) – was away attending the general chapter at Northampton, Paschal intruded himself as abbot again, sealing leases and other documents with the conventual seal and pawning the abbey jewels. The abbot of Beaulieu as visitor put Pecche back in possession. Paschal is subsequently recorded in 1447 as an attorney for the abbot of Coggeshall (*Cal Pap Letters*, vii, 319; *Rot Parl*, iv, 312; *Cal Pat R*, 1446–51, 50; TNA: PRO, SC 8/6733; SC 6/917/16; C 1/9/357–61; BL, Campbell Ch X.iv.27). In 1426–7 Pecche wrote to the king that the house had been impoverished by the mismanagement of his predecessors (TNA: PRO, SC 8/6733).

John Pecche ceased to be abbot in 1430 (*Cal PM R*, iv, 248; *Cal Pat R*, 1436–41, 483–4; 1446–51, 109; *Cal Close R*, 1422–9, 211; TNA: PRO, SC 8/6733; SC 2/191/48, ms 1–2; E 213/31). He was followed in the middle years of the century by a succession of men about whom nothing more is known than their names (Table 7). John Langton became abbot in 1483, and served until 1513 (*Cal Pap Letters*, xvi, 166–7; *L and P Hen VIII*, i, no. 438(3), m 16; *Cat Anc Deeds*, i, 545; ii, 320; *Cal Pat R*, 1476–85, 466: TNA: PRO, SC 2/190/18; SC 2/191/50, ms 2–11, /51, ms 2–3, /52, ms 1–2, /57, m 6, /58, ms 1–4; E 303/10/307, 354; BL, Harley MS 6953, pp 10, 30; Add Ch 39405). John Langton was replaced by Richard Pest or Prehest, another short-lived abbot. In 1516 the sub-prior, John Palmer, stole the abbey keys from his deathbed, shut the other monks out of the chamber and took £200 from the abbey chest; he then absented himself from the abbey and lived 'unreligiously' (*L and P Hen VIII*, ii(1), no. 1861; TNA: PRO, SC 2/191/52, m 3; E 303/10/297; C 1/426/49).

Henry Moore was the last abbot, being in office at the suppression. His brother John Moore was buried in the abbey church in 1529, and there was also a monk called Thomas Moore in the abbey at this time, mentioned as a rent-collector in 1523 and again in 1538, who may have been another relative. Abbot Henry received a pension of 100 marks (£67 6s 8d) per annum and a further gift of 50 marks. He continued to be paid the pension for the remainder of Henry VIII's reign, but later exchanged the pension for a rent of £45 a year received from Coggeshall, until such time as he could be found a non-resident clerical sinecure of the same value. Unlike the abbot of the London Charterhouse (Barber and Thomas 2002, 2–3), there is no evidence to suggest that Henry Moore resisted the fate of his monastery. The grant of leases noted previously (above, 3.5) suggests that he made the best of it (*L and P Hen VIII*, xiv(2), no. 236; xi, no. 392; xiv(1), no. 688; xvi, no. 745; xvii, no. 258; xviii(1), no. 436; xviii(2), no. 231; xix(1), no. 368; xx(1), no. 557; xxi(1), no. 643; xxi(2), no. 775; TNA: PRO, SC 2/191/59, mm 1–4; E 303/10/354; C 1/426/49; SC 12/11/43; PROB 11/23/10; BL, Harley MS 6955, p 74; GL, MS 9531/9, fo 64).

The monks and officers

The abbey started with less than the full complement of monks. By April 1358 the abbot had five monks in the 'chapel', possibly that of Holy Trinity (B1; Chapter 2.3). In this month Edward III granted the annuity of 40 marks (£27 13s 4d) to provide for an additional monk (*Cal Pat R*, 1358–61, 34). In February 1365 the bequest of Walter Stodele (Table 12) secured another and in January 1376 the land left by Nicholas de Loveyne funded two more (although his will had specified three) (TNA: PRO, E 326/5595; *Cal Pat R*, 1374–7, 213–14; LPL, Reg Sudbury, fo 87v). The founding of a chantry in July 1375 was on condition that there should be five monks professed as priests in the abbey (GL, MS 25121/953; TNA: PRO, E 326/5599). There were seven monks in 1379, six in 1381 and 11 in 1391, when 11 pairs of shoes and 12 pairs of stockings were bought for the abbot and convent (McHardy 1977, nos 13, 195; TNA: PRO, SC 6/1258/1). In 1398 and 1400 the abbey petitioned for the grants of the Kent and Audley manors to increase their numbers, according to the provision of Edward III's will. Another petition in 1417 threatened that they would have to reduce their number by half if they lost the Audley manors again (TNA: PRO, C 81/666/881; SC 8/E.711A and B). In 1513 there were seven monks and at the Dissolution nine, including the sub-prior (*L and P Hen VIII*, xiv(1), no. 688). It seems improbable that the abbey ever achieved the numbers of a single convent, let alone the double convent intended by Edward III. The names of a substantial proportion of these monks are known (Table 8).

From the reign of Richard II onwards the house also had a prior. The names of only two priors are known: William of Wendover became abbot of Meaux in 1399, while Ranulph was prior in 1400 and 1417 before becoming abbot of St Mary Graces, probably in the latter year (*Cal Pat R*, 1399–1401, 397; *Cat Anc Deeds*, i, 212; *VCH* 1909, i, 463; TNA: PRO, C 1/9/358; E 303/10/354; BL, Royal MS 17.B.xlvii). There were also sub-priors, apparently two in 1379: John de Forda and Roger Ykham, the latter probably becoming abbot in 1412 (McHardy

Table 8 Monks of St Mary Graces

Monk	Office/comment	Dates	References
John Benet	sub-deacon	1365	LPL, Reg Sudbury 35, 36
Thomas Benet	acolyte	1365	LPL, Reg Sudbury 35, 36
Thomas atte Hale	acolyte	1365	LPL, Reg Sudbury 35, 36
Jordan de Biggleswade	deacon and priest, farmer of St Giles, papal chaplain; became intrusive abbot of Dore, 1396	1364–92	*Reg Sudbury*, 23, 28; McHardy 1977, nos 13, 195; *Cal Close R*, 1392-6, 528; *Cal Pat R*, 1396-9, 30; *Cal Pap Letters*, iv, 275; TNA: PRO, SC 6/1258/1
Semanus de London or Passtheneye	sub-deacon, deacon, priest	1365–81	*Reg Sudbury*, 36, 46, 58; McHardy 1977, nos 13, 195
John de Forda	sub-prior	1379–81	McHardy 1977, nos 13, 195
Thomas de Ledys		1379–81	McHardy 1977, nos 13, 195
Nicholas Drayton		1379	McHardy 1977, nos 13, 195
Roger Ykham or Greeneway	sub-prior, sacristan, abbot	1379–1415	McHardy 1977, no. 13
Roger Hitcham (? as above)	papal chaplain	1400	*Cal Pap Letters*, iv, 310
Thomas Dene		1379	McHardy 1977, nos 13, 195; BL, Harley Ch 111.A.35
Richard	transferred from Rufford	1379	McHardy 1977, nos 13, 195; BL, Harley Ch 111.A.35
Richard Passtheneye	? same as above	1381	McHardy 1977 nos 13, 195; BL, Harley Ch 111.A.35
? Giles		1391	TNA: PRO, SC 6/1258/1
John Sautre		1391	TNA: PRO, SC 6/1258/1
Philip Northwych		1391	TNA: PRO, SC 6/1258/1
Thomas Bewleu		1391	TNA: PRO, SC 6/1258/1
John de Byrton	papal chaplain	1395	*Cal Pap Letters*, v, 292
William of Wendover	prior, became abbot of Meaux, 1399	pre-1399	*Cal Pat R*, 1399–1401, 397
Ranulph	prior, later abbot	1400–17	*Cat Anc Deeds*, i 212; *VCH* 1909, 463; TNA: PRO, C 1/9/358; E 303/10/354; BL, Royal MS 17.B.xlvii
Ralph de Byker	transferred from Swinehead	1401	*Cal Pap Letters*, v, 346–7
Thomas Hylle		1405	*Cal Pap Letters*, vi, 13
Nicholas Sampson		1411	*Cal Pat R*, 1408–13, 320
Thomas Broun		1411	*Cal Pat R*, 1408–13, 320
John Stacey		1412	*Cal Close R*, 1409–13, 344, 400; TNA: PRO, C 1/9/358
John London		1412	*Cal Close R*, 1409–13, 344, 400; TNA: PRO, C 1/9/358
William Mone		1417	*Cal Close R*, 1409–13, 344, 400; TNA: PRO, C 1/9/358
John Pecche		1417	*Cal Close R*, 1409–13, 344, 400; TNA: PRO, C 1/9/358
Pascal Gilot	abbot in 1419	1412	*Cal Close R*, 1409–13, 344, 400; TNA: PRO, C 1/9/358
William Ponde		1425–6	TNA: PRO, SC 6/917/16
John Grene		1491	*Cal Pap Letters*, xv, no. 727
John Palmer	sub-prior	1516	*L & P Hen VIII*, ii(1), no. 1361; TNA: PRO, SC 2/191/52, m 3; E 303/10/297
Thomas Austen	? bursar	1523–8	TNA: PRO, SC 12/11/43
Thomas Moore	rent-collector	pre-1523, 1538, 1539	*L & P Hen VIII*, xiv(1), no. 688; TNA: PRO, SC 12/11/43
William Simpson		1533	TNA: PRO, E 135/22/48
William Withyngton		1533	TNA: PRO, E 135/22/48
Roger Coventry		1533	TNA: PRO, E 135/22/48
William Dankaster		1533	TNA: PRO, E 135/22/48
Thomas Epphurth		1533	TNA: PRO, E 135/22/48
Richard Laveroke		1533, 1539	*L & P Hen VIII*, xiv(1), no. 688; TNA: PRO, E 135/22/48
Richard Lawrence		1533, 1539	*L & P Hen VIII*, xiv(1), no. 688; TNA: PRO, E 135/22/48
William Smyth	sub-prior	1539	*L & P Hen VIII*, xiv(1), no. 688
William Harper		1539	*L & P Hen VIII*, xiv(1), no. 688
William Robinson		1539	*L & P Hen VIII*, xiv(1), no. 688
Richard Davye		1539	*L & P Hen VIII*, xiv(1), no. 688
Matthew Davye		1539	*L & P Hen VIII*, xiv(1), no. 688
Charles Mapson		1539	*L & P Hen VIII*, xiv(1), no. 688

1977, no. 13). John Palmer was sub-prior in 1516 and William Smyth at the Dissolution (*L and P Hen VIII*, xiv(i), no. 688). Several of the monks were priests and/or papal chaplains (Table 8), and the layout of the church suggests that provision was made for a number of altars. Jordan de Biggleswade appears to have been a relatively long-lived and ambitious monk. He is first attested as a deacon and priest in 1364, early in William de Warden's abbacy. He made a great many journeys on abbey business, is mentioned as a papal chaplain in 1390, and became the farmer of the disputed St Giles Hospital in 1391–2. At the height of the abbey's influence during the Great Schism (below, 3.9), Jordan twice intruded himself as abbot of Dore before the general chapter meeting in his own abbey pronounced in favour of the other candidate (*Reg Sudbury*, 23, 28; McHardy 1977, nos 13, 195; *Cal Close R*, 1392–6, 528; *Cal Pat R*, 1396–9, 30; *Cal Pap Letters*, iv, 275; TNA: PRO, SC 6/1258/1).

Early in the monastery's life there was another Cistercian monk living in the vicinity at the hermitage called the Swan's Nest, near the Crash Mills. Brother John Ingram of Wroxton was a former monk of Medmenham, Buckinghamshire, whose grant of this refuge by Sir William de Pulteney was ratified by the king in 1370. In 1371 he was given protection from the jurisdiction of the bishop, and he was still at the Swan's Nest in 1375 (*Cal Pat R*, 1367–70, 463; 1370–4, 51; *Cat Anc Deeds*, ii, 94).

An unnamed novice is mentioned in 1391 and the acolytes in 1365 may also have been novices (*Reg Sudbury*, 35; TNA: PRO, SC 6/1258/1). There is no definite reference to lay brothers, formerly an essential element of a Cistercian community. In 1391 eight black pelts were bought for *seculares*; in 1422 a papal indulgence was granted to the monks and lay brothers of the abbey (*Cal Pap Letters*, vii, 319); and Sir Thomas Montgomery's will of 1489 refers to lay clerks helping to sing in the choir (TNA: PRO, PROB 11/10/22). None of these is sufficient to confirm the presence of lay brothers, nor do there seem to have been buildings in which to house them.

The abbey had a number of officers to conduct its business, and monks sometimes filled these positions (Table 9). There was a steward who administered the monastery's lands and presided over the manorial courts. The bailiff of East Smithfield carried out the orders of these courts and may have collected local rents. There was also a receiver or rent-collector for the abbey properties in London. The abbey's main financial officer was the bursar in 1391. The rent-collector's account of 1425 refers to the black paper book in the bursary, so the office must have continued. It was perhaps the position held by Brother Thomas Austen in 1523–8 when he received each year's takings from the rent-collector. In 1391 there was also a purveyor called Walter, who travelled to Stratford, Rotherhithe, Romford and *Merscham* (Merstham) to buy food, and accompanied the abbot and some of the monks on a journey to Beaulieu (TNA: PRO, SC 6/917/16; SC 6/1258/1).

The servants

The abbey had a number of servants (Table 10). In 1368 these were referred to as *familiares*. The 1391 account provides a complete list of the servants at this time, and additional servants are mentioned in 1425, 1525 and at the Dissolution. In 1391 six caps with grey fur, one beaver hat, one cloak bag, one towel of

Table 9 Officers of St Mary Graces

Name	Office	Dates	References
William Burton	steward	1479–92	TNA: PRO, SC 2/191/49, 50, 57, 58
George Treheyron	steward	1508–15	TNA: PRO, SC 2/191/52
Richard Staverton	steward	1522	TNA: PRO, SC 2/191/59
Sir Thomas Lovell	steward	d 1524	TNA: PRO, E 315/100, fo 281
Sir Edmund Walsingham	steward	1533–9	*Val Eccl*, i, 399; TNA: PRO, E 315/100, fo 281; SC 6/HenVIII/2396
John Sterne	sub-steward	1533–9	*Val Eccl*, i, 399; TNA: PRO, E 315/100, fo 231v
Henry Chamberleyn	bailiff of East Smithfield	1535	*Val Eccl*, i, 399; TNA: PRO, C 1/714/32; E 315/98, p 138
William Basker	bailiff of East Smithfield		TNA: PRO, SC 6/HenVIII/2397, m 54v
Philip Willde	bailiff of East Smithfield	1540	TNA: PRO, SC 6/HenVIII/2397, m 54v
? Walter	purveyor	1391	TNA: PRO, SC 6/1258/1
Richard Olyver	receiver or rent-collector	1391	TNA: PRO, SC 6/1258/1
William Est	receiver or rent-collector		TNA: PRO, SC 6/917/16
John Lovell	receiver or rent-collector		TNA: PRO, SC 6/917/16
William Ponde	receiver or rent-collector; monk	1425–6	TNA: PRO, SC 6/917/16
Thomas Moore	receiver or rent-collector; monk	pre-1523	TNA: PRO, SC 12/11/43
Richard Beerde	receiver or rent-collector	1523–8	TNA: PRO, SC 12/11/43
Hugh Losse	receiver or rent-collector; remained in office after the Dissolution	1539	Rosenfield 1961, 298–303; TNA: PRO, E 315/98, pp 13b, 42; E 303/10/314; LR 2/262, fo 8; SC 6/HenVIII/2383; 2384; 2396, m 42; 2397, m 40; 2398; 2427

16 yards, and cup cloths were bought for the servants, clerks and boys (*Reg Sudbury*, 83; TNA: PRO, SC 6/1258/1).

Table 10 Servants of St Mary Graces

Name	Position	References
1391		
William Holy	butler	TNA: PRO, SC 6/1258/1
Thomas Sakevyle	?	TNA: PRO, SC 6/1258/1
Walter Sondeye	?	TNA: PRO, SC 6/1258/1
Giles Frаunceys	?	TNA: PRO, SC 6/1258/1
Robert	cook	TNA: PRO, SC 6/1258/1
Richard	porter	TNA: PRO, SC 6/1258/1
Richard Taylor	launderer	TNA: PRO, SC 6/1258/1
?	pages of the kitchen	TNA: PRO, SC 6/1258/1
?	barber	TNA: PRO, SC 6/1258/1
William Ketel	keeper of the postern	TNA: PRO, SC 6/1258/1
1425		
William Holy	?	TNA: PRO, SC 6/917/16
John Yngelond	worked in hospice	TNA: PRO, SC 6/917/16
John Benet	?	TNA: PRO, SC 6/917/16
James	kitchen boy	TNA: PRO, SC 6/917/16
John de Messendon	?	TNA: PRO, SC 6/917/16
William Crull	?	TNA: PRO, SC 6/917/16
1525		
Three unnamed servants		*L & P Hen VIII*, iv(1), no. 1299
1539		
William Wryght	?	TNA: PRO, SC 6/HenVIII/2427; E 315/100, fo 342v; E 315/104, fo 130v
Griffith ap Howell	?	TNA: PRO, SC 6/HenVIII/2427; E 315/100, fo 342v; E 315/104, fo 130v

The corrodians

The abbey was also obliged to provide a corrody – an arrangement whereby, usually for life, a lay person was provided with lodging, food and clothing within the monastic precinct – for one of the king's servants, which consisted of an annuity of 40s and a robe per annum, as well as possibly accommodation. In 1391 five ells of ray-coloured cloth were bought to make furred robes for the corrodians. In the 15th century the abbey seems to have found this a burden, and drew up a petition and a draft grant linking the corrody to the Audley manors of which it had lost control, and thereby excusing itself from the obligation (TNA: PRO, E 135/22/46; E 211/380). Several of the corrodians appointed by the king are known by name (Table 11).

The patrons

The most important patron of the abbey was the founder, Edward III, and the abbey continued to enjoy royal patronage under Richard II until the end of the 14th century. The grants and bequests of property, and the problems attendant on these, have already been discussed (above, 3.4), but royal patronage also took the form of obits and chantries (Table 12). In 1398 Richard II ordered obits for Sir Simon Burley, Sir James Berners, Sir John Salisbury and Queen Anne. A chantry for Burley was already in existence, having been arranged by Baldwin de Raddington in 1394 (*Cal Pat R*, 1396–9, 348). Obits were also instituted for other members of the royal family: for Queen Isabella in 1361 and 1369, for Queen Philippa in 1369, on Christmas Day 1400 for Henry IV (arranging his own obit in advance) and his deceased wife Mary, Countess of Derby, and his father John of Gaunt, and for Cardinal Henry Beaufort in 1447 (*Cal Pat R*, 1367–70, 323–4; 1399–1401, 457; *Cal Close R*, 1360–4, 179; 1399–1402, 325–6; TNA: PRO, E 328/381; E 326/5591). The abbey also received 5 marks (£3 6s 8d) a year from 1504 for its part in the chantry of Henry VII (*Cal Chart R*,

Table 11 Corrodians and pensioners of St Mary Graces

Corrodian/pensioner	Office/position	Dates	References
John Maudelayn	Keeper of the King's Robes	1387–94	*Cal Close R*, 1385–9, 439; TNA: PRO, SC 6/1258/1
William Serle	groom of the King's Robes	1394–9	*Cal Close R*, 1392–6, 295
William Flaxman	?	1399–1412	*Cal Close R*, 1399–1402, 98
William Rodelle	?	1412–?	*Cal Close R*, 1409–13, 362–3
Ralph Bakelowe	Clerk of the Signet Office	1412–?	*Cal Close R*, 1409–13, 323–9
Walter Myddilton	mason	1412/15–?25	TNA: PRO, SC 6/917/16
William Frenygham	?	?–1444	*Cal Close R*, 1441–7, 220–1
Hugh Kyngeston	?	1444–?	*Cal Close R*, 1441–7, 220–1
William Walker	?	1461–?	*Cal Close R*, 1461–8, 99
John Bell	?	?	*L & P Hen VIII*, i, no. 5243
Ralph Jenet	valet of the Wardrobe	?–1514	*L & P Hen VIII*, i, no. 5243
John Siggewike	page of the Wardrobe of Beds	1514–39	*L & P Hen VIII*, i, no. 5243; *Val Eccl*, i, 399; TNA: PRO, SC 6/HenVIII/2396, m 52; LR 2/262, fo 8v

Table 12 Bequests, obits and chantries

Name	Type	Dates	References
Joanna Cros	bequest for building work	1352	*Cal Husting Wills*, i, 665
Queen Isabella of France	obit	1361 & 1369	*Cal Close R*, 1360–4, 179; *Cal Pat R*, 1367–70, 323–4
Walter Stodele	bequest for additional monk	1365	TNA: PRO, E 326/5595
Henry de Yerdelee	chapel of Holy Trinity in the 'new cemetery'	1368	*Cal Husting Wills*, ii, 131
Queen Philippa of Hainault	obit	1369	*Cal Pat R*, 1367–70, 323–4
John de Kennington	at the altar of All Saints	1375	TNA: PRO, E 326/5599
Arnold de Pynkeney	obit	1375	*Cal Pat R*, 1374–7, 109
Richard Rothyng	bequest to establish chantry	1375	TNA: PRO, E 210/8264
John Shirbourne	bequest on the altar	1375	*Cal Husting Wills*, ii, 182
Sir Nicholas Loveyne	bequest for three additional monks plus 20s & seven robes for the poor on the anniversary of his death	1376	*Cal Pat R*, 1374–7, 213–14; TNA: PRO, SC 6/917/16
Countess Marie de St-Pol	bequest of 100 marks	1377	Jenkinson 1915, 432–5
Robert de Denton	obit	1380	TNA: PRO, E 210/9947
Simon de Mordon	bequest	1383	*Cal Husting Wills*, ii, 243
William de Lincoln	bequest	1393	*Cal Husting Wills*, ii, 301–2
Sir Simon Burley	masses said for his soul in return for manor of Parrock, & obit	1394/8	*Cal Pat R*, 1396–9, 348
Sir James Berners	obit	1394	*Cal Pat R*, 1396–9, 348
Sir John Salisbury	obit	1394	*Cal Pat R*, 1396–9, 348
Queen Anne of Bohemia	obit	1394	*Cal Pat R*, 1396–9, 348
Countess Mary of Derby	obit	1400	*Cal Pat R*, 1399–1401, 457; *Cal Close R*, 1399–1402, 325–6; TNA: PRO, E 328/381
King Henry IV	obit	1400	*Cal Pat R*, 1399–1401, 457; *Cal Close R*, 1399–1402, 325–6; TNA: PRO, E 328/381
John of Gaunt	obit	1400	*Cal Pat R*, 1399–1401, 457; *Cal Close R*, 1399–1402, 325–6; TNA: PRO, E 328/381
Robert Somersete	bequest	1400	*Cal Husting Wills*, ii, 349
Robert FitzRobert	bequest to celebrate divine service, & rent of 10s per annum as pittance for expenditure on refectory	1422	
Matilda Aston	bequest	1436	*Cal Husting Wills*, ii, 502
Thomas Chynnore	chantry in chapel of St Anne in lieu of debt	1442	*Cal PM R*, iv, 248; TNA: PRO, PROB 11/1/15
Cardinal Henry Beaufort	obit	1447	TNA: PRO, E 326/5591
John Norman	bequest	1467	*Cal Husting Wills*, ii, 564
Sir Thomas Montgomery	chantry – six poor men to pray for him, & the mayor, sheriffs, recorder & sword-bearer of London to attend his anniversary	1494	*Val Eccl*, i, 399
King Henry VII	chantry worth 5 marks from Westminster Abbey	1504	*Cal Chart R*, 1500–9, 368(viii), 389(x); TNA: PRO, SC 6/HenVIII/2383, m 25d; 2396, m 48v; SC 12/29/22
Elizabeth Rollysley or Rowley	obit	1513	Madox 1702, 440
John Sedley	in the chapel of St Anne	1528	TNA: PRO, E 303/10/354

1500–9, 368(viii), 389(x); TNA: PRO, SC 6/HenVIII/2383, m 25d; 2396, m 48v; SC 12/29/22).

Royal patronage was vital to the foundation, construction and continued existence of the abbey, but it could be both a blessing and a curse, depending upon the king's enthusiasm for the project and his other commitments at any given time. As a result, St Mary Graces was often in dire straits financially, but fortunately it had a number of other patrons. Two important early benefactors were Sir Nicholas Loveyne (d 1375) and Countess Marie de St-Pol (d 1377). Loveyne was a prominent royal servant, ambassador to the Holy See in 1361, governor of Ponthieu in 1367, and brother-in-law to Aubrey de Vere, Earl of Oxford, as well as being the lord of East Smithfield after the death of Sir John de Pulteney, a former lord mayor of London, in 1349 (Nichols 1826, i, 98–9; *Cal Close R*, 1349–54, 296–7; *Cal Inq PM*, xiv, no. 172; Blair 1980; LPL, Reg Sudbury, fo 86). Marie de St-Pol was the widow of Aymer de Valence, Earl of Pembroke, who was one of Edward I and Edward II's principal military commanders. The reversion of the manors she held for life came to the abbey via the king, but she left the abbey 100 marks for building work in her will (Jenkinson 1915, 432–5). A third potential early benefactor, Sir Andrew Cavendish, a knight of Suffolk and a son of Sir John Cavendish, the Lord Chief Justice, was buried in the chapel of St Anne in 1394. He had served Edward III in France in 1374 (TNA: PRO, PROB 11/2/45). All these people had royal connections, and may have been displaying a degree of political acumen in their pious assistance with the finances of a troubled royal foundation. After the deposition of Richard II in 1399 the abbey appears to have lost its royal patronage, finding scant favour with Henry IV and his successors, and undergoing a series of financial and disciplinary crises in the early 15th century.

However, by the latter half of the 15th century the abbey had attracted a number of wealthy patrons who were associated with the Court, but were more noticeably prominent landowners in Essex, tied to one another by bonds of family and friendship. The earliest of these was Sir Lewis John, who died in 1442 leaving the inning of Woolwich Marsh (land which he had previously reclaimed from the river) to the abbey. A native of west Wales, he is first recorded in London in 1402 when he was appointed deputy in the port of London to the king's chief butler. He appears to have lived in the Vintry in 1412, being listed as a goldsmith and entertaining Henry, Prince of Wales (subsequently Henry V) at his house. In 1413 he married Alice, daughter of Aubrey de Vere, Earl of Oxford (Margaret de Vere, her aunt, had been married to Sir Nicholas Loveyne), and was appointed Keeper of the King's Exchange in London and Calais, and Keeper of the King's Mint in the Tower and Calais. In July 1414, John was sufficiently wealthy and well-connected to own 300 acres in West Horndon, Essex. This he enclosed and built a lodge on with a licence to crenellate. In 1416 he was sheriff of Hertfordshire and Essex, and he became sheriff of Essex again in 1420, and a commissioner of array for that county in 1419 and 1421. Alice was dead by 1433, and he remarried, this time to Anne, daughter of John Montague, Earl of Salisbury. He became a member of the king's council and was also in the service of Cardinal Beaufort. He was appointed commissioner of the peace in Essex in 1435, 1437, 1440 and 1441. He sat as a Member of Parliament for that county on a number of occasions, the last being in 1439. Sir Lewis John had connections with another prominent Essex family, the Montgomerys, who were also patrons of the abbey. In 1430 he was bonded for 1000 marks (£667 6s 8d) with Sir John Montgomery to retrieve Sir Thomas Montgomery from France where he was a hostage. Previously, in 1421, he had given Sir John Montgomery and others power of attorney over his estates during his absence (Carr 1967).

Sir Thomas Montgomery, an associate of Sir Lewis John's, and possibly a friend or protégé, was a major patron of the abbey, having paid for the construction of the Lady chapel at some point before 1489. As noted above, he was ransomed from France in 1430 by Lewis John and by his own brother, John Montgomery. He followed Lewis John as a Warden of the Mint in 1449, was knighted in 1461 by Edward IV at the Battle of Towton, and shortly thereafter became sheriff of Norfolk and Suffolk. He was a Knight of the Body in 1469 and king's councillor in 1483, and fought for Richard III at Bosworth in 1485. His principal manor was at Falkbourne in Essex, where his first wife Dame Philippa was buried until her body was translated to St Mary Graces. He was also steward of the Duke of Buckingham's lands in Essex. He was buried in the Lady chapel in 1495, along with his first wife, his second wife Dame Lore in 1501, other members of his family, and other Essex notables like William Belknap, lord of Knoll. Belknap, like Montgomery, was a nephew of Ralph Butler, Lord Sudeley. Sir John Montgomery was buried in the chapel of St Anne before 1489. All of these may have been patrons of the abbey (BL, Add MS 29608, m 3; *Cal Inq PM*, Henry VII (i), no. 1040; Griffiths 1981, 298, 339, 363, 369; Ross 1981, 57 n39, 111, 156; *Rot Parl*, v, 193; *Cal Pat R*, 1446–52, 84, 305; BL, Harley MS 433, fo 248v; Rawcliffe 1978; TNA: PRO, PROB 11/10/22).

The Montgomerys, and to a lesser extent the family of Sir Lewis John, were connected to the Stafford dukes of Buckingham, and a number of minor members of the Stafford family were also buried in St Mary Graces: Dame Joan Stafford, daughter of Duke Humphrey; Dame Elizabeth Ratcliffe, daughter of Duke Edward, who was executed for treason in 1521; and her son George (Wagner 1956, 143–4; Rawcliffe 1978). Thus the abbey may have enjoyed the patronage of the much more powerful Staffords in the late 15th and early 16th centuries, and it may have been the influence of the Staffords, and perhaps the de Vere earls of Oxford which recommended patronage of the abbey to these lesser, but prominent, Essex families.

The abbey also enjoyed a certain amount of patronage from wealthy merchants and other citizens of London (Table 12). It remembered the deaths of Joanna Cros, widow of the Henry who had sold the property on which the chapel of Holy Trinity was built; of Walter Stodele in 1365 and of Henry de Yerdelee, fellmonger, in 1368 (he was buried in the chapel of Holy Trinity); of Richard Rothyng, a fishmonger who left a bequest to establish a chantry, John de Kennington, clerk (at the altar of All Saints), John Shirbourne and Arnold de Pynkeney, all of whom died in 1375; Robert de Denton, chaplain, in 1380; of Simon de Mordon, stockfishmonger, in 1383; of William de Lincoln, saddler, in 1393; of Robert Somersete, draper, in 1400; and of Matilda Aston in 1436 (Clapham 1915, 256; *Cal Pat R*, 1374–7, 109; *Cal Husting Wills*, i, 665; ii, 131, 182, 243, 349, 301–2, 502, 564; TNA: PRO, SC 6/917/16; E 210/8264; E 210/9947; E 326/5595; E 326/5599). Both Stodele and Denton were also admitted to the spiritual benefits of the Fraternity of St Benedict. In 1422 Robert FitzRobert, a grocer, left a bequest to celebrate divine service and 10s to be used on the refectory, while Thomas Chynnore, a fishmonger, who had a house in St Katherine's precinct, established a chantry in the chapel of St Anne in lieu of a debt in 1442 (TNA: PRO, PROB 11/1/15; *Cal PM R*, iv, 248). In the 16th century Elizabeth Rowley or Rollysley left a pittance for each monk to pray for her soul in 1513 and was later buried in the church (below, 3.7; Madox 1702, 440). In 1528 John Sedley of Kent, an abbey tenant and auditor of the King's Exchequer, set up a chantry in the chapel of St Anne (TNA: PRO, E 303/10/354). Another London grocer, John Walden, was buried in the church in 1464. He had been a sheriff of London in 1453, an alderman in 1454, and master of the Grocers' Company in 1455–6. His wife Elizabeth, buried beside him, was the daughter of Richard Rich, also a sheriff of London (TNA: PRO, PROB 11/1/15; *Cal PM R*, iv, 248; Thrupp 1962).

3.7 The church and cemetery burial populations

It is probable that the majority of those interred in the western cemetery, the area possibly reserved for later epidemic burials before *c* 1400 (OA2), were from the lower strata of society, while those in the eastern cemetery (OA9, closer to the church) were potentially and those in the church certainly from the higher. This is difficult to prove from the excavated skeletal assemblages, of which a total of 378 skeletons were available for analysis (from 443 graves excavated), comprising 199 skeletons from the western, possible later epidemic cemetery (from 221 graves excavated; OA2, period B2) dated to 1350–*c* 1400, 78 from the eastern cemetery (from 91 graves excavated; OA9, period B3) dated to *c* 1400–1539, and 101 from the abbey church and cloister (from 131 graves excavated, including three empty graves; periods B2–B3), dated to 1361–1539 (the subsamples are detailed further in Chapter 5.10, 'Introduction'). Mean height of a cemetery population is frequently taken as an indicator of nutrition or the lack of it, and thus to some extent social status. The mean height of those buried in the western cemetery (OA2) was 1.70m for males and 1.64m for females, for those buried in the eastern cemetery (OA9) it was 1.73m for the males, with no statistics available for females, and for those in the church it was 1.70m and 1.63m respectively. The average stature for males in the church was actually lower than that for the later ?epidemic burials (OA2) and the eastern cemetery (OA9), and below the mean average for Britain in the period *c* 1050–*c* 1550 (1.71m: Roberts and Cox 2003, 248), but the samples from the church and the eastern cemetery were small, and much smaller than that from the western cemetery. At St Mary Spital the average stature within the church was 1.73m for males and 1.59m for females, but in an external cemetery area the averages were 1.69m and 1.54m (Conheeney 1997, 223). At the nearby Cistercian house of St Mary Stratford Langthorne the mean height from pooled data for all areas was found to be 1.73m, and of those buried specifically in the north transept slightly higher at 1.75m (White 2004, 173). The figures from St Mary Graces do not provide evidence for a generally poorer diet nor, therefore, lower social status for those buried in either the later ?epidemic burial ground or the eastern cemetery when compared to the church.

Nevertheless, the names of a number of those buried in the presbytery and chapels of the monastic church are known; these include several knights, their relatives, and minor sons and daughters of the nobility. While there is little documentary evidence for those buried in the nave, given the relative cost of burial there it is unlikely that the very poor were often interred there. Equally it is highly probable, given the ratios of males to females buried in each, that the burial selection criteria for the eastern cemetery (OA9) were different from those for the western cemetery (OA2), and those buried in the eastern cemetery were perhaps not dissimilar in status to those buried in the church (Figs 67–9). In general the ratio of males to females from the external burial area (including both OA2 and OA9) was 1.8:1 (Chapter 5.10). A substantial portion of the external cemetery area was excavated, albeit not the total number buried there, but no further clear evidence for zoning was detected in either burial area beyond the possible concentration of children (<12 years) to the south in the western cemetery (OA2). Nevertheless, if the external burials are broken down by area it becomes clear that the higher ratio of males to females exists closer to the church (OA9), and not to the west (OA2), the reused Black Death cemetery area (Fig 28). In the western cemetery (OA2), 60 burials were identified as male (46% of the total) and 39 as female (19.6%), giving a ratio of 1.54:1, but in the eastern cemetery (OA9) 36 burials were male (46%) while only 13 were female (17%), giving a ratio of 2.8:1. An assemblage from a predominantly lay cemetery should have an even ratio, like those from the underlying Black Death cemetery (1.77:1), St Nicholas Shambles, London (1.27:1), St Helen-on-the-Walls, York (0.86:1), and the pre-monastic cemetery at St Andrew, Fishergate, York (1.4:1) (Grainger et al 2008, 26, 55; White 1988, 29–30; Dawes and Magilton 1980, 11, 65; Stroud and Kemp 1993, 252). The ratio found in the eastern cemetery (OA9) is more in keeping with a monastic site, but nothing of the order recorded at other London monastic sites. At Cistercian Stratford Langthorne the overall male to female ratio was 19.1:1, at St Mary Merton 11.2:1 and at St Saviour Bermondsey 17.1:1 (White 2004, 160; Conheeney 2007, 267; Dyson et al 2011, 130–1). Beyond London similar ratios have been recorded at monastic sites, for example at Guildford Blackfriars (6.3:1), the Dominican friary in Oxford (8.5:1), the Oxford Greyfriars (16.1:1) and the Gilbertine priory (formerly St Andrew's), Fishergate, York (15.7:1) (Hicks and Hicks 2001, 341, table 57; Stroud and Kemp 1993, 254, table 55). Nevertheless, more equal ratios at monastic sites, similar to those recorded in lay cemeteries and for the western cemetery (OA2), are found at Chelmsford Blackfriars (1.5:1), Hartlepool Greyfriars (1.2:1), Hartlepool Franciscans (1.1:1) and Guisborough Priory (1.1:1) (Hicks and Hicks 2001, 341, table 57).

Only two named burials are possibly recorded for the external cemetery area as a whole; they are both of men, John Galeys in 1358 and John Shirbourne (who may, however, have been buried in the church) in 1375 (*Cal Husting Wills*, ii, 160, 182). Monks of St Mary Graces may have been buried close to the church (OA9) though there is no means of detecting their presence from the available evidence. There was probably also a right of burial in this eastern area for the abbey servants and officers. St Mary Graces appears to have been a predominantly male establishment, and those servants known to have worked in the abbey do not include a single female (Table 10), though at least two women are known to have been resident within the precinct: the wife of William Ketel the gatekeeper in 1391, and Katherine Somers in 1405 (TNA: PRO, SC 6/1258/1, m 1; *Cal Close R*, 1422–7, 211; TNA: PRO, SC 6/917/16).

The status of the cemetery as a whole may be another factor. The parochial rights belonged to Holy Trinity Aldgate, as proprietor of St Botolph Aldgate, and these were retained outside the precinct. Those resident in the parish would not normally be buried at St Mary Graces without a special dispensation, and the same would apply to adjacent parishes. A higher proportion of transient dead (ie those not belonging to a local parish) could have been buried in the cemetery, particularly if found on abbey property, but these were as likely to be male as female under normal circumstances. Immigrants to London were also as likely to be male as female, as noted in the hospital cemetery of St Mary Spital, and such immigration should produce significantly greater numbers of young adult deaths than appears to be the case here (Thomas et al 1997, 112; Conheeney 1997, 230). Though the cemetery population may have included 'strangers', the abbey was not a hospital, and therefore neither likely nor obliged to bury large numbers of such people. One source of more male transients may have been the extensive properties on St Mary Graces' riverside at Wapping (above, 3.5), which was an integral part of the medieval port of London, but again the most likely burial place for these (at least before *c* 1400) was to the west (OA2) – if the eastern cemetery (OA9) was reserved for monks, servants and other individuals connected to the abbey. Another possible parallel with the London Charterhouse should also be noted in this context. The Pardon churchyard, the northern part of the West Smithfield Black Death cemetery, was purchased for the Carthusians in 1370 and added to their precinct. This, like the western cemetery (OA2) at St Mary Graces, was the furthest part of the original cemetery from the new church, and was used until the 17th century for 'burying of such as desperately ended their lives or were executed for felonies' (Barber and Thomas 2002, 12–13; Stow 1603, i, 82). Although there is nothing to confirm the hypothesis that these same unfortunate classes of people were also buried in the western cemetery (OA2), the parallel does support the use of a burial area within the precinct for individuals with little or no connection to the abbey either as personnel or patrons.

The age profiles of the two skeletal assemblages from the western and eastern cemetery areas did produce dissimilar results with regard to the number of infants and juveniles buried in each area. To the west (OA2), 40 children (<12 years old), or 20% of the total, were identified (although there was a marked absence of those in the youngest category); to the east (OA9) nine were found, or 11.5% of the total. If all subadults (<18 years old) are included the figure rises to 36.2% for the western cemetery (OA2) and 18% for the eastern cemetery (OA9). The 11.5% closer to the church (OA9) is significantly lower than that observed to the west (OA2). These figures could easily be the result of chance and archaeological survival but the western cemetery (OA2) *may* have continued to be used largely or solely for the burials of victims of later 14th-century epidemics, particularly those outbreaks of the plague which occurred every decade or so after 1350. These subsequent outbreaks, like the *Pesta Secunda* of 1361, were noted in the documentary sources for the number of children they killed (Orme 2003, 107) and the figures provide some evidence to suggest that more children (ie those unlikely to have built up a resistance to subsequent outbreaks of the plague) were buried in the western cemetery (OA2). However, the age distribution at death here also shows an increase from 18 years onwards, only declining in the ≥46 years group, the groups that should show some resistance to fresh outbreaks of the disease, while even in an ordinary medieval lay cemetery at St Andrew's, Fishergate, York, subadults made up 36% of the total sample (Stroud and Kemp 1993). It is possible that the lack of infants (<1 year old) is a reflection of a living population (Waldron 1994, 16), as generally observed in a catastrophe cemetery (Chamberlain 2006, 79). During a catastrophic event such as the plague in 1597–8 in Penrith, Cumberland (Scott and Duncan 1998), and in London in 1603 (Hollingsworth and Hollingsworth 1971) the pattern, however, clearly showed a high level of infant deaths and a gradual decrease in mortality with age. It is possible that what is seen in the later ?epidemic burials at St Mary Graces is a reflection of prior events, since a high level of infant deaths during the years 1348–9 would have decreased the number of births and child mortality during the years immediately after the catastrophic event. It is, of course, also possible that if this area was still being used as an emergency burial ground, it was not – as has also been observed for the underlying Black Death cemetery (Grainger et al 2008, 9–12) – used until the existing parish cemeteries and churches could no longer cope. In this event it is perhaps conceivable that younger victims of the epidemic, being the ones more likely to succumb early to the disease, would be buried in those parochial burial grounds. Nevertheless, even if the figures from both external burial areas are valid and not the result of uneven or partial survival of the evidence, they may only prove that it was comparatively more difficult for younger people to be buried closer to the church in Open Area 9.

It is possible that there were external burial areas in many monasteries where the selection criteria for burial – if any – mimicked that of a parish cemetery, and other areas where they did not. This may have happened at St Mary Graces, with two formal and distinct areas of burial. However, such a division may only exist in the interpretation of the excavated remains and may never have done so in the minds of the monks. They may have regarded their cemetery as all one, with burial as close as possible to the cemetery cross a more expensive but 'informal' option. And here, where only the ratio of male to female burials suggests such a division, even close to the church (OA9) and within the church (see below), St Mary Graces appears a lot less exclusive in this respect than many other houses. This may be due to the abbey's late foundation date and urban location. St Mary Graces was founded after 1350, and the other houses in the 11th, 12th and 13th centuries. Though there were variations between orders, in general the rules governing the burial of patrons, women and children were gradually relaxed or more frequently ignored as the centuries progressed. The composition of the cemeteries of St Mary Stratford Langthorne and St Mary Merton, which can to a greater or lesser extent be phased by cemetery area and were altogether more rural, may reflect this (Barber et al 2004, 107–14; Miller and Saxby 2007, 146–8).

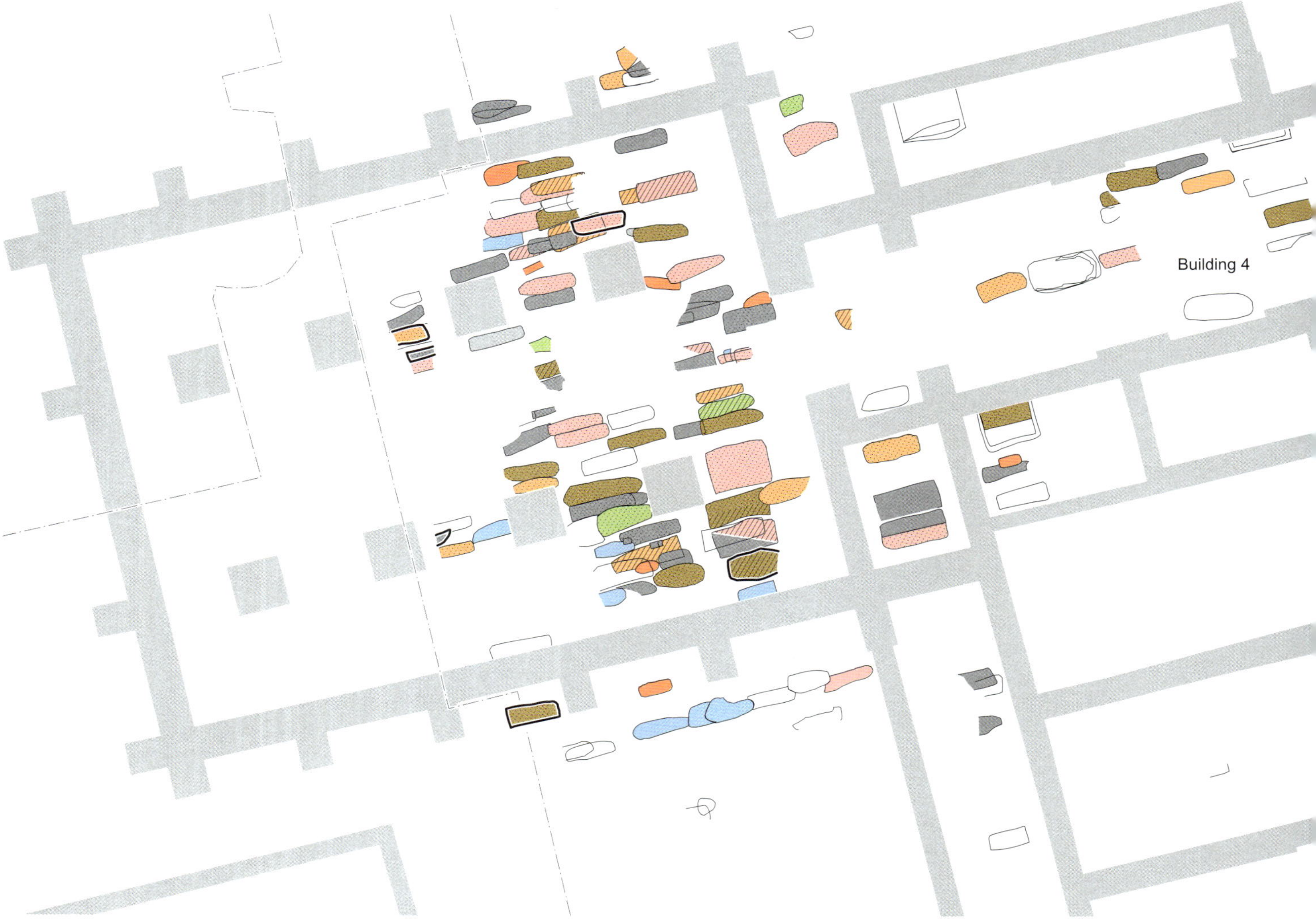

Fig 67 Age and sex distribution in the church and cloister, 1361–1539 (periods B2 and B3), with cases of DISH also shown; burials immediately to the north and east of the church are also included (see Chapter 5.10, 'Introduction') (scale 1:250)

In the church the male to female ratio was 2.6:1, which is not dissimilar to that found in the eastern cemetery (OA9), although of the 39 male burials found within the church and cloister eight were only probably male, and of the 15 females six were only probably female. Of these, one identified male was buried within the timber pentice (B18). However, in either case the sample is a small one and must be treated with caution. A total of 131 burials were excavated in the church and cloister, including empty graves, but only 101 survived to be recorded on to the database: 48 from the nave to the west of the rood screen (Chapter 2.4), 45 to the east in the chapels, porch and presbytery, and eight in the cloister. In the nave the graves excavated are likely to represent 50–60% of the original total – if, as suspected, St Mary Graces had a five-bay nave – or more if burial close to the rood screen was more popular. In the choir, presbytery and chapels, the total excavated is likely to be much closer to the number originally buried, perhaps 70–80%. Of the 48 recorded burials in the nave, 20 (41%) were male or possibly male and six (12.5%) were female or possibly female, a ratio of 3.3:1. Those aged <18 years accounted for 16.5% of the burials (eight) while the adults, including unsexed adults, accounted for 83% of the total buried. Of the adults, seven males (11%) but only one female were aged ≥46 years. In the presbytery, porch and chapels, of the 45 burials recorded on the database, 17 (38%) were male or possibly male and ten (22%) female or possibly female, a ratio of 1.7:1. There were five children aged <18 years, 11% of the total of 45 burials, as against 40 adults (including unsexed adults) (89%). Of the adults buried, six of the males were aged ≥46 years (13%) whereas only two of the females fell into this age group (4.5%). Of the eight recorded individuals buried in the cloister, four were subadults (<18 years old) and one an adult male, while the remaining individuals were indeterminate adults.

The data described above suggest, after making due allowance for the vagaries of evidence survival and interpretation, that burial in all parts of the church was largely a male prerogative, but by no means exclusively so. The documentary evidence (the 'Visitations of Clarenceux'; below, 3.8) indicates that the burial of women to the east of the rood screen was rather more frequent than the archaeological evidence suggests.

The burial of women in a Cistercian, or indeed any, monastic church was not unusual by the 14th century, and had already occurred in the 12th and 13th centuries despite the Order's ambivalent attitude to women (Williams 1991, 113–15). These women were probably wealthy patronesses of the abbey or the relatives of patrons, and their right to burial in the church virtually automatic (above, 3.6; Table 13). It was rarer for subadults (<18 years old) to be buried anywhere in the church and cloister. They made up only 15.8% of the assemblage, less than that found in the eastern cemetery (OA9). Their occasional burial in the church probably occurred at the request of patrons or members of the monastic community. As with the western cemetery (OA2), it is possible that one area, the north alley of the church cloister (B18), was set aside for the burial of younger people, but, with only ten burials found, the sample is a small one. Of the identified burials, four were aged <18 years (one 7–11 months, one 6–11 years, and two 12–17 years), and only two positively identified as adult, one a male aged ≥46 years.

The pathology of those buried externally and within the church presents a mixed picture when the different areas are compared. Cribra orbitalia, which may be an indication of iron deficiency anaemia and a deficiency in diet, occurred in 64 skeletons (32.2%) from the western cemetery (OA2) and fewer (7.1%) from the eastern cemetery (CA9), compared to 42 (41.6%) in the church. Four cases of tuberculosis were noted among those buried outside, two from each area, but none from the church. Dental disease was fairly common in both the western and eastern cemeteries and in the church, where caries prevalence was higher than average for the late medieval period. Diffuse idiopathic skeletal hyperostosis (DISH), a condition associated with obesity and increasing age, and possibly with the monastic life specifically (Rogers and Waldron 2001), was found in seven cases (6.9%) in the church, but none were identified in the cemetery as a whole. The prevalence of DISH in a monastic church is consistent with the findings from other London monasteries, with figures of 20% at St Mary Spital (Conheeney 1997, 228), 8.7% at St Mary Stratford Langthorne (White 2004, 176), 8.6% at Merton Priory (Miller and Saxby 2007, 149) and 7.8% at St Saviour Bermondsey (Dyson et al 2011, 131). In all these cases the disease predominantly affected males aged ≥46 years.

3.8 Burials and burial practices

The study of burial practices at St Mary Graces is based upon the examination of the 312 graves found in the external cemetery areas (OA2 and OA9), and the 131 graves (of which three were empty) found in the church and cloister. For the purposes of this discussion identified graves containing no skeleton are included. All of the graves can be assigned to the period 1350–1539. A number of graves within the church may be tentatively assigned to the late 14th century, and it is probable that the western cemetery (OA2) went out of use as a burial ground at the turn of the 15th century. In certain individual cases of burial within the church it is possible to suggest an identity for the skeleton and thus a date for the burial.

General patterns

All or part of the southern portion of the western cemetery (OA2) had ceased to be used for burial by 1405, but it is impossible to know the extent of this area. A tenement existed to the north of the 'great court' and the church door, probably Building 22 (Chapter 2.5), by that date when it belonged to William and Katherine Somers. It included a garden that took in part of the cemetery (*Cal Close R*, 1422–7, 211; TNA: PRO, SC 6/917/16). This garden would have occupied at least part of the western cemetery and possibly all of it. The western cemetery may never have been regarded as part of the cemetery proper, but used or seen as an area primarily for the burial of individuals who died during the later 14th-century epidemics. It may not have been used for burial for several years before the tenement and garden were established, since the later outbreaks killed significantly fewer people. It is equally possible that the

Fig 68 Age and sex distribution in the western (later ?epidemic) cemetery, 1350–c 1400 (OA2, period B2) for burials planned in detail (scale 1:250)

Cistercians may simply have decided that what remained of the cemetery was sufficient for their needs, and that the renting out of the tenement and garden was likely to be more lucrative. However, there is no proof either that the original Black Death cemetery (OA2: Grainger et al 2008, 31) continued to be used only or at all for epidemic burials, or that the tenement and garden took up a significant proportion of the area, so burial could easily have continued there until the suppression, as it did in the eastern cemetery (OA9).

The pattern of burial within the external cemetery area as a whole seems to have evolved slowly from the orderly pattern of the original Black Death burial area to a more untidy pattern in which graves were cut haphazardly wherever space was, or appeared to be, available. Such a pattern, with multiple

Fig 69 Age and sex distribution in the eastern cemetery, c 1400–1539 (OA9, period B3) for burials planned in detail (scale 1:250)

intercutting and disturbance of earlier burials, is frequently the norm within medieval churchyards. In some cases such intercutting, clustering or nucleation may represent familial or other social groupings. However, in medieval churchyards multiple burial in the same place or cyclically across the churchyard was normal; burials frequently exhumed earlier ones, even of those buried within living memory. Even in the case of double graves, where two individuals were laid in the same cut, a familial or social connection need not have existed (Harding 1989, 116). Only in the case of those graves nucleated around the possible cemetery cross (S1, OA9; Chapter 2.5), and those nestling up against the north wall of the abbey church, can a phenomenon be suggested that is not simply a product of overcrowding or economy.

Burial types

Grave cuts

St Mary Graces produced a considerable variety in the shape of grave cuts, and there was little if any evidence of standardisation within the external cemetery area. The deciding factor appears to have been the habits of the gravedigger. Within the church some regularity and order appears to have been imposed, particularly in the presbytery and chapels. As noted at St Mary Stratford Langthorne, this may have been done to minimise the disturbance of tiled floors, but is more likely to reflect the use of memorial slabs and other markers (Barber et al 2004, 105–7). The church contained six large rectangular cuts, four in the chapel of ? St Anne (room 6a) and two in the porch (B8), which, with one exception, produced no evidence for linings or monuments. Three of these graves contained two burials each, and in each case the later burial disturbed the earlier. This suggests that the graves were marked by removable slabs and intended for reuse. They may have belonged to individual families – one double grave in the chapel had a male and a female interred in it, and another a male and an unclassified adult – or, in the case of the porch (B8), perhaps represent the burial of monks. Those graves of similar size, but with only single burials in them, may also have been dug with multiple burials in mind. The exception to this was burial [13823] in the chapel of ? St Anne (Chapter 2.5), which was sealed beneath mortar with the remains of a monument above that (Fig 34). Double burials within a single grave cut also occurred in the external cemetery area, but only to the west (OA2). These were 'normal' sized cuts and may represent a continuation of the practice noted for the underlying Black Death cemetery (Grainger et al 2008, 13), involving epidemic burials rather than familial or social connections between those buried.

No graves were found with carved head-niches, nor were any demonstrably cut to resemble a coffin.

Grave alignment

The graves were aligned broadly east–west as was the common medieval practice, and the alignment of individual graves was, as frequently found elsewhere, often apparently influenced by nearby topographical features. This was most noticeable near the church (OA9) where the alignment of the grave rows swung from north-west to south-east in the west to north–south in the east, suggesting alignment on either the abbey church or the cemetery cross (S1). To the west (OA2) the grave alignment was almost certainly influenced initially by the layout of the underlying Black Death cemetery (Grainger et al 2008, 12). Nevertheless, over time that alignment was as likely to be dictated by the adjacent property boundaries, which probably also influenced the layout of the underlying cemetery. A few graves in this area deviated sufficiently from this norm to suggest that they were aligned on features no longer extant, or that other, unknown factors, perhaps no more than the whim of the gravedigger, were involved. Within the church the alignment of graves appears to be dictated by the alignment of the building and its individual walls and structures, but one grave, of a juvenile in the retrochoir (room 6b), departed sufficiently from this pattern to suggest other, unknown factors governing its alignment.

Shrouds and clothing

Only in one case, burial [13530] within the 'chapel without the quire on the south side' (B16; Chapter 2.5), was textile evidence for the use of a shroud found. Such isolated survival, as at St Mary Spital (Thomas et al 1997, 121), was entirely a matter of chance and does not preclude the more general use of shrouds both within the church and in the external cemetery area. No shroud pins were positively identified, and the skeletons' positions were not studied for 'tightness of posture' as an indicator, as suggested at St Mary Stratford Langthorne (Barber et al 2004, 99). One piece of corroborating evidence for the use of shrouds comes from the late 15th-century tomb slab with indents for shroud brasses found in the vicinity of the church (Fig 48). The use of copper-alloy penannular buckles or brooches as evidence for burial in a shroud or clothing has been discussed at length in the preceding companion volume (Grainger et al 2008, 21–2), and the balance of evidence suggests that the brooches or buckles indicate burial in clothing. No other evidence was found to suggest that burial in a shroud or clothing occurred but, given the rarity of such survival in the archaeological record, there is no reason to suppose that the majority of dead were buried naked.

Coffins

No examples of lead or stone coffins were found in the church or external cemetery area. This is perhaps atypical for a monastic church, where at least one or two examples of either or both are usually found, as at Stratford Langthorne (Barber et al 2004, 100). This absence may simply be a matter of chance non-survival, particularly in the case of lead coffins, which may have been stripped out after the suppression; at least one, and possibly two, prominent tombs appear to have been robbed at that time.

The use of wooden coffins was not uncommon in both the external cemetery area and the church, but does not appear to have been standard. In many cases traces of timber survived to indicate the presence of a coffin, and in others the pattern of nails within the grave was taken to indicate a coffin, although this only represents the position where the nails had fallen as the coffin timber decayed, and not the shape or structure of the coffin itself.

In the western cemetery (OA2), 102 potential wooden coffins were identified, representing 64% of interments, and in the eastern cemetery (OA9) only 28 coffins (37%) were potentially identified. In the church (not including the cloister), 50 potential wooden coffins (43.5%) were identified. This shows a rough parity between the number of such interments in the east (OA9) and in the church, but not with the west (OA2). On this evidence, there appears to be no link between the use of a coffin per se and higher status. However, there is no way, from the archaeological evidence, of judging the quality of the coffins used in each area, and the vagaries of archaeological survival and interpretation must always be borne in mind. The use of coffins was not as rare as at St Mary Stratford Langthorne, where only 1.5% of interments in the north-eastern cemetery were positively identified as being in coffins and 27.3% in the church (Barber et al 2004, 100). Only one coffin was detected in the St Mary Graces cloister.

The church, eastern cemetery (OA9) and western, later ?epidemic cemetery (OA2) all produced examples (four, one and one respectively) of 'charcoal' burials. Several of these were found in the earlier Black Death cemetery, and they are discussed in full in the companion volume (Grainger et al 2008, 20–1) and extensively elsewhere (Daniel 1997, 158–60; Barber et al 2004, 103; Miller and Saxby 2007, 155). The six examples from St Mary Graces can add little to the debate, but they do confirm that the practice continued in London after 1350 and possibly into the 15th and 16th centuries. They also suggest that the use of charcoal had little to do with economic status, given the practice being at least as or more likely to occur in both external burial areas as in the church, and apparently just as prevalent in the underlying Black Death cemetery (OA2). Some examples in the church and external cemetery area may represent the burials of Cistercian monks in light of the documented practice of placing dying monks on sackcloth and ashes (Daniel 1997, 30). However, at least one example in the external cemetery area was the burial of an infant or juvenile, and the examples from the Black Death cemetery and St Nicholas Shambles are unlikely to be Cistercian or solely ecclesiastical burials (White 1988, 18–19).

One burial practice was confined to the church, namely the use of crushed chalk or lime to line the coffin. Two burials of this type were found, in both cases a supine extended adult male in a timber coffin lined with the mixture. Crushed chalk or lime may have been used in the coffin for reasons similar to those behind the charcoal/ash-lined burials. As both of these individuals must have been of reasonably high status, it is possible that their coffins were on display in the church for some time before burial. However, burial [13530] argues against this, as the corpse appears to have been crammed into a chalk- or lime-lined coffin too small for it, making any open-coffin display a potentially grotesque spectacle (Fig 38). It is conceivable that the chalk or lime had a practical purpose in counteracting the side-effects of putrefaction, by soaking up the liquids produced, in an attempt to preserve the corpse. The coffins may have been brought a considerable distance from the place of death to the church, or these burials may represent the re-interment of individuals buried elsewhere who for some reason were transferred to this church. There is one record of this happening at St Mary Graces: the corpse of Philippa, first wife of Sir Thomas Montgomery, was translated from his manor of Falkbourne in Essex so that she could lie beside him in the Lady chapel (TNA: PRO, PROB 11/10/22). In such a case the packing may have been intended to prevent bone tumble in the coffin. However, from a purely practical standpoint there were lighter ways of packing a coffin for this purpose. As suggested for a similarly used Reigate stone deposit at Stratford Langthorne (Barber et al 2004, 104), the white colour may be significant, but if so the meaning is lost.

Tombs, vaults and cists

Despite the truncation of certain areas of the presbytery and choir, it is clear from the stratified remains and a small number of *ex situ* architectural fragments that St Mary Graces housed a number of fine tombs and/or monuments. Three, possibly four, vaults were located. These varied in detail but were essentially the same in construction, and appear from their construction and some corroborating documentary evidence to be of 15th-century date (below). The most complete, for burial [13530] (Fig 38) in 'the chapel without the quire door on the south side' (B16), appeared either to be poorly designed for the eventual occupant, whose identity may not have been foreseen at the time of construction, or designed to accommodate a number of further interments. This may imply that it was intended as a long-term family vault or to be used for the interments of whoever could afford the privilege of burial in the chapel. This latter possibility suggests a degree of financial risk in the construction of the vault and perhaps the chapel, in the sense that the vault was not paid for in advance by a patron but speculatively constructed in the hope of generating sufficient future revenues from it to make a profit. The brick vault [16011] (Fig 32) in the presbytery (B4) contained a male and female buried side-by-side in coffins, and was probably designed specially for a husband and wife.

Burial [16042] (Fig 31) occupied a central position in the presbytery and appears to have been marked by a tomb or monument above. This rested on chalk foundations and included a cavity above the grave fill, which may indicate an above-ground tomb chest. The mortar surface and tiles placed on edge above [13823] (Fig 34) also suggest the presence of a tomb chest, though of somewhat different construction. One such tomb is known to have existed at St Mary Graces, a near copy of the Black Prince's tomb at Canterbury built for Sir Nicholas Loveyne in 1377 (Fig 71; Blair 1980). A number of *ex situ* Purbeck marble slabs with rivet holes (eg Fig 86) may have come from such tombs rather than the floor.

The robbed grave [12477] (Fig 29) contained a chalk and mortar lining which appears to have been a variation on the cist graves frequently found in other medieval cemeteries. Thirty-six such cists were identified at St Mary Merton, constructed of a variety of materials (Miller and Saxby 2007, 152–4), and 22 burials in lined graves at St Saviour Bermondsey (Dyson et al 2011, 132–3), far greater numbers than found on other London sites such as St Mary Spital where only one was recorded (Thomas et al 1997, 122) and St Mary Stratford Langthorne where no cist burials were recorded among 647 burials excavated (Barber et al 2004, 101). At St Mary Merton 14 of the cists were found in the chapter house and are considered to be the burials of senior monks. However, the use of cists is not confined exclusively to male or ecclesiastical burials. A few of the Merton cists were empty, as with the St Mary Graces example; this might suggest the deliberate robbing of graves (especially if they were clearly marked) because they were believed to contain valuables, or the removal of bodies for subsequent re-burial elsewhere.

Further *ex situ* evidence for monuments comes from the fragments of decorated tomb canopies (Fig 30; Fig 83) and the numerous fragments of tomb slabs (eg Fig 48; Fig 86). Three tomb slabs were found reused as door thresholds in monastic buildings (Fig 15; Fig 19). That within the threshold of the porch (B8) may have come from a grave in the church or cemetery, though this seems unlikely; but the slabs from the kitchen thresholds (B11) were identified on site by the Monumental Brass Society as early 14th-century and pre-dating the abbey, and were clearly brought to the abbey as building material. Provision was also made in wills for grave slabs for Alice Spice (post-1489) in the Lady chapel, Walter Havard (1504, gravestone and hearse) at the choir door, and Robert Wolf (1520), and for a hearse for John Moore before the rood screen on the south side of the church (TNA: PRO, PROB 11/14/12; 11/19/31; 11/23/10; 11/10/22).

Cistercian monks' burials

The number of burials in the church alone, to say nothing of the external cemetery area, indicates that they cannot represent only the Cistercian monks of St Mary Graces. There is no documentary evidence for their burials; indeed we can only be certain that one abbot, Richard Pest or Prehest, died in office at St Mary Graces (TNA: PRO, C 1/426/49). A number of lay burials are recorded in the church (below) and cemetery, and a large number of the archaeologically recorded burials, the majority even, must represent secular individuals. Regrettably, though St Mary Graces has a number of well-defined areas of burial and what may be regarded as a reasonable sample recovered of those buried, it is not possible to identify distinct separate groups of lay or ecclesiastical burials, or (for the most part) sort them by date, as hoped for by researchers (Coppack 1990, 60). Barber has shown in his recent work on Stratford Langthorne (Barber et al 2004, 114–16) how no specifically Cistercian burial rite could be archaeologically identified there, and such has proved to be the case at St Mary Graces as well.

Neither the distribution of adult males nor of those individuals suffering from DISH can be used to pinpoint an area reserved for monks. No area within the church produced only positively identified adult male burials. Only three areas had no positively identified female burials, but of these the 'chapel without the quire door on the south side' (B16) contained only three burials (one an infant aged 1–6 months), the porch (B8) four burials (including two indeterminate adults), and the timber pentice (B18) one adolescent, one juvenile and two infant burials. There was no unequivocal evidence that any burial took place in the chapter house (B9), although two features there hinted that it did. This building was traditionally, but not always exclusively, reserved for the burial of abbots, priors and senior obedientiaries, as at Boyle (Ireland), Rievaulx and St Mary Merton (Stalley 1987, 205; Peers 1967, 8–10; Miller and Saxby 2007, 148; see also discussion in Barber et al 2004, 112–16). By the 14th and 15th centuries there was a growing trend for them to be buried in the presbytery. Far more burials were found to the east of the rood screen than are mentioned in the 'Visitations of Clarenceux' (below), which was solely concerned with secular burials, and the burial of senior Cistercian monks in the presbytery would be anticipated. Burial [16042] (Fig 31), a male aged 36–45 years, and the robbed burial [12477] (Fig 29) might be those of abbots, as might the unsexed adult burial [16104] aged ≥46 years. Possible candidates for such prominent burial locations include the early abbots, particularly William de Warden, although burial [16042] was clearly too young to be him (Table 7), and his is quite possibly burial [16104] which was immediately before the high altar.

It is possible that a number of monks were buried in the traditional location for a monks' cemetery, to the east of the church (OA10). Black Death victims were interred there before the abbey was built (OA3: Grainger et al 2008, 30, fig 21), and some potentially later indeterminate burials were found there. It is also possible that a number of monks were interred to the east of the chapel of Holy Trinity (B1) in the cloister enclosure/garth (OA4) (Chapter 2.4 and 2.5). One reference exists to a chapel in the 'monks' cemetery' in 1425–6, which may be referring to the chapel of Holy Trinity (TNA: PRO, SC 6/917/16). Only two heavily truncated burials were recovered from this area, and neither could be aged or sexed. It is tempting, therefore, to suggest that many of the monks were buried to the north of the church (OA9) along with abbey servants and less wealthy patrons.

Lay burials and the 'Visitations of Clarenceux'

Rather more can be said of the church with regard to lay burials. As with the identification of monks' burials, no area can definitely be said to have been reserved for lay folk or non-Cistercians. A large number of those buried in the nave were probably not major patrons of the abbey or of particularly high status, but are probably a reflection of the constant sale of burial places to bolster the monastic revenues. The use of the nave for the burial of lesser patrons in the 14th century is paralleled at Roche Abbey in Yorkshire (Coppack 1998, 82). The primary function of the nave and aisles, and perhaps of the timber pentice to the south of the nave, appears to have been as a burial area. There was a clear tendency towards interment in the north or south aisle rather than the central vessel. This may indicate the presence of altars against the rood screen in these aisles, and suggest that the burials were in chapels and connected by familial, household, or organisational links. A similar emphasis on burial in the aisles compared to the nave has been noted at the Chester and Oxford Blackfriars (Ward 1990). The lack of a substantial north cloister walkway, and the presence of a number of subadult burials in the pentice constructed instead, suggests that major patrons were not buried there as at Fountains in Yorkshire and possibly Hulton in Staffordshire (Gilyard-Beer 1970, 46; Wise 1985, 2).

The more important patrons of the abbey were buried in the presbytery and the various chapels east of the rood screen. St Mary Graces is fortunate in the survival of a remarkable document, the 'Visitations of Clarenceux', which lists and in part locates some of the more notable lay burials in these areas (Wagner 1956, 143–4). If no single area can be said to have been solely for the burial of laity, it is often possible with the aid of this document and occasionally other sources to suggest, with varying degrees of uncertainty, that specific burials correspond to named individuals. On 3 September 1532 and 27 March 1533, the royal herald Thomas Benolt, Clarenceux King of Arms, visited the church of St Mary Graces. The purpose of his visits was to check the tombs and monuments to ensure that none bore heraldic devices or titles to which their occupants were not entitled. The pertinent information from the document is given in Table 13.

As a means of identifying specific burials this document has its limitations. Clarenceux was only interested in those graves which bore heraldic devices, and even in the area to which he largely confined himself, to the east of the rood screen, there were clearly far more burials than he mentions. Moreover, he was concerned with the monuments rather than the burials themselves, and the location given for the former may differ from the latter. Nevertheless, it is still a document which, when taken in conjunction with other historical sources, can usefully be compared with the excavated remains. Assuming that the interpreted layout of the church is broadly correct, and that Clarenceux methodically drafted his report in the order in which he identified monuments, it is feasible to follow in his footsteps (Fig 70).

Clarenceux devotes the entire record of his first visitation to, and begins his second with, a description of the Lady chapel on the north side of the church. If Building 17 has been correctly identified as this space, little of the Lady chapel survived modern truncation (Chapter 2.5; above, 3.6). The fragmentary tomb found there ([12034], Fig 28; Fig 39) may represent the vault of Sir Thomas Montgomery, the patron of

Table 13 The location of lay burials in the church recorded in the 'Visitations of Clarenceux' of 1532 and 1533 (Wagner 1956, 143–4)

Name	Date of death	Location	Comments	Additional references
Sir Thomas Montgomery	1495	Lady chapel	Lady chapel on the N side of the church	TNA: PRO, PROB 11/10/22
Dame Lore, Countess of Ormonde	before 12.1501	Lady chapel	wife of Sir Thomas Montgomery	
William Belknap esquire, lord of Knoll	after 1480	Lady chapel	an heir of Ralph Butler, Lord Sudeley Treasurer of England	
A daughter of Sir Thomas Montgomery		Lady chapel	married to a Mortimer	
Alice Spice	after 1489	Lady chapel, by Sir Thomas Montgomery's tomb	sister & heir to Sir Thomas Montgomery, first married to Clement Spice of Blake Notely, Essex	TNA: PRO, PROB 11/14/12
Sir Nicholas Loveyne, lord of East Smithfield	1375	S side of the choir		Nichols 1826, 98–9; LPL, Reg Sudbury, fo 86
1) Margaret de Bereford, or possibly 2) Margaret de Vere (name not given by Clarenceux)	1) 1370 2) 1397	in floor by Sir Nicholas Loveyne	wife of Sir Nicholas Loveyne: 1) daughter of Sir William Poultney, also married Sir John Pekebrygg; 2) second wife, sister of Aubrey de Vere, Earl of Oxford	
Dame Elizabeth Ratcliffe	1529x1532	before the high altar in the choir	wife of Lord Robert Ratcliffe, Lord Fitzwater, Earl of Sussex, & daughter of Edward Stafford, Duke of Buckingham	
George Ratcliffe	1529x1532	beside Dame Elizabeth Ratcliffe	son of Dame Elizabeth Ratcliffe, who died without issue	
Dame Joan Stafford (Clarenceux calls her Jane)	after 1485	on the other side of Dame Elizabeth Ratcliffe, right before the high altar under a stone	daughter of Humphrey, Duke of Buckingham, & wife of Sir William Knyvet	
Sir Lewis John	1442x1444	in a tomb on the N side of the choir		TNA: PRO, PROB 11/1/14
Alice de Vere (name not given)	1433	in tomb with Sir Lewis John	wife of Sir Lewis John daughter of Aubrey de Vere, Earl of Oxford	
Eleanor		beside the tomb of Sir Lewis John	daughter-in-law of Sir Lewis John, married successively to John Whyte, Sir William Tyrell, Sir Henry FitzLewis, & Thomas Gaithe, treasurer to Edward Duke of Buckingham	
Sir Thomas Charles	before 1475	chapel outside the choir door on the S side	Lieutenant of the Tower of London	
Walter Haward	1504	at the choir door	secretary to the Lord Treasurer of England	TNA: PRO, PROB 11/14/12
Elizabeth Rowley		at the choir door	gentlewoman	
Sir John Montgomery	before 1489	chapel of St Anne, on the S side of the church in a tomb	older brother of Sir Thomas Montgomery	TNA: PRO, PROB 11/10/22
Sir Andrew Cavendish	1394	chapel of St Anne, on the S side of the church	son of Lord Chief Justice killed in 1381	TNA: PRO, PROB 11/2/45
Dame Rose Cavendish	1419	chapel of St Anne, on the S side of the church	wife of Sir Andrew Cavendish	
John Walden esquire	1464	on the N side	grocer, mayor of London, alderman, master of Grocers Company	
Elizabeth Walden	before 1464	on the N side	wife of John Walden	

the chapel who died in 1495, Lady Philippa his first wife (not mentioned by Clarenceux), whose body was translated there from Falkbourne, Essex, in 1494 (Nichols 1826, 396), and Lore or Laura, Countess of Ormond, who died before December 1501 (Cokayne 1910–59, ix, 338; x, 132–3). The tomb could also have been for William Belknap, lord of Knoll in Essex, who died after 1480, or for Alice Spice, sister of Sir Thomas, although she had a grave slab above her burial (TNA: PRO, PROB 11/14/12), or that of an unnamed daughter of Sir Thomas.

On leaving the Lady chapel to investigate the area around the high altar, Clarenceux appears to have either missed or ignored one important burial, that of Sir Simon Burley (Table 14). Burley was a rich, respected and influential favourite of Richard II, who was beheaded for treason on Tower Hill by the Merciless Parliament on 5 May 1388, and his corpse taken for burial to St Mary Graces (Lewis 1937, 668–9). Burial [16052] (period B2, Chapter 2.4) was a decapitated adult, interred against the north wall of the presbytery, close to the high altar. While it is possible that this was not Burley, no other burial of an execution victim is known at St Mary Graces. In 1392 John of Gaunt contributed £10 towards the cost of his tomb (TNA: PRO, DL 28/3/2), and his nephew Baldwin de Raddington established a chantry at St Mary's for his soul in 1394 (*Cal Pat R*, 1396–9, 348), so a prominent monument might be expected. It

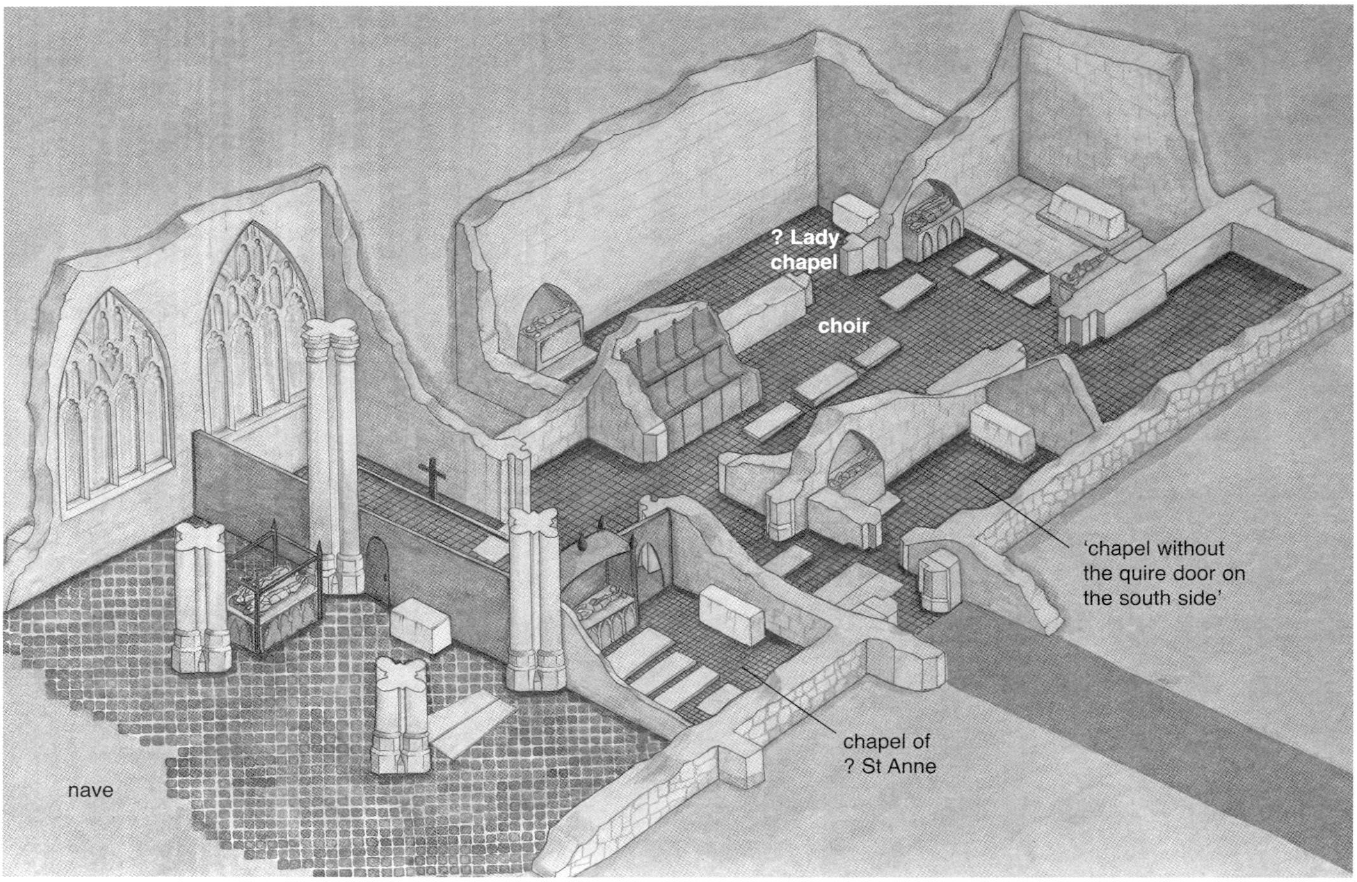

Fig 70 Reconstruction of the possible interior layout of the church in the 1530s, based on the 'Visitations of Clarenceux' of 1532 and 1533 (Wagner 1956, 143–4) (no scale)

is possible that a tomb was constructed but stood in the way of the entrance to the Lady chapel, which was constructed some time before 1489 (Nichols 1826, 396), and was removed to make way for it. Clarenceux may simply have walked over Burley without realising he was there.

The identification of the tomb and burial place of Sir Simon Burley at St Mary Graces conflicts with the alternative view that his tomb was in St Paul's Cathedral. In Dugdale's history of St Paul's of 1658, he and his engraver Wenceslaus Hollar identified a tomb on the north wall of the choir of the medieval cathedral as that of Simon Burley (Dugdale 1658, 104). This identification was first disproven by Belz in the mid 19th century and latterly by Lewis in 1937. The tomb in St Paul's is in fact that of Sir Richard Burley, his nephew, also a Knight of the Garter, who died one year before Simon, in 1387 (Belz 1841, 257–9; Lewis 1937, 668–9). (This will be dealt with in more detail in the forthcoming publication of the archaeology of the medieval St Paul's Cathedral (Schofield in prep)).

Clarenceux next mentions the tomb of Sir Nicholas Loveyne, lord of East Smithfield, who died in 1375 and was buried on the south side of the choir (Nichols 1826, 98–9). Immediately after this Clarenceux deals with a number of burials around the high altar, implying that Loveyne's tomb was in a prominent position close to these. A contract for the construction of the tomb by the marbler Henry Lakenham exists, giving detailed instructions about the work required, and from this John Blair has reconstructed the tomb (Blair 1980, 66–74) (Fig 71). Unfortunately, the area to the south of the high altar was severely truncated and no trace of such a tomb was found. It may be that [13554], a burial which was not analysed, represents the interment of Loveyne or Margaret de Bereford (or possibly de Vere), Loveyne's wife who died *c* 1370 (Sheppard 1965–8). Though it is central to the presbytery and choir, burial [16042], beneath a possible tomb chest, is also a possibility for Loveyne (Fig 28; Fig 31).

Next, three burials are described by Clarenceux as being close to the high altar: those of Dame Joan or Jane Stafford who died after 1485 (Cokayne 1910–59, ii, 63), Dame Elizabeth Ratcliffe who died between 1529 and 1532, and George Ratcliffe who was also dead by 1532 (ibid, xii(1), 519–20). Burial [16104] was an indeterminate adult aged ≥46 years and is most likely, given its central position, to be that of Joan Stafford who 'lies right before the high altar, under a stone' (Wagner 1956, 143–4). Joan Stafford was married as early as 1454 and was therefore certainly a mature adult by the time she died. However, as suggested above, this burial might also be that of William de Warden, abbot from 1360 until 1411, who must have been a very old man when he died. No other female burial was identified in this area, but Elizabeth Ratcliffe could have occupied the empty grave on the south side of burial [16104].

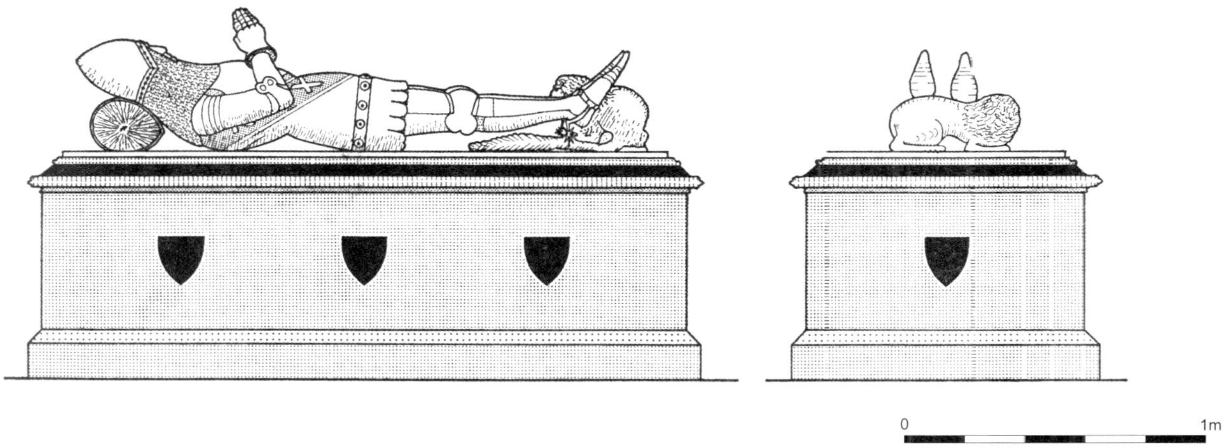

Fig 71 Reconstruction of the tomb of Sir Nicholas Loveyne, lord of East Smithfield (Blair 1980, 69 fig 1) (scale 1:25). Reproduced by kind permission of the Society of Antiquaries of London from Antiquaries Journal, *© reserved*

The burial place of her son, George, at her other side, was then probably lost to the south of that. However, it is possible that burial [16073], that of a male aged ≥46 years, represents his interment. George Ratcliffe was married between 1527 and 1529 but died without issue by 1532.

The next tomb described is that of Sir Lewis John and his wife on the north side of the choir. The brick vault [16011] containing burials [16098] and [16102] was directly to the north of the burials described above, against the north wall of the presbytery (Fig 28; Fig 32). Burial [16098] was a male aged 36–45 years with evidence of DISH, and [16102] that of a female 26–35 years old. Sir Lewis John may have been born as early as 1385, and is certainly recorded as early as 1402 when he was appointed deputy to the king's butler in the port of London. He died between 1442 and 1444, which would suggest that he was at least in his fifties when he died, making burial [16098] perhaps a little too young to be him if the skeletal evidence has been correctly interpreted. His wife Alice de Vere, whom he married in 1413, was dead by 1433, suggesting that the tomb was constructed then and was certainly in existence before Lewis John died (Carr 1967, 260–70). The area immediately to the south of this was truncated and no trace of the burial of his daughter-in-law Eleanor was found. Clarenceux wrongly describes her as Lewis John's daughter; in fact Sir Henry FitzLewis, one of her husbands, was his son (ibid, 269).

Clarenceux next moves to a chapel on the south side of the church 'withowt the quire door, on the south side' (Wagner 1956, 143–4). Only one burial of importance is described in this chapel, that of Sir Thomas Charles, Lieutenant of the Tower of London, who died before 1475 (*Cal Pat R*, 1461–71, 110). The choir door referred to was probably that at the north end of the porch (B8) and thus Building 16 the chapel described (Chapter 2.5); here the only burial of apparent importance remaining was a male aged ≥46 years within tomb [13530] (Fig 28; Fig 38). Sir Thomas Charles's age at death is unknown, but he was presumably adult. At the choir door Clarenceux then notes two burials, those of Walter Haward (or Havard), secretary to the Lord Treasurer, who may have died in 1504, and Elizabeth Rowley or Rollysley, gentlewoman, who died after 1513 (*Cal Pat R*, 1485–9, 369; TNA: PRO, PROB 11/14/12; Madox 1702, 440). If the choir door has been correctly identified, no definite female burial was found in this area. Nevertheless, burial [13545] (not analysed) to the north of the proposed doorway, or one of the indeterminate burials [13778] and [13849] within the porch, may be that of Elizabeth, while burial [13935], an adult male aged 26–35 years immediately to the south of the choir door, may have been Walter Haward. However, if the area has been correctly identified, Walter Haward could be represented by any of the burials within the porch.

The second chapel that Clarenceux visits is that of St Anne on the south side of the church. Even if the chapel of St Anne has been correctly identified as room 6a in the nave, far more people were interred there than are mentioned by him. Sir John Montgomery was buried there before 1489, as were Sir Andrew Cavendish and his wife Rose, in 1394 and 1419 respectively (Nichols 1826, 201, 396). Conceivably burial [13825], a male aged 26–35, was Sir John Montgomery. A probable late monument [13856] above the burial formed part of the north wall of the chapel (Fig 28; Fig 34). The grave [13667] containing burials [13670] and [13747], respectively a female and a male both aged ≥46 years, was not that of the Cavendishes; the papal bulla of Clement VIII (1423–9) (<S46>) found with [13670] is of too late date to have been buried with either. Grave [13542] contained two bodies, burial [13633] of an unclassified adult beneath burial [13724], of a female aged 36–45. These may have been the Cavendish burials, particularly if, as appears to be the case, grave [13667] cut grave [13542].

The two final burials noted by Clarenceux were on the north side of the church. Possibly he had finished his work in the choir and chapels and was now in the nave proper. Burial [12414] of a male (Fig 28; Fig 35) and indeterminate burial [12489] between the columns of the north nave arcade may have had a monument above them. These may have been John Walden, a grocer who died in 1464, and Elizabeth his wife who apparently predeceased him (Beaven 1908, 10); it is noteworthy

Table 14 Other documented burials at St Mary Graces

Name	Date of death	Location	References
John Galeys	1358	in the churchyard, or New Church, Hawe	*Cal Husting Wills*, ii, 160
John Shirbourne	1375	in the church or churchyard	*Cal Husting Wills*, ii, 182
Sir Simon Burley	executed 5 May 1388	in the choir	Lewis 1937, 668–9; TNA: PRO, DL 28/3/2
Roger Coryngham	1412	in the monastery	TNA: PRO, PROB 11/2/24
Nicholas Barnet	1443	in the monastery, or St Martin's, Tower Hill	GL, MS 9171/4, fo 114v
Robert Wolf, priest	1520	in the church	TNA: PRO, PROB 11/23/10
John Moore	1529		TNA: PRO, PROB 11/23/10

that burial [12414] slightly cut burial [12489].

One further burial in the nave, not dealt with by Clarenceux, is independently located. According to his will of 1529, John Moore desired to be buried before 'the rood on the south side' (TNA: PRO, PROB 11/23/10) (Table 14). Assuming that his wish was carried out, it is likely that one of the later burials in the south aisle of the nave is Moore. However, there are several to choose from, although the most likely candidates are burials [13622], [13678], [13774], [13840] or [13848].

3.9 A London and Cistercian house: the abbey in its wider context

The London context

St Mary Graces' importance to medieval London is difficult to assess. Edward III may well have had grandiose plans for his new royal foundation, but he lacked the will or the money to see them fulfilled. Certainly for the first decade or more of the monastery's life the overriding impression is one of poverty, and although the abbey did have the third-highest net value of the English and Welsh Cistercian houses in 1535, there seldom seem to have been periods when it was not in financial difficulties. It therefore probably did not have the wealth, or the authority that wealth confers, to make a significant impact on the life of the capital.

The Cistercians were not a preaching order like the friars, and it is unlikely that the nave was used for this purpose, although the status of the chapel of Holy Trinity is uncertain and the laity may have had access to it for services. St Mary Graces did have a number of priests (Table 8) and it is likely that the nave, where the lay brothers would have worshipped in earlier times, was divided into chantry chapels where masses could be said for the souls of dead patrons (Table 12), as at Rievaulx, Fountains, Hailes, Byland and Jervaulx (Coppack 1998, 81–2). It is possible, as suggested by Barber, that St Mary Graces – as a new royal foundation closer to the City – took some of the patronage of the urban and Essex elite still inclined to support the Cistercians away from St Mary Stratford Langthorne, but the proof of this is lacking (Barber et al 2004, 130). St Mary Graces did sufficient work for the poor and sick by the Dissolution to merit a plea to keep it open from Richard Gresham, the mayor of London (Chapter 2.6). However, we do not know the extent of this work or how long St Mary Graces had such a reputation prior to 1539. The abbey's short-lived and ill-tempered acquisition of the leper hospital at St Giles in the Fields between 1391 and 1399 smacks not so much of any desire to care for the sick, but rather to increase the abbey's shaky revenues.

Many Londoners who dealt with the abbey probably did so as tenants of its urban properties. On the death of Edward III, St Mary Graces received property in 30 parishes scattered across the City, in addition to the land and tenements it had already received in the immediate vicinity, and by the Dissolution still had property in 20 parishes. The abbey appears to have been a reasonable landlord where records survive (above, 3.5). These properties provided a significant proportion of the abbey's income, and it is tempting to see it as a largely urbanised institution living off these rents. Nevertheless, St Mary Graces did have a large number of rural properties and appears to some extent to have farmed them directly (above, 3.5). The abbey does not appear, however, to have significantly managed the marshland that it owned in the immediate vicinity, despite the Cistercians' reputation for the cultivation of marginal land. The land adjacent to their precinct was still not drained at the Dissolution (above, 3.5). Despite this, the abbots were still included in the commissions to inspect local riverbanks and ditches in 1448, 1467, 1480, 1483, 1497, 1499 and 1511 (Honeybourne 1952). From 1375 the abbey owned the manor of East Smithfield and from 1397 that of Poplar. As lord of these suburban manors the abbey presided over the manorial courts through its steward, and had its will enforced by the bailiff. Individual abbots also occasionally played a more significant role in London affairs. William de Warden was a collector of the Poll Tax in 1381 for the archdeaconries of London and Middlesex, and of the clerical subsidies for the archdeaconry of London in 1399 and 1406 (TNA: PRO, E 179/42/10a).

The decline in the agricultural economy, with the consequent demise of the lay brothers and the buildings required to house them, led to space being created in many

Cistercian precincts and the need to find alternative sources of income. Many precincts, like Beaulieu, housed lay tenants (Hockey 1976, 169). St Mary Graces, her most urban daughter, was no exception to this, and also benefited from the apparent desire of rich people to have their dwellings near to a monastic church. Sir Lewis John, a patron of the abbey who was buried in the choir, had a house in the precinct in the 1420s and 1440s (*Cart Holy Trinity*, no. 995).

Occasional vignettes show St Mary Graces more generally involved in London life. In October 1377 men-at-arms and archers mustered for a foreign expedition at the abbey and at Ratcliff. On Shrove Tuesday 1392 the parish clerks of London performed a stage play in the abbey. We do not know if this was a regular event or an isolated occurrence, but if the play took place indoors it may well have been performed in the refectory. The royal council held a meeting at the abbey in 1419 to instruct ambassadors being sent to negotiate with the Genoese; this does appear to have been an isolated event for the abbey.

The Cistercian context

St Mary Graces should not have been an important Cistercian abbey as far as the Order was concerned; it was a small, late foundation and at times ill-disciplined. What prominence it gained within the Order was the result of two inter-related external factors: royal patronage and proximity to London and the seat of government.

St Mary Graces temporarily achieved a prominent position in the affairs of the Order during the Great Schism of 1378–1409. Since France gave allegiance to the pope at Avignon and England to the pope in Rome, the English Cistercian houses were cut off from the head of the Order at Cîteaux in northern France. In or before 1394 the Roman pope, Boniface IX, made new arrangements for the Order in England, Wales and Ireland. The abbots of Boxley, Stratford Langthorne and St Mary Graces were to convoke the general chapter of these lands to meet at St Mary Graces. They were to appoint two visitors to govern the abbeys and supervise their elections at each meeting, and to do all that the abbot of Cîteaux would do at the general chapter of the whole Order (Graham 1929, 377–8; Knowles 1955, 168–9; *Cal Pat R*, 1391–6, 557). Placing the supervision of the Order in the hands of the youngest member, a royal foundation, and two small houses near London, against all normal Cistercian observance of a hierarchy based on seniority, shows the influence of Richard II on the papal decision. Indeed the pope revoked this order in 1397 but without immediate effect, for the English chapters continued to meet at St Mary Graces until 1400 (Graham 1929, 378–9, 383; Knowles 1955, 169; *Cal Pap Letters*, v, 9). In 1401 a new papal command gave the direction of the English Cistercians to the two senior foundations, Waverley and Furness (Graham 1929, 385, 387; Knowles 1955, 169). In 1409 the ending of the Schism at the Council of Pisa reunited the Order under the abbot of Cîteaux. During St Mary Graces' brief period of prominence the English Cistercians were troubled by scandalous disputed elections at Beaulieu in 1394, at Meaux in 1396, and at Dore, where Jordan de Biggleswade, a monk of St Mary Graces, twice intruded himself as abbot before the chapter meeting at his own abbey pronounced in favour of his rival. Armed force was used in all of these conflicts (Graham 1929, 380–2; *Cal Pat R*, 1389–92, 30). At this time the abbot of St Mary Graces also served on a number of minor papal commissions (*Cal Pap Letters*, iv, 512; v, 349; *Cal Close R*, 1389–92, 479).

The abbey's prominence was ended by the usurpation of Henry IV. It lost the custody of St Giles and the holding of the general chapter, and before long it was suffering from internal disputes and serious financial difficulty. In November 1410 the custody of the abbey was given over to a panel of councillors and Cistercian abbots, including the abbot of Stratford Langthorne (*Cal Pat R*, 1408–13, 268; TNA: PRO, C 1/75/80). Matters did not improve under the mismanagement of William de Warden's successors, and the same measure had to be taken again in 1427 (*Cal Pat R*, 1422–9, 394; TNA: PRO, SC 8/6733). Nevertheless, its proximity to London still afforded the abbey a leading place in the English Cistercian Order in the 15th and early 16th centuries. It is likely that other Cistercian abbots visiting London on business stayed at the abbey (Honeybourne 1952, 21). In the 15th century Cîteaux appointed supervisors and visitors for the English abbeys, and the abbots of Fountains, Stratford Langthorne and St Mary Graces served almost continually in this capacity (Knowles 1959, 29). In 1520 the abbey was the venue for a meeting of the English abbots to reform the Order, convened at the behest of Cardinal Wolsey (TNA: PRO, E 135/21/14; E 135/2/47).

4

Conclusions

The Royal Mint project was essentially an archaeological rescue excavation of the 1980s, and as such the research aims at the time of excavation were basically limited to the recovery of whatever information could be rescued. This process has provided a wealth of data to which research questions have been addressed after the event.

The excavations of the 1980s successfully recovered some two-thirds of the overall ground plan of the core of the abbey within its precinct and allowed for other parts of that plan to be conjectured with reasonable confidence. The recovered plan reflects the need to adapt to a constrained suburban site and the influence of contemporary late 14th-century monastic trends – particularly mendicant design for both the church and cloister – on the patron, the Cistercians and the master mason. It also reflects the influence of the site's most recent past, that is, its use as a burial place for victims of the Black Death and the need to commemorate the catastrophe. In this respect the archaeological work suggested further parallels with the Carthusian establishment of Charterhouse in West Smithfield, also a commemorative foundation of the immediate post-plague years. The ground plan of St Mary Graces was essentially a product of the years 1353–92, and very little appears to have been added later, beyond the Lady chapel and the 'chapel without the quire door on the south side'. But the excavations also indicate a ground plan that contained elements, like the large and expensive north–south aligned refectory, that would not (perhaps surprisingly at this late date) have looked out of place in a Cistercian house built in the 12th century. The post-excavation analysis has also to a large extent allowed the process of construction to be recovered, and again indicates that the monks of St Mary Graces followed a course that would have been easily recognisable to their forebears, albeit one adapted to their circumstances and the times. As with earlier monastic houses, before the monks were able to achieve *stabilitas* and construct a permanent church, cloister and other buildings necessary for conventual life, they first occupied temporary buildings while they raised the funds to build their monastery proper. The differences detectable in this process at St Mary Graces – the use of stone, rather than timber, for the 'temporary' buildings, the construction of a cloister, and the retention of those buildings for the lifetime of the abbey – are only differences of detail and in keeping with 14th-century monastic construction.

The overriding impression of the abbey gained from the remains is of a small and utilitarian house. The interior wall faces were rendered with limewash, the exterior ones were of hammer-dressed Kentish ragstone, the church cloister was unfinished, and the chapter house small and plain. Here simplicity and economy appear to have been the virtues of necessity, a function of poverty and a cramped site, rather than any unlikely attempt to return to the rigour of the early 12th century. The *ex situ* architectural fragments to some extent contradict this picture, at least where the church is concerned, and along with the documentary sources and a few richer finds like the miniature sceptre (<S41>, Fig 96) hint at the Perpendicular beauty that was destroyed after the suppression.

The abbey may never have achieved lasting financial security (Chapter 3.4). From the documentation available, the various crises can be traced to a variety of specific causes: the delayed endowment by the king, the greed of powerful nobles, and the incompetence and mendacity of individual abbots (Chapter 3.6). However, all of these factors were in play against the background of the problems for medieval society as a whole created by the Black Death and subsequent outbreaks of the plague. Many monastic building programmes suffered from the lack of skilled labour after 1350. This was particularly the case where masons are concerned; their numbers appear to have been particularly badly depleted by the Black Death, and the problem was compounded by the king's monopolisation of many of those left for his building works at Windsor (Platt 1997, 141). This state of affairs may have hit St Mary Graces harder than most, given that it was an entirely new project and reliant on the king to provide the skilled men needed to construct the necessary buildings, but it did not make its problems unique. A large number of existing monasteries, Cistercian or otherwise, lost monks in the Black Death and subsequent outbreaks of the plague, and they struggled to maintain their numbers. St Mary Graces' failure to muster even the 12 monks required for a single convent should also be seen in that light (Chapter 3.6), and initially at least, during the 1350s, the Cistercians may not have been able to spare monks to found a new house, irrespective of Edward III's demands. The reliance on rents, particularly urban rents, rather than direct farming may have been more pronounced in the case of a new and very urban monastery, but this trend had already begun in the Cistercian Order before the plague, as shown by the gradual disappearance of the lay brothers and their associated buildings, and the Black Death merely accelerated the process for all.

What the excavation did not achieve was to find and map to any great extent the outer precinct, the ancillary non-conventual buildings, and the economic infrastructure of the abbey. There are a number of reasons for this. These structures, when found, were frequently truncated and fragmentary, surviving only as isolated foundations, or clearly having been reused after the suppression. In a number of cases such buildings lay in areas yet to be investigated, particularly to the west on the Tower Hill frontage. There are also few references to such buildings in the documentary sources, which may imply that they lay elsewhere, if they existed at all. St Mary Graces may have relied on the City to supply most of its needs, preferring to rent out much of the vicinity to tenants. Many of the structures excavated close to the conventual buildings suggest domestic occupation rather than specific industrial functions. It is from these that the only sizeable finds and environmental assemblages come; the conventual buildings produced little, having been intensively reused during the post-medieval period, or apparently kept clean during their monastic usage.

The human skeletal remains show some traits typical of other monastic assemblages: better general health, greater longevity, a higher incidence of DISH in the church, and a preponderance of adult males over women or subadults. If anything, however, the male domination of the assemblages is less pronounced than in other London monasteries, which probably reflects the abbey's late foundation and urban location. The various well-defined areas of burial allowed for the examination in detail of the effects of patronage on burial practice in a late Cistercian church. The numbers of lay patrons buried can to some extent be quantified, the web of patronage that led to their choice of St Mary Graces partly reconstructed, and in certain cases even specific individuals tentatively identified. It was not possible to identify areas reserved for the burial of monks, which means that St Mary Graces can add nothing to the debate concerning Cistercian burial practices except in the negative. No burial practices leaving evidence in the ground that were specific to the Cistercians could be identified. In all probability no area within the church or outside it was reserved exclusively for the monks, the power and necessity of patronage proving too great, with the burial practices of the monks being indistinguishable from those of the laity lying alongside them and from medieval practice in general. In this respect St Mary Graces confirms the evidence from St Mary Stratford Langthorne (Barber et al 2004, 112–16).

The chronology of events at the Dissolution and their effect on the various buildings of the abbey is difficult to pin down. The manor house period was a short one of only 22 years, and transitional in terms of both history and archaeology. It is impossible to be certain how long the church remained standing after 1539. The evidence suggests, equivocally, that full demolition did not occur until after 1560, but to what extent the church was left untouched and derelict before that is a matter of conjecture. Equally there can be no absolute proof that the former kitchen (B11) and house and chamber or abbot's hospice (B14), converted at some point in the 16th century, were not altered after 1560 for the victualling yard rather than earlier.

Ultimately the value of the abbey to the archaeological study of Cistercian monasteries, and to Cistercian studies in general, lies in the tension between its traditional and untraditional elements. It was the last Cistercian house to be founded in England by some 70 years, the only one built entirely in the 14th century, and the only one established adjacent to a major city. Yet, despite all the expected influences of the late 14th century, there are components that remain recognisably Cistercian. One final point is perhaps worth making. Elements of St Mary Graces still survive to be visited, though the remains are difficult to see, do not have the setting or grandeur of the great rural Cistercian houses, and are not listed in any tourist guide for those interested in monastic sites. Overshadowed by the nearby Tower of London and heavily disguised by a pedestrian underpass, a number of walls from the church (Fig 14), chapter house (Fig 17), refectory (Fig 21), infirmary (Fig 23), kitchen, and house and chamber (Fig 18) have been preserved in the basement of Murray House, part of the Royal Mint development of the 1980s.

5

Specialist appendices

5.1 Architectural fragments

Mark Samuel

Introduction

During the 1984 and 1986–8 excavations, great quantities of loose stone from the demolition of the abbey were found. Post-excavation analysis commenced in 1991. Thirty-seven stones were discovered during the 1984 trial trenching (MIN84), of which nine merited publication. During the main excavations a further 865 architectural worked stones were numbered and marked; of these 637 stones merited retention and further study (including the 1984 material) but relatively few are sufficiently distinctive to be mentioned here.

Methodology

All potentially worked stone was retained, being either individually accessioned or else (in the case of the many small fragments) by the bagful. The post-Dissolution demolition layers contained many tiny fragments of stone, the 'debitage' of the demolition process.

Interpretable isolated stones and the best examples of duplicated stones were categorised as 'typestones'. There were fewer than 80 'true' typestones, and the bulk of these are published. Typestones were grouped according to demonstrable relationships into stone 'groups'. For example, it is possible for very different parts of a window (such as the arch and sill) to have the same moulding; the two typestones would be 'related' to form a 'group'.

The identification of groups does allow a phase of construction to be recognised even where advanced reconstruction is impossible. The various mouldings present in the group can be shown to belong together in a particular style fixed in time and space. At St Mary Graces, it is possible to identify broader stylistic connections between groups, even though their mouldings vary in detail. These groups are dated, as far as possible, by moulding style. Where broader stylistic similarities are also apparent (eg <A2>–<A10>) the implication is that the groups all derive from a single period of construction. The relationship these apparent phases of construction may have to the documentary evidence is discussed in Chapter 3.3. The criteria by which they are defined are of course highly subjective, and take into consideration such factors as the type of stone and the tooling techniques.

Individual stones occur which bear no relationship to any others (eg <A59>–<A60>). In such a case, the individual blocks are treated as a typestone and a single-stone 'group'. In the three instances where relatively complete reconstruction is possible (<A17>–<A21>, <A36>–<A42>, <A61>–<A70>), geometrical information played an important role in unifying the surviving elements. Great care was therefore needed to record the short lengths of arc that were preserved on the surviving stones. The published reconstructions were drawn manually, before CAD became generally available.

Catalogue

<A1> Ashlar with devotional inscription (Fig 37)
<3634>, [13453]; period B3, B16
This complete ashlar was discovered in the foundations of the chapel (B16) and is described in detail in Chapter 2.5. The stone is a typical ashlar block and the clawtooling of the borders indicates that it was surrounded by others of the same type. The flat-batted back indicates that the ashlar served little structural purpose, acting as a veneer for the mortar wall core. The front was fine-combed and then carved with a succession of symbolic figures and epigraphy. To carve the cross and circles, a series of arcs were first described with a compass. Once the carving was completed, the surface of the stone was polished down to remove the scribe lines (traces of which remain). The ashlar is dressed from Reigate stone. To dress the margins a clawtool with a blade *c* 3.5cm wide and with six teeth was used.

<A2>–<A5> Trefoil window tracery (Fig 72)
<A2>, <3074>, [+]
<A3>, <3743>, [13072]; Grainger and Phillpotts 2010, period C1, OA14
<A4>, <3747>, [13032]; Grainger and Phillpotts 2010, period C1, OA14
<A5>, <3748>, [13032]; Grainger and Phillpotts 2010, period C1, OA14
Both <A2> and <A3> were found in the area of the demolished church. Two others, <A4> and <A5>, may merit further study, but they do not affect the published partial reconstruction. Fragment <A2> probably comes from a larger block, but <A3>, although heavily trimmed for reuse, is essentially complete; the stone is very fresh, only the external elevation being lightly weathered. Fragment <A3> is the junction between the archlets at the head of two main window lights. It is probable that the lower bed was the level of the arch springing line. Although the archlets appear symmetrical, the location of their centres indicates that they were in fact slightly asymmetrical. This was apparently intentional (below). Both fragments are dressed from Reigate stone of a dense and hard type. The surviving bed on <A3> is coarsely combed and there are no clawtool marks. A small cross was scored on the face after the combing was completed, while a straight line marks the moulding's axis of symmetry and presumably forms part of the original 'setting-out'. This type of moulding was very common, but the overall proportions, the tooling and the petrology all indicate that the group is related to <A7>–<A10> (below). To reconstruct the light width, it was assumed that the lost median line of the light bore the same relation to the archlet centres (74% of the distance of the centre from the surviving block). This suggests that the lights were slightly narrower than in the <A7>–<A10> window. The reconstruction shows a wide light, but a narrower light would produce a better-proportioned trefoil; Fig 72 therefore shows only one of two possible reconstructions. The surviving evidence indicates that the cusps were very large, dividing each light head into a very heavy trefoil. Like the archlet radius, the radii of the surviving cusps were asymmetrical. Unlike the archlet centres, the cusp centres (not illustrated) were aligned on the bed. The taller archlet may have been at the centre of the window, being flanked by two slightly lower archlets. The overall size of the window is unknown. The presence of a small cusp among other fragments suggests that there may have been other archlets decorated with more conventional septfoils or cinquefoils. The jamb fragment <A2> indicates that the window had no external casement and was sheltered by a hood-mould; the <A7>–<A10> hood-mould was probably common to both groups. The main arch of the window is conjectural, and for this reason no overall reconstruction of this window has been attempted. The internal casement, like that of <A7>–<A10>, was probably shallow and flat. The internal (unweathered) elevation of <A3> retains, on the fillet, the setting-out lines (not illustrated) whereby the mason worked out the geometry of the stone before cutting. A compass was used to describe the median lines of the archlets. The carefully executed geometry supports the contention that the subtle asymmetry was intentional.

The affinity of this group with <A7>–<A10> has already been noted. The moulding is a 'scaled-up' (but otherwise identical) version of the <A6> moulding. Fragments <A2>–<A10> all date from the same phase of construction. Good parallels exist for this moulding and the unusual trefoil; the simple moulding was, however, widely used over a long period and is an unreliable dating tool, occurring as late as 1414 (by ? William Colchester) in the Old Library at York Minster (Harvey 1978, 260). An early occurrence is in the west window of the south walk at Chichester Cathedral (*c* 1400). The large trefoil is paralleled at the Archbishop's Palace, Mayfield (*c* 1325) (Wood, M E, 1965, 353).

<A6> Cinquefoil window tracery (Fig 72)
<1982>, [4527]; Grainger and Phillpotts 2010, period C2, B12
This near-complete moulded stone was found in the post-medieval backfill of the storeroom (B12). The internal elevation is largely broken away, but the external elevation is mostly present. Weathering is slight but no paint survives. Enough survives of the internal moulding (identified by the position of the glazing rebate) to indicate that it was the same as the external moulding. The element was part of a cinquefoil archlet which almost certainly formed the head of a main light. Part of a supermullion stood on the apex of the archlet. The centre of the archlet could be accurately determined from the curvature of the surviving fillet. The two joint beds pointed to the two centres of the archlet, but their survival was not essential to the reconstruction. The light was 0.705m wide. The foils and cusps were sufficiently well preserved for their centres to be determined. The lower joint bed also pointed to the centre (not illustrated) of an intermediate foil. It is assumed that the missing side of the foil was a mirror image of the surviving side. Only the lowest foil is conjectural. The absent side of the archlet mirrors the surviving side. The implied tracery pattern is straightforward and robust. It is probable that the mullions continued upwards to subdivide the lights at either side of the

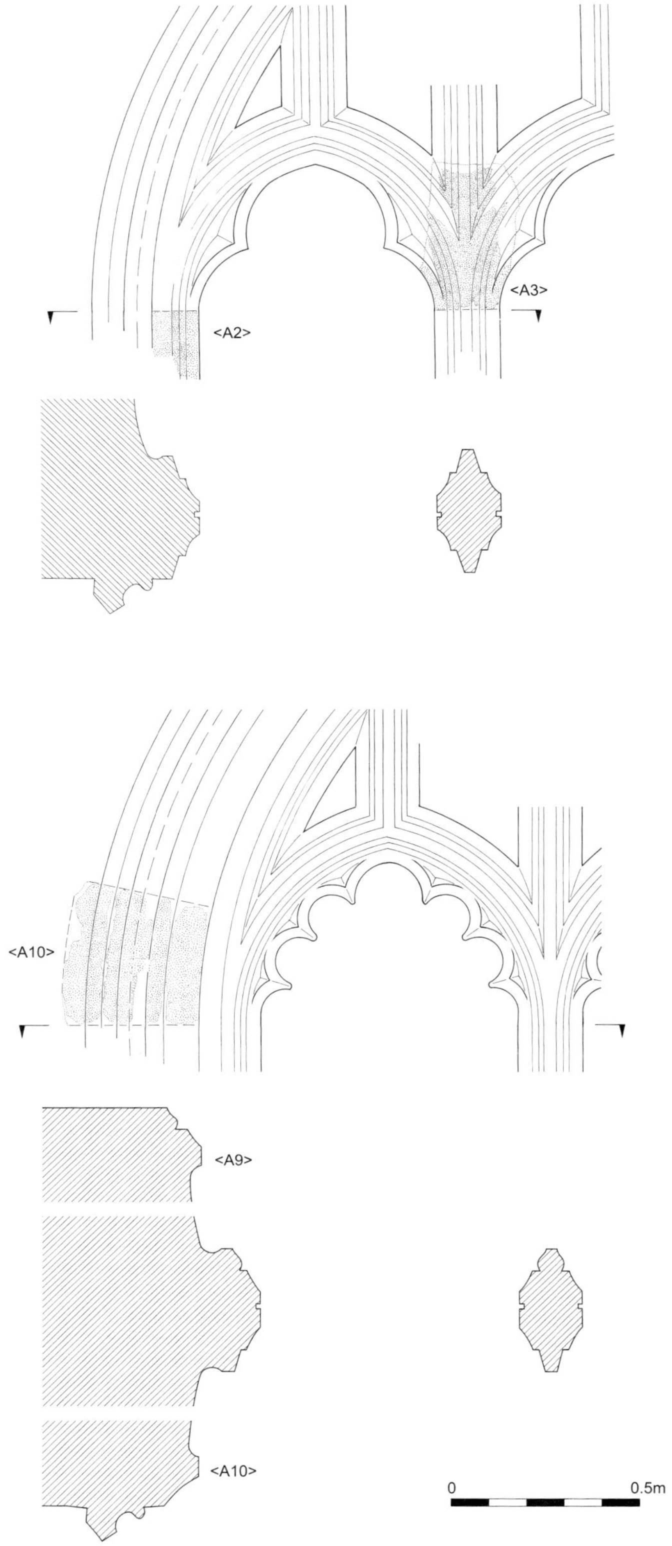

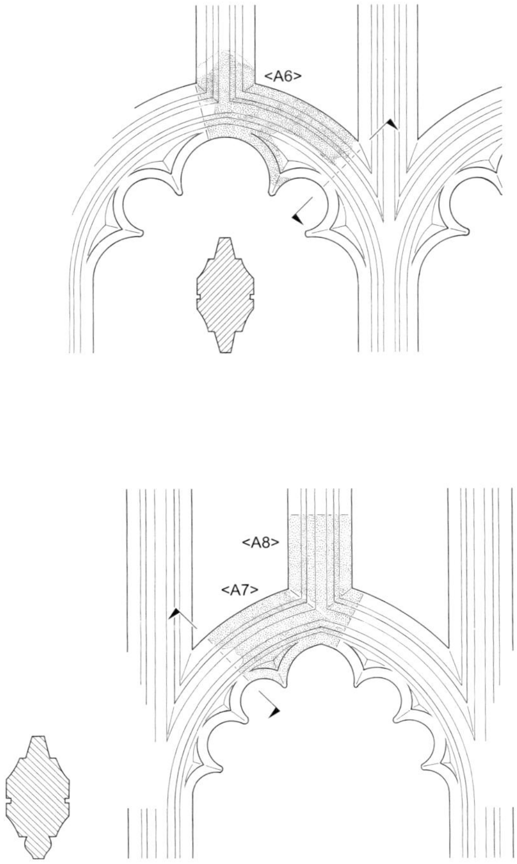

Fig 72 Reconstructed window tracery, possibly from the chapel of Holy Trinity or the presbytery: <A2> and <A3>; <A6>; <A7> and <A8>; <A9> and <A10> (scale 1:20)

archlet supermullion. All lights were glazed. The size of the window is unknown, but the employment of only a single order implies that it was not very large. The archlet was dressed from a very hard variety of Reigate stone. The beds were dressed with regular, diagonal rows of clawtooling; the lower bed was slightly concave. The visible surfaces were finely combed to a smooth finish.

In style, jointing and dressing technique, and the type of stone used, this window clearly relates to <A2>–<A5> and <A7>–<A10> and derives from the same phase of construction. The moulding is a 'scaled-down' but otherwise identical version of the <A2>–<A5> moulding. The use of a cinquefoil is more conventional than the great trefoils of group <A2>–<A5>. Although the moulding is lighter than that of <A7>–<A10>, the light width was very similar (0.705–0.68m). The asymmetrical way in which the archlet was jointed is another characteristic of this phase of construction. The mason in charge favoured a wide variety of cusping arrangements in archlets of much the same size. The wider stylistic affinities of this window are the same as for <A2>–<A5>, but the cinquefoil heads (with the near-circular central foil) are reminiscent of the cloisters at New College, Oxford, built after 1396 by William Wynford (Harvey 1978, 131). The New College cloister differs in employing two orders of moulding, although strongly resembling the tracery of <A6>–<A10>.

<A7>–<A10> Septfoil window tracery (Fig 72)
<A7>, <309>, [691]; Grainger and Phillpotts 2010, period C1, B28
<A8>, <331>, [691]; Grainger and Phillpotts 2010, period C1, B28
<A9>, <332>, [691]; Grainger and Phillpotts 2010, period C1, B28
<A10>, <333>, [691]; Grainger and Phillpotts 2010, period C1, B28

Broken in two at the time of reuse in Building 28, fragments <A7>–<A8> fit together to form a complete moulded stone. Although obscured by mortar and chemical concretions, the stones were not battered and only slightly weathered. The good preservation allows the local context and light width to be reconstructed. The stone incorporates an archlet and the supermullion that stood at the apex. The archlet was septfoil and almost certainly formed the head of a main light. The tracery seems to have been simple. The main light and the tracery lights above it were glazed. The ogival fillet is fresher than the straight fillet, which implies that it was internal. The displacement of the glazing groove (so as to further shelter the glass) is an important means of recognising the external components of the moulding. The visible surfaces were combed to a high finish, but the beds were finished with very regular parallel rows of clawtooling. The Reigate stone employed is a hard, dense variety which is less vulnerable to weathering than is normally the case.

Two more important fragments were found in the same post-medieval wall. The casement hollow <A9> was broken, though substantially complete. The visible surface was slightly weathered, but the surviving bed was fresh. Fragment <A10> was intact and unweathered. Both mouldings retained traces of white paint and incorporated the outer part of very similar window casements. The chief difference was the presence of a window hood-moulding on <A10>. It is likely that the two derive from the internal and external casements of the same window. The survival of both beds allowed the radius of <A10> to be accurately measured (1.439m). The radius of <A9> was slightly greater (*c* 1.83m); this is a less reliable reading (being made from the curvature) and the two were probably the same. This curvature is important because it is the only clue to the overall scale of the window arch. The two casement mouldings are dressed from the same hard, dense variety of Reigate stone as the archlet.

The moulding was virtually identical to <A3> (above) with the exception of the use of an ogival fillet. The archlets were of much the same size but the cusping was very different. The simultaneous reuse and the general stylistic similarity (the heaviness of detail and the broad, shallow, hollow chamfers) strongly suggest that all derive from the same window. The casements were broad and shallow, making it impossible to reconstruct their length (Fig 72 reflects this uncertainty). Although no window jamb elements survived, their moulding can be predicted. It would have closely resembled the surviving jamb moulding of <A11>–<A12> (below), the chief difference being that there was an external casement. This window also closely relates to the <A6> window (above), which was identical in style and proportions but 'scaled-down'. The moulding is closely paralleled by the mullions of the south walk at the cloister of Chichester Cathedral, thought to date to *c* 1400 (Harvey 1978, 248).

<A11>–<A12> Arch (Fig 73)
<A11>, MIN84 <52>, [+]
<A12>, <1658>, [71]; Grainger and Phillpotts 2010, period C1, B28

Fragment <A11> was recovered during the 1984 trial trenching and was comparatively well preserved. The surviving stone probably represents 75% of the original element. Fragment <A12> is more fragmentary, and was probably part of a much larger block; it was broken up for reuse in the rubble foundations of Building 28. Both were unweathered, implying an internal context. Although the two elements share no common length of moulding, indirect evidence suggests that they derived from the same structure. Fragment <A11> was an arch voussoir. The loss of the bed and the slightness of the surviving curvature made the radius difficult to measure. The apparent measurement (*c* 4.155m) merely suggests the great size of the arch. The use of double ogees characterised this arch; <A11> was the minor order. If the assumption is made that the arch was two-order and with a symmetrical moulding, the lost part of the moulding should also be a double ogee. Fragment <A12> has a similar double ogee next to a casement, presumably the same as that partially preserved on <A11>. The slight radius has the predicted direction. It is probable that the two fragments originally belonged together, but because the size and depth of

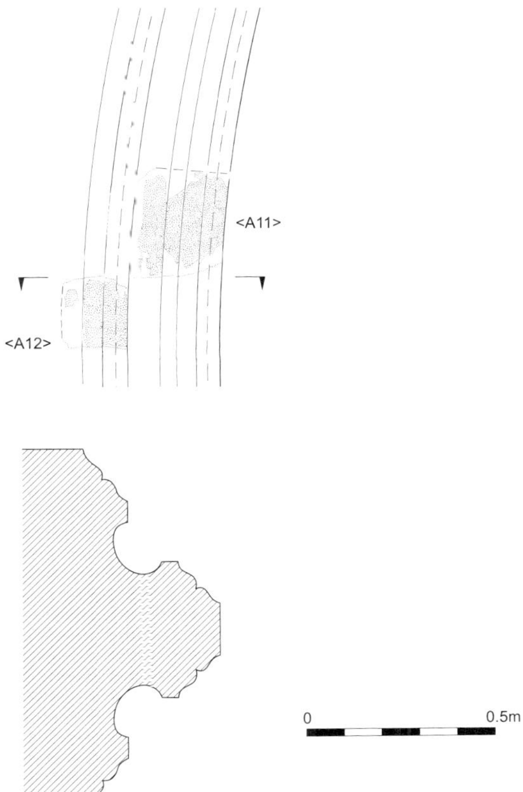

Fig 73 Fragments of arch <A11>–<A12> (scale 1:20)

the casement are unknown, the mouldings' exact relationship remains uncertain. The visible surfaces are finely combed, but the inward faces are roughly batted, suggesting that the surrounding wall fabric was mortar faced with rubble. The radius suggests that the arch was *c* 7–8m wide. The nave had a central vessel *c* 7m wide (Chapter 2.4) so it is conceivable that this arch spanned it; but if the model for the church was generally mendicant, with a timber roof, a high transverse vault rib seems unlikely.

Double ogees long remained a favourite stylistic device of the Perpendicular and are of little use for dating. An early occurrence of the moulding of the minor order <A11> is in the staircase tower of the Vicars' Close (1348) at Wells Cathedral in Somerset (Harvey 1978, 256). However, the St Mary Graces group could be a hundred years later.

<A13>–<A21> Perpendicular subarcuated alternate tracery with ogeed fillets (narrow moulding) (Fig 74)
<A13>, MIN84 <47>, [+]
<A14>, MIN84 <49>, [+]
<A15>, MIN84 <50>, [+]
<A16>, MIN84 <71>, [+]
<A17>, <307>, [691]; Grainger and Phillpotts 2010, period C1, B28
<A18>, <477>, [947]; Grainger and Phillpotts 2010, period C1, B28
<A19>, <4322>, [691]; Grainger and Phillpotts 2010, period C1, B28
<A20>, <3180>, [13288]; Grainger and Phillpotts 2010, period C1, B26
<A21>, <662>, [+]

Several stones associated with the apex of a window arch were recovered. Fragments <A17> and <A19> were found in Building 28 and <A20> in the area of the church. Fragment <A21> was unstratified but derived from this part of the window. The mullion <A15> came from a post-medieval dump and could have derived from several positions in the window but fits the bed on the underside of <A20>. The glazing groove is very marked. Although no fragments survived from the separate 'minor order' central element, the moulding can be inferred from the 'stooling' on <A17>. The opposing side mirrors the surviving elements. A 'best fit' radius of 3.545m was averaged from the different estimates of the radii (which were difficult to measure due to the great size of the arch and the shortness of the surviving elements). The arch moulding <A21> was separated from the window mouldings by a large casement, and their exact relationship is uncertain. It is probable that the inner and outer casements were the same. Reigate stone of intermediate hardness was used. The moulding was combed to a smooth finish. No paintwork was observed, but weathering was slight and confined to the external elevation. The beds were neatly dressed with parallel diagonal rows of clawtooling. The other concealed surfaces were dressed more irregularly with clawtooling. The tool had nine teeth per 5cm of blade. The bands were separated by ridges creating a 'wave effect'. A 'figure-of-eight' mason's mark was graven on a visible surface of <A19>. The jamb mouldings were integral with deep casements that framed the window, unlike the tracery mouldings <A16>, incorporating parts of the inner and outer casements. The junction between the casements and wall faces would have shared the moulding of the arch fragment <A21>. The depth of the casement is uncertain. The thickness of the wall in which the window was situated was approximately 0.85m. Fragment <A18> was probably trimmed for reuse in the foundations of Building 28. The vertical jamb met a cusped archlet below the springing line of the window and then continued above the tracery arch. The arch was approximately twice the width of the cinquefoils at the apex of the window. The mullion <A15> could have been employed in many locations, including the position depicted (Fig 74). Fragments <A16> and <A18> are dressed from the same building stone and in the same manner as <A17> and <A19>–<A21>.

Fragment <A13> is a substantial portion of a large tracery element. The minor order has foils and cusps of a size intermediate between <A17> and <A19>–<A21>, and <A15>–<A16> and <A18>. It is difficult to identify an appropriate setting for this tracery element. The radiusing of the main order (2.39m) is comparable to that of the main arch of the window, which suggests that the tracery was subdivided by curving continuations of the mullions. This sort of tracery is called 'subarcuated'. The surviving bed is assumed to be horizontal, but the stone could have been orientated in a variety of ways. Although reconstructed as part of a septfoil arch, it is equally possible (if differently orientated) that the block was part of an 'inverted dagger'. If the septfoil interpretation is correct, <A18> would have rested upon a mullion with the same moulding as <A15>; that stone could have had a variety of different applications.

A fragmentary tracery element <A14> showed no evidence of reuse. The orientation was probably vertical. The element seems to incorporate part of a mullion, implying that it derives from the tracery's lower margin. One side of the mullion continues upwards while the other is apparently a cusped arch. The radiusing of the arch is similar to that of <A18>, but the surviving cusp is much smaller and the two cannot have matched. Because no other related element survives, the stone's position within the tracery is unknown.

The suggested width of the light is based upon the known width of the paired lights <A17> and <A19>–<A21>. A narrow light is assumed.The frequency of these mouldings suggests that there was more than one window of this class. The incompatibility of some of the tracery fragments bears this out. Fig 62 shows how <A17> and <A19>–<A21>, and <A15>–<A16> and <A18> may have inter-related; the exact roles of <A13> and <A14> are unknown. They imply that even if these windows were all of the same size, they were provided with at least two tracery patterns. The missing areas can be reconstructed by other means. The likely stylistic context of <A17> and <A19>–<A21> is shown by the aisle windows of the west front of the ante-chapel at New College, Oxford, by William Wynford (1380–6) (Harvey 1978, pl 59). In the surviving windows, the eyelet and paired cinquefoils <A15>,

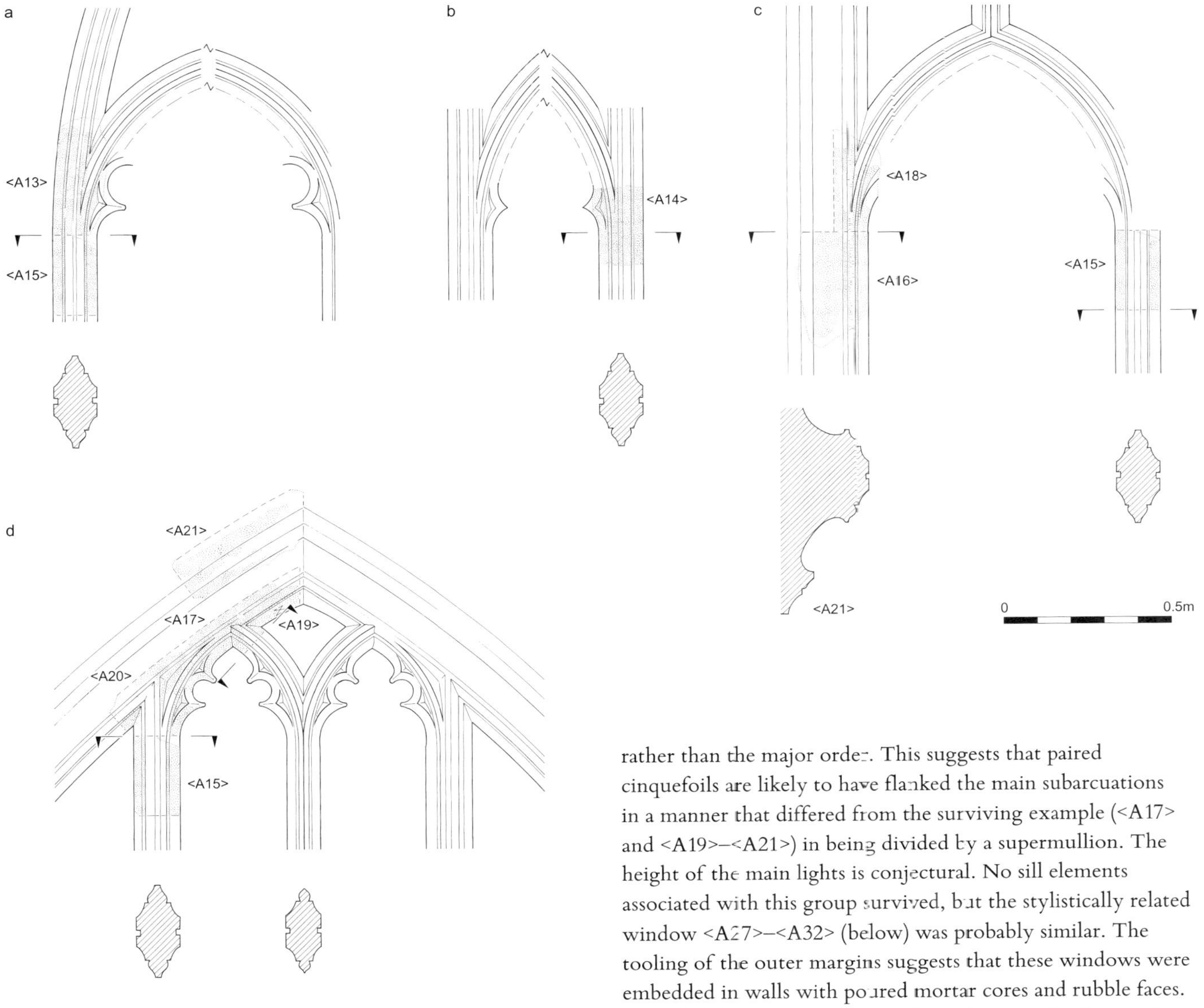

Fig 74 Reconstructed window tracery, possibly from the nave: <A13> and <A15>; <A14>; <A15>, <A16>, <A18> and <A21>; <A15>, <A17> and <A19>–<A21> (scale 1:20)

<A17> and <A19>–<A21> stood over a 'dagger'; plain triangular lights closed off by arcuated continuations of the central mullion were on either side of the mullions. The centres of the two-centred window arch were level with the springing line. If the centres of the arches are known, as well as the angle of their junction, it is possible to predict the width of the window. There were four main lights. Each light was of the same width as the known light in the window apex (which is subdivided by a minor-form mullion). Elements <A17>, <A19>–<A21>, <A15>–<A16> and <A18> can be reconstructed as a large cinquefoil (an interpretation borne out by the largeness of the surviving cusp). The New College window has a horizontal row of such arches along the lower margin of the tracery. The St Mary Graces window differed from this in several minor respects. The large cinquefoils were below the springing line (in Fig 62 they are shown immediately below it, but they could have been further down). They were framed by the minor order rather than the major order. This suggests that paired cinquefoils are likely to have flanked the main subarcuations in a manner that differed from the surviving example (<A17> and <A19>–<A21>) in being divided by a supermullion. The height of the main lights is conjectural. No sill elements associated with this group survived, but the stylistically related window <A27>–<A32> (below) was probably similar. The tooling of the outer margins suggests that these windows were embedded in walls with poured mortar cores and rubble faces. The moulding was widespread throughout England over a long period and is therefore not particularly diagnostic of stylistic attribution or date.

<A22>–<A26> Glazed Perpendicular tracery with ogeed fillets (intermediate moulding) (Fig 75)
<A22>, MIN84 <48>, [+]
<A23>, <3710>, [13485]; period B4, B16
<A24>, <354>, [691]; Grainger and Phillpotts 2010, period C1, OA7
<A25>, <3092>, [13251]; Grainger and Phillpotts 2010, period C2, B31
<A26>, <3124>, [13289]; Grainger and Phillpotts 2010, period C2, B32
A near-complete tracery fragment <A26> was reused in the area of the church. It is unweathered (there are no signs of paint) and very similar to <A20>, but the distance between the glazing reveals is significantly greater. Although one elevation is entirely broken away, the moulding had two-way symmetry. For this reason the element probably derived from a similar context to <A20> and is reconstructed accordingly. Although the direction could be determined, it was not possible to

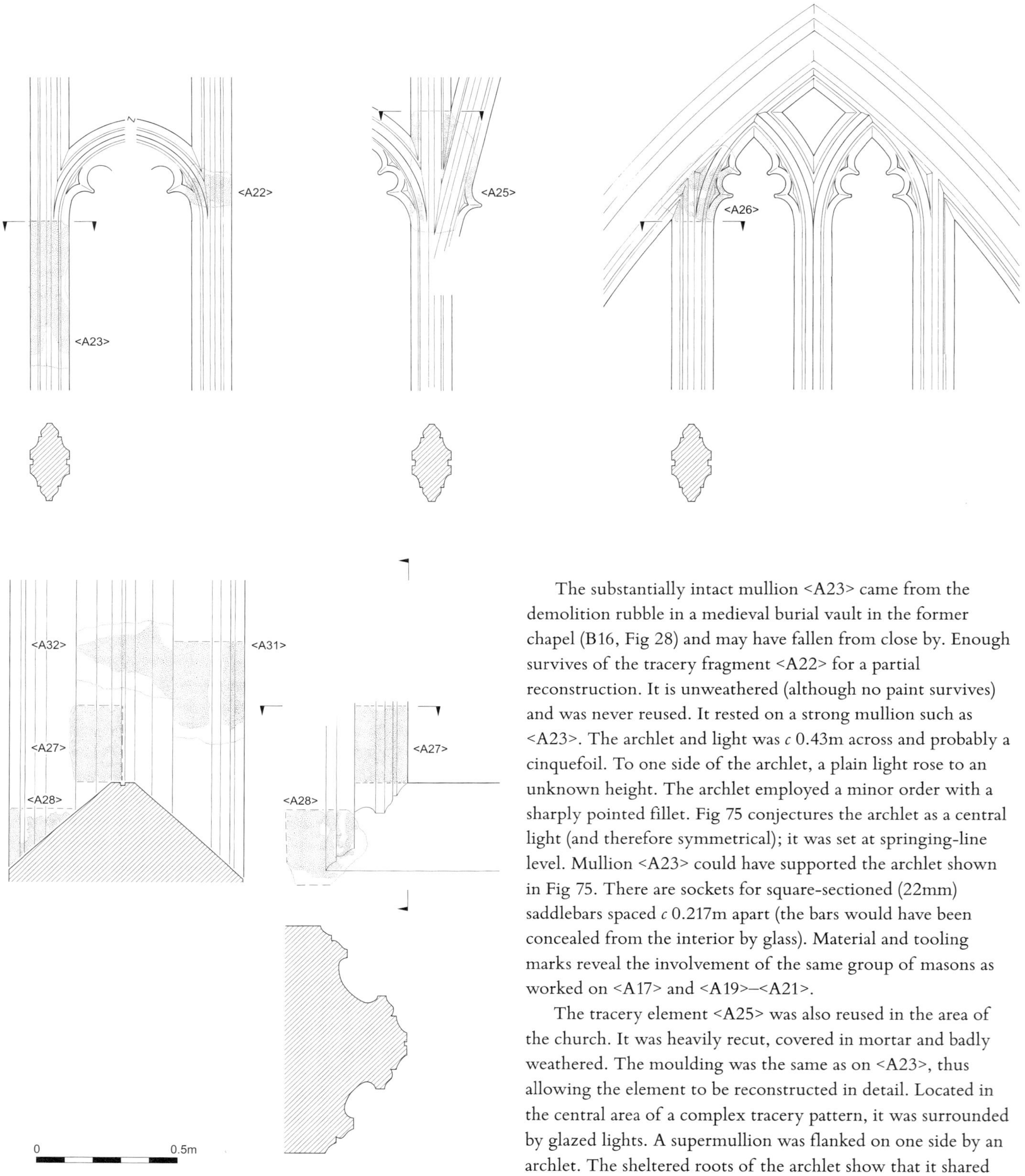

Fig 75 Reconstructed window tracery <A22> and <A23>, <A25>, <A26>, and jamb and sill <A27>,<A28>, <A31>, <A32>, possibly from the chapel of Holy Trinity or the presbytery (scale 1:20)

measure the distance of the arch centre with accuracy. The element is dressed from the same type of Reigate stone as <A17>–<A21>. The surviving bed is clawtooled in regular rows.

The substantially intact mullion <A23> came from the demolition rubble in a medieval burial vault in the former chapel (B16, Fig 28) and may have fallen from close by. Enough survives of the tracery fragment <A22> for a partial reconstruction. It is unweathered (although no paint survives) and was never reused. It rested on a strong mullion such as <A23>. The archlet and light was *c* 0.43m across and probably a cinquefoil. To one side of the archlet, a plain light rose to an unknown height. The archlet employed a minor order with a sharply pointed fillet. Fig 75 conjectures the archlet as a central light (and therefore symmetrical); it was set at springing-line level. Mullion <A23> could have supported the archlet shown in Fig 75. There are sockets for square-sectioned (22mm) saddlebars spaced *c* 0.217m apart (the bars would have been concealed from the interior by glass). Material and tooling marks reveal the involvement of the same group of masons as worked on <A17> and <A19>–<A21>.

The tracery element <A25> was also reused in the area of the church. It was heavily recut, covered in mortar and badly weathered. The moulding was the same as on <A23>, thus allowing the element to be reconstructed in detail. Located in the central area of a complex tracery pattern, it was surrounded by glazed lights. A supermullion was flanked on one side by an archlet. The sheltered roots of the archlet show that it shared the geometry of the paired cinquefoils in <A17> and <A19>–<A21>, which strongly suggests that the archlet had a cinquefoil of the same pattern. The light width would therefore have been the same. The reconstruction in Fig 75 assumes the cinquefoil to be the central light of the window. An alternative possibility is that there were paired cinquefoils to one side of the surviving element, divided by a minor-order mullion. The other side is more problematic. A strong mullion met the vertical mullion at an acute angle. The presence of a cusp and glazing groove indicates that there was an oculus here, perhaps three-sided. The lower edge of the oculus would have been closed by another element, perhaps another archlet. Because no trace of this survives the area has been left blank (Fig 75). The divergence of the vertical and sloping mullions suggests that there was a glazed dagger between them (not illustrated). The technical details are similar to those of <A17> and <A19>–<A21>. The one surviving bed has an axial scribe line.

Stylistic features as well as the building stone and the dressing techniques are indistinguishable from <A17> and <A19>–<A21>. Only greater moulding width distinguishes this group (the difference is too marked and consistent to be put down to error in workmanship). The size was more suitable for very large windows. As the <A13>–<A21> windows were four lights wide, these windows were presumably larger. The rarity of these mouldings implies that the large windows were few. The context of mullion <A23> suggests that these windows lit the clerestory of the presbytery. They formed part of an extensive structural phase with <A13>–<A21> and <A23>. A typestone from this group (<A24>, not illustrated) retains an internal axial termination painted red, and it is probable that all axial terminations were picked out in red. Like <A13>–<A21>, the moulding parallels that of the Norwich Cathedral presbytery clerestory (*c* 1362) (Harvey 1978, fig 21).

<A27>–<A32> Large window jamb and sill (Fig 75)
<A27>, <3746>, [13032]; Grainger and Phillpotts 2010, period C1, B28
<A28>, <356>, [691]; Grainger and Phillpotts 2010, period C1, B28
<A29>, <2454>, [5419]; Grainger and Phillpotts 2010, period C2, B39
<A30>, <2455>, [5419]; Grainger and Phillpotts 2010, period C2, B39
<A31>, <2864>, [+]
<A32>, <2876>, [+]
Fragment <A28> was reused in Building 28, and <A27>, <A29> and <A30> in the area of the demolished church. Although <A28> was fresh, the painted casement framing it (<A29>) had a slightly weathered moulding. Fragment <A27> was exceptionally fresh and retained a single coat of white paint. The complete moulding of a glazed window and its casements is represented. The moulding employed an ogee hollow casement in the jambs (turned through 90°) and again at the junctions between the casements and the wall face. This use of common moulding profiles allowed the stones to be related. The surviving perpends demonstrated how the elements fitted together. The line of the glazing was a favoured position for the joint between the external and internal casement elements. However, to provide additional strength the joint line was sometimes at 90° to the wall line. Fig 75 is a composite reconstruction. One casement was deeper than the other and may have been external. The wall was *c* 0.833m thick and enough survives of the sill for the profile to be determined. The rough perpends indicate that the wall had a mortar core and was faced with random rubble.

The moulding is larger than on <A13>–<A26>. The glazing reveal and group are identical; the hollow chamfers are only slightly longer but the axial terminations are deeper and heavier. The surviving jamb implies that they were *c* 0.047m wider than those of <A22>–<A26>. The clawtooling demonstrates that this group is contemporary with the phase of construction represented by <A13>–<A26>. The enlarged moulding indicates a larger window. Because the smallest version of this moulding (<A13>–<A21>) was associated with a window four lights wide, the implication is that this window was larger still. The <A22>–<A26> window almost certainly was part of the presbytery, so this window probably also lit the presbytery. The parallels for <A13>–<A21> indicate a date in the second half of the 14th century, and the window here is similar to window fragments excavated at St Mary Spital, possibly from the south wall of the Lady chapel and again dated to after 1350 (Samuel in prep). Masons of the St Mary Graces lodge are likely to have carried out the renewal of windows at Holy Trinity Priory, Aldgate, because <A27> and <A32> are exactly paralleled in form and dimensions at Holy Trinity Priory (Schofield and Lea 2005, 214, fig 193, <A35> and <A36>).

<A33> Cloister tracery paired cinquefoils (Fig 66)
<3152>, [13028]; Grainger and Phillpotts 2010, period C2, B38
The battered fragment <A33> was reused in the church area. The surviving facing is fresh and unweathered. The fragment incorporates part of an archlet. The reconstructed moulding is characteristic of a window but has no glazing groove. The position of the foils and the sharp curvature of the archlet suggest that the archlet was cinquefoil, but the width of the light is unknown. The stumps of a second archlet survive. The remnants fitted the radius already determined for the better-preserved side. The element was symmetrical with an open light above. The apices of the archlets presumably supported supermullions (not shown in Fig 66). The absence of glazing indicates that this element may have derived from the tracery of a cloister. The moulding is closely related to that of <A27>–<A32> (above). The masons who built the large tracery windows of the church (<A13>–<A32>) probably also built a cloister, whereby they had simply to omit the glazing groove from the <A27>–<A32> group moulding template. The paired cinquefoils suggest the possible architectural context (not illustrated) of this group. The minor-order mullion below <A33> may have divided a larger light flanked by strong mullions. In that case, the light above <A33> was an eyelet below the apex of the arch. These lights were wider than those of <A13>–<A21>. The cloister apparently represented by this group may be the earlier (B3) of the two cloisters (but see Chapter 3.3). The moulding also shares the same parallels as <A27>–<A32>.

<A34>–<A35> Quatrefoil screen (Fig 76)
<A34>, <2882 >, [+]
<A35>, <3723 >, [13199]; Grainger and Phillpotts 2010, period C1, OA14
Fragment <A34> was found near the church and <A35> was

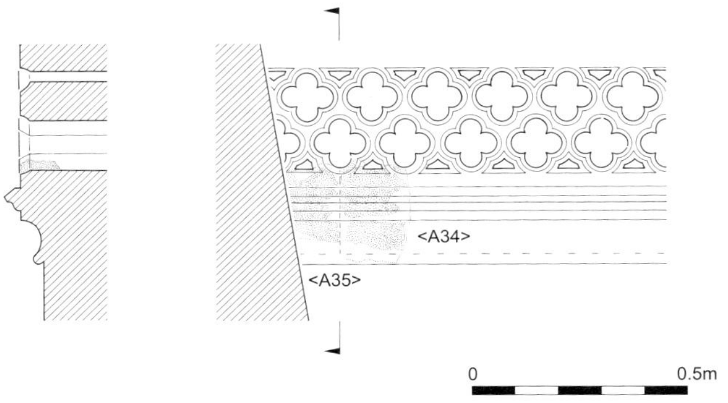

Fig 76 Reconstruction of the quatrefoil screen, possibly from the nave, based on architectural fragments <A34> and <A35> (scale 1:20)

reused in the church area. Both were broken up for reuse. The surviving surfaces are very fresh, implying an internal context. Despite their fragmentary condition, the stones retain the broken stumps of integral 'openwork' and a drip-mould, and below it a hollow casement. The moulding was developed for such positions as roof eaves. Similar mouldings from the 15th-century Leadenhall garner (Samuel 1989) indicate that a horizontal roll to form a cornice completed the moulding. Here it was being used in a miniaturised, purely decorative context. The two stones form part of the repeated standard elements that formed the lower border of a decorative quatrefoil screen, two tiers of holes high. Knowing this, it is possible to reconstruct the geometry of the quatrefoils from the surviving evidence. The visible surfaces were coarsely combed; the beds were clawtooled and then combed.

The quatrefoil screen resembles the balustrade below the east window of Exeter Cathedral by Robert Lesyngham in 1390 (Harvey 1978, 112). The pattern was widespread and had a long history. It is possible that the St Mary Graces fragments derive from a similar context. The opening allowed the viewer to see the east window's sill through it.

<A36>–<A42> Nave arcade (Fig 63; Fig 77)
<A36>, <67>, [1561]; Grainger and Phillpotts 2010, period C2, B45
<A37>, <302>, [691]; Grainger and Phillpotts 2010, period C1, B28
<A38>, <325>, [691]; Grainger and Phillpotts 2010, period C1, B28
<A39>, <352>, [691]; Grainger and Phillpotts 2010, period C1, B28
<A40>, <3222>, [+]
<A41>, <4142>, [13199]; Grainger and Phillpotts 2010, period C1, OA14
<A42>, <4144>, [13199]; Grainger and Phillpotts 2010, period C1, OA14
A pier drum <A36> was recut for reuse in an 18th-century wall and <A37> comes from Building 28. The complete pier base element <A41> was used as part of the blocking of the south door of the porch (B8) and formed part of a free-standing pier base. The surviving perpends show that four such elements supported a pier with four engaged shafts. The sub-plinth is missing but the height can be estimated. The setting-out lines on the top and bottom beds allowed the stone to be orientated as these lines correspond to the axes of symmetry. Although there was much abrasion of the upper bed, enough survived to show that it supported a shaft with the <A36> and <A37> moulding. The shafts were separated by hollow chamfers of quadrant section. The lower part of the pier is cut to form a continuous hollow chamfer over the sub-plinth. The block also incorporates the base moulding of the engaged shafts. Pier drum <A36> survives to its full height and was sheared off the body of the pier moulding. The lower bed may have rested on the pier base, but the upper bed was stepped diagonally to the pier's axis of symmetry. Fragment <A37> incorporates enough of the pier moulding to prove the association with the base element <A41>. It too has a large diagonal step in its surviving bed. The stepped beds may have enhanced the pier's strength by providing keying. A friable variety of Reigate stone was used. On the shafts the combed finish was quite rough, and was probably intended to key a thick coat of whitewash. The beds were covered in regular rows of clawtooling marks; on the underside of <A41> these were subsequently removed by combing.

Capital fragments <A38> and <A39> were found in Building 28, <A40> probably in or near the church, and <A42> in the blocking of the Building 8 door (not illustrated, but see Fig 63). The surviving parts of the pier capital, though fragmentary,

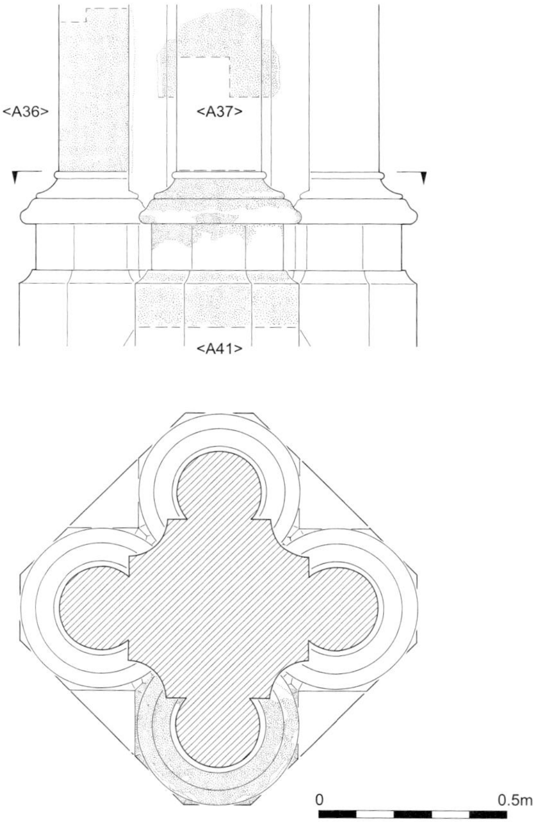

Fig 77 Reconstructed pier base and shaft <A36>, <A37> and <A41> from the nave arcade (scale 1:20)

have a very fresh appearance. The moulding of the pier shaft <A42> was engraved in the upper surface alongside an engraving in the moulding of the arch that rested on the capital. This allowed <A42> to be orientated to the pier base. The base showed that there were four capitals. The plan of the pier base supplied the overall dimensional framework to reconstruct the plan of the capital impost. The arch minor form survived in part on <A42>, while the complete form was preserved by <A39> and <A38>; these shared the moulding scribed on to the capital. The same arcade arch moulding turned through 90° indicates the position of the arcade arch major order (Fig 77). The engraved schema provides additional important clues about the relation of the pier and the arch mouldings. The arch centre was approximately determined from a voussoir <A38> with a large radius (2.216m). The complete moulding survived on <A39> and accorded with the moulding scribed on the impost of <A42>. Another capital fragment <A40> (not illustrated) provides evidence that the lower part or bell of the capital was cylindrical rather than polygonal. Fragment <A41> is closely paralleled by a pier base fragment found at St Mary Spital (Samuel in prep).

The pier, capital and arch form an arcade almost certainly from the nave, and it is possible to relate the arcade to *in situ* foundations (Chapter 2.4). The bay interval can be determined to within a few centimetres. The foundations suggest that the bay interval was *c* 5.05m wide, or one perch (16.5ft), a widely employed unit of measurement in English medieval architecture as is illustrated by the recent reconstruction of the Guildhall chapel (Samuel 2007, 373). The reconstructed elevation (Fig 63) shows the possible appearance of one of the nave arches based upon this bay interval and employing the radius of <A38> (*c* 2.216m) which is compatible with this spacing (the depicted arches have this radius). The missing sub-plinths are based on parallels. The heights of the piers are unknown.

<A43> Window mullion from precinct building (Fig 78)
MIN84 <75>, [+]
The internal moulding <A43> is well preserved but covered by many coats of whitewash. Weathering destroyed the external elevation during the life of the building of which the stone formed a part. The building in question may be one of those that are known to have survived the Dissolution (Fig 64). This window mullion survives to full height, and one of the beds has a groove for a saddlebar passing through the mullion. It is probable that the external moulding was the same. The height of the mullion corresponds to the spacing between saddlebars. The visible surfaces and the beds were finely combed; the beds were then keyed for the mortar with a broad-bladed chisel. At the same time, a simple cross was inscribed on the bed. Such marks are very common and probably indicate the completion of a piece.

The presence of an axial roll flanked by widely separated beads suggests that this was a strong mullion of a complex traceried window. The minor form can be predicted (the axis of symmetry would correspond to the median line of the flanking beads).

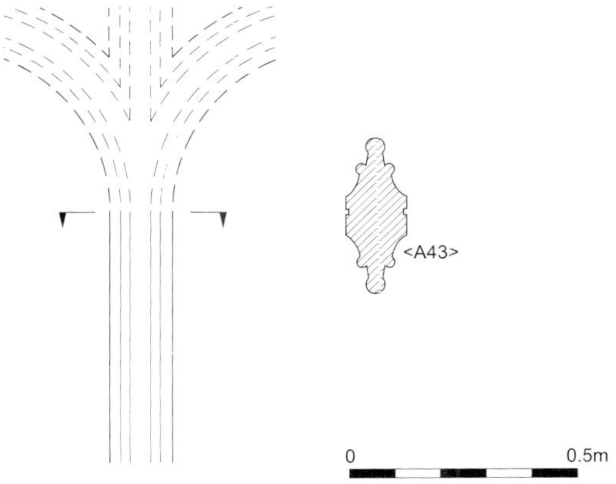

Fig 78 Window mullion <A43>, possibly from the refectory (B13) or infirmary (B15) (scale 1:20)

<A44>–<A45> Pinnacles from ?tomb (Fig 79)
<A44>, MIN84 <3>, [+]
<A45>, <1722>, [2950]; Grainger and Phillpotts 2010, period C1, B28
Fragment <A44> was found during the 1984 trial trenching and <A45> in layers below Building 28. Both fragments, though battered, represent *c* 75% of the complete element; both are unweathered (implying an internal context) but bear no paint. The two elements are decorative pinnacles of virtually identical pattern. Although <A44> is the better-preserved of the two, <A45> (not illustrated) features technical differences worthy of description. The surviving joint bed on <A44> indicates that the

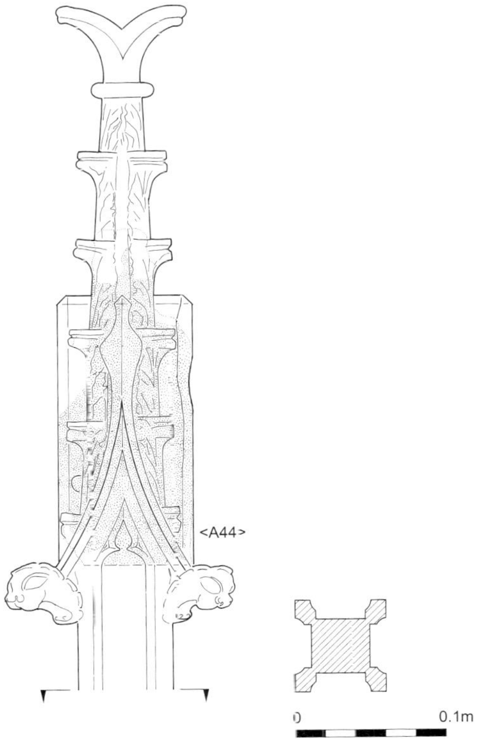

Fig 79 Pinnacle fragment <A44> from a tomb canopy or chantry chapel, c *1390 (scale 1:5)*

pinnacle fitted on a thin shaft of unknown height. The point of contact was very slight. A bullet-shaped hole (not shown) was therefore drilled in the bed and presumably in the shaft below it. Four pointed grooves were then carved in both beds, radiating from the central hole. A hole was then drilled in one of the corners of the pinnacle to reach the central hole. An iron bar was probably placed in the hole to unite the two elements and molten lead then poured into this hole. The grooves in the beds would also fill with metal, making it impossible to rotate the pinnacle. Such metal fixings would have been extracted at the time of demolition. Pinnacle <A45> omitted various details present on <A44>. The original intention was to carve all four faces with the same detail, and the necessary guide lines were scored on the bed; however, two sides were left blank. This pinnacle also lacked the radiating channels for the poured metal present on <A44>. The two pinnacles were one mason's handiwork, identical in every respect, and perhaps indicating the use of a special set of templates. It is possible that the blank faces were in a corner where the client would not see them. The Reigate stone used was fine-grained and of intermediate hardness, and a special variety was probably selected for such minutely modelled work.

These pinnacles derive from the interior of the church, and may have formed part of a reredos, screen or sedilia, for a tomb, chantry chapel or other monumental feature. Broadly similar pinnacles decorate the choir stalls in Chester Cathedral, built *c* 1390 by Hugh Herland (Harvey 1978, 104). The point of the pinnacle and the small animal heads in the reconstruction are based on that parallel. The form of the pinnacles is a widespread one; other examples survive at Westminster Abbey (R Lea, pers comm). A photograph of <A44> has previously been published (Mills 1985, 74).

<A46>–<A47> Cloister mullion (Fig 66)
<A46>, <363>, [691]; Grainger and Phillpotts 2010, period C1, B28
<A47>, <374>, [691]; Grainger and Phillpotts 2010, period C1, B28
Six stones (including duplicates) from this group were reused in Building 28. Weathering was slight or absent, and one of the stones retained traces of paint. The window moulding lacks a glazing groove. At least two mullions seem to be represented. Fragment <A47> was the top of a mullion and incorporated ornamental capitals on both elevations (one of which survives). A continuous saddlebar at the springing line reinforced the tracery but the lights were otherwise apparently unobstructed. Moulding outlines scribed on the capitals indicate that the same moulding was used for the mullion and tracery. The absence of glazing indicates use in a cloister. A coarse Reigate stone was used. The visible surfaces of the mouldings are combed and the beds are finished with a clawtool.

<A48>–<A49> ? Mullion capital and base moulding (Fig 80)
<A48>, <3426>, [13343]; Grainger and Phillpotts 2010, period C2, B38
<A49>, <3644>, [+]
Fragment <A48> was found in the area of the demolished church. Though fragmentary, both stones have a fresh appearance, and <A48> retains faint traces of red paint. Stone <A48> is a fragment of a ?mullion capital that was similar although not identical to the capital incorporated in mullion <A46>–<A47> (above). The form of the capital could be reconstructed thanks to the medieval technique of engraving moulding profiles and the axis of symmetry on the impost; however, full reconstruction was only achievable by comparison with surviving parallels, such as those within the porch of the London Guildhall. The typical three-unit capital had a polygonal abacus and a round bell (Fig 80). The engraved profile shows that the colonette shaft is of three-quarters round section. The round base moulding is essentially complete and has a typical double-ogival profile. Although the two surviving elements share the same moulding, they had different architectural contexts. The base moulding was engaged to a flat surface, but immediately below it the polygonal base is askew (Fig 80). This suggests that it comes from the base of a moulded window casement, possibly a sloping sill, and although it may derive from the cloister it seems a little large for this (G Coppack, pers comm). Comparison with contemporary tracery in the presbytery of St Mary Spital allows the architectural context to be better understood (Samuel in prep). The capital and base probably adorned a shaft in the casemented embrasure of a large window.

There is a strong stylistic link with the nave arcade <A36>–<A42> (above), of which <A48>–<A49> is essentially a scaled-down version, and it is possible that they derive from the same building campaign. Similar bases survive in the presbytery clerestory of Norwich Cathedral (*c* 1362) (Harvey 1978, 254), and parallels for the capital are widespread.

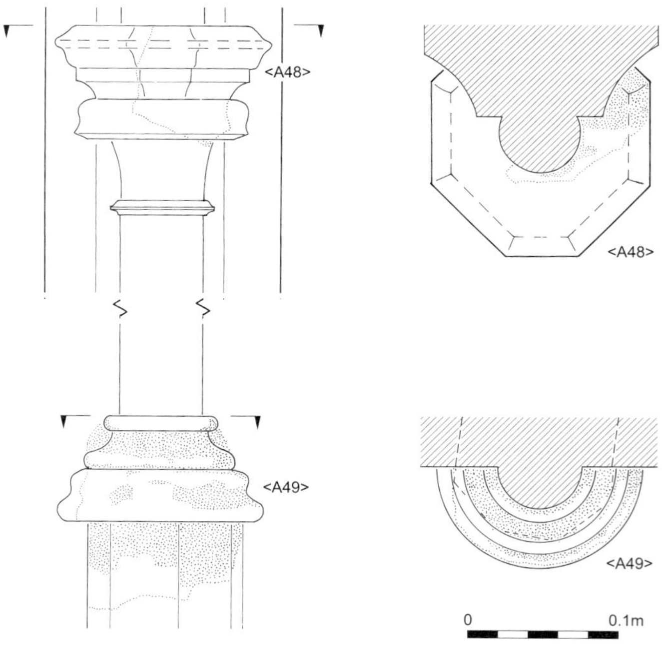

Fig 80 ? Mullion capital and base moulding <A48>–<A49> (scale 1:10)

<A50>–<A51> Two-light shuttered window (Fig 81)
<A50>, <1677>, [4017]; Grainger and Phillpotts 2010, period C1, B28
<A51>, <1698>, [4017]; Grainger and Phillpotts 2010, period C1, B28
Both fragments were reused in Building 28. They were fragmentary but unweathered, and there was no trace of paint. Fragment <A51> formed part of a window archlet. The surviving jamb allowed the fragment to be orientated, while the preservation of the original compass-drawn setting-out lines permitted the centre of the archlet to be precisely determined. This in turn allows the median line of the light to be predicted reasonably accurately. A less literal but more probable reconstruction (not illustrated) would have the spandrels closed by the horizontal upper margin of the window casement (R Lea, pers comm). The mullion fragment <A50> indicates a window at least two lights wide. The surrounding wall was probably constructed of random rubble with a mortar core. Timber shutters, when closed, would have been firmly held in square rebates and were hinged at the jambs; when open they would have lain against the splayed reveal of the window embrasures. Saddlebars on the exterior secured the glazing.

The presence of shutters and the absence of tracery lights and casements suggest that this window was domestic, perhaps no more than two lights wide, and lit one of the conventual buildings. The moulding bears no relationship to any of those associated with the church. No documented parallels are known, but the form is broadly similar to windows in the possible vestry at St Bride's, Fleet Street (Samuel 1997).

<A52>–<A54> Vault rib junction with foliate decoration (Fig 82)
<A52>, <1799>, [+]
<A53>, <197>, [2553]; Grainger and Phillpotts 2010, period C3
<A54>, <198>, [2553]; Grainger and Phillpotts 2010, period C3
Fragments <A53> and <A54> are two halves of the same well-preserved vault rib, and were found in a post-victualling yard, very late 18th-century context. The element <A52> incorporates the apex between two wall ribs and a ridge rib, the latter being at a higher level. The junction is concealed by carved vine leaves. The two half-ribs and the ridge rib incorporate rebates for supporting the vault webs. Fragments <A53>–<A54> (not illustrated) are a continuation of the ridge rib moulding. The joint surfaces of the vault ribs were cut with a clawtool but the reverse is scappled. The bed for the ridge rib is deeply scored with a large point to provide additional keying for the mortar. The visible surfaces are finely combed. A Reigate stone of intermediate hardness was used.

This is the only extant vault element from the site. Its architectural provenance is unknown. The moulding shows affinities with groups <A13>–<A21>, <A22>–<A26> and <A27>–<A32>.

<A55> Fan vault tomb canopy (Fig 83)
<2978>, [16010]; Grainger and Phillpotts 2010, period C2, B33
This fragment was part of a much larger element that had been broken up. White paint and gold leaf survived (below). It is a 'toy' fan vault, in which the ribs and webbing are all carved from a single block. The ribs have narrow but flat fillets flanked by hollow chamfers. The fragment can be orientated and the architectural context reconstructed. The surviving perpend butted against a wall face, or was slightly inset in it. The element carried two wall ribs and nine tierceron ribs; they and the webs were painted white, but the fillets (including part of the hollow chamfers) were decorated with strips of gold leaf. The space enclosed was no more than *c* 0.52m wide. The canopy of a free-standing tomb within the church is represented, and this imposes orders of size on any putative reconstruction. Fig 83 is based on the assumption that the tomb chest was rectangular. The element may have been arranged to form three square bays (of which one and a half are illustrated) *c* 1.9m long and *c* 0.63m wide. No evidence survives for the flat areas between the fans (these are left blank in the reconstruction) but they may have been the sites of pendants. A high-quality Reigate stone facies was selected for a very high finish. High tolerances were demanded for such prestigious tombs and monuments. The level of specialised craftsmanship is indicated by documentary evidence for the construction of one tomb in the church by Henry Lakenham (Blair 1980, 66).

This tomb may have stood on a brick vault ([16011]) against the north wall of the presbytery, possibly that of Sir Lewis John and his wife constructed in the 1420s or 1430s (Fig 32; Chapter 3.8). The fragment was found above the tomb, but in a much later 18th-century context. The element formed part of a decorative canopy distinct from the vault below. Such a canopy would have covered reclining effigies of the two people buried in the vault. Fan vaults like this have a wide date range (*c* 1350–*c* 1550). The use of a 'toy' vault suggests that this is not the tomb referred to in the contract of 1376 (Blair 1980, 66).

<A56>–<A58> Partial reconstruction of free-standing tomb monument (Fig 30)
<A56>, <3172>, [12482]; period B4, B4
<A57>, <3173>, [12482]; period B4, B4
<A58>, <3496>, [13314]; Grainger and Phillpotts 2010, period C1, OA14
Fragments <A56> and <A57> were found in the rubble backfill of robbed grave [12477] along with many other tiny fragments, and <A58> was found in the rubble of the demolished church. The small 'toy' fan vault fragment <A57> incorporates parts of four ribs and is similar to <A55> (above), while <A56> incorporates the inner and outer mouldings of an arch. A fan vault was immediately behind the arch and shared its geometry. On the exterior there is a trace of a field above the arch. A foliate vault boss shielded the junction between the wall ribs and a ridge rib (not illustrated). The tomb canopy was divided into a series of pointed openings, and it is possible to estimate the profile of the fan vault at the springing line by comparison with the other canopy fragments (<A55>, above). The present fragments derive from the corner of a tomb chest or some other internal furnishing of the church. A small fragment of panel tracery with part of a cinquefoil cannot be located with

Fig 81 Domestic window fragment <A50>–<A51> with (facing page) internal shuttering (scale 1:10)

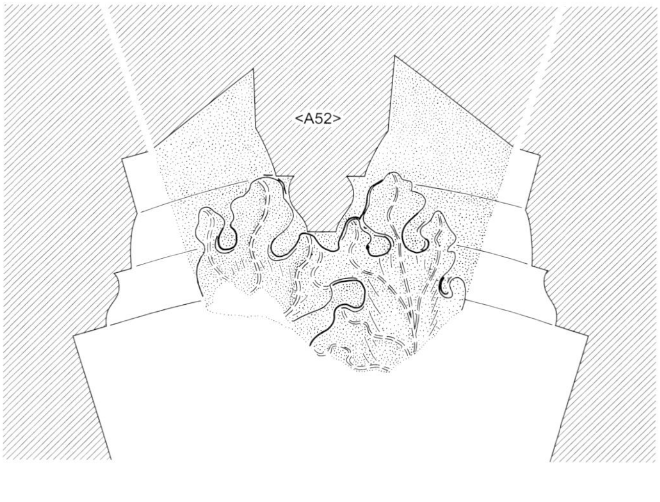

Fig 82 Vault junction with foliate decoration <A52> (scale 1:5)

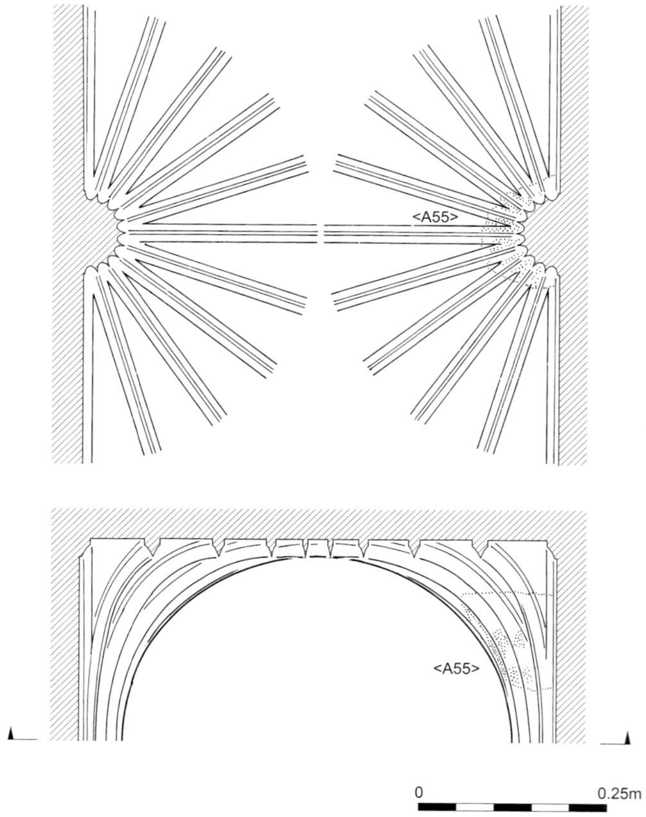

Fig 83 'Toy' fan vault <A55> from a tomb (scale 1:10)

certainty. Traces of paint on <A58> show that this tomb structure featured bright polychromy.

The free-standing tomb was lavishly ornamented, but can only be broadly dated (*c* 1350–1539). (Empty grave [12477], located in the central presbytery area, is assigned to period B3, but this tomb may have covered another burial: Chapter 2.5; Fig 29.)

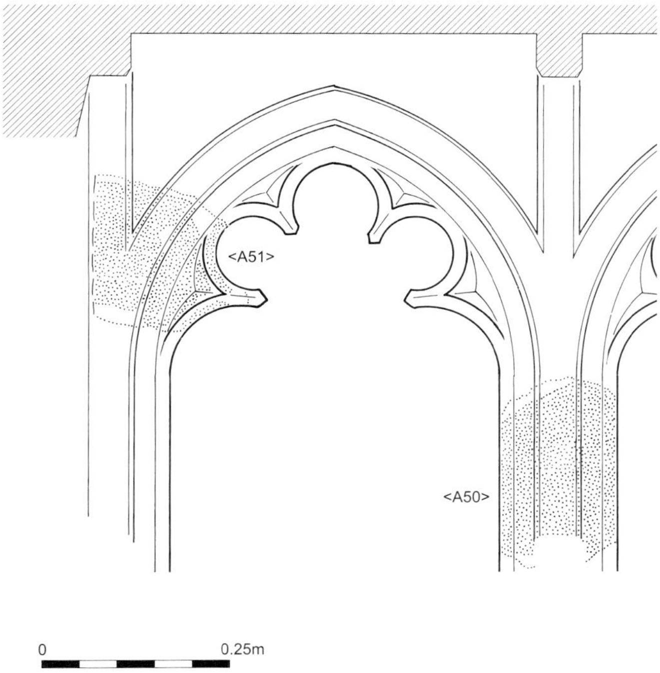

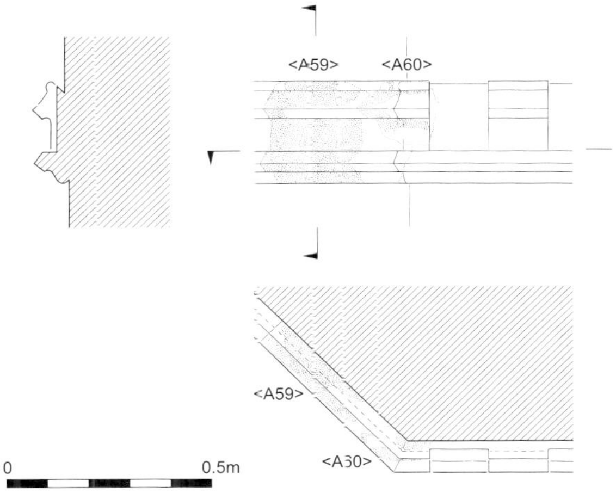

Fig 84 Ornamental cresting <A59>–<A60> from a tomb (scale 1:20)

<A59>–<A60> Ornamental cresting from tomb (Fig 84)
<A59>, <3726>, [16028]; Grainger and Phillpotts 2010, period C1, OA14
<A60>, <3451>, [13299]; Grainger and Phillpotts 2010, period C1, OA14
Fragment <A59> was found among the pieces blocking the southern door of the porch (B8) after the demolition, and was substantially complete; <A60> was found within the area of the church. The two are composites of two different mouldings used here in a purely decorative manner to form a cresting or coping. In fragment <A59> the coping was continuous, but in <A60> it was interrupted, probably by crenellations to form brattishing (ie decorative work along the coping, cornice, screen, etc of a building, generally of openwork). Fragment <A60> may represent the junction between runs of plain and crenellated brattishing. In plan, the two runs meet at an angle of 135°. The surviving fragments show that this brattishing was extensively employed throughout the church. The roughly scappled back of <A59> shows that it was set in a thick wall with a mortar core. The careful clawtooling of the upper and lower margins (at the wall face) indicates that this wall was faced with a 'veneer' of ashlar. The finish and building stone are slightly inferior to corresponding work in the individual tombs.

The fragments probably formed parts of a screen resembling the one separating the chapel of St Nicholas from the presbytery in Westminster Abbey; the cresting is strikingly similar. Extant wall-painting fragments from St Stephen's Chapel, Westminster (British Museum), show that a similar moulding was employed as a form of dado.

<A61>–<A70> Flamboyant open tracery framed by panel tracery (Fig 61; Fig 85)
<A61>, MIN84 <68>, [+]
<A62>, <9>, [+]
<A63>, <312>, [+]
<A64>, <348>, [691]; Grainger and Phillpotts 2010, period C1, B28
<A65>, <467>, [947]; Grainger and Phillpotts 2010, period C1, B28
<A66>, <469>, [947]; Grainger and Phillpotts 2010, period C1, B28
<A67>, <554>, [+]
<A68>, <1662>, [4017]; Grainger and Phillpotts 2010, period C1, B28
<A69>, <1679>, [4017]; Grainger and Phillpotts 2010, period C1, B28
<A70>, <4080>, [+]
These fragments derived from a window. Stone <A61> was uncovered during the 1984 trial trenching, while the fragmentary <A65> and <A66> were reused as part of the foundations of Building 28. Fragment <A70> (Fig 85) formed the junction of the window arch with the window jamb. The arch and the cusped archlet did not share the same springing line. A small eyelet between the greater and lesser arches flouted the geometrical laws of the window; it was cut into the volume that should have been occupied by the minor arch. The missing

side of the eyelet was restored with an inverted dagger over the archlet. The overall reconstruction is, however, very uncertain and the elevation shown is minimal. Three fragmentary minor-form typestones of this group (<A62>, <A64>, <A69>; not illustrated) are incompatible with the reconstruction. Differential weathering indicated that the casement was external. The casement seems to have been small and tightly curved, perhaps round, but no direct evidence survives except at the point where it met the tracery. Internally, there was no casement; instead, the window moulding edged a complex pattern of panel tracery that shared the plane of the glazing in the window. Part of a cusped panel survived. The other side was closed off by an apparently straight moulding, which ran into the arch moulding at an acute angle. It is not certain whether this was a major or minor form (the reconstruction shows the former option). This panel tracery was probably confined to the spandrel of the window.

Stone <A61> (Fig 85) is of considerable complexity. This fragment revealed the window to be of 'subarcuated intersecting' form, but much experimentation was required to show the probable relation of the two tracery fragments. The key to relating them was the common window arch. The light width can be determined because <A61> incorporates one of the apices of the sub-arcuations. The curvature of the window arch suggests that it was three lights wide. Fragment <A66> (not illustrated) mirrors <A61> and may come from the opposite side of the same window. The lights were probably 2ft wide. Fragment <A61> also preserved part of a falchion light. The width of the main light shows that there were as many as eight small cusps in its archlet. No mullions survived apart from the small fragment <A67> (not illustrated). Fragmentary minor forms, one of which is illustrated (<A65>, Fig 85), hint at the complexity of the unknown central area of tracery, which may have differed significantly from the one depicted in the reconstruction. The Reigate stone used was distinct but tooling did not differ from the norm. The window was surrounded by closely jointed freestone dressings on all sides.

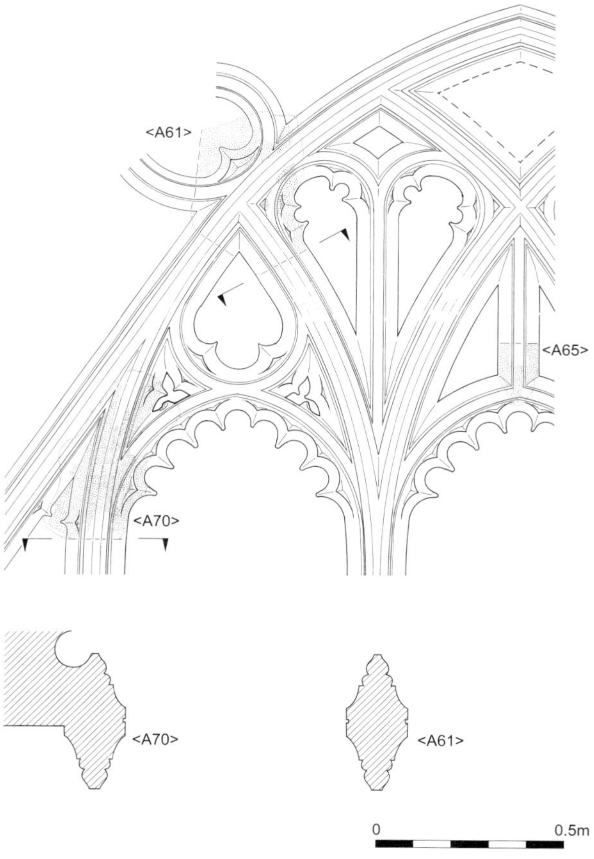

Fig 85 Reconstructed Decorated-style window tracery <A61>, <A65> and <A70>, possibly from the chapel of Holy Trinity or the presbytery (scale 1:20)

Fragment <A68> (not illustrated) was found in the rubble foundation of Building 28 and certainly derives from the same window. It is relatively complete (comprising *c* 50% of the original element), though <A63> (below) is fragmentary. The mullion/casement is the same but the presence of panel tracery suggests that they come from below the lost sill of the window. The back of the stone is carefully shaped, suggesting that it was set in an ashlar wall. The surviving jamb <A63> (not illustrated) indicates that the panel was significantly taller than it was high. Restoring the full form of the trefoiliated archlet was straightforward enough. The presence of the casement moulding demonstrates that it was part of panel tracery below the window lights. The mullions continued downwards to subdivide the panels with two trefoils between each mullion division, with a minor-order mullion to divide the two. The division between the strong mullions (?2ft) was unchanged. Small patches of white paint survived on the blind or panel tracery. Moulding surfaces were combed to a very smooth finish. The beds between mouldings show the parallel marks of the clawtool, diagonal to the mouldings' axis of symmetry. There were eight teeth to each 5cm of the clawtool blade. A crude cross was scribed on one of the beds (<A61>); this was probably a completion mark, as these are invariably present on tracery fragments on joints. The other surfaces of the stones were more roughly cut with a clawtool. All vertical relationships in the reconstruction are conjectural but the plan is secure. The sill probably coincided at the tips of the axial terminations of the mullions; there are stylistic precedents for this (see below). The lower border of the panel tracery presumably met another weathering of unknown form which is assumed to have extended to the external wall face, so that water dripping from the window sill would be thrown clear of the wall. The presence of small cusps in the spandrels of the archlets is evidence of a further subdivision in the upper tier of panels, but no attempt has been made to depict this. It is probable that a hood-mould covered the window (not illustrated).

The possible three-light window was the most elaborate in St Mary Graces (Fig 61). The surround of panel tracery shows that the entire fabric of the structure was built to the highest standards. All the stonework was painted; although only white paint was noted, other colours may also have been used. The panel tracery surrounding the internal elevation of the window suggests that it may have fitted inside a gable wall (R Lea, pers comm). The idiosyncratic moulding and tracery are quite distinct in terms of size and elaboration. It is loosely similar to Decorated style windows at Frampton, Lincolnshire (Fletcher 1943, 454, T), but no surviving parallel is known. The window may therefore be from the presbytery or the chapel of Holy Trinity, perhaps the east/gable end. It is possible that the casement was divided by sub-mouldings as at Frampton, in which case a much thicker wall could be employed. A similar moulding occurs in the windows of Henry VII's chapel in Westminster Abbey (R Lea, pers comm), but the tracery's use of subarcuated intersections appears too early for the 1490s.

Paviors and tomb slabs

The excavation (MIN86) produced 35 stone paviors (paving slabs) or tomb slabs, all incomplete or consisting of fragments (<A71>–<A82>, Table 15), together with three slabs left *in situ* on site (Fig 15; Fig 19). Some were obviously tomb slabs as they incorporated features such as indents and grooves for brasses, while others were just paviors. Demolition material in the church area included two Purbeck marble tomb slabs, one with grooves for shroud brasses of the type popular in the later 15th century (MIN84 [+] <87>; Fig 48) and the other with a hole drilled through it. Many of the fragments were reused in later features. Doorway thresholds [13096], [4718] and [164] incorporated Purbeck marble tomb slabs with indents for brasses (eg Fig 19). In the victualling yard two Purbeck marble paviors with rivet plugs, similar to <A72> (Fig 86), were found capping well [10041], while the base of a sump and the roof of one of the drains incorporated many large fragments of Purbeck marble, Purbeck limestone, and a grey and white marble with purple veining (period C1: Grainger and Phillpotts 2010).

Table 15 Paviors and tomb slabs <A71>–<A82>

Cat no.	Acc no.	Context	Description and size
<A71>	<3075>	[16011]	limestone pavior, 550 x 310 x 85mm
<A72>	<3452>	[13299]	Purbeck marble pavior/tomb slab, 1.50+m x ? x 1.10m (Fig 86)
<A73>	<3642>	[13474]	Purbeck marble ?pavior/tomb slab, 174 x 71 x 28mm; demolition pit
<A74>	<2887>	[12383]	Purbeck marble tomb slab with indents for brasses, 400+ x 380+ x 100mm
<A75>	<3519>	[12383]	Purbeck marble ?pavior/tomb slab, 380+ x 225+ x 110mm
<A76>	<4160>	[1331]	Purbeck marble pavior, 630 x 320 x 55mm
<A77>	-	[767]	Purbeck marble pavior, 211 x 205 x 50mm
<A78>	<124>	[767]	grey and white marble with purple veining; the rebate suggests that it is part of the side of a sarcophagus
<A79>	<3077>	[12456]	Purbeck marble pavior, 530 x 290 x 50–80mm
<A80>	<503>–<511> <513>–<524> <526>–<528>	[77]	8 fragments of Purbeck marble, 15 fragments of Purbeck limestone, fragment of shelly oolitic limestone
<A81>	<3081>	[+]	Purbeck marble pavior, 705 x 400 x 60mm
<A82>	<3183>	[+]	Purbeck marble pavior, 50mm thick

Fig 86 Purbeck marble pavior with rivet plug holes <A72> (0.5m scale)

5.2 Ceramic building material

Decorated medieval floor tiles

Elizabeth Eames

Introduction

A total of 284 decorated medieval floor tiles and fragments were recovered, 24 in 1984 and the rest in 1986. Two large areas of pavement were found *in situ* in the kitchen (B11) and the house and chamber or abbot's hospice (B14) (Chapter 2.6). Both pavements were post-medieval in their existing form but included reused tiles from medieval floors. Other medieval tile floors survived in the presbytery (B4) and nave (B6) in small patches where some tiles were reset in a new position (Chapter 2.4 and 2.5). Several areas of paving were recorded *in situ* though with not all tiles in their original position. Many of the decorated tiles recovered were scattered finds. The areas south of the church yielded large numbers of such tiles. Many plain glazed tiles were also present. Most of these disturbed tiles were found in the demolition debris.

The majority were of the type manufactured at Penn in Buckinghamshire in the 14th century. This was one of the most successful commercial tileries known from the medieval period and is fortunately well documented. From the 1350s to the 1380s royal clerks of works were buying Penn tiles, and both orders and payments have survived in royal records. Penn tiles were distributed in Buckinghamshire and neighbouring counties, as well as throughout the middle Thames valley and Essex and the nearer parts of Kent.

Only seven decorated tiles from other industries were recovered. Three tiles were French imports (designs <T3> and <T4>), two were possibly made in Essex (designs <T1> and <T2>) and two belonged to the series known as 'Westminster' (designs <T5> and <T6>). In addition, a large number of tiles were too worn or fragmentary for any decoration to be certainly identified, although some were undoubtedly Penn fabric as were some of the plain glazed tiles.

It comes as no surprise that in the third quarter of the 14th century the church of St Mary Graces and other important monastic buildings were paved with Penn tiles. The Penn tilers had the monopoly of decorated tile production in the region at that time. Nor is it surprising that a little later the French tiles were being imported. It is, however, more difficult to see how the slip-painted and 'Westminster' examples came to be used on the site. It is possible that they were already old and were used as rubble when St Mary Graces was built. The destruction levels included so much heavily disturbed material that it is quite possible that these pieces had never been part of a pavement on this site.

Sixty-three tile designs are illustrated (Fig 12; Fig 13; Fig 87). Fifty-seven of these occur on Penn tiles and of these designs 52 have previously been published (either in Hohler

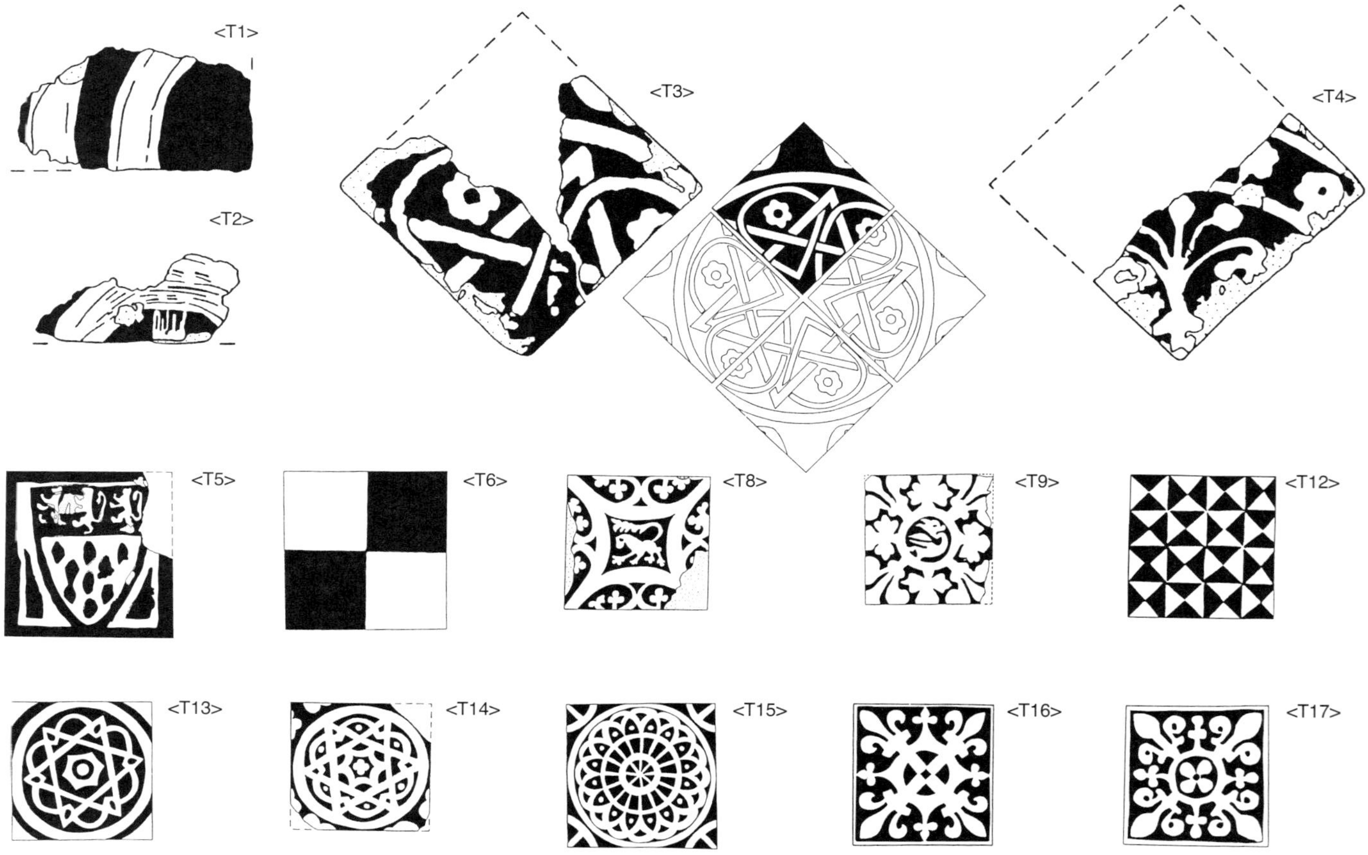

Fig 87 Ex situ *medieval decorated floor tile designs from St Mary Graces: Penn except for slip-painted <T1> and <T2>, French <T3> and <T4>, and 'Westminster' type <T5> and <T6> (scale 1:6 diagrammatic, 1:3 pictorial)*

<T18>
<T19>
<T21>
<T22>
<T23>
<T24>
<T25>
<T26>
<T27>
<T28>
<T30>
<T31>
<T32>
<T33>
<T34>
<T35>
<T36>
<T37>
<T38>
<T41>
<T42>
<T43>
<T44>
<T45>
<T46>
<T48>
<T49>
<T50>
<T51>
<T53>
<T54>
<T55>
<T56>
<T57>
<T58>
<T61>
<T62>
<T63>

Table 16 Concordance of decorated medieval floor tile designs from St Mary Graces

Cat no.	Acc no.	Context	Eames no. (W no.)	Hohler no.	Fig no.
Slip-painted/ stencilled					
<T1>	-	[13787]	-	-	87
<T2>	<3418>	[14122]	-	-	87
French series					
<T3>	<3784>	[14320]	-	-	87
<T4>	<2113>	[3756]	-	-	87
'Westminster' type					
<T5>	-	[+]	(W32)	-	87
<T6>	<3853>	[13546]	2015 (W46)	-	87
Penn designs					
<T7>	<2859>	[+]	1407	P2	13
<T8>	<601>	[1640]	1803	-	87
<T9>	<423>	[2652]	1952	P72A reverse	87
<T10>	<584>	[1640]	2025	-	13
<T11>	<3813>	[13559]	2028	-	12
<T12>	<1744>	[2950]	2037	-	87
<T13>	<3841>	[13448]	2070	P94	87
<T14>	<2061>	[2950]	2072	P93	87
<T15>	<1528>	[1908]	2074	P92	87
<T16>	<1750>	[2950]	2199	P71 no border	87
<T17>	<1729>	[2950]	2200	P69	87
<T18>	<3856>	[13526]	2340	P67	87
<T19>	<1295>	[1640]	2220	P51	87
<T20>	<2174>	[6071]	2221	P51≠	12
<T21>	<617(b)>	[1640]	2225	P48	87
<T22>	<2682>	[9577]	2226	P50	87
<T23>	<670>	[964]	2230	P52	87
<T24>	<2468>	[7498]	2231	P54	87
<T25>	-	[+]	2232	P44	87
<T26>	<3761>	[12402]	-	P55	87
<T27>	<3257>	[13172]	-	-	87
<T28>	<1468>	[1908]	2353	P58	87
<T29>	<612>	[1640]	2326	-	13
<T30>	<2705>	[9592]	2355	-	87
<T31>	<3794>	[14320]	2377	P101	87
<T32>	-	[14383]	-	-	87
<T33>	<3666>	[13377]	2394	-	87
<T34>	<3827>	[13405]	2390	P63	87
<T35>	<2721>	[9799]	2395	P62	87
<T36>	<1736>	[2950]	2396	P76	87
<T37>	<421>	[2587]	2409	P66	87
<T38>	<3473>	[13299]	2426	P86≠	87
<T39>	<3479>	[13299]	-	P86	12
<T40>	<4100>	[13405]	2460	P107	12
<T41>	<3253>	[16051]	2535	P88	87
<T42>	<2062>	[2950]	2553	P82	87
<T43>	<593>	[1640]	-	P81	87
<T44>	<588>	[1640]	-	P81≠	87
<T45>	<1437>	[1908]	2560	-	87
<T46>	<2127>	[3577]	1925	P125	87
<T47>	-	[13275]	-	P124	12
<T48>	<3066>	[14169]	-	-	87
<T49>	<3358>	[13299]	2834≠	P131	87
<T50>	<672>	[964]	2837	-	87
<T51>	<1432>	[1908]	-	-	87
<T52>	<20>	[86]	2819≠	P139≠	12
<T53>	<3579>	[13395]	2840	P144	87
<T54>	<1732>	[2950]	2842	P134	87
<T55>	<3758>	[15202]	1831	P110	87
<T56>	<1731>	[2950]	1833	P109	87
<T57>	-	[13253]	1837	P112	87
<T58>	<1738>	[2950]	1838	-	87
<T59>	<3476>	[13299]	1848	LB15	13
<T60>	<3463>	[13299]	1846≠	P153≠	12
<T61>	<1483>	[1908]	-	P155	87
<T62>	<1754>	[2950]	1827	P73	87
<T63>	-	[+]	-	-	87

Key:
Eames no. = Eames 1980; W no. = Betts 2002; Hohler no. = Hohler 1942
P = Hohler's Penn design series; LB = Hohler's Little Brickhill design series (St Mary Graces examples of LB15 are on tiles made of Penn fabric); ≠ = slight variation of the design as previously published

1942 or Eames 1980, a number of them being illustrated in both publications). Designs <T27>, <T32>, <T48>, <T51> and <T63> are not identical with any in either publication (Fig 87). Two different conventions are employed in the design illustrations. The British Museum designs (Eames 1980) are diagrammatic, most having been composed from the decoration on a number of different tiles, many of them fragmentary. The Museum of London house style is pictorial. Design <T60> is here published both in diagrammatic and pictorial form (Fig 12).

All the details of the decorated tile designs recovered are included in Table 16. Tiles on which the design could not be certainly identified have been omitted from this tabulation.

Slip-painted tile designs <T1> and <T2>

It is not known exactly how the white clay which formed the decoration of the Penn tiles was applied to the surface, but it is certain that it went into cavities pressed into the surface of the tile. The decoration of designs <T1> and <T2> (Fig 87) was applied in thick white slip to the surface of the tiles, probably through a stencil.

The British Museum's collections include five examples (Eames 1980, ii, 6–12), all from sites in Essex. Other examples have been found elsewhere in East Anglia, but this type of decoration is rare. Similar tiles were used in two London parish churches, St Matthew Friday Street and St Dionis Backchurch, and a further example has been found during excavations at Plantation House, Great Tower Street (FER97) (I Betts, pers comm; Betts 1994, 134–5). It is possible that the fragments found at St Mary Graces were made in Essex. A slip-decorated floor tile dating to the late 14th to mid 16th centuries has been found at the pottery and tile production site at Weald View, Noak Hill, Essex (Sabel 2002–3, 19–20, fig 11, no. 16).

This group may date from the late 13th to the early 14th centuries. One fragment was recovered from the nave south aisle (B6) and the other from the church cloister (B10). If these tiles were used for the first time at St Mary Graces, which was not founded until 1350, the slip-stencilled tiles may be a little later than had been thought.

French tile designs <T3> and <T4>

Three fragments of tiles of this type (Fig 87) were recovered, two from the church cloister (B10) and the third from the kitchen (B11). Norton (1993) has identified this group of tiles as having been manufactured in Normandy.

Other examples have been found in London and the south-east, particularly in Sussex, where it was thought that they had been made. They have also been found in York as well as in Dublin and Drogheda in Ireland. There is very little dating evidence for the tiles in this group, with the exception of two sites in Sussex, Poynings and Arundel, where the tiles seem to date to the last quarter of the 14th or the very beginning of the 15th century (Norton 1993, 85). The tiles average 103 x 102 x 20mm in size. The fabric is well prepared and the glaze a fairly dark reddish brown over an oxidised body. Examples have been found in the church of St Thomas in Winchelsea, Sussex. This suggests that some St Mary Graces paving was possibly laid in the 1390s when Penn tiles had ceased to be available.

'Westminster' type tile designs <T5> and <T6>

Only two examples of this type of tile were recovered (Fig 87). 'Westminster' tiles were made in London, but also elsewhere, from the mid 13th to the early 14th century. Many examples have been found, though not *in situ*, in datable contexts during London excavations (Betts 2002). The piece of tile decorated with design <T5> (ibid, W32) from St Mary Graces has no recorded find location but that of design <T6> (ibid, W46) came from the church area.

Table 17 Plain glazed and unglazed floor tile fabrics

Fabric no.	Size (mm)	Comment
1678	? x 220 x 45	
	? x 222 x 36	
	115 x 114 x 24	
	125 x 125 x 29	
	206 x 206 x 28	
	220 x 220 x 30	
	258 x ? x 40	
	278 x 276 x 45	
	280 x 280 x 40	calcium carbonate, Low Countries fabric
1810	110 x 107 x 27	coarse sandy, Penn fabric
1977	?	silty, Low Countries fabric
2194	127 x 127 x 31	
	180 x 180 x 36	
	220 x 217 x 46	coarse sandy fabric
2318	104 x 104 x 21	silty, Low Countries fabric
2322	115 x 113 x 29	
	130 x 126 x 30	
	190 x 185 x 30	fine sandy fabric
2323	224 x 222 x 45	
	255 x 255 x 42	
	273 x 270 x 54	
	275 x ? x 55	calcium carbonate, Low Countries fabric
2324	115 x 115 x 26	
	218 x 217 x 45	
	180 x 180 x 31	
	222 x 220 x 27	fine sandy fabric
2497	179 x 179 x 40	calcium carbonate, Low Countries fabric
2504	?	calcium carbonate, Low Countries fabric
2850	127 x 126 x 28	
	160 x 160 x 25	
	180 x 177 x 42	silty, Low Countries fabric

Plain glazed and unglazed floor tiles

Naomi Crowley and Elizabeth Eames

The majority of the plain glazed tiles used appear to have been manufactured using techniques common in the Low Countries during the 14th to 16th centuries (Fig 13; Table 17). These tiles can be identified by the presence of small nail holes sometimes visible under the surface of the glaze; since many of the tiles have very worn surfaces, these nail holes are easy to spot. The holes are due to the manufacturing techniques employed by the Low Countries tilers. After the initial shaping of the clay into squares using a frame, and after a period of drying, a block was placed over the tile. This block had small nails in the corners in order to grip the tile while the tiler trimmed the edges around the block. These tiles are also in distinct fabrics with silty or calcium carbonate inclusions. Where the glaze survives it has a glassy quality and is easily chipped. This is due to the fact that the tiles were biscuit-fired then glazed and fired a second time. English-produced tiles went through only one firing so that the glaze was fused to the tile surface. The glazes are lead glazes in yellow, green and dark green. The yellow colour is achieved with a lead glaze over a white firing clay slip. The green colour has copper added to the lead glaze, again over a white slip, and the dark green colour is a copper-rich lead glaze directly over the red earthenware tile surface.

The small plain glazed English tiles, in the same fabric as the decorated Penn tiles, were probably manufactured in the 14th century at the Penn kilns in Buckinghamshire. The imported tiles from the floors in the claustral buildings and from the post-Dissolution floors in the former kitchen (B11) and house and chamber or abbot's hospice (B14) (Chapter 2.6) were probably manufactured between the 14th and 16th centuries.

Bricks

Naomi Crowley

During the monastic phases small fragments of brick in MOL fabrics 3031 and 3033 begin to appear (Table 18). These bricks are generally poorly made, with uneven surfaces and occasionally misshapen. The bricks in fabric 3031 have chamfered headers or stretchers. The dating is based on dimensions and surface features of the bricks. Many of the bricks in fabric 3033 have sunken margins. This is due to the method of manufacture and is common on 15th- to 16th-century bricks. After the Dissolution fabrics 3031 and 3033 are still present, although fabric 3031 only occurs as rubble. Fabric 3046, a fabric similar to fabric 3033, first appears at this time.

Table 18 Brick fabrics and dimensions

Fabric no.	Size (mm)	Date
3031	203 x 94–103 x 47–57	Low Countries-type, 15th century
3033	228 x 115–121 x 54–55	'local', 16th century
	205–211 x 95–100 x 48–53	'local', 15th/16th century
3046	215 x 105 x 55	'local', 16th century

Continental stove-tile fragments

Lyn Blackmore, David Gaimster and Richenda Goffin, with scientific analysis by Michael Cowell and Ian Freestone

Introduction

This report summarises previously published work which considers more fully the cultural significance of the stove-tile fragments in the social and art-historical context of the European tile-stove tradition, and provides a detailed scientific analysis of the fragments (Gaimster et al 1990; Gaimster and Hughes 1999).

The stove-tile fragments were all found in period C1 deposits (Grainger and Phillpotts 2010, 23) but date to the early 16th century. Three fabric types are present, one tin-glazed and two lead-glazed; a minimum of 25 tiles are represented. The tin-glazed tiles are almost certainly from the Netherlands and form a previously unrecognised element of the early tin-glazed wares produced in the Low Countries. The lead-glazed tiles could also have been produced in the Low Countries, although stylistically they most closely match ones produced in the lower Rhineland, notably in the Cologne area.

The two types of (contemporaneous) stove-tile (polychrome tin-glazed and monochrome lead-glazed) represent either two separate stoves or a single 'combination' stove. But the context of the stove-tile fragments found at St Mary Graces poses problems of interpretation and dating, for although found in localised concentrations (notably the 149 recovered from the fill of a cellar in the former kitchen, B11; Chapter 2.6) they were scattered widely across the site. Mortar and sooting were generally absent but the quantity of the different tile types found implies that they derive from a stove (or stoves) and were not just souvenirs. On stylistic and technological grounds it is argued that the tiles date to the pre-Dissolution, early 16th-century, period, after which ceramic stove iconography and form changed dramatically in north-west Europe.

The stove-tile fragments

A total of 177 stove-tile fragments were found (3.94kg), which derive from a minimum of 25 tiles. A few fragments show some slight evidence of sooting on the reverse. The fragments were first examined macroscopically and divided into three fabric groups. These groups were subsequently confirmed by petrological and neutron activation analysis undertaken at the British Museum Research Laboratory by M Cowell and I Freestone (Gaimster et al 1990, 37–46). Within these fabric groups a number of different form types were identified, as described below and summarised in Table 19. The different tile types are described in the order in which they appear in Fig 88.

FABRIC 1

This is typically cream, but localised areas can be slightly pink in colour. The overall colour ranges from white/pale yellow (Munsell 2.5Y 8/2.4) to very pale brown (Munsell 10YR 8/3.4) or reddish yellow (Munsell 5YR 7/6). The decoration comprises relief moulding under a tin glaze with polychrome over-painting. One crenellation fragment <1821> and two niche-tile fragments (<253>, <1940>) were submitted for thin-section and neutron activation analysis (Gaimster et al 1990, 42).

a) Bastion (Fig 88, nos 1–2)

Thirteen fragments were recovered, from a minimum of four tiles. These have a height of *c* 113mm and a maximum width of 54mm across the top, tapering slightly to the base. The thickness varies from 3mm to 6mm. The front is tin-glazed; droplets and dribbles also run the length of the reverse faces. The tiles are convex and faceted, with four crenellations at the top. These and the arrow slits are defined in blue; other architectural features are picked out in yellow. Each tile has a perforation *c* 5mm in diameter towards the lower edge. One example (no. 1) has been

Table 19 Distribution of the stove-tile fabric and form types, with weight

Stove-tile form	Fabric 1		Fabric 2		Fabric 3	
	Fragment count	Weight (g)	Fragment count	Weight (g)	Fragment count	Weight (g)
Bastion	13	123				
Rosette	4	91				
Crenellation	25	347				
Niche-tile	23	594	43	1342		
Separator (a)	2	127			7	129
Separator (b)					29	679
Tile-hanging cornice					31	508
Total	**67**	**1282**	**43**	**1342**	**67**	**1316**

subjected to sufficient heat to cause the glaze to blister; however, it is impossible to say whether this occurred while the tile was in place on the stove, or post-deposition.

b) Rosette (Fig 88, no. 3)

Only one rosette was found (four joining fragments), which measures 100mm in diameter. This has 12 petals alternately yellow and orange in colour, which stand out in sharp relief from the white background. At the centre is a perforation 6mm in diameter, encircled by a smaller rosette of five yellow petals. There are several dribbles of glaze on the reverse, which is knife-trimmed around the perforation.

c) Crenellations (Fig 88, nos 4–8)

Twenty-five fragments were found from a minimum of four tiles. The maximum dimensions are on average 180 x 98mm, with a thickness of 6mm. The relief moulding comprises a repeating pattern reminiscent of Gothic tracery; this is covered by a white tin glaze which does not completely cover the reverse. The main design is over-painted in yellow, with a blue border around the edges; the crenellations and perforations are also defined in blue.

d) T-sectioned separator (Fig 88, no. 9)

Only one example of this form is present. It comprises an elaborately moulded column mainly in white with yellow bands against a blue background. There is very little glaze on the reverse apart from at the lower edge. The width is 42–44mm, with a maximum depth of 43mm; the width of the spine is 8mm.

e) Niche-tiles (Fig 88, nos 10–15)

Eleven fragments (203g) from the niches of at least three tiles were found together with a further 12 flange fragments (391g), possibly from the same tiles. The main fragment (no. 10) derives from a niche-tile with overall dimensions of *c* 275 x *c* 180mm. The tile has two vertical flanges and a third horizontal flange at the lower edge; the upper edge is flat, with a slight cut-away at each corner to fit neatly under the lower flange of the tile positioned above it. The central relief consists of two male figures against a plain background, standing on a sward of green. The larger figure wears a yellow doublet with voluminous sleeves and a white hose. In the right hand is an ornate cup or chalice; the left hand rests on a dagger suspended from the hips. The head and lower part of the legs are missing. To the left of this figure is a smaller fair-haired one, possibly a servant or boy, who wears a blue doublet; the facial features are crudely rendered. The right hand holds a long thin object with bulbous lower end, perhaps a musical instrument, which rests against the right shoulder. The rest of this figure is missing apart from the lower part of the left leg. On both figures the finer details are depicted in blue or highlighted by relief moulding. Two stylised classical columns in blue frame the niche with double torus mouldings at the base. The decoration on the flanges comprises a continuous border of yellow vine leaves. The details on the leaves and the outer edge of the flange are outlined in blue. There is very little tin glaze on the reverse of these fragments. The various aspects of the profile are represented by the flange fragments: no. 13 from the top left-hand corner, no. 14 from the left side, and no. 15 from the bottom right-hand corner. These are all decorated in blue and yellow as described above. Six other niche-tile fragments may belong either to the above or to another in the same series. These include the head of a male figure with ginger hair and beard, wearing a yellow garment (no. 11). Another fragment shows a large yellow hat or turban, outlined in blue, with possibly the edge of a hand holding it aloft (no. 12).

FABRIC 2

This combines a typically red-brown backing and a layer of white clay or slip over most of the outer surface. The backing ranges from very pale brown (Munsell 10YR 8/4) to reddish yellow (Munsell 7.5YR 8/6 or 5YR 7/6,8). The decoration comprises relief moulding on the white-slipped area, under a bright green glaze (Michel dark yellow green and dark olive green). Four sherds were submitted for thin-section analysis (<1953>, <1845>, <4114>, <4181>).

a) Niche-tiles (Fig 88, nos 16–18, 31–2)

Sherds from a minimum of three tiles were found of which the most complete has a width of *c* 212mm; if this tile had the same proportions as that in fabric 1, the original height was probably *c* 320mm. Like the tin-glazed niche-tiles, these are flanged on three sides only, the upper edge being flat so as to fit under the flange of the tile above. The reverse is knife-trimmed, with occasional splashes of glaze.

The most substantial fragments derive from the upper parts of two different tiles, each with a double baldachin canopy in the form of elaborate Gothic-style vaulting and tracery (nos 16 and 17). This springs from the capitals of the columns which frame the niche, which are surmounted by highly decorated finials. The relief decoration on the flanges comprises scrolling vine foliage similar to that on the T-shaped separators, except that in this case the leaves are smaller and are not entwined around a central stem. These fragments are probably of two-mould construction, one for the main tile and one for the baldachin canopy.

The third example comprises two sherds from the lower part of a tile with relief decoration on the niche recess itself which shows the lower half of a large bird with plumage and tail feathers (no. 18). The head is missing, but the bird may represent an eagle or a phoenix. The columns and flanges are the same as those described above.

In addition to the above there are several slightly concave fragments which derive from the niches of these tiles or others like them. Two of these have foliate designs (Fig 88, nos 31–2).

FABRIC 3

This is an off-white ware, quite different in character from fabric 1. The decoration comprises a green glaze ranging from pale to dark (Michel dark yellow green and dark olive green). One T-shaped separator fragment (<1723>) was submitted for thin-section and neutron activation analysis.

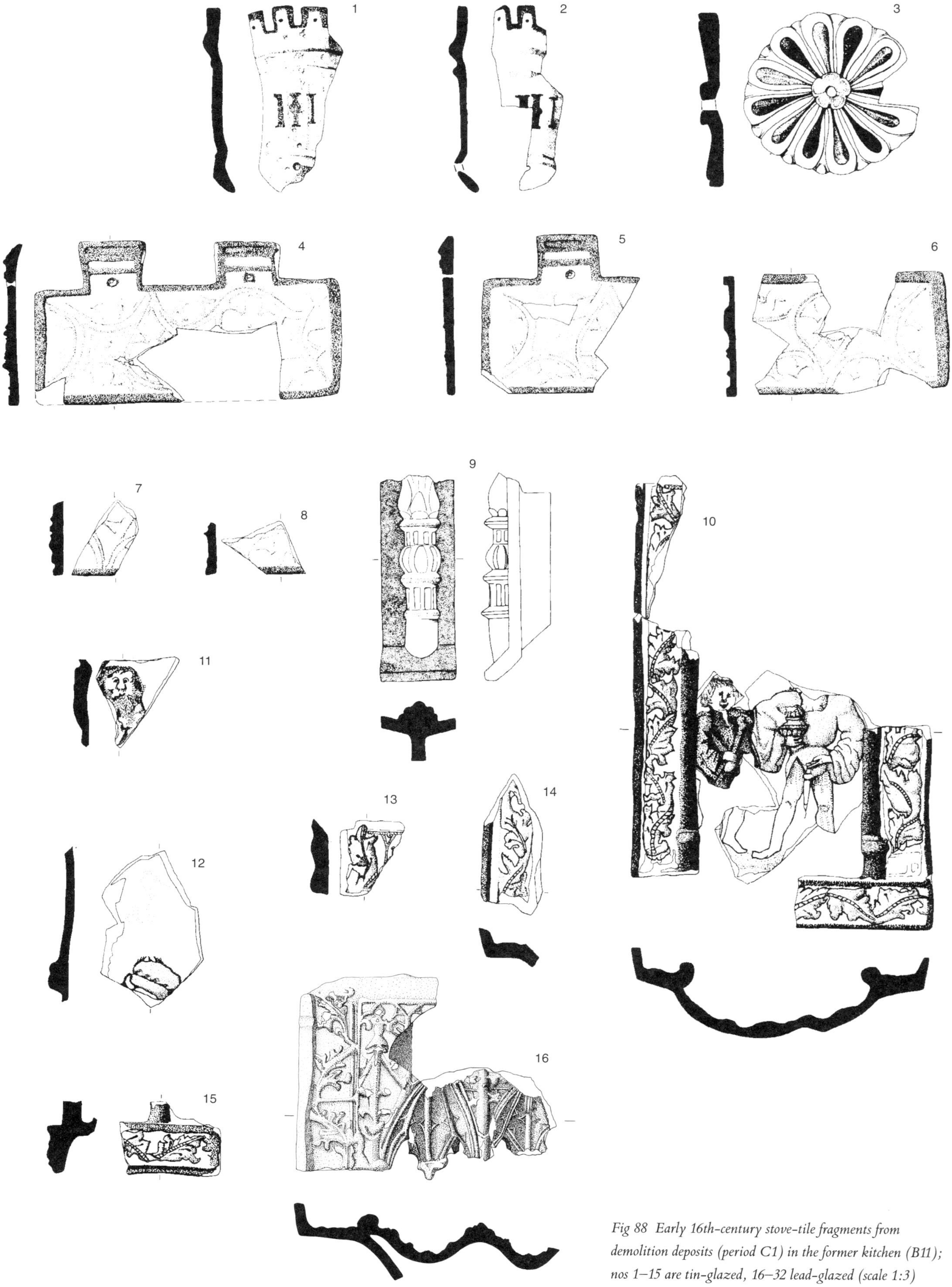

Fig 88 Early 16th-century stove-tile fragments from demolition deposits (period C1) in the former kitchen (B11); nos 1–15 are tin-glazed, 16–32 lead-glazed (scale 1:3)

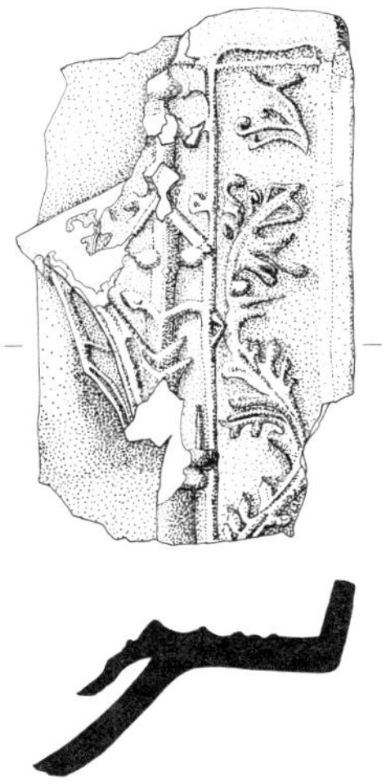
17

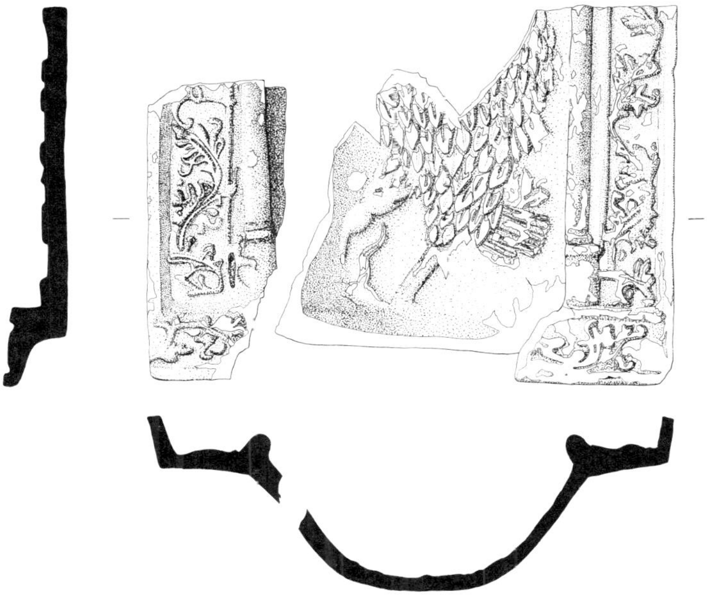
18

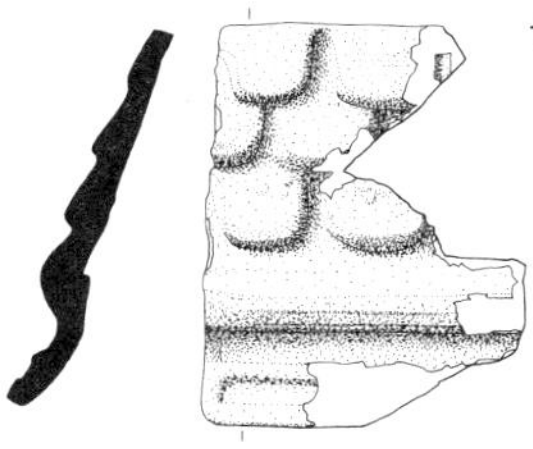
19

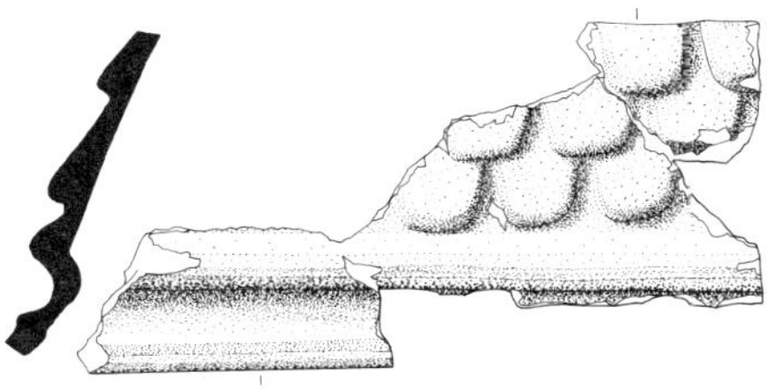
20

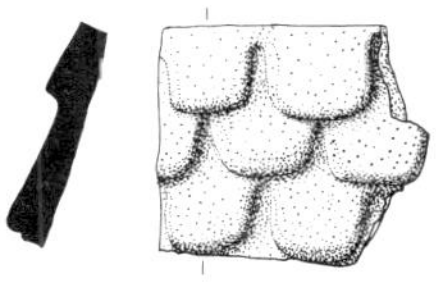
21

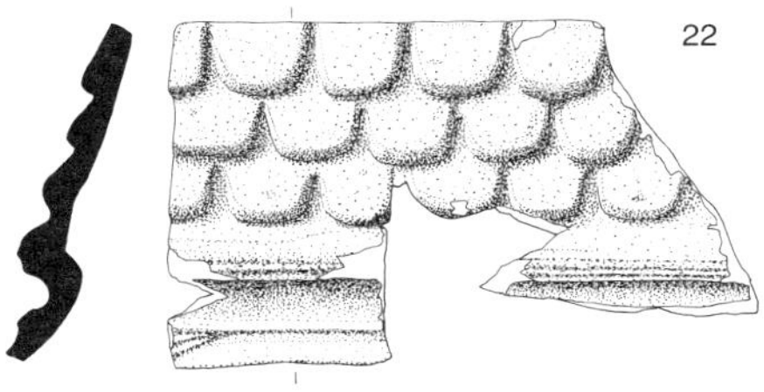
22

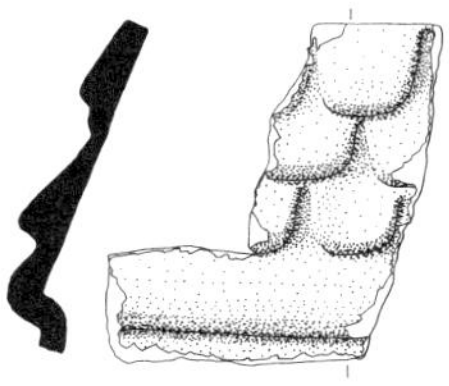
23

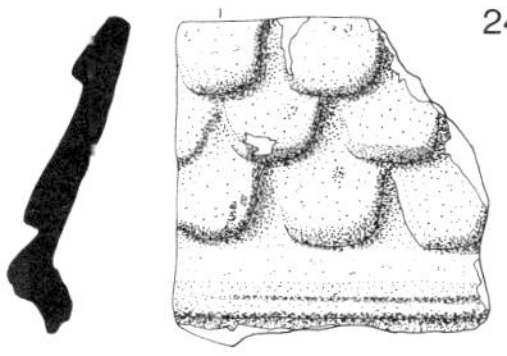
24

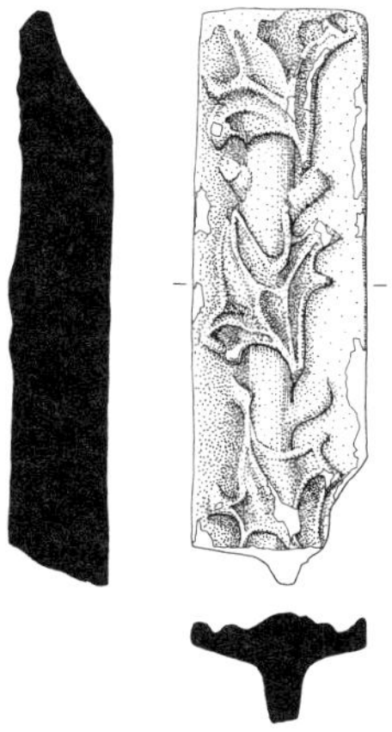
25

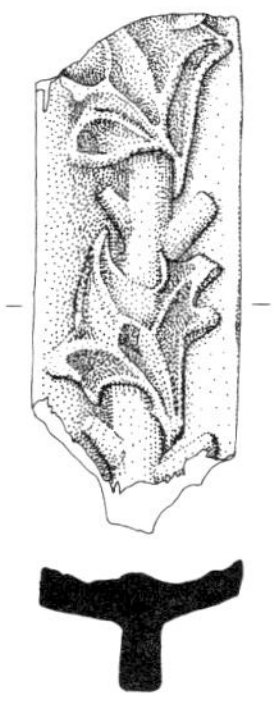
26

27

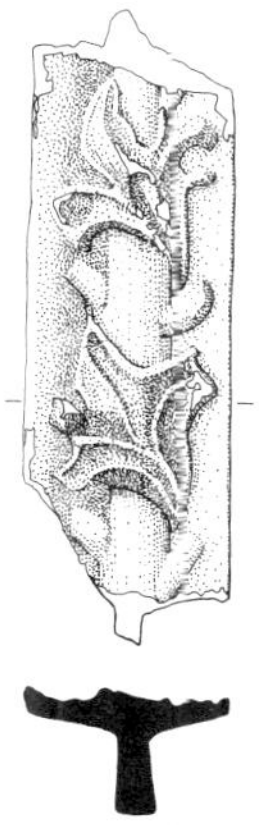
28

29

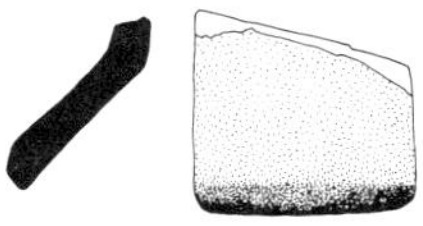
30

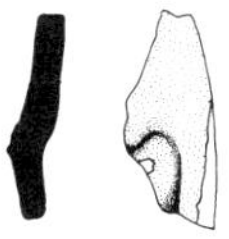
31

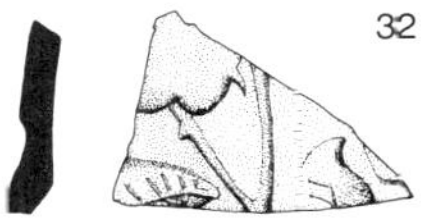
32

a) Tile-hanging cornice (Fig 88, nos 19–24)

Fragments from a minimum of four tiles are present. There are no complete examples, but the depth is *c* 80mm so the width should correspond to that of the niche-tiles. The moulded decoration comprises three rows of overlapping roof tiles, with a gully at the lower edge representing the gutter. The upper surface and edges are covered with a green glaze which extends patchily over the heavily knife-trimmed reverse surfaces.

b) T-sectioned separators (Fig 88, nos 25–30)

This group comprises two sub-types of separator.

A total of 29 fragments (679g) with moulded decoration are from a minimum of three tiles. The decoration comprises a scrolling vine entwined around a stem or pole, under a green glaze which also extends over the edges (nos 25–9). Some tiles are heavily knife-trimmed around the spine. Patches of glaze are also present on the reverse faces. The width of these separator fragments is 40mm; the original height would have been the same as that of the niche-tiles. The depth, including the spine, is 25mm. The spine is 7mm wide and is neatly chamfered at the upper end, which is 25mm below the main edge of the separator (no. 25). No fragments with the lower edge were found.

Seven fragments (129g) appear to be from similar T-shaped separators, but are distinctly wider (42–44mm) and thicker (8mm) than those described above. Several of them display a clear change in angle (no. 30), showing that these separators are like the polychrome example (no. 9, above). They must have been designed for the upper junction of this part of the stove and the support plate, or for the lower junction of the stove and the plinth. These fragments are covered with a green glaze which spreads over the edges and around the peripheries of the reverse, which is knife-trimmed.

5.3 Pottery

Lyn Blackmore (imported wares), Richenda Goffin (medieval assemblages), Roy Stephenson (Dissolution-period assemblages), with David Gaimster (stonewares)

Introduction and methodology

The English medieval pottery assemblage was recorded, quantified and analysed by Richenda Goffin, and the Dissolution-period assemblages by Roy Stephenson; the imports were studied by Lyn Blackmore. A brief summary of the imports, prepared in January 2001, follows the English medieval pottery summary (edited and added to in 2001 by Lyn Blackmore); more details of all the finds are available in the site archive, and it is hoped to publish the imports more fully elsewhere. The stonewares were examined by David Gaimster, and are not considered in detail in this text, although mention is made of some individual pieces; aspects of the assemblage have been touched on in his publication on German stonewares (Gaimster 1997).

All the pottery was classified in 1989–90 using fabric and form codes established by the Museum of London (Chapter 1.4) and the archive reports on the different imported and domestic wares were written in 1990. The pottery was quantified by weight and sherd count; estimated vessel equivalents (EVEs) were recorded for both rims and bases, although only rims have been used in this report. Selection for illustration was limited to sherds unusual in either fabric or form, the details of which are given in Table 20 (context numbers of illustrated pottery included there are not repeated in the text). The collection is considered by land use and the discussions of individual pottery groups are included in the relevant land-use text (Chapter 2.3–2.6). For the imported pottery, the original quantified data were checked and transferred to an Excel spreadsheet so that the trends could be ascertained, but the data on the stonewares remain more or less as they were when first recorded by Goffin and Stephenson.

The English pottery

Summary

The archive report covers pottery dating from *c* AD 970 to *c* 1500. This end date nearly coincides with the suppression of St Mary Graces in 1539, and is taken as a dividing line in the phasing of the site, between medieval and post-medieval activity. Although all the medieval pottery was identified and quantified, very little of this material was worthy of detailed statistical analysis, in contrast to the post-medieval assemblage. This was usually because well-stratified medieval deposits did not survive in any quantity; the material was often contaminated by later pottery and/or the features were heavily truncated. No substantial closed contexts such as rubbish pits or cesspits survived that can definitely be placed within the bounds and lifetime of the abbey. This degree of disturbance is reflected in the large quantity of residual medieval material, which makes up nearly a third of the total assemblage. The period associated with the abbey is therefore poorly represented in the pottery record, although small quantities of material do provide useful dating evidence. Little ceramic evidence for the preparation and consumption of food and drink was found that could be directly related to the abbey through primary contexts. The few slightly more substantial groups of material were from pits beyond the abbey precinct in Open Area 12 (Chapter 2.5).

The imported pottery

Introduction

In all, 1976 sherds of imported pottery were recovered from the site (*c* 50kg, 60.8 EVEs; Blackmore and Goffin 2008; Blackmore 2010, 98). Of these, 220 sherds (6803g, 12.3 EVEs) came from deposits associated with the abbey and the Dissolution period, the majority being stonewares. All three sherds from period B1 (1350–61) and three of those from period B2 (1361–*c* 1400) were stratified, but ten sherds from period B2 were intrusive. Most of

Table 20 Details of illustrated pottery <P3>–<P37>

Cat no.	Context	Land use	Period	Fabric code	Form	Fig no.
<P3>	[3055]	OA7	B2	SPGR/MAGR	jar	22
<P4>	[12836]	OA2	B2	MG	bowl/cooking pot	27
<P5>	[12836]	OA2	B2	KING	bowl	27
<P6>	[9592]	OA2/OA12	B3	CBW	puzzle jug	45
<P7>	[9592]	OA2/OA12	B3	?CBW	mammiform costrel	45
<P8>	[9592]	OA2/OA12	B3	?CBW	baluster jug	45
<P9>	[9592]	OA2/OA12	B3	CBW	bowl	45
<P10>	[9592]	OA2/OA12	B3	CHEA	pipkin	45
<P11>	[13395]	B6	B4	ANDAL	dish	47
<P12>	[13048]	B6	B4	FREC	jug with applied medallion	47
<P13>	[4603]	B11	B4	SNTG	vase with decoration including hindquarters of hare	49
<P14>	[3998]	B12	B4	PMSR	jug	53
<P15>	[3998]	B12	B4	PMSR	jug	53
<P16>	[3998]	B12	B4	PMSR	jug	53
<P17>	[3998]	B12	B4	BORD	plate	53
<P18>	[3998]	B12	B4	BORD	condiment dish	53
<P19>	[3998]	B12	B4	PMR(E)	chamber pot	53
<P20>	[3998]	B12	B4	BEAU1	dish with border of two types of stylised leaf separated by obliquely combed lines	53
<P21>	[3998]	B12	B4	BEAU1	dish with border of obliquely combed lines & incised diamond-shaped lozenges	53
<P22>	[3998]	B12	B4	RAER	standard drinking jug	53
<P23>	[3998]	B12	B4	RAER	jug with collared rim form	53
<P24>	[3998]	B12	B4	?DUTSL	skillet	53
<P25>	[11852]	OA11	B4	DUTR	pipkin with arcaded slip decoration	55
<P26>	[3357]	OA13	B4	SIEG	shallow drinking bowl	55
<P27>	[1707]	B45	C2	SAIN	base sherd (*sgraffito*)	89
<P28>	[3817]	OA17	C1	SNTG	vase with 'IHS' insignia	89
<P29>	[4535]	B14	C1	SNTG	dish with central medallion with 'IHS' insignia	89
<P30>	[3666]	B11	C1	SIEG	jug (*Jacobakanne*)	89
<P31>	[1481]	B14	C1	RAER	drinking jug	89
<P32>	[3817]	OA17	C1	RAER/LANG	jug with rouletted decoration	89
<P33>	[14051]	OA14	C1	RAER/LANG	large base with thumbing on underside	89
<P34>	[13282]	OA14	C1	KOLS	oak-leaf jug	89
<P35>	[6033]	OA29	C2	KOLS	jug with facemask	89
<P36>	[14288]	OA15	C1	KOLS/FREC	jug with applied acanthus leaves & medallions	89
<P37>	[4682]	OA5	B2	KOLS/FREC	jug medallion reused as counter	89

the 48 sherds from period B3 do fall within the period's date bracket of *c* 1400–1539, although some of these wares continued in use beyond this date; the 18 sherds of Frechen and Westerwald stoneware (FREC, WEST), however, must derive from activity in period C1 (victualling yard, 1560–*c* 1660). A total of 169 sherds are from deposits assigned to period B4 (1539–60). A few of these are residual medieval wares, while others, such as Weser slipware (WESE), the Spanish starred costrel (STAR) and Chinese porcelain (CHPO), are later types. Most of the group, however, fits with a mid 16th-century horizon. In addition, there are some 16th-century wares found in period C which could well have been used in periods B3 or B4, or in period C1; these are discussed with the later material (Blackmore 2010).

Although not large, the collection from the period *c* 1350–*c* 1560 includes a sample of most of the major fabrics traded in the late medieval and early post-medieval periods, and most of the main forms are represented here (Fig 89). The assemblage also includes a few complete or near-complete vessels. Approximately half the material comprises German stonewares, with the remainder coming from Spain, Italy, France, Germany and the Low Countries.

Italy and the Mediterranean

No archaic maiolica or white-slipped red earthenware was found. The former is very rare in London, while white-slipped Italian earthenwares, though also rare, have been found nearby in late 15th- to earlier 16th-century contexts at the Tower postern (Blackmore 1994, 40; 2006; in prep a) and in the Broad Arrow Tower (Nelson in prep).

FAENZA/MONTELUPO TIN-GLAZED WARES (ITGW, MLTG)

Four sherds are from small jugs or vases typical of the period *c* 1480–*c* 1550. These are of the type formerly assigned to Faenza (Platt and Coleman-Smith 1975, fig 209, no. 1348), but which are now thought to be from Montelupo (Clark 1979, fig 27, no. 203; M Milanese, pers comm); other possible sources are Deruta or another centre in Umbria (Wilson 1987, 91). Recent scientific analysis of sherd material from London sites has suggested that many similar jugs and vases previously classified as Netherlandish are in fact Italian (Blake 1999; Hughes and Gaimster 1999).

Stratigraphically the earliest of these wares are from period B3 (Chapter 2.5). The first is a single sherd from a vase with 'ladder' medallion found in context [98]. The second is a base

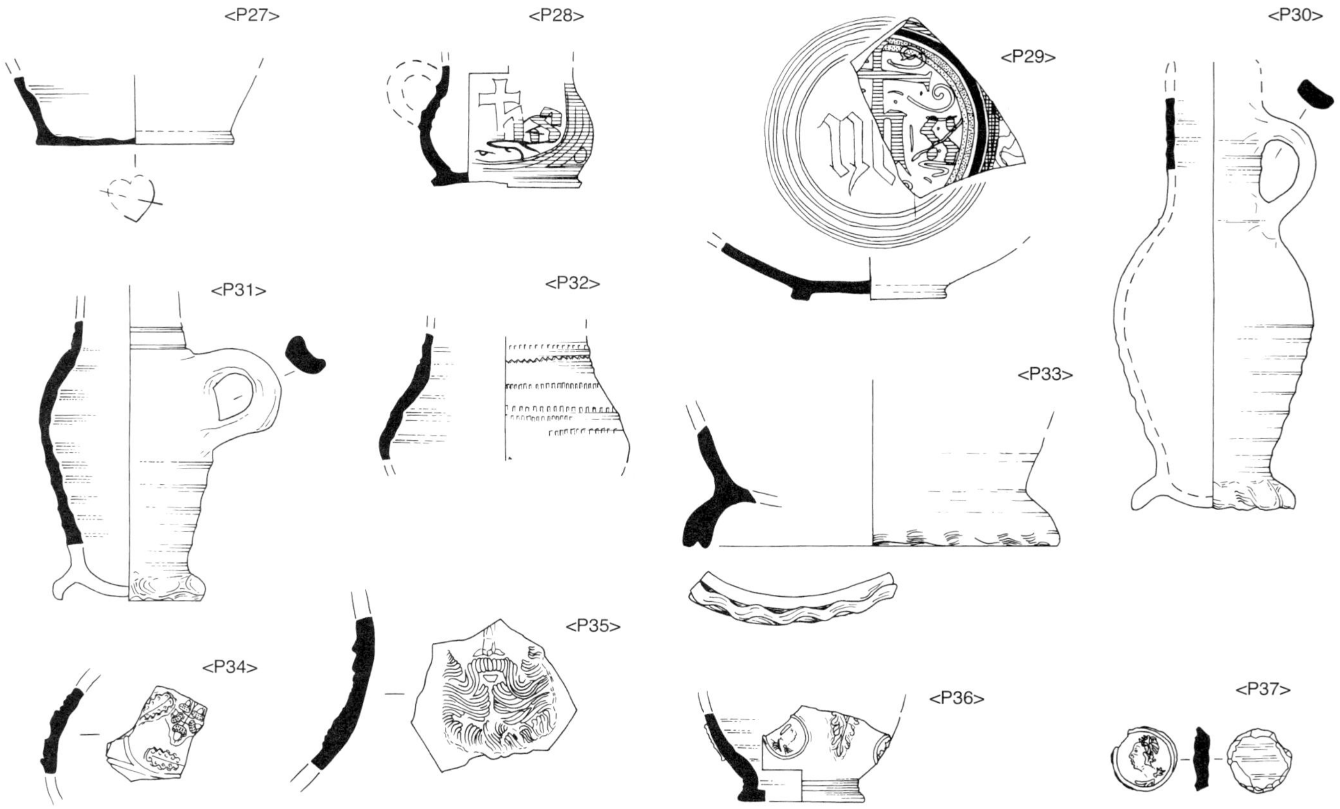

Fig 89 Medieval and 16th-century imported pottery <P27>–<P37> from contemporary and later contexts (see Table 20 for contexts, land uses and period) (scale 1:4)

sherd with a panel design outlined in pale and dark blue with yellow, and a vertical 'herringbone' panel ([5374]). Two other sherds are from similar jugs, but are residual in later contexts. Similar jugs/vases have been found in several late 15th- to mid 16th-century contexts across the country (Gaimster 1999). Findspots in London include Holy Trinity Priory (Blackmore 2005; Blake 1999), St John and St Mary Clerkenwell (Blackmore 2004; in prep b), Barking Abbey (Jennings nd) and at the Tower postern (Blackmore 2006; in prep a). Examples have also been found on several sites on the south bank of the Thames (Blackmore 2002). Some of the other 16th-century Montelupo wares found in later deposits could be from pre-1560 contexts, but are discussed with the finds from period C (Blackmore 2010).

Spain

The earliest Spanish and Mediterranean wares from the City are from waterfront contexts dated to the late 13th century (Vince 1985, 54; 1995, 330; Blackmore 1994, 38–9; 1999, 51; 2002). They are, however, rare until the late 14th century. The only find from period B2 (Chapter 2.4) is a rim sherd from a green-glazed jar that could be Spanish (SPGR) or Maghrebi-type ware (MAGR) from North Africa <P3> (Fig 22). Although rather small, this might have contained sugar, manna, treacle, spices or other exotic products used in the abbey (Childs 1993, 37).

Four sherds were found in period B4 deposits (Chapter 2.6). Of these, part of a late Andalusian lustreware (ANDAL) dish <P11> (Fig 47) and two sherds of olive jar are not out of place in a Dissolution-period context, but a small sherd with a thin tin glaze ([13048]) appears to be from a jar or starred costrel (STAR) and is probably intrusive.

LATE ANDALUSIAN AND VALENCIAN LUSTREWARE (ANDAL, VALE)

Andalusian wares are characterised by their pinkish tone and the presence of tabular fragments of reddish-brown schistose metamorphic rock (Hurst 1977, 76–84). Valencian wares have a fine creamy buff fabric of finely divided calcium carbonate and anisotropic minerals with sparse quartz, iron ore, chert and limestone (ibid, 84–9; Vince 1982; 1985, 59, 64; Hurst et al 1986, 40–2). The dish fragment <P11> (Fig 47) is more calcareous than the normal Andalusian wares but much coarser than the usual Valencian wares; it is also unlike the Paterna wares that have been found in London. This piece, which has a thin glaze and decoration in pale blue, is similar in style to pedestal jugs and dishes from the Tower postern and to finds from elsewhere in the City, all of which occur in late 15th- and early 16th-century contexts (Blackmore 2006; in prep a). A similar ware has been found in Southampton and dated to the same period (Platt and Coleman-Smith 1975, fig 207, no. 1330).

It is possible that two sherds found in periods C1–C2 (Grainger and Phillpotts 2010) contexts are from Valencian lustreware (VALE) bowls used in the abbey. The first is a rim with decayed lustre decoration ([5413], period C1) (cf Hurst et al 1986, fig 19, no. 40; fig 20, no. 48) which may be of 14th- or 15th-century date. The second, probably of late 15th- or 16th-century date, has a copper lustre decoration of leaves inside and horizontal bands outside ([7498], period C2) (Grainger and Phillpotts 2010; cf Hurst 1977, fig 30, no. 34).

France

A total of 58 sherds (1559g, 2 EVEs) of French pottery are from period B contexts, of which 37 are from period B4. Most finds are contemporary with the phase, but part of a late 16th- or 17th-century chafing dish found in period B2 ([10429]) is intrusive from period B4 or C1. In addition there are 11 sherds of Saintonge ware from later contexts (mainly period C1: Blackmore 2010, 101–2) which are probably residual. Other important groups have come from the nearby site of the Tower postern (Blackmore 2006; in prep a), from sites downstream from the Royal Mint, and from Southwark.

SAINTONGE WARES

These wares first reached London with cargoes of wine from Gascony, and were the main import between *c* 1270 and *c* 1350 (Chapelot 1983; Hurst 1974; Hurst et al 1986, 76–99). Importation continued until the mid 17th century. A range of medieval jugs, pitchers and mortars are found, albeit in small quantities, across the whole of the London area (Pearce et al 1985, 19; Vince 1985, 59, 79; Blackmore 1994, 34–5).

A total of 22 sherds from jugs and pitchers (*pégaux*) were found in period B contexts; most are from period B4 deposits, and are probably residual. Indeed, some sherds from periods B and C could be from jugs discarded in period A (Grainger et al 2008, 35). These include a sherd with applied rouletted strips ([3616]). An unphased jug sherd ([8231]) has polychrome decoration of applied ribs and pellets very like that seen on Kingston-type wares, but the fabric is much finer and whiter; it is uncertain whether this vessel is from northern or southern France. Finds of note from period B4 include a sherd of Saintonge polychrome ware (SAIPL) and the complete base of a tall straight-sided jug (cf Chapelot 1983, fig 5.2, no. 120) which is blackened both inside and out. Of particular note is a base sherd (<P27>, Fig 89) found in period C2, apparently from a pear-shaped jug, with an owner's mark (a heart with an arrow through it) inscribed after firing; this jug is externally sooted and also has an internal deposit.

A problematic find is a narrow strap handle with all-over dark green glaze from period B2 ([98]) (Chapter 2.4). The fabric is not dissimilar to 'Tudor Green' (TUDG) and early Surrey-Hampshire border ware (EBORD), but the form is atypical for Surrey; it is uncertain whether this find is English or French.

BEAUVAIS EARTHENWARE AND STONEWARE

From the late 15th century until *c* 1700, a range of earthenwares (both plain and slip-decorated) were produced in a fine white-firing clay at Beauvais (Hurst 1971, 7; Hurst et al 1986, 105–16). The peak of production seems to have been *c* 1500–50, and these wares are not uncommon in Dissolution-period groups. Finds from the period B4 contexts at St Mary Graces comprise 30 sherds from up to five vessels (1176g, 1.48 EVEs).

One of these is a jug handle with an amber glaze ([13462]); cf Hurst et al 1986, fig 50, no. 157). In London similar pieces have been found in Dissolution-period deposits at St Mary Clerkenwell (Blackmore in prep b) and in mid 16th-century deposits at Guy's Hospital (Hurst 1971, figs 5–11; Hurst and Clark 1979, 53, fig 12, nos 216–20). The other sherds are from dishes found in the Dissolution and manor house period organic rubbish deposit [3998] in the former storeroom (B12) (period B4; Chapter 2.6). Two of these are single *sgraffito* ware (BEAU1) dishes that have the 'IHS' insignia at the centre, suggesting that they should date to before 1539. One (<P20>, Fig 53) has a border design comprising two types of stylised leaf separated by obliquely combed lines. The other (<P21>, Fig 53) has a repeating pattern of four obliquely combed lines and incised diamond-shaped lozenges made up of overlapping angled lines, which are alternately hatched or contain a single wavy line; the same pattern has been found at Plymouth, Devon (Clark 1979, 29, fig 19, no. 106). The fact that <P21> joins with sherds from a later context ([3817], OA13, period C1) suggests that some of the other nine *sgraffito* wares found in later contexts (165g, 0.03 EVEs; period C1: Grainger and Phillpotts 2010) were used on the site before *c* 1550.

The Low Countries

LOW COUNTRIES GREYWARE (LCGR)

Three unglazed sherds (51g, 0.15 EVEs) are in a very hard, fine, dark grey ware with fused surfaces. One is from period B2, while the others were probably residual in periods B4 and C1. It is likely that all are from the same large jug or pitcher vessel (cf Janssen 1983, fig 9.9; Bruijn 1979, fig 64, no. 6) and date to the later 14th century. Possible sources include Haarlem (Janssen 1983, 123, 127, 143), Utrecht (Bruijn 1979; Janssen 1983, 143–5), Leiden or Lampernissese (Verhaeghe 1983, 69, 80–1, 83).

SOUTH NETHERLANDS MAIOLICA (SNTG)

The most common SNTG form found in England is the small vase or altar vase, which was probably used for private devotion as well as in religious houses, especially those with the 'IHS' monogram (Hurst et al 1986, 117); numerous examples have been found in Dissolution-period groups across the country (although some might now prove to be of Italian origin). The five sherds that were stratified in the period B4 organic rubbish deposit [3998] (Chapter 2.6) include a body sherd with ring handle. Sherds from three other such vases found in periods C1 and C2 may also have been used in the abbey. The most complete example is represented by the base and lower body with the 'IHS' insignia (<P28>, Fig 89); the other pieces comprise two small body sherds from period C1 ([2951], [3964]), and a rim sherd from period C2 ([7575]).

The only other find from period B4 is from a vase on which the design incorporates the hindquarters of a hare (<P13>, Fig 49). Animal motifs such as this are more typical of the later 16th century, and so this piece could date to *c* 1550–60 (Korf 1981, pl opp p18; Hurst et al 1986, 121, col pl VIII).

Two other finds from period C could also have been used in period B4. The first is a small polychrome vase with a geometric border around the rim; a rim of similar form was found at St

John Clerkenwell (Sloane and Malcolm 2004, fig 175, <P79>). The second is a dish with a central medallion containing the letters 'IHS' (<P29>, Fig 89) (cf Korf 1981, 207, no. 581; 209, nos 585–6). The raised footring is perforated for suspension on the wall, although this would have resulted in the lettering being viewed on its side with the 'S' at the top. Production of 'IHS' dishes continued in Antwerp after 1600, but this piece is more likely to have been used in the abbey or a private house than in the victualling yard.

DUTCH RED EARTHENWARES (DUTR, DUTSL)

Compared to other sites in London (Vince 1985, 58, 79; Blackmore 1994, 37), Dutch red earthenwares are rare in pre-Dissolution contexts; only two definite sherds are from period B4 deposits. In addition, there is a complete ? Dutch slipped red earthenware (?DUTSL) skillet with pinched feet (<P24>, Fig 53). The carinated profile resembles a hybrid of two types found at Utrecht (Bruijn 1979, fig 38, no. 3, with applied feet; fig 38, no. 6, with pinched feet).

Slip-decorated dishes, pipkins and other forms were produced in Utrecht and other centres in the Netherlands from the 14th century onwards (Bruijn 1979; Hurst et al 1986, 146–9). The earliest finds from St Mary Graces probably date to the first half of the 15th century. They comprise a pipkin with arcaded slip decoration (<P25>, Fig 55) (cf Hurst et al 1986, fig 60, no. 191) found in a period B4 context (Chapter 2.6), but probably derived from period B3, and sherds from two dishes found in period C1.

Germany

EARTHENWARES

No German earthenwares were stratified in period B contexts, and the few sherds of Werra and Weser slipware (WERR, WESE) from period B4 are intrusive from period C1. An intriguing find from period C2 is the spout of a yellow-glazed vessel in a fine whiteware fabric with occasional large iron-rich inclusions ([3359]) (Grainger and Phillpotts 2010). The ware is more like Badorf-type ware than Saintonge or Beauvais wares, and it is possible that this piece is from the area of Langerwehe, where spouted baby-feeders were made in the 15th century (Hurst et al 1986, 228–9, fig 110, nos 343–4). If this identification is correct, the piece may have been used in the refectory or the infirmary.

STONEWARES

The pattern of medieval stoneware imports to London has been considered by Vince (1985; 1988), Blackmore (1994, 35–7; in prep c) and Gaimster (1987), and the documentary and archaeological evidence for London has been discussed in greater detail by Gaimster (1997, 78–87). The chronology of the different stoneware forms found in London, based on the waterfront sequences, agrees well with that in the Netherlands and the Rhineland (Vince 1985, 58–9; Blackmore 1994), and excavations elsewhere in London are confirming and amplifying this picture (Gaimster 1987; 1997, 84–7). The earliest type is Siegburg stoneware (SIEG), which appeared *c* 1350 and was followed *c* 1400 by Langerwehe stoneware (LANG). Raeren stoneware (RAER) and Cologne stoneware (KOLS) date from *c* 1480 and *c* 1500 respectively, while Frechen stoneware (FREC) was introduced *c* 1550.

The sample from St Mary Graces is too small for the period before 1480 to make valid comparisons with other sites. One tiny sherd of SIEG was found in a period B1 context ([7543]) but this can be considered intrusive as two small sherds of RAER and FREC were found in the same context. The numbers increase slightly in period B3, with a total of 44 sherds of stoneware. Of these, 12 are of FREC while six are of Westerwald stoneware (WEST), but they are not associated with any of the other stonewares, which should be stratified. The latter comprise 13 sherds of SIEG, five of LANG, seven of RAER and one of KOLS.

In period B4 there is a further rise in the amount of stoneware (121 sherds, 3415g, 6.89 EVEs); of these, however, 84 sherds are of RAER. Some of the FREC (20 sherds, 294g) may be intrusive, while some of the SIEG (17 sherds, 364g) is probably residual. The latter include the rim of a *Jacobakanne* drinking jug ([3347]) (cf Hurst et al 1986, 179, fig 88, no. 263) and a shallow bowl <P26> (Fig 55) (cf ibid, 178, fig 88, no. 257). It is also likely that much of the RAER found in this phase was used in the abbey (84 sherds, 2757g, 5.61 EVEs). The most common form is the standard drinking jug, several examples of which were found in the organic rubbish deposit [3998] (eg <P22>, Fig 53). Of note is a near-complete RAER jug with collared rim form (<P23>, Fig 53) from the same context. No KOLS was stratified in a period B4 context, but part of a FREC jug with applied medallion was found (<P12>, Fig 47).

Residual finds of SIEG from period C include a near-complete *Jacobakanne* (<P30>, Fig 89) and three complete small, undecorated beakers (*Trichterhalsbecher*) from [4830] and unphased contexts (cf Hurst et al 1986, pl 30); one of these has a perforation in the wall of the body.

Residual finds of RAER/LANG include the lower body of a funnel-necked drinking jug (<P31>, Fig 89), a jug with rouletted decoration (<P32>, Fig 89) and a large base with thumbing on the underside (<P33>, Fig 89); two very similar bases were found in the Tower postern (Blackmore 2006). KOLS finds include an oak-leaf jug (<P34>, Fig 89), while KOLS/FREC includes a very fine facemask (<P35>, Fig 89) and sherds from jugs with applied acanthus leaves and portrait medallions (eg <P36>, Fig 89). The most notable of these is a medallion that has been chipped around the edges to form a gaming counter (<P37>, Fig 89). These jugs are most typical of the mid 16th century (Hurst et al 1986, 210–15) and they could have been used late in period B3 or in period B4. It is not impossible that some of the globular jugs were also used in period B4, but these are noted in period C (Blackmore 2010, 104).

Discussion

Like the other religious houses of the day, St Mary Graces lay somewhat beyond the City fringes. The fact that it was Cistercian may also have had a bearing on the range of pottery used on the site, but imports are extremely rare at all the religious houses of London which have been studied in detail. At St John and St Mary Clerkenwell, imports amount to only a tiny proportion of the 14th- to 15th-century assemblages, and are still rare even in the 16th century (Blackmore 2004; in prep b; in prep c); it is only in the post-Dissolution levels that the range increases. The same applies to Bermondsey Abbey (Pearce in prep). In the case of Cistercian St Mary Graces, the overall scarcity of 14th-century and earlier 15th-century imports could reflect the slump in trade experienced as a result of the Black Death or the strictures of the Order. Indeed, there is a lack of obviously displayable material from any context earlier than *c* 1500. This could also reflect efficient rubbish disposal within the precinct. Another possibility is that any displayable pieces were carefully curated, and not used, broken or discarded along with the general mass of domestic wares.

The obvious dominance of stonewares in periods B3 and B4 reflects the fact that until *c* 1500 the development of London's trade was dominated by the Hanse. This was particularly the case in the 15th century: between 1422 and 1474 up to 85% of the Hanseatic trade with England was controlled by the merchants of Cologne. This probably also accounts for the presence of Dutch red earthenwares in relatively early groups on the site (Blackmore and Goffin 2008, 36). The second most common type is Saintonge ware, which probably came to the abbey with purchases of wine. The scarcity of other types before *c* 1500 probably reflects the fact that during the 14th and earlier 15th centuries most English overseas trade was conducted by foreign merchants in Continental towns such as Bruges and Antwerp, which served as entrepots for goods from the south (Childs 1993). Trade with Iberia and the Mediterranean increased in the mid 15th century (ibid), but the scarcity of such wares at St Mary Graces suggests that they reached the abbey as gifts, donations or personal possessions.

There is an increase in the number of imports from late 15th- and 16th-century contexts, consistent with the trend across London as a whole; this partly reflects increased wealth, the growth of the consumer market and the increasing number of immigrants to London. Although groups of this date are relatively few within the City itself (Vince 1995, 330–1), excavations outside the city wall have uncovered several important 16th-century assemblages which include high proportions of imports (Dawson 1979; Glanville 1989, 270; Malcolm 1997; Whittingham 2009). In addition, Dissolution-period groups from the sites of most religious houses in London yield sherds of Italian and Spanish pottery, Beauvais earthenware, south Netherlands maiolica (notably the 'altar vases') and Dutch red earthenwares. All these assemblages offer comparative material for the finds from St Mary Graces, although some have yet to be published.

5.4 Vessel glass

John Shepherd

Introduction and methodology

The excavations produced a total of 855 pieces of vessel glass. Virtually all of this material is very fragmentary. By far the greater volume of glass comes from the post-Dissolution periods C1 and C2 (Shepherd 2010) and especially from the late 17th century onwards.

All the glass from the Royal Mint site was catalogued primarily according to form and metal and secondarily according to metal alone. The latter, being just body fragments from indeterminate forms, account for the bulk of the catalogue (360 fragments). All these fragments are included in a full archive report of the glass available at the Museum of London (Chapter 1.4). This published report includes a limited catalogue of the more important fragments that date to the monastic and immediate post-Dissolution periods of the site's use.

The assemblage

Glass vessels of medieval date, in particular from the 13th century onwards, are recognisable among the general Royal Mint assemblage. A number of fragments appear to be residual, but as there is little evidence that soil containing ceramics and glass was brought in from elsewhere, it can probably be assumed that the vessels found here were originally deposited on the site prior to later disturbance. Both specific vessel types and metals are represented here, and are as follows.

Three small fragments from vessels made in an opaque red ('sealing-wax') glass were recorded, but unfortunately they are too small to permit a proper identification of their forms (<G2>). During the 13th and 14th centuries metal would appear to have been popular used either on its own, as here for solid opaque red vessels, or in the form of trails or prunts for decorating colourless or natural-green vessels. Fragments in solid opaque red glass are known from London, notably fragments of a flask from Watling House, Watling Street, which were found in 1954 together with French ceramics of the late 13th century (Hume 1957, 104, fig 1); and a number of examples can be cited for Britain generally (Charleston 1980, 69, who refers to 13th-century fragments from Maison Dieu, Arundel, Sussex; 14th-century ones from Northampton Castle; and 12th- to 14th-century ones from Woodperry, Oxfordshire). It is possible that this type of glass was made in England. A late medieval crucible containing such a metal was found on the Lower Chaleshurst site at Chiddingfold, Surrey (Kenyon 1967, 161, pl III). However, there is also a lot of evidence for its manufacture in Italy (Harden 1966, *passim*) and Greece (Davidson 1940, 306, for evidence from Corinth).

The lamp with a flared rim and a pointed, tapering stem is frequently depicted in medieval manuscripts and sculpture, both in this country and on the Continent, and is often found on monastic sites. It was a purely functional form which, when not being held in the hand, would have been suspended from a harness. A complete lamp has been found at Winchester, probably of 13th-century date (Harden 1969, fig 4) but examples are invariably identified only by the thick stub ends of the base (<G3>–<G6>; Fig 52). They have been recorded in an early 14th-century context at Southampton (Charleston 1975, 205, 216, no. 1502; see also 205, n11 for reference to a 13th- to 14th-century example from Goldsborough, Yorkshire, and an example in a context dated *c* 1350–70 at Northolt Manor, Middlesex) and a probable 14th-century context at Winchester, Hampshire (Charleston 1980, nos 9–10).

The urinal was another type of medieval glassware which was often depicted in contemporary manuscripts and sculpture and, just like the lamp, fulfilled a wholly specialist function (<G7>–<G17>; Fig 52). Made with a rounded base, very thin walls and a wide mouth with a horizontal rim, they were used both as utensils in the science of uroscopy and, but perhaps less commonly, as simple *vases de nuit*. As Charleston points out, 'from carvings and manuscript illuminations of the 13th and 14th centuries to the graphic arts of the 15th, 16th and 17th centuries, the theme of the doctor holding up his urinal to the light is universal' (Charleston 1984, 32). Such weak and fragile vessels would have had to have been carefully stored when not in use.

Those characteristic features of this type of vessel, namely the out-splayed, horizontal rim and the thickened, rounded base tend to be the parts which survive to be recorded in the archaeological record. The thin bodies seldom survive and hence the scarcity of complete or reconstructable examples. A virtually complete example comes from St Swithun's House, Walbrook, excavated in 1954 and dated to *c* 1500. Examples are numerous from the City in contexts dating from the mid 13th century onwards.

There are nine fragments of particularly interesting glass (<G18>–<G19>) from contexts in period B3 and therefore broadly contemporary with the abbey (1350–1539). Eight fragments of natural green glass come from the body of a flask or bottle that has been flattened on one side but remains bulbous on the other (<G19>). This body form matches a type commonly used as pilgrim flasks and known by that name. Two handles were located in the angle of the neck and shoulder of the flask so that it could be suspended. Only one other example is known from this country, from Kings Langley, Hertfordshire (Charleston 1973, 69, fig 20, no. 5). This vessel came from a cellar dated by documentary evidence to between 1291–2, when it was built, and its damage by fire and subsequent decay in 1431. Charleston (ibid) noted that the light green and slightly bubbled glass was of a fine quality and, as a medieval vessel, it could not have been of English manufacture but was a foreign import; he speculated that its place of manufacture was in France or elsewhere in northern Europe. Subsequent research on the full repertoires of the north European glasshouses during the medieval period (Baumgartner and Krueger 1988; Foy and Sennequier 1989) does not reveal or involve discussion of any comparative vessels.

In addition to these body fragments, there is also the neck fragment <G18> with a 'bulb' or swelling. This fragment is of the same metal as the other eight and comes from an associated context; it is most likely, therefore, to be part of the same vessel as the body fragments. It is not possible to say whether it originally had handles. The metal of these fragments and the swelling in the neck fragment make it directly comparable with a group of eight bottle neck fragments in the Museum of London (MOL acc nos 2271, 2273 and 78.52/12, 2276, 2281, 2597, 12707, 14539 and 78.52/11, 17869, A13382). Three of these have at least two swellings; all except one handle-less vessel have two handles, and the surviving body fragments for two of these show that their forms were not simply bulbous but partially or totally flattened.

Apart from the fragmentary two-handled, partially flattened pilgrim flask from the medieval cellar at Kings Langley, these enigmatic bottles would appear to have no other parallels. However, they are strikingly similar in many details to a well-documented group of gilded and enamelled Islamic pilgrim flasks, the products of Ayyubid and Mamluk Syria (W Evans, pers comm) and lesser-known, but seemingly common, plain Islamic bottles of the 11th to 15th centuries also from the Levant region. It must be stressed that there is no evidence whatsoever that any of the London examples had ever been gilded or enamelled. More research is needed to identify the source of these plain vessels, but it is possible that they represent vessels made in an Islamic tradition in a country closer to late medieval England, Spain for example.

The site produced a total of 57 fragments (representing a minimum of 15 and a maximum of 27 vessels) in opaque white glass (*lattimo*) or colourless but with opaque white decoration, 18 of which come from the St Mary Graces phase of the site (<G20>–<G23>). This style of glass is well-attested among the Venetian repertoires of the 16th and 17th centuries, where it undoubtedly originated and developed, as well as in other north European glasshouses, for example in France, the Low Countries and England, which produced glass in *façon de Venise*.

The most common decorative technique is the use of *lattimo* canes laid or gathered on to a paraison and reworked (as in all the examples here). This technique originated in Venice during the second quarter of the 16th century and was in use throughout the 17th century. Three different types of decoration are represented in the St Mary Graces assemblage, employing both plain opaque white canes (*vetro a fili*) and twisted opaque white threads on a colourless core (*vetro a retorti*). These are:

a) *vetro a fili* – a colourless vessel with decoration combining opaque white and blue canes (<G20>, Fig 91).
b) simple *vetro a retorti* – a colourless vessel decorated with rods of opaque white spirals on colourless cores (<G21> (Fig 92) and G22).
c) *vetro a fili* and *vetro a retorti* together – the two types of cane used on the same vessel (<G23>).

The forms represented by these fragments are well-attested ones, namely cylindrical beakers or vases. The profile of the foot fragment <G21> (Fig 92), which probably comes from a jug, can be seen on a 'chalcedony' glass jug of *c* 1500 (Tait 1979, 105, no. 167). Unfortunately, the majority of the fragments here are far too small to enable a positive identification of their respective forms, but it is probable that they come either from the aforementioned forms or from stemmed drinking glasses or *tazze* (ibid, *passim*). Such glass in *façon de Venise* was also being made elsewhere, including London. Excavations at the Wingate Centre, 62–64 Aldgate High Street (site code AL74) examined an area that had been used in the mid 17th century as a dumping ground for refuse from a nearby slaughteryard and a glass factory. Waste debris there included *lattimo* material (Charleston and Grew in prep). It is interesting to note that the Royal Mint assemblage also includes a small quantity of glassworking debris. Among this material is a distorted object, 'decorated' with *lattimo* rods, which probably came from the end of a paraison once the rods had been gathered and marvered on to it.

The earliest identifiable drinking vessel form recorded on this site is the tall, almost cylindrical beaker (<G24>–<G41>) fashioned with a pushed-in base forming a pedestal foot (<G35>–<G41>) (Fig 93; Fig 94). This form, according to Charleston (1981, 88), should be regarded as a type-fossil on glassmaking sites dating to the end of the 16th and the beginning of the 17th centuries, such as Rosedale and Hutton in Yorkshire (Charleston 1972, 136–41, fig 61, nos 23–6; fig 64, nos 64–82; fig 65, nos 83–4, 87–92), Woodchester, Gloucestershire (Daniels 1950, pl VII, nos 48–53), and many Wealden sites (Kenyon 1967, pl XIV, a; pl XVI, i; pl XVII, g–h). Such beakers were probably designed for drinking beer (Charleston 1972, 133–6, fig 64, no. 64). Many of them have low-relief decoration, usually vertical or diagonal ribs or diamonds/ovals in a diaper pattern, formed by the paraison being blown into a mould early in the fashioning process and subsequently reinflated. Examples of the common decorations, found also on those sites referred to above and frequently recorded in London, are represented here by fragments <G25>–<G34>.

Bulbous-bodied bottles (<G42>–<G47>) with tapering necks, out-splayed rims, bases with low domed kicks, and plain bodies, or spiral, low-relief mould-blown ribs ('wrythen') on the bodies, were common in the second half of the 16th and the first half of the 17th century. Examples come from London (Hume 1957, 106, nos 5, 7), Basing House, Hampshire (Charleston 1971, 66, nos 28–9, fig 28), Southampton (Charleston 1975, 223, nos 1573–7), Chichester, Sussex (Charleston 1981, 224, no. 11, fig 8.54) and Linacre Garden, Canterbury (Shepherd 1990, 212–14, nos 241–7, 250, 264–72). It would not be unreasonable to say that this form, 200–270mm high and with some smaller and larger variations, can be taken as being the standard medieval glass bottle. Among the earliest occurrences of this form are the fragments from the early 14th-century glasshouse site at Blunden's Wood, near Hambledon, Surrey (Wood, E S, 1965, 65–7). The earliest datable London example was found on a site in Milk Street (MIL72 [502a] <112>) in a context dated to the second half of the 14th century. Examples in late 17th-century contexts at Nonsuch Palace show that this was a long-lived, functional type. Finds from numerous Wealden glasshouses (Kenyon 1967, pls XII–XIII), including Blunden's Wood, and St Weonard's, Herefordshire (Charleston 1975, 213), suggest that the manufacture of this form of bottle was widespread.

Catalogue

Catalogue number <G1> has already been used to catalogue a fragment of Roman glass in the preceding companion volume (Grainger et al 2008) so this catalogue begins with <G2>.

<G2> Red glass vessel
[3713]; Grainger and Phillpotts 2010, period C1, B30
[1911]; Grainger and Phillpotts 2010, period C1, OA17
Three fragments of free-blown opaque red glass from thin-walled, bulbous-bodied vessels. 13th or 14th century.

<G3> Hanging lamp
[4590]; Grainger and Phillpotts 2010, period C1, B30
The rounded base of a lamp. Free-blown; natural green glass with deep surface decomposition. Pontil scar visible. 13th to 16th centuries.

<G4>–<G6> Hanging lamps (Fig 52)
<G4>, <3887>, [3998]; period B4, B12
<G5>, <3067>, [14117]; Grainger and Phillpotts 2010, period C1, OA14
<G6>, [7121]; Grainger and Phillpotts 2010, period C2, OA29
Base fragments as for <G3>

<G7> Urinal
[3998]; period B4, B12
Fragment from the rim and neck of a urinal. Free-blown; natural green glass with a deep surface decomposition layer. The rim is simply fire-rounded and out-splayed with a small, vertical lip. 13th to 16th centuries.

<G8>–<G11> Urinals
<G8>, [3998] x 2; period B4, B12
<G9>, <2014>, [3998]; period B4, B12
<G10>, <2090>, [14117]; Grainger and Phillpotts 2010, period C1, OA14
<G11>, <3414>, [14274]; Grainger and Phillpotts 2010, period C1, OA15
Fragments as for <G7>. Natural green glass.

<G12> Bottle or urinal (Fig 90)
<111>, [72]; Grainger and Phillpotts 2010, period C1, B30
Fragment from the base of a round-bottomed bottle or urinal. Free-blown; natural green glass with a deep surface decomposition layer. Pontil scar visible. 13th to 16th centuries.

<G13>–<G17> Bottle or urinal (Fig 52)
<G13>, [3998]; period B4, B12
<G14>, <2012>, [3998]; period B4, B12
<G15>, <2023>, [3998]; period B4, B12
<G16>, <2050>, [3998]; period B4, B12
<G17>, [4644]; Grainger and Phillpotts 2010, period C1, B14
Fragments as for <G12>. Natural green or greenish-blue glass.

<G18> Flask or bottle
<2702>, [9589]; period B3, OA2/OA12
Fragment from the neck of a flask or bottle. Free-blown; natural green glass with numerous small and elongated air bubbles. The neck has been constricted in two places to form a swelling or bulb. 13th to 16th centuries.

<G19> Flask or bottle
<2731>, [9589]; period B3, OA2/OA12
Eight fragments from the body of a flask or bottle. Free-blown; natural green glass with many small and elongated bubbles. The form of the body is not symmetrical: one side is convex, the other flattened as for pilgrim flasks. Probably part of <G18>. 13th to 16th centuries.

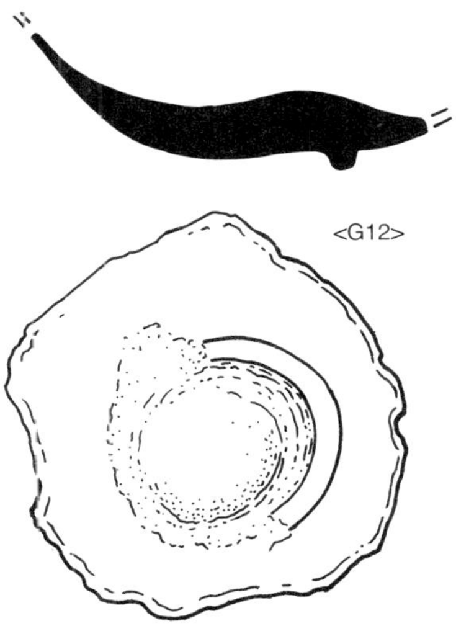

Fig 90 Round-bottomed glass bottle or urinal fragment <G12> (scale 1:1)

<G20> Vase or goblet (Fig 91)
<2152>, [6033]; Grainger and Phillpotts 2010, period C2, OA29
Eleven fragments from the rim and side of a vase or goblet. Free-blown; colourless glass with a decoration comprising two opaque white rods alternating with a rod of blue on an opaque white core (*vetro a fili*). 16th century.

<G21> Jug or tazza (Fig 92)
<2521>, [7967]; period B4, OA2/OA9
Fragment from the base of a jug or tazza. Colourless glass decorated with colourless glass rods with opaque white spiral decoration (*a retorti*). Lip of foot fire-rounded and folded up and over to make a triangular section. Late 16th or early 17th century.

<G22> Decorated glass
<2493>, [7957]; Grainger and Phillpotts 2010, period C2, OA31
<3466>, [13299]; Grainger and Phillpotts 2010, period C1, OA14
<3549>, [13299] x 2; Grainger and Phillpotts 2010, period C1, OA14
Fragments of free-blown colourless glass decorated with colourless rods with opaque white spiral decoration (*a retorti*). 16th or 17th century.

<G23> Cup or tazza
<2666>, <2667>, <2668>, [9508]; period B4, OA2/OA9
Three fragments from a cup or tazza. Colourless glass decorated with opaque white rods (*a fili*) and colourless rods with opaque white spiral decoration (*a retorti*) gathered on the paraison before full and final inflation. 16th or 17th century.

<G24> Beaker
[378]; Grainger and Phillpotts 2010, period C1, OA19
Fragment from the rim of a beaker. Natural green glass with surface decomposition. Fire-rounded rim. 15th to early 17th centuries.

<G25> Beaker (Fig 93)
<2675>, [9570]; Grainger and Phillpotts 2010, period C2, OA29
Fragment from the rim of a beaker. Mould-blown and reinflated ('optic-blown'); natural green glass with surface decomposition. Body decorated with spiralling low-relief ribs ('wrythen'). Rim fire-rounded. 15th to early 17th centuries.

<G26> Beaker (Fig 93)
<247>, [1911]; Grainger and Phillpotts 2010, period C2, OA31
Fragment from the rim and part of the side of a beaker. Technique and metal as for <G25>. Body decorated with long ovals, slightly 'wrythen'. Rim fire-rounded. 15th to early 17th centuries.

<G27> Beaker
<2552>, [7908]; Grainger and Phillpotts 2010, period C2, OA31
Fragment from the side of a beaker. Technique and metal as for <G25>. Decorated with ovals in diaper. 15th to early 17th centuries.

<G28> Beaker
<3099>, [14137]; Grainger and Phillpotts 2010, period C2, OA25
Fragment from the rim and side of a beaker. Technique and metal as for <G25>. Decorated with ovals in diaper. 15th to early 17th centuries.

<G29> Beaker (Fig 93)
<410>, [1764]; Grainger and Phillpotts 2010, period C1, OA17
Fragment from the rim and side of a beaker. Technique and metal as for <G25>. Body decorated with long diamonds in diaper. 15th to early 17th centuries.

<G30> Beaker (Fig 93)
<4283>, [+]
Fragment from the rim and side of a beaker. Technique and metal as for <G25>. Body decorated with high-relief diamonds in diaper. 15th to early 17th centuries.

<G31> Beaker
<2083>, [4590]; Grainger and Phillpotts 2010, period C1, B30
Fragment from the rim and side of a beaker. Technique and metal as for <G25>. Body decorated with relief vertical ribs. 15th to early 17th centuries.

<G32> Beaker
<268>, [+]
<511>, [9570] x 2; Grainger and Phillpotts 2010, period C2, OA29
Three fragments as for <G31>. 15th to early 17th centuries.

<G33> Beaker
[6455]; Grainger and Phillpotts 2010, period C2, OA29
Fragment as for <G31> but with a very deep surface decomposition. 15th to early 17th centuries.

<G34> Beaker (Fig 93)
<2256>, [7115]; Grainger and Phillpotts 2010, period C2, OA29
Fragment from the rim and part of the side of a beaker. Technique and metal as for <G25>. Body decorated with 'nip't' diamond waies. 15th to early 17th centuries.

<G35> Beaker
<409>, [1764]; Grainger and Phillpotts 2010, period C1, OA17
Fragment from the base of a beaker. Blown; natural green glass

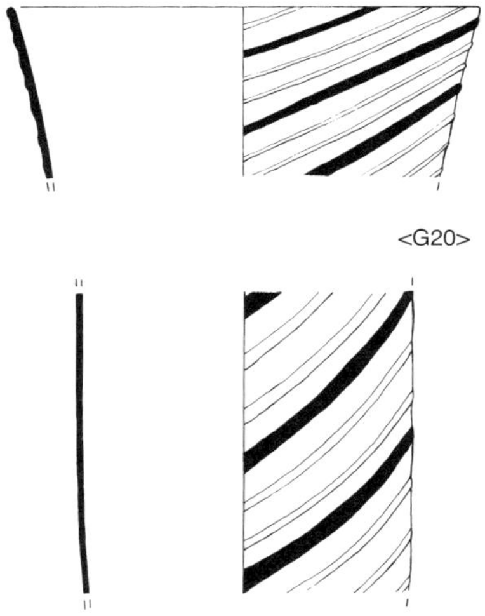

Fig 91 Vase or goblet <G20> (scale 1:2)

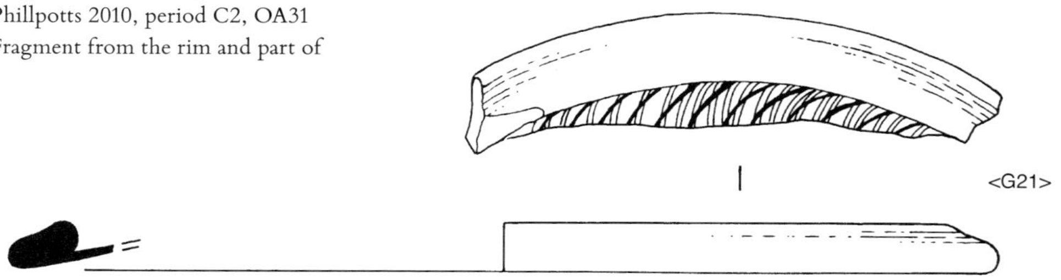

Fig 92 Part of glass jug or tazza <G21> (scale 1:1)

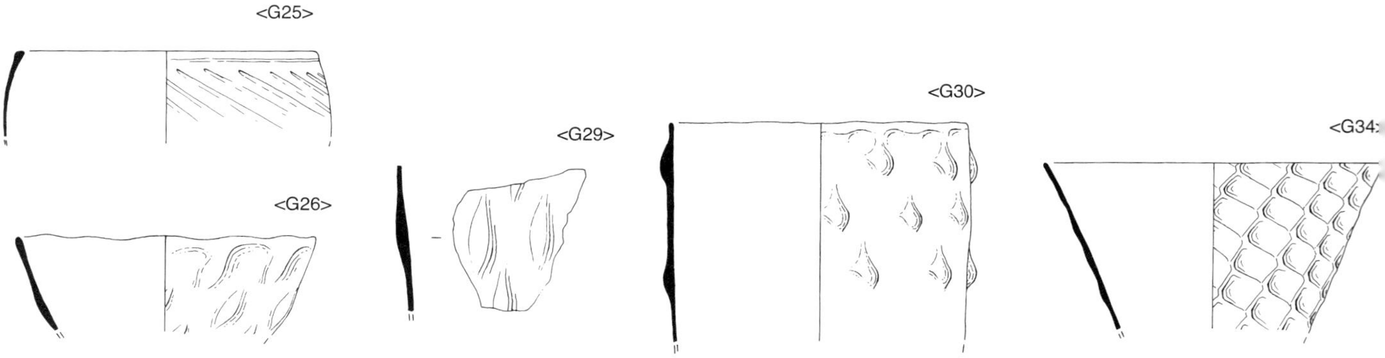

Fig 93 Rims of beakers <G25>, <G26>, <G29>, <G30> and <G34> (scale 1:2)

with surface decomposition. Pushed-in, pedestal base. 15th to early 17th centuries.

<G36>–<G41> Beaker (Fig 94)
<G36>, <2270>, [378]; Grainger and Phillpotts 2010, period C1, OA19
<G37>, [378]; Grainger and Phillpotts 2010, period C1, OA19
<G38>, [14137]; Grainger and Phillpotts 2010, period C2, OA25
<G39>, <2676>, [9570]; Grainger and Phillpotts 2010, period C2, OA29
<G40>, <3433>, [13006]; Grainger and Phillpotts 2010, period C3, -
<G41>, [10301]; Grainger and Phillpotts 2010, period C1, OA20
Six fragments, as for <G35>. Fragment <G41> decorated with low-relief, mould-blown vertical ribs. 15th to early 17th centuries.

<G42> Bottles
<2701>, <2572>, [9589]; period B3, OA2/OA12
A very large number of fragments (in excess of a thousand) from a group of bottles (minimum of ten). Both free-blown (at least four) and mould-blown 'wrythen' (at least four) are represented. Rims knocked-off and flared on a tapering neck. Bulbous bodies with pushed-in base. 14th to early 17th centuries.

<G43> Bottle
<2101>, [+]
Fragment from the knocked-off, flared rim and tapering neck of a bottle. Free-blown; natural green glass with surface decay. 14th to early 17th centuries.

<G44> Bottle
<2167>, [+]
[72]; Grainger and Phillpotts 2010, period C1, B30
[4644]; Grainger and Phillpotts 2010, period C1, B11
[8622] x 2; Grainger and Phillpotts 2010, period C2, OA31
<2558>, [7950]; Grainger and Phillpotts 2010, period C2, OA31
<2746>, [208]; Grainger and Phillpotts 2010, period C2, OA26
<2260>, [6019]; Grainger and Phillpotts 2010, period C2, OA29
Eight fragments, as for <G43>.

<G45> Bottle
[+]
[378]; Grainger and Phillpotts 2010, period C1, OA19
Two fragments, as for <G43> but in natural greenish-blue glass.

<G46> Bottle
[+]
Fragment from the pushed-in, domed base of a bulbous-bodied bottle. Natural green glass with surface decay. Pontil scar visible. 14th to early 15th centuries.

<G47> Bottle
[+] x 2
[4644] x 3; Grainger and Phillpotts 2010, period C1, B11
<257>, [4644]; Grainger and Phillpotts 2010, period C1, B11
[583]; Grainger and Phillpotts 2010, period C2, B37
[378] x 4; Grainger and Phillpotts 2010, period C1, OA19
[367]; Grainger and Phillpotts 2010, period C1, OA19
Twelve fragments, as for <G46>.

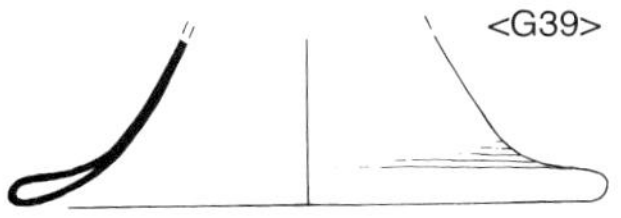

Fig 94 Fragment of base of beaker <G39> (scale 1:2)

5.5 Window glass

Jill Channer

A small quantity of very fragmented and deteriorated 15th-century painted glass was recovered from within the former south aisle of the nave, from rubble deposits associated with the *c* 1560 demolition of the church (period C1: Grainger and Phillpotts 2010). The glass was found in an area identified as immediately below the window in the second bay (from the east) of the south aisle, that is, the bay to the west of the chapel of ? St Anne (room 6a) (Chapter 2.5). The fragments laid out contiguously would just about cover two sheets of A3 paper, or an area of *c* 590 x 840mm.

The base glass is all white with bold, cursive paint, backpainting and yellow stain where the surfaces survive. It is much perished: hardly any is translucent, and the surfaces are obscured by both the accretion of demolition detritus and deterioration resulting from burial. No glazing construction debris or coloured glass was recovered. None of the glass shows signs of glaziers' sorting marks, heat damage, exterior corrosion or lead shadows where the came would have protected the surface, which indicates that the glass was not *in situ* for long enough for either to impact on the surface. The context and condition of the glass are consistent with its having been smashed out to enable the valuable lead to be asset-stripped.

The designs are consequently all very incomplete, with few surviving defining grozed edges and not one single intact piece. The repertoire includes architectural, background, floor, border and drapery designs; there are no discernible heads, hands, feet, or heraldic or iconographic attributes to indicate the subject matter, but there are pieces depicting hair and one distinctive fragment of blackletter inscription '(?h)om'. These remnants would indicate the common 15th-century design type of figures set beneath and/or within an architectural framework, with canopies at the apex, a tiled floor and inscriptions at the base set against a background of foliage designs or decorative quarries. The techniques deployed are also typical of the 15th century, including two-tone washes to articulate the third dimension, backpainting to emphasise depth, designs picked out of matte washes, and yellow stain applied to the exterior.

The cursive and imprecise application of the paint, combined with the thickness of the glass (2–5mm), indicates that this is not high-quality, expensive glazing – which is disappointing as we have such meagre survivals of medieval painted glass from City sites. It is perhaps unexpected to find glass of such disappointing quality, which may reflect a dearth of high-worth donors at this stage of the foundation's development (Chapter 3.6 and 3.9). It might seem surprising to find figurative glass in a Cistercian monastic church, but Cistercian glass of any date is extremely rare in the UK, including 14th- and 15th-century (and thus figurative) glass (Marks 1986).

The most substantial survivals of all the discernible designs are illustrated in Fig 95, with the grozed edges shown with a dotted line and the broken edges with a broken line where discernible; washes are indicated by stippling. Distinguishing the paint lines from the surface damage and accretions was difficult.

Fragment <GW1> is the blackletter inscription and <GW2> is a 'seaweed-type' background foliage design. Fragments <GW3> and <GW4> are related foliage designs, and <GW5> is a distinct quarry design with four foliate fronds radiating from a central

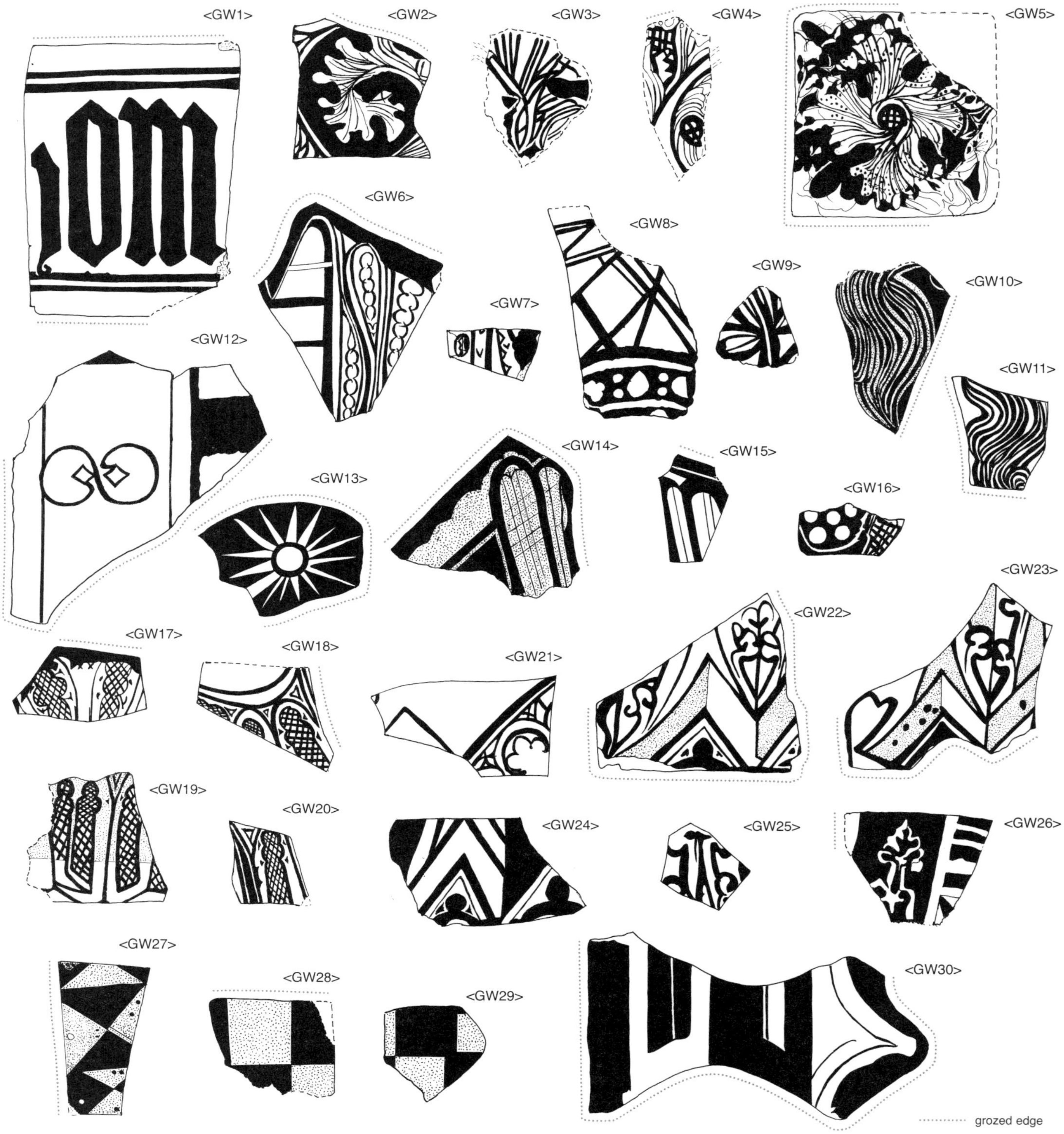

Fig 95 Selected window glass <GW1>–<GW30> from the south aisle of the nave (B6) (scale 1:2) (drawings courtesy of English Heritage)

cross-hatched circle – an interesting addition to the typology. Pieces <GW6>–<GW8> are fragments of draperies with decorative borders: <GW6> has pronounced backpainting to emphasise the depth of the folds and could perhaps be part of a sleeve, while <GW9> could be either a small fragment of drapery or a stem and veined leaf design. Fragments <GW10> and <GW11> are pieces with hair. Fragment <GW12> is a large-scale border design and <GW13> is a spiky star design, imprecisely picked out of a matte wash radiating from an unpainted central circle; this could be from a heraldic device. Fragments <GW14> and <GW15> are related designs set within a cusped border. Piece <GW16> is a very fragmented decorative design incorporating circles. Fragments <GW17>–<GW20> are unusual, small-scale, precisely painted, fictive trefoil-headed windows with reticulated glazing and cusped interstices. The design function of these fragments and that of <GW21> has not been ascertained. Fragments <GW22>–<GW26> are all crocketted gables from canopy or border designs with the third dimension articulated by washes. Fragments <GW27>–<GW29> are two tiled floor designs, one of triangles and the other of squares. Fragment <GW30> is the most complete find, a bold architectural design painted on thick (2–3mm) glass with two-tone washes.

5.6 Accessioned finds

Judy Stevenson (metal) and Richenda Goffin (antler and bone) with Alison Nailer (leather)

The assemblage

Only 29 metal objects came from monastic period contexts and fall within the lifespan of St Mary Graces; items of this date found in later contexts are included here. Several more objects overlap the period of the late monastery (period B3, *c* 1400–1539), the Dissolution and manor house (period B4, 1539–60) and early victualling yard (period C1, 1560–*c* 1660). Four of the objects are noteworthy: a gilded miniature sceptre <S41> (Fig 96), two similar gilded book cover strapends <S42> and <S43> (Fig 97) found in different areas of the site, and a lead papal bulla <S46> from a grave within the church. The miniature gilded sceptre was possibly held in the hand of a small wooden statue, probably standing in the church. Such a statue may have been of the Virgin in Majesty but is more likely to have been that of a king, either a saint-king or Edward III. The gilded book clasps are similar to other examples found in London, Oxford, Salisbury and Colchester. They all terminate in a suspension ring and were probably fastened by means of a peg which fixed into a hole at the back of the clasp. The clasps were attached to the end of a book strap; one of our examples retains traces of a leather strap, the other of a textile strap. They are late 14th-century in date.

The graves produced a number of items of dress. The copper-alloy annular brooches/buckles from the monastic phase are stylistically inseparable from those from the Black Death cemetery (Stevenson 2008, 37–41). Two pairs were recovered, one matching pair <S97> and one non-matching pair <S96>. A more interesting annular brooch decorated with spiralled wire <S95> (Fig 25) was the single find from a child's grave. Spiralled wire decoration on medieval and post-medieval jewellery and toiletry items was probably a cheap means of producing ornamentation. A small rectangular single-loop shoe buckle <S106> (Fig 102) was found at the foot of a skeleton. A second buckle of copper alloy <S105> (Fig 102) is a type usually found in the latter half of the 14th century. A copper-alloy hooked strap mount <S121> (Fig 104) was a single find in one of the graves. Other belt fittings include a copper-alloy eight-petalled floral belt mount <S119> found with several plain 'spangle' fragments, and a copper-alloy bar belt mount <S120>. Further dress fittings from the monastic period burials include two spherical buttons <S127> and <S128> found in grave fills. Two padlocks were found in the graves: a brazed iron barrel padlock cylinder <S78> and an iron barrel padlock <S79>, possibly with an unusual mechanism.

Other late medieval copper-alloy objects include a knife handle chape <S140> of late 15th- to early 16th-century date with incised male and female figures and traces of the wooden handle; three small copper-alloy single-loop buckles, two with buckle plates (<S98>, <S103>) and one without (<S105>), all dating to *c* 1350–*c* 1450; and a domed thimble <S153> also belonging to the first half of the monastic phase. A piece of folded copper-alloy sheet <S56> may be a mending piece. Three iron door keys <S85>, <S89> and <S90> of approximately 14th-century date, and the two barrel padlocks <S78> and <S79> (above), one of which is probably also 14th-century, belong to the abbey phase. Five pieces of iron mail with riveted links <S172> appear to be of 15th-century European type. Mail tends to have a long lifespan as the time and effort required to produce it prolongs secondary usage, and scraps such as these were almost certainly being reused for purposes other than the original military one. Finally, half a pair of iron shears <S146>, probably dating to the early to mid 15th century, may represent the only datable tool associated with the industrial life of the abbey.

As the 16th century includes the final monastic, Dissolution and manor house, and early victualling yard phases, it is rarely possible to assign the finds from this century to any one of those phases. Two toilet instruments recovered from a Dissolution context are dated from the 14th to 16th centuries. One of these (<S152>) may have been used on the ears, nails and teeth. Such an object found at Battle Abbey (Geddes 1985, 162, fig 52, no. 77) has been compared with a 16th-century French example. A second toilet instrument found in the same context is a copper-alloy cosmetic spoon or scoop (<S151>). This may date from earlier than the 16th century as scoops with twisted shanks occur in 14th-century contexts from the City of London (Egan and Pritchard 1991, 379, fig 251, nos 1758–62). Two thimbles (<S154>, <S155>) from unstratified contexts date from the mid 15th to 16th century; the ring thimble <S155> may be the earlier of the two.

Five groups of cast lead cames (<S66>, <S71>, <S72>, <S74>, <S75>) may be all that remains of the abbey window lead, as lead would have been melted down during the Dissolution period and later. Group <S72> from period B4 (B16) includes not only cast cames but also lead cames of the type milled in a toothless mill (type D), and possibly manufactured during the 16th century; this may suggest the use of type D cames in the later abbey phases.

The excavations recovered a fairly small number of leather items, mostly from victualling yard contexts (periods C1–C2: Grainger and Phillpotts 2010, 108–9). Only a few leather items (eg <S65>) were recovered from the Dissolution and manor house phase (period B4, 1539–60), and none from earlier phases of the abbey.

Catalogue numbers <S1>–<S40> are used in the preceding companion volume (Grainger et al 2008), so the sequence in the following catalogue begins with <S41>. Abbreviations of dimensions used in the catalogue are as follows: L (length); W (width); Diam (diameter); Th (thickness); H (height); D (depth). Other abbreviations used are: max (maximum); ext (external); int (internal). This report is substantially that written in 1990–1.

Items associated with institutional use/religion

Statue fitting

<S41> Silver-gilt miniature sceptre (Fig 96)
<1899>, [3964]; Grainger and Phillpotts 2010, period C1, B11
Square-sectioned body with pedestal-and-knop terminals. Half of the body is plain and the other half ribbed, with a raised coronet design separating the two halves. Small sections of the outer gold casing are missing, around one terminal and at the centre, but this loss cannot account for any method of fixing. L 32mm, section 2.54mm.

The object has no means of attachment, and is therefore an isolated item, probably from a statue. It was presumably held in the hand of a standing or seated wooden statue no more than about 30cm high, and likely to have been a figure of royalty. The Virgin is often seen seated in majesty holding a sceptre in 12th- to 13th-century representations, but the design of the sceptre along with the abbey's date would tend to suggest that the effigy was not the Virgin. The greater likelihood of a royal figure may suggest Edward III or a later king, or possibly an earlier saint-king such as Edward the Confessor or St Edmund (J Cherry, pers comm).

The construction of the miniature sceptre is uncertain. X-ray fluorescence (XRF) analysis in 1990 (by Michael Heyworth, Ancient Monuments Laboratory) determined that the object may have a silver metal core and a mercury-gilded exterior. The gilding may have been in the form of gold leaf applied with mercury (the mercury since fused into the leaf). The sceptre now has a largely hollow interior with only a double strip of metal (presumably silver) running down its length diagonally from one corner of the shank to the other. There is no base left for the gilded surface to adhere to. A brown resinous substance on the interior may be a corrosion product of the silver core (M Heyworth, pers comm). The object was presumably fashioned by a silversmith and is possibly of 14th- to 15th-century date.

Fig 96 Gilded miniature sceptre <S41> (scale 2:1)

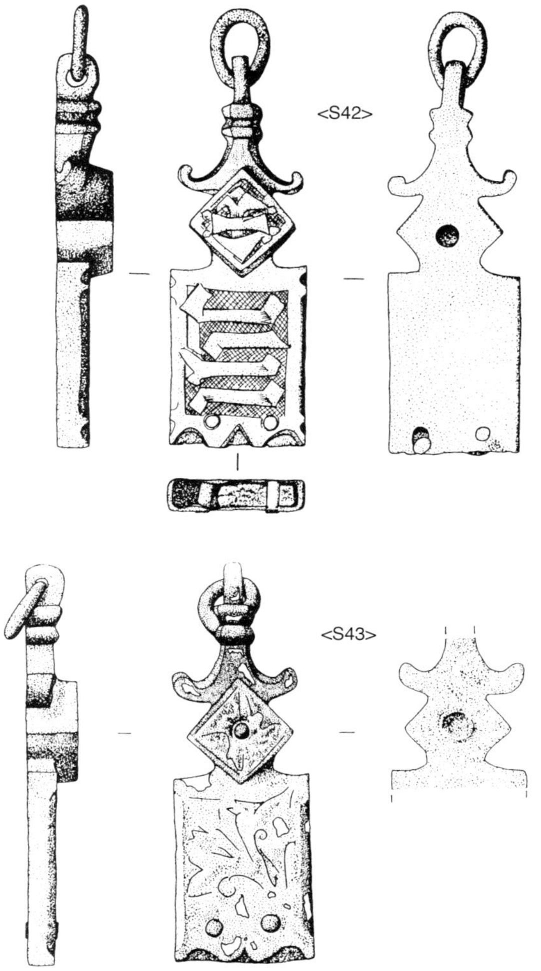

Fig 97 Medieval book clasps <S42> and <S43> (scale 1:1)

Book clasps

<S42> Gilded copper-alloy book clasp (Fig 97)
<15>, [367]; Grainger and Phillpotts 2010, period C1, OA19
Extensive gilding of the copper alloy, including on the reverse side. Strap plate engraved with 'ihc', the first three letters of the Greek form of the name Jesus, alternatively written as 'IHS' and interpreted as 'I(esus) H(ominum) S(alvator)' – 'Jesus saviour of mankind' (Murdoch 1991, 108, no. 201). The lozenge-shaped boss bears the sacred monogram 'MARIA'. Remains of leather strap. L 59mm, W 18mm, Th 6mm. Late 14th century.

<S43> Gilded copper-alloy book clasp (Fig 97)
<1939>, [4590]; Grainger and Phillpotts 2010, period C1, B12
Gilded copper alloy. Main body engraved with a fleur-de-lys, the lozenge-shaped boss with a quatrefoil design. Remains of tabby weave textile strap. L 55mm (originally 59mm), W 18mm, Th 6mm. Late 14th century.

<S44> Copper-alloy book clasp
<2065a>, [3998]; period B4, B12
Small book clasp. Splayed terminal, and single-split and rolled hooked end. No decoration except for concentric rings around the rivets. L 28mm, W 8mm. Late medieval to early post-medieval.

<S45> Copper-alloy book clasp
<2282>, [+]
Fragment. Splayed terminal with three triangular notches scalloped into the end. A central band of incised decoration runs down the clasp, consisting of a border groove on each side of the band and a central groove which divides opposed oblique lines. Two iron nail/rivet holes survive. The middle and upper section of the clasp as well as its hook attachment are missing. L 13mm, W 17mm, Th 1.3mm. (A second fragment of plating of approximately the same thickness and with one original edge may also be from this clasp. This piece has three incised lines which form part of a larger pattern. A regular, albeit slight, curve in the piece casts some doubt on its identification, but the fragment is included under the same accession number as the identified book clasp fragment. L 13.8mm, W 9.8mm, Th 1.3mm.) Such book clasps usually date from the late 15th to 17th centuries.

Papal bulla

<S46> Lead bulla
<3826>, [13670]; period B3, room 6a
Papal bulla probably of anti-pope Clement VIII (?1424–9). The obverse of the seal shows '..VIII' (possibly 'PPVIII') on the base line but the name of the pope is illegible. The reverse depicts the heads of St Peter and St Paul with the lettering 'SPASPE' running across the top. The horizontal alignment of these letters is a feature of bullae pre-dating Innocent VIII (1484–92) (A Prescott, pers comm). Diam *c* 43mm.

Tuning peg

<S47> Bone tuning peg (Fig 98)
<2128>, [3989]; Grainger and Phillpotts 2010, period C1, B30
Fragment of lower half with rectangular head. When complete, the other end would have been perforated with a hole or slit for a string to pass through. The shaft is knife-trimmed, with no wear marks of strings apparent to the naked eye and no evidence of any staining from metallic strings. L 44mm, W 5mm, shank Diam 5mm.

A tuning peg like this would probably have belonged to an instrument whose peg-board was accessible from either side for threading or tensioning the strings, such as a frame harp, lute or fiddle (Henig 1977). Such bone artefacts are not uncommon in medieval levels, or among Dissolution-period deposits at religious houses. A similar tuning peg came from Dissolution-period debris at St Augustine's Abbey, Canterbury (Henig 1988, 184). Excavations at Battle Abbey produced 12 tuning pegs from post-Dissolution contexts, not all of this design

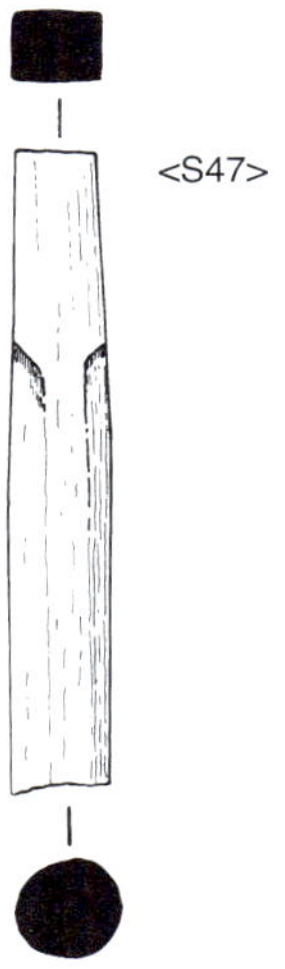

Fig 98 Bone tuning peg <S47> (scale 1:1)

(Lawson 1985). Another example has been recovered from excavations at Merton Priory (Miller and Saxby 2007, 126, fig 154, <S29>; Egan 2007, 223). Page (1978) lists four London harpmakers and lutemakers from 1416–34, including John Bore who supplied harps to Henry V.

Fixtures, fasteners and fittings

Mounts and box or furniture fittings

<S48> Copper-alloy mount (Fig 25)
<2723>, [9890]; period B2, OA2
Small cruciform mount. Each arm has a lateral knop on either side, and the middle of the cross has a depressed lozenge with raised centre. One arm is incomplete and the opposite arm has a small attachment hole. The delicacy of this mount may suggest use on a strap or some other item of attire, or alternatively it may have been a decorative mount on a small box. Original dimensions 16 x 16mm.

<S49> Iron mounts
<4024a>, <4024b>, <4024c>, [4542]; period B2, B3
Three mounts, possibly tinned, probably box fittings. a) Disc mount attached by means of a shank positioned slightly off-centre. Diam 23mm. b) Strip with flared lobed terminal; pierced towards the plain end which may be broken. L 30mm, W 6–8mm, W of terminal 16mm. c) Square mount pierced near the centre; possibly originally rectangular. Dimensions 18 x 21mm.

<S50> Copper-alloy lion mount
<10013>, [16575]; period B2, B3
Circular mount. Embossed sitting lion with embossed ropework perimeter. No visible means of attachment. Diam 25mm. Probably 16th to 17th centuries.

<S51> Iron fastener
<4016c>, [4542]; period B2, B3
Ring-headed fastener. Diam of head 18mm.

<S52> Iron ring
<4016b>, [4542]; period B2, B3
Oval section. Diam 22mm (ext), 15mm (int).

<S53> Copper-alloy mount
<2960>, [13809]; period B2, B6
Plain staple mount for upholstery. Concave-sectioned bar, with the staple arms bent at the ends. L (max) 17.5mm, W 22mm.

<S54> Copper-alloy casket mount
<2093>, [4789]; period B2, B11
Flat square casket mount with an extension on one edge. Perforation in the centre of the square. Overall L 46mm, square 25 x 27mm, extension 20 x 15mm.

<S55> Iron handle
<3300a>, [9589]; period B3, OA2/OA12
Movable handle from drawer or box. Narrow hooked terminals which hooked through loops attached to furniture and allowed free movement of the handle. Angular bridging (bridge L 125mm (ext), 110mm (int)). Overall L 160mm.

<S56> Copper-alloy mending piece
<2572>, [9589]; period B3, OA2/OA12
Folded angular copper-alloy plating, formed by bringing two ends together and then doubling them back. Dimensions 34 x 15mm.

<S57> Iron box fitting
<2055>, [3998]; period B4, B12
Part of ? box or box fitting. Rectangular, with three edges bent up straight to form an enclosed area, the other side and edge broken. Wood remaining within the container. L 66mm (incomplete), W 75 mm, max edge H 17mm (incomplete).

<S58> Copper-alloy chain
<2803>, [9508]; period B4, OA2/OA9
Chain formed from S-shaped wire links (L 12–14mm). Unfolded L *c* 65mm.

Pintles, staples, nail and stud

<S59> Iron pintle
<4016a>, [4542]; period B2, B3
Both arms of equal L 40mm.

<S60> Iron pintle
<3109>, [13434]; Grainger and Phillpotts 2010, period C1, OA14
? Small pintle; arm L 26mm (complete), 32mm (broken).

<S61> Iron staple
<3300b>, [9589]; period B3, OA2/OA12
Square cross-section. Both points broken. W 22mm (int), 33mm (ext), L 65mm (incomplete). Found with other fittings, possibly from a box.

<S62> Iron staple
<3708>, [12350]; period B4, B16
Small hooped staple of square cross-section. L 45mm, ext W 25mm.

<S63> Iron nail
<2662>, [9212]; period B2, B1
Very large nail with a curled, clenched end. Square domed head. L 195mm (250mm when straightened), section 15 x 15mm.

<S64> Copper-alloy domed stud (Fig 99)
<2067>, [4553]; period B4, B11
Large and heavy stud with domed head cast with a segmented design. Heavy, blunt-ended shank. Diam 30mm, shank L 25mm.

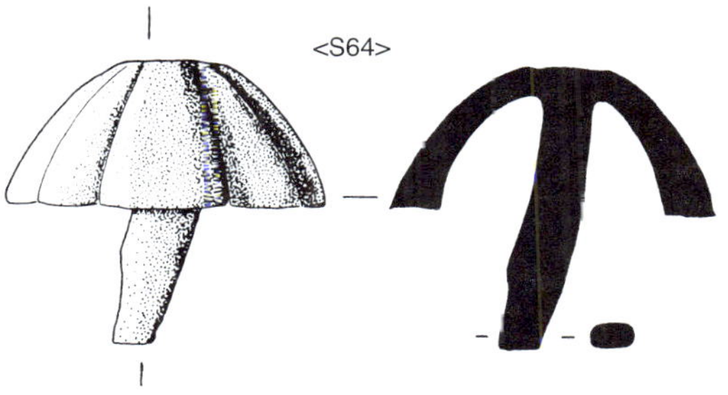

Fig 99 Large copper-alloy domed stud <S64> (scale 1:1)

Leather strap

<S65> Leather strap
<2006>, [3998]; period B4, B12
Part of a thick strap most probably used for heavy work; surviving L 221mm, W 59mm. One end has been cut straight across but the other has been torn off. Six single rows of small stitch

holes run across the strap, presumably to act as a strengthening and to secure other layers of leather.

Window fittings

The typology of lead cames is that employed for the finds from Battle Abbey, Sussex (Knight 1985).

<S66> Lead window came
<2448>, [5366]; period B3, OA10
Type C, cast, with the casting flash shaved flush. Copper corrosion spots suggest a lead/copper alloy. Small chips of green ?glass retained in the came.

<S67> Lead window came
<2066>, [3998]; period B4, B12
Type D, milled in a toothless mill. L *c* 210mm.

<S68> Lead window came
<2017>, [3998]; period B4, B12
Type D, milled in a toothless mill; in pieces. L (max) 105mm.

<S69> Lead window came
<2038>, [3998]; period B4, B12
Type D, milled in a toothless mill.

<S70> Lead window came
<2388>, [3998]; period B4, B12
Type D, milled in a toothless mill. L 90mm.

<S71> Lead window came
<3675a>, [13350]; period B4, B16
Type A, cast in a two-piece mould. Found with lead sheeting.

<S72> Lead window came
<3699a>, [12350]; period B4, B16
Lead came fragments, of three types. One piece is milled type D, two pieces are cast type A, and two pieces are probably cast type C, but possibly milled type D. Found with <S73>, four other lead objects, probably all window fittings.

<S73> Lead window fitting(s)
<3699b>, [12350]; period B4, B16
Pierced lead bar, L 63mm (incomplete), W 10mm, Th 3mm; lead ? window catch, dimensions 45 x 16 x 20mm; lead strip or offcut; corroded lead object.

<S74> Lead window came
<3236>, [13252]; Grainger and Phillpotts 2010, period C1, OA14
Type A, cast in a two-piece mould; in three pieces.

<S75> Lead window came
<3499a>, [13252]; Grainger and Phillpotts 2010, period C1, OA14
Type A, cast in a two-piece mould. Found with a corroded lead rod.

Lead cap

<S76> Lead cap
<2422>, [7524]; period B3, OA11
Roughly square-shaped cap with perforations and nails around the border. Turned down along three and a half edges to form a roughly circular, flat top. Nails entered from the convex side. One corner has diagonal slashes cut along its edge, presumably to ease folding. This object was probably used for capping a wooden post or pole. Dimensions 73 x 82mm, Th 2mm.

Lead plating

<S77> Lead plating
<2021>, [3998]; period B4, B12
Rectangular lead plating with one long edge bent at right angles. The fold is at one-third of the width. Pierced from the convex side by wide disc-headed nails at three corners, the other corner broken. L 248mm, W 81mm (with fold at *c* 25mm), Th 2.5–4mm. Probably used for waterproofing.

Security equipment

Padlocks

<S78> Iron padlock
<2308>, [7001], period B3, OA9
Probable barrel padlock cylinder. Copper alloy traces probably indicate brazing, a fairly common practice on iron locks. Ridged barrel cylinder. Dimensions 17 x 15mm.

<S79> Iron padlock
<2264>, [6386]; period B3, OA9
Part of barrel padlock. Possibly with unusual lock mechanism, although the preservation is not good. L 90mm, W 54mm.

<S80> Iron padlock
<3545>, [13346]; Grainger and Phillpotts 2010, period C1, OA14
Barrel padlock with copper alloy traces suggesting brazing. Dimensions 50 x 50mm. 13th to 15th centuries.

<S81> Iron padlock bolt (Fig 100)
<3670>, [13434]; Grainger and Phillpotts 2010, period C1, OA14
T-shaped bolt with two spines each with double leaf spring. Brazed iron.

<S82> Iron padlock (Fig 100)
<2844>, [+]
Barrel padlock case with longitudinal rods, fin and tube. Copper-alloy plating fixed over part of the tube, perhaps as reinforcement; other copper alloy traces on the barrel rods and elsewhere suggest brazing. Rectangular or T-shaped keyhole across end plate and underside. L 53mm, W 58mm wide, barrel Diam 26mm. Medieval.

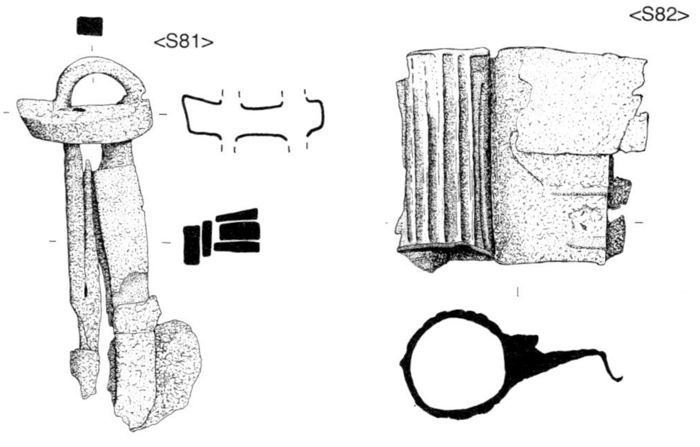

Fig 100 Iron T-shaped padlock bolt <S81> and barrel padlock case <S82> (scale 1:2)

Door latch

<S83> Iron door latch
<3894>, [3718]; Grainger and Phillpotts 2010, period C1, OA17
Perforated arm (L 40mm), pin arm is broken. L 85mm. Found with a rod with one end flattened and broken (L 91mm).

Keys

<S84> Iron key
<2240>, [5131]; period B3, OA10
Key with kidney-shaped bow. L 80mm (complete), bow W 29mm, bit W 23mm.

<S85> Iron key
<4273>, [93]; period B4, OA5
Key with thick stem and bow folded into an unusual form. The bow resembles an example from London Wall (Ward-Perkins 1940, pl XXXI, no. 48). L 81mm, bow W 43mm, bit W 36mm.

<S86> Iron key
<1781>, [3932]; period B4, B11
?Chest key with oval bow with thickened top. L 60mm, bow W 22mm, bit W 18mm.

<S87> Iron key
<2361>, [9508]; period B4, OA9
Door key with slightly kidney-shaped bow and symmetrical bit. L 145mm (complete), bit L 35mm, bit W 29mm.

<S88> Iron key
<3528>, [13252]; Grainger and Phillpotts 2010, period C1, OA14
Key with kidney-shaped bow and broken or corroded bit. L 90mm, bow W 37mm, bit W 30mm.

<S89> Iron key
<162>, [1829]; Grainger and Phillpotts 2010, period C1, OA17
<4278>, [1986]; Grainger and Phillpotts 2010, period C1, B11
Door key with circular-sectioned shank, oval bow and symmetrical bit. L 150mm, bow W 50mm, bit W 48mm. Found in two pieces in two different contexts, although the break is fairly recent (<162> is the bow, <4278> the shank and bit). ?Late medieval.

<S90> Two iron door keys
<1967a, b>, [3989]; Grainger and Phillpotts 2010, period C1, B30
a) Complete key with oval bow and symmetrical bit. L 195mm, bow W 58mm, bit W 42mm. b) Incomplete key with D-shaped bow and symmetrical bit. L 120mm (originally *c* 135mm), bow W 40mm, bit W 30mm. Late medieval, 14th century.

Dress accessories

Shoes and related fittings

<S91> Shoe leather
<2020>, <2041>, [3998]; period B4, B12
There are five fragments of topbands and three fragments of uppers from adult shoes; two of these have butt seams along one edge, and one has been cut up for reuse. There are two other pieces, neither showing any signs of reuse, but they could again be fragments of uppers.

<S92> Iron shoe buckle
<3783>, [14321]; period B2, B10
Annular. Diam 12.5mm (ext), 8mm (int) (ie max strap width).

Pins

<S93> Iron pin
<1901>, [3998]; period B4, B12
Pin with conical corrugated head; the wide end of the cone-shape is the top of the head. Five ridges possibly formed from coiled wire. Incomplete shank. In the X-radiograph the shank appears to pass through the top of the head. Surviving L 60mm, L of head 10mm, max Diam of head 10mm.

<S94> Bone pin or weaving tool (Fig 101)
<483>, [3912]; Grainger and Phillpotts 2010, period C1, B30
Perforated pin fragment made from a pig fibula. Undecorated. L 121mm, W 12mm, Th 6mm, perforation Diam 5mm. This object could have been used to secure an item of clothing. Although perforated like a needle, it has a wide, untrimmed head which would have limited its use in textile working, unless it was for something that was loosely sewn, or for netmaking. Alternatively it may have been a weaving tool (Rogerson and Dallas 1984, 167). Such objects are usually associated with the late Saxon and early medieval periods in England (MacGregor 1989). Other examples come from excavations at Melbourne Street, Southampton (Holdsworth 1980, 76), and a perforated bird bone of mid 13th-century date from High Street site C (Harvey 1975, 272).

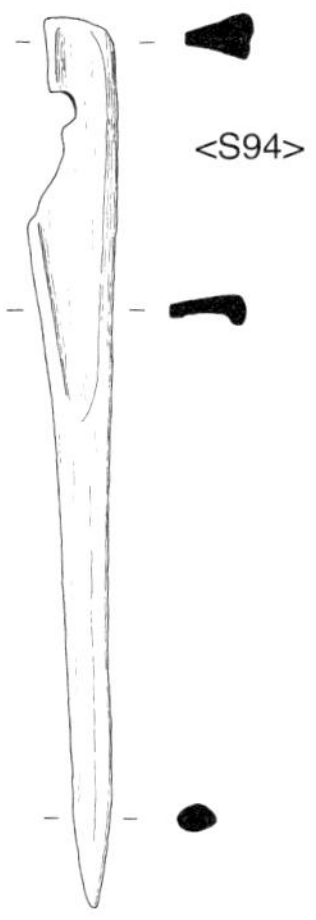

Fig 101 Bone pin or weaving tool <S94> (scale 1:2)

Brooches and buckles

<S95> Copper-alloy coiled wire brooch (Fig 25)
<2828>, [12674]; period B2, OA2
Small decorated annular brooch. Fine wire coiled around slightly thicker-gauge wire, which in turn is coiled around the thin ring of the brooch (cf Egan and Pritchard 1991, 256, fig 164, nos 1339–40). Pin with pointed end. Diam *c* 20mm.

<S96> Copper-alloy brooches/buckles
<2431>, <2435>, [7472]; period B2, OA2
Circular frames. Non-matching pair. <2431> Semi-plain pin, stepped shoulder; Diam 51mm. <2435> Plain pin; Diam 39.5mm.

<S97> Copper-alloy brooches/buckles
<2820>, <2819>, [12530]; period B2, OA2
Circular frames. Matching pair. <2820> Semi-plain pin, single groove. ?Textile traces on part of frame. Diam 46mm. <2819> Mineralised textile on pin shank (Table 23). Diam (ext) 42mm.

<S98> Copper-alloy buckle and buckle plate (Fig 25)
<2826>, [11895]; period B2, OA2
Small single-loop buckle and buckle plate. Elongated D-shaped loop with large decorative frontal knop. Rectangular buckle plate with single rivet. Pin missing. Overall L 42mm, buckle L 21mm, buckle W 12mm. *c* 1350–*c* 1400.

<S99> Copper-alloy buckle
<414>, [711]; period B3, OA6
Plain figure-of-eight-shaped buckle. L 22mm, W 18mm.

<S100> Copper-alloy buckle/brooch pin
<2832>, [13909]; period B3, OA9
Fragment of a pin from either a buckle or a brooch. L 8mm.

<S101> Copper-alloy buckle
<2757>, [9900]; period B3, OA9
Buckle, broken, probably figure-of-eight-shaped loop. L 11mm, W 14mm.

<S102> Copper-alloy buckle (Fig 102)
<2674>, [9386]; period B3, OA9
Small rectangular single-loop ?shoe buckle. Trapezoidal-sectioned frame. Iron pin. L 15mm, W 14mm.

<S103> Copper-alloy buckle and buckle plate
<2054a>, [3998]; period B4, B12
Figure-of-eight-shaped buckle and buckle plate. Semicircular extensions in the centre of each end bar with unclear moulded decoration. Overall L 37mm,

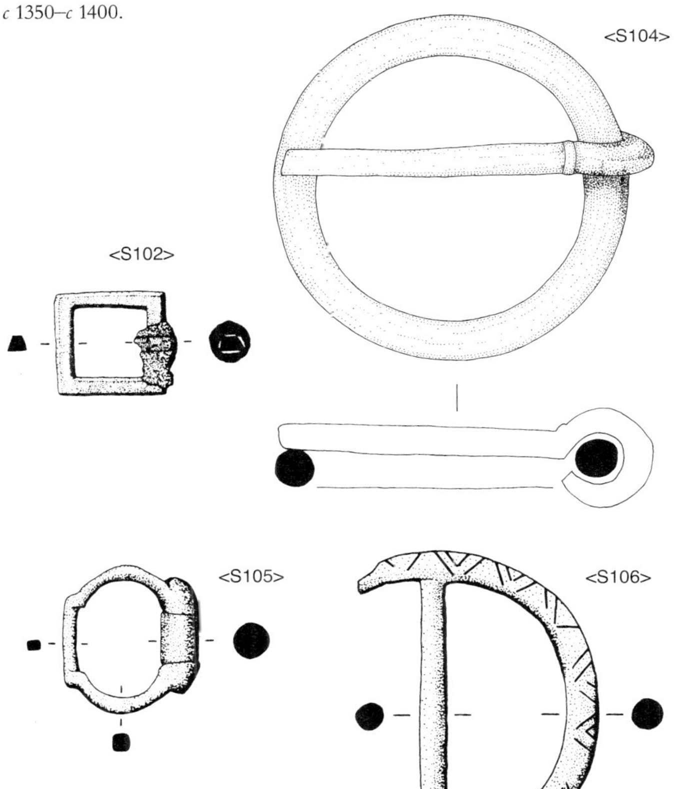

Fig 102 Copper alloy ?shoe buckle <S102>, brooch/buckle <S104> and buckles <S105> and <S106> (scale 1:1)

buckle L 29mm, buckle W 19mm, buckle plate L 20mm. *c* 1350–*c* 1450.

<S104> Copper-alloy brooch/buckle (Fig 102)
<2184>, [6073]; period B4, OA2
Circular frame. Semi-plain pin, stepped shoulder. Diam 47mm.

<S105> Copper-alloy buckle (Fig 102)
<2525>, [8195]; period B4, OA2
Single-loop buckle, roughly circular with a ribbed copper-alloy strip wound around the knopped frontal bar. L 20mm, W 18mm. *c* 1350–*c* 1450.

<S106> Copper-alloy buckle (Fig 102)
<2732> [6073]; period B4, OA2
Large decorated circular buckle with double loop, of circular cross-section. Incised decoration of double zigzag lines. Diam 43mm.

<S107> Copper-alloy buckle
<21>, [367]; Grainger and Phillpotts 2010, period C1, OA19
Blackened D-shaped buckle. Iron pin, now missing. The ends of the 'D' have short extensions as does the bar. The blackening of buckles was a common practice during the medieval and later periods. L 26mm, W 20mm.

<S108> Copper-alloy buckle
<1683>, [2581]; Grainger and Phillpotts 2010, period C1, OA18
Small figure-of-eight-shaped buckle with iron pin and slightly concave curvature. Knops on either end of the central bar. L 20mm, W 15.5mm. Late medieval.

<S109> Copper-alloy buckle
<1840>, [4644]; Grainger and Phillpotts 2010, period C1, B11
Single-loop oval buckle. Elongated oval with enlarged tubular frontal bar. Pin missing. L 21mm, W 17mm, strap W <10mm. Possibly 13th to 14th centuries.

<S110> Copper-alloy buckle and buckle plate
<227>, [1361]; Grainger and Phillpotts 2010, period C2, OA26
Rectangular single-loop buckle and buckle plate. Broadened frontal bar with three centrally placed grooves and two ridges on each arm. The pin is small and tapered. Long, plain buckle plate with single rivet at end. Overall L 42mm, W 14mm, buckle L 15mm. Possibly *c* 1350–*c* 1450.

<S111> Copper-alloy brooch/buckle
<2204>, [6071]; Grainger and Phillpotts 2010, period C2, OA29
No pin. Possible textile traces. Diam 41mm.

<S112> Copper-alloy buckle and buckle plate
<157>, [1805]; Grainger and Phillpotts 2010, period C2, B11
Buckle plate and part of the buckle. Buckle plate has rectangular upper plate and forked underplate (similar construction to many strapends). L 36mm (incomplete), W 21.5mm. 13th to 14th centuries.

<S113> Copper-alloy buckle
<431>, [2535]; Grainger and Phillpotts 2010, period C2, B30
Decorated pin, ribbed platform.

<S114> Copper-alloy buckle and buckle plate
<2186>, [+]
Buckle plate construction as <S112> (above). Buckle loop slightly pointed at front. L 41mm, W 21mm. 13th to 14th centuries.

Strapends, strap mounts and tags

<S115> Copper-alloy mount or chape
<64>, [1076]; period B1, B3
Possibly a strapend. Double plating of oval form with broken rectangular extension from one side. Small riveted plate on opposite side. L 45mm, W 38mm.

<S116> Copper-alloy strap mount
<2765>, [9987]; period B3, OA2
Rod with central cylindrical orifice, possibly intended for an inset, and circular pierced terminals with rivets *in situ*. L 32mm. This type of strap mount is also a common find in earlier medieval material (cf a belt from Wein with four apparently identical mounts, and dated to the early 13th century, illustrated in Bock 1866; and Egan and Pritchard 1991, 213, fig 134, nos 1154–8). The effigy of Gilbert Marshall, 4th Earl of Pembroke (d 1241), in the Temple church, London, has this style of mount spaced along his belt.

Fig 103 Copper-alloy hinged pendant strapend <S117> (scale: 1:1)

<S117> Copper-alloy strapend (Fig 103)
<10015>, [1930]; period B3, OA5
Small hinged pendant strapend with pierced end. Main body is roughly circular, pierced in the centre, with a ring of decorative circular indentations around the hole. At the hinged end two arms hold the pivot-pin, and in the extended terminal is a hole for a further attachment. L 23mm, W 10.5mm, strap W 5mm.This form of strapend may be a book fastener. It has been found elsewhere in late 14th- to 15th-century contexts (Egan and Pritchard 1991, 154, fig 101, nos 720–6; MOL acc no. 85.580/7).

<S118> Copper-alloy strapend
<2735>, [11475]; period B3, OA9
Undecorated strapend, with an expanded fold possibly for a hinged secondary plate. Five rivets. Leather extant between the plates. L 35mm, W 15mm.

<S119> Copper-alloy strap mount
<2764>, [9974]; period B3, OA9
Strap mount of floral design, consisting of eight petals and central perforation. Diam 17mm. Floral strap mounts were very popular during the later medieval period, and such finds are fairly common; for example, a leather strap found at Newgate, London, has six-petalled studs mounted by means of perimeter rivets (MOL acc no. A3691; Ward-Perkins 1954, fig 63, no. 7). 14th century.

<S120> Copper-alloy bar mount
<3882>, [13840]; period B3, B6
Fragment of small lobed bar mount. The end lobe has a rivet. L 10mm (incomplete), W 4.5mm.

<S121> Copper-alloy hooked strap mount (Fig 104)
<19>, [367]; Grainger and Phillpotts 2010, period C1, OA18
Hooked strap fitting. Tinned surface. Plain, flat, elongated oval body, bounded at the top and the bottom by transverse rectangular bars with a median groove; beyond these are a suspension ring at the terminal end and at the other end a long looped hook running down the back of the mount. All edges are chamfered, with a single slight notch on either side of the oval central element. Irregular-surfaced flat back, possibly suggesting a one-piece mould. L 57mm, W 21mm. Possibly 15th to 16th centuries.

<S122> Copper-alloy ? plate fitting
<2097>, [4789]; period B2, B11
Rectangular strip with large perforation towards one end. L 23mm, W 9mm.

<S123> Copper-alloy plate
<2793b>, [11474]; period B3, OA9
Very small rectangular plate with large perforation. Dimensions 6.5 x 4mm.

<S124> Copper-alloy tag
<2427>, [8101]; period B3, OA9
Triangular tag formed of folded sheet metal. L 16mm, W 10mm.

<S125> Copper-alloy tag
<2766>, [9974]; period B3, OA9
Fragments of triangular tag with two small pierced plating fragments.

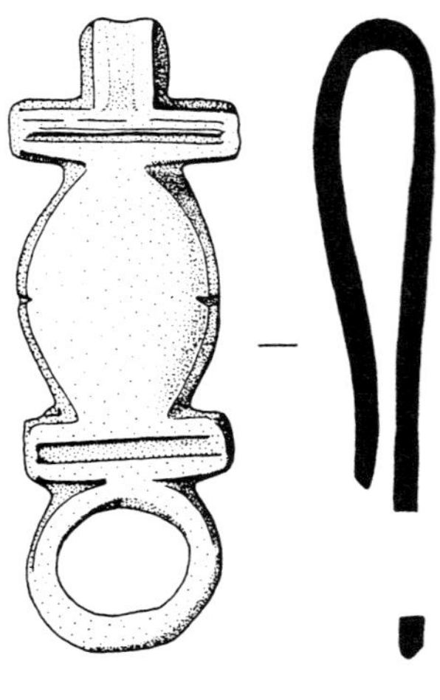

Fig 104 Copper-alloy hooked strap mount <S121> (scale 1:1)

Buttons

<S126> Copper-alloy button
<2095>, [4789]; period B3, B11
Part of spherical button. Max dimension 12.5mm.

<S127> Copper-alloy button
<2310>, [7020]; period B3, OA9
Spherical button with suspension loop. Diam 12mm.

<S128> Copper-alloy button
<2836>, [12756]; period B3, OA9
Spherical button with suspension loop. Small, slightly squashed. Diam 6–8mm.

<S129> Copper-alloy button
<3101>, [13047]; Grainger and Phillpotts 2010, period C1, OA14
Flattened spherical button; no suspension loop evident. Diam 7–9mm.

<S130> Copper-alloy button
<293>, [1911]; Grainger and Phillpotts 2010, period C1, OA17
Spherical button with traces of suspension loop. Diam *c* 10mm.

Household items

Knives and handles

<S131> Iron knife
<4522>, [14380]; period B3, B18
Blade with whittle tang. Triangular section. Overall L 108mm, blade L 80mm, blade W *c* 13mm.

<S132> Iron knife
<4186>, [14297]; period B4, OA8
Complete un-edged blade. The tang is a thickened scale or a wide whittle type, and is not complete. In three pieces, the short, wide blade appears in part to have differential metal weld with three densities of metal, although this is not certain. Additionally the blade may have a ridged back and/or a groove along the back edge. Curved shoulder to blade line. Overall L 98mm; blade L 90mm, W 24mm, Th at back 5–6mm; tang L 11mm, W 4–5mm.

<S133> Iron knife
<4027>, [3890]; period B4, B11
Blade with scale tang. Incomplete. Blade and tang both of triangular section. Overall L 83mm, blade W 12mm.

<S134> Bone knife handle
<2054b>, [3998]; period B4, B12
Fragment of small bone knife handle with iron tang and corroded copper-alloy end cap and copper-alloy rivets through the remains of the bone scale. L 31mm, W 14mm. Late medieval, second half of the 15th to the 16th century.

<S135> Iron knife
<1710>, [3861]; period B4, B14
Knife blade with incomplete whittle tang. Triangular section. Overall L 83mm, blade W 9mm.

<S136> Iron knife
<3676>, [12350]; period B4, B16
Knife blade with part of scale tang. Triangular section. The blade is coated in a layer of copper corrosion. Copper rivets. Overall L 95mm, blade W 10mm.

<S137> Iron knife
<3540>, [13252]; Grainger and Phillpotts 2010, period C1, OA14
Scale tang with copper-alloy rivets, from knife. Broken at both ends. L 21mm, W 10mm, Th 2.5mm. Found with section of thick copper-alloy rod.

<S138> Iron knife
<3590>, [13434]; Grainger and Phillpotts 2010, period C1, OA14
Blade with scale tang, wooden handle traces, a shoulder band, copper-alloy rivets, two large suspension holes reinforced with copper-alloy rings, and a copper-alloy plating chape. Knife blade broken; triangular section; possible remnants of a ring-like maker's mark. Overall L 124mm; blade W 16mm, Th 3mm; Diam of suspension rings 6–7mm.

<S139> Iron knife
<3576>, <3577>, [13382]; Grainger and Phillpotts 2010, period C1, OA14
Blade, of uncertain type, with scale tang. Possibly differential metal welding evidenced in X-radiograph. Triangular section. Overall L 143mm (incomplete); blade W 16mm, Th 5.5mm. Scatter of copper-alloy fragments around the blade.

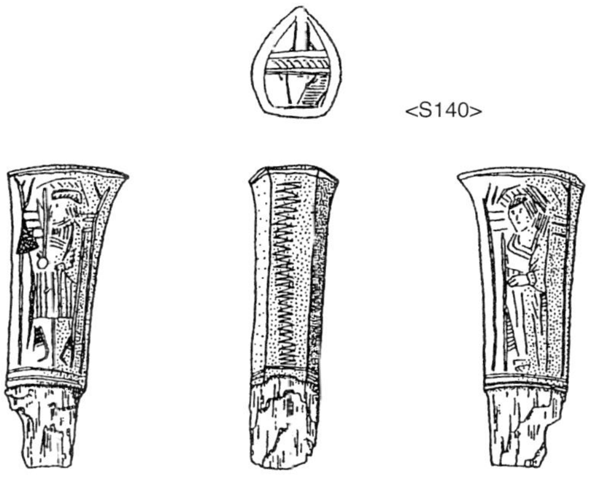

Fig 105 Decorated copper-alloy knife handle chape <S140> (scale 1:1)

<S140> Copper-alloy knife handle chape (Fig 105)
<3532>, [14200]; Grainger and Phillpotts 2010, period C1, OA15
Decorated knife handle chape. The incised decoration depicts a male figure on one side and a female figure on the other, with a zigzag pattern running down the flat, straight-edged back; the end plate also has incised decoration. The sides are formed from a single sheet soldered together, with a separate drop-shaped piece soldered on as the end plate (the point corresponding to the ridge between the figurally-decorated faces). Remains of the wooden handle are attached to the iron whittle tang. Overall L 34mm; chape L 25mm, max W (at end) 13mm. A few knife chapes of identical form and similar style come from the Thames foreshore in the City of London, notably from Billingsgate and Hackney Docks (MOL acc nos 86.102/6, 80.406/1, 85.488/1). Late 15th to early 16th centuries.

<S141> Bone knife handle
<1897>, [4644]; Grainger and Phillpotts 2010, period C1, B11
Bone knife handle fragment with remains of organic material. Iron tang with corroded copper-alloy end cap. Probably from a small table knife. L 33mm, W 13mm. Second half of the 15th to the 16th century.

<S142> Iron knife
<2426>, [7397]; Grainger and Phillpotts 2010, period C2, OA29
Blade with whittle tang and maker's mark. Triangular section. The mark consists of an oval centre with two projections from each end. Possibly pattern-welded. Overall L 86mm (incomplete), blade W 11mm. Possibly late 14th century.

<S143> Iron knife
<3029>, [2449]; Grainger and Phillpotts 2010, period C2, B13
Blade with scale tang and maker's mark. Triangular section. The mark is triple-pronged on two sides; the closest parallel for this is on a knife found at the Billingsgate Lorry Park excavations in London and dating to the late 14th century (Cowgill et al 1987, 21, 98, fig 6, no. 173). Overall L 134mm (tip missing); blade W 18mm, Th 4mm. Post-13th century.

Spoon

<S144> Copper-alloy spoon
<2247>, [6299]; Grainger and Phillpotts 2010, period C2, OA29
Spoon bowl, fig-shaped. L 61mm, W 50mm. 15th to 16th centuries.

Tools

<S145> Iron scissors
<2984>, [3998]; period B4, B12
Pair of scissors with circular pivoting plate. Badly preserved. Blade tips broken. Overall L 93mm, L of handle arms 62mm. Medieval or later.

<S146> Iron shears
<2203>, [6455]; Grainger and Phillpotts 2010, period C2, OA29
Half a pair of shears. Straight-backed narrow blade with angled tip (L 80mm, W 10mm). Plain bow, double recess with notched point between the recesses at the arm/blade junction. Overall L 133mm. The shape of these shears may indicate an early to mid 15th-century date.

<S147> Iron tool
<3744>, [13880]; period B4, B6
Large implement with pointed end and wedge-shaped terminal. Mostly square-sectioned. W (wedge end) 38mm, Th *c* 17mm.

<S148> Iron shank
<3546>, [13338]; Grainger and Phillpotts 2010, period C1, OA14
Shank with right-angled bend at one end and a small copper-alloy collar near the bend. Both ends appear to be pointed. Long arm L 60mm, short arm L 18mm.

<S149> Antler ?weaving tool (Fig 106)
<2297>, [7518]; Grainger and Phillpotts 2010, period C2, OA31
Implement with pointed ends. One end is tapered to a broad flat point, the other end is crudely sharpened to a second point. L 135mm, W 11mm. This could possibly be a weaving tool such as a pinbeater, or it could be a leather-working tool. A similar antler tool, of medieval date, came from excavations at St Peter's Street, Northampton (Oakley 1979, 312).

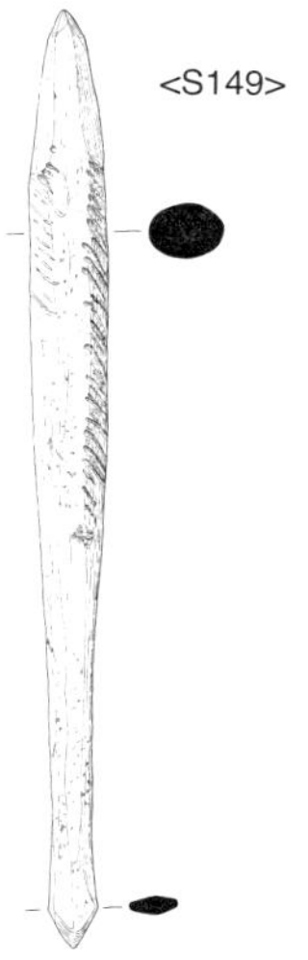

Fig 106 Antler ?weaving tool <S149> (scale 1:2)

Personal equipment

Comb

<S150> Bone and antler comb
<258>, [3077]; period B4, OA13
Fragment of a composite single-sided comb, with the remains of two toothplates. One complete toothplate is 25mm in length. The sideplates and toothplates are attached at both ends of the toothplates with iron rivets. The toothplates are made from antler, while the sideplates are made of bone. All the teeth have been broken off, leaving a few remnants only 3–4mm in length. The cut marks on the sideplates indicate that the teeth were cut after the different parts of the comb had been assembled and riveted together. The toothplate has a small repair, in which a new piece has been inserted to replace two of the teeth, wedged in position with two further fragments (these fragments are presumably also made of antler, although this has not been confirmed). Undecorated. L 53mm, W 17mm, Th 10mm.

This comb is of particular interest because, rather than being discarded when the teeth were broken, one of the toothplates had been carefully repaired. There are examples of repaired combs from archaeological excavations, such as a single-sided composite decorated comb with one replaced toothplate (Butler 1974, 92–3, fig 6, B4). The repair to <S150> consists of the insertion of two new teeth into the remains of the original toothplate. This has been effectively done, and would perhaps have been hardly noticeable from the underside or tooth side of the comb. Such composite combs were not uncommonly made of antler and bone combinations. The use of antler rather than bone in the toothplate would have been logical, given the superior strength of antler and its ability to withstand stress.

Toilet implements

<S151> Copper-alloy ? ear scoop (Fig 107)
<1859>, [3960]; period B4, B14
Cosmetic scoop with twisted shank and flattened square end. L 47mm. Possibly used as an ear scoop although the bowl might appear to be rather large for such a function. Combined ear scoops and toothpicks from the City of London and dated to the 14th century (Egan and Pritchard 1991, 379, fig 251, nos 1758–62) are very similar in style to this object, apart from the pointed toothpick ends. The flat end of <S151> may have been functionless, or may have served as a spatula, nail cleaner or cuticle pusher. From the same context as <S152> (below). Possibly 14th to 16th centuries.

<S152> Copper-alloy toilet implement (Fig 107)
<1873>, [3960]; period B4, B14
Toilet implement (now bent in a U-shape) with scoop at one end, two splayed picks/probes at the other, and knotted wirework on the handle. Original L 52mm. These toilet items have been found elsewhere in London, for example at the Thames Exchange site (Egan and Pritchard 1991, 379, fig 251, TEX88 acc no. 3753), as well as at other locations in Britain such as St Augustine's Abbey, Canterbury (Henig and Woods 1988, 214, 216, fig 69, no. 59), and at Battle Abbey (Geddes 1985, 162, fig 52, no. 77), where it is described as being for ears, teeth and nails and paralleled with a 16th-century French example (Pichon 1879, 36, no. 207; Gay 1887, 526). However, a 14th-century date can be ascribed to these implements. From the same context as <S151> (above). 14th to 16th centuries.

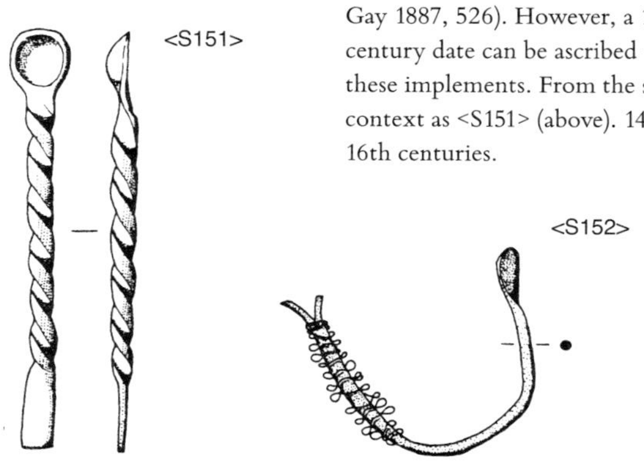

Fig 107 Copper-alloy toilet implements <S151> and <S152> (scale 1:1)

Thimbles and needle

<S153> Copper-alloy thimble (Fig 108)
<456>, [3713]; Grainger and Phillpotts 2010, period C1, B30
Domed thimble. Light indentations cover the surface apart from the apex of the crown, hand-punched in vertical lines. H 15mm, Diam 15mm. Probably *c* 1350–*c* 1450.

<S154> Copper-alloy thimble
<2000>, [+]
Domed thimble. Flat crown. Indentations large and formed in a spiral. Used for coarser cloth or leather. H 20mm, Diam 18.5mm. Probably 16th century.

<S155> Copper-alloy thimble
<2172>, [+]
Ring thimble. Thin copper-alloy sheet with a brazed join soldered together using an internal copper-alloy strip. Medium-sized indentations, hand-punched in

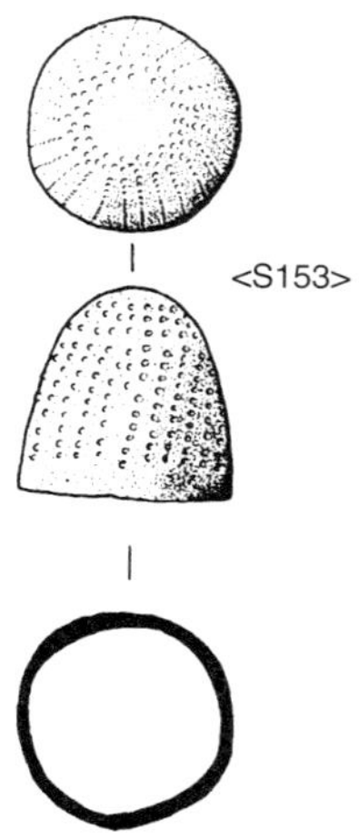

Fig 108 Copper-alloy domed thimble <S153> (scale 1:1)

vertical lines and set between an upper and lower groove. Inaccurately executed. H 15mm, Diam 18mm (base), 15mm (top). After *c* 1450 and probably no later than the 16th century.

<S156> Copper-alloy needle
<2213>, [6181]; period B3, OA9
Eye appears as a stretched split shank (cf Goodall 1980, 186, fig 26, no. 89). Pointed end missing. Surviving L 53mm.

Horse equipment

Horseshoes

<S157> Iron horseshoe
<3798>, [14297]; period B4, OA8
Half of a horseshoe with three holes. Web W 22mm. Late 14th to early 15th centuries.

<S158> Iron horseshoe
<4061>, [6073]; period B4, OA9
Half of a horseshoe with four rectangular holes and thickened heel. One nail in place. Mid 14th to early 15th centuries.

<S159> Iron horseshoe
<3932>, [6085]; Grainger and Phillpotts 2010, period C2, OA29
Horseshoe with a slight angle on the internal edge. Probably an oval front-foot shoe hammered into shape from a rounder-shaped shoe. Three rectangular holes on one side, one with the nail in place. Web W *c* 26mm. 14th to early 15th centuries.

<S160> Iron horseshoe
<2355>, [7121]; Grainger and Phillpotts 2010, period C2, OA29
Horseshoe with few identifiable features remaining. L 150mm+, W *c* 130mm, web W 38mm. A large shoe, unusual before *c* 1400 but not large enough to be 17th-century. 15th to 16th centuries.

<S161> Iron horseshoe
<2627>, [7528]; Grainger and Phillpotts 2010, period C2, OA31
Horseshoe, complete. Eight rectangular holes with rectangular-headed nails. L 140mm, W 120mm, max web W 43mm. 16th century.

<S162> Iron horseshoe
<2534>, [7978]; Grainger and Phillpotts 2010, period C2, OA31
Part of a horseshoe with rectangular holes and a clenched nail in place. 16th century.

Spurs

<S163> Iron spur
<2846>, [12836]; period B3, OA12
Rowel spur, most of body and terminals missing. Medium shank and six-point rowel. L 70mm.

<S164> Iron spur
<2261>, [6019]; Grainger and Phillpotts 2010, period C2, OA29
Half of a rowel spur; broken at terminal ring. Eight-point rowel. Overall L 135mm, L of shank and rowel 50mm.

<S165> Iron spur
<2576>, [+]
Part of a rowel spur. Probably tinned. Rowel and terminals missing. Shank and body lie on the same plane. Short shank, L 23mm.

<S166> Gilded copper-alloy spur buckle (Fig 109)
<2654>, [8464]; Grainger and Phillpotts 2010, period C2, OA29
Probable spur buckle cast in one piece, with long bridging strip and hooked end. Lateral zigzag decoration (cf Egan and Pritchard 1991, 78, fig 48, nos 320–1). Pin missing. L 53mm, W 16mm. Medieval.

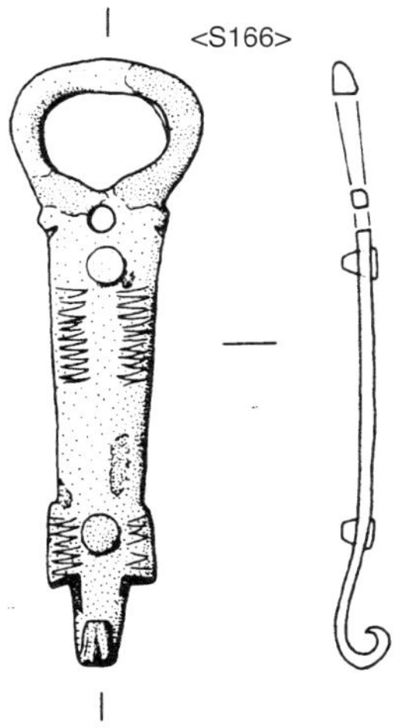

Fig 109 Gilded copper-alloy spur buckle <S166> (scale 1:1)

Rumbler bells

These could be attached to personal attire and animal harness.

<S167> Copper-alloy rumbler bell
<2716>, [9589]; period B3, OA2/OA12
Fragments of a rumbler bell, with central flange Diam 25mm.

<S168> Copper-alloy rumbler bell
<130>, [378]; Grainger and Phillpotts 2010, period C1, OA19
Rumbler bell, fragmentary. Two hemispheres soldered together along a central flange. Diam 23.5mm, H 10mm.

<S169> Copper-alloy rumbler bell
<2747>, [10341]; Grainger and Phillpotts 2010, period C1, OA20
Part of a rumbler bell possibly formed in one piece. Traces of suspension loop and slot. Max dimension 12mm.

<S170> Copper-alloy rumbler bell
<2372>, [7071]; Grainger and Phillpotts 2010, period C2, OA29
Possible rumbler bell. Lightly domed hemisphere with internal flange. Diam 25–27mm, H 8mm.

Arms and armour

<S171> Bone dagger handle (Fig 110)
<2150>, [6033]; Grainger and Phillpotts 2010, period C2, OA29
Dagger handle fragments, highly decorated with an incised design.

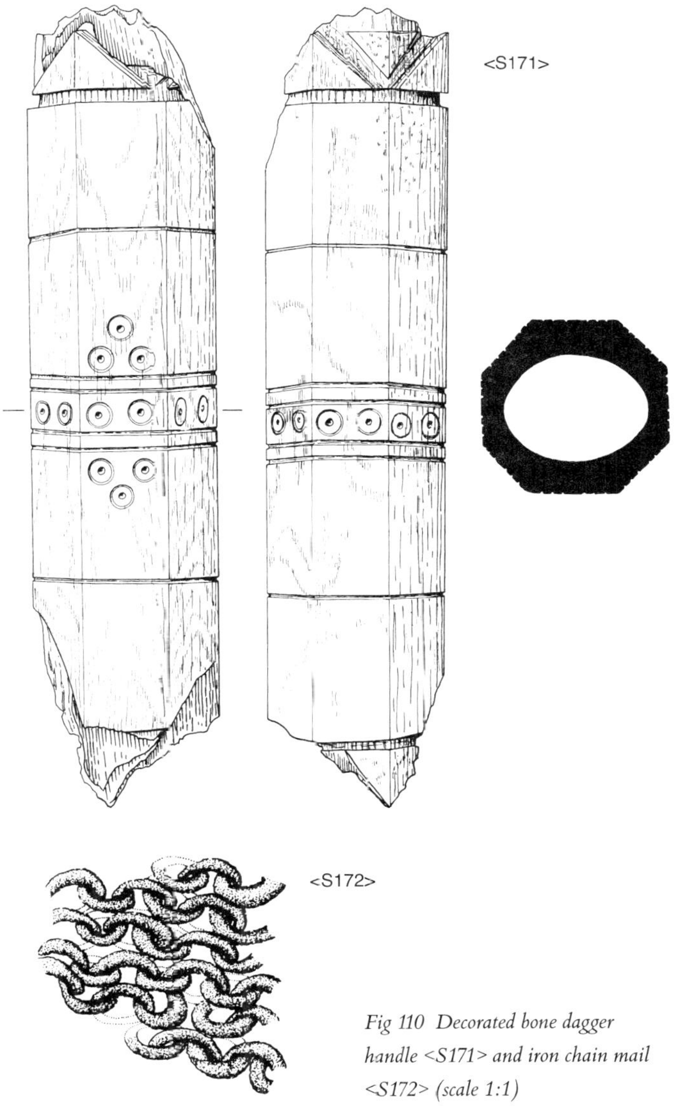

Fig 110 Decorated bone dagger handle <S171> and iron chain mail <S172> (scale 1:1)

The two joining fragments are octagonal in section and slightly tapering. The decoration consists of lines and dot-and-circle motifs with a more deeply incised design at either end. L 109mm, W 25mm. These fragments are dated to the first half of the 16th century, *c* 1540 (T North, pers comm).

<S172> Iron chain mail (Fig 110)
<3714>, [13198]; Grainger and Phillpotts 2010, period C1, OA14
Five pieces of riveted mail, with 8–9mm size links. Th of wire *c* 1.5mm. The X-radiograph shows one copper-alloy link (Diam *c* 9mm, Th of wire *c* 1mm) within the largest sample. This copper-alloy link is not obviously positioned along the edge as might be expected, since brass mail was sometimes used as a decorative border on iron mail suits; however, it may be lying loose on, or within, the iron links. The largest of the five pieces measures 75 x 65mm. European, 15th century.

Miscellaneous objects

<S173> Copper-alloy bar
<443>, [3077], period B4, OA13
Curved bar with moulded ribbing on the convex upper surface. One square-sectioned end ?broken, and one flattened pierced end with adjacent rivet. L 127mm, W 6–7mm.

<S174> Polished, tapered bone object
<3126>, [13252]; Grainger and Phillpotts 2010, period C1, OA14
The shaft is flat on the reverse side, and the obverse has a narrow groove (W *c* 3mm) running the length of the object. One end has a small perforation in the centre, while the tapered end comes to a gentle point. L 14mm, W 15mm, D at widest end 6mm. This object was attached to something else, but its function is unclear. An object of similar shape made from copper alloy was recovered from the post-Dissolution layers at Battle Abbey (Geddes 1985, 165), but its identification is also uncertain.

<S175> Copper-alloy ferrule
<3482>, [13348]; Grainger and Phillpotts 2010, period C1, OA14
Cylindrical open ferrule with flanged edge. Flange formed of six cut and pierced sections. L 30mm, max W *c* 36mm.

Bone waste

<S176> Bone waste
<2301>, [9058]; period B4, OA2
Fragment of bone waste from the manufacture of circular objects such as beads or buttons *c* 13mm in diameter. The interior of the cutouts indicates that the bone objects were drilled out first from one side and then the other. L 61mm, W 11mm, Th 5mm. Archaeological examples of this kind of bone waste are quite common; a similar fragment came from excavations at the Customs House Site (Tatton-Brown 1974, 198).

5.7 The plant remains

John Giorgi

Introduction and methodology

During the excavations sediment samples were systematically collected as part of the environmental research design. When processed these produced both organic and inorganic material. This report is concerned with the analysis of the plant macro-remains recovered from these samples and the extent to which they might shed light on diet and activities carried out during the monastic and the Dissolution and manor house periods (periods B1–B3 and B4) and provide more general information on the economy of London during this time.

The criteria for selection were that the deposit should be datable and part of a well-stratified sequence. A further consideration for selection could be the potential of a particular deposit for environmental study. Contexts from a range of feature types were sampled from different areas and periods of the site. A number of feature types were sampled more than once, to investigate spatial variation in sample composition. Samples were collected in varying quantities from nearly all areas of the site. The victualling yard provided 78% of all the samples collected (Grainger and Phillpotts 2010, 115–20). The abbey and manor house periods accounted for just 7% and 14% respectively of all the samples collected.

A total of 221 sediment samples were collected, from which 102 were selected for an assessment to establish the preservation, frequency and diversity of the plant macro-remains from the different areas of the site. The assessment report (Giorgi 1991) recommended that virtually all the samples should be used in the analysis, with the exception of those that either could not be well dated or were highly contaminated. It was further proposed that the material should be scanned rather than quantified owing to the nature of the preservation. Thus 203 samples were analysed for the post-excavation programme. The sediment samples were processed almost entirely by flotation using a Siraf tank with sieve sizes of 250 and 500 microns for recovering the flot and residue respectively. Sample size was variable from 5 to 42 litres (with an average of 15 litres). Samples obviously rich in organic material were stored wet and sorted in water.

The flots were sorted under a binocular microscope and material identified with the aid of the MOLA reference collection and a number of seed manuals. The author is indebted to Mark Robinson of the Oxford University Museum and John Letts for the species identification and verification of some of the more exotic species. The *Prunus* species may belong to a number of varieties of plum, cherry and the like, but neither time nor the size of the *Prunus* samples allowed a detailed study based on the size of the stones. Thus the *Prunus* species were catalogued following the categories in the MOLA database. The residues were sorted by eye, with the exception of the smallest fraction (0.5–1mm), and relevant environmental material extracted. A scanning record was made of the waterlogged and mineralised material because it was considered that the quantitative analysis of this material would do little to facilitate the interpretation of the samples. For example, many of the more frequent species were from high-seed-producing plants such as fig (*Ficus carica*), which may produce up to 2000 seeds per fruit. Furthermore, a much larger number of samples could be analysed using a scanning sequence, thereby increasing the possibility of detecting trends and changes spatially over the site, and recovering the rarer species. Although absolute numbers were not recorded, the relative frequency of individual species was noted. An exception was made for charred material, as it was considered that quantified results might in this case provide information on crop-processing activities.

The results were stored on the botanical database system together with the archaeological information for the production of tables and analytical manipulation of the remains. Virtually all the samples from the site produced variable quantities of plant macro-remains. The plant remains were mainly preserved either by their survival in waterlogged (anaerobic) conditions or as the result of mineralisation (by which calcium phosphates replace the cell tissue of the seed). A relatively small quantity of plant remains had been preserved by charring. Overall the plant remains recovered were from a wide range of species, exceeding well over a hundred. If assigned to broad categories, the samples included cereals, legumes, fruits and nuts, and an array of 'other plants', a number of which may have been utilised for food, commercial or industrial purposes.

The range of plant remains

The results for the abbey and manor house are summarised by period in Table 21 and Table 22; periods B1 and B2 produced no plant remains.

The abbey, *c* 1400–1539 (period B3)

Fourteen samples were recovered from this phase, but few were collected from the main building complex, while several samples may belong to the early post-medieval period (below). The results from ten samples are summarised in Table 21, comprising four from two pits in OA6 (fills [4132] and [4156]; fills [2544] and [2546]), one from chalk-walled pit [98] within the projected area of Building 2 (fill [100]), two from the chalk-

Table 21 The plant remains from period B3

		Land use	OA6	OA6	OA6	OA6	B2	OA11	OA11	OA2/OA12	OA12	OA12
		Context no.	[4132]	[4156]	[2544]	[2546]	[100]	[6812]	[7682]	[9592]	[9649]	[9671]
Species		Sample no.	{349}	{350}	{136}	{145}	{24}	{601}	{644}	{843}	{861}	{864}
Latin name	Common name	Habitat/use										
Charred plant remains												
Triticum aestivum type	bread/club wheat	FI	2		1							
Brassica/Sinapis spp	-	ABFGHI	2									
Agrostemma githago L	corncockle	AB	1									
Medicago/Trifolium spp	medick/clover	ABDI	3									
Cerealia	indet cereal	FI			1			1				
Leguminosae indet	-	-				1						
Mineralised plant remains												
Rubus fruticosus/idaeus	blackberry/raspberry	CFGH		+								
Malus/Pyrus spp	apple/pear	CFI		+								
cf *Malus/Pyrus* spp	?apple/pear	CFI		+								
Ficus carica L	fig	FGI		+								
Indeterminate	-	-	+	++								
Waterlogged plant remains												
Ranunculus flammula L	lesser spearwort	EG										+
Ranunculus spp	-	ABCDEG			+							
Papaver somniferum L	opium poppy	BGHI										+
Chelidonium majus	greater celandine	BC	+		+			+				+
Fumaria sp	fumitory	ABC							–			
Brassica/Sinapis spp	-	ABFGHI										+
Agrostemma githago L	corncockle	AB				+						
Stellaria media gp	chickweeds	ABCDE										+
Spergula arvensis L	corn spurry	ADF							–			
Caryophyllaceae indet	-	-							–			
Chenopodium hybridium L	maple-leaved goosefoot	AB							–			
Chenopodium sp	goosefoot	ABCDFH							–+		+	
Vitis vinifera L	grape	FI	+				+		–+++	+	+++	+
Rubus fruticosus/idaeus	blackberry/raspberry	CFGH			+			+	–+	++++	++++	+++
Fragaria vesca L	wild strawberry	CDF						++			++	++
Potentilla/Fragaria spp	-	BCDEFGH									++	
cf *Malus/Pyrus* spp	?apple/pear	CFI									+	
Rosaceae indet	-	-										+
Humulus lupulus L	hop	CGHI									+	
Ficus carica L	fig	FGI				+	++	++	–	++++	++++	+++
Morus nigra	mulberry	FHI									+	
Hyoscyamus niger L	henbane	BDG					+		–			
Solanaceae indet	-	-									+	

Table 21 (cont)

Species		Land use	OA6	OA6	OA6	OA6	B2	OA11	OA11	OA2/OA12	OA12	OA12
		Context no.	[4132]	[4156]	[2544]	[2546]	[100]	[6812]	[7682]	[9592]	[9649]	[9671]
		Sample no.	{349}	{350}	{136}	{145}	{24}	{601}	{644}	{843}	{861}	{864}
Latin name	Common name	Habitat/use										
Labiatae indet	-	-							+			
Sambucus nigra L	elder	BCFGH	+				+		++	+	+	
Onopordum acanthium L	scotch thistle	ABC							+			
Leontodon sp	hawkbit	BDF						+				
Carex spp	sedge	CDEH							++			
Indeterminate	-										3	

Key:
+ = 1–10 seeds; ++ = 11–50 seeds; +++ = 51–100 seeds; ++++ = 101+ seeds
habitat/use codes: A = segetals, weeds of cultivated ground; B = ruderals, weeds of disturbed ground and waste places; C = plants of woods, scrub, hedgerows; D = plants of grassy places; E = aquatic and damp ground plants; F = edible plants; G = medicinal and poisonous plants; H = other uses, eg fibre, dyeing; I = cultivated plants

Table 22 The plant remains from period B4

Species		Land use	B6	B6	B6	B6	B11	B11	B12	B12	B12	B12
		Context no.	[13401]	[13464]	[13503]	[13503]	[4554]	[4633]	[3998]	[3998]	[3998]	[3998]
		Sample no.	{1268}	{1281}	{1314}	{1315}	{357}	{372}	{265}	{273}	{277}	{282}
Latin name	Common name	Habitat/use										
Charred plant remains												
Triticum aestivum type	bread/club wheat	FI									1	
Secale cereale L	rye	FI										
Brassica/Sinapis spp	-	ABFGHI					1					
Agrostemma githago L	corncockle	AB					1					
Medicago/Trifolium spp	medick/clover	ABDI					5					
Carex spp	sedge	CDEH					1					
Bromus secalinus/mollis	rye-brome/lop-grass	ABD					1					
Triticum secale sp	wheat/rye	FI										
Hordeum sativum L	barley	FI										
Lolium sp	rye grass	BI										
Mineralised plant remains												
Berberis vulgaris L	barberry	CFH										
cf *Berberis vulgaris* L	?barberry	CFH										
cf *Raphanus raphanistrum*	?wild radish/charlock	A										
Vitis vinifera L	grape	FI							+		++	+++
Malus/Pyrus spp	apple/pear	CFI							+			+
cf *Malus/Pyrus* spp	?apple/pear	CFI										
Prunus spp	-	CFGI										
Rosaceae indet	-	-							+			++
Ficus carica L	fig	FGI										
Waterlogged plant remains												
Ranunculus sceleratus L	celery-leaved crowfoot	E				+						
Ranunculus spp	-	ABCDEG				+				+	+	
Chelidonium majus	greater celandine	BC										
cf *Chelidonium majus*	?greater celandine									+		
Fumaria sp	fumitory	ABC										
Brassica/Sinapis spp	-	ABFGHI								+		
Viola sp	violet	ABCDG										
Silene spp	campions/catchflies	ABCDF								++		
Agrostemma githago L	corncockle											
Stellaria media gp	chickweeds	ABCDE										
Stellaria graminea type	lesser stitchwort	CD								+		

lined well in the Pineapple garden (OA11) (fills [6812] and [7682]), and one from a pit (fill [9592], OA2/OA12) and two from a well (fills [9649] and [9671], OA12) both in the north-west part of the precinct.

The majority of the plant remains were preserved by waterlogging, but seed frequency and species diversity were generally low. The most frequent species were the small-seeded fruits – fig (*Ficus carica*), grape (*Vitis vinifera*), elder (*Sambucus nigra*) and blackberry/raspberry (*Rubus fruticosus/idaeus*). Charred remains included several bread wheat (*Triticum aestivum*) grains, possible arable weed (corncockle (*Agrostemma githago*) and *Brassica/Sinapis* spp) and legume (medick/clover (*Medicago/Trifolium* spp, Leguminosae) seeds. The mineralised seeds consisted of fruit species (blackberry/raspberry, fig and apple/pear (*Malus/Pyrus* spp)), while the waterlogged assemblage consisted of a similar range of fruits plus wild strawberry (*Fragaria vesca*) and mulberry (*Morus nigra*). Other potential useful plants included hop (*Humulus lupulus*), opium poppy (*Papaver somniferum*) and henbane (*Hyoscyamus niger*), although the low frequencies of these seeds in mixed assemblages suggest that they are probably just weeds. There was a high incidence of potential food plants; the high number of wood/hedgerow/scrub species in the habitat groups is indicative of the overall predominance of fruit species. This may reflect the local environment or imported foodstuffs, or both. It is probable that at least some of the fruit species may have been grown near or within the monastic complex, although the abbey may also have been importing some foodstuffs from its estates north and east of London and in Kent.

The Dissolution and manor house, 1539–60 (period B4)

Thirty samples were collected from period B4 and the results are summarised in Table 22. These samples included four from the demolition of the church (B6), two from the former kitchen (fills [4554] and [4633], B11), 21 from an organic

	B12	B12	B12	B12	B12	B12	B12	B12	B12	B12	B12	B12	B12	B12	B12	OA12	OA12	OA12
98]	[3998]	[3998]	[3998]	[3998]	[3998]	[3998]	[3998]	[3998]	[3998]	[3998]	[3998]	[3998]	[3998]	[3998]	[3998]	[9798]	[11852]	[11852]
4}	{288}	{290}	{291}	{299}	{337}	{340}	{342}	{355}	{359}	{363}	{364}	{365}	{371}	{372}	{297}	{903}	{966}	{973}
																3		
																1		
																2		
															1	1		
										+	+							
									+									
						+												
			++	+++	+	++			+++	+	+++		+					
				+				+	++	+								
												+						
						+				+	++							
						+												
			++			+++			+++				+					
																++		
			+								+							
			+						+									
											+							
									+									
								+				+						
		+							+							+		
		+							+							+		

Table 22 (cont)

Species		Land use	B6	B6	B6	B6	B11	B11	B12	B12	B12	B12	B
		Context no.	[13401]	[13464]	[13503]	[13503]	[4554]	[4633]	[3998]	[3998]	[3998]	[3998]	[
		Sample no.	{1268}	{1281}	{1314}	{1315}	{357}	{372}	{265}	{273}	{277}	{282}	{
Latin name	**Common name**	**Habitat/use**											
Stellaria spp	chickweed/ stitchwort	ABCDEG											
Spergula arvensis L	corn spurrey	ADF				+					+		
cf *Spergula arvensis*	?corn spurrey	ADF											
Carophyllaceae indet	-	-								+			
Montia fontana spp *Chondrosperma* L	blinks	AE									+++		-
Chenopodium album type	fat hen	ABFH											
Chenopodium hybridum L	maple-leaved goosefoot	AB									+		+
Chenopodium spp	goosefoot etc	ABCDFH				+				++	++		+
Chenopodium/ Atriplex spp	Goosefoots/ oraches	ABFGH								+			
Vitis vinifera L	vine	FI							+	++++	+++		+
Rubus fructicosus/idaeus	blackberry/raspberry	CFGH	+					+		+++	+++		+
Fragaria vesca L	wild strawberry	CDF									++		+
Potentilla/Fragaria spp	-	BCDEFGH			+								
Prunus spinosa L	sloe/blackthorn	CFG								+			
Prunus domestica L	plum/bullace	CFI								++			
Prunus persica (L) Batsch	peach	FI											
Prunus spp	-	CFGI								+			
Malus domestica/sylvestris	apple/crab apple	CFHI							+	++			
Malus/Pyrus spp	apple/pear	CFI							+		+		
Coriandrum sativum L	coriander	FGI								+			
Aethusa cynapium L	fool's parsley	A											
cf *Aethusa cynapium*	?fool's parsley	A											
cf *Carum carvi*	?caraway	BFGI								+			
Bryonia dioica Jacq	bryony	CG								+			
Euphorbia helioscopia L	sun spurge	AGI									+		+
Euphorbia peplus L	petty spurge	AB											
Polygonum persicaria L	persicaria	ABEH								+			
Polygonum aviculare agg	knotgrass	ABG											
Polygonum spp	-	ABCDEFG											
Rumex acetosella agg	sheep's sorrel	AD				+				+			
Rumex spp	docks	ABCDEFG								+			
Polygonaceae indet	-	-									+		
Urtica dioica L	stinging nettle	BCDEFGH				+					+		
Ficus carica L	fig	FGI	+	++	+	+	++			++++	++++		+
Morus nigra	mulberry	FHI								++			
Hyoscyamus niger L	henbane	BDG					+			++	++		
Stachys sp	woundwort	ACEG								+			
Solanum cf *nigrum*	?black nightshade	BF								+			
Verbena officinalis L	vervain	BG									+		
Lycopus europaeus L	gipsy wort	EH				+							
Stachys palustris L	marsh woundwort	AE								+			
Ballota nigra L	black horehound	CG			+								
Lamium sp	dead nettle	ABC				+							
Lamium purpurem	red dead nettle	AB			+								
Marrubium vulgare L	white horehound	BG				+							
cf *Marrubium vulgare*	? white horehound	BG				+							
Labiatae indet	-	-			+	++				+	+		+
Sambucus nigra L	elder	BCFGH		+	+	+				+			
Sambucus spp	elder	BCFGH				+					+		
Anthemis cotula L	stinking mayweed	ABGH				+							
Taraxacum spp	dandelion	BCDEFGH			+								
Alisma plantago-aquatica L	water-plantain	EG											
Eleocharis palustris/uniglumis	spike-rush	E											
Carex spp	sedges	CDEH				+				+			
Cyperaceae indet	-	-			+								
cf Cyperaceae indet	-	ABCDEFI								+			
Indeterminate	-	-				1					12		

Key: see Table 21

3]	B12 [3998] {288}	B12 [3998] {290}	B12 [3998] {291}	B12 [3998] {299}	B12 [3998] {337}	B12 [3998] {340}	B12 [3998] {342}	B12 [3998] {355}	B12 [3998] {359}	B12 [3998] {363}	B12 [3998] {364}	B12 [3998] {365}	B12 [3998] {371}	B12 [3998] {372}	B12 [3998] {297}	OA12 [9798] {903}	OA12 [11852] {966}	OA12 [11852] {973}
		+									+							
						+												
	+	++	++			++			++		++	+						
						+												
	+		+			+												
		+	++			+		+	+		++							
	+	+	++			+	+	++++	+++		+	+						
	++	+	+++			++	+++	++	+++	+	+++	++				+		+
			++				+		++		++	+						
		+										+						
									+									
							+	++	+									
					+													
								++	+									
								++	+									
								++										
						+								+				
									+		+							
	+	+	++			+			+		+	+						
		+	++			+												
			+						+									
			+															
																+		
									+									
									+		+							
	+					+			++		+					+	+	
-	+++	+++	++++			++	+++	++++	++++	++	++++	+++				+		+
			+					+										
+	++	+	++			++		++	+++	+	++	+						
											+							
-																		
		+																
		+	+			+	+				+					+		
		+	+			+	+			+	++	+				+	+	
																+		
	+																	
			+								+			+			+	
									+		+					++		
			2					2	2									

rubbish deposit within a former storeroom ([3998], B12), and three from two rubbish pits (fills [11852] and [9798], OA12).

Waterlogged seeds provided the bulk of the evidence in terms of both species diversity and seed frequency. The small fruit species – fig, grape, blackberry/raspberry and elder – are the most common finds. Charred remains represented very small quantities of cereal grain, consisting of bread wheat, barley (*Hordeum sativum*) and rye (*Secale cereale*), plus a number of possible arable weed seeds (corncockle, *Brassica/Sinapis* spp and rye-broom/lop-grass (*Bromus secalinus/mollis*)). Calcified seeds consisted of the small fruit species (grape, apple/pear, fig and barberry (*Berberis vulgaris*) and an arable weed, wild radish/charlock (*Raphanus raphanistrum*). The waterlogged assemblages comprised the small-seeded fruit species mentioned above plus wild strawberry, mulberry and a number of fruit stones – sloe/blackthorn (*Prunus spinosa*), plum/bullace (*P domestica*) and peach (*P persica*). Other potentially useful plants included coriander (*Coriander sativum*) and caraway (*Carum carvi*) as well as henbane, although the low frequency of these and other species in mixed assemblages makes it difficult to ascertain whether they were used or were simply weeds or escapees from cultivation.

In summary, food taxa are the most frequent, while wood/hedgerow/scrub taxa are the best-represented of the habitat groups, indicative of the predominance of fruit species in the samples.

5.8 Textiles

Frances Pritchard

Textiles were recovered from a burial in the western cemetery (period B2, OA2, [12530]), from a burial vault within the church (period B3, B16, [13530]) and from an organic rubbish deposit within a former storeroom (period B4, B12, [3998]). Details of these textiles are given in Table 23. Discussions of the textiles from the cemetery and the burial vault are included in Chapter 2.4 and 2.5, and that from the post-Dissolution rubbish deposit in Chapter 2.6.

5.9 Animal bone

Discussion of the bird bone is included in Chapter 2.6; details of large mammals and birds recovered from the Royal Mint site as a whole can be found in the assessment report (West 1992; see also West 2010).

Eggshell

Jane Sidell

Methodology

The samples were cleaned in an ultrasonic tank, air-dried and weighed. Each sample was then scanned under a stereo microscope and sorted into superficial types. The thickness range and pore count were measured using an eyepiece graticule at a magnification of x20. Representative pieces were then mounted on aluminium stubs and gold-coated for scanning electron microscopy (SEM). The mammillae count and surface description were carried out under SEM at magnifications between x100 and x1500. Full description of all these methods may be found in Sidell (1993).

Results

Superficial examination of the eggshell showed one main type, buff or 'colourless' (ie complete absence of the cuticle layer) with a well-defined mammillae layer. All other pieces were classed as type 2. In some cases the material was badly mineralised and identification was impossible. Traces of the organic membrane were found in some of the samples; some were mineralised, which explains the unusual preservation. Where the membrane obscured the entire surface of the fragments, identification was either difficult or impossible. Two samples containing eggshell were recovered from period B3 (*c* 1400–1539). The shell from pit fill [2777] in the kitchen yard (OA6) was only tentatively identified as chicken due to the membrane obscuring the surface. A second pit fill from period B3 ([9592], OA2/OA12) yielded a very rich deposit, all identified as chicken, with a fragment of what appears to be a

Table 23 Mineralised textiles from periods B2–B4

Period	Land use	Context	Comment	Acc no.	Fibre	Twist of yarn	Fabric structure	Threads/stitches per cm	Dye tested
B2	OA2	[12530]	on buckles <S97>	<2819> <2820>			tabby		-
B3	B16	[13530]	burial ?shroud	<3765> <3829>	flax	Z/Z	tabby		-
B4	B12	[3998]		<2125>	?hemp	Z/Z	tabby	8–10/8–10	-
B4	B12	[3998]		<2125>	?flax	Z/Z	tabby	17/16	-
B4	B12	[3998]		<2008>	wool	Z/S	tabby	12/12	yellow
B4	B12	[3998]		<2405>	wool	Z/S	tabby	14/14	-
B4	B12	[3998]		<2042>	wool	Z/Z	2.2 twill	29/24–29	negative
B4	B12	[3998]		<2027>	wool	SS	knitted	2–3	-

malformed egg that could not be assigned to any species (Chapter 2.5).

The deposits associated with period B4 (1539–60) yielded a series of samples, particularly [3998], an organic rubbish deposit in the former storeroom (B12), which produced shell from seven different samples (Chapter 2.6). All identifiable fragments bar one were identified as chicken. The final piece compared favourably with modern turkey, but this would be a remarkably early find as the feature dates to the 16th century, which is just when the turkey was being introduced to England. A drain fill ([4633]) in the former kitchen (B11) produced chicken eggshell. A pit fill ([9799]) associated with period B4 in Open Area 2 also contained chicken shell, as did a fill of pit [11851] (OA2), which was an extremely rich deposit with large amounts of chicken shell plus a few fragments that compare favourably with goose (Chapter 2.6).

Small mammals

Helen Hibberd

Introduction and methodology

Small mammals were recovered from period B2–B4 samples, and were identified with reference to Lawrence and Brown (1974) and Hillson (1986) as well as by comparison with the reference collection at the Museum of London. The speciation of the rat material was based on tooth morphology (Miller 1912) though most of the samples were too worn and eroded to be identified to anything other than being similar to an actual species.

Results

With the construction of St Mary Graces, the presence of people and their rubbish began to attract pests such as house mouse, feral cat and black rat. Many of these individuals are juveniles or subadults which, like the amphibia, are more often found in pitfall traps while the adults actively avoid them. No other species were recovered dating to the monastic period. After the suppression in 1539, rats remained in the vicinity, and mice, rabbits and hares were also found in the organic rubbish deposit [3998] in the former storeroom (B12). The rabbits were juveniles and may have been bred on site, but were more likely purchased.

Amphibia

Helen Hibberd

Introduction and methodology

Eleven samples produced bone fragments thought mostly to be from four species: common and warty newt, and the common frog and toad (Table 24). The species identification was carried out with reference to Böhme (1977), Holman et al (1990), Holman and Stuart (1991) and a personal reference collection. The main identifying criteria for the tail-less amphibians, the *Anura*, are the ilia and the pterygoid, but most of the remains in this assemblage consist of the vertebrae and long bones. Consequently, many of the identifications are to genera, not to species, whereas the newts were identified to species by their vertebrae.

Table 24 Species representation in the amphibian remains from periods B3 and B4

Period	Context	Sample no.	Latin name	Common name
B3	[2777]	{307}	*Triturus vulgaris*	smooth newt
B3	[4132]	{349}	*T vulgaris*	smooth newt
B3	[4156]	{350}	*T vulgaris*	smooth newt
B4	[3798]	{231}	*T vulgaris*	smooth newt
B4	[3998]	{282}	*Rana* sp	frog
B4	[3998]	{291}	*Rana* cf *temporaria*	common frog
B4	[3998]	{342}	*Rana* sp	frog
B4	[3998]	{363}	*Rana* cf *temporaria*	common frog
			Bufo bufo	common toad
B4	[3998]	{371}	*Triturus cristatus*	warty newt
B4	[4633]	{372}	*T vulgaris*	smooth newt
			Rana temporaria	common frog
			Triturus cristatus	warty newt
B4	[4633]	{377}	*T vulgaris*	smooth newt
			T cristatus	warty newt

Results

The earliest remains (*c* 1400–1539, period B3) were of common newts from the refectory (B13) and the kitchen yard (OA6) (which contained Drain 1, which may have been their route of access). Newts have terrestrial and aquatic phases in their life-cycle, and so their presence here does not necessarily mean that there was clean, fresh water in the abbey complex. However, the local ecology at this time must have featured hedges or grassland as well as ponds or ditches for the newts to mate and hibernate in.

After the suppression in 1539, the former storeroom (B12) was used for rubbish disposal and again probably acted as a pitfall trap for frogs, toads and the warty newt (1539–60, period B4). They may have fallen in while migrating from the spawning waters in late spring in search of shaded summer feeding grounds, especially the toads and newts which are commonly found under stones and which actively search out damp, shady areas in open buildings. Conversely, they may have fallen in while on migration from summer feeding grounds or in the early spring, en route to the spawning waters. The ecology at this time would have been similar to that of the earlier phase, with grassland, hedgerows, pastures and slow-moving streams, ponds, or ditches.

Fish

Alison Locker

Fish bones were recovered largely by wet-sieving soil samples, which ensured the recovery of the very smallest species; a small proportion of the bones were recovered by hand collection on

Table 25 Species representation in the fish bones from periods B1, B3 and B4 (fragment count by period)

Latin name	Common name	Period B1	Period B3	Period B4
Rajidae	ray indet		9	12
Raja clavata	roker		3	5
	elasmobranch indet			4
Anguilla anguilla	eel		830	1091
Conger conger	conger eel		1	4
Clupea harengus	herring	1	107	298
Sprattus sprattus	sprat		304	62
Clupea harengus/Sprattus sprattus	herring/sprat			18
Salmonidae			6	
Osmerus eperlanus	smelt		97	231
Esox lucius	pike		2	
Cyprinidae			9	2
Barbus barbus	barbel			1
Tinca tinca	tench		1	
Leuciscus leuciscus/cephalus	dace/chub		3	1
Rutilus rutilus	roach		10	3
Gadus morhua	cod		78	89
Melanogrammus aeglefinus	haddock		2	30
Merlangius merlangus	whiting		84	130
Gadidae indet			3	21
Trigla sp	gurnard			18
Liza ramada	thin-lipped mullet			1
Scomber scombrus	mackerel			5
Merluccius merluccius	hake		1	
Pleuronectes platessa/Platichthys flesus	plaice/flounder		34	84
Pleuronectidae	flatfish indet		3	4
Total		1	**1587**	**2114**

Table 26 Eel skull lengths (measured largely from branchial arcs: Libois et al 1987, 6)

Size (mm)	No.
20	6
22	1
27	1
28	11
30	3
40	1

site. The contrast between recovery levels serves as a good illustration of the importance of sieving to recover the full range of species. A total of 8606 fish bones were identified to species or group level from the site as a whole. Species representation is shown in Table 25, and the size of eel from this site in Table 26. Detailed discussion is included in Chapter 2.5 and 2.6 (periods B3 and B4).

5.10 The human bone

Jelena Bekvalac and Tania Kausmally

Introduction

The human remains sample from the entire Royal Mint site (MIN86) has been redefined as the 1012 articulated skeletons currently (2011) curated in the Rotunda store at the Museum of London, 150 London Wall, London EC2Y 5HN, and entered on to the MOL Oracle electronic database. The 634 skeletons (of 759 excavated) of the victims of the Black Death (1348–50) are described in the preceding monograph (Grainger et al 2008). So far as the later burials at St Mary Graces are concerned, a total of 378 were available for analysis (from 443 graves excavated), split into three subsamples: a sample of 199 from the western, later ?epidemic cemetery (OA2, period B2) dated to 1350–*c* 1400 (Fig 9; Fig 68) (this OA2 sample includes a skeleton ([5785]) from the area south-east of the church presbytery (B4), shown on Fig 67; see Chapter 2.5, OA10); 78 single inhumation burials from the eastern cemetery (OA9, period B3) dated to *c* 1400–1539 (Fig 28; Fig 69) (this OA9 sample includes a small number of skeletons (seven) from eight graves immediately north and east of the church presbytery (B4), shown on Fig 67); and 101 from the abbey church, dated to 1361–1539. This church sample comprises the church with presbytery (B4), nave (B6), south porch (B8), a 'chapel without the quire door on the south side' (B16) and the ? Lady chapel (B17), and the cloister with east cloister alley (B10) and timber pentice (B18), from which two and six skeletons respectively were available for analysis (Fig 9; Fig 28; Fig 67). Data on the total sample may be obtained by accessing the Wellcome Osteological Research Database (WORD), available through the Museum of London website (http://www.museumoflondon.org.uk/English/Collections/OnlineResources/CHB/Database). Any previously examined sample from the MIN86 site has thus been superseded by the early 21st-century work described here.

Recording

From October 2003 onwards a team of human osteologists in the Centre for Human Bioarchaeology at the Museum of London recorded skeletons directly on to the appropriate section of the MOLA Oracle relational database. Training and coding for the human bone analysis were carefully controlled in order to exert quality control of data and to minimise inter-observer variation during the recording process.

Methodology

The analysis rigidly followed the manual for rapid data capture that accompanies WORD (Connell and Rauxloh 2003). The methodology for recording the individuals was dictated by the WORD database, following those guidelines. Age at death of adults was based on morphological changes on the pubic symphysis (Brooks and Suchey 1990), the auricular surface of the ilium (Lovejoy et al 1985) and the sternal portion of the ribs (Iscan et al 1984; 1985). For subadults, age was based on the length of the long bone diaphyses (Maresh 1970; Scheuer et al 1980), development and eruption of teeth (Gustafson and Koch 1974; Smith 1991) and epiphyseal fusion (Scheuer and Black 2000). The age categories were divided into 12 stages which are more coherent than the published age ranges used hitherto and are consistent with MOLA practice and the majority of UK scoring standards.

Sex determination for the adults was established from morphological features of the skull and pelvis (Phenice 1969; Ferembach et al 1980) and was scored on an ascending five-point scale: male, possible male, intermediate, possible female and female (Buikstra and Ubelaker 1994). Sex determination for subadults was not attempted. Metric and non-metric data were recorded following guidelines by Brothwell (1981) and Buikstra and Ubelaker (1994). Tooth measurements were based on Buikstra and Ubelaker (ibid) and Hillson (1996). Pathological changes were recorded following Roberts and Connell (2004), with reference to Aufderheide and Rodríguez-Martín (1998), Ortner (2003), and Roberts and Manchester (1995) *inter alia*.

Reporting

With the worldwide availability of the WORD databank it was seen as unnecessary to download material exhaustively for publication here. Thus, palaeodemographic data are presented here on the burial subsets by land use and summarised overall. However, metric data are left for those researchers with a particular interest in craniometry (fewer than ten skulls were intact) or in measures of physique (humeral, meric, cnemic indices, etc), the exception being stature (female and male) computed from measured maximum femoral length using standard regression formulae (Trotter 1970).

Similarly, no data on non-metric variation are presented in this report. The value of non-metric traits is not fully understood, and although they may contribute to estimation of biological distance involving archaeological populations, or in the analysis of possible family groups of burials, their precise significance remains elusive (Tyrell 2000). A suite of non-metric traits was recorded for MIN86 on the database and the interested reader is referred to the online route for these (above).

There are also photographs of various pathologies online: http://www.museumoflondon.org.uk/English/Collections/OnlineResources/CHB/Resources/Photographs/stmarygraces.htm.

The western cemetery (OA2): later ?epidemic burials

Preservation

Preservation was assessed as 'good', 'medium' or 'poor' (Connell and Rauxloh 2003). The overall preservation of the skeletal remains in this area was good, with only 5.6% of subadults and 1.6% of adults being poorly preserved (Table 27). The overall completeness in terms of the integrity of the skeletons was poor, with 51% of adult skeletons and 71% of subadult skeletons being less than 50% complete.

Table 27 Preservation of skeletons in the later ?epidemic cemetery (OA2) sample

Preservation	Adults	Adults (%)	Subadults	Subadults (%)
Good	90	70.3	39	54.9
Medium	36	28.1	28	39.4
Poor	2	1.6	4	5.6
Total	128		71	

Age and sex distribution

A total of 199 individuals were recovered from the later ?epidemic cemetery (OA2). These were distributed among 12 rows and four clusters. Overall the distribution was 36.2% subadults and 63.8% adults. There were 60 males and probable males (30.2%), 39 females and probable females (19.6%), 28 adults of unknown sex (14.6%) and 72 subadults (36.2%) (Table 28; Fig 67; Fig 68). The sex ratio was 1.54:1. The age distribution showed a gradual increase of deaths between the 18–25 age group and the 36–45 age group for both sexes, followed by a decline in the proportion aged ≥46 years. The dramatic decline in number of deaths in the elderly age category appears to follow the trend described by Dyer (1989, 142), though it may be explicable as an artefact of osteological ageing techniques rather than genuine demographic variation. Males exceeded females in all adult age categories over the age of 25.

In the urban parochial cemetery of St Nicholas Shambles, London, the male to female sex ratio was 1.27:1 (White 1988, 29), whereas in the rural cemetery at Wharram Percy, Yorkshire, it was 1.58:1 (Mays 1998, 71–2), comparable to that for the later ?epidemic cemetery. The age distribution at St Nicholas Shambles revealed a peak in the 26–35 years age category. This tends to suggest that the individuals in the later ?epidemic cemetery had a higher average age at death than those buried at St Nicholas Shambles.

Table 28 Demography of the later ?epidemic cemetery (OA2) sample

Age	Male No.	Male %	Probable male No.	Probable male %	Intermediate No.	Intermediate %	Probable female No.	Probable female %	Female No.	Female %	Unsexed No.	Unsexed %	Grand total No.	Grand total %
Perinatal											1	1.4	1	0.5
1–6 months											1	1.4	1	0.5
7–11 months											0	-	0	-
1–5 years											22	30.6	22	11.1
6–11 years											16	22.2	16	8
12–17 years											15	20.8	15	7.5
<18 years (subadult)											17	23.6	17	8.5
Total subadults											**72**		**72**	
18–25 years	6	14.3	3	16.7	1	3.6	3	21.4	6	24			**19**	**9.5**
26–35 years	12	28.6	7	38.9	1	3.6	6	42.8	6	24			**32**	**16.1**
36–45 years	17	40.5	5	27.8	2	7.1	4	28.6	9	36			**37**	**18.6**
≥46 years	6	14.3	2	11.1	1	3.6	0	-	3	12			**12**	**6**
>18 years (adult)	1	2.4	1	5.6	23	82.1	1	7.1	1	4		**27**		**13.6**
Total adults	**42**	**33.1**	**18**	**14.2**	**28**	**22.0**	**14**	**11.0**	**25**	**19.7**			**127**	
Total all individuals	**42**	**21.1**	**18**	**9.0**	**28**	**14.0**	**14**	**7.0**	**25**	**12.6**	**72**	**36.2**	**199**	

The age distribution within the subadult group revealed that the majority were aged 1 year or older. The age group 1–5 years accounted for the highest proportion with 22 (30.5%), followed by a gradual decrease in deaths with 16 (22.2%) for the 6–11-year-olds and 15 (20.8%) for the 12–17-year-olds. The apparent mortality of newborn children was remarkably low at just two (2.8%), whereas the death rate among the youngest members of the population would be expected to be higher, around 25% (Orme 2003, 113).

Stature

Stature is believed to provide an indication of dietary status, though genetics is always to be considered a contributory factor (Roberts and Cox 2003, 248). It was possible to calculate the average stature based on 34% of females and 38% of males (Table 29). When compared to collected data on average stature in Britain during the 'late medieval' period (defined as *c* 1050–*c* 1550: ibid, 248), the mean stature for males fell comfortably within the maximum and minimum ranges. The females were taller than the medieval average and this is reflected in the range of stature for this part of the Royal Mint site.

Pathology

CONGENITAL ABNORMALITIES

Congenital abnormalities or malformations are those that are present from birth, produced by pathological changes during normal intra-uterine development (Aufderheide and Rodríguez-Martín 1998, 51). The effect of such conditions may vary significantly depending on the severity of the abnormality and which part of the skeleton is affected (Ortner 2003, 453).

Border shifts

The number of presacral segments in the spine may vary from the normal count of 24, made up of seven cervical, 12 thoracic and five lumbar vertebrae (Barnes 1994, 78). These variations are asymptomatic in the living person and are not uncommon. The most frequent of all border shifts are at the lumbosacral border and usually consist of a supernumerary lumbar vertebra or sacralisation of the fifth lumbar vertebra. In this population two males had a supernumerary lumbar vertebra (L6), with complete sacralisation in [12520] and [12716]. A further five individuals (two males and three females) displayed complete sacralisation of the fifth lumbar vertebra with a prevalence of

Table 29 Stature calculations for the later ?epidemic cemetery (OA2) sample compared to average stature in late medieval Britain (Roberts and Cox 2003, 248)

Sample	Sex	Sample size	Ave height (m)	Min height (m)	Max height (m)
Britain c 1050–c 1550	Male	8494	1.71	1.67	1.74
	Female	7929	1.59	1.54	1.65
St Mary Graces (OA2)	Male	23	1.70	1.67	1.74
	Female	12	1.64	1.60	1.68

2/38 (5.26%) for males and 3/27 (11.1%) for females. Another two males displayed partial sacralisation of the fifth lumbar vertebra (5.26%) and one female incomplete lumbarisation of the first sacral segment (4%). One male also displayed an anterior cleft between the first and second sacral segment (2.9% of possible cases). This is normal in younger individuals as a process of fusion, but in some adults there is a failure of fusion in later life. A sacrocaudal shift occurred only in one female, who exhibited sacralisation of the first caudal vertebra (25% of possible cases), but these vertebrae were present in very limited numbers and would therefore not be entirely representative of the true distribution.

Spondylolysis is the separation of the neural arch from the vertebral body, and most commonly occurs in the fifth lumbar vertebra and more rarely in the fourth lumbar vertebra (Ortner 2003, 148). The aetiology of this condition has been debated; although it is now generally accepted as being caused by a stress fracture in childhood or adolescence (Crawford Adams and Hamblen 2001, 205), it has also been associated with congenital weakening (Roberts and Manchester 1995, 78). Clinically it is often asymptomatic but may occasionally be the cause of deep lumbar back pain (Crawford Adams and Hamblen 2001, 205). No strong predisposition by sex has been found, although a slight bias towards males is evident (Aufderheide and Rodríguez-Martín 1998, 63). Two females, [8268] and [12687], had bilateral spondylolysis of the fifth lumbar vertebra. The latter was elderly (≥46 years old) and the former was a young (18–25-year-old) woman who also showed spondylolysis of the fourth lumbar vertebra (though it was not possible to establish whether this was bilateral, owing to post-mortem damage). The modern prevalence of this condition is around 3% (Roberts and Manchester 1995, 79), which is consistent with the overall prevalence in this population. This represents 3% of possible cases, when calculated against the number of fifth lumbar vertebrae present (67).

Extra-spinal anomalies

Congenital hip dysplasia (CHD) is believed to be caused by genetic factors, though it has also been seen at higher rates in infants born in the breech position. There is a clear genetic predisposition in girls, who are affected six times more often than boys, and it is bilateral in a third of all cases (Crawford Adams and Hamblen 2001, 306). Unilateral congenital hip dysplasia was present in a female 26–35 years of age [12648], evidenced by the shallow configuration of the acetabulum. The outer margin of the acetabulum displayed extra cortical bone growth as a reaction to the condition. Unfortunately, the femoral head was absent post-mortem, which made further observations on the condition impossible.

Congenital malformations of a single skeletal element were seen in a female aged 26–35 years [9843]. She displayed congenital shortening of the neck in the right calcaneum. This had not affected any of the adjacent bones such as the talus, and did not appear to have affected the individual to any great degree as there was no sign of stress.

DEGENERATIVE JOINT DISEASE

Schmorl's nodes

Schmorl's nodes are lesions on the vertebral body and are the result of herniation of the *nucleus pulposus*. This condition is commonly found in elderly individuals but may also been seen in adolescents. They are believed to be the result of extensive physical activity, falls from great heights and heavy lifting (Mann and Hunt 2005, 95).

The overall prevalence was 17.8%, with males (22%) affected twice as often as females (11%). In both sexes, the lower thoracic region was the most commonly affected, at 44–65% in males and 18–35% in females. Interestingly, the youngest adult age category of 18–25 years displayed the highest prevalence of 21%, followed by age group 36–45 years (20.5%). If younger individuals were more prone to developing Schmorl's nodes it would be expected that the increase with age would be gradual. As the prevalence rate in the younger age category was highest, the individuals who developed Schmorl's nodes at a young age were more likely to die young too. Whether this is related to heavy physical activity is unclear. The prevalence rate of Schmorl's nodes displayed here (17.8%) was comparable to the 16.6% seen in pooled medieval samples (Roberts and Cox 2003, 197).

Intervertebra disc disease (IVD)

This condition results from the rupture of the fibrous capsules situated in the disc spaces between the vertebral bodies, stimulating a bony reaction. This results in either IVD or osteophytosis. Females were affected by IVD only to a slightly higher degree than males (14.1% and 12% respectively) and it showed a gradual increase with age from 8.7% in the 18–25-year-olds to 14.5% in the elderly age categories.

Osteophytosis (OP)

Osteophytes occur along the margins of the vertebral body and result from stimuli similar to those implicated in IVD. The OP trend was similar to that seen in IVD, with females (12.8%) showing a slightly higher prevalence than males (12%). This condition also appeared to increase gradually with age, from 6.5% in the 18–25-year-olds to 16.3% in the elderly.

Fusion

Congenital fusion of vertebrae was only noted in one unsexed individual aged 36–45 years (0.05%). The fusion observed here was between the first and second lumbar vertebrae.

Spinal osteoarthritis (OA)

Osteoarthritis of the spine was recorded through the presence of eburnation. The cause of OA is not clear-cut: though it is a degenerative condition, caution should be observed in linking it to specific types of occupation (Waldron and Cox 1989). The presence of OA was remarkably low in this population, with only 0.3% of males and no females displaying any eburnation. Only the two older age groups showed any degenerative changes related to OA, with the highest in the ≥46 years category at 0.9%.

Extra-spinal osteoarthritis

Osteoarthritis in the extra-spinal joints occurred with a very low prevalence (crude prevalence rate (CPR) 2.3%). Two males, one in the 36–45-year-old category [9662] and one aged ≥46 years [9543], exhibited OA of the left and right distal ulna respectively. No females displayed any joint eburnation, while one unsexed 36–45-year-old [8210] had eburnation on the left distal fourth and fifth metatarsal joint surfaces.

TRAUMA

Fractures

There was a distinct paucity of fractures in this assemblage, with a prevalence of 4.7%. Since only males were affected, this rises to 10% of the males. The fractures were mainly situated in the upper body (83.3%), with only one healed fracture found in the lower limbs (16.7%). In the upper body, fractures were seen in the left clavicle [8102] (1/124 or 1.1% of possible cases), the left scapula [9987] (1/128 or 0.78% of possible cases), two ulnae (2/137 or 1.45%), two radii (2/139 or 1.43%) and a single rib (1/126 or 0.79%).

All fractures were well-healed, with only one ulna [12757] exhibiting misalignment in the distal portion of the shaft. The femoral fracture [11025], situated on the proximal shaft, was only slightly misaligned. Generally, with fractures of the femur, treatment is required to avoid shortening of the shaft, as the large muscles in this area will pull together and shorten the shaft significantly. The fact that the femur fracture was well-reduced suggests that the individual had received some form of treatment, probably by the application of a splint.

Projectile injury

Projectile injuries are a direct indication of conflict in a population. Presumably they result from action in battle, rather than casual inter-personal violence (Roberts and Cox 2003, 275). One elderly male [7314] had a projectile point embedded in the fifth thoracic vertebra, penetrating the left inferior facet. The projectile had entered at an angle, penetrating the vertebra from the upper direction. The margins of the injury were sclerotic and showed evidence of healing, suggesting that he did survive the injury for some time. The exact nature of the projectile was not established precisely but was a small ferrous object and most likely an arrowhead.

Sharp force and multiple trauma

Sharp force injury was evident in the cranium of a young male [12525]. The wound crossed the right lambdoid suture, affecting both the occipital and right parietal bone. The area measured 48mm wide by 14mm deep and exhibited marginal healing with rounded edges.

Multiple injuries were only noted in one elderly male [7102]. He had a 'parry' fracture of the left ulna and radius. Usually parry fractures are of the ulna only, suggesting that this individual received a substantial blow to the arm. He further displayed an avulsion injury to the knee and a soft tissue injury to the proximal medial portion of the tibia, which would most likely have been associated with the avulsion injury. Parry fractures are generally seen to be associated with inter-personal violence as in defending against a blow to the head (Roberts and Manchester 1995, 77), and it is not unlikely that this individual had sustained his injuries through acts of aggression.

INFECTIOUS DISEASES

Non-specific periosteal infections

Non-specific periostitis is common in medieval populations but is poorly understood. It is believed to be an effect of trauma or blood-borne infections such as syphilis and tuberculosis (Roberts and Cox 2003, 235) but has also been associated with more benign conditions, such as varicose veins (Mann and Hunt 2005, 183). Non-specific infections are characterised by the periosteal reactions which occur in bone without being firmly associated necessarily with a specific bacterium or condition.

A total of 26 individuals displayed non-specific infections. The infections were predominantly recorded in the tibiae, fibulae, femora and maxillary sinuses. The tibiae were the most commonly affected and this was seen predominantly in males (14/77 or 18.2% of cases). The prevalence in females was much lower (3/55 or 5.5%). Bilateral infection of the tibiae was seen in five out of nine males (55.5% of possible cases) – two of whom also showed infection of the fibulae – and in one of three females (33.3%). Three subadults also had infection of the tibiae (4/88 or 4.5%), with one juvenile having both tibiae affected.

The overall rate of non-specific periostitis of the tibiae was 10.6% (24/226). Compared with other sites from the late medieval period (14.1%) this was slightly below average, though the latter figure was calculated against number of individuals rather than number of bones present (Roberts and Cox 2003, 235).

Maxillary sinusitis has been associated with atmospheric pollution (Roberts and Cox 2003, 233). This condition was present in four males (10.5%) and one female (4.2%), affecting 8% of the individuals with maxillary sinuses readily available for inspection (via cranial damage). It should be stressed that this apparent prevalence rate may be somewhat reduced, since observations were made purely on a macroscopic basis, requiring the skull to be sufficiently fragmented. Compared to an overall CPR of 13.3%, based on other late medieval sites (Roberts and Cox 2003, 233), this was relatively low. It might have been assumed that living in a densely populated London, with a large amount of atmospheric pollution through burning of fuels, would have produced a higher prevalence rate than, for instance, at rural Wharram Percy in Yorkshire (ibid). However, this was not the case, since the Wharram Percy site revealed a prevalence of 50.9%, more than six times higher than in the later ?epidemic cemetery population at St Mary Graces. However, this may not be comparing like with like. At Wharram Percy, a rural site, the available fuel was timber only, whereas in London alternative fuels such as coal were available from at least the 14th century onwards, and this would have had a bearing on nasal infections.

Non-specific osteomyelitis

Non-specific osteomyelitis differs from non-specific periosteal reaction in that it is an infection which affects the bone marrow. This can be caused by a number of factors such as trauma, soft tissue injury or by a haematogenous route from a remote septic focus predominantly caused by the bacterium *Staphylococcus aureus* (Ortner 2003, 181).

One young female [8173] showed osteomyelitis of the right proximal femur displaying enlargement and thickening of the shaft, with reactive bone formation producing an irregular surface of pitting, cavities and plaques of new bone. An older female [9956], 26–35 years of age, displayed a swelling of the midshaft on the left tibia.

Tuberculosis (TB)

Tuberculosis is a specific infection that can be acute or chronic, infecting soft tissues and bone, and caused by the spread of one of the two species of *Mycobacterium tuberculosis* (Aufderheide and Rodríguez-Martín 1998, 118). The infection in humans usually occurs through the respiratory tract, but much more rarely it may also occur through ingestion of cattle products entering the system through the intestinal wall and mesenteric lymph nodes (Ortner 2003, 227). In the skeleton, the spine is the most commonly affected area, with the lower spine the primary focus (ibid, 231). The infection usually commences in the anterior portion of the vertebral body near the intervertebral disc and may involve several spine segments. This may eventually lead to collapse of the spine, also known as Pott's disease (Crawford Adams and Hamblen 2001, 186).

Tuberculosis was recorded in two adolescents (both *c* 15 years old), [11436] and [12696]. Both displayed the classic infectious lesions in the vertebrae, with the former exhibiting kyphosis of the spine (Pott's disease). A male [10177] had earlier been shown to exhibit tuberculosis of the left wrist joint (T Waldron, pers comm) and ancient DNA analysis further revealed the presence of the TB organism *Mycobacterium*, but it was impossible to identify to species, whether *M tuberculosis or M bovis* (Taylor et al 1996). An adolescent [9901] was also earlier identified with a lytic condition of the first and second lumbar vertebrae, apparently suggestive of tubercular infection. DNA analysis confirmed the presence of *Mycobacterium,* although again it was uncertain whether the human or bovine form of the disease was present (Taylor et al 1996). (The wrist [10177] and vertebrae [9901] were unavailable for further study as not part of the MOL collection.) The nature of the disease is such that it may well have affected many other individuals than were identifiable, but, with its contagion and rapidity, macroscopically identifiable bony lesions may well not be observable. The condition is seen to generate an osteological response in only *c* 10% of cases (Roberts and Cox 2003, 229).

Tuberculosis prevalence was calculated against the number of individuals at risk in the assemblage. As TB may affect any bone element, it was recorded as a percentage of the entire population (199), producing a CPR of 1%, consistent with the prevalence (0.88%) in other late medieval skeletal assemblages (Roberts and Cox 2003, 231).

METABOLIC DISORDERS

Cribra orbitalia

Cribra orbitalia is represented by porous pitting in the orbital roof. It is not necessarily pathological per se but has been linked to conditions such as scurvy, malnutrition, iron deficiency anaemia and chronic gastrointestinal bleeding (Mann and Hunt 2005, 31; Roberts and Manchester 1995, 165; Stuart-Macadam 1989, 212). In most cases the condition is bilateral.

The overall prevalence was 34.1%, with subadults most commonly affected (43.3%). A peak was observed in the 6–11 years age group (66.7%), though it should be noted that no observation was possible in infants, of course. Among the adult population, females showed a higher prevalence (36.8%) than males (24.4%). Females tended to be more affected as younger adults, whereas males showing the condition were slightly older (Table 30). The prevalence of cribra, at 34.1%, appeared high compared to the quoted CPR for later medieval sites of 10.8%,

Table 30 Prevalence rates of cribra orbitalia in the later ?epidemic cemetery (OA2) sample

All individuals	N = 82	n = 28	% = 34.1						
Age		Subadults			Male			Female	
	N=	n=	%	N=	n=	%	N=	n=	%
Perinatal	1	0	-						
1–6 months	0	0	-						
7–11 months	0	0	-						
1–5 years	12	5	41.7						
6–11 years	6	4	66.7						
12–17 years	9	3	33.3						
Subadults not aged	2	1	50.0						
Total subadults	30	13	43.3						
18–25 years				4	1	25.0	8	4	50.0
26–35 years				11	3	27.3	7	2	28.6
36–45 years				14	4	28.6	3	1	33.3
≥46 years				5	0	-	1	0	-
Total adults				34	8	24.4	19	7	36.8

Key: N = number of individuals with observable orbital roof; n = number of individuals with cribra orbitalia but the trend revealed that overall females were affected more often than males (Roberts and Cox 2003, 235).

CIRCULATORY DISEASES

Osgood Schlatter disease

Osgood Schlatter disease is a childhood affliction which sees apophysitis of the tibial tubercle. The tubercle becomes temporarily enlarged and undergoes strain from the pull of the patellar tendon (Crawford Adams and Hamblen 2001, 373). A possible case of this condition was noted in one young male aged 18–25 years [7039], though an alternative diagnosis was an avulsion injury.

Osteochondritis dissecans

This is a localised disorder of the convex joint surface in which a segment of subchondral bone becomes avascular and slowly separates from the surrounding bone. This condition mainly occurs in younger individuals and may cause irritation of the joint, possibly resulting in 'locking' of the joint (Crawford Adams and Hamblen 2001, 136).

This condition affected three males, [7202], [8012] and [11867] (CPR 5%), one female [6360] (CPR 2.6%), one unsexed individual [11452] (CPR 3.6%) and one adolescent [11436] (CPR 6.7%). Two males were aged 25–35 years and one 36–45 years, the female 18–25 years, the adolescent 12–17 years, and the unsexed person was also unaged. The overall prevalence including all five individuals was 3%. Among the males, two were affected in the knee joint and one in the talocrural joint, whereas both the female and the adolescent were affected in the talocrural joint. The unsexed individual was affected on the left femoral head.

MISCELLANEOUS DISEASES

Paget's disease (Osteitis deformans)

Paget's disease is idiopathic, though it has been suggested recently to be the result of a viral infection (*Paramyxovirus* family) in the osteoclasts of the affected bone. It is a slow progressive disorder of one or several bones. The affected bones become spongy and thickened in nature. The condition rarely begins before the age of 40 years and mainly affects males. It is often asymptomatic but it may, owing to thickening of the cranium, damage the optic or auditory nerves (Crawford Adams and Hamblen 2001, 52).

Paget's disease was noted in one unsexed individual aged 36–45 years [8210], giving a CPR of 0.7%. The cranial vault was thickened, though with no sign of a porous surface. The thickening appeared most significant on the endocranial portion surface (average thickness of bone 10.3mm at the level of the parietals). Paget's disease seen in other late medieval populations varies in prevalence from 0.21% to 1.66%, with an average of 1.16% (Roberts and Cox 2003, 284), consistent with the rate noted here.

DENTAL PATHOLOGY

The late medieval period saw the revival of ideas as to how best to treat dental ailments. It was recommended by Guy de Chauliac in Montpellier, France, in 1343 that dental hygiene should be maintained by cleaning teeth in a mixture of honey, salt and vinegar (Roberts and Cox 2003, 257). It is clear, however, that any dental care proved of little value to overall dental health. Dental health provides an excellent indication of the general health and wellbeing of a population, and provides information not only on diseases but also on diet and dental treatment.

Dental diseases include caries, calculus, periapical lesions, periodontal disease and dental enamel hypoplasia. These conditions would have affected the rate of ante-mortem tooth loss and serve as a reflection of the overall state of dental health seen in the population. Subadult dental health was evaluated for the presence of caries, calculus and dental enamel hypoplasia, in both permanent and deciduous dentition.

Ante-mortem tooth loss is an indication of general dental health and hygiene, and is recognised by the subsequent closure of the tooth socket. Alveolar resorption may occur following the atrophied state of the bone once the tooth is gone. Most teeth are lost following other dental diseases (below).

The overall prevalence of ante-mortem tooth loss in this population was 10.1% for males and 3.6% for females. The trend revealed the expected gradual increase in tooth loss with age, with 40.7% of all elderly males and 7.5% of all elderly females suffering ante-mortem loss. The greatest loss occurred in the molar dentition in general. This is not uncommon as the fissures of the crown are prone to retain food residue and thereby provoke caries. The most affected tooth was the first molar, which is as expected since this is the first permanent tooth to erupt. There was no obvious variation in ante-mortem tooth loss when comparing maxillary with mandibular dentition.

Comparing the overall ante-mortem loss of 9.3% with other sites from the late medieval period, it becomes apparent that the prevalence is well below the average (19.4%); Merton Priory by contrast revealed an average tooth loss of 16% (Roberts and Cox 2003, 263). By calculating tooth loss against age and sex, it is clear that the rate of loss is highly influenced not only by age but also by sex. This may in part explain the variations seen between sites such as this one and Merton Priory, where a large proportion of the individuals were mature and older adult males (Conheeney 2007, 266–7).

Caries

Dental caries is a destruction of tooth enamel, dentine and cement caused by acid production by bacteria in the dental plaque (Hillson 1996, 269). The prevalence of caries was higher in males (8.7%) than in females (5.4%). For males the highest caries prevalence rate was seen in the two middle age groups (26–35 and 36–45 years), while for females the highest prevalences were in the youngest age group (18–25 years) and then again at the age of 36–45 years. Taking the dental caries prevalence for the first molar alone, this was still higher in the younger population than the older.

Dental caries prevalence in subadults was at a very low level (3/354 teeth or 0.8%), affecting the first and second molars of the permanent dentition. In the deciduous dentition only one individual had caries, and this was in the first maxillary molar (0.4%).

Comparing the prevalence of dental caries in this population with other later medieval sites, the overall rate of 8.9% was above the average figure of 5.6% (Roberts and Cox 2003, 258).

Calculus

Calculus is mineralised plaque which accumulates at the base of living plaque deposits and is attached to the surface of the tooth (Hillson 1996, 255). This is one of the most common diseases to affect the dentition once the tooth has erupted, and it is responsible for high rates of tooth loss (ibid, 254). Calculus prevalence tends to increase with age and to affect males more than females (ibid, 260).

In this population, over half of all dentition recorded was affected by calculus, with a roughly even distribution between males (56.1%) and females (56.4%); the trend towards calculus accumulation increased with age in both sexes. Again, the first molar was the most commonly affected. The overall calculus prevalence (51.7%) was similar to that (54%) seen at other later medieval sites in Britain (Roberts and Cox 2003, 262). The prevalence of calculus in subadult permanent dentition was lower at 28.2%, affecting primarily the first and second molars, which would have erupted at the age of 6 years and 12 years respectively. Calculus was noted in only three deciduous teeth, all mandibular first or second molars, at a rate of only 1.4%.

Periapical lesions

Periapical lesions occur as inflammation of the jaws, when bacteria enter the pulp of the tooth, through attrition or fracture. Once triggered, the inflammatory response generates a discharge, which if confined within the tooth increases the pressure and may ultimately lead to the death of the tooth. Thereafter, the infection passes down the root canal to inflame the periodontal tissue (Hillson 1996, 285). Acute abscesses develop from periapical granulomas and cysts, and leave a fistula or broad pit around the root of the apex (ibid, 286).

The prevalence of periapical lesions observed in this population was very low at 0.6%. That in males (1.3%) was slightly higher than that seen in females (0.4%). The most commonly affected teeth were the jaw regions adjoining the first and second molars in males and second molars in females. In males the 26–35 years age group was affected more frequently (2.7%) while in females the youngest adult age group (17–25 years) revealed the highest prevalence rate (1.4%). The overall prevalence of 0.6% was low when compared to other contemporary sites, with an average of 3.1% (Roberts and Cox 2003, 260); a total of 12 sites were evaluated and only one site (Ysgol Twm o'r Nant, Denbigh, Clwyd) had a lower average of 0.33%.

Periodontal disease

Periodontal disease seen in the archaeological record is the final stage of the inflammation of the gums. The first three stages are classed as gingivitis and are not expressed in the bone; the last stage is periodontitis and is a deeper lesion involving the periodontal tissues. Bone loss occurs, exposing cement on the root surface and allowing sub-gingival plaque to form. This condition is very common in adults over the age of 30 (Hillson 1996, 262). Bone loss may occur vertically and horizontally. The vertical bone loss tends to be symmetrical and affects mainly the first and second molars while the horizontal bone loss involves reduction in the height of the walls surrounding the tooth roots. Teeth are eventually lost when all the surrounding alveolar bone has vanished (ibid, 265).

In the later ?epidemic cemetery males were affected over four times more frequently than females (32.4% and 6.8% respectively) The prevalence of periodontal disease increased dramatically from the younger age groups (17–35 years) to the older age groups (36–45 and ≥46 years). In males the distribution was seen to be more even, with a high incidence of bone loss across all dentition, averaging 34%. This may suggest that females were more prone to 'vertical periodontitis' whereas the males were more susceptible to 'horizontal periodontitis'.

The overall prevalence was 23.1%, which compared to other late medieval sites (37.5%) was relatively low. It should, however, be stressed that the comparative site calculations were based on number of individuals and not number of teeth; furthermore, the sites included in the overall average had very variable rates of prevalence (Roberts and Cox 2003, 260).

Dental enamel hypoplasia

Hypoplasia of the dental enamel is a deficiency of the enamel thickness, disrupting the contour of the crown surface, initiated during enamel matrix secretion (Hillson 1996, 165). The presence of enamel hypoplasia is an indication of disrupted growth during the time of crown formation. The location in the dentition provides an indication of the period in which the individual was affected and generates information on periods of disrupted growth in childhood, which could be caused either by disease or malnutrition (Hillson 1996, 166).

The teeth most commonly affected are the canines, which may show hypoplasia on any portion of the crown surface, depending on the age of development during the period of stress. Again, males were affected more frequently at 62.2%, as compared to 46.2% in females, with an almost even distribution between the mandibular and maxillary dentition. In the subadults with erupted permanent canines present, the prevalence was lower at 27.8%, affecting the mandibular canines more than twice as often as the maxillary teeth (Table 31).

In both males and females the central portion of the crown was most commonly affected in both the maxillary and mandibular dentition. No deciduous dentition displayed any dental hypoplasia.

The overall prevalence of adults with dental enamel hypoplasia was 41 of 76 possible cases (53.9%) and in children 27.8%, based on the canines only. The general late medieval prevalence noted by Roberts and Cox (2003, 264) was 35.4% but was based on all dentition. This overall prevalence was perceptibly higher in comparison with their 'early medieval' period (defined as AD *c* 410–*c* 1050) (CPR 18.8%, based on the number of individuals with hypoplasia). Comparing the results from this assemblage did pose some problems owing to differential methods of analysis used, which may have inflated

Table 31 Dental enamel hypoplasia in the later ?epidemic cemetery (OA2) sample

	Male			Female			All adults		
	N=	n=	%	N=	n=	%	N=	n=	%
Maxilla location									
Crown	40	1	2.5	24	2	8.3	68	3	4.4
Mid	40	12	30.0	24	5	20.8	68	18	26.5
Distal	40	11	27.5	24	1	4.2	68	12	17.6
Mandible location									
Crown	44	1	2.3	25	1	4.0	74	0	-
Mid	44	14	31.8	25	5	20.0	74	2	2.7
Distal	44	8	18.2	25	2	8.0	74	2	2.7
Total	**45**	**28**	**62.2**	**26**	**12**	**46.2**	**76**	**41**	**53.9**

Key: N = number of individuals with one or more observable canines; n = number of individuals with DEH of one or more canines
Total % = total number of individuals with hypoplasia on any location of the maxillary or mandibular canines

the figure slightly by including canines only. It is, however, apparent that there was a dramatic increase in individuals with hypoplasia in the later medieval period, and it is not unlikely that these were the individuals who suffered during the great famine of 1315–18, which was one of the worst of the millennium (Dyer 1989, 265–7).

OVERALL DENTAL HEALTH

All dental diseases recorded proved to have a higher prevalence rate in males than females, apart from calculus, while females appeared to be affected at an earlier age than males. The overall dental health of the adults in this assemblage proved to be better than average when compared to other sites from the later medieval period.

The eastern cemetery (OA9)

Preservation

The bone quality of the majority of the skeletons in the eastern cemetery was rated as 'good', with only 9.4% being poorly preserved (Table 32). However, truncation of the skeletons occurred frequently, with no more than 60% completeness in this cemetery. This is perhaps not particularly surprising for a cemetery in continual use, especially given that during this period the intercutting of burials was a common occurrence (Roberts and Cox 2003, 222). Nevertheless, the impact of skeletal preservation and integrity becomes more apparent in relation to the detail achieved in the osteological analysis of the skeletal material.

Table 32 Preservation of skeletons in the eastern cemetery (OA9) sample

Preservation	Adults	Adults (%)	Subadults	Subadults (%)
Good	46	71.9	13	92.8
Medium	12	18.7	1	7.1
Poor	6	9.4	0	-
Total	**64**		**14**	

Age and sex distribution

Of the 78 individuals recorded, 64 (82.1%) were adults and 14 (17.9%) were subadults. There were 36 males, 13 females and 15 unsexed adults (Table 33; Fig 67; Fig 69). The male to female sex ratio therefore was 2.77:1. There was a fairly even spread across the age ranges for the 49 adults of known sex, but 15 individuals could be classed only as adults over 18 years of age. As there were more males than females, the numbers relating to death rates in the age categories are slightly biased. The derived mortality figures for males and females in each of the age groups 18–25 years, 26–35 years and ≥46 years were roughly equal and contrasting with the slightly higher number of males in the age category 36–45 years.

Among the 14 subadults, no infants were present and the youngest individual was in the 1–5 years age category, with the majority (eight) being in the 6–11 years age category. As in other cemetery groups there are many variables to account for apparent low infant mortality, including burial practice and poor survival of subadult skeletal material. An excavation will, at best, produce only a sample of the population as a whole, and in this instance the numbers within that sample are small, so that it would be difficult to draw any statistically valid conclusions. In contrast, and as a matter of interest, a comparison of the Bills of Mortality for London during the 16th and 17th centuries suggest that about 40% of deaths were of those aged under 5 years while the deaths of those aged 6–20 years were as low as 6–7% (Roberts and Cox 2003, 304).

The time span for the skeletal material in the eastern cemetery is broad, covering nearly 200 years and a period that was marked by the aftermath of the Black Death, other plague outbreaks and the great famine of 1437–40. These are clearly important factors to be considered, particularly in terms of the population structure represented by this assemblage.

Table 33 Demography of the eastern cemetery (OA9) sample

	Male		Probable male		Intermediate		Probable female		Female		Unsexed		Grand total	
Age	No.	%	No.	%	No.	%	No.	%	No.	%	No.	%	No.	%
Perinatal											0	-	0	-
1–6 months											0	-	0	-
7–11 months											0	-	0	-
1–5 years											1	7.1	1	1.3
6–11 years											8	57.1	8	10.3
12–17 years											4	28.6	4	5.1
<18 years (subadult)											1	7.1	1	1.3
Total subadults											14		14	
18–25 years	3	13.6	2	14.3	0	-	0	-	2	18.2	1	7.1	8	10.3
26–35 years	3	13.6	3	21.4	0	-	1	100	3	27.3	2	14.3	12	15.3
36–45 years	8	36.4	3	21.4	1	100	0	-	1	9.1	0	-	13	16.6
≥46 years	6	27.3	0	-	0	-	0	-	4	36.4	0	-	10	12.8
>18 years (adult)	2	9.1	6	42.9	0	-	1	100	1	9.1	11	78.6	21	27
Total adults	22	34.4	14	21.9	1	1.6	2	3.1	1	17.2	14	21.9	64	
Total all individuals	22	28.2	14	17.9	1	1.3	2	2.6	11	14.1	28	35.9	78	

Stature

Stature estimation was based upon the maximum femoral length using regression formulae (Trotter 1970). The paucity of intact bones for measurement meant that estimation was only possible for five individuals, all of whom were males. The average stature estimated was 173.41cm, slightly above the average stature for Britain in the later medieval period (Roberts and Cox 2003, 248); however, the numbers involved are small and the resulting figures must be seen in this light.

Pathology

Twenty-two (28.2%) of the individuals from the eastern cemetery manifested macroscopically observable pathological changes, and of these five (17.8%) had one or more pathological lesions.

CONGENITAL ABNORMALITIES

Seven individuals (8.9%) showed congenital abnormalities. Only males and subadults were affected, but as there were no markedly severe congenital conditions in the skeletons they would have been asymptomatic in their expression. One 6–11-year-old child [9310] had a supernumerary tooth between the left maxillary first and second molars along with other congenital defects expressed in the vertebrae and in the feet. In one male aged 18–25 years [9373], the eleventh thoracic vertebra was a 'butterfly vertebra'. This is an uncommon finding and, as in the case of this individual, generally only affects one vertebra and more commonly males (Aufderheide and Rodríguez-Martín 1998, 62).

Spina bifida occulta

The condition known as spina bifida occurs when the spinal chord is exposed due to incomplete fusion of the sacral posterior neural arch(es). There are two types, but the less severe and more commonly found in archaeological material, and known to have a less debilitating effect, is spina bifida occulta (Ortner 2003, 468). Spina bifida occulta was present in one male aged 36–45 years [10145] who also had a sacralised extra lumbar vertebra and may have suffered from tuberculosis of the spine.

DEGENERATIVE JOINT DISEASE

Osteoarthritis (OA)

Diseases of the joints are generally the most predominant disease identified in archaeological skeletal material, with the most common of these being osteoarthritis. In clinical terms OA may be identified through joint pain and diminished joint space. In skeletal material it is generally characterised by both subtle and fully developed morphological changes in and around the joint, affecting one or more joints with the definitive condition of eburnation (Ortner 2003, 545).

Perhaps surprisingly, only two individuals (2.6%) in the eastern cemetery revealed pathological changes associated with osteoarthritis. Both exhibited changes to the knee joint, with the adult male [9327] manifesting bilateral changes to the patellae and femora with osteophytic lipping, sub-chondral surface breakdown and eburnation. Degenerative changes of both hip joints were also observed in this male. The older female aged ≥46 years [9334] showed changes only to the right femur with slight osteophytic lipping and a small area of eburnation.

Rotator cuff injury

Rotator cuff injuries are associated with the muscles that control the rotation of the shoulder joint and which can be exposed to stresses from the action of throwing or lifting the arm above the head. In one study they have been identified as a natural correlate of ageing (Milgrom et al 1995).

One individual [9403], a male aged 36–45 years, had a possible rotator cuff injury to the right shoulder, with a smooth, rounded depression and osteophytic lipping visible within the area for the muscle attachment *subscapularis*. The muscle stabilises the glenohumeral joint and rotates the joint medially (Stone and Stone 2003, 115). This male also showed eburnation between the vertebral bodies of the fifth and sixth cervical vertebrae, which might tentatively be linked to the cuff injury with regard to the association and relation to the muscle.

Spinal osteoarthritis

There has been an attempt sometimes to link osteoarthritis to occupation, but caution should be exercised as there are many factors involved. Age-related degeneration is also a frequent factor identified with spinal and extra-spinal osteoarthritis.

There was a very low prevalence of spinal osteoarthritis (0.5%) in both the males and the females in the eastern cemetery. The vertebrae affected in males were the cervical while in the females it was the lumbar. The numbers involved were very small but this may be an indication of a certain variation in either posture or possibly activity. Osteoarthritis has been linked to the ageing process and, where present here, occurred in the age categories 26–35 and 36–45 years but not in the ≥46 years age group. This is perhaps a little surprising but probably not unduly so, as the majority of individuals were in the 36–45 years age category, which may account for the higher rate.

Schmorl's nodes

Schmorl's nodes were more prevalent in the males (11%) compared to the females (6.1%). Since they have been associated with load bearing and lifting this might be an indication of a difference in roles carried out by the males and females. The higher incidences were seen in the age categories 18–25 years (10.7%) and ≥46 years (13.2%), possibly linking them in part to age. The vertebrae most commonly affected were the thoracic, and generally the mid to lower thoracic vertebrae.

Intervertebral disc disease (IVD)

Intervertebral disc disease is identified with bony changes to the vertebral body surface that may include increased porosity and pitting of the surface. The males (15.7%) were three times more affected than the females (5.5%), with the prevalence increasing with age. The prevalence was highest (at 25.6%) for individuals in the age category 36–45 years.

The males had observable changes in all the vertebrae, with the fifth and sixth cervical vertebrae (31.8%) and the fourth and fifth lumbar vertebrae (31.8%) the most commonly affected. This could be associated with the natural curve of the spine and the areas more commonly affected by general degeneration.

Osteophytosis (OP)

Osteophytosis is observed as marginal bony outgrowths of the vertebral bodies which may be slight to severe and in some instances may lead to fusion. The condition was more than twice as prevalent in the males (9.3%) compared to the females (4.4%), but in part this may be attributable to there being fewer female vertebrae available for study. The incidence of osteophytosis increased through the age categories, with the lowest rate observed in the 18–25 years category and, as with intervertebral disc disease, the highest rate observed in the 36–45 years age category. The thoracic vertebrae were the most frequently affected in both the males and females.

Fusion

There were no observed instances of vertebral fusion in any of the individuals from the eastern cemetery.

TRAUMA

Fractures

A total of three individuals (3.8%), two males and one female, showed evidence of trauma. One male aged 36–45 years [10102] had a well-healed fracture of the proximal shaft of the right femur, with a remodelled callus (Fig 111). There was no indication of infection, suggesting that it was a closed fracture, and there were no secondary joint changes evident. Neither was there any misalignment or angulation of the fracture, with the only noticeable alteration being a slight (anterior/posterior) bowing of the femur which may indicate weight being placed on the bone in the early stage of healing. The other male, aged ≥46 years [10420], had a healed hairline fracture of the fifth proximal phalange of the right hand. The older female, aged

Fig 111 Posterior view of a fracture of the right femur [10102] (OA9) (scale c 1:2)

≥46 years [9334], revealed a compression fracture of the fifth thoracic vertebra with slight kyphosis. The advanced age of this female, the type of fracture and the indication of scoliosis may well allow the attribution of osteoporosis as the predisposing condition.

There were no individuals with multiple traumata, and cranial trauma was not observed. However, the aforementioned degree of truncation to the skeletons and the absence of skulls for analysis are factors that need to be borne in mind.

Soft tissue trauma

A soft tissue injury (myositis ossificans) is observed where an injury to the muscle produces calcification or new bone formation (Roberts and Manchester 1995, 67). Evidence for soft tissue injury was found in two individuals (2.6%) both of whom were males, [10058] and [10348]. The former was a young individual showing changes to the right humerus, and the latter an older man with changes to the distal end of the right tibia.

INFECTIOUS DISEASES

Non-specific periosteal infections

The most frequently observed pathological lesion was inflammatory periosteal bone reaction (active and healed) on the diaphyseal shafts of the tibiae and fibulae. Eight individuals (10.2%) were affected, none of whom were female, which is probably attributable to the truncation and overall poorer bone preservation of the females. This type of bone inflammation may be attributed to low-grade infections possibly associated with minor trauma, stress or varicose venous problems, and are commonly observed in archaeological skeletal material.

Non-specific osteitis and osteomyelitis

Osteitis and osteomyelitis are both inflammatory processes in bone whereby osteitis primarily affects the inner structures of compact bone and osteomyelitis involves the marrow (Ortner 2003, 51–5). One case of non-specific osteitis was identified in a male 36–45 years old [10058] with a smooth swelling of the cortical bone of the right tibia and left fibula. The one case of non-specific osteomyelitis was identified in an adult individual [10145] where no specific age or sex criteria were present. The bone most affected was the right acromion, with a large rounded abscess and drainage hole to its posterior superior aspect. Bony changes were also evident in the right clavicle.

Venereal syphilis

Venereal syphilis and its presence in Britain during this period continue to cause controversy, but there is a growing body of evidence that it existed in Europe before the final decade of the 15th century (Roberts and Cox 2003, 272). One individual, a male aged 26–35 years [9395], had manifest postcranial skeletal changes with a distribution (left elbow, left femur and tibia) and bony responses that were closely indicative of a treponemal infection. There was widespread sub-periosteal new bone formation, partially remodelled new bone masses with 'snail tracking', and destructive gummatous foci combined with a lack of joint involvement. Unfortunately, there was no skull present and so it was not possible to determine whether there were any changes in the skull or the presence of caries sicca, a key diagnostic feature of tertiary syphilis.

Tuberculosis (TB)

One individual, [10145], had a lesion in the spine that could possibly have been caused by a tuberculous infection. Interestingly, this 36–45-year-old male also had spina bifida occulta. The sacralised sixth lumbar vertebra manifested a deep destructive opening with nodular bony growths, probably caused by the infection which may have been exacerbated by the presence of the sacral defects. Tuberculosis is known to have been prevalent at this period, affecting males more than females and generally identified in the over-30s (Roberts and Cox 2003, 229). These criteria would appear to fit this individual, and the location and bony lesions make tuberculosis a plausible diagnosis.

METABOLIC DISEASE

Cribra orbitalia

The prevalence of cribra orbitalia in the skeletons from the eastern cemetery was 7.4%, which was low for the late medieval period (Roberts and Cox 2003, 235). However, the number of observable orbital areas of skulls was rather low, applying to only about one-third of the assemblage, and included no females or subadults (Table 34).

DENTAL PATHOLOGY

Among the 64 adults examined from the eastern cemetery there were 482 observable maxillary teeth and 616 mandibular teeth. Ante-mortem tooth loss was more prevalent in the males than the females but this is probably attributable to the state of preservation of the female skeletons and there being fewer of them in total. The most frequently lost teeth in the males were in the mandibular dentition and predominantly the molars. The first molar was the most commonly lost tooth ante-mortem, a circumstance affecting males in all age categories, with the higher frequency in the age categories 36–45 and ≥46 years.

Caries

As there were more males than females in the sample examined, it is perhaps not surprising that there were more instances of dental caries observable in males than in females. The females with observable teeth showed caries solely in the maxillary dentition, with the highest prevalence in the 18–25 years age group. The apparent absence of mandibular dental caries was probably not significant, most likely being attributable to differential preservation of the skeletal material. Males exhibited caries in both the maxillary and mandibular dentition, increasing with age at death, with the maxillary second premolar and molars being the most commonly affected teeth. The highest caries prevalence was seen in the first maxillary (33.4%) and mandibular molars, with the highest of all in the left first mandibular molar (40%). The overall prevalence of dental caries for the eastern cemetery was higher than for the later medieval sites included in the calculation of the mean caries prevalence of 5.6% by Roberts and Cox (2003, 258–9).

Table 34 Prevalence rates of cribra orbitalia in the eastern cemetery (OA9) sample

All individuals	N = 27	n = 2	% = 7.4						
Age		Subadults			Male			Female	
	N=	n=	%	N=	n=	%	N=	n=	%
6–11 years	3	0	-						
12–17 years	1	0	-						
Total subadults	**4**	**0**	**-**						
18–25 years				2	0	-	0	0	-
26–35 years				4	1	25.0	1	0	-
36–45 years				5	0	-	0	0	-
≥46 years				6	1	16.7	2	0	-
>18 years (adult)				2	0	-	1	0	-
Total adults				**19**	**2**	**10.5**	**4**	**0**	**-**

Key: N = number of individuals with observable orbital roof; n = number of individuals with cribra orbitalia

Calculus

The presence, severity and location of dental calculus is generally a good indication of the dental hygiene of a population, with the frequency and extent of deposits increasing with age (Beiswanger et al 1989). Calculus was present in all the age categories for both the males and females, with the highest prevalence in males (60%) and females (81%) aged 26–35 years at death. It occurred in both the maxillary and mandibular dentition, and in both males and females the anterior dentition was affected most often. In both males and females the mandibular dentition was more frequently affected, with the mandibular left and right central incisors in males showing a very high prevalence of 76.9% and 84.1% respectively. Males also showed in the mandibular teeth an increase in calculus prevalence with age.

Periodontal disease

Predominantly the males in the age category 36–45 years exhibited the greatest degree of periodontal disease, with the maxillary and mandibular premolars and molars most commonly affected. The left maxillary premolars in the males were the most affected teeth.

Abscesses

Few abscesses were observed, involving a total of 13 teeth from males in the age categories 36–45 and ≥46 years, most frequently the maxillary right anterior teeth and left molars. The root of a single right maxillary canine was affected in an adult female.

Dental enamel hypoplasia

Enamel hypoplasia was observed in 11 males and two females, with the overall prevalence of adults with dental enamel hypoplasia being 14 of 35 possible cases (31.4%) based on the canines only. The canine in both the males and females was the most commonly affected tooth, with the changes most often observed in the males in the mid section of the mandibular canine (29.2%) (Table 35). All the males had more than one tooth affected, and one male aged 36–45 years [9411] had enamel defects on 11 teeth, predominantly in the middle crown

Table 35 Dental enamel hypoplasia in the eastern cemetery (OA9) sample

		Male			Female			All adults	
	N=	n=	%	N=	n=	%	N=	n=	%
Maxilla location									
Crown	21	0	-	3	0	-	26	0	-
Mid	21	3	14.3	3	0	-	26	3	11.5
Distal	21	3	14.3	3	0	-	26	0	-
Mandible location									
Crown	24	0	-	4	0	-	30	0	
Mid	24	7	29.2	4	1	50.0	30	8	26.7
Distal	24	1	4.2	4	1	25.0	30	2	6.7
Total	**28**	**11**	**39.3**	**5**	**2**	**40.0**	**35**	**14**	**40.0**

Key: N = number of individuals with one or more observable canines; n = number of individuals with DEH of one or more canines
Total % = total number of individuals with hypoplasia on any location of the maxillary or mandibular canines

area. This individual also exhibited considerable deposits of periosteal new bone formation on his lower long bones from an inflammatory response that was both active and remodelled from healing. These two pathological changes are potentially linked with this individual undergoing a period of marked stress. One of the females [9362] had four teeth affected, all mandibular in the mid crown area.

Enamel hypoplasia may be caused by a number of factors related to both disease and environment; however, the most common cause is considered to be malnutrition (Aufderheide and Rodríguez-Martín 1998, 407). This is of particular interest, as the period of use of the eastern cemetery coincides with famines and most notably the severe famine of 1437–40 (Roberts and Cox 2003, 228).

SUBADULT DENTAL DISEASE

The number of instances of dental disease in subadults was small, with only five such individuals (35.7%) showing any disease. Among the 14 subadults only 32 maxillary and 34 mandibular teeth (including both deciduous and permanent teeth) were present and observable. Only a single individual, [10082] aged 6–11 years, had carious lesions identified (left mandibular molars). Calculus was evident in the deciduous dentition of two subadults and in [9320] on the deciduous and permanent dentition.

Hypoplasia was evident in the permanent dentition of three subadults (42.9%), with one individual, [10060] aged 12–17 years, having seven teeth affected, generally in the mid to lower crown area. As with the adults, these enamel defects may be an indication of a period of marked stress, such as childhood disease or malnutrition, suffered earlier in life by this adolescent.

The church

Preservation

Most of the human bone was reasonably well preserved, with 55.4% of adults and 61.1% of the subadults being in the highest category of preservation ('good') and only 9.6% of adults and 11.1% of subadults judged to be in a poor state of preservation (Table 36). However, truncation of skeletons (with at most *c* 85% completeness) meant that some areas were not available for inspection and some measurements could not be made.

Age and sex distribution

Of the 101 individuals recorded, 83 (82.2%) were adults and 18 (17.8%) were subadults. There were 39 males, 15 females and 29 unsexed individuals (Table 37; Fig 67). The sex ratio for the sample from the church was thus 2.60:1, which was rather similar to that for the eastern cemetery outside (2.77:1). Among the 54 sexed adults there were only a handful of individuals in the age categories 18–25 and 26–35 years, with the highest numbers in the 36–45 and ≥46 years age categories. There were more males than females present, with the deaths of two-thirds of the males (66.6%) being concentrated in the 36–45 and ≥46

Table 36 Preservation of skeletons in the church sample

Preservation	Adults	Adults (%)	Subadults	Subadults (%)
Good	46	55.4	11	61.1
Medium	29	34.9	5	27.7
Poor	8	9.6	2	11.1
Total	83		18	

Table 37 Demography of the church sample

	Male		Probable male		Intermediate		Probable female		Female		Unsexed		Grand total	
Age	No.	%	No.	%	No.	%	No.	%	No.	%	No.	%	No.	%
Perinatal											0	-	0	-
1–6 months											1	5.5	1	1
7–11 months											1	5.5	1	1
1–5 years											5	27.8	5	4.9
6–11 years											4	22.2	4	3.9
12–17 years											5	27.8	5	5
<18 years (subadult)											2	11.1	2	2
Total subadults											18		18	
18–25 years	0	-	1	12.5	0	-	0	-	1	10	1	3.8	3	2.9
26–35 years	4	12.9	2	25	0	-	4	80	3	30	1	3.8	14	13.9
36–45 years	13	41.9	1	12.5	0	-	1	20	3	30	1	3.8	19	18.8
≥46 years	13	41.9	1	12.5	1	33.3	0	-	3	30	0	-	18	17.8
>18 years (adult)	1	3.2	3	37.5	2	66.7	0	-	0	-	23	88.5	29	28.7
Total adults	31	37.3	8	9.6	3	3.6	5	6	10	12	26	31.3	83	
Total all individuals	31	30.7	8	7.9	3	2.9	5	4.9	10	9.9	44	43.6	101	

years age groupings. Female deaths were also more prevalent in the 36–45 years age category (46.6%).

Among the 18 subadults there were two infants, one aged 1–6 months and the other 7–11 months. There was a fairly equal distribution across the range from the early childhood age category 1–5 years through to the adolescent age category 12–17 years.

There was a fairly even spread across the adult age categories among the individuals buried in the different parts of the church and in terms of males and females. In accordance with the general age distribution the majority were in the 36–45 years age category. As there were more males than females altogether, it is not surprising that there were more males present in all the defined areas of the church. There was also a large proportion of unsexed adults throughout the church.

Stature

The completeness of the femora available for measurement was limited, and estimation was only possible for seven males and three females. The average stature estimate for the males was 169.93cm, slightly below the mean stature (171cm) for late medieval Britain, while the female average stature was 163.03cm, slightly above the late medieval mean stature (159cm) (Roberts and Cox 2003, 248). The tallest male (175.7cm) in the church was from the chapel of ? St Anne (room 6a), with the shortest male (161.6cm) coming from the nave (B6). However, the number of individuals available for stature estimation was small, as was the case with the eastern cemetery, and these estimates should therefore not necessarily be seen as representative of the stature of this population overall.

Pathology

Forty-seven (46.5%) of the individuals from the church exhibited macroscopically observable pathological changes, and of these 18 individuals (38.3%) had one or more pathological lesions.

CONGENITAL ABNORMALITIES

Scoliosis

Two males, [12414] and [13530] (both period B3; Chapter 2.5 and 3.8), the former 36–45 years old and from the nave west of the rood screen (room 6c), and the latter aged ≥46 years and from a vault in the 'chapel without the quire door on the south side' (B16), showed scoliosis, a lateral curvature of the spine. The first individual had curvature of the fourth to eighth thoracic vertebrae towards the left side. Extensive osteophytic lipping was also present on the sixth to eighth vertebrae, probably as a response to the abnormal alignment of the spine. The older individual was similarly affected in the same thoracic region but the curvature was towards the right side. Osteophytic lipping of the vertebrae was also evident, with partial fusion occurring between the third and tenth thoracic vertebrae, and the fourth to seventh fully fused. The type of fusion was similar to that observed in DISH, with its location on the right side, and given that the individual was an older male. However, the facets were fully fused which is not typical of DISH. Fusion of the facets is generally seen in ankylosing spondylitis but with fusion occuring from the lumbar vertebrae upwards, creating a 'bamboo spine' (Aufderheide and Rodríguez-Martín 1998, 103). It is possible that the curvature of the spine promoted the severe osteophytic response, but DISH should not be ruled out.

Spondylolysis

Spondylolysis is a common congenital malformation where a congenitally weak vertebra separates into two parts, and generally occurs at the fifth lumbar vertebra. It may be caused by the recurrent stress of lifting with a bent back or by an injury to an already weak bone (Roberts and Manchester 1995, 78).

Four individuals (3.9%) showed spondylolysis. Two females and one male had bilateral spondylolysis while a child aged 6–11 years [13765] from the chapel of ? St Anne (room 6a) had a possible right unilateral spondylolysis.

Miscellaneous congenital conditions

One male aged ≥46 years ([13530], B16) had fusion of two ribs, which is commonly associated with thoracic vertebral anomalies. A female aged 18–25 years ([13872], in the retrochoir, room 6b) possibly had sarcoidosis (below) and also had an additional facet on the anterolateral aspect of the left navicular. This congenital anomaly was also observed in two individuals from the eastern cemetery (OA9, [9411] and [10063]).

Bathrocrany

One male aged 36–45 years [13825] from the chapel of ? St Anne (room 6a) exhibited possible bathrocrany, whereby there is an abnormal occipital projection or 'bun' on the back of the head (Brothwell 1981, 169).

DEGENERATIVE JOINT DISEASE

Osteoarthritis (OA)

Eleven (10.9%) adult individuals from within the church exhibited pathological changes attributable to osteoarthritis; of these five were males, one was female and five were unsexed.

In this admittedly small sample there was an even distribution of the major joints affected in the upper and lower extremities, with involvement of the hands (predominantly the thumb joint) and the feet. A female aged 36–45 years [12497] from the nave (room 6c) had diffuse bilateral osteoarthritis of the hands that was particularly severe in the thumb, with subchondral damage and eburnation. Osteoarthritis of the hands is a common finding in the modern population and also affects females more frequently than males (Roberts and Manchester 1995, 114).

Involvement of the hip joints was observed in two individuals, a male aged ≥46 years [12493] from the nave (room 6c) and another male aged 36–45 years [16042] from the presbytery (B4). The older male showed pronounced changes of the right acetabulum with severe porosity, eburnation and enlargement of the joint (Fig 112). The changes to the right femoral head were also severe, with marginal osteophytic lipping, subchondral destruction, eburnation and the early stages of ankylosis of the joint at the inferior margin of the acetabulum. These joint changes to the right hip were associated with the male having congenital hip dysplasia. The man from the presbytery had bilateral osteoarthritis of the hip joints with osteophytic lipping, subchondral changes and eburnation of the acetabulae and superior aspect of the heads of the femora. This individual also had osteoarthritis of both thumb joints.

Osteoarthritic changes of the shoulder joint are generally seen to be associated with trauma, while involvement of the acromioclavicular and sternoclavicular joints is seen predominantly in today's elderly population (Roberts and Manchester 1995, 114). Two males were affected in the shoulder joint, one being again the older male [12493] from the nave (room 6c), perhaps indicating a traumatic event in his life. The other, [16009], also aged ≥46 years and from the nave (room 6c), showed porosity and eburnation of the acromioclavicular joint of the right clavicle. This male also had degenerative changes to the right patella and the distal ends of the left and right tibiae and the right fibula. The observed changes probably represent age-related degeneration.

Secondary osteoarthritis from trauma was identified in an unsexed adult individual [13778] from the porch (B8). The individual was heavily truncated, with only the legs present, and had a healed fracture of the distal right fibula with secondary infection. The osteoarthritic changes were observed in the bilateral involvement of the lateral aspect of the anterior femorotibial articulation surface with the presence of eburnation. The change of gait and shift in weight from the fracture might be an explanation for the presence of osteoarthritis found in relation to trauma. A male [13975] from the nave (room 6c) also exhibited secondary osteoarthritis to the tibial plateau of the left femur, probably following trauma.

Spinal osteoarthritis

The prevalence rate for spinal osteoarthritis was relatively low among the individuals interred in the church. The main difference was the females being more markedly affected (7.2%) compared to the males (1.3%), particularly when taking into consideration that there were fewer female vertebrae available for examination. The cervical and lumbar vertebrae of the females were the most affected, with the highest prevalence (28.6%) observed in the lower cervical vertebrae.

The incidence of spinal osteoarthritis showed a marked increase (20.7%) in the age category 26–35 years, which was surprisingly high compared to the older age category ≥46 years with a decidedly low prevalence of 1.5%. This is a marked contrast as there were nearly three times as many observable vertebral joints available for examination in the older age group. Such a noticeable difference would appear to be a reflection of something happening within this age group that was clearly impacting upon the spine. Such changes could possibly be linked to an activity or occupation, or a distinct variation in the roles of the males and females. The fact that these individuals were buried within the church, suggesting a higher social status, also

Fig 112 Osteoarthritis of the right hip with congenital hip dysplasia [12493] (B6, room 6c) (scale c 1:2)

adds to the interest of this marked variation. However, further investigation would be needed to pursue such enquiries, and the small size of the assemblage must also be considered.

Rotator cuff injury

One adult male individual [16332] in the central vessel of the nave (room 6c, period B3) exhibited marked changes to the left shoulder joint that could be attributed to a rotator cuff injury. This individual also had degenerative changes of the left hip joint and possible diffuse idiopathic skeletal hyperostosis (DISH).

Ankylosis

Ankylosis is the fusion of skeletal elements and may be seen to be a precursor to other pathological changes such as ankylosing spondylitis (AS) and DISH. There were two male individuals (1.9%) showing ankylosis, both with involvement of the sacroiliac joint. The older male [13663] from the nave south aisle (B6, period B2) was one of the most complete individuals and exhibited bilateral ankylosis of the sacroiliac joints. The presence of the sacroiliac fusion and the individual's age and sex could be a very good indication of this male potentially suffering from ankylosing spondylitis. The vertebral involvement, however, was inconclusive as there was no fusion of the lumbar vertebrae, with fusion only occurring between the sixth and seventh vertebrae. There was marked osteophytic lipping of the spine and intervertebral disease of the cervical vertebrae but this could also be attributable to the older age of the individual.

Diffuse idiopathic skeletal hyperostosis (DISH)

DISH is generally associated with older males, producing the classic 'dripping candle wax' fusion of the vertebrae on the right side but without intervertebral disc involvement (Aufderheide and Rodríguez-Martín 1998, 97). It is often linked to a high calorific diet and obesity that can cause late-onset diabetes, and in the archaeological record it is frequently observed in monastic communities (Rogers and Waldron 2001).

Seven individuals (6.9%), five males ([16332], [12480], [16344], [16098], and from the pentice (B18) [16304]), a female aged ≥46 years ([13518], chapel of ? St Anne, room 6a) and one unsexed adult ([16311]) showed skeletal changes associated with DISH (Fig 67). Of these, four (3.9%) had the more classic indications of the disease. Interestingly, a male aged 36–45 years [16098] from a brick vault [16011] in the presbytery (B4, period B3; Chapter 2.5 and 3.8) also showed hyperostosis frontalis interna (HFI), which is also associated with obesity and involved the thoracic vertebrae and enthesopathies (ossification of the muscle insertions (entheses)) of the iliac crests of the pelvis and Achilles tendon that are often found in association with DISH. What were possibly the early stages of the disease were seen in the unsexed adult [16311] from the nave (room 6c, period B3), with right-sided fusion of thoracic vertebrae T9 and T10. A male adult [16332] from the nave (room 6c, period B3), although fragmented, had a 'dripping candle wax' fusion of at least four mid-thoracic vertebrae and the presence of enthesopathies.

Two males both in the age category 36–45 years exhibited more marked changes, with one male, [12480] in the nave north aisle (B6, period B2), having pronounced osteophytic lipping of the right side of the thoracic vertebrae from T2 to T11 with fusion of T6 to T8. The other male, [16098] from the presbytery brick vault, had right-sided fusion of the thoracic vertebrae T7 to T12 with no intervertebral disc involvement and marked enthesopathies of the iliac crests and Achilles tendon.

The youngest male to manifest changes associated with DISH came from the nave ([16344], room 6c, period B3) and was in the age range 26–35 years. He had fusion on the right side of six of the upper thoracic vertebrae, producing the classic 'dripping candle wax' appearance. This is quite unusual, as the disease is normally associated with older male individuals, and could be an indication of this individual's over-indulgence in food or a predisposition to the disease and its subsequent manifestations.

Sarcoidosis

Sarcoidosis is a disease of the joints most often seen in the bones of the hand with small nodular granulomatous foci of inflammation (Aufderheide and Rodríguez-Martín 1998, 114). One individual, a young female [13872] from the retrochoir (room 6b), possibly had lesions that could be identified as sarcoidosis, as they were small lytic lesions affecting the scaphoid and capitate bones of the left wrist.

Intervertebral disc disease (IVD)

Males were slightly more affected (15.8%) by intervertebral disc disease when compared to the females (13.1%). Apart from the first two cervical vertebrae, all the vertebrae in both the males and females were affected to some degree by the condition.

The incidence of intervertebral disc disease increased with age and was most prevalent (18.2%) in the older age category of ≥46 years, with the sixth and seventh cervical vertebrae most commonly affected (64.3%).

Osteophytosis

There were high rates of osteophytosis observed in both the males and females but the male prevalence rate was higher at 32.1% compared to the females at 22%. The incidence of osteophytosis, as with intervertebral disc disease, increased with age and was most prevalent in the older age group ≥46 years (38.4%). The increase in age also saw osteophytosis to some degree in all vertebrae, particularly in the age categories 36–45 and ≥46 years and predominantly in the mid-thoracic region. Such changes could be linked to many factors and attributed to age, sex, activity and posture. It was interesting, however, that these individuals were markedly more affected than those from the eastern cemetery (OA9).

Fusion

There was a low prevalence rate of vertebral fusion, and when observed it was in the age categories 36–45 years (0.3%) and ≥46 years (0.7%). In all instances the thoracic vertebrae were affected but with the females having a prevalence rate (1.8%) twice that of the males (0.9%).

TRAUMA

Fractures

A total of seven individuals (6.9%), five males and two unsexed adults, exhibited fracture-related trauma in the upper and lower extremities. One male aged ≥46 years ([12493], room 6c) had a compression fracture of the third thoracic vertebra which may have been an accidental injury. Four of the individuals, [13675] (south porch, B8), [13778] (B8), [13975] (nave, room 6c) and [16332] (room 6c), had healed fractures while two, [16060] (room 6c) and [16076] (presbytery, B4) had fractures at different stages of healing. The male adult [16332] from the nave (room 6c, period B3) was the only one to exhibit any rib fractures. This might be due to the condition of the skeletal material and the fragmented nature of many of the skeletons. In this instance there was post-mortem damage and the ribs were fragmented, but at least two of the fragments showed evidence of well-healed fractures. This male also suffered from a possible rotator cuff injury and it is possible that they could represent the same traumatic event.

One unsexed adult [13778] had a healed fracture to the distal end of the right fibula that exhibited bony changes indicative of a secondary infection. Such changes would suggest that the injury had been an open fracture, allowing bacteria to infect the individual and producing the periosteal changes identified on the bone surface of the fibula.

The other two individuals with healed fractures were both males in the age range 36–45 years. The male from the porch, [13675], had a well-healed and aligned fracture to the midshaft of the right ulna, while the other male, [13975] from the nave, had a possible compression fracture across the tibial plateau of the left tibia and affecting the lateral condyle. The integrity of the bone length was not affected but there was osteophytosis of the intercondylar eminence and increased porosity of the medial condyle with secondary osteoarthritis.

There were also two individuals with non-united fractures at different stages of healing. One male aged ≥46 years [16076] had a non-united fracture of the right clavicle where there was an indication of healing with an attempt of the two parts to begin to reunite, with the presence of some callus formation. When fitted together there was about a 1cm overlap of the two parts (Fig 113). Trauma of the clavicle and the muscles associated with it often cause the misalignment of fractures to this bone. The other non-united fracture was identified in a male aged 36–45 years [16060]. The fracture was an oblique one to the neck of the right femur with compression of the femoral head into the area of the greater trochanter and proximal shaft (Fig 114). There were three non-united bone segments that were all well-healed and fitted together well when placed anatomically in position. There was a bony response to the trauma, with woven bone at the site of the fracture with proliferative bony changes, but the femur as a whole was not atrophied and so indicated that the leg had still been in use, even if reduced in its normal biomechanical function.

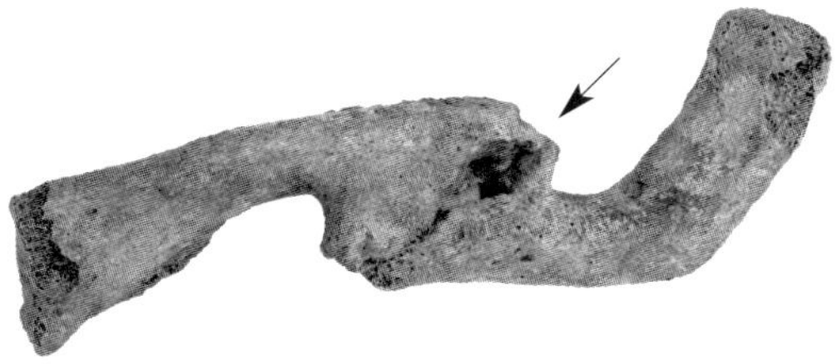

Fig 113 Anterior superior view of a non-united fracture of the right clavicle [16076] (B4); the arrow indicates pseudo-facet formation at the point of fracture (scale c 1:2)

Fig 114 Anterior view of a non-united fracture of the neck of the right femur [16060] (B6, room 6c) (scale c 1:2)

Soft tissue trauma

Soft tissue trauma was observed in eight (7.9%) individuals within the church, with the upper and lower extremities affected. Two male individuals, [13774] and [13848] from the nave (room 6c), both had soft tissue trauma to the right hand.

Sharp force trauma

The most dramatic example of sharp force trauma was the beheading in 1388 of Sir Simon Burley ([16052]), who was buried in St Mary Graces. Originally the excavated remains of adult [16052] in the presbytery (B4, period B2; Chapter 2.4 and 3.8) comprised the left humerus and bones of the left hand, the left patella, and the bones of the ankles and feet, together with

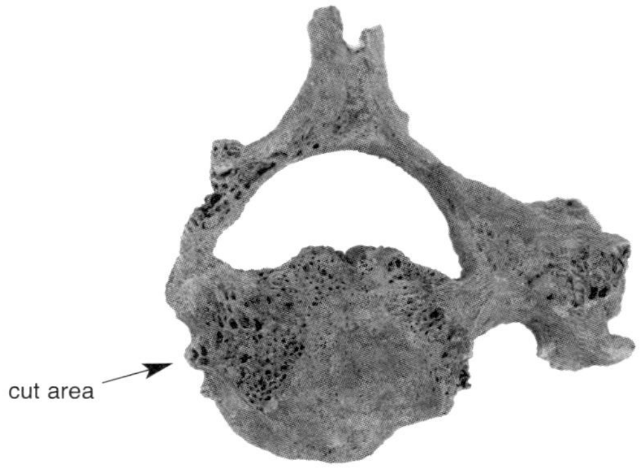

Fig 115 Fourth cervical vertebra [16052] (B4) showing marks of decapitation (scale c 1:1)

some rib and vertebral fragments (T Waldron, pers comm). Unfortunately, all that remains now to represent such a violent and traumatic end is the fourth cervical vertebra showing the decapitation cut (Fig 115).

One other individual, a male [13622] aged 25–36 years from the nave (room 6c), had evidence of a healed sharp force trauma to the right supraorbital ridge possibly resulting from inter-personal violence. However, the interpretation of such traumata can be problematical in terms of distinguishing between accidental causes and inter-personal violence. In this case it is more weighted towards inter-personal violence by reason of the trauma being caused by a sharp-edged implement.

METABOLIC DISEASE

Scurvy

Scurvy is caused by a deficiency of vitamin C. Ascorbic acid is essential for collagen formation, and a deficiency can lead to haemorrhaging from minor trauma and inflammation, with skeletal manifestation being most marked in infants (Ortner 2003, 384).

Two (1.9%) possible cases of scurvy were identified in the subadults, both from the nave. One, a child aged approximately 1 year [13711] (room 6c), revealed lesions most closely resembling those found in scurvy. However, the pathognomic feature of woven bone (Ortner and Ericksen 1997) of the sphenoid could not be observed as it was not present for analysis. The child also showed severe cribra orbitalia in both orbits, another indication of stress being placed upon the system, and possibly – if suffering from scurvy – as a result of the vitamin deficiency.

The other case was a child of 6 years [13887] (room 6c) who showed new bone periosteal lesions of both tibiae, new bone within the right maxillary sinus and squamous temporalis bone but without an indication of any bony responses of the sphenoid bone. This child also had severe cribra orbitalia and hypoplastic enamel defects in the not fully-erupted permanent dentition. The combination of these changes might suggest that the child suffered from scurvy, malnutrition or some other disease.

Cribra orbitalia

The prevalence rate for cribra orbitalia in the St Mary Graces church sample was 35.3% (Table 38), which is considerably higher than the general prevalence rate for the later medieval period (Roberts and Cox 2003, 235) and five times higher than that observed in the eastern cemetery (OA9) (Table 34).

Both males and females were affected (prevalence rates of 23.8% and 28.6% respectively), although the number of females was small. The prevalence among the subadults was very high at 83.3%, with the peak seen in the 1–5 years age category (66.7%), but again the numbers were small.

INFECTIOUS DISEASES

Leprosy

Leprosy is a chronic infectious disease caused by *Mycobacterium leprae* that affects the skin, nasal tissue, peripheral nerves and bone (Aufderheide and Rodríguez-Martín 1998, 141). The

Table 38 Prevalence rates of cribra orbitalia in the church sample

All individuals	N = 34	n = 12	% = 35.3						
Age		Subadults			Male			Female	
	N=	n=	%	N=	n=	%	N=	n=	%
7–11 months	1	1	100.0						
1–5 years	3	2	66.7						
6–11 years	1	1	100.0						
12–17 years	1	1	100.0						
Total subadults	**6**	**5**	**83.3**						
18–25 years				1	0	-	1	0	-
26–35 years				5	1	20.0	4	1	25.0
36–45 years				8	3	37.5	1	1	100.0
≥46 years				5	1	20.0	1	0	-
>18 years (adult)				2	0	-	0	0	-
Total adults				**21**	**5**	**23.8**	**7**	**2**	**28.6**

Key: N = number of individuals with observable orbital roof; n = number of individuals with cribra orbitalia early medieval period in Britain was the time most affected by leprosy; the disease had a huge impact on the population and the subsequent response from society and the Church was stigmatisation and exclusion (Roberts and Cox 2003, 268).

An unsexed adult [14321] from the east cloister alley (B10, period B3) exhibited bilateral periosteal bone changes to the diaphyseal shaft surfaces of the tibiae and fibulae with reactive changes evident on both first metatarsals and proximal phalanges. Such periosteal bone changes of the long bones are not uncommon in leprosy and are usually bilateral and symmetrical (Aufderheide and Rodríguez-Martín 1998, 154). It is quite feasible that some of the periosteal bone reactions observed as being non-specific may well be a precursor not only to other systemic infections but possibly leprosy. However, although the changes in the feet are predominantly bilateral they could not be described as symmetrical (ibid, 151). Unfortunately, there was no skull and so it was not possible to look for any further diagnostic features that could imply leprosy. For the period concerned and the changes evident, leprosy remains a plausible diagnosis but further analysis would need to be conducted for a more conclusive result.

A very tentative suggestion of leprosy could be made for a male individual, [12400], with pathological lesions of the skull and ribs that might be an indication of the infection. The man, who died aged 36–45 years, was buried in the retrochoir (room 6b, period B3), and his skull exhibited an area of increased porosity and subperiosteal bone response in the region of the glabella on the frontal bone, with periosteal bone lesions of both zygomatic bones. There were changes in some of the ribs, observed as destructive lesions of the tubercle facets with a cystic destructive lesion on the left first rib. Differential diagnosis would not rule out that these pathological changes could be attributed to tuberculosis. Both of the putative leprosy cases could be subjected to a DNA analysis in order to distinguish the *Mycobacterium* species responsible for the pathology observed.

Non-specific periosteal infections

The most frequently observed pathological lesions were inflammatory periosteal bone reactions, both active and healed, commonly observed on the diaphyseal shafts of the tibiae and fibulae. Nineteen adult individuals (18.8%) were affected by periosteal bone reactions, and of these 13 were males and three were females. Four subadults had periosteal changes of the long bones, where two were possibly attributable to changes identified in scurvy. Those affected were identified from most of the areas within the church.

Maxillary sinusitis

Two male individuals, [12403] and [16332], both from the retrochoir (room 6b), had inflammatory bone lesions of the frontal sinuses. Such inflammation has been attributed to environmental pollutants such as smoke from fires (Roberts and Manchester 1995, 131), suggesting that these individuals were exposed to a smoky environment.

Non-specific osteomyelitis/osteitis

One young female aged 18–25 years [13872] from the retrochoir (room 6b) exhibited a bony lesion associated with a non-specific bone infection such as osteomyelitis or osteitis. There was a smooth swelling on the midshaft of the right fibula with only slight periosteal changes to the bone surface.

NEOPLASTIC DISEASE

One adolescent of approximately 17 years of age [14421] from the timber pentice (B18) had a smooth elongated protuberance on the posterior distal metaphysis of the right femur that was identified as an osteochondroma. They are a common benign tumour and the location of this osteochondroma was where they are most frequently encountered (Aufderheide and Rodríguez-Martín 1998, 381). Interestingly, this young individual also had very pronounced large Schmorl's nodes, possibly suggesting an occupational experience of heavy stress and load-bearing on the spine.

MISCELLANEOUS DISEASE

Hyperostosis frontalis interna (HFI)

HFI is a condition that is generally most commonly associated with elderly females and identified with outgrowths of bone on the inner surface of the skull, predominantly the frontal bone (Ortner 2003, 416). There are seen to be three stages, with the first identified as small nodules of bone leading to the third that is more exuberant with smooth undulating thickened bone. Only one individual manifested such changes, an older female [13518] aged ≥46 years from the chapel of ? St Anne (room 6a). Interestingly, this female also exhibited changes in the thoracic vertebrae, with smooth bony bridging of the vertebral bodies, that were similar to those identified in the DISH more commonly associated with males. This female also manifested degenerative changes of the knees and periosteal bone reactions of the lower legs and feet, with the pathological changes in the feet being bilateral and having fine woven periosteal bone. This periosteal response of the lower legs and active inflammation of the feet could possibly be associated with the diabetes which has been linked with HFI (Aufderheide and Rodríguez-Martín 1998, 342).

DENTAL PATHOLOGY

Among the 83 adults examined in the St Mary Graces church sample there were 454 observable maxillary teeth and 572 mandibular teeth. Ante-mortem tooth loss in the males was most frequently observed in the maxillary and mandibular dentition, with the incidence increasing with age and reaching its highest rate in the 36–45 years age category. Molars, perhaps not surprisingly, were the most frequently lost teeth, with the mandibular first molars the most common tooth affected. For the females tooth loss was observed more in the mandibular dentition but also predominantly in the age category 36–45 years.

Caries

The overall incidence of carious lesions was not very high in either the male or female dentition, but perhaps not surprisingly the males had more carious lesions than the females. Males in the age category 25–36 years were those most affected. The prevalence rate for dental caries was 7.6%, still slightly higher than the quoted later medieval mean of 5.6% (Roberts and Cox 2003, 258). Of the teeth involved, the maxillary teeth were more commonly affected both in the males and the females, and in the younger females especially. In males, the first premolar was the tooth with the highest recorded incidence of carious lesions.

Calculus

Calculus was evident in the maxillary and mandibular dentition of males and females alike, but as with caries the males were more frequently affected, although again this is probably attributable to differential preservation. The greatest prevalence of calculus in females was seen in the age category 25–36 years, while the males were affected in all age categories with the highest prevalence in the 36–45 years age category. There was also a slight increase in calculus in the mandibular teeth with age for males.

Periodontal disease

Periodontal disease affected both the maxillary and mandibular dentition of the males and females alike, but with the incidence of periodontitis occurring most frequently, as with calculus, in the females in the age category 25–36 years. The males in the age category 36–45 years exhibited the most periodontal disease, with the molars being the teeth most affected, and above all the left second mandibular molar.

Abscesses

Very few abscesses were observed, with a total of only ten teeth in males affected, the majority of these in the maxillae in the age category 25–36 years and most frequently on the right side. Only four teeth in females were affected, with three of them in the mandible.

Dental enamel hypoplasia

Enamel hypoplasia affected nine males and four females, involving both the maxillary and mandibular dentition and with the canine teeth the most frequently affected (Table 39). The overall prevalence in adults was 14 of 29 possible cases (48.3%) based on the canines only. For the males the mid crown area was the most commonly affected in both the mandibular (25%) and maxillary (20%) canines. All the males and females concerned had more than one tooth affected, with one male aged 36–45 years [12400] from the retrochoir (room 6b) having eight teeth affected, predominantly in the mid crown area. The hypoplastic defects of the teeth of this male indicate a period of stress from either infection or poor nutrition at the time when the teeth were developing, which could be linked to the period featuring episodes of plague and famine. The four females with hypoplastic defects of the teeth were all in the age category 25–36 years and were affected predominantly in the mid crown area of the tooth (14.3%).

SUBADULT DENTAL DISEASE

There were only 18 subadults in the church sample, with a mix of deciduous and permanent dentition observable (29 maxillary and 25 mandibular deciduous teeth, and 38 maxillary and 44 mandibular permanent teeth). Only four of the subadults displayed any dental disease. Of two in the age category 6–11 years, one child [13887] from the nave (room 6c) had slight calculus and the other child [13765] from the chapel of ? St Anne (room 6a) had a hypoplastic defect of the left lateral mandibular permanent canine. The two subadults in the age category 12–17 years displayed hypoplasia, carious lesions and an abscess. The subadult with the abscess, [14421] from the timber pentice (B18), had a carious lesion on the occlusal surface of the first left maxillary permanent molar, the abscess being related to this. The subadult [12410] from the nave (room 6c) had four teeth affected by carious lesions, all of them the permanent molars; this adolescent also had slight hypoplastic defects in the mid crown area of the mandibular permanent canines. The evidence suggests that there was a deficiency in the diet of these young people, either from stress or disease, and possibly that the poor diet was the cause of the carious lesions.

Table 39 Dental enamel hypoplasia in the church sample

	Male			Female			All adults		
	N=	n=	%	N=	n=	%	N=	n=	%
Maxilla location									
Crown	15	0	-	7	0	-	25	0	-
Mid	15	3	20.0	7	1	14.3	25	4	16.0
Distal	15	2	13.3	7	1	14.3	25	3	12.0
Mandible location									
Crown	16	0	-	7	1	14.3	27	1	3.7
Mid	16	4	25.0	7	1	14.3	27	6	22.2
Distal	16	1	6.3	7	2	28.6	27	3	11.1
Total	**18**	**9**	**50.0**	**7**	**4**	**57.1**	**29**	**14**	**48.3**

Key: N = number of individuals with one or more observable canines; n = number of individuals with DEH of one or more canines
Total % = total number of individuals with hypoplasia on any location of the maxillary or mandibular canines

General observations on the St Mary Graces samples

The severe truncation of skeletons and the generally poor quality of bone preservation militated against extracting comprehensive palaeodemographic and palaeopathological data from the human remains buried in the Cistercian abbey of St Mary Graces. In the case of the former, it meant a high proportion of the adults resisting exhaustive sex assignment, as key areas of the skull and pelvis used in sexing were often missing. Moreover, skulls were few and mostly fragmented, so that even simple measurements such as maximum cranial length and breadth could not be made.

The distribution of the sexes among the western, later ?epidemic cemetery (OA2), the eastern cemetery (OA9) and the church showed a predominance of male burials in each of the three areas (the church sample includes eight individuals from the cloister). The burials in the church constitute a special case, where a distinct bias in the demography of the burials could have been expected. Unfortunately, though, since a large proportion of individuals proved impossible to age or sex, this expected demographic bias could not be demonstrated in practice.

The sex ratio of 1.54:1 evident in the later ?epidemic burials (OA2) was much closer to equivalence of the sexes than was seen in the eastern cemetery or the church, with 2.77:1 and 2.60:1 respectively. For the two external cemetery areas (OA2 and OA9) combined, the sex ratio was 1.85:1. For the church and the later ?epidemic burials, the proportions of known males to females were equal among the young adults (18–25 years) but in all older age categories males exceeded females in the sample. When the sexed adults from the two cemetery areas were combined, males exceeded females in every adult age category without exception. The slight preponderance of males among the burials thus mirrors that seen at other monastic sites, but is lower than that recorded from other Cistercian houses (Chapter 3.7; Barber et al 2004, 86).

In all three areas and thus for the site as a whole, there was a dearth of infants, that is of children who died under the age of 1 year. This is unusual from a historical and empirical perspective. Whether it was caused by intrinsic factors such as the young, under-mineralised skeletons being less well preserved in the cemetery soil, or by extrinsic factors such as the infant burials being made in a specially designated part of the cemetery as yet unexcavated, it has skewed the age range of the sample(s) towards the higher levels. This was a phenomenon also observed among the Black Death victims at the Royal Mint site, where it caused potentially greater problems (Grainger et al 2008, 25–6). To a lesser extent the other subadult burials were also fewer in number than expected and this, too, remains unexplained.

The largest sample, from the later ?epidemic cemetery (OA2), is dated to 1350–*c* 1400 – a period of stress immediately following the years of the plague epidemic of 1348–50, with the population not beginning to recover for more than a century (Dyer 1989, 140). The life expectancy for 20-year-old males in the late 14th century was on average 32.5 years in rural populations (ibid, 182). Infant mortality was generally high, records from a slightly later period (1540–99) revealing a death rate of 27% during the first year of life and an overall subadult death rate of 42.5% (Orme 2003, 107). However, the archaeological record again failed to reflect the expected high subadult mortality rate.

Comparing these results with those from the St Mary Graces church and eastern cemetery (OA9) samples, it was evident that the subadult mortality was twice the rate in the later ?epidemic cemetery (36.2%) than in either the church (17.8%) or eastern cemetery (17.9%) samples, dated to 1361–1539 and *c* 1400–1539 respectively. However, the mortality pattern within the subadult population proved similar as individuals below the age of one were under-represented in all three areas. The proportion of the 1–5 years age category was similar among the church and later ?epidemic burials but markedly lower in the eastern cemetery, which in turn revealed a high proportion of individuals in the 6–11 years age category.

The average stature for males at the St Mary Graces site was 170.5cm, slightly lower than the late medieval average height of 171cm, but that for women (163.7cm) exceeded the mean (159cm) late medieval height (Roberts and Cox 2003, 248). By comparison, 64 males from the Black Death cemetery at the Royal Mint site had an average stature that was significantly lower at 168.7cm, and 24 females had an average height that was lower at 157.6cm (Grainger et al 2008, 23).

The overall prevalence of pathological conditions was low, in particular that of degenerative ones such as osteoarthritis. This may in part be explained by the composition of the excavated population, with a relatively low representation of elderly individuals. Osteoarthritis and osteophytosis were much more prevalent among those buried in the church than in the two cemetery areas. Trauma (usually healed fractures) was observed in a number of individuals, but only males. Some displayed direct evidence of inter-personal violence.

The pathologies observed varied between the different areas of the site but more pathological processes were identified in the individuals in the church sample. Most notable were the infectious diseases tuberculosis, venereal syphilis and leprosy. Tuberculosis and leprosy were two diseases that were prevalent at the time but are not always represented as such in the skeletal record, with the CPR of 1% for tuberculosis clearly an under-representation of the disease (Roberts and Cox 2003, 230). The most common and frequent pathological lesions identified in males and females from all three assemblages were periosteal bone reactions. Non-specific periosteal infections were common in this period and affected many people, with a CPR of 14% (ibid, 235).

Diseases associated with nutritional deficiencies such as rickets or scurvy were not observed in the later ?epidemic burials or in the eastern cemetery but, perhaps surprisingly, possible cases of scurvy were identified in the skeletal remains of subadults buried in the nave of the church. Similarly, there was no indication of the diffuse idiopathic skeletal hyperostosis (DISH) often associated with over-indulgence in the diet (Roberts and Manchester 1995, 120) in either of the two external cemeteries, but it was evident in several of the individuals from within the church (including one in the adjoining pentice, B18). The condition may be a reflection of social position or access to protein-rich foodstuffs. It should be noted that two individuals from the underlying Black Death cemetery in Open Area 2 also exhibited the classic symptoms of this condition (Grainger et al 2008, 45).

Dentition revealed a higher prevalence of dental conditions in males than females, contrary to what is generally seen in later medieval populations. The rate of dental enamel hypoplasia was high and reflects a rise in such defects from the early medieval period onwards. The increase is believed to be a reflection of the stress the later medieval population endured: first from the great famine and later from the Black Death. Dental caries in all three areas of the site was higher than in contemporary sites. The highest caries prevalence was observed in the eastern cemetery (OA9), where the rate was in double figures, reminiscent of post-medieval sites (Roberts and Cox 2003, 326) rather than the single figures for late medieval samples, and perhaps reflects its relatively late date.

FRENCH AND GERMAN SUMMARIES

Résumé

Elisabeth Lorans

L'abbaye cistercienne de St Mary Graces fut établie en 1350 par Edouard III dans le quartier d'East Smithfield, à Londres, et fut fermée en 1539. St Mary Graces fut le dernier fondé des 62 établissements cisterciens d'Angleterre. En outre, il fut créé immédiatement après la Grande Peste et, de manière inhabituelle pour un monastère cistercien, dans un environnement urbain et selon un plan qui ne correspondait pas aux normes de cet ordre mais caractérisait beaucoup d'autres fondations monastiques du XIVe siècle. Tous ces éléments associés lui donnent une importance d'envergure internationale, à la fois sur le plan des études cisterciennes et de l'archéologie monastique et médiévale en général. Les circonstances de la fondation de St Mary Graces sont comparables à celles de la Chartreuse de Londres, légèrement plus tardive, en relation avec la piété grandissante à la cour d'Edouard III. Toutes deux furent établies comme chapelles cimétériales et devinrent des mausolées pour de riches familles et toutes deux introduisirent en milieu urbain des ordres traditionnellement implantés en milieu rural, amorçant en Angleterre une pratique qui avait commencé avant la Grande Peste sur le continent.

La fouille du site de l'ancienne Monnaie Royale fut conduite de 1983 à 1988 et cette publication de synthèse rend compte de toutes les transformations de l'abbaye. Ainsi, l'ouvrage a pour ambition de fournir une meilleure compréhension de l'histoire du site en combinant les données stratigraphiques, textuelles, mobilières et environnementales. Ce volume est le deuxième d'une série de trois ouvrages consacrés à l'étude archéologique de ce site. Sa publication fait suite à celle de deux autres monographies publiées par MoLAS/MOLA, l'une consacrée au cimetière de la Grande Peste de 1348-1350 (Grainger et al 2008), l'autre aux magasins d'approvisionnement de la Marine utilisés de 1560 à 1785 (Grainger and Phillpotts 2010).

A la suite de l'introduction (chapitre 1), une présentation chronologique fait état de tout ce qui est connu du site avant l'abbaye, pendant son existence et immédiatement après sa fermeture, lorsque ses bâtiments furent réutilisés comme manoir. Les sections 2.1 et 2.2 présentent les caractéristiques géologiques du terrain et les grandes lignes de l'occupation du site jusqu'à la Grande Peste, en introduction à l'analyse topographique du monastère. Le chapitre 2.3 tente de montrer comment et pourquoi les moines utilisèrent la chapelle de la Sainte-Trinité, érigée dans le cimetière de catastrophe de la Grande Peste, comme leur premier lieu de culte. Le chapitre 2.4 concerne la principale période de construction, montrant que l'essentiel de l'église et des bâtiments conventuels fut édifié entre 1361 et 1392. Les XVe et XVIe siècles (chapitre 2.5) furent une période de faible activité architecturale, hormis la construction de deux petites chapelles, mais il convient d'y rattacher la majorité des 131 inhumations pratiquées dans l'église et dans le cloître et des 305 tombes situées à l'extérieur. Le dernier chapitre présentant les données stratigraphiques porte sur la suppression de l'abbaye et sa conversion en résidence seigneuriale, alors que l'église et de nombreux autres bâtiments furent conservés à l'état de ruines.

Une série de chapitres thématiques examine ensuite l'abbaye dans un cadre plus large. La section 3.1 analyse l'origine du monastère et propose des explications à l'établissement par les cisterciens d'une nouvelle abbaye aussi proche de la ville, environ 70 ans après la dernière fondation en Angleterre. L'organisation topographique du monastère est étudiée dans le chapitre 3.2 qui établit clairement l'influence des couvents de frères de la même époque, associée à des éléments d'inspiration cistercienne plus traditionnels, mais aussi les simples adaptations aux contraintes du terrain. Le style essentiellement perpendiculaire de l'église et des principaux bâtiments conventuels est étudié dans le chapitre 3.3. Les aspects politiques et la dotation du monastère sont également analysés (chapitre 3.4), pour mettre en évidence les revenus de l'établissement et son histoire financière ainsi que les éléments qui les ont affectés. Le chapitre 3.5 est consacré à l'économie du monastère au moment où il avait des difficultés à survivre après la Grande Peste. Dans la section 3.6, le personnel de l'abbaye est étudié à partir des sources écrites et des données anthropologiques provenant de l'église et des zones d'inhumation ; l'état sanitaire est présenté et le déséquilibre entre hommes et femmes, habituel dans un monastère, est commenté. Les pratiques funéraires et les différents espaces d'inhumation, bien définis, sont décrits et la question de la distinction entre les différentes catégories de religieux et de laïcs est abordée. A noter l'intérêt particulier d'un document intitulé « Les inspections de Clarenceux », qui énumèrent et même localisent, jusqu'à un certain point, des sépultures de laïcs à l'intérieur de l'église. Le dernier chapitre thématique place St Mary Graces dans un cadre plus large pour établir son impact sur Londres et inversement et pour évaluer l'importance de cette maison pour l'ordre cistercien.

La conclusion (chapitre 4) récapitule la signification des découvertes à la lumière des débats académiques actuels, suggère de nouvelles orientations de recherche et indique le potentiel archéologique subsistant. Les annexes spécialisées (chapitre 5) fournissent le corpus des preuves sur lequel sont fondées les interprétations avancées dans les chapitres précédents.

Zusammenfassung

Manuela Struck

Die Zisterzienserabtei St. Mary Graces wurde 1350 von Edward III. in East Smithfield, London, gegründet und 1539 aufgelöst. St. Mary Graces war die letzte Gründung von 62 Zisterzienserabteien in England. Sie entstand außerdem unmittelbar nach der Pest, war – untypisch für englische Zisterzienserhäuser – eine städtische Anlage und mit einem für Zisterzienser uncharakteristischen Grundriss ausgestattet, der aber nichts desto trotz typisch für viele andere Klosterbauten des 14. Jhs. war. All diese Faktoren zusammengenommen verleihen dem Kloster internationale Bedeutung, mit Sicherheit im Rahmen zisterziensischer Forschungen sowie klösterlicher und mittelalterlicher Archäologie allgemein. Die Umstände der Gründung von St. Mary Graces können mit denen der etwas späteren Londoner Kartause verglichen werden, die viel mit der tieferen Frömmigkeit am Hofe Edwards III. zu tun hatte. Beide Komplexe gingen aus Friedhofskapellen hervor und bestanden als Mausoleen wohlhabender Gönner weiter. Beide brachten darüber hinaus traditionell ländliche Orden in das städtische Umfeld, wodurch sie in England zum ersten Mal einen Trend initiierten, der auf dem Europäischen Kontinent schon vor der Pest eingesetzt hatte.

Die Ausgrabungen an der Stelle der ehemaligen Königlichen Münze fanden zwischen 1983 und 1988 statt. Der vorliegende umfassende Bericht berücksichtigt alle Informationsarten zur Entwicklung der Abtei. Durch die Kombination stratigraphischer und dokumentarischer sowie von Umwelt- und Kleinfundinformationen soll so ein besseres Verständnis der Geschichte des Fundplatzes erreicht werden. Dieser Band ist der zweite einer dreiteiligen Publikation zur Archäologie des Fundplatzes. Seine Publikation folgt den MoLAS/MOLA-Monographien zum Pestfriedhof von 1348–50 (Grainger et al 2008) und zum Provianthof der Königlichen Marine von 1560–1785 (Grainger and Phillpotts 2010).

Nach der Einleitung (Kapitel 1) werden in einem umfassenden chronologischen Abriss die Informationen zum Fundplatz vor und während der Zeit der Abtei und unmittelbar nach ihrer Säkularisierung, als die Gebäude ein weltliches Herrenhaus wurden, vorgelegt. Kapitel 2.1–2.2 behandeln Geologie sowie Geschichte und Archäologie bis zum Schwarzen Tod, wodurch der Grundriss der Abtei in seinem Zusammenhang gesehen wird. Kapitel 2.3 versucht zu erläutern, wie und warum die Mönche die Pestfriedhofskapelle der Dreifaltigkeit als ihre erste Kirche nutzten. Kapitel 2.4 gilt der Hauptbauperiode, wobei gezeigt wird, dass Kirche und Konventsgebäude zum großen Teil zwischen 1361 und 1392 errichtet wurden. Das 15. und 16. Jh. (Kapitel 2.5) war eine Zeit mit offenbar geringer Bautätigkeit, die nicht über zwei kleine Kapellen hinausging, in der jedoch die meisten der 131 Gräber in Kirche und Kreuzgang sowie 305 Gräber in den äußeren Friedhöfen angelegt wurden. Der Schlussabschnitt zur Stratigraphie behandelt die Auflösung der Abtei und deren Umwandlung zum weltlichen Herrenhaus; die Kirche und viele andere Gebäude waren zu der Zeit offenbar aufgelassen und verfallen.

Anschließend wertet eine Reihe thematischer Abhandlungen die Abtei in größerem Kontext aus. Kapitel 3.1 beschäftigt sich mit ihrer Gründung und schlägt Erklärungen für eine zisterziensische Neugründung so nahe an der Stadt und ungefähr 70 Jahre nach ihrer letzten englischen Gründung vor. Die Grundrissanalyse der Abtei in Kapitel 3.2 verdeutlicht den Einfluss der Grundrisse zeitgenössischer Bettelordenshäuser im Zusammenspiel mit eher traditionellen zisterziensischen Elementen und einfacher Anpassung den Gegebenheiten des Ortes. Die grundsätzlich im Perpendikularstil gestaltete Architektur der Kirche und wichtigsten Konventsgebäude wird in Kapitel 3.3 untersucht. Die Politik und Dotierung der Abtei kommen in Kapitel 3.4 zur Sprache, indem zusammengestellt wird, was zur finanziellen Grundlage und finanziellen

Geschichte des Klosters sowie deren Einflussfaktoren bekannt ist. Kapitel 3.5 analysiert die Informationen zur klösterlichen Wirtschaft, denn das Haus kämpfte nach der Pest ums Überleben in der Welt. Dem Personal der Abtei ist Kapitel 3.6 gewidmet, wozu die schriftliche Überlieferung und das Skelettmaterial von Kirche und Friedhöfen herangezogen werden; Indizien für Gesundheitszustand und Krankheit werden besprochen und das Ungleichgewicht von männlichen und weiblichen Bestattungen unterstrichen, wie es typisch für Fundplätze von Klöstern ist. Bestattungssitten und die vielen gut definierten Bestattungsareale werden beschrieben, wobei das Problem der Unterscheidung zwischen den Gräbern von Mönchen und Laien zur Sprache kommt. Von besonderem Interesse sind dabei die „Visitationen des Clarenceux", ein Schriftstück, das eine Reihe von Laiengräbern nennt und bis zu einem gewissen Maße innerhalb der Kirche lokalisiert. Der abschließende Themenkomplex (Kapitel 3.9) versucht, St. Mary Graces in einen weiteren Kontext zu stellen, einerseits um den gegenseitigen Einfluss von Abtei und Stadt London zu beleuchten und andererseits die Bedeutung dieser Abtei für den Zisterzienserorden zu ermessen.

Die Zusammenfassung (Kapitel 4) würdigt die Ergebnisse vor dem Hintergrund der aktuellen wissenschaftlichen Diskussion, zukünftige Forschungsgebiete werden vorgeschlagen und auf das Potential weiterer Ausgrabungen hingewiesen. Die Anhänge der Spezialisten (Kapitel 5) liefern schließlich notwendige Angaben, welche die Ausführungen der vorangegangenen Kapitel untermauern.

BIBLIOGRAPHY

Manuscript sources

British Library, London (BL)

Add Ch 39405 inspeximus of charters of St Mary Graces, 1511

Add MS 29608, m 3 accounts of the treasurer of the household of the Duchess of Buckingham, 1472–4

Campbell Ch X.iv.27 lease in Holsworthy, Devon, from Abbot Paschal, 1421

Cotton MS Cleopatra E.iv, fo 222 petition of Sir Richard Gresham, mayor of London, to the king, asking for the hospitals of St Mary Spital, St Bartholomew and St Thomas, and the abbey of St Mary Graces to be handed over to the City authorities for the continued care of the poor and sick, August 1538

Harley Ch 43.E.7 royal licence for the abbey to acquire lands in St Michael le Querne and other parishes, 3 April 1375

Harley Ch 75.G.7 lease from St Mary Graces in Elmley, Kent, to Sir William and James Crowmer, 1527

Harley Ch 111.A.35 bull of Pope Urban VI to the abbot of Stratford Langthorne concerning the transfer of the monk Richard from Rufford to St Mary Graces, January 1379, with lead bulla attached

Harley Ch 111.C.36 lease from St Mary Graces to John Stanes in St Margaret Moses parish, 1532

Harley MS 433, fo 284v Privy Council records, 1483–5: grant by Richard III to Sir Thomas Montgomery

Harley MS 6953, pp 10, 30 notes of the institutions of John Langton, abbot of St Mary Graces, as vicar of Gedington, 28 August 1494, and Stoke Daubney, 2 May 1498 (both in Northants, the latter by the presentation of Sir Thomas Lovell)

Harley MS 6955, p 74 Henry Moore professed as abbot of St Mary Graces, 7 May 1516

Harley Roll N.18 court rolls of St Mary Graces' Hertfordshire manors, temp Edward IV to 1511

Royal MS 17.B.xlvii, fo 131v lands held of St Mary Graces in Gracechurch Street, 15th century

Sloane MS 3254A, no. 1 survey of the parish of St Katherine by the Tower, by John Ogilby, 1686

Guildhall Library, London (GL)

MS 10890 lease by St Mary Graces to John Meryfelde of a tenement and yard in Fenchurch Street, 2 October 1538

MS 25121/953 St Paul's deeds: confirmation of the grants of tenements in the parishes of St Michael le Querne and St Dunstan in the East to St Mary Graces, for masses for the soul of John de Kenyngton, clerk, 7 July 1375

MS 25121/1761 St Paul's deeds: agreement between Holy Trinity Priory and the rector of Stepney, equally dividing the tithes of the Crash Mills and its river walls, 11 March 1234

MS 9171/4 will register of the Commissary Court of London, 1438–50

MS 9531/9 register of Richard FitzJames, Bishop of London, 1506–22

Lambeth Palace Library, London (LPL)

Reg Sudbury register of Simon Sudbury, Archbishop of Canterbury, 1375–81

London Metropolitan Archives (LMA)

CLA/023/DW/01 deeds and wills enrolled in the Court of Husting, City of London, 13th to 16th centuries

The National Archives, Public Record Office, London (TNA: PRO)

ADMIRALTY

ADM 114/14 Navy Board and Admiralty: Victualling Board: deeds etc, 1701–65

CHANCERY

C 1/9/357–61 Chancery proceedings: John Holand, Earl of Huntingdon, v Pascall Gylot, former abbot of St Mary Graces, and Robert Boydon, concerning a forged document, 1432–43

C 1/75/80 Chancery proceedings: abbot of St Mary Graces v prior of Leeds and John Boton, concerning Bykenore Priory, 1386–1486

C 1/426/49 Chancery proceedings: Henry More, abbot of St Mary Graces, v John Palmer, sub-prior, concerning the theft of keys and embezzlement of money, 1515–18

C 1/714/32 John and Christine Apryce v abbot of St Mary Graces, concerning expulsion from the liberty of Tower Hill, 1532–8

C 66/250 and /305 patent rolls, 30 Edward III (1356–7) and 3 Richard II (1379–80)

C 66/712, /723 and /742 patent rolls, 34 Henry VIII part 3, 35 Henry VIII part 2, 36 Henry VIII part 3 (1542–4)

C 81/666 Privy Seal writs, 4–7 Henry V (1416–19)

CROWN ESTATES

CRES 38/1683 Crown Estates Commissioners: Swedeland Court conveyances, 1756–1936, with reports on earlier surveys

DUCHY OF LANCASTER

DL 25/1032/(i), (ii), (iii) deeds concerning land in Poplar, Stepney and Ratcliff, late of the abbey of St Mary Graces, 27 April 1551 and 9 May 1555

DL 28/3/2 accounts of the receiver general of the Duke of Lancaster, 15–16 Richard II (1391–2)

EXCHEQUER

E 40 Treasury of Receipt: ancient deeds, series A

E 42 Treasury of Receipt: ancient deeds, series AS

E 135 miscellaneous ecclesiastical documents

E 178 special commissions of enquiry

E 179 King's Remembrancer: lay subsidy rolls

E 210 King's Remembrancer: ancient deeds, series D

E 211 King's Remembrancer: ancient deeds, series DD

E 213 King's Remembrancer: ancient deeds, series RS

E 303/10/292–354 Court of Augmentations: conventual leases of St Mary Graces

E 310/3/17 particulars for Crown leases in London in the reign of Elizabeth I

E 310/3/18 Court of Augmentations: particulars for Crown leases in London and Middlesex

E 310/19/94 particulars for Crown leases in Middlesex from Philip and Mary to James I

E 311/29 counterparts of Crown leases, 28 Elizabeth I (1585/6)

E 314 Court of Augmentations: miscellanea

E 315 Augmentation office: miscellaneous books

E 318 Court of Augmentations: particulars for Crown grants

E 321 Court of Augmentations: proceedings

E 326 Augmentation office: ancient deeds, series B

E 328 Augmentation office: ancient deeds, series BB

E 329 Augmentation office: ancient deeds, series BS

LAND REVENUE

LR 2/262 surveys and rentals: surveys of religious houses in Middlesex and Hertfordshire, including rental of St Mary Graces, 1546/7

LR 11/78/904 court roll extracts of Poplar and East Smithfield manors, 31 Henry VIII (1539–40)

LR 14 ancient deeds, series E

MAPS AND PLANS

MPB 1/4 two plans of the Pineapple garden in East Smithfield and Nightingale Lane, *c* 1590

MPF 1/158 plan of the King's Storehouses on Tower Hill and the fields to the east, 1623

MPHH 1/56 plan of the Tower of London and adjacent parts, 1726

MAPS AND PLANS (ROLLED STORAGE)

MR 1/106 plan of the naval victualling yard on Tower Hill, 1635

PREROGATIVE COURT OF CANTERBURY

PROB 11 will registers

SPECIAL COLLECTIONS

SC 2/190/17–18 and 191/48–59 court rolls of the manor of Stepney, 2 Richard II (1378–9) and 9 Henry V to 26 Henry VIII (1421–1535)

SC 6/917/16 ministers' and receivers' accounts: lands of St Mary Graces, 3–4 Henry VI (1424–5)

SC 6/972/11 reeve's account of West Lydford manor, Somerset, 1447/8

SC 6/1258/1 ministers' and receivers' accounts: St Mary Graces bursar's account, 14–15 Richard II (1390–1)

SC 6/HenVIII/2382–5, 2396–8, 2427 ministers' and receivers' accounts: possessions of St Mary Graces, 30–34 Henry VIII (1538–42)

SC 8 ancient petitions

SC 11/455 rentals and surveys, rolls: valor of possessions of St

Mary Graces, temp Henry VIII
SC 12/11/13 rentals and surveys, portfolios: valor of possessions of St Mary Graces, temp Henry VIII
SC 12/11/43 rentals and surveys, portfolios: Middlesex rent rolls, 16–20 Henry VIII (1524–8)
SC 12/26/32 rentals and surveys, portfolios: valor of East Smithfield manor, 7 James I (1609/10)
SC 12/29/22 rentals and surveys, portfolios: valor of the former possessions of St Mary Graces, 33 Henry VIII (1541–2)

Printed and other secondary works

Alexander, J, and Binski, P (eds), 1987 *Age of chivalry: art in Plantagenet England 1200–1400*, Roy Acad Arts exhibition catalogue, London

Allen Brown, R, Colvin, H M, and Taylor, A J, 1963 *The history of the King's Works: Vols 1–2, The Middle Ages*, London

Aufderheide, A C, and Rodríguez-Martín, C, 1998 *The Cambridge encyclopedia of human paleopathology*, Cambridge

Baily, J W, 1868 [Proceedings of the Association, June 10th] Two woollen burgess's flat caps, time about Henry VII, from an excavation in Finsbury, *J Brit Archaeol Ass* 1 ser 24, 289

Barber, B, and Thomas, C, 2002 *The London Charterhouse*, MoLAS Monogr Ser 10, London

Barber, B, Chew, S, Dyson, T, and White, B, 2004 *The Cistercian abbey of St Mary Stratford Langthorne, Essex: archaeological excavations for the London Underground Limited Jubilee Line Extension Project*, MoLAS Monogr Ser 18, London

Barber, R, 1978 *Edward, Prince of Wales and Aquitaine: a biography of the Black Prince*, London

Barnes, E, 1994 *Developmental defects of the axial skeleton in paleopathology*, Niwot, Colo

Baumgartner, E, and Krueger, I, 1988 *Phönix aus Sand und Asche: Glas des Mittelalters*, Munich

Beard, D, 1986 The infirmary of Bermondsey Priory, *London Archaeol* 5(7), 186–91

Beaven, A B, 1908 *Aldermen of the City of London* (2 vols), London

Belz, G F, 1841 *Memorials of the Order of the Garter*, London

Beiswanger, B B, Segreto, V A, Mallatt, M E, and Pfeiffer, H J, 1989 The prevalence and incidence of dental calculus in adults, *J Clinical Dentistry* 1, 55–8

Bettey, J H, 1989 *The suppression of the monasteries*, London

Betts, I M, 1994 Medieval floor tiles in London churches, in Schofield, J, Saxon and medieval parish churches in the City of London: a review, *Trans London Middlesex Archaeol Soc* 45, 133–40

Betts, I M, 2002 *Medieval 'Westminster' floor tiles*, MoLAS Monogr Ser 11, London

Blackmore, L, 1994 Pottery, the port and the populace: the imported pottery of London 1300–1600 (part 1), *Medieval Ceram* 18, 29–44

Blackmore, L, 1999 Aspects of trade and exchange evidenced by recent work on Saxon and medieval pottery from London, *Trans London Middlesex Archaeol Soc* 50, 38–54

Blackmore, L, 2002 Further discussion of the pottery, in Ayre, J, and Wroe-Brown, R, *The London Millennium Bridge: excavations of the medieval and later waterfronts at Peter's Hill, City of London, and Bankside, Southwark*, MoLAS Archaeol Stud Ser 6, 90–1, London

Blackmore, L, 2004 The pottery, in Sloane and Malcolm 2004, 331–55

Blackmore, L, 2005 The pottery, in Schofield and Lea 2005, 227–47

Blackmore, L, 2006 The pottery, in Whip, D, *The medieval postern gate by the Tower of London*, MoLAS Monogr Ser 29, 39–48, London

Blackmore, L, 2010 Imported pottery, in Grainger and Phillpotts 2010, 97–106

Blackmore, L, in prep a Medieval and later imported pottery from the postern by the Tower, City of London, *Medieval Ceram*

Blackmore, L, in prep b The pottery, in Sloane, B, *Excavations at the nunnery of St Mary* de fonte clericorum, *Clerkenwell, London*, MOLA Monogr Ser

Blackmore, L, in prep c Pottery, the port and the populace (part 2), *Medieval Ceram*

Blackmore, L, and Goffin, R, 2008 The pottery, in Grainger et al 2008, 35–6

Blair, J, 1980 Henry Lakenham, marbler of London, and a tomb contract of 1376, *Antiq J* 60(1), 66–74

Blake, H, 1999 *De Nomine Jhesu*: an Italian export ware and the origin of Renaissance maiolica pottery making in the Netherlands, in Gaimster 1999, 23–56

Blatherwick, S, and Bluer, D, 2009 *Great houses, moats and mills on the south bank of the Thames: medieval and Tudor Southwark and Rotherhithe*, MOLA Monogr Ser 47, London

Bock, F, 1866 *Geschichte der liturgischen Gewänder des Mittelalters, Bd 2*, Bonn

Böhme, G, 1977 Zur Bestimmung quartarer Anuran Europas an Hand von Skelettelementen, *Wissenschaftliche Zeitschrift der Humboldt-Universität zu Berlin, Mathematik-Naturwissenschaft* 26, 283–300

Boyle, N E, 1951 *Old parish churches and how to view them*, Skeffington

Brooks, S T, and Suchey, J M, 1990 Skeletal age determination based on the os pubis: comparison of the Acsádi-Nemeskéri and Suchey-Brooks methods, *J Hum Evol* 5, 227–38

Brothwell, D R, 1981 *Digging up bones: the excavation, treatment and study of human skeletal remains*, 3 edn, Oxford

Bruijn, A, 1979 *Pottersvuren langs de Vecht: aardewerk rond 1400 uit Utrecht*, Rotterdam Pap 3, Rotterdam

Buglass, J, 1991 Marine shell at the Royal Mint, unpub MOL rep

Buikstra, J E, and Ubelaker, D H (eds), 1994 *Standards for data collection from human skeletal remains: proceedings of a seminar at the Field Museum of Natural History*, Arkansas Archaeol Survey Res Ser 44, Fayetteville, Ark

Butler, L A S, 1974, Medieval finds from Castell-y-Bere, Merioneth, *Archaeol Cambrensis* 123, 78–112

Butler, L A S, 1984 The houses of the mendicant orders in Britain: recent archaeological work, in *Archaeological papers from York presented to M W Barley* (eds P V Addyman and V E Black), 123–36, York

Cal Chart R *Calendar of the charter rolls, 1226–1516*, Public Rec Office, 1903–27, London

Cal Close R *Calendar of the close rolls*, Public Rec Office, 1892–1975, London

Cal Feet of Fines *A calendar to the feet of fines for London and Middlesex* (eds W J Hardy and W Page), 2 vols, 1892–3, London

Cal Husting Wills *Calendar of wills proved and enrolled in the Court of Husting, London, AD 1258–AD 1688, preserved among the archives of the Corporation of the City of London at the Guildhall* (ed R R Sharpe), 2 vols, 1889–90, London

Cal Inq PM *Calendar of inquisitions post mortem*, Public Rec Office, 1904–74, London

Cal Pap Letters *Calendar of entries in the papal registers relating to Great Britain and Ireland: papal letters: Vol 4, 1362–96* (eds W H Bliss and J A Twemlow), 1902; *Vol 5, 1396–1404* (eds W H Bliss and J A Twemlow), 1904; *Vol 6, 1404–15* (ed J A Twemlow), 1904; *Vol 7, 1417–31* (ed J A Twemlow), 1906; *Vol 15, 1484–92* (ed M J Haren), 1978; *Vol 16, 1492–1503* (ed A P Fuller), 1986, London

Cal Pat R *Calendar of the patent rolls*, Public Rec Office, 1894–1974, London

Cal PM R *Calendar of plea and memoranda rolls preserved among the archives of the Corporation of the City of London at the Guildhall: Vols 1–4, 1323–1437* (ed A H Thomas), 1926–43, Cambridge

Carr, A D, 1967 Sir Lewis John: a medieval London Welshman, *Bull Board Celtic Stud* 22, 260–70

Cart Holy Trinity *The cartulary of Holy Trinity Priory, Aldgate* (ed G A J Hodgett), London Rec Soc Pub 7, 1971, Leicester

Cat Anc Deeds *A descriptive catalogue of ancient deeds*, Public Rec Office, 1890–1915, London

Chamberlain, A, 2006 *Demography in archaeology*, Cambridge

Chapelot, J, 1983 The Saintonge pottery industry in the later Middle Ages, in Davey and Hodges 1983, 49–53

Charleston, R J, 1971 The glass, in Moorhouse, S, Finds from Basing House, Hampshire, *c* 1540–1643 (part 2), *Post-Medieval Archaeol* 5, 63–70

Charleston, R J, 1972 The vessel glass from Rosedale and Hutton, in Crossley, D W, and Aberg, F, Sixteenth-century glassworking in Yorkshire, *Post-Medieval Archaeol* 6, 128–50

Charleston, R J, 1973 The glass, in Neal, D S, Excavations at the palace and priory at Kings Langley, 1970, *Hertfordshire Archaeol* 3, 67–72

Charleston, R J, 1975 The glass, in Platt and Coleman-Smith 1975, 204–26

Charleston, R J, 1980 Glass of the high medieval period (12th- to 15th-century), *Bulletin de l'Association Internationale pour l'Histoire du Verre* 8, 65–76

Charleston, R J, 1981 Medieval and post-medieval glass from the north-west quadrant, in Down, A, *Chichester excavations 5*, 222–8, Chichester

Charleston, R J, 1984 *English glass and the glass used in England, c 400–1940*, London

Charleston, R J, and Grew, F, in prep The post-medieval glass from Aldgate

Childs, W, 1993 Imports of Spanish pottery to England in the later Middle Ages, *Medieval Ceram* 17, 35–8

Clapham, A W, 1910 The topography of the Carmelite priory of London, *J Brit Archaeol Ass* 2 ser 16, 15–31

Clapham, A W, 1915 On the topography of the Cistercian abbey of Tower Hill, *Archaeologia* 66, 353–64

Clapham, A W, and Godfrey, W H, 1913 *Some famous buildings and their story, being the results of recent research in London and elsewhere*, Westminster

Clark, A, 1979 The pottery, in *Plymouth excavations: Castle Street* (ed C Gaskell-Brown), Plymouth Mus Archaeol Ser 1, 26–47, Plymouth

Cokayne, G E, 1910–59 *The complete peerage of England, Scotland, Ireland, Great Britain and the United Kingdom: extant, extinct or dormant* (ed V Gibbs), 13 vols in 14, London

Coldstream, N, 1986 Cistercian architecture from Beaulieu to the Dissolution, in Norton and Park 1986, 139–59

Colvin, H, and Foister, S, 1996 *The panorama of London c 1544 by Anthonis van den Wyngaerde*, London Topogr Soc Pub 151, London

Conheeney, J, 1997 The human bone, in Thomas et al 1997, 218–31

Conheeney, J, 1999 Reconstructing the demography of medieval London from studies on human skeletal material: problems and potential, *Trans London Middlesex Archaeol Soc* 50, 78–86

Conheeney, J, 2007 The human bone, in Miller and Saxby 2007, 255–77

Connell, B, and Rauxloh, P, 2003 *A rapid method for recording human skeletal data*, unpub MOL rep

Coppack, G, 1990 *English Heritage book of abbeys and priories*, London

Coppack, G, 1991 *Mount Grace Priory, North Yorkshire*, London

Coppack, G, 1998 *The white monks: the Cistercians in Britain 1128–1540*, Gloucester

Coppack, G, 2003 *Fountains Abbey: the Cistercians in northern England*, Stroud

Coppack, G, 2006 *Abbeys and priories*, Stroud

Coppack, G, Hayfield, C, and Williams, R, 2002 Sawley Abbey: the architecture and archaeology of a smaller Cistercian abbey, *J Brit Archaeol Ass* 3 ser 155, 22–114

Cowgill, J, de Neergaard, M, and Griffiths, N, 1987 *Knives and scabbards*, HMSO Medieval Finds from Excavations in London 1, London

Crawford Adams, J, and Hamblen, D L, 2001 *Outline of orthopaedics*, 13 edn, Edinburgh

Crowfoot, E, 1979 Baynard's Castle: early 16th-century textiles, preliminary catalogue, unpub MOL rep

Daniel, C, 1997 *Death and burial in medieval England*, London

Daniels, J S, 1950 *The Woodchester glasshouse*, Gloucester

Davey, P, and Hodges, R (eds), 1983 *Ceramics and trade: the production and distribution of later medieval pottery in north-west Europe*, Sheffield

Davidson, G R, 1940 A medieval glass factory at Corinth, *American J Archaeol* 44, 297–324

Davison, B K, 1972 Trial work at the Royal Mint, unpub MOL rep

Dawes, J D, and Magilton, J R, 1980 *The cemetery of St Helen-on-the-Walls, Aldwark*, The Archaeology of York 12/1, London

Dawson, G J, 1979 Excavations at Guy's Hospital, 1967, in *Surrey Archaeol Soc Res Vol 7*, 27–65, Guildford

DGLA, 1989 Department of Greater London Archaeology, London post-excavation review, unpub MOL rep

DNB, 1894 *Dictionary of National Biography, Vol 13*, repr 1937–8, London

Dugdale, W, 1655–73 *Monasticon anglicanum* (eds J Caley, H Ellis and B Bandinel), 6 vols, 1817–30, London

Dugdale, W, 1658 *A history of St Paul's Cathedral, London*, London

Dyer, C, 1989 *Standards of living in the later Middle Ages: social change in England* c *1200–1520*, Cambridge

Dyson, T, 2009 Historical background [Rotherhithe], in Blatherwick and Bluer 2009, 15–17

Dyson, T, Samuel, M, Steele, A, and Wright, S M, 2011 *The Cluniac priory and abbey of St Saviour Bermondsey, Surrey: excavations 1984–95*, MOLA Monogr Ser 50, London

Eames, E S, 1980 *Catalogue of medieval lead-glazed earthenware tiles in the Department of Medieval and Later Antiquities, British Museum* (2 vols), London

Egan, G, 2007 The non-ceramic finds, in Miller and Saxby 2007, 219–35

Egan, G, and Pritchard, F, 1991 *Dress accessories,* c *1150–*c *1450*, HMSO Medieval Finds from Excavations in London 3, London

English Heritage, 1991 *Management of archaeological projects*, 2 edn, London

Ferembach, D, Schwidetsky, I, and Stloukal, M, 1980 Recommendations for age and sex diagnoses of skeletons, *J Hum Evol* 9, 517–49

Fletcher, B F, 1943 *A history of architecture on the comparative method for students, craftsmen and amateurs*, 11 edn, London

Flower, C T (ed), 1923 *Public works in medieval law, Vol 2*, Selden Soc Pub 40, London

Foy, D, and Sennequier, G (eds), 1989 *A travers le verre du moyen-âge à la Renaissance*, Musée Départemental des Antiquités de la Seine-Maritime, Rouen, exhibition catalogue, Nancy

Fry, G S (ed), 1896 *Abstracts of inquisitions post mortem relating to the City of London returned into the Court of Chancery: Part 1, 1485–1561*, Brit Rec Soc Pub 15, London

Gaimster, D, 1987 The supply of Rhenish stoneware to London 1350–1600, *London Archaeol* 5(13), 339–47

Gaimster, D, 1997 *German stoneware 1200–1900: archaeology and cultural history*, London

Gaimster, D (ed), 1999 *Maiolica in the north: the archaeology of tin-glazed earthenware in north-west Europe* c *1500–1600*, Brit Mus Occas Pap 122, London

Gaimster, D, and Hughes, M, 1999 The earliest maiolica stove in north-west Europe: re-anaylsis of the Dissolution finds from the abbey of St Mary Graces, London, in Gaimster 1999, 185–8

Gaimster, D, Goffin, R, and Blackmore, L, with Cowell, M, and Freestone, I, 1990 The Continental stove-tile fragments from St Mary Graces, London, in their British and European context, *Post-Medieval Archaeol* 24, 1–49

Gay, V, 1887 *Glossaire archéologique du moyen-âge et de la Renaissance*, Paris

Geddes, J, 1985 The small finds, in Hare, J N, *Battle Abbey: the eastern range and the excavations of 1978–80*, HBMCE Archaeol Rep 2, 147–77, London

Gilyard-Beer, R, 1970 *Fountains Abbey, North Yorkshire*, London

Giorgi, J, 1991 An assessment of the plant remains from the Royal Mint excavations, unpub MOL rep

Given-Wilson, C, 1978 Richard II and his grandfather's will, *Engl Hist Rev* 93, 320–37

Glanville, P, 1989 The crafts and decorative arts, in *The Cambridge guide to the arts in Britain: Vol 3, Renaissance and Reformation* (ed B Ford), 268–300, Cambridge

Goodall, A R, 1980 Copper alloy and lead, in Palmer, N, A Beaker burial and medieval tenements in The Hamel, Oxford, *Oxoniensia* 45, 183–8, fiche 2 B13

Graham, R, 1929 The Great Schism and the English monasteries of the Cistercian Order, *Engl Hist Rev* 44, 373–87

Grainger, I, and Hawkins, D, with Falcini, P, and Mills, P, 1988 Excavations at the Royal Mint site 1986–8, *London Archaeol* 5(16), 429–36

Grainger, I, and Phillpotts, C, 2010 *The Royal Navy victualling yard, East Smithfield, London*, MOLA Monogr Ser 45, London

Grainger, I, Hawkins, D, Cowal, L, and Mikulski, R, 2008 *The Black Death cemetery, East Smithfield, London*, MoLAS Monogr Ser 43, London

Griffiths, R A, 1981 *The reign of King Henry VI: the exercise of royal authority, 1422–61*, London

Gustafson, G, and Koch, G, 1974 Age estimation up to 16 years of age based on dental developments, *Odontologisk Revy* 25, 297–306

Harden, D B, 1966 Some glass fragments, mainly of the 12th–13th century AD, from northern Apulia, *J Glass Stud* 8, 70–9

Harden, D B, 1969 Medieval glass in the west, in *Proceedings of the 8th International Congress on Glass, London, 1–6 July 1968* (eds R J Charleston, W Evans and A E Werner), 97–111, Sheffield

Harding, V, 1989 'And one more may be laid there': the location of burials in early modern London, *London J* 14(2), 112–29

Harvey, J H, 1961 The architects of St George's Chapel: Part I, The 13th and 14th centuries, *Rep Soc Friends of St George's Chapel, Windsor Castle* 4(2), 48–55

Harvey, J H, 1978 *The Perpendicular style, 1330–1485*, London

Harvey, J H, 1984 *English mediaeval architects: a biographical dictionary down to 1550*, rev edn, Gloucester

Harvey, Y, with Goodall, I, and Biek, L, 1975 The small finds: catalogue, in Platt and Coleman-Smith 1975, 254–93

Harward, C, Holder, N, McKenzie, M, Pitt, K, Thomas, C, Aitken, R, and Bowsher, D, in prep *Medieval Spitalfields: the priory and hospital of St Mary Spital and the Bishopsgate suburb*, MOLA Monogr Ser

Haslam, J, 1988 Parishes, churches, wards and gates in eastern London, in *Minsters and parish churches: the local church in*

transition 950–1200 (ed J Blair), 35–43, Oxford
Hedges, J W, 1984 The medieval and post-medieval textiles, in Allan, J P, *Medieval and post-medieval finds from Exeter, 1971–80*, Exeter Archaeol Rep 3, 334–6, Exeter
Henig, M, 1977 Bone instrument pegs, in Durham, B, Archaeological investigations in St Aldates, Oxford, *Oxoniensia* 42, 163–6
Henig, M, 1988 Small finds from excavations, 1960–5, in Sherlock and Woods 1988, 177–87
Henig, M, and Woods, H, 1988 Small finds from excavations, 1976–8, in Sherlock and Woods 1988, 201–31
Hicks, M, and Hicks, A, 2001 *St Gregory's Priory, Northgate, Canterbury: excavations 1988–91*, The Archaeology of Canterbury ns 2, Canterbury
Hillson, S, 1986 *Teeth*, Cambridge
Hillson, S, 1996 *Dental anthropology*, Cambridge
Hinton, P, and Thomas, R, 1997 The Greater London publication programme, *Archaeol J* 154, 196–213
HMC Salisbury Calendar of the manuscripts of the Marquis of Salisbury preserved at Hatfield House, Hertfordshire: Vol 6, 1596, Hist Manuscripts Comm 9, 1895, London
Hockey, S F, 1976 *Beaulieu: King John's abbey, 1204–1538*, Southampton
Hohler, C, 1942 Medieval paving tiles in Buckinghamshire, *Rec Buckinghamshire* 14, 1–49, 99–132
Holdsworth, C J, 1992 Royal Cistercians: Beaulieu, her daughters and Rewley, in *Thirteenth-century England IV: proceedings of the Newcastle-upon-Tyne conference, 1991* (eds P R Coss and S D Lloyd), 139–50, Woodbridge
Holdsworth, P, 1980 *Excavations at Melbourne Street, Southampton, 1971–6*, CBA Res Rep 33, London
Hollingsworth, M F, and Hollingsworth, T H, 1971 Plague mortality rates by age and sex in the parish of St Botolph's without Bishopsgate, London, 1603, *Population Stud* 25, 131–46
Holman, J A, and Stuart, A J, 1991 Amphibians of the Whitemoor Channel early Flandrian site near Bosley, east Cheshire: with remarks on the fossil distribution of *Bufo calamita* in Britain, *Herpetol J* 1, 568–73
Holman, J A, Stuart, A J, and Clayden, J D, 1990 A middle Pleistocene herpetofauna from Cudmore Grove, Essex, England, and its paleogeographic and paleoclimatic implications, *J Vertebrate Paleontol* 10, 86–94
Honeybourne, M B, 1929 Two plans of the precinct and adjoining property of St Mary Graces, *Trans London Middlesex Archaeol Soc* ns 6(1), 199–204
Honeybourne, M B, 1930 The extent and value of the property in London and Southwark occupied by the religious houses (including the prebends of St Paul's and St Martin's-le-Grand), the inns of the bishops and abbots, and the churches and churchyards before the Dissolution of the monasteries, unpub MA thesis, Univ London
Honeybourne, M B, 1952 The abbey of St Mary Graces, Tower Hill, *Trans London Middlesex Archaeol Soc* ns 11(1), 16–26
Hughes, M, and Gaimster, D, 1999 Neutron activation analysis of maiolica from London, Norwich, the Low Countries and Italy, in Gaimster 1999, 57–91
Hume, I N, 1957 Medieval bottles from London, *The Connoisseur* (March), 104–8
Hurst, J G, 1971 Sixteenth-century Beauvais drinking jugs, *Groupe de Recherches et d'Etudes de la Céramique du Beauvaisis* 3, 6–12
Hurst, J G, 1974 Sixteenth- and 17th-century imported pottery from the Saintonge, in *Medieval pottery from excavations: studies presented to Gerald Clough Dunning* (eds V I Evison, H Hodges and J G Hurst), 221–55, London
Hurst, J G, 1977 Spanish pottery imported into medieval Britain, *Medieval Archaeol* 21, 68–105
Hurst, J G, and Clark, P V, 1979 Other imported pottery, in Dawson 1979, 51–3
Hurst, J G, Neal, D S, and van Beuningen, H J E, 1986 *Pottery produced and traded in north-west Europe 1350–1650*, Rotterdam Pap 6, Rotterdam
Iscan, M Y, Loth, S R, and Wright, R K, 1984 Age estimation from the rib by phase analysis: white males, *J Forensic Sci* 29, 1094–1104
Iscan, M Y, Loth, S R, and Wright, R K, 1985 Age estimation from the rib by phase analysis: white females, *J Forensic Sci* 30, 853–63
Jamroziak, E, 2006 St Mary Graces: a Cistercian house in late medieval London, in *The use and abuse of sacred places in late medieval towns* (eds P Trio and M de Smet), Mediaevalia Lovaniensia Ser I, Studia 38, 153–64, Louvain
Janssen, H, 1983 Later medieval pottery production in the Netherlands, in Davey and Hodges 1983, 121–85
Jenkinson, H, 1915 Mary de Sancto Paulo, foundress of Pembroke College, Cambridge, *Archaeologia* 66, 401–46
Jennings, S, nd The medieval and later pottery from Barking Abbey, unpub Passmore Edwards Mus rep
Kenyon, G H, 1967 *The glass industry of the Weald*, Leicester
Knight, B, 1985 Lead cames, in Geddes 1985, 154–6
Korf, D, 1981 *Nederlandse maiolica*, Haarlem
Knowles, D, 1955 *The religious orders in England: Vol 2, The end of the Middle Ages*, Cambridge
Knowles, D, 1959 *The religious orders in England: Vol 3, The Tudor age*, Cambridge
Knowles, D, 1976 *Bare ruined choirs*, Cambridge
Lambert, F, 1921 Some recent excavations in London, *Archaeologia* 71, 55–112
L and P Hen VIII Letters and papers, foreign and domestic, of the reign of Henry VIII (eds J S Brewer, J Gairdner and R H Brodie), 22 vols in 35, 1864–1932, London
Lawrence, C H, 1984 *Medieval monasticism*, London
Lawrence, M J, and Brown, R W, 1974 *Mammals of Britain: their tracks, trails and signs*, London
Lawson, G, 1985 Musical instrument pegs, in Geddes 1985, 151–4
Levey, S M, 1968 Illustrations of the history of knitting selected from the collection of the Victoria and Albert Museum, *Textile Hist* 1, 183–205
Lewis, N B, 1937 Simon Burley and Baldwin of Raddington, *Engl Hist Rev* 52, 662–9

Libois, R M, Hallet-Libois, C, and Rosoux, R, 1987 *Eléments pour l'identification des restes crâniens des poissons dulçaquicoles de Belgique et du Nord de la France: 1, Anguilliformes, Gastérostéiformes, Cyprinodontiformes et Perciformes*, Fiches d'ostéologie animale pour l'archéologie: Série A, Poissons (3), Juan-les-Pins

Linford, P, and Linford, N, 1991 Archaeomagnetic dating: the Royal Mint, London, unpub AML rep 40/91

Lovejoy, C O, Meindl, R S, Pryzbeck, T R, and Mensforth, R P, 1985 Chronological metamorphosis of the auricular surface of the ilium: a new method for the determination of age at death, *American J Phys Anthropol* 68, 15–28

MacGregor, A, 1989 Bone, antler and horn industries in the urban context, in *Diet and craft in towns* (eds D Serjeantson and T Waldron), BAR Brit Ser 199, 107–28, Oxford

McHardy, A K, 1977 *The Church in London, 1375–92,* London Rec Soc Pub 13, London

Madox, T, 1702 *Formulare anglicanum: or, a collection of ancient charters and instruments of divers kinds … to the end of the reign of King Henry the VIII*, London

Malcolm, G, 1997 Excavations at Island Site, Finsbury Pavement, London EC2, *Trans London Middlesex Archaeol Soc* 48, 33–58

Mann, R W, and Hunt, D R, 2005 *Photographic regional atlas of bone disease: a guide to pathologic and normal variation in the skeleton*, 2 edn, Springfield, Ill

Maresh, M M, 1970 Measurements from roentgenograms, in *Human growth and development* (ed R W McCammon), 157–200, Springfield, Ill

Margary, H, 1981 *A collection of early maps of London 1553–1667*, Margary in assoc Guildhall Library, Kent

Marks, R, 1986 Cistercian window glass in England and Wales, in Norton and Park 1986, 211–27

Martin, A R, 1937 *Franciscan architecture in England*, London

Mays, S, 1998 *The archaeology of human bones*, London

Mellor, J E, and Pearce, T, 1981 *The Austin Friars, Leicester*, CBA Res Rep 35, London

Milgrom, C, Schaffler, M, Gilbert, S, and van Holsbeeck, M, 1995 Rotator-cuff changes in asymptomatic adults: the effect of age, hand dominance and gender, *J Bone and Joint Surgery – Brit Vol* 77-B, 296–8

Miller, G S, 1912 *Catalogue of the mammals of western Europe (Europe exclusive of Russia) in the collection of the British Museum*, repr 1966, London

Miller, P, and Saxby, D, 2007 *The Augustinian priory of St Mary Merton, Surrey: excavations 1976–90*, MoLAS Monogr Ser 34, London

Mills, P, 1983 The Cistercians and their London house, *London Archaeol* 4(8), 217–19

Mills, P, 1985 The Royal Mint: first results, *London Archaeol* 5(3), 69–77

Murdoch, T (ed), 1991 *Treasures and trinkets: jewellery in London from pre-Roman times to the 1930s*, MOL exhibition catalogue, London

Nelson, S, in prep The pottery from the Broad Arrow Tower

Nichols, J (ed), 1780 *A collection of all the wills of the kings and queens of England*, London

Nichols, J, 1826 *Testamenta vetusta*, London

Norton, C, 1993 The export of decorated floor tiles from Normandy, in *Medieval art, architecture and archaeology at Rouen* (ed J Stratford), Brit Archaeol Ass Conf Trans 12, 81–97, London

Norton, C, and Park, D (eds), 1986 *Cistercian art and architecture in the British Isles*, Cambridge

Oakley, G E, 1979 The worked bone, in Williams, J H, *St Peter's Street, Northampton: excavations 1973–6*, Northampton Devel Corp Archaeol Monogr 2, 308–18, Northampton

Oppenheim, M, 1896 *A history of the administration of the Royal Navy and of merchant shipping in relation to the Navy*, Aldershot

Orme, N, 2003 *Medieval children*, New Haven and London

Ortner, D J, 2003 *Identification of pathological conditions in human skeletal remains*, 2 edn, San Diego

Ortner, D, and Ericksen, M, 1997 Bone changes in the human skull probably resulting from scurvy in infancy and childhood, *Int J Osteoarchaeol* 7, 212–20

Page, C, 1978 String-instrument making in medieval England and some Oxford harpmakers, 1380–1466, *Galpin Soc J* 21, 44–67

Pearce, J, 2011 The pottery, in Dyson et al 2011, 214–36

Pearce, J E, and Vince, A G, 1988 *A dated type-series of London medieval pottery: Part 4, Surrey whitewares*, London Middlesex Archaeol Soc Spec Pap 10, London

Pearce, J E, Vince, A G, and Jenner, M A, 1985 *A dated type-series of London medieval pottery: Part 2, London-type ware*, London Middlesex Archaeol Soc Spec Pap 6, London

Peers, C, 1967 *Rievaulx Abbey, Yorkshire*, London

Phenice, T W, 1969 A newly developed visual method of sexing the os pubis, *American J Phys Anthropol* 30, 297–302

Pichon, J, 1879 *Catalogue des objets de curiosité*, Paris

Platt, C, 1984 *The abbeys and priories of medieval England*, London

Platt, C, 1997 *King Death: the Black Death and its aftermath in late medieval England*, London

Platt, C, and Coleman-Smith, R, 1975 *Excavations in medieval Southampton, 1953–69: Vol 2, The finds*, Leicester

Ponting, K G, 1979 Knitted caps, *Bulletin de Liaison du CIETA* 49, 78–81

Pritchard, F, 1991 Textiles from excavations at Cutler Street, London (CUT78), unpub MOL rep

Rawcliffe, C, 1978 *The Stafford earls of Stafford and the dukes of Buckingham, 1394–1521*, Cambridge

Reg Chichele *The register of Henry Chichele, Archbishop of Canterbury, 1414–43* (ed E F Jacob), Canterbury and York Soc Pub 42, 45–7 (4 vols), 1937–47, Oxford

Reg Edward Black Prince *Register of Edward, the Black Prince: preserved in the Public Record Office* (eds M C B Dawes and H C Johnson), 4 vols, 1930–3, London

Reg Sudbury *Registrum Simonis de Sudbiria, diocesis Londoniensis, 1362–75* (ed R C Fowler), Canterbury and York Soc Pub 34, 38 (2 vols), 1927–38, Oxford

Roberts, C A, and Connell, B, 2004 Palaeopathology, in *Guidelines to the standards for recording human remains* (eds M Brickley and J I McKinley), IFA Pap 7, 34–9, Reading

Roberts, C A, and Cox, M, 2003 *Health and disease in Britain from prehistory to the present day*, Stroud

Roberts, C A, and Manchester, K, 1995 *The archaeology of disease*, 2 edn, Stroud

Robinson, D (ed), 1998 *The Cistercian abbeys of Britain: far from the concourse of men*, London

Rogers, J, and Waldron, T, 2001 DISH and the monastic way of life, *Int J Osteoarchaeol* 11, 357–65

Rogerson, A, and Dallas, C, 1984 *Excavations in Thetford 1948–59 and 1973–80*, E Anglian Archaeol Rep 22, Gressenhall

Rosenfield, M C, 1961 The disposal of the property of London monastic houses, unpub PhD thesis, Univ London

Rot Parl Rotuli Parliamentorum ut et petitiones et placita in Parliamento: tempore Edward I–Henry VII, 6 vols, 1783, London

Rutt, R, 1987 *A history of hand knitting*, London

Sabel, K, 2002–3 The tiles, in Meddens, F, Sabel, K, Ackeroyd, A, et al, The excavation of a medieval ceramic production site and tile kiln at Weald View, Noak Hill, Essex, *Medieval Ceram* 26/27, 3–43

Samuel, M, 1989 The 15th-century garner at Leadenhall, London, *Antiq J* 69(1), 119–53

Samuel, M, 1997 Worked stone, in Milne, G, *St Bride's church, London: archaeological research 1952–60 and 1992–5*, Engl Heritage Archaeol Rep 11, 69–81, London

Samuel, M, 2007 The 15th-century Guildhall chapel, in Bowsher, D, Dyson, T, Holder, N, and Howell, I, *The London Guildhall: an archaeological history of a neighbourhood from early medieval to modern times*, MoLAS Monogr Ser 36, 369–73, London

Samuel, M, 2009 Architectural fragments from Rotherhithe, in Blatherwick and Bluer 2009, 159–65

Samuel, M, in prep The architectural fragments, in Harward et al in prep

Scheuer, J L, and Black, S M, 2000 *Developmental juvenile osteology*, London

Scheuer, J L, Musgrave, J H, and Evans, S P, 1980 The estimation of late foetal and perinatal age from limb bone length by linear and logarithmic regression, *Ann Hum Biol* 7, 257–65

Schofield, J, in prep *St Paul's Cathedral before Wren*

Schofield, J, and Lea, R, 2005 *Holy Trinity Priory, Aldgate, City of London: an archaeological reconstruction and history*, MoLAS Monogr Ser 24, London

Scott, S, and Duncan, C J, 1998 *Human demography and disease*, Cambridge

Shepherd, J, 1990 The glass, in Driver, J C, Rady, J, and Sparks, M, *Excavations in the cathedral precincts, 2 Linacre Garden, 'Meister Omers' and St Gabriel's chapel*, The Archaeology of Canterbury 4, 206–16, Maidstone

Shepherd, J, 2010 Vessel glass, in Grainger and Phillpotts 2010, 106–8

Sheppard, W L, 1965–8 Sir Nicholas de Loveyne and his two wives, *Genealogists Mag* 15, 251–5

Sherlock, D, and Woods, H, 1988 *St Augustine's Abbey: report on excavations, 1960–78*, Kent Archaeol Soc Monogr 4, Maidstone

Sherlock, R L, 1960 (1935) *British regional geology: London and Thames valley*, 3 edn, London

Sidell, E J, 1993 *A methodology for the identification of archaeological eggshell*, MASCA Res Pap Sci Archaeol suppl to vol 10, Philadelphia, Pa

Sloane, B, and Malcolm, G, 2004 *Excavations at the priory of the Order of the Hospital of St John of Jerusalem, Clerkenwell, London*, MoLAS Monogr Ser 20, London

Smith, B H, 1991 Standards of human tooth formation and dental age assessment, in *Advances in dental anthropology* (eds M A Kelly and C S Larsen), 143–68, New York

Stalley, R, 1987 *The Cistercian monasteries of Ireland: an account of the history, art and architecture of the White Monks in Ireland from 1142 to 1540*, London and New Haven

Stevenson, J, 2008 Earlier medieval accessioned finds / Accessioned finds from the Black Death cemetery, in Grainger et al 2008, 36–41

Stone, R J, and Stone, J A, 2003 *Atlas of skeletal muscles*, 4 edn, Boston, Mass

Stow, J, 1603 *A survey of London* (ed C L Kingsford), 2 vols, 1908 repr 1971, Oxford

Stroud, G, and Kemp, R L, 1993 *Cemeteries of the church and priory of St Andrew, Fishergate*, The Archaeology of York 12/2, London

Stuart-Macadam, P L, 1989 Nutritional deficiency diseases: a survey of scurvy, rickets and iron-deficiency anaemia, in *Reconstruction of life from the skeleton* (eds M Y Iscan and K A R Kennedy), 201–22, New York

Tait, H, 1979 *The golden age of Venetian glass*, London

Tatton-Brown, T, 1974, Excavations at the Customs House Site, City of London, 1973, *Trans London Middlesex Archaeol Soc* 25, 117–219

Taylor, G M, Crossey, M, Saldanha, J, and Waldron, T, 1996 DNA from *Mycobacterium tuberculosis* identified in mediaeval human skeletal remains using polymerase chain reaction, *J Archaeol Sci* 23, 789–98

Thomas, C, Sloane, B, and Philpotts, C, 1997 *Excavations at the priory and hospital of St Mary Spital, London*, MoLAS Monogr Ser 1, London

Thrupp, S L, 1962 (1948) *The merchant class of medieval London, 1300–1500*, 2 edn, Ann Arbor, Mich

Trotter, M, 1970 Estimation of stature from intact limb bones, in *Personal identification in mass disasters* (ed T D Stewart), 71–97, Washington, DC

Tuck, J A, 1973 *Richard II and the English nobility*, London

Tyrell, A, 2000 Skeletal non-metric traits and the assessment of inter- and intra-population diversity: past problems and future potential, in *Human osteology in archaeology and forensic science* (eds M Cox and S Mays), 289–306, London

Val Eccl Valor ecclesiasticus tempore Henrici VIII, auctoritate regia institutus (eds J Caley and J Hunter), 6 vols, Rec Comm, 1810–34, London

VCH, 1909 *The Victoria History of the counties of England: London, Vol 1*, London

VCH, 1974 *The Victoria History of the county of York: Vol 3*, London

Verhaeghe, F, 1983 Medieval pottery production in coastal

Flanders, in Davey and Hodges 1983, 63–94

Vince, A G, 1982 Medieval and post-medieval Spanish pottery from the City of London, in *Current research in ceramics: thin section studies* (eds I Freestone, C Johns and T Potter), Brit Mus Occas Pap 32, 135–44, London

Vince, A G, 1985 The Saxon and medieval pottery of London: a review, *Medieval Archaeol* 29, 25–93

Vince, A G, 1988 The date and frequency of German imports in the City of London from the 10th to 15th centuries, in *Zur Keramik des Mittelalters und der beginnenden Neuzeit im Rheinland – Medieval and later pottery from the Rhineland and its markets* (eds D Gaimster, M Redknap and H-H Wegner), BAR Int Ser 440, 241–2, Oxford

Vince, A G, 1995 Spanish medieval pottery from the City of London, in *Spanish medieval ceramics in Spain and the British Isles* (eds C M Gerrard, A Gutiérrez and A G Vince), BAR Int Ser 610, 329–31, Oxford

Wagner, A, 1956 *Heralds and heraldry in the Middle Ages*, Cambridge

Waldron, T, 1994 *Counting the dead: the epidemiology of skeletal populations*, Chichester

Waldron, T, and Cox, M, 1989 Occupational arthropathy: evidence from the past, *J Ind Med* 46, 420–2

Ward, S W, 1990 *Excavations at Chester: the lesser medieval religious houses, sites investigated 1964–83,* Grosvenor Mus Archaeol Excav Survey Rep 6, Chester

Ward-Perkins, J B, 1940 *Medieval catalogue*, London Mus Catalogues 7, London

Ward-Perkins, J B, 1954 *Medieval catalogue*, London Mus Catalogues 7, corrected repr, London

Watson, B, 1990 Excavations at 54/55–66 Carter Lane, 1–3 Pilgrim Street and 25–33 Ludgate Hill, City of London (PIC87), unpub MOL rep

Watson, B, and Thomas, C, 2010 The mendicant houses of medieval London: an archaeological and architectural review, in *The friars in medieval Britain: proceedings of the 2007 Harlaxton Symposium* (ed N Rogers), Harlaxton Med Stud 19, 265–97, Donington

West, B, 1992 Birds and mammals from the Royal Mint, unpub MOL rep

West, B, 2010 Large mammals and birds, in Grainger and Phillpotts 2010, 121–5

Wheeler, A H, 1978 *Key to the fishes of northern Europe*, London

White, B, 2004 Human bone, in Barber et al 2004, 158–79

White, W J, 1988 *Skeletal remains from the cemetery of St Nicholas Shambles, City of London*, London Middlesex Archaeol Soc Spec Pap 9, London

Whittingham, L, 2009 Pottery from Southwark, in Blatherwick and Bluer 2009, 177–95

Wilkinson, K, 1991 The non-marine molluscs from the Royal Mint, unpub MOL rep

Williams, D H, 1991 Layfolk within Cistercian precincts, in *Monastic studies: the continuity of tradition II* (ed J Loades), 87–118, Bangor

Wilson, T, 1987 *Ceramic art of the Italian Renaissance*, London

Wise, P J, 1985 Hulton Abbey: a century of excavations, *Staffordshire Archaeol Stud* ns 2, 1–142

Wood, E S, 1965 A medieval glasshouse at Blunden's Wood, Hambledon, Surrey, *Surrey Archaeol Collect* 62, 54–79

Wood, M E, 1965 *The English mediaeval house*, London

INDEX

Compiled by Ann Hudson

Page numbers in **bold** indicate illustrations and maps
Personal names in Tables 7–13 are indexed only if they also appear in the main text
All street names and locations are in London unless specified otherwise
County names within parentheses refer to historic counties